W9-BMK-506

B + T 6266 (Sweringen)

MODERN GERMAN HISTORY

CORONATION OF ARCHDUKE OTTO OF BAVARIA

German view of German history.   The ceremony took place in 1180 when Count Otto VI
of Wittelsbach became Duke of Bavaria.   This is how an artist of the late seventeenth
century imagined the scene

MODERN
GERMAN HISTORY

RALPH FLENLEY
Professor Emeritus, University of Toronto

**WITH TWO ADDITIONAL CHAPTERS (XIII and XIV)
COVERING THE WAR OF 1939–45 AND THE POST-
WAR YEARS**

by
ROBERT SPENCER
Associate Professor of History, University of Toronto

*Illustrated with
sixteen pages of photographs,
ten maps, and other drawings in the text*

LONDON: J. M. DENT & SONS LTD
NEW YORK: E. P. DUTTON & CO. INC

TO
D. H. F.

PREFACE

THERE WERE two main reasons for writing this book. The first is, that although much has been written in English on German history, there is a real lack of surveys which, within reasonable length, go sufficiently far back to give an adequate historical explanation of modern developments in that complicated field. And whilst a number of histories of Germany written by German historians have appeared in English recently, yet despite their learning and skill they naturally do not look at such developments with the same perspective as a non-German. The second reason, bound up with the first, is the desire to lay more emphasis than has often been done on the social, economic, and not least the intellectual and cultural factors which have been of such great importance in German history. It is not, of course, that German historians have been unaware of such aspects. But in the formative stage of their historical writing in the earlier years of the nineteenth century first the philosopher-historian Hegel laid down the principle that, as he put it: 'The State is the Divine Idea as it exists on Earth,' and so, 'It is to the State that change in the form of History indissolubly attaches itself.' Then the great master of the historian's art, Ranke, both emphasized in his works the importance and power of the State, and also formulated the doctrine which became known as that of 'the primacy of foreign policy' (*Primat der Aussenpolitik*) in history. These views, as a recent writer has remarked,[1] 'permeated the academic study of history in Germany to an amazing degree.' Whilst Treitschke in his great history transcended them to a considerable extent for the years before 1848, yet the preoccupation with the problem of political unity, the continuance of the Prussian tradition, and the Bismarckian emphasis on foreign policy, all tended to preserve such views and interests to the subordination of other aspects, as Professor Gerhard Ritter of Freiburg acknowledged in his inaugural address[2] to the first congress of German historians held after the recent war.

The book is, I hope, written at the level both of the university student engaged in the study of German and European history, and the so-called general reader anxious for light on 'the problem of Germany.' It is based on both primary and secondary authorities, German, French, and English, with a very limited use of illustrative footnotes and references. In order to make clear the factors which have contributed to make the Germany of our own day I have been obliged to go back to the Reformation, and even before in an introductory way. Yet to cover so large and complicated a field in one moderate-sized volume has necessitated the use both of seven-league boots and rigorous selection. As the table of contents makes clear,

[1] T. H. Von Laue, *Leopold Ranke, the Formative Years* (Preface), Princeton University Press. 1950.
[2] Printed in the *Historische Zeitschrift*, June 1950, vol. clxx, pp. 1–22.

however, the main emphasis is on the modern period which concerns us most.   A select bibliography has been added at the end of the volume.

I am much indebted to the University of Toronto for a year's leave of absence which enabled me to complete the book, as also to the Canadian Social Science Research Council for a grant to the same end.   I owe warm thanks to colleagues in the university, notably to Professors Barker Fairley and T. A. Goudge, for aid in a number of matters dealing with German literature and philosophy, and to Professor E. W. McInnis for reading some of the later chapters.

R. F.

UNIVERSITY OF TORONTO.
 February 1953.

PREFACE
TO THE SECOND EDITION

THE volume has now been brought more up to date by the addition of two chapters, dealing respectively with the war of 1939–45 and the post-war years.

1959.   R. F.

PUBLISHER'S NOTE
TO THE THIRD EDITION

IN order to bring the volume up to date and to take account of recent literature on the subject, two new chapters (XIII and XIV) dealing with the Second World War and the post-war period have been added ·by Professor Robert Spencer of the Department of History, University of Toronto.

1964.

CONTENTS

		PAGE
Preface		vii

CHAP.

I.	The Reformation Era and its Results	1
II.	The Rise of Prussia—I (to 1713)	29
III.	The Rise of Prussia—II (1713–86)	51
IV.	The Intellectual and Literary Revival of the Eighteenth Century	77
V.	The Remaking of Germany through the French Revolution and Napoleon	108
VI.	Conservatives, Liberals, and Nationalists, 1815–40	136
VII.	The Revolution of 1848–9	161
VIII.	The Unification of Germany	200
IX.	Economic, Social, and Cultural Trends in the Middle of the Nineteenth Century	241
X.	The Bismarckian Empire: I. 1871–90	269
XI.	The Bismarckian Empire: II. 1890–1918	301
XII.	The Weimar Republic and the Nazi Dictatorship, 1918–39	346
XIII.	Triumph and Catastrophe, 1939–45	388
XIV.	The German Phoenix, 1945–63	430
	Select Bibliography	473
	Index	479

ILLUSTRATIONS

PLATES

Coronation of Archduke Otto of Bavaria *frontispiece*

Maurice of Saxony; Luther; Albert of Branden- *facing page*
burg installed as Hereditary Duke of Prussia 18

Typical North German Towns; Osnabrück;
Wesel; Bremen 21

King Frederick I of Prussia; Prince Eugene of
Savoy; Bach; Handel 52

The Elector Frederick William I; Frederick the
Great; Hamburg Town Hall in the Eighteenth
Century 57

Eighteenth-century Court Life 80

Frederick William II; Lessing; Herder; Wieland 97

Gellert; Gottsched 104

Klopstock; The Young Goethe; Queen Louise of
Prussia; Beethoven 117

Taking the Oath of Allegiance to Frederick
William IV 148

Schiller at Carlsbad: E. T. A. Hoffman; E. M.
Arndt; Duke Charles Augustus of Weimar 181

Bismarck; Ludwig II; King George V of Hanover 212

Frederick William III; Emperor Frederick III 309

Hamburg Warehouses; Industrial Scene, Upper
Silesia 340

Hitler and Mussolini reviewing troops; Field
Marshals Rommel and Goering 405

Chancellor Erhard; Willi Brandt; President
Heuss; Former Chancellor Adenauer 420

In the Text

PAGE

The Emperor and Seven Electors, from bronze door knocker, Lübeck town hall   *title-page*

Nobles and Peasants about 1500   7

Town Wall and Moat, Nürnberg   10

Title-page of Luther's Bible (New Testament), printed in 1523   15

The Electresses Magdalene and Hedwig, first and second consorts of Joachim II   32

Goethe   96

Schiller   100

Uhland   148

Heine, aged thirty-two   163

August Campe   164

Bebel   251

Wagner   262

Nietzsche   299

William II   309

Bernhardi   334

Hindenburg   341

Maps

The Growth of Prussia to 1795   61

Germany in 1815   130

Prussia, 1815–71   173

The Unification of Germany   228–9

Industry in Germany   250

Agriculture in Germany   252

The Frontiers of Versailles   356–7

World War II, Western front [1]   420

World War II, Eastern front [1]   421

Post-War Germany   434

[1] From H. Stuart Hughes: *Contemporary Europe: A History*, reprinted by permission of Prentice-Hall Inc., Englewood Cliffs, New Jersey, U.S.A.

CHAPTER I

THE REFORMATION ERA
AND ITS RESULTS

*Introductory — Germany before the Reformation — The Results of
the Reformation Era*

I. INTRODUCTORY

THE HISTORY of modern Germany begins with the era of the Reformation. True, this was preceded by other changes marking the transition from medieval to modern, such as the change to a money economy and the introduction from Italy of the revived classical learning. But it was the era of the Reformation, extending from Luther's appearance to the close of the Thirty Years War, which completed the transition, and brought in its train other developments which were to determine the pattern of German life and history through much of the modern period. The nature of these developments may be briefly indicated here.

By the Reformation, Germany was permanently divided into two camps in the all-important matter of religious faith. The one part stood by the old Church, with its allegiance to Rome, the other broke with that to form a new Church, that of Luther. The growth of Calvinism in Germany shortly brought a third rival, whose divisions with Lutheranism were for a time to be almost as fateful for the country as that between Lutheranism and Roman Catholicism. There were, in addition, other Protestant sectarians, notably the Anabaptists, but these did not affect the general situation. While the importance of the divisions between the rival Protestant faiths was gradually to decline, the broad division between Protestant and Catholic was to remain of abiding importance in German history.

In this period came also the establishment of the sovereignty and virtual independence of the more important German princes, at the expense on the one hand of the imperial authority and national unity, on the other of claims to or hopes of a share in the business of government either by existing local assemblies or Estates (*Landstände*) or the German people in general. While this development was in train before the Reformation opened, it was both fostered and given a wider base by the political and religious developments of the time, and was to be even more fateful than the religious divisions for the future of the country.

This period saw also a steady decline in Germany's economic position, both absolutely and in relation to other western nations. On the eve of the Reformation Germany was in a highly prosperous condition. 'The German nation,' wrote no less an authority than Aeneas Sylvius in 1458, 'takes the

1

lead of all others in wealth and power.' That favourable situation was due above all to the economic activities and growth of the cities, especially the free imperial cities. Whilst it is true that the greatest days of the northern Hansa cities were over before 1500, some of them, as Cologne and Hamburg, were still rich and important. And the cities of the Upper Rhine and Upper Danube were at the height of their prosperity through the trade with Italy and the east. The new age was, however, slowly to sap that prosperity and to lead to a steady decline in their fortunes. One major cause of this, the opening of the new oceanic trade routes and the shrinking of the trade along the old routes to the east, had nothing directly to do with the Reformation. But the religious and civil disturbances in Germany, the wide divisions, the turn to armed force, especially in the Thirty Years War, the increase in the power of the princes, all contributed to diminish the resources and the power of the cities. Earlier, with the decline of the empire, they had constituted a sort of dualism with the princes in control of the destinies of Germany; now they became definitely inferior to them. And as they had represented the chief part of the economic prosperity of Germany, with their decline the country lost to its rivals along the western coast of Europe the pre-eminence it had formerly enjoyed.

Finally, this decline of the cities of the south-west brought with it another change in this period, the loss of the old supremacy of that region in the general and not least the cultural life of the country. Long after the old Franconia and Swabia had ceased to be the seats of imperial authority, the region fertilized by the upper valleys of the two great rivers, Rhine and Danube, had preserved its predominance in German life, thanks largely to the stimulus of its busy city life, its easy contacts with both Italy and France, and its own cultural achievement. It had not lost that to Vienna, despite the establishment of the imperial seat there. But in the era of the Reformation, greatly influenced by its course as by the rise of the greater territorial states away from the south-west, this old supremacy was lost, and that permanently. The leadership of the south-west had been a true cultural leadership, rather than one based on political or military power. But henceforth leadership in Germany was to be centred in other regions, to be based on other forces, and to be exercised in different ways.

II. GERMANY BEFORE THE REFORMATION

We cannot attempt to follow the long and complicated history of Germany before about 1500: the early settlement of the tribes, their contact with Rome (which Ranke, the greatest German historian, considered the most fruitful in German history), the organization of Charlemagne's Empire, the separation and reorganization of the more purely German part of that empire under the Saxon and succeeding emperors, the setting up of the Italian connection and the long struggle with the Papacy, ending with the victory of the Popes and destruction of the Hohenstauffen Empire, the steady growth, notwithstanding, of every side of German life in country and town. But before attempting to measure what the Reformation and its wars did to Germany we must present some brief sketch of what Germany was like before Luther precipitated the religious revolution.

Germany in 1500 was organized politically as the Holy Roman Empire, although after Frederick III (1440–93) its emperors were no longer crowned in Rome. The boundaries of the empire were none too clearly established.[1] To the east Bohemia was partly in, partly out, of the *Reich* or Commonwealth; to the south there were imperial lands and claims in Italy; to the west Alsace, the County of Burgundy (Franche Comté), Lorraine, Luxemburg, and the eastern and northern part of the Netherlands were still within the empire. Internally the outstanding feature of the political arrangements of the empire was an intricate confusion. The major secular principalities composing it were Austria (with its adjoining territories), Bavaria, Wurtemberg, the Palatinate, Hesse, Saxony (recently divided into two parts), and Brandenburg. But there were many minor principalities, from Brunswick or Mecklenburg downwards, until the long hierarchy of the German nobility closed with the Imperial Knights. A large part of German territory, estimated at one-third, belonged to the Church, whose archbishops, bishops, abbots, and priors ruled over domains of widely varying size, wealth, and influence. And, dotted all over, but especially numerous in the south-west, were the Imperial Cities, owing allegiance only to the emperor, and often ruling over adjacent areas. This confusion, reflected in a wide variety of titles, and unmatched elsewhere in Europe, was the product of long evolution. Like the confusion of the waves of the sea, it was never still, but always changing and evolving into new forms or combinations.

By the so-called Golden Bull of Emperor Charles IV (1356), the first attempt at a written constitution for the empire, the emperor was elected by a special Electoral College composed of the archbishops of Mainz, Trier, and Cologne, and the lay princes of the Palatinate, Saxony, and Brandenburg, with the King of Bohemia. Curiously enough, neither the Habsburg rulers of Austria, nor the Wittelsbach princes of Bavaria, possessed electoral votes. Nevertheless, the Habsburg family had secured possession of the imperial throne, though not without election and even severe opposition as was shown in 1519. This Habsburg family had emerged from the Swiss part of the old Swabia, had gained possession of the 'East Mark,' i.e. Austria, and around it had built up a domain of 'hereditary lands,' including Carinthia, Styria, Carniola, and Tyrol. Beyond these they had asserted claims to the thrones of Bohemia and Hungary, both of which were to be permanently won later, and had claims to lands in Italy and to territories west of the Rhine. There the rise of the house of Burgundy in the fifteenth century had threatened the unity of the empire. But the marriage of Maximilian, son of Emperor Frederick III, to the heiress of the Burgundian territories, and his election as emperor in 1493, had brought most of these lands back

---

[1] H. Treitschke, *History of Germany in the Nineteenth Century* (trans.), vol. i, p. 11: 'No one could say where the boundary stones of the Holy Roman Empire stood.'

within the orbit of the empire, although Maximilian was unable to win control of their rich resources.

As emperors the Habsburgs could and did continue to assert their universal authority. As late as 1440 the emperor claimed to be 'head protector and governor of all Christendom.' Actually, since they were no longer crowned in Rome, they were but kings of the Romans; but Maximilian got over this by getting from the Pope the title of Emperor Elect. Yet whilst they might retain the title and its pretensions, they were in fact being pushed back in this period to their position as rulers in Germany; Maximilian indeed assumed the title of King of Germany. The assumption of this title did not, however, clear up the confusion which existed between his dual roles in Germany. Ironically enough, the imperial claims to universal sovereignty tended to weaken the Habsburg position as German kings, since the other princes of Germany claimed to interpret their allegiance in imperial terms rather than as members of a national monarchy. The emperor was in theory the fountain of justice for the empire, the guardian of its peace, the commander of its army, the confirmer of its laws. But the empire lacked any working administrative, financial, or military system. There were few imperial resources, as such. The older sources of imperial revenue had declined, and the emperors were obliged to rely very largely on the revenues from their 'hereditary lands,' which were mountainous and poor. They had the greatest difficulty in securing aid from the empire to meet the threat caused by the Turkish advance up the Danube.

And the Habsburg emperors themselves made little serious attempt to transpose themselves into national German kings. Their position, whether as emperors or kings, had suffered a steady decline during the long reign of Frederick III (1440–93), when the emperor had been reduced to living for a time on monastic charity. The succession of Maximilian I in 1493, however, seemed to presage a new era. Maximilian was indeed a striking and romantic figure, with high gifts and higher ambitions (he was ready to add the papal to the imperial crown), a medieval knight touched by the Renaissance, eloquent, daring, and optimistic. But he proved to be as lacking in statesmanship as he was in financial resources. Instead of making any serious attempt to build a modern national state as his contemporaries in France, England, and Spain were doing, he spent his energies in the pursuit of imperial and family interests. 'He lived,' says Ranke,[1] 'in the interests of his House.' Maximilian's successor, Charles V, emperor 1519–56, was, it is true, a far more solid character. But to him Germany was but one of his many possessions, the most troublesome and the least remunerative. He did not speak its language (save, it was said, to his horse), he never regarded it as his home, and for years together he never visited it. His latest biographer [2] sums him up in much the same terms as Ranke used of Maximilian: 'He knew but one passion, his dynasty and its power.' These Habsburgs, indeed, provided the most shining, and, up to a

---

[1] *History of the Reformation* (trans.), vol. i, p. 138.
[2] K. Brandi, in *Die deutsche Reformation*, vol. i, p. 298.

point, the most successful example of the rising force of dynasticism, which was becoming a more active political force everywhere. The other German princes followed the example of the emperors, and elsewhere in Europe the same trend was manifest. The Habsburg failure to rise above it was one of the major reasons why Germany in this period failed to attain real political unity.

Yet this period before and during the Reformation was of critical importance for the political organization of Germany. The old tribal dukedoms round which medieval Germany had been built up, Saxony, Franconia, Bavaria, Swabia, and Lorraine, had disintegrated or declined by the fifteenth century, like the medieval empire itself. New families such as the Habsburgs and Hohenzollerns, new combinations as in divided Saxony, new forces, such as the Imperial Cities, had emerged or were emerging in their place. Some of the outlying portions of the empire had fallen away or were falling away, as Switzerland, Italy, and the Netherlands. Despite the traditional and persistent strength of localism in Germany it might have been possible to work out a system of political and administrative unity had the Habsburgs thought more in terms of Germany as a whole and less in terms of their Austrian lands and their European claims and position.

The focus for such unity existed in the Imperial Diet or *Reichstag* in which most of Germany was represented; the exceptions were the Imperial Knights and the peasants, who had no direct representation. Early in the fifteenth century, stirred by the Conciliar movement and the restless energy of Emperor Sigismund, the Diet had shown signs of life, but in the long reign of Frederick III it had slumbered again. The emperor might call Diets, but he never attended any for thirty years. And the Diet was by no means a fully organized body. There were no established rules as to who should be called, or even who should call it, where and how often it should meet, how it was to be organized when in session, what its procedures and above all what its powers were. It had come in the fifteenth century to be divided into three bodies. These were the College of Electors, as defined by the Bull of 1356; the College of Princes, the former feudal assembly of both secular and clerical lords, in which the greater lords or princes had individual votes, the remainder group votes; and finally the representatives of the many Imperial Cities. But the exact relation of these bodies to each other, and their relation in turn to both emperor and *Reich*, lacked any kind of clear definition. The Golden Bull of 1356 had been almost entirely concerned with the election of the emperor.

Towards the end of the fifteenth century, however, new winds began to blow. Other countries were setting their houses in order, why should not Germany do the like? The need for this had long been evident, and Nicolas of Cusa (d. 1464), reformer, philosopher, and Cardinal Bishop, had made specific proposals for the reform and strengthening of the Diet. These received new stimulus with the succession of Maximilian as emperor in 1493, backed by a new reformer, Archbishop Berthold of Mainz (d. 1504). The *Reichstag* became more active than ever before, and for a time it almost seemed that it might develop into a real national assembly clothed with authority to control both emperor and country. When the emperor was forced to appeal to the Diet for aid against the advancing Turks, the Diet responded, as in parallel cases elsewhere, by demands for reform. The Diets held at Worms in 1495 and the following years sought to end the endemic disorder in the realm by outlawing private war and proclaiming a public peace. To aid this they created an imperial supreme court (*Reichs-kammergericht*) and added an imperial tax (the Common Penny) to finance an imperial army. The Diet also aspired to establish a sort of permanent executive council (*Reichsregiment*). To provide the necessary administrative control, Germany was to be divided into areas known as Circles (*Kreise*), at first six, then ten. Finally the *Reichstag* was to meet annually.

Although these measures, save that setting up a supreme court, failed to come into effective operation, the activity of the *Reichstag* continued through the first half of the sixteenth century. The disputed election of Charles V gave the Electors the opportunity to secure pledges from him to govern in accordance with the laws of the Diet and with its aid. The imperial council was revived and functioned for a time during the absence of the emperor. And the issue of the Reformation gave fresh importance to the meetings of the *Reichstag*, from the historic Diet of Worms of 1521 to that of Augsburg which established a compromise peace in 1555. Yet in fact the efforts to make of the *Reichstag* an effective and real national assembly controlling the destinies of Germany had ended in failure before the Diet of 1555, which the emperor did not attend in person. The issue raised by Luther both split the Diet in two, from the Electoral College downwards, and proved beyond its powers to settle finally. And even without the Reformation issue it is very doubtful whether the *Reichstag* could have evolved into a working national parliament, so great were the obstacles in the way. The emperors showed no desire for any such development, Maximilian regarding any efforts in that direction as encroachments on his own rights, Charles measuring it solely by its help or hindrance in his worldwide imperial and dynastic interests. The Diet itself, and even its separate colleges, were far from united in any attempt to strengthen the *Reichstag*. Princes, high and low, and even the Imperial Cities, followed only too closely the example of the emperors in pursuing their own separate or individual interests, with little regard for the interest of the nation, even when threatened by aggression from the Turks or the French. The Diet was to crystallize before the seventeenth century into a permanent body, a sort of closed corporation. But its permanence was a sign rather of its impotence than of its strength. It could survive a Protestant secession such as that which occurred ten years before the Thirty Years War broke out, but it had lost all possibility of ruling the *Reich*, and the failure may have helped to discredit the whole idea of parliamentary government in Germany, as a recent German historian suggests.[1] National issues in Germany were to be decided by other hands and other weapons than those of a national assembly.

[1] V. Valentin, *The German People*, 1946, p. 224.

In the pursuance and triumph of local and individual interests the Imperial Diet reflected only too well the nature of German society at the close of the Middle Ages.   That society was not merely locally particularist, but also highly stratified.   The stratification was, of course, medieval, feudal, and not confined to Germany.   But whereas elsewhere in western Europe this was being modified by the forces of the new age, in Germany it was still very strong, and was to remain so for centuries.   Apart from the imperial court the major elements of that society were the territorial nobility, the Church, the cities, and the peasantry.   And although there was some intermingling,

Nobles and peasants about 1500.   Illustration to a satirical (anti-noble) broadsheet, attributed to Hans Sachs

e.g. between nobility and higher clergy, the class feelings and interests were decidedly marked.

The German nobility, using that term in the broadest sense, ranged from the greater princes to the simple knights and lords.   It was clerical as well as secular, but the Church can best be looked at separately.   The greater secular nobility were in process of building up, on the ruins of the medieval empire, the principalities which were to provide the framework of modern Germany.   This process of consolidation, expansion, and repudiation of any external authority within their territorial limits had been favoured by the weakness of the imperial authority and the general disorders of the fifteenth century, but it was by no means completed when the sixteenth century opened.   Alliance between the emperor and the lesser nobility and the cities might have checked it, but failing that it continued.   Hence Saxony, Brandenburg, Bavaria, the Palatinate, Hesse, and Wurtemberg were to emerge at the end of the Reformation period as sovereign powers, the real masters (in rivalry with Austria) of Germany.   Below them were middle-sized states such as Mecklenburg and Brunswick; in the south-west, where the old imperial authority survived, the process of consolidation took longer.

These greater and middle-sized principalities were emerging as dynasties, with the pretensions of ruling families, and it was they rather than the emperor who were to personify in Germany Machiavelli's definitions of princely rule. Their claims to authority were strengthened by the introduction of Roman legal concepts and practices into Germany in the fifteenth century. The universities now provided them with legal officials trained in Roman law, with its emphasis on the power of the prince; the old German law and popular rights were in eclipse. 'The Roman lawyers are overwhelming us,' wrote Wimpheling early in the sixteenth century. These princes could better afford to buy and use the new weapon of artillery against castles or city walls, and were likewise better able to hire the professional soldiery, the *Landsknechte*, who were becoming almost a separate class in Germany.

Below these relatively few great princes there stretched out in descending order the wide range of lesser nobles of varying rank, possession, and power. Perhaps two hundred or so of these had some claim to importance, and that rather local than national. Ten times more numerous were the Imperial Knights (*Reichsritterschaft*), claiming dependence upon the emperor alone, and clustered mainly in the south-west. They had asserted their independence as a class in the fourteenth century, but were by this time in decline, and their revolt, led by Sickingen in 1523, was no more than a vain and despairing protest against the decay of their position. Many were to be absorbed into the general territorial system, others were to remain as archaic survivors of a bygone age, until one of the last of them, the great statesman, Karl Freiherr vom und zum Stein (1757–1831), gave them a dying glory.

While the future was to belong to the territorial princes of Germany, in 1500 their power was at least rivalled by that of the Church. One-third of German land was in clerical hands, and certainly a proportionate share of the national wealth: the German Church was in fact the richest in Europe. There were over a hundred bishops and abbots of major importance. The three ecclesiastical electorates of Mainz, Cologne, and Trier were matched in the wide extent of their lands by the sees of Magdeburg, Salzburg, and Würzburg, while those of Bamberg, Münster, Augsburg, Strassburg, Speier, Paderborn, and Halberstadt were not far below. The great abbeys of Fulda, Kempten, St. Gall, and Quedlinburg headed the long list of monastic foundations which spread thickly over the hills and valleys of Germany. Many of these bishoprics and abbeys were headed by members of the German nobility, and shared some of the interests of the secular aristocracy. But the Church was better organized and more closely integrated than secular German society, and its influence reached into every nook and cranny of German life.

The relations of the Church in Germany to Rome had been the subject of much and stormy debate during the Conciliar period, especially during the Council of Basel, but Frederick III had made a concordat with the

Pope which confirmed or restored many of the papal claims. The Pope was allowed to make appointments to clerical offices in Germany, cases were called to Rome for judicial decision, and the first year's income of bishops was paid to the Pope. The Pope drew from Germany far more in the way of revenue than the emperor, and his powers there were greater. His legate sat in the *Reichstag*, even opened it in the absence of the emperor, and the imperial coronation oath included a pledge of obedience to the Holy See, as well as pledges to uphold the Catholic faith and protect the German Church.

Yet there was much criticism of papal rights and claims in Germany through the fifteenth century, and with it was coupled criticisms of the Church and clergy in general there, of the abuse of clerical privilege, the laxity of clerical life, both regular and secular, the ignorance, wealth, and exactions of the clergy. There was, in fact, considerable need for reform. But that is not to say that there were not pious and devoted clergy in Germany before the Reformation, or that religion was notoriously in decline among the laity. There is, in fact, ample evidence of religious activity; without it there would have been no Reformation. Not merely was there a zest for pilgrimages and the collection of relics—the Electors of Saxony and Brandenburg had thousands of these—but there was religious activity of a deeper kind both in individuals and groups, in town and country, amongst both rich and poor. Criticism of the clergy did not necessarily imply criticism of the existing faith. The new printing presses poured out a growing stream of religious books, sermons, injunctions to piety (among these over fifty editions before 1500 of Thomas à Kempis's *Imitation of Christ*), and editions of parts or the whole of the Bible both in Latin and German. Art, down to and including the great Dürer, reflected a like pre-occupation with religious subjects. The early humanists, such as Agricola, were men of deep religious faith. While the growth of the universities during this period, with nine new ones founded between 1456 and 1506, testified to the growing interest in both secular and religious learning, the educational activities of the Brethren of the Common Life in their schools in north-western Germany were more specifically religious in character. Yet abuses continued, and it was because a young scion of the house of Brandenburg, already the holder of two bishoprics, needed money to pay for a papal permit to succeed also to the great see of Mainz, that indulgences were sold in Germany in the way which so aroused Luther and precipitated the religious revolution.

Next in importance to nobles and clergy were the city folk. Whilst the early Germans, Tacitus tells us, disliked the confinement of towns, by the fourteenth century Germany possessed a remarkably large number of cities, many of them Imperial or Free Cities, subject only to the emperor, and in many respects city republics. They were not large by modern standards, the largest numbering about twenty thousand inhabitants, and they were small in area and rather crowded within. They were as a rule fortified with walls, contained fine churches and public buildings, and possessed considerable wealth. If Germany was the wealthiest country in Europe it was her cities which made her so. These cities were highly organized communities with mayors or burgomasters, councils which regulated every side of city life, and numerous guilds both for the various industries and for social and religious purposes. They had extended their control over the adjacent countryside: Rothenburg, with only six thousand inhabitants, had fifteen thousand peasants on its surrounding lands. In the fifteenth century the cities had won recognition as a separate college in the Imperial Diet, and there and in the country at large they represented, though somewhat vaguely and impotently, the traditions of imperial unity.

Town wall and moat, Nürnberg

These cities had risen to their high position by the energy of their burghers in exploiting their central position in Europe for trade in every direction, across the Baltic and North Seas, up and down the numerous rivers, especially the Rhine and the Danube, westward to France, eastward to Poland and Russia, over the Alpine passes to Italy and the Mediterranean. They had likewise developed industries such as textiles, metal, and wood; the recent invention of printing in a German city provided a new industry. With much effort they had freed themselves from feudal and clerical control, and for the defence and extension of their trade they had formed unions of cities, such as the short-lived Rhenish and Swabian leagues, and the more permanent and more important Hanseatic League of the Baltic and North German cities. This German Hansa included at one time or another nearly one hundred cities, had trading factories and privileges in London, Bruges, Bergen, and Novgorod, and in the fourteenth century was strong enough to wage war against and defeat a king of Denmark.

And when in the latter part of the fifteenth century the Hansa fell into decline, the cities of south-west Germany, more industrial than the Hansa athough busy traders as well by Rhine and Danube, as over the Alps, rose to the zenith of their wealth and importance. It was their citizens, such as the well-known Fugger family of Augsburg, who developed the new techniques of large-scale capitalist finance in northern Europe, extending their interests far outside Germany, and accumulating fortunes of a magnitude hitherto unknown there. Never had the cities of Germany seemed, or been, more prosperous. In an imperial levy of 1520 three of them (Cologne, Nürnberg, and Ulm) were assessed at the same highest rate as the rich electoral princes; three more (Lübeck, Augsburg, and Frankfurt on Main) were ranked with the greater princes, ten with the major bishops and dukes, forty with the middle nobles, twenty with the lesser nobility and minor bishops.[1]

Yet despite this prosperity, when the Reformation opened the German cities were at or past the turn of their fortunes. Some of the causes of the decline of the Hansa were special and local, such as the decline of the Baltic herring fisheries. But there were more general causes in operation by this time which were to affect both northern and southern German cities in varying degree. The rise of national feeling, national organization, and national economic interest in the countries adjacent to Germany lessened their trading position abroad. The oceanic discoveries and the opening of the new trade routes to America and Asia, with the advance of the Turk both up the Danube and in the Mediterranean, reduced the advantages of their central position in Europe, in particular those derived from their close relation with Italian and Mediterranean trade. The steady weakening of the imperial power on the one hand, and the rise of the territorial princes on the other, threatened to undermine their independent position. They had always been subject to internal strife as new classes or groups sought to share the privileges which the upper ruling class enjoyed. So far from joining with the lesser nobility or gentry as in the English House of Commons, they were usually at odds with the local nobility, especially with the impoverished Imperial Knights, who envied them their wealth, and in the absence of any authority strong enough to keep the peace frequently attacked them and raided their convoys, or hindered their trade by the imposition of excessive local tolls on the rivers. The peasants found them harsh landlords, and had no love for them. Their wealth, the luxury it engendered, the concentration of financial power in the hands of a few, and its use to establish monopolies in trade and industry, aroused widespread jealousy, criticism, and hostility. In the Imperial Diets held after 1500 there were petitions against such practices, and as the decrees passed against them were ineffective, the feeling continued. They had managed to hold their own against the disorders of the fifteenth century, but the growing strife of the new age was to expose them to greater trials. Divided and isolated as they were, they could not hope to maintain themselves against the weight of warlike princely power which the sixteenth century, and still more the seventeenth, were to see arrayed in battle and plunder through the length and breadth of Germany. Their trade and industry inevitably suffered, and although there was no

[1] K. Brandi, op. cit., vol. i, p. 95.

sudden decline, and many of them played a notable part in the Reformation itself, nevertheless, there was a steady diminution in their weight and influence in the life of the nation as the period went on.   And by its close they had permanently lost the once proud position they had formerly held.

The largest but least regarded class in the social hierarchy of Germany was that of the peasants.   Some, mostly in the east (Pomerania), were serfs (*Leibeigene*); the majority were personally free but bound to the land, subject to dues (or rent) in money or kind, services (*Fronen*) and tithes (of three kinds), and special dues to the Church.   During the fifteenth century their position seems to have been improving steadily, and there is evidence of rural prosperity and good living.   But with the turn into the next century we begin to hear more of their grievances and of a worsening of their conditions.   The truth seems to be that on the one hand the peasantry, as a result of improved conditions, had become more conscious of their feudal burdens and more urgent to get rid of them.   In this aim they were encouraged in south-western Germany, where discontent became most rife, by the successful example of the Swiss peasants.   'We would be as the Swiss,' said the peasants round Speier in 1502.   On the other hand, their position was, in fact, worsened at this time by a number of developments beyond their control.   The rise in prices after 1500 hurt them.   An increase in population led to a reduction in the size of their holdings.   The extension of territorial sovereignty threatened their common lands, which some lords now claimed as their own.   This was bound up with the introduction of Roman legal concepts, and the efforts of the lawyers to reduce the endless variety of peasants' services to a more uniform but at the same time a more rigid system.   There were complaints against the greed for land of the city merchants, the high rates of interest on mortgages, and heartless foreclosure.

Already, before 1500, local risings of peasants had occurred: in 1476 near Würzburg; in 1491 against the Abbey of Kempten in Bavaria; two years later against the Bishop of Strassburg; all three against clerical landlords. The years 1502, 1512, and 1514 saw fresh risings, all anticipatory of the more general rising of 1525.   The famous Twelve Articles of that year provide the clearest definition of what the peasants or their leaders desired, though it is to be remembered that by this date the Lutheran movement was exerting its influence.   They wanted to elect (and if necessary depose) their priests, and to get rid of other tithes than that on grain; they wished to be free of serfdom and of excessive services; the common lands were to be restored, with the old rights of free woodcutting; rents were to be reduced, and the preservation of game for the lord's hunting to be abolished; the new (Romanized) laws were to go.   Moderate as most of this programme seems now, its demands, and the alarming spectacle of the humble diggers of the soil rising to demand their 'rights,' was too much for established society, whether of the old or the new faith, save for a few radicals.   The revolt was crushed with great severity, Luther adding his voice to the chorus of condemnation, and with its crushing any hopes of improvement in the conditions of the peasants vanished for many a long day.   The lot of the peasant worsened, his hopes of freedom were indefinitely postponed, and he was to share with the cities in the devastation of the Thirty Years War.

The strength and permanence of these class divisions and interests did not imply the lack of any national feeling, or of the elements of a national state. Germany by 1500 had a common language, and if her literary achievement in that language was as yet inferior to that of the other western nations, the Reformation through Luther was shortly to mark a notable progress here. She had traditions which were national as well as imperial, and Hutten's passionate outbursts, and indeed the whole Reformation, were to reveal the existence of a fund of national feeling which could be drawn upon. The printing press, a German invention, was to give voice to this; to Fichte, looking back from the age of Napoleon, it was the most important instrument of the Reformation. It was in the fifteenth century that the Holy Roman Empire became the 'Holy Roman Empire of the German nation.' The new learning seeping into Germany from Italy took on a national as well as a religious colouring in the universities and elsewhere.

But while the elements of national unity were present, there was a real failure to organize this identity in terms of political unity. The 'lack of governance' from which Germany suffered had existed also in both France and England after the Hundred Years War. In both those countries, however, the period of anarchy or confusion was followed by one of growing unity under a national monarchy. In Germany the opportunity for this, if one existed, was lost, for reasons we have indicated. Instead the divided country was plunged into a period of religious and civil strife which confirmed and strengthened those divisions, and destroyed all hope of political unity for centuries. Further, the crystallizing of political evolution at this stage into the autocratic and multi-state form which triumphed at the Peace of Westphalia in 1648 was to delay indefinitely the political evolution of the German people, and render them incapable of the revolution which France achieved to break the bonds of absolutism.

III. THE RESULTS OF THE REFORMATION ERA

The Reformation in Germany may be regarded as having come to a close in 1555. But adequately to estimate the results of the movement we must go further on, through the half-century and more of uneasy peace which followed, which was also the period of the Counter-Reformation or Catholic Reformation, and into and through the period of the Thirty Years War, which dragged out its interminable length to the settlement of Westphalia in 1648. That makes, from Luther's challenge to the papal indulgences in 1517, 131 years, four generations of leaders and led, covering all or part of the reigns of eight Habsburg emperors (and nineteen Popes) from Maximilian I to Ferdinand III. Here we are concerned not to follow the course of events, but from a general view over the whole period to estimate what had happened to Germany, what were the results of so much effort, strife, and war, on one of the major nations of Europe.

So brief a survey as this can take small account of individuals, yet the personality and influence of Martin Luther were too important to be omitted. For Luther gave a stamp to the Reformation in Germany and to the Lutheran Church, which it never lost, and which was all important for Germany as a whole. By any measurement, the peasant-miner's son of Eisleben in Saxony was one of the great men of history, who by no means had greatness thrust upon him, but from sheer conviction and with indomitable courage first stood forth against a religious abuse, then led a large percentage of the people of Germany in opposition to papal authority and to the rejection of certain doctrines and practices of the Catholic Church, finally establishing a new faith and a new church in his native land. He had helpers and protectors, of course, not all of them stirred by the highest or purest of motives. And he had obvious defects and limitations of character, being at times too violent and impetuous, presenting indeed an extraordinary mixture of revolutionary and conservative. He also made mistakes, like every other leader of men. But of the force and great influence on Germany of Luther's appeal, defined in the three famous pamphlets of 1520 and in his many later writings, there is no possible doubt. It has been estimated that by 1570 some seventy per cent of Germany's population (including Austria) was Protestant, the great majority of these Lutheran; and there were many Lutherans outside Germany. The new invention of printing was immensely helpful to Luther in the dissemination of his views; but it was Luther himself who first made the German language the instrument of wide popular use.

The Lutheran Church was not created by Luther alone. Philip Melanchthon, a greater scholar, drew up the Augsburg Confession of 1530, its first and fundamental definition. Yet Luther remained the acknowledged leader of the new faith as it spread over Germany, particularly in the north which was largely Protestant when he died in 1546. And Luther did much to determine the all-important matter of the relations of the new Church to society, above all to the State. Here the contradictions of his character came in. On the one hand he revolted against the authority of the Pope and the Catholic Church. 'The just shall live by faith'; the individual conscience based on the Scriptures was to be the guide of man's relation to God. But Luther the monk had been long under authority. In 1520 he appealed for princely support in the *Address to the Christian Nobility of the German Nation*. One of these princes, the Elector Frederick the Wise of Saxony, responded by whisking him secretly away from danger at the famous Diet of Worms (1521) to hide in the Thuringian forests at the Wartburg. The almost immediate outburst of religious radicalism led by Münzer and Carlstadt, the revolt of the Imperial Knights led by Sickingen, above all the revolt of the peasants in 1525, all frightened Luther. He became increasingly conservative in some of his theology, and increasingly ready to accept the authority of princes as the representatives of God. Such authority, he declared, 'is a sign of the Divine grace.' 'When the magistrate punishes, God himself punishes,' records his *Table Talk*.

Princely authority over the new faith was indeed to go far beyond Luther's

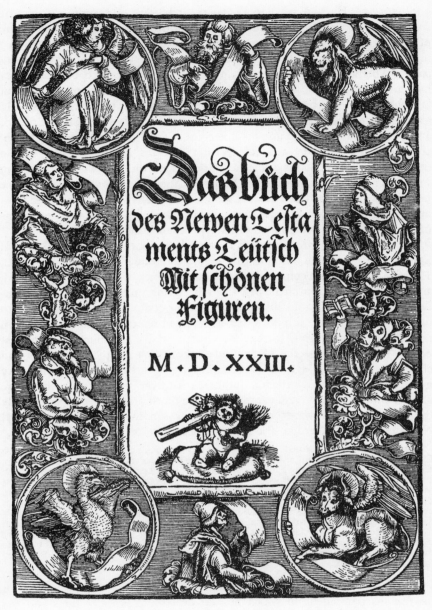

Title-page of Luther's Bible (New Testament), printed in 1523

conceptions. He had tried to define the relations of church and secular rule in 1523, exempting faith and conscience from lay control, but the nature of the age and the course of events moved inexorably towards wider princely influence. The divisions and controversies between the Protestants themselves, whether in the Lutheran Church or outside, which continued for half a century and more, invited and indeed compelled the intervention of lay authority. The Imperial Diet, in the very year after the Peasants' Revolt, left the states (i.e. the princes) to decide on the enforcement of its Edict of 1521, condemning Luther and his doctrines. The Peace of Augsburg (1555) confirmed this attitude with its decision that the prince or ruler should decide the religion of his subjects. Those who did not wish to conform were to go elsewhere; only in the Imperial Cities was toleration of difference in religious faith provided for. Lutheran Germany came to be organized in territorial churches (*Landeskirchen*), each working out its own problems under the direction and control of its own secular ruler.

That control had already begun to take shape in a state such as Electoral Saxony as soon as the old authority of the Catholic Church was destroyed. There, in the resultant confusion, the electoral prince, with Luther's approval, supervised the erection of the new Church, setting up bishops or superintendents in place of the old bishops, organizing commissions of visitation to oversee local pastors, administering confiscated church property, setting up new bodies, consistories, to regulate church affairs in general. These last bodies indeed became the recognized authorities over the local Lutheran churches. And although the exact nature and degree of princely authority exercised in and through them naturally varied from state to state, they were and remained the agent and expression of that authority, reflecting inevitably the general trend towards princely autocracy in the seventeenth century. As an historian of German Protestantism puts it:

The territorial prince ruled absolutely. He proclaimed as princely ordinances the Church regulations affecting every branch of Church life, organization, form of worship, and doctrine. He named the Church officials down to the pastors, appointed the Church authorities, and supervised their work. The Visitations were made in his name, the reports made to him, and the necessary orders given by him, to be carried out by his commission, by the next Visitation, or by the subordinate officials. All complaints were brought before and decided upon by him, whether in the consistory courts, or over their heads directly by him, including matrimonial cases. The whole financial system of the Church was controlled in this way, all appeals for increases of salary were laid before him, either by the Visitations commissions or more rarely by the Superintendents. He had to make the requisite money available. Disciplinary power over the clergy lay in his hands, indeed the whole legal position of the Church was there concentrated.[1]

Thus did Luther's *Liberty of a Christian Man* (to use the title of one of his famous pamphlets, in which he had declared: 'We are kings and the freest of men') come to be regulated by the State, and Lutheranism became a recognized pillar of German territorialism, a contributor to the system of local autocracy which was to stamp Germany for so long. The instrument of freedom became the tool of authority, and the Protestant influence and example encouraged Catholic princes in Germany to make similar if less complete invasions of ecclesiastical authority. And by its alliance with the

[1] E. Sehling, *Geschichte der protestantischen Kirchenverfassung*, 1913, p. 21.

princes and its condemnation of religious radicalism and efforts at peasant liberation Lutheranism had separated itself from and even alienated some of the forces available for social and political progress. The support of the middle class was important, but of less account politically because its members lived largely in the separated cities, and these were declining in importance. Hence the Reformation in Germany did less than might have been expected to emancipate the German mind and spirit. It would have been too much to expect that it should bring an immediate recognition of the principle of religious toleration. That was foreign to the age. The new Church, like the old, believed that only in its own faith was salvation to be found, and looked to secular authority to enforce the true faith; only slowly did the idea of toleration emerge. But whereas in England the setting up of a Protestant state church was followed by a movement which through civil war temporarily overthrew both State and Church, and had profound effects on the development of political liberty in England, in Germany a parallel civil war only fastened more tightly on the country the bonds of princely authority. The movement which had begun as a demand for spiritual freedom failed to develop into a movement for political or civil freedom, a factor of much importance in explaining the slowness of German political development. It is true that Calvinism, with its theories of local self-government, and its more highly developed organization, in which the laity shared, was to spread into Germany. But neither this, nor the advent of other Protestant creeds, appreciably changed the general situation. The rulers of Prussia were wise enough, when they turned Calvinist early in the seventeenth century, to leave undisturbed the Lutheran faith of their subjects.

The Reformation split the Holy Roman Empire, in the matter of religion, into two not very clearly divided parts. Very roughly the north became Protestant, and the south, after becoming partly Protestant, swung back, or was pulled back, into the Catholic fold. Large parts of the northern Rhineland, however, remained Catholic. This process took a long time to work out, and the settlement of the religious boundaries was the major preoccupation of German history from the Diet of Worms in 1521 to the Peace of Westphalia in 1648. Thus while France, England, and Holland (as she became), despite their religious conflicts, were reaching out across the seas to establish trading routes, trading factories in Asia and colonies in America, Germany was still wrestling with the problems of religion. And with that the whole of German life became entangled, so that what began as a question of religious faith—though it was never solely that—became increasingly one of political issues, with wide and deep social and economic as well as cultural significance and results. And this German issue, never wholly German by any means, became in the seventeenth century a European one, with Germany the battle-field and the victim both.

At first the new faith seemed to have it much its own way, spreading in country and town from the southern provinces of Austria to the North and Baltic Seas, from across the Rhine to the Polish frontiers and beyond, linking up with the Hussite movement in Bohemia, and reaching into Hungary. It fell to a new emperor, Charles V, to meet this spreading tide, and Charles, with his wide interests in Catholic Europe, held to the old faith both from conviction and interest. He strove, in his infrequent visits to Germany, to check the movement. His first attempt, in and after the all-important Diet held at Worms in 1521, was a failure; Protestantism continued to spread through the empire. And although he won an outstanding success in the first religious war (that of the Schmalkaldic League, 1546–7), and subdued or won over the leading Protestant princes, he was unable either to complete or to maintain that success. A new Protestant rising, led by the faithless Maurice of Saxony, proved a complete check to him, and the ensuing Peace of Augsburg of 1555 marked the recognition by the emperor and the country of the permanent division of Germany into Lutheran and Catholic sections. The Peace indeed represented a considerable triumph for the Protestant cause, and a Venetian observer a year after the Peace went so far as to say: 'Were I to record my conviction, I would say that this land of Germany will shortly be completely alienated from the Roman Church.'

The Peace of Augsburg did indeed put an end to open conflict for a time. But it did not finally settle the boundary lines between the two faiths. The princes were to decide the religion of their lands. But the boundaries of these lands were not immutable; ambitious princes were always trying to extend their territories, and such extensions might involve the question of the religion of the added portion. In particular, what was to happen in the matter of the lands of the Catholic Church held or seized by Protestant princes, or where a Catholic bishop turned Protestant? The treaty provided that lands seized after 1552 were to be returned to the Church, and that where a bishop or abbot turned Protestant in the future he was to be replaced by a Catholic; in fact the Protestants continued to hold on to at least seven north German bishoprics supposed to be returned to their former owners. Finally the treaty made no provision for the Calvinist or Reformed Protestant faith. Yet Calvinism already had its disciples in Germany, and it continued to spread into the Rhineland, and as far east as Hungary. It came to be accepted by the electoral prince of the important Rhenish Palatinate, and later by the Elector of Brandenburg. Its coming increased the division already present amongst Lutherans on doctrinal matters. And although the Lutherans managed in 1580 to arrive at a Formula of Concord amongst themselves, the issue between them and the Calvinists remained, the Calvinists uncompromising and provocative, the Lutherans bitter and resentful. The breach seriously weakened the whole Protestant position.

And within a few years of the Peace of Augsburg the Catholic forces in Germany were ready to take advantage of such weakening. The Council of Trent had indeed failed to reunite western Christendom, but it revived the Catholic Church, redefined its faith, strengthened the Papacy, and made the Jesuits the leaders of the Counter-Reformation. Disunited Protestantism in Germany had little to offer comparable to the single-minded devotion and zeal of the Jesuit Fathers there, nor did the princely guardians of Protestantism there display the same energy as the Catholic rulers of Austria and Bavaria.

MARTINVS   LVTHERVS

MAURICE OF SAXONY   LUTHER
From contemporary prints

ALBERT OF BRANDENBURG INSTALLED AS HEREDITARY DUKE OF PRUSSIA
From a picture by the nineteenth-century Polish romantic painter, Jan Matejko

The Jesuits were able to extend their activities, and with marked success, into both Catholic and Protestant Germany, as into neighbouring countries such as Poland.   In north-western Germany they had their headquarters in Cologne, in the south-east they won the support of the Habsburgs, who rooted out Protestantism from their hereditary lands.   In the south-centre the Wittelsbach rulers of Bavaria emerged to importance as leaders of the Catholic revival, making that faith as valuable an aid to their own authority as had the Protestant princes.   The Prince Bishop of the great diocese of Würzburg combined reform of his clergy with the expulsion of Protestants, and other south German bishops followed his example.   Thus by the end of the sixteenth century the Catholic Church in Germany had recovered an appreciable amount of its lost ground.   And although in the law and constitution of the empire the balance established by the treaty of 1555 (which had curiously enough never been ratified) remained, actually this settlement was being steadily undermined by the greater unity and initiative, and the more effective leadership, of the Catholic party.

Out of this disturbance of a balance resting on insecure foundations and always rather precarious came the Thirty Years War.   There were, of course, particular circumstances and occasions within the empire which led up to the war.   There was strife between Protestants and Catholics in the Imperial City of Donauwörth on the Danube (1608), ending in a Catholic victory over a Protestant majority thanks to the intervention of the Duke of Bavaria; there was a succession dispute in the Rhineland (the Kleve-Jülich affair); and there was the problem of Bohemia, predominantly Protestant but greatly divided religiously, nationally, and socially.   There was the prospect that an old, weak, and ailing emperor, Matthias (1612–19), one of a number of ineffective emperors during this period, would be succeeded by a zealous Catholic, Archduke Ferdinand, a product of Jesuit education, who had already driven the Protestants out of his lands of Styria.   And beyond Germany the lists were being set for the decisive struggle between the Habsburgs and the French Bourbon kings.   The whole of Europe, indeed, was concerned over the problem of Germany, which the emperor's chief adviser at this time declared Solomon himself could not have solved.

The conclusion of the long war which distracted and dislocated Germany for a generation offered no new solution.   For the Peace of Westphalia in 1648 but reaffirmed the principle of 1555, save that Calvinism was now recognized as equal in status to the other two religions: church offices, lands, and faiths were to stand as they did in 1624.   Despite the success of Ferdinand II in establishing Catholicism in Bohemia, in the victory over the Swedes at Nordlingen, in securing a favourable peace at Prague (1635), his successor was forced in the end to accept a settlement which finally destroyed all hope of restoring either imperial authority or religious unity in the empire. Germany remained divided into a Protestant north and a Catholic south, with the lower Rhineland, however, more definitely Catholic.   The Imperial Diet was henceforth to be divided into two bodies, a Catholic and a Protestant, for religious matters.   And outside Germany the star of the Spanish Habsburgs, the former champions of the old faith, had almost burnt itself out. France, its successful rival, had finally won recognition of her ownership of the former German bishoprics of Metz, Toul, and Verdun, as well as of parts of Alsace. Sweden had taken western Pomerania and Bremen. The separation of Switzerland and Holland from the empire was formally recognized.

Much of this suggests that by 1648 whatever of religion there had been in the origins of the war had disappeared. Certainly the French intervention on the Protestant side, arranged by a cardinal of the Catholic Church, Richelieu, showed how national and dynastic interests had come to override religious affiliations. Even the Pope on one occasion denied that the war was a religious one; he later protested against the settlement. But the religious factor must not be forgotten in Germany itself, and the permanence of the confessional division between north and south had profound effects on every side of German life through the succeeding centuries. True, the differences between Prussia and Bavaria (to take the outstanding examples of Protestant and Catholic faith in modern Germany) were not due solely or perhaps even primarily to religion. It can indeed be argued that the difference of religion was itself the result and expression of deep and abiding divergence between the two. But whether effect or cause, or both, the confessional difference long contributed materially to separate north and south, to colour their respective political views and loyalties, to affect their cultural outlook and expression and indeed their lives from cradle to grave, in a wide variety of ways.

Yet in certain important respects the political pattern of the Germany which emerged from the long struggle of the Reformation era did not differ so markedly from north to south. Both Catholic and Protestant Germany had exhibited the same trend towards the weakening of the imperial power and the unity of the empire, had pursued the same goal of princely independence. It was a sign of their success that the empire as a whole was not even represented in the peace negotiations which ended the Thirty Years War. The Imperial Diet remained, indeed, but any hopes of its development into a real national assembly had faded completely and finally. It continued to meet, and since the Diet which met at Regensburg in 1663 was never dissolved, it became a permanent body. But that was rather a symbol of weakness than of strength. The princes no longer attended in person, but sent representatives, rather as ambassadors. Nor did the *Reichstag* display any particular desire to support the emperor, who had tried to make it subserve Habsburg ends and to reduce its position. Only for the smaller states of the south-west did it retain any real importance. They made attempts to organize defence against the French danger through it, using the old Circles, and the greatest German thinker of the century, Leibnitz, put forward in 1670 proposals of his own to the same end. But the attempt met with little support from the greater princes, and failed to provide protection against the French invader towards the end of the century. The Imperial Supreme Court at Speier to 1689, then at Wetzlar, likewise declined steadily in importance despite attempts at its reform and revival. The

Osnabrück, late seventeenth century

Wesel, late seventeenth century

Bremen, sixteenth century.   The buildings labelled, not in High German, but in the local
Platt-deutsch dialect

TYPICAL NORTH GERMAN TOWNS

princes strove to evade its jurisdiction, the emperor made more use of a rival court, the *Reichshofrat* or Aulic Council, in Vienna. To the inquiring mind of Puffendorf, the greatest German authority on legal historical matters in the later seventeenth century, the empire seemed a monstrosity, and indeed it had something of the appearance, and the qualities, of an antediluvian survivor of the flood-tides of revolution and war. The active political life of the country was to be found elsewhere, most obviously in the major principalities which were now rising to their height.

The rise of the chief territorial states to almost complete sovereignty was in fact the outstanding political result of the era of the Reformation. It had begun before Luther as we have seen, and it proceeded, despite interruptions by temporary resurgences of imperial authority, to secure full recognition in the settlement of 1648. For by its terms the states were given the right to make their own alliances and conduct their own foreign policies, subject only to the proviso that these were not to be against emperor or *Reich*. The rulers of Bavaria, Brandenburg, Saxony, and Wurtemberg had made gains in territory, and Bavaria at last had won an electoral seat. The long wars and the inevitable emphasis on military power had strengthened their position and weakened that of the scattered and divided cities, who with the peasantry had been the worst sufferers from devastation and rapine. Their states were becoming more consolidated by the abandonment of the old division of their lands at death, in favour of the succession of a single heir. We have already seen how the religious settlement had given them new powers, primarily in the Protestant states but reflected also in Catholic ones. And this implied not merely control over the Church and matters formerly in the hands of the Church, such as education and social conditions, but also an enhanced idea of their position as the representatives of God, shading into a Divine Right to absolute rule.

For princely sovereignty did not merely imply independence of the emperor, it also meant to a steadily increasing extent autocratic rule over their subjects. That too was growing before the Reformation, but it developed further both before and after 1648. An obvious sign of this was the growth during the sixteenth century in the larger principalities of the machinery of government and administration, of princely councils, of bodies of officials charged with judicial and financial work. This process brought in many cases the absorption of the lower nobility into the services of the greater princely houses. The legislative activities and powers of the princes were enlarged by concessions wrung from the emperors at elections (*Wahl-kapitulationen*), or taken over from the weakening hands of the Imperial Diet (e.g. in the raising of levies for war against the Turks), or simply assumed as part of the princely duties. But this in many cases involved conflict with the local Estates, which claimed joint legislative rights with the prince, at least in matters involving taxation. The rights and constitutional position of these local Estates naturally varied from state to state, and the story of their relations with the respective princes similarly differed in detail over the period. But in general the whole era, and particularly the years of

B

warfare, showed a steady decline of their powers and influences, and a corresponding increase in princely authority. The Estates did not disappear, and in some cases, as in Wurtemberg, could continue to put up a stiff fight against princely efforts at encroachment on their rights. Yet such opposition was in general on behalf of a particular local class, nobles or burgesses, rather than for the people as a whole, and scarcely relieved the general stagnation of political life in the individual states as in the *Reich*. The Estates and princes of Germany found their model not in the evolving parliamentary struggle in England, but in the nearer and more splendid absolutism of France. From there, after the Thirty Years War, the court of Louis XIV at Versailles provided them with their models of government, of court life, as of manners and morals. In this the smaller states aped the larger ones, elevating their titles, pretensions, and extravagances, with as little regard to the realities of power as to the interests of their subjects. For Germany as a whole it was a sad outcome of a period which had begun with such promise and such effort.

On the economic and social life of Germany the period as a whole had likewise unfortunate results. There seemed at first no reason why this should be so. Germany was prosperous, both absolutely and relatively to her neighbours, when the period opened. The Reformation represented an outburst of new energy, and Protestantism, with its emphasis on individuality, seemed peculiarly fitted to harmonize with the economic changes of the age, its encouragement of commercial enterprise, its development and use of capital in finance, in industry, in trade. It had its share in those impulses to which so much, perhaps too much, has been attributed by Weber and his disciples in the growth of the modern capitalistic system. And for a time cities and citizens of Germany, more especially south-German cities such as Augsburg and Nürnberg, did continue to grow in wealth and importance. The outstanding example of the new capitalists was, of course, the Augsburg house of Fugger, the Rothschilds of the sixteenth century, who from earlier profits in the textile industry and trade added ownership of the mines of Tyrol, became the bankers of the Emperor Charles V and other princes, had enterprises and agents all over Europe, and engaged largely and for a time profitably in the Spanish trade with the New World. They were by no means the only capitalists or international bankers of Augsburg, but so outstanding were they that they could be described as 'the glory of Germany.'

The second half of the sixteenth century saw a change, however. Some of the causes for this had been at work for some time, and have already been referred to in speaking of the general conditions of Germany when the Reformation opened. But their effects were now more evident, especially when conjoined with other factors. The rise of national sentiment in such countries as France and England had already hurt the fortunes of the Hansa towns. Now emerged a new nation, Holland, in control of the mouth of the Rhine and trading into the Baltic. This, with the fall of the great port of Antwerp through which they had done much of their trade and business, hindered the outlet for the main trade route, the Rhine, while at the other end of that route the decline of Venice and the old connection through the Mediterranean with the east brought a parallel loss. And the new routes overseas were being exploited by rival nations, with easier access to the Atlantic and a new spirit of economic enterprise unmatched in Germany. The connection with Spain ceased to be profitable as Spain fell into decline, and the Spanish kings proved bad debtors. The vast fortunes of the Fuggers largely disappeared, and this was symptomatic of the economic decay of the formerly bustling and prosperous German cities.

The religious wars of the sixteenth century had hindered trade, but the long war and foreign invasions of the early seventeenth had far more devastating results. The extent of the damage has been the subject of much controversy, and the older view of complete or widespread depopulation and destruction, generalizing from contemporary and often local accounts, and attributing to the war the results of forces at work before it began, has been modified by later research. Whether Germany really lost eight millions of population (from twenty-one to thirteen) immediately as a result of the war, seems doubtful, unless we take into account the territories formally separated at the Peace (e.g. Holland and Switzerland). But it is obvious enough that the war disrupted trade, destroyed or damaged certain cities, ravaged the countryside, destroyed resources, involved many cities in debt, and was in general most harmful to the economic life of the country. The populations of Wurtemberg and Thuringia sank to a fifth of their size; the sack of Magdeburg in 1631 was but the most outstanding example of the damage done to many other German cities.

The cities and the peasantry indeed bore the main burden of suffering in the war, as they were least able to defend themselves from foreign or imperial armies, and it was their economic position which was most obviously worsened by it. The free Imperial Cities did not disappear, but they did not recover their former economic or political importance, save in a few instances such as Hamburg; in economic as in political life the initiative passed to the territorial state, to be exercised in accordance with the doctrines of the new faith of Mercantilism. The peasantry had seen their villages burnt, their crops seized or destroyed. Some of them had grasped the opportunity to escape from serfdom, but with the return of peace laws were passed, as in Saxony, to compel their return, and there was no lightening of the yoke which the reaction after their revolt in 1525 had fastened more securely on their shoulders. Thus the era of the Reformation as a whole saw a worsening rather than a betterment of their condition for a time.

The continuance of serfdom was in conformity with the continuance of the social stratification marked in Germany at the close of the Middle Ages. Here indeed the Reformation era and the Thirty Years War brought not more change or freedom but rather increased rigidity. That, like so much else, was bound up with the triumph of territorialism. The princes and the nobility surrounding them and dependent upon their favour tended to form a caste, delicately graded and distinguished in the most meticulous degree by honours and privileges, above all by titles, forming a pyramid with the princes at the top, and descending through the nobility to the burgesses, to rest at its bottom on the tillers of the soil.   While the system was influenced by the example of French society of the *ancien régime*, it was less elastic and, as events showed, more lasting.   Here, no doubt, as in other matters, the influence of the rising star of Prussia must be taken into account.   But it was more general than merely Prussian in character.   And it was much more than a subject for easy ridicule, for it played an important part in hindering the social and political development of Germany through the seventeenth and eighteenth centuries, and into the nineteenth, despite the shocks given to it by both the French and the Industrial Revolutions.

The cultural life of Germany immediately before the Reformation may be regarded as running in two main though partly connected channels.   On the one hand there was the growing humanist movement, much indebted to Italy, marked by the zest for learning, the study of the ancient languages both in and outside the universities, led by men like Reuchlin, Celtis, and Hutten, with the great figure of Erasmus in the offing.   On the other was the more popular and more purely native growth primarily associated with the rich and colourful life of the cities at the height of their prosperity, especially those of the south and west.   This was expressed rather in architecture and the arts than in literature, with the invention and spread of printing and engraving as characteristic.   Very properly it was the most outstanding of these cities, Nürnberg, 'the eye and ear of Germany' as Luther called it, that produced the incomparable genius of Albrecht Dürer, Germany's greatest painter, who by his debt to Italian painting shows the connection between the two channels, but in his religiosity and his versatile mastery of craftsmanship illustrates the highest qualities of German civic life at this time.   And in a more general way Dürer may be taken as an example of the heights reached by German cultural achievement before the storm of the Reformation engulfed the country.   When he died in 1528, Luther himself said of him prophetically that he was happy since 'Christ had taken him in the midst of this time of trouble and from greater troubles to come.'

The Reformation, and the controversies and wars that followed, inevitably affected profoundly the whole cultural life of Germany, and in many respects for the worse.   One service, indeed, Luther performed for all Germany. His writings, and above all his translation of the Bible, created a common German language for writing, a vehicle for a national literature to come. But, apart from that, the division of the country into two parts checked the flow of cultural interchange and increased the existing cultural differences between north and south, cutting off the former from the Italian and Catholic influences which had played so great a part in the past.

In the long run, the Reformation was to foster religious toleration.   But for the time being it exercised a narrowing effect, not merely in religion but in most aspects of cultural life.   While this was true of both sides in the struggle, it was most obvious at first in Protestantism, where the preoccupation with the new way to salvation, with theology, dogma, and counter-dogma,

became all absorbing.   If the heavens were opened, part of the earthly scene
was closed.   Humanism suffered, so that Erasmus could declare that where
Lutheranism reigned, culture perished.   Lutheran vehemence and Calvinistic
rigidity were both extremely intolerant, and not merely in matters of faith,
though Germany was spared the excesses of Geneva.   This narrowing and
intolerance was not, of course, confined to Germany, but it was more marked
and continued longer there, so that its results were more serious.   As Germany was shut off from the New World now opening to the western European
nations, so did her absorption in the religious struggle tend to lessen her
interest and her share in the intellectual activities of the modern western
world during a critical creative period, since the necessary freedom was lacking.
The single genius, such as Kepler, could rise superior to circumstances, but
in general the atmosphere was inimical to speculation or creative thought,
to great literature or great art.   Apart from the vigour of Luther's or other
theological writings, no great literature was produced in Germany during
this period.   The reputation of Opitz, with his reforms of versification during
the Thirty Years War, was largely due to the paucity of rivals.   There was
little room for the encouragement of art, so that Holbein was driven to
England to find a livelihood, and art in Germany, like literature, suffered a
steady decline.   The thought of the one German philosopher of the period,
Böhme (d. 1624), was mainly compounded (if not confounded) of Protestant
theology.

The attitude of the time in Germany to the new astronomy, and to witches,
furnish illustration of the temper of the time.   When Copernicus on his
deathbed in 1543 published his new theory of cosmology, making the sun
instead of the earth the centre of the universe, Luther, Melanchthon, and
Calvin all in turn condemned it.   The Catholic Church, if more cautious
or less concerned for a time, later repudiated it, burnt Bruno, and drove
Galileo to recantation.   In fairness to Lutheranism it should be added that
some of the earliest adherents to the new scientific faith were Lutherans.
And Kepler of Wurtemberg was a Lutheran parson, though suspected of
Calvinist leanings, who was driven from his university of Grätz by Catholic
persecution, to find under a tolerant emperor the freedom to justify and
round out with his own discoveries the work of his two great predecessors,
Copernicus and Tycho Brahe.   The monstrous wave of witch-hunting which
spread over all Europe in the second half of the sixteenth century reached its
height in Germany, with both Protestants and Catholics sharing in the
responsibility for sending thousands of innocent victims to torture and death
in a single year, nearly a thousand in one Catholic bishopric alone, of both
sexes and all ages from infancy to old age.   It was a tragic commentary
on the age.

Yet the cultural picture of Reformation and Counter-Reformation
Germany was not all dark.   Luther loved music, and by his love of it,
enshrined in his hymns and made an essential part of the Lutheran religious
service, he helped to develop the art of sacred music in Germany.   And this,
through the later hymns of Gerhardt, was carried on to the day of Sebastian

Bach.   More obviously important was the contribution of the Reformation to education.   Luther early appreciated the need for schools to train the young in the new faith and to prepare pastors for the flock.   'Good schools,' he wrote in 1524, 'are the tree from which grows all good conduct in life.' Under his urgings and influence new schools were set up in Saxony and elsewhere in Protestant Germany.   The State now took over this earlier function of the Church, sometimes applying confiscated church funds therefor, and in these new State high schools religion and the classics were the main subjects of study.   Under Melanchthon's influence six new universities were founded in Protestant Germany, Marburg and Jena the chief, these also dependent on princely authority.

Thus the Reformation fostered schooling, at any rate for the middle and higher classes, and the Counter-Reformation followed its example.   For the Jesuits similarly attached great importance to educational work, and from the foundation of the German College in Rome (1552) they set about the establishment of schools and colleges in Germany.   Ingolstadt became as important for the Counter-Reformation as Wittenberg had earlier become for Luther's work.   With extraordinary skill they adapted their methods to the problem of combining sound general education with the inculcation or revival of the Catholic faith, and the results rewarded their labours.   Nor was this their sole contribution to the cultural life of Germany, for it was they who imported from Italy the 'Jesuit' or baroque style of architecture. Adapting itself to German soil it became deeply rooted in the cities and countryside of Catholic Germany.   Classical and Renaissance in origin and outward form, its exuberance of decoration and colour in the interiors of its churches was in marked contrast to Lutheran and Calvinist simplicity.

Yet neither educational efforts nor baroque architecture could save the country from the dire effects of the Thirty Years War, which, however we may estimate its results, could not but be harmful to the cultural as to the political and economic life of the country.   Grimmelshausen's story *Simplicissimus* may be exaggerated in its details, but its general picture certainly contains much that is true of the vagabondage and lawless conditions that prevailed over large parts of the empire during the war, and such conditions were necessarily unfavourable to the arts of peace.   We may admire the way in which the lawyer-scientist Guericke, driven out of Magdeburg after its devastation in 1631 to become a soldier, returned to his native city both to aid in its restoration and to pursue his fruitful researches in physics.   But individual examples such as his, or that of Kepler, and indeed others, cannot negate the general conclusion both about the period of the war itself, nor for some time after.   Nor was the triumph of territorialism, in and after the war, making the local princes the arbiters not merely of peace and war, of justice and well-being, but of religion and education, of manners and taste, necessarily favourable in general to cultural life, since so much depended on the individual and the local circumstances.

Two general changes of importance in the cultural life of Germany may be remarked as having been fostered by the religious strife, although other forces in the whole period also had their effect. There was in the first place a gradual but steady shift in what has been termed the cultural centre of gravity in Germany, away from the south and west towards the north and east. The focusing of the Reformation itself in Saxon Wittenberg was significant; and it was Leipzig, the later rival and successor to Wittenberg as the cultural centre of Saxony, that gave birth to Leibnitz, just as the Thirty Years War was drawing to a close. The Habsburg city of Vienna had never been the real capital of the empire, but for long the cultural leadership of Germany had centred in the cities of the south and west, where indeed most of the Diets had been held, and where the medieval empire had reached its height in Hohenstauffen days. Now, not merely had Saxony given leadership, but Brandenburg-Prussia began to exert more influence, Silesia to play a part, and Hamburg to emerge as a cultural centre in a way the old Hansa had never done. The old supremacy of the south and west was over, and was not to return. A Goethe might be born there, but he was to find a career elsewhere for his talents. And Weimar was on the way to Berlin.

The other broad cultural development associated with the post-Reformation period was a marked increase in foreign and more particularly French cultural and indeed general influence in and upon Germany. Such foreign influences had, of course, always played their part in Germany, as elsewhere, for good or ill, or both. French influence in the Middle Ages had in part given way to Italian influence at the time of the Renaissance. Charles V had brought Flemish and Spanish influences in his train, and the rise of Spain to its height in the latter part of the sixteenth century had been reflected in Germany in fashions in dress, in military life, in social habits. North Germany had felt the influence of both Flemish and the rising Dutch national spirit in architecture. French influence was revived through Burgundy as through Calvinism, and German travel to France increased it. And when Germany lay open to Europe in the division and weakness of the Thirty Years War it was above all the French influence and the example of its increasingly splendid monarchy, which became all important for the German princes and their courts, for the manners and morals of polite society, for language and literature, even for thought, reaching its height in the eighteenth century.

German nationalists of a later age, from the Romantics on, girded at this Gallic influence, blaming it for the backwardness, weakness, or vices of German society in the seventeenth and eighteenth centuries. Certainly the French influence was not all good, particularly when transferred to the petty stages of the minor principalities of Germany, and expressed in a dissolute court life. But difficult, indeed impossible, as it is to strike a final balance in the measurement of the influence of one nation or culture upon another, it is probably true to say that the civilizing effects of French culture in Germany far outweighed the less desirable results.[1] We cannot tell how

[1] F. Paulsen, in his history of German university education (*Geschichte des gelehrten Unterrichts auf den deutschen Schulen und Universitäten*, 1885, p. 339), asserts that the excessive drinking at German courts, and later in the universities, was reduced by French example.

Germany would have fared without it, but there seems no reason to believe that she would have emerged of herself more quickly or more fortunately from the low estate in which the long struggle of her religious wars left her.

For the tragedy of the Reformation era in Germany was not so much that it ended in subjection to foreign influences, not that it did not remain German enough. Rather was it that it was in a sense *too* German. It helped to prevent a natural evolution towards a greater degree of national unity when such unity might have been attained by less violent means than were finally to be employed by Bismarck. It ended what hopes there were of evolving any widely based political life. It crystallized and hardened trends already in existence, whether towards the triumph of territorial autocracy or the perpetuation of social regimentation. And it was accompanied by a century and a half of civil strife which had deplorable effects on economic and cultural conditions. Thus it prepared the way for many of the significant developments of later German history. The first and not least of these, the rise of Prussia, was already under way when the period closed, and the rise of Prussia was the key to many things in the German future.

CHAPTER II

THE RISE OF PRUSSIA—I (TO 1713)

Introductory — Brandenburg — East Prussia — The Great Elector—
King Frederick I

I. INTRODUCTORY

THE STATE of Prussia affords the prime example of the rise and triumph of the principle of territorial sovereignty in Germany through and' after the Reformation period. Composed of three separate parts, Brandenburg, Prussia proper, and Rhenish Prussia, it was in the later part of this period, immediately before the Thirty Years War, that these parts were drawn together under the central rule of Brandenburg and its Hohenzollern princes. (The title of Prussia as applied to the whole came later, when in 1701 the emperor agreed that the Elector of Brandenburg should assume the title of King, but from a province outside the bounds of the empire.) Thus Prussia, and even Brandenburg-Prussia before the monarchy, was a modern not a medieval creation, and since each of its parts had its own history and traditions, much effort was required to weld them together into one state. It is true that the two eastern and more dominant portions, Brandenburg and Prussia proper, had similar origins as border and colonial areas, and that all three parts were spread along that northern European plain stretching from Flanders far into Russia. But Rhineland Prussia had its own long, deep, rich traditions and local connections, whilst even the eastern provinces had centuries of separate existence behind them ere they were joined together under one rule. And any geographical likeness between the parts was partly offset by the lack of natural frontiers, although this was a factor which could be turned to advantage when the state was ready for expansion, and when opportunity offered (as in the decline of Poland) for the incorporation of lands dividing the separate parts of the kingdom. Further, the very effort required to hold the lands together developed certain qualities of organization and military strength which were to be fundamental and characteristic of Prussia. We are not here concerned with the details of the earlier, or indeed the later, history of the separate units of the future kingdom, but it is necessary to refer briefly to the origins and growth of the various parts, in order to appreciate their local position and problems, their special developments, and their contribution to and place in the unified state.

II. BRANDENBURG

The central and most important part of the future Prussian state was the province of Brandenburg, in origin a border region, a *Mark* or March, first sketched out by Charles the Great, but defined more clearly by Otto I as the North Mark (later the Old Mark) along the lower Elbe. Its eastern limits were necessarily vague in the flat lands of the lake, marsh, and forest where

29

flowed the Spree and the Havel rivers, and further east to the Oder, where the Slavic Wends lived a pastoral, semi-nomadic life. The Nordmark as a political unit emerges more clearly when Albert the Bear, from Ballenstedt in the region of the Harz mountains, became its ruler in 1134. For Albert was both one of the outstanding figures in twelfth-century Germany, the rival and enemy of Henry the Lion, and the founder of a line of rulers in the Nordmark, the Ascanian line, which was to last there for nearly two hundred years (to 1320). During that time these Ascanian dukes absorbed or supplanted the Wends, and introduced colonists from the Rhineland and the Netherlands, peasants and townsfolk, with a sprinkling of nobility. They extended the eastern limits of their rule across what came to be known as the Ukermark to the Oder, and even into Pomerania, as well as south-east into Lusatia. Under their rule the land gradually became Germanized (though Slavic elements remained), with small towns such as Brandenburg and Berlin-Coelln, bishoprics and abbeys, villages and widespread farm lands. As border rulers they were more independent of imperial or other outside authority, and for a time kept a firm grip on their subjects. Their growing importance was recognized when in the thirteenth century they became accepted as Electors to the imperial throne, the highest rank amongst the German princes. But in their later years their rule weakened, their towns began to assert themselves, and there was a beginning of organized provincial Estates.

The fourteenth century saw the end of the Ascanian line and a further decline of the Electorate. The formerly promising margravate fell into a 'time of troubles' which threatened to break up its lands, reduce its shrinking remains to anarchy, and completely destroy the work of the earlier Ascanian rulers. During this period Brandenburg lost territory to the north-east and south-east. It became an apanage first of the Wittelsbachs of Bavaria, then of the house of Luxemburg. A few years of firmer rule under the outstanding emperor of that house, Charles IV, were followed by years of divided sovereignty, misrule, and neglect under his sons. Finally, the last of these, Emperor Sigismund, handed over the margravate to a faithful supporter, Frederick of Hohenzollern, who was invested as Elector of Brandenburg in 1417. The date marked the beginning of a new era in the history of Brandenburg.

The importance of the change took some time to appear, however. In the swirling confusion of feudalized Germany the Hohenzollerns were of no special importance. Frederick's branch of this Swabian family had been imperial representatives (Burggraves) in the Free City of Nürnberg, and therefrom had managed to build up a heritage of lands round Ansbach and Bayreuth in eastern Franconia. Frederick (of Ansbach) had attached his fortunes to those of Sigismund, had fought for him, saved his life in battle, played a crucial part in Sigismund's election as emperor, and rendered him outstanding service at the Council of Constance. Now he had his reward. But the new Elector had no intention of burying himself in the rude and remote forests of the north, and when hopes of wider advancement were disappointed he withdrew from the Mark to end his days in the gentler Ansbach. Yet it was worthy of note that in this age, when national states were emerging more plainly in western Europe under monarchical rule, a new dynasty should establish itself in northern Germany, and this at a time when the empire, despite the efforts of Sigismund, was about to fall into irremediable decay.

It was the first successor of Frederick of Ansbach, Elector Frederick II, who really began to identify his line with the Mark. As he put it: 'My father had many lands; I have but one.' So he set about making that one into an orderly principality. He restored princely authority over both nobles and towns, subjugated Berlin and made it his capital, and held the pretensions of the Church in check, making his own concordat with the Papacy. No less important, he began to extend the boundaries of his Electorate. 'All Hohenzollerns,' remarked Bismarck once to his more reluctant master, 'have been enlargers of the State,' and this Frederick set the pattern by recovering the New Mark lost to the Teutonic Order, adding lands in lower Lusatia, nibbling at Mecklenburg and Pomerania to the north. His successor Albert Achilles in turn continued the nibbling, being indeed, says the historian of Prussia,[1] 'the most quarrelsome German prince of his day.' This third Brandenburg Hohenzollern also made a famous decree: that Brandenburg was to go to the first-born, and that it was not to be divided. The decree marked a step in the evolution of the Electorate towards a state and in its separation from Hohenzollern lands in southern Germany.

The age of the Renaissance and the Reformation was one of growth for the Electorate, with both profit and loss for its rulers. Brandenburg was hardly a friendly or fruitful soil as yet for the intellectual or artistic movement of the time, despite the high-sounding title of Cicero later bestowed upon the last Elector of the fifteenth century. Nor had the two Joachims who successively ruled Brandenburg during the crisis of the Reformation any claims to leadership in that movement. The first won the opprobrious title of 'Father of all Avarice' for his unscrupulous readiness to be bought by both of the contestants in the imperial election of 1519 in turn. In the end he voted for Charles V, and supported his policy against Luther. But he was mainly concerned with his own local interests, repressing disorders, adding a little territory, fostering the study of Roman law as advantageous to his rule. Nor did the second Joachim, weaker in mind and will, make any change in religious policy for a time.

The new faith was, however, bound to spread into Brandenburg from adjacent Saxony, borne on the waters of their common river, the Elbe. The Brandenburgers displayed, said Melanchthon, 'a wondrous thirst for the pure doctrine,' and in the end Joachim II entered the Lutheran camp, though he refused to join any Protestant alliance against the emperor. He found profit in the greater control he could exercise over the new Church and in the gain of episcopal lands; the wealthy archbishopric of Magdeburg, of the greatest strategic and economic importance, became a dependency of the

[1] H. Prutz, *Preussische Geschichte*, vol. i, p. 161.

Electorate, to be absorbed in due course.   His successor was a more ardent
adherent of the new faith, and under him the Electorate both escaped the
controversies which the Counter-Reformation was reviving elsewhere and
began to emerge as the leading Protestant state in the empire in succession
to Saxony.   At the same time, however, the authority of the Electors was
being weakened in their own land by the growing claims of the local Estates,
now rising to the height of their importance, and taking advantage of princely
extravagance and consequent financial embarrassment to assert themselves.
At the same time the nobility were tightening their grip over the peasantry.

The Electress Magdalene of Brandenburg,   The Electress Hedwig of Brandenburg,
       first consort of Joachim II   second consort of Joachim II

   The early seventeenth century brought some improvement in the fortunes
of the Electors.   Still straitened at home, they won two pieces of territory
abroad, which were to be of immense importance in the future.   To the
west, after lengthy and tedious controversies, Elector John Sigismund secured
by the convention of Xanten (1614) the Duchy of Kleve, the Counties of
Mark and Ravensberg, and the lordship of Ravenstein, i.e. a hold on the
lower Rhine.   To the east the same Elector entered into the heritage of
Prussia (1619).   Likewise important for the future were two more domestic
events of this same period.   One was the organization in 1604 of a privy
council which was to become an instrument for electoral authority and the
centralization of power.   The other was the turn of the Electors to the
Reformed (Calvinist) faith, done partly with an eye on the Kleve-Jülich
succession, but a breach with their Lutheran subjects, and duly protested
against.   Yet that too was to bring its profit, and not merely on the Rhine.
For from it there came a degree of religious toleration novel at that time,
whereby Brandenburg-Prussia was to become a land of asylum to the persecuted in Germany, and indeed more widely.   It required, however, a

greater figure than any of the Electors of the sixteenth or the early seventeenth century to take advantage of these changes; that was to be the work of the Great Elector, Frederick William I, who ranks with Frederick II and Bismarck among the makers of Prussian history.

III. EAST PRUSSIA (PRUSSIA PROPER)

The conquest of Prussia, the region east of the lower Vistula where the southern shores of the Baltic begin to curve northwards, by the crusading German or Teutonic Order in the thirteenth century was the most dramatic episode in the eastward expansion of the German people. It did not indeed stand alone: apart from the growth of Brandenburg itself, the push along the Baltic coast was already taking German traders further and further east to tap the resources of Lithuania and Russia, whether by the activities of the emerging Hansa, or the particular efforts which led to the founding of Riga (1201), Reval, and Dorpat. But the work of the Teutonic Order, absorbing the earlier Knights of the Sword, had a more organized and unified quality; the historian Marcks [1] calls it the greatest achievement of medieval Germany. Like the work of the Hansa it was accomplished independently of the support of the emperor or any of the greater princes of Germany, though the land won was later to be absorbed by one of these, and indeed was to give its name of Prussia to the resultant monarchy. And the gain of Prussia was to strengthen that monarchy in its military and aristocratic quality, and in its emphasis on the State.

The Teutonic Order was in its origin a crusading hospital Order driven out of the Holy Land by the rising tide of Saracenic conquest, and finding in the unoffending but heathen Prussians opportunity for Christian missionary work nearer home. But from its first entry into the coastal area east of the Vistula the Christianizing motive seems to sink into the swamps abounding there; and the de-heathenized Prussian fishermen, shepherds, and bee-keepers, after bitter resistance found themselves serfs at best, slaves (Slavs) in social position as they were in race. That was not unique in such efforts. What was more remarkable was the rapid emergence of the 'Order-State,' based on the organization of knight-monks under the elected Grand Master; the seat of the Order was transferred to Prussian Marienburg from Venice in 1309. The relatively few knightly members of the Order were established as local administrators, forming an aristocratic caste, warriors but still under a monkish rule. These were joined by a trickle of nobles from Germany and elsewhere seeking fame and fortune. And no less important was a large flow of colonists proper, peasants and townsfolk from western Germany, many of whom settled in villages which quickly grew into small towns. Thus Kulm, Thorn, Marienburg, the central fortress, Koenigsberg, and Memel, were all established and given civic privileges by about the middle of the thirteenth century, but all under central control, and all subject to military service in this military state.

[1] *Ostdeutschland in der deutschen Geschichte*, 1920, p. 19.

Thus organized, the Teutonic Order preserved enough of its original impetus to expand still further through the fourteenth century. Without perceptible stop it pushed its dominion up the east coast of the Baltic as far as the Gulf of Finland, while to the west of the Vistula it won Pomerelia (the later West Prussia), and even acquired the New Mark from Brandenburg. It reached out into the Baltic with its ships to win possession of the island of Gothland. Its agriculture prospered, it undertook the draining of swamps, the finances of the Order flourished from the profits of the trade it carried on, free in this matter from the restraints generally imposed on monastic orders. Its cities, now including Danzig, shared in the profits of the Hanseatic League. Although there were bishoprics within its lands exempt from the jurisdiction of the Order, its fusion of Church and State made it largely independent of papal control. Under Winrich von Kniprode, Grand Master from 1351 to 1382, the Order-State reached the peak of its power.

From that peak, however, the Order was soon to decline, and that swiftly and permanently. There was something incongruous, at all events outside the Mediterranean, in the spectacle of a religious Order establishing not merely a state but a military state; and that incongruity became more evident as the modern age emerged. The Order itself plainly showed the marks of secularizing influences, and the discrepancy between vows of monastic asceticism and a life of baronial privilege and even luxury weakened the Order itself and fostered criticism of its rule both within Prussia and outside. Like its neighbour the Hansa, the Order did little for cultural advancement. The townsfolk of Prussia resented its trading activities and monopolies; serfs and nobles not members of the Order alike suffered from its closed aristocratic rule. Outside, political changes were taking place in the Baltic area, as the Hansa was finding to its cost. The Teutonic Order had expanded into lands claimed by both Lithuania and Poland. Now Lithuania became Christian, which took away an excuse for conquering it, and was joined to Poland under the Jagellonian kings, forming a Slav ring round a large part of the Order's lands. Tension between Poland and the Order was followed by war, and in the battle of Tannenberg (1410) the Order's successes of nearly two hundred years were wiped out. The legend of the invincibility of the Knights of the Order was destroyed in what Treitschke (in Bismarck's day) described as 'the first great victory gained by the Slavs over our people.' [1] Nor was this the end. Internal strife continued within the Ordensland, accompanied by economic decay, and from without Polish pressure increased until after a second and long-drawn-out war (1454–66) the Order was reduced to a vassal state of the kingdom of Poland, to which state it also lost West Prussia and Danzig. The day of the Order was over, its power broken, and the Slav had inflicted what seemed a decisive defeat to German expansion eastward along the Baltic coast.

The sixteenth and early seventeenth centuries, however, brought a number of developments which modified the situation, and were to decide the fortunes of Prussia (or East Prussia, as it became) for the next three centuries.

[1] *Das deutsche Ordensland, Preussen, Ausgewählte Schriften*, p. 106.

First came the transformation of the Order-State into a secular principality. By treaty with Poland (1525) the Order was suppressed in Prussia, its black cross was replaced by a black eagle, and the last Grand Master there became the first Duke of Prussia, though still the premier vassal of Poland. And this Duke of Prussia was a Hohenzollern, kin to the rulers of Brandenburg. Next came the change by which Prussia adopted the Lutheran faith. Thereby a link was forged between Prussia and the other north German Protestant states, a link which became of greater importance when the victory of the Counter-Reformation in Poland added the difference of religion to that of race between this kingdom and its Prussian vassal. Last and most important was the union of Prussia with Brandenburg. This took place in 1618, when the male line of the dukes of Prussia died out, and by virtue of a family arrangement made half a century earlier the Electors of Brandenburg succeeded to the province which they had long hoped to secure. The union marked a new era not merely in the history of the former crusading state but, most importantly, in that of Brandenburg itself, thus enlarged in the very year of the opening of the Thirty Years War, its eastern frontier now deep in the land of the Slavs.

IV. THE GREAT ELECTOR, FREDERICK WILLIAM

It was a calamity for the newly enlarged Brandenburg-Prussia that during most of the long and momentous Thirty Years War, from 1619 to 1640, the Electorate was ruled over by a prince who by general agreement was one of the least able of the long line of Brandenburg rulers. For George William, though well meaning, was weak, and left too much of the conduct of affairs in these critical years to his ministers, above all to the greedy, Catholic, and pro-Austrian Schwarzenberg. True, he showed a willingness unusual amongst Hohenzollerns to consult the local Estates, but this proved hardly a help in time of war. His general desire and policy was to avoid being drawn into the conflict. But this from the beginning was difficult, and it became impossible as the scale of the conflict widened and the Baltic powers were drawn in. Especially was this true when Sweden, under its able and ambitious ruler Gustavus Adolphus, entered the conflict, since Brandenburg lay directly in his path to the heart of Germany. And George William lacked the military strength and resources to hold his frontiers either to north or to south.

The result was that Brandenburg was invaded, plundered, and laid waste by both sides, by Wallenstein and Gustavus in turn. Driven then, after the dreadful sack of Magdeburg by the imperialists (1631) to take the Swedish side, the Elector was treated as a mere vassal, forced to find support for the Swedish armies, and to see his hopes of the promised succession to Pomerania (where the last of the reigning dukes had now died) challenged by the northern invader. Turning to the imperial side under Schwarzenberg's influence, after the death of Gustavus Adolphus, he found little relief or betterment of his position, as both sides pillaged his unhappy land with

almost equal impartiality. When he died in 1640 Brandenburg seemed to
have belied the hopes raised so recently by her accessions of territory to
east and west, and to have sunk back into a time of troubles comparable
to those of two hundred years earlier.

Thus it was to a weak and prostrated Electorate that the young Frederick
William, aged twenty, succeeded, to reign for forty-eight years. The population of the whole Electorate, small before, had shrunk to that of a good-sized
modern city, perhaps 600,000. The central province of Brandenburg had
suffered most, Prussia least. In Brandenburg both towns and country bore
the marks of pillage and destruction, the former reduced to half their size,
the latter in places wholly deserted. Food was so short that we even hear
of cannibalism. What remained of the Electorate's military forces was in a
state of complete demoralization, preying on the land as the foreign armies
had done. The resources of the government were almost non-existent.
Whilst most of Germany had suffered parallel damage, the south had suffered
less than the north, so that the position of the Electorate was relatively
worsened in the empire. And with such limited resources, its recuperation
promised to be a slow and difficult process, even when the war should come
to an end.

Frederick William's claim to the title of the Great Elector rests on the fact
that in the next half-century he successfully rebuilt his state, aided and
witnessed its restoration from the losses of the war, united its several parts,
fostered its economic development, equipped it with the best if not the
largest army in Germany, and made it the undisputed master in northern
Germany, the successor to Saxony as leader of the Protestant forces in the
empire, a serious rival to Austria, and a power to be reckoned with in Europe.
He is the one prince of the seventeenth century in Germany to be compared
with the other great European rulers of the age, with Richelieu and Louis XIV,
Cromwell and William of Orange, with Peter the Great of Russia, and this
despite the relatively small scale of his activities. Prussian patriotism of a
later age has sometimes exaggerated his achievements, trying to make of
him, what he was not, a national German figure. But he was, even above
Frederick the Great, the maker of Prussia.

His achievement was in part aided by circumstances. If Brandenburg-
Prussia was exhausted and poor, so was the rest of Germany. He had no
outstanding rival there, from the Habsburg emperors downwards; these had
the Turk still on their back, the rising Bourbon ascendancy to the west.
The Peace of 1648 finally established the sovereignty of the German princes
at the expense of both emperor and empire, and there was no rival state to
Brandenburg in northern Germany. Poland was in decline, and the threat
from Sweden, though still present and strong enough to prevent Frederick
William from gaining the desire of his heart, the possession of all Pomerania,
was in fact slowly diminishing. To the east, Russia was not yet ready to
cast her shadow over central Europe. And finally the Elector had nearly
half a century in which to carry out his work.

Undoubtedly the greatest asset the Elector possessed was his own character and personality.   Like Louis XI of France after the Hundred Years War, he was determined to restore, reunite, and add to his lands: everything was subordinated to that.   He was not a particularly attractive figure; he had little of geniality or broad human sympathy.   Like Frederick the Great he had a great distrust and suspicion of others.   The times were hard, and he shared some of their quality.   Family affection he had, and a steady religious (Calvinist) faith, which did not, however, prevent him from being unscrupulous in his diplomacy.   He firmly believed in the divine quality of his position as prince, the father of his people, and responsible to God.   But he was the judge of that responsibility, and though he used advisers, he made decisions himself, at times in opposition to their advice.   Of the popular will, or any share of the people in government, he had no thought, finding the claims of the Estates to control of taxation or other matters mere obstruction, to be evaded or destroyed.   He was ruthless in his persecution of those who opposed his will, as in the Estates of East Prussia.   Yet he was tolerant in religion, both to his Lutheran subjects and to others.   In the all-important matter of foreign policy he veered about just as much as his father had done. But he had learnt from bitter experience the dangers of trying to be neutral in a war in which his neighbours were engaged.   In such case, as he put it, 'even under the best conditions one is ill-treated.'   To remedy this and to serve his ends, he began the creation of the Prussian standing army, and led it himself in battle, finding there an outlet for a natural impetuosity held in check elsewhere by his iron will.

The first clear revelation of his character and aims, and of the tenacity with which he was to pursue them, came in the lengthy negotiations leading up to the Peace of 1648.   Freeing himself from the alliance with the emperor he played for his own hand, above all pushing his claims to Pomerania, promised to the Hohenzollerns by the last ruler of that wide-stretching Baltic duchy.   But Sweden was no less tenacious of her claims there, and since neither the emperor nor France saw any reason to favour the Elector's ambitions, in the end he had to content himself with the larger but less valuable Eastern Pomerania.   His claims to compensation elsewhere were also whittled down.   But he did well enough, winning the broad lands of the bishoprics of Halberstadt and Minden, and the promise of the larger Magdeburg when the administrator there died.   Minden on the river Weser was a valuable stepping-stone between Brandenburg and the Rhineland.   Less selfishly, Frederick William also worked for and won the recognition of Calvinist freedom alongside that of Lutheran and Catholic, gaining thereby the leadership of Protestantism in Germany.   All in all the Peace of Westphalia marked a very sensible increase of the position of Brandenburg-Prussia in the empire, the more marked since this same Peace signalized the defeat of Austria and of Spanish Habsburg ambitions along the Rhine.

The Peace of Westphalia hardly inaugurated a period of peace and quiet for Prussia.   Periods of peace there were in the forty years of life and rule that remained to the Elector, and they were used to good effect in the organization of his state.   But there were wars as well, into which he was drawn in part in defence, in part by his restless ambition to increase the power and extent of his Electorate. In East Prussia he sought to free himself from vassalship to Poland. For Brandenburg, Sweden's possession of Western Pomerania, with easy access to the heart of the Mark, was a constant irritation, so that Frederick William was even ready on one occasion to exchange his Rhenish lands therefor. Since those Rhenish possessions lay open to a French push eastwards, Holland was the natural ally for the Elector there. But although he was connected with the house of Orange by his marriage to the aunt of the future William III of England, he proved no ally to be counted upon. Within Germany his frontiers marched with those of many of the lesser princes, and he also was one of the eight electoral princes. But whilst he once declared that 'I am a true German, as it beseems an Elector of Brandenburg to be,' in practice he displayed little concern for the affairs of the *Reich*, save as they directly affected the interests of Brandenburg. For the Habsburgs he had as little love as they for him. The court at Vienna had no desire to see, as someone put it, a new Vandal kingdom arising in the north of Germany, and ever strove, in Puffendorf's phrase, to bridle the wild Brandenburg charger. And Frederick William responded by being ready, at one time, to support a French candidate to the imperial throne.

The twelve years immediately following the Peace of 1648 showed both the alternations of peace and war, and the oscillations of the Elector's alliances. He had seven years of peace, briefly interrupted by a vain attempt to push his claims on the Rhine, followed by five years of conflict in the first Northern War, between Sweden and Poland. Herein he fought first as the ally of Sweden against Poland, winning renown for himself and his small army in the victorious battle for Warsaw; and then by a complete turn as the ally of Poland against Sweden. By the Peace of Oliva (1660) he failed to win Swedish Pomerania as he hoped, but gained the freedom of the Duchy of Prussia from Poland. Henceforth Prussia was his in full sovereignty, and Brandenburg-Prussia began to emerge as a Baltic power, a rival to declining Sweden in that area, not yet disturbed by the appearance of a new rival to Baltic supremacy, Russia.

For the remainder of Frederick William's reign his main concern abroad was his relation to the rising tide of French ascendancy, now flowing north and east towards the Low Countries and the Rhine. Herein he followed a policy of shifts and twists which on the whole brought him little profit and less credit. For the most part he preferred to ally with France, getting solid subsidies and hoping for support for his own ends, but periodically he was driven into the opposite camp for a shorter or longer time. Thus he made a secret treaty with Louis XIV in 1669, disregarding the danger to Holland until the French swept through that country in 1672. Then he reversed his stand, but soon abandoned his Dutch ally to make a separate peace with France. Within a year, however, he was fighting alongside the imperial forces against France in Alsace, with little success, however, in part from the lack of unity between his own and the Austrian forces. The entry of Sweden into the war as an ally of France, and the Swedish invasion of the Mark, aroused him to more vigorous action nearer home. He defeated the Swedes in his greatest military success at Fehrbellin (1675), overran Swedish Pomerania, and drove the Swedes out of East Prussia in a hard midwinter campaign. Once again, however, he was thwarted in his desire to gain Swedish Pomerania, largely because France wished to preserve Swedish strength in the Baltic.

This did not prevent the Elector from turning again to make another treaty of alliance with Louis, in 1679, a treaty enlarged in the following years. For a time Berlin became the focal point of French domination in Germany, from which the French ambassador, Rebenac, exercised his master's influence through the *Reich*. But in the middle of the eighties the pendulum of Frederick William's foreign policy began once more to swing. The French alliance brought subsidies, but no territorial gain, or hope of it. The succession of the Catholic James II in England reminded him that he was the head of the Protestant cause in Europe. The growing intolerance of the French monarch towards his Huguenot subjects alarmed him, and he answered the Revocation of the Edict of Nantes by one of his boldest and most admirable measures, an Edict of Potsdam which opened his domains to the persecuted French Protestants. He renewed his alliance with Holland and his nephew William of Orange, joined hands, if not hearts, with Austria, and even allied with his old enemy Sweden, like Prussia a Protestant state. But although he planned a campaign against France, and became a confidant and even a party to the preparations of William of Orange to invade England, he nevertheless preserved the semblance of amity with the French king. The turn in England he was not to see, for he died six months before William's invasion. He had made one territorial gain in these latest years, that of the great archbishopric of Magdeburg, a rich if at first unwilling prize which greatly strengthened the Prussian hold along the middle Elbe.

The chequered record of Frederick William's diplomacy was not so different in kind from that of his contemporaries, of the emperor or the other princes of Germany, of the 'Sun King' of France, or Charles II of England. Yet it differed in degree, being more consistently inconsistent in its alliances and counter alliances. And whilst over all the profits were greater than the losses, it may be questioned whether the gains were proportionate to the efforts put forth, to say nothing of the loss in reputation. Apart from the successes in battle at Fehrbellin and Warsaw, the Elector's title of Great rests more properly upon his achievements as a ruler within his scattered dominions, though both parts of his activity contributed to make him the founder of the Brandenburg-Prussian state.

Frederick William's aims in the domestic field were simple: he strove to weld the three portions of his divided realm into a whole, controlled from the centre; to remove any obstacles to his own authority; to build up his army; and to develop the economic life of his state and people. All these, and especially the first three, were closely connected, and in pursuing them the Elector reflected the absolutist theories of Divine Right common to rulers

of the age.   He was indeed no theorist, but he had a simple immovable
faith in his own right and duty to rule and to determine what was best for
his people.   His Calvinism did not prevent him from adopting Lutheran
views of princely authority.   But if his aims were simple the attainment of
them was by no means easy.   For in addition to the separate history and
traditions of the three parts of his divided state, each had its local liberties
embodied in the local assemblies, the Estates.   In Brandenburg, as we have
seen, the representative Estates had managed to increase their powers in the
period before Frederick William became Elector.   And in the recently
acquired Prussia and Kleve-Mark the local Estates were even more strongly
entrenched.   But Frederick William found it intolerable that such bodies
should limit his authority, above all in the matter of raising money for the
army.   'The more you rely on such bodies,' he warned his son in his political
testament of 1667, 'the more you lose your authority, since the Estates are
always trying to weaken your sovereign powers.'

Hence there arose a bitter struggle between the Elector and the Estates
from Koenigsberg to the Rhine, a struggle paralleled elsewhere in Germany
during the same period.   Of all these struggles, however, that in Brandenburg-
Prussia was the most intense and the most prolonged, and the ultimate
victory of the Elector the most significant for both Prussia and the *Reich*.
Since the struggle there was for local liberties and to a considerable extent
for the class interests of the nobility, it differed materially from the contemporary struggle being waged in England.   Yet in both cases the struggle
was one against princely autocracy, and the victory of the Crown in Prussia
was as important for that country as the ultimate triumph of the Parliament
was for England.   In Brandenburg-Prussia the conflict was waged separately
in its three parts, most bitterly in East Prussia, but it was sharp and long
drawn out in all three regions.   In Brandenburg and Kleve-Mark the Elector
was helped by class divisions between nobles and townsfolk, which played
into his hands.   In all three the questions at issue were the rights of the
Estates to control taxation, to meet without electoral permission, and, in
Prussia and the Rhineland, to have their affairs administered by their own
people.   The provision for and quartering of troops was likewise an issue.
In Brandenburg the most severe crisis came in 1652-3, when a general
Landtag had to be prorogued six times ere it granted the money the Elector
wanted for his new standing army.   Even then he only secured it by important concessions, confirming the hold of the nobility over the peasants and
accepting the local liberties of the towns.   Nor did the struggle end then.
Only in his latest years could Frederick William feel that he had finally
defeated the claims of the Brandenburg Estates in taxation, and substituted
the authority of his own officials for theirs.

In Kleve-Mark the remoteness from Berlin, the proximity of the free
communities of Holland, and the lack of any historical connection with the
Hohenzollerns, naturally strengthened the independent attitude of the local
Estates.   They strongly resisted the Elector's attempts to establish his
authority there according to his ideas and by his agents, to quarter troops

upon them, and to levy taxes without their consent.   They even appealed to the imperial *Reichstag* over his head (1653) and got a decision of the Aulic Council in their favour.   But they were too small to continue the struggle alone, and the interests of nobles and townsfolk were divided.   So that although in 1661 Frederick William recognized the right of the Estates to meet when they desired, and to vote taxes, they in turn were forced to make concessions, and by steady pressure their rights were steadily whittled away until the supremacy of the government at Berlin was assured.

The stiffest fight of all came in Prussia, furthest away, never part of the *Reich*, with a tradition of stiff-necked independence among both its land barons and its townsfolk in Koenigsberg and elsewhere, and able to look for sympathy and support from Poland.   Lutheranism too was stronger and less tolerant of a Calvinist prince there.   There was continuous and growing opposition during the fifties, as Frederick William strove steadily to increase his authority, disregarding local protests about taxation, the right to have local-born administrators, and the burden of the army.   The decisive struggle came when Frederick William had secured the freedom of East Prussia from Polish suzerainty in 1660.   Sovereignty to him meant not merely freedom from vassalage to Poland, but complete control over all his East Prussian subjects.   Matters came to a head with the meeting of the 'Great *Landtag*' of 1661–3, when the Prussians found leaders to present their grievances and fight for their liberties.   These were Roth, a tough and determined citizen of Koenigsberg, for the townsfolk, and the two Kalck-steins, father and son, for the nobility.   The crisis was resolved only by the Elector's marching to Koenigsberg with overwhelming force.   Roth was seized and sent to drag out sixteen years in captivity; the younger Kalckstein later paid for his opposition with his life, being seized and carried off by Frederick's orders from the Polish capital to be tried, tortured, and executed. The end of the Great *Landtag* saw certain concessions on both sides, with the Elector promising to recognize the rights of the Estates in taxation and other matters.   But in fact the power of the Estates, and with it the local independence of Prussia, was broken, and as with Kleve-Mark, the eastern province came increasingly to depend on the will of the sovereign and the centralized authority of Berlin.

The work of centralizing such authority in and from Berlin went on step by step with the destruction of the rights of the local Estates.   Behind it, and fundamental to it, was the reorganization in 1651 of the central Privy Council into departments, largely on a territorial basis for the whole realm, with various inner committees for foreign affairs, and later finance, justice, and economic matters, all under the Elector himself.   The evolution of this body took time to work out, and suffered changes, but it steadily extended its activities and authority from Brandenburg outwards until it became 'the great machine which set everything in motion.' [1]   Although Frederick William reserved to himself the right to final decision, and used it, notably in foreign policy, as time went on he relied more and more on the advice of

[1] A. Waddington, *Histoire de Prusse*, 1911, vol. i, p. 357.

his council. Of his many ministers, the name of Otto von Schwerin, a
Pomeranian noble, stands out as most faithful, wisest, and longest in power.

Connected with the work of this council, and essential for the establishment
of centralized control, was the supersession of locally appointed officials by
directly appointed electoral agents, and the setting up of bodies appointed
by and controlled from the centre for judicial, fiscal, economic, and religious
matters. These gradually absorbed the former powers in such matters. In
place of the locally appointed official there now began to grow and flourish
that bureaucracy of officialdom which was to be an essential part of the
Prussian system of government. Here too Frederick William may be termed
a founder, on whose work later rulers were to build. Like other rulers
elsewhere, he preferred as agents men of the middle class, being more sure
of their obedient devotion, and he continued throughout his reign to follow
their work closely, reviewing their decisions, and in general keeping a firm
grip on local administration, even to directing the choice of officials in
supposedly free civic elections. In all this process the length of his reign
and the increasing firmness of his will were of account. '*Das ist unser Wille*'
(That is our will) became for him the final word to his people from Niemen
to Rhine.

Frederick William's work in building up a standing army, in place of the
former feudal levy and local militia, has been mentioned already. This
army was only seven or eight thousand strong before 1648, but rose to over
three times that number in the first Northern War, and to forty thousand in
the second. Between wars its numbers naturally decreased; but of its permanence, its large size relatively to the total population, and its undisputed
control by the Elector alone, there was no question. Its recruitment,
organization, housing, and relation to the civil population were matters of
constant concern to him. As a fighting force in time of war it acquired a
reputation for discipline and courage equal to that of any army in Europe;
superior, indeed, to most. How to finance it was an ever-present problem,
to which every kind of tax the Elector or his advisers could raise was applied,
supplemented by the subsidies received in both war and peace from France,
Spain, and Holland, as well as loans when they could be raised. To raise
money for this end and for the growing expenses of government was indeed
one of the major problems of the reign, and there was never a surplus,
usually a deficit. The old idea persisted that the Elector should 'live of his
own,' but whilst the electoral domain was large it was quite inadequate for
the expenses of a military state.

Frederick William indeed made great efforts to increase the general
prosperity of the State and people. He had been much influenced by the
wealth and prosperity he saw in Holland during the years spent there in his
youth, and for the rest of his days Holland, then at the height of its power
and reputation, remained a model to him in that respect. 'The most certain
wealth and growth of a country comes from its trade,' he declared in old age;
and again, in an Edict of 1686: 'Trade and shipping are the foremost pillars of
a state.' Hence arose, in part, his strong desire for Swedish Pomerania,

with Stettin and the mouth of the Oder, instead of his poor port facilities in Eastern Pomerania.   Hence too his efforts to build up a mercantile marine, to start a navy, using Dutch or other agents therefor, and hence also his attempts to imitate the Dutch and other western states at this epoch in founding an overseas empire.   After various schemes had been adumbrated, including one for the founding of an imperial East India Company, in 1680 he sent an expedition to the Guinea Coast of West Africa, followed by two others, and by the founding of an African Company.   But his schemes brought little result.   The Dutch regarded them with jealousy, and partially wrecked them.   He found much opposition from his advisers and little or no backing from his subjects.

The fact was that, as Schwerin and others pointed out to the ambitious Elector, Brandenburg was not ready for such schemes.   She had neither the capital, the ships, the sailors, nor the spirit of commercial enterprise for such undertakings.   Frederick admired the Dutch achievement, but he completely failed to realize that the enterprise and success of the Dutch in trade, which made them 'the bourgeois of western European history *par excellence*,' [1] were bound up with a tradition of political freedom, and that there was a profound incompatibility between his efforts to reduce his people to an absolutist system, and his hope at the same time of seeing them display the individualist energy of the freer Dutch.   Efforts to build up a marine, both for war and for peace, brought little result, although they testify to the energy of the ageing Elector.   More successful were his attempts to build up the internal trade and economy of his lands.   After 1648, and again after his later wars, he strove with success to restore the damage these wars had done to agriculture.   He invited settlers from abroad, from Holland, from other parts of Germany, from Switzerland, and not least from France. This last immigration, the largest in his reign, was primarily religious in origin.   The Calvinist prince offered asylum to refugees of his own faith from France, where they were suffering under the intolerance of the later years of Louis XIV.   Immigration began in the sixties, to reach its height after the Revocation of the Edict of Nantes, and added a valuable element to the population of both the countryside and the towns, above all, Berlin.   The capital was further favoured by the building of a canal connecting the trade of the Oder with that of the Elbe.   'It was,' we are told,[2] 'the origin of its commercial prosperity.'   There were also other public works to further trade both in Brandenburg and Prussia.   Industry too received its share of attention, with some slight modification of the rigidly exclusive control by the guilds, and regulation of all branches of industry, particularly minute in the case of the major wool and cloth industry.

In all this Frederick William followed closely the principles and practice of the prevailing mercantilist trend.   With the triumph of local territorialism in Germany, and the absence of any national economic control or policy, it lay with the princes to formulate and carry out policies which elsewhere

[1] E. F. Heckscher, *Mercantilism*, 1935, vol. i, p. 353.
[2] A. Waddington, op. cit., vol. i, p. 396.

were of a national character, and the Elector's conception of his position
and duties made it natural for him to follow the pattern of the time.   Thus
he regulated trade and industry within his realm in view of what he regarded
as the national or state interest, forbidding imports or exports as they seemed
to conflict with that.   But such regulation inevitably had at times an inhibiting
effect on the economic life of the realm.   Nor did he get so far as to bring
about freedom of trade within his own domains.   The endless tolls which
choked the river and road trade of Germany were not abolished in Brandenburg-Prussia, partly because of the vested interest of the towns, and in part
because he himself drew revenue therefrom.[1]   So that, although trade and
industry, and with them the prosperity of his country, increased in the later
and more peaceful years of his reign, it was in part despite, as well as owing
to, the Elector's well-meant efforts.

The social order inherited by Frederick William in all his possessions was
one of ranks and classes, and this he firmly believed in and maintained to
the best of his ability.   He even stiffened it in a number of ways.   Thus he
gave it a military and bureaucratic quality, something indeed of a police
nature, with himself as the chief policeman of his realm.   By the agreement
of 1653 with the Brandenburg nobility he fastened the institution of serfdom
on the peasantry for the next hundred and fifty years.   'Where serfdom
exists and is customary it must by all means remain.'   And remain it did,
until the emancipation of 1807; he defined more closely than before the
boundaries between the nobility and the townsfolk, the townsfolk and the
peasantry.   The peasantry, indeed, came off badly in his reign.   With no
desire to tyrannize over them, and occasionally even protecting them, and
treating them rather better on his own lands than they were treated elsewhere,
he nevertheless riveted them more firmly in their place of subjection, from the
so-called 'free' peasants, who were, however, not free to leave their hereditary
holdings, down through the various grades to the serf-slaves.   The services
to be rendered by them to their lords were redefined, if not increased, in a
number of decrees late in his reign.

The townsfolk in his realm were similarly graded, from the smallish
number of patrician urban families, through the larger body of merchants
organized in their guilds and enjoying a monopoly for their wares, the few
Jews who by special licence engaged in finance, down to the mere workmen.
The burgesses provided many of the electoral officials, including the jurists,
and were protected from competition by the nobility in trade and manufacture.   The nobility for their part, as natural supporters of the Elector
and his regime, enjoyed a partial exemption from taxation, officered the army,
held local and central offices of state, and as landlords had the prerogative
of many rights of a feudal nature over their subjects.   But over both the
greater landlords and the lesser squires the Elector established, by force at
times, the superior weight of his own authority, from the *Junkers* of Prussia
to the nobles of the Rhenish provinces.   By the close of his reign their
interests were sufficiently identified with those of the Hohenzollern house.

[1] E. F. Heckscher, op. cit., vol. i, p. 70 seq.

That house had grown considerably in stature and power when the Great Elector ended his days in 1688, and it had been from first to last a growth of his own making. The founding of the Brandenburg-Prussian state was indeed his main task. A Calvinist, he had set a remarkable example of religious toleration, even towards Roman Catholics and Jews. He had done something for higher if not for lower education, fostering the universities of Frankfurt (on the Oder) and Koenigsberg, and founding a new if very small one for his Rhenish provinces at Duisburg. He had drawn the eminent Puffendorf to Berlin as electoral historiographer, and had in his later years shown marked interest in the general cultural development of his somewhat backward state. His capital, Berlin, had grown not merely in size and prosperity but also in cultural importance; he had built a library as well as an army. Yet there was no question as to which came first in his mind, and we may seek in vain in his realm for any national achievement in thought, literature, or art comparable in any degree to those of a Leibnitz, a Milton, a Racine, or a Rembrandt. Despite the failure of his more ambitious schemes of commercial advancement, his state had more than made good the losses of population and material resources suffered during the long wars. It remained, however, his greatest achievement that of an inheritance which at his death contained only a million and a half people he had made a State with a reputation for military strength far beyond what would have seemed possible, with so small a population and such limited resources. In achieving this, by hard and unremitting effort, he had stamped the Brandenburg-Prussian state with a certain impress and certain qualities; and also with certain obvious limitations for a developing society. Both the qualities and the limitations were to remain, and to produce their fruits, long after the founder of modern Prussia had passed away. His outstanding legacy to Prussia was, as the modern historian of the Hohenzollerns puts it,[1] 'the ambitious drive to be a great power.'

V. KING FREDERICK I

The two greatest rulers of Brandenburg-Prussia enjoyed long reigns: the Great Elector forty-eight years and Frederick the Great forty-six years. Between them came two rulers with twenty-five and twenty-seven years of rule respectively. Thus the Hohenzollern line, like that of the early Capetians in France, had the great advantage of a steady succession of relatively long-lived princes, and no lack of an heir. Indeed the situation was rather the other way at times, with too many electoral or royal princes, often of different mothers, crowding the stage. It was a curious lapse for so ardent a state builder as the Great Elector that he should have threatened the success of his whole work by creating what were in effect feudal apanages for his younger sons, in defiance of the famous decree of Albert Achilles (1473) establishing primogeniture for Brandenburg, and in disregard of the lesson of so much German history. And it was at first sight surprising that a ruler

[1] O. Hintze, *Die Hohenzollern und ihr Werk*, 1913, p. 254

so much weaker as his successor, Frederick (1688–1713) proved to be, should have had the temerity to disregard these paternal intentions, expressed in two successive testaments.

The explanation, however, provides the key to the central aim and ambition of Frederick's mind, the 'knot,' as Frederick the Great called it, of his policy.   He wished to raise his electoral dignity to that of a king, and for that even the partial division of authority designed by his father would have been an additional obstacle.   Frederick lacked the solidity of mind and purpose of his predecessor.   He was neither warrior nor creative statesman. He had, indeed, other qualities, being in some ways a more attractive personality, gentler and less ruthless, more rather than less pious, more interested in the arts of peace.   He was also a lover of forms and ceremonies, a quality which showed itself in the tenacity with which he pursued his quest for a crown and in the elaboration of etiquette with which he surrounded his acquisition and enjoyment of it.   There was no particular reason why this scattered state of but one and a half million inhabitants, little if any larger than Saxony or Bavaria, should require a king at this moment, and there was certainly no desire, whether in Vienna or in Germany generally, to distinguish the thrusting ambition of Brandenburg-Prussia in this way.

Yet Frederick could find reasons enough.   Monarchy, as exemplified in the dazzling pre-eminence of the court at Versailles, was at its apogee in Europe.   Two of his immediate neighbours had won crowns: William of Orange that of England, the wild and irresponsible Frederick Augustus (the Strong) of Saxony that of Poland (1697).   Closer still the divided lands of Brunswick-Lüneburg were being united by Guelph princes who looked back to the great days of their forbear Henry the Lion, and who won both the creation in 1692 of a new Electorate, that of Hanover, in the very middle of the electoral lands, and in due course a claim to the throne of England. Similarly in South Germany the ruler of Bavaria became both Governor of the Spanish Netherlands and a claimant for the succession to the moribund Spanish king.   And kings, new or old, the sensitive Frederick discovered, to his discomfiture, reclined in arm-chairs to dine, while lesser princes, even Electors, sat on stools.   It was an age of etiquette where each man, not least in Germany, clung to his rank and titles, and was to a considerable extent rated accordingly; and Frederick, in this at least, was a full child of his age.

It was in part this respect for traditional rank and title which made him accept the fact that he must have the consent if not the approval of the Habsburg emperor ere he could take the title of king, and thereafter the recognition of the *Reich* and all the crowned heads of Europe.   He was also committed by secret promise, made in his father's reign, to restore to Austria a small territory (Schwiebus) in Silesia.   Hence in the first thirteen years of his reign, until his accession to the rank of king in 1701, he was more closely allied with Austria than ever his father had been.   True, the Great Elector had moved towards Austria and against France in his latest years, and Frederick in a sense followed his policy.   But he went further to get even less in solid gain.   He joined the Grand Alliance against France in 1690,

and electoral troops fought and maintained their good repute in the Netherlands, in Italy, and also against the Turk for the emperor in Hungary.   But
as their aid was paid for by the subsidies of the other allies, and they were
thus divided and not led by their own ruler as before, Frederick received less
consideration as an ally (and less money) than he thought proper.   The
Peace of Ryswick (1697), which temporarily closed the struggle, brought him
nothing save, as he said in dudgeon, 'the fact that I am included.'   However,
he shared in the general measure of relief at the check to the ambitions of
Louis XIV.   Meanwhile he had pursued a policy of peace with his northern
and eastern neighbours, flirting with Denmark in the hope of gaining Swedish
Pomerania, but professing friendship with Sweden, seeking the goodwill of the
new ruler of Russia, the great Peter, as also that of the new king of Poland.

In due course, after interminable secret and tortuous diplomatic efforts
at Vienna, and payment of hard cash, Frederick got his royal crown.   It was,
understandably enough, the Austrian need of Frederick's aid to east and
west, and the desire to ensure the Habsburg succession to the empire, which
had moved the unwilling Emperor Leopold to agree.   Catholic agents,
hopeful of winning still another Elector to their side (as the Elector of
Saxony had recently turned Catholic to aid in securing election as King of
Poland) had also used their not inconsiderable influence at the imperial
court.   The title was to come from Prussia, where the Elector was full
sovereign, and not from inside the *Reich*.   He was splendidly crowned, by
himself, in Koenigsberg, having studied the coronation of Charles II in
Scotland, and he established his court in Berlin after the fashion of that of
Louis XIV at Versailles, privately inquiring as to the shape and size of the
wig worn by that supreme example of monarchy.   So Brandenburg-Prussia
attained the highest rank (save the empire) in princely dignity, and Frederick
proceeded to hedge himself about with the trappings of royalty.   The title
of king 'in' Prussia soon came to be applied to the whole realm; in word, if
not in fact, Prussia swallowed Brandenburg, and as kings of Prussia the
Hohenzollerns were to rule and make their mark to the end of the chapter.
And when, thanks to Bismarck, they did in fact attain to the even higher
title of emperor, the kingship of Prussia remained the central and controlling
symbol of their power.   In his famous lectures on *Politik*, Treitschke even
claimed that 'an impartial judgment must admit that since the time of the
Great Elector, the political history of Germany is wholly contained within
that of Prussia.'   The new dignity did not bring any immediate accession of
power, though it may have helped in the slow but steady unification of the
scattered units of the new monarchy.   It remained for later and greater
figures than that of the first king to fill out the title.   The greater Frederick's
judgment was that his grandfather secured the title of king before he had the
power to sustain it, and the verdict is sound enough.

For the crown had to be paid for.   Frederick had already expended
much, overmuch, of his strength, and bent or warped his foreign policy to
attain his Grand Design.   And the years following his accession to the
Crown, which were also those of the Spanish Succession War and the

Northern War between Charles XII of Sweden and Peter of Russia, saw Frederick pursuing the same policy as before of active intervention alongside Austria against France in the west, as part of the pledge given for his crown, and neutrality towards the struggle in the east. Again, Prussian troops fought in the Low Countries, on the Danube, and in Italy, as well as on the middle Rhine, and again they won fame, as at Blenheim and elsewhere, but again they fought as paid (or sometimes unpaid) subordinates of the greater allies, by whom Frederick himself was not particularly regarded or trusted. In the general peace negotiations of Utrecht he played a minor role and received little reward.

It was the Prussian historian Droysen's harsh judgment that whereas Frederick had an army and no policy in the west, in the east he had a policy but no army. The epigram, as is usual, over simplifies the facts. East and west were not so separate as all that. His western policy was based partly on a natural anti-French interest, and his eastern policy was not so markedly superior, being more negative than positive. Admittedly, then as later, there was more room for an ambitious Prussian king to expand eastwards than westwards, with Poland already plainly in decline. The question of a partition of this kingdom, first raised by the Great Elector with Sweden, was raised again just at this time. But the prime reason why Frederick's soldiers fought where they did and were not available for eastern adventuring was that they were largely maintained by the allies fighting in the western war. Frederick could not maintain them himself, and there was no guarantee that similar paymasters would be available in the east. The meteoric rise, ambitions, and successes of Charles XII of Sweden caused him ceaseless alarm and concern during the years in which Charles defeated Denmark, Russia, and Poland in turn, and he went so far at the height of Charles's fortunes as to make a 'perpetual' alliance with him (1707). He had refused Russian invitations to an alliance, though maintaining friendly relations, and even after Peter the Great crushingly defeated his Swedish rival at Pultawa (1709) he still feared the Swedish lion too much to engage in open hostilities against him and thereby won the distrust and reprobation of the tsar. So although Frederick still cast eyes on part of Prussian Poland he was unable to get any support for his hopes of it. Thus there, as in the west, his policy failed to bring any of the accessions of territory expected of a Prussian king. There too, however, his critics forgot that he had at least survived what was to be the last Swedish tempest.

More serious than his failure to add to his territory (though he did add two small territories, one in Westphalia by purchase, and Neufchâtel in western Switzerland by succession) was the way in which his concentration on the quest for a crown, and thereafter the maintenance of the royal dignity, led to the neglect of the welfare of his people. Allowance must certainly be made for the long wars, which if they did not ravage Prussia, touched her, and more, to east and west, and drew off both manhood and resources. But Frederick lacked both the interest and the capacity to pursue an active economic policy, and although his first chief minister, Danckelmann, did something, after his fall the maladministration of Wartenberg and his associates led to a steady worsening of economic conditions as the financial needs of the court and the war, and the accompanying corruption, swallowed up all available resources of taxation. The nobility took advantage of the weaker grip of the ruler, and the peasantry suffered under the burdens of the revived serfdom. A general inquest of 1710 revealed the bad conditions which prevailed from one end of the realm to the other, and revealed also the growing opposition of the Crown Prince Frederick William to the extravagant regime of his father.

King Frederick was indeed more interested in the religious and cultural life of his state than in its economic growth. His Calvinism was of a more rigid cast than that of the Great Elector, and led him to impose strict regulations for the observance of Sunday. Yet he continued the policy of toleration for other creeds than his own, and despite the continued antagonism of Lutheran and Calvinist in his realm, of which he had personal experience in the fanatical Lutheranism of his third wife, he zealously adopted proposals put forward by Leibnitz from Hanover for the union of the two Protestant faiths. He built churches for both Calvinists and Lutherans, and issued decrees for the instruction of all children every Sunday afternoon in the elements of religion. He was even ready at one time to follow the counsels of his Bohemian court preacher, Jablonski, and find a basis for wider union in the compromise of the Church of England. It hardly needs saying that his well-meant efforts here failed to bear fruit.

In another way, however, this period of Frederick's reign was of considerable importance in the history of the religious life of Prussia and indeed of Protestant Germany. One of the actions of the Elector which may be approved without any question is his foundation of the University of Halle in 1694. If the idea was not his, at least he gave it effective support. Halle was a State university, directly dependent upon State support and so fitting into the emergent pattern of Brandenburg-Prussian development. And, although it was Lutheran, it was less rigidly attached to one creed. There was room for the enlightened Thomasius, driven from Leipzig by Lutheran intolerance, to become renowned for his insistence on using his own language for purposes of instruction, as against the prevalent Latin. Halle also found room for the newer studies of science and history. But what gave the new foundation its special pre-eminence at the turn of the century was its share in promoting the religious revival known as Pietism.

Pietism was not in origin, or indeed in development, a purely or specially Prussian movement. It bears obvious relation to Quakerism in England, as to other attempts at religious revival in Germany and elsewhere. Nor were its two leading exponents or founders, Spener and A. H. Francke, products of Prussia. But it is a tribute to the tolerant spirit of the Great Elector and his son that both these men found refuge there from Lutheran intolerance in Saxony, Spener to be a preacher in Berlin, Francke to be a pastor and professor in Halle. Spener had defined the aims of the new movement in a book of 1675, *Pia Desideria*, calling for deeper spiritual life,

a lessened emphasis on controversial dogma and ritual, and a wider practice
of the Christian virtues. Halle and its university became the centre of the
new influences, which were to affect profoundly both the religious and the
general life of Prussia and Protestant Germany. Whilst Spener until his
death poured out a stream of writings and sermons which were widely read,
Francke, returning to Luther's zeal for popular education, set up a school
for poor children in Halle, and extended his efforts to include the wide range
of philanthropic efforts associated with his name. The growth of popular
education in Prussia was to owe not a little to the Pietist movement. The
movement also came to represent a protest against the prevailing emphasis
on class divisions, by its reminder of the equality of men in the sight of God,
and a protest likewise against both the dominant Gallicism and the later
rationalism of the eighteenth century. It was to form one of the elements
out of which Fichte and others created the German nationalism of the
nineteenth century.[1]

This is to carry the movement far beyond any interest or desire of the
well-meaning Frederick, who despite a certain interest in the religious
education of his people was hardly a Pietist. He must, however, be given
some credit for the general encouragement of the cultural life of the nation,
centring round his capital and court in Berlin. In this his Hanoverian
(second) wife, Sophia Charlotte, and no less her mother Sophia, Electress
of Hanover, played a notable part, as did the ever-present example of the
French king. Brandenburg had not so far been distinguished in thought
or the arts. Now for the first time there came a stirring in this direction.
And although only the name of the sculptor Schlüter survives as of the first
rank of artists from this period of Prussian history, at least the winds were
stirring in the bleaker north German atmosphere. The greatest German
thinker of this age, Leibnitz, cannot be tied with Prussia in any permanent
way, yet in Frederick's reign he visited Berlin frequently from neighbouring
Hanover, and began in Berlin what he hoped would be the first instalment
of a national German enterprise. This was the founding in 1700 of an
Academy of Sciences, of which Leibnitz became the first president, and
which he encouraged and cherished through its earliest days by his frequent
presence and the power of his mind and pen, despite discouragements. His
presence gave the later years of Frederick's reign a lustre perhaps greater
than they deserved. Such lustre was to suffer a marked sea-change after his
death, when the budding Athens of the north became a more real Sparta.

[1] See Koppel S. Pinson, *Pietism as a Factor in the Rise of German Nationalism*, 1934.

CHAPTER III

THE RISE OF PRUSSIA—II (1713–86)

Frederick William I — Frederick the Great

I. FREDERICK WILLIAM I

WHEN THE first King of Prussia died in 1713 the divided parts of the new monarchy had begun to attain a certain unity and uniformity. Not that the people of the Rhineland felt that they were Prussians, or vice versa. But both Rhinelanders and East Prussians acknowledged the authority of the common centre, Brandenburg, or rather of its ruler in Berlin. That authority had grown steadily since the accession of the Great Elector in 1640, and now expressed itself in every side of the life of the State and people, following the pattern of royal rule prevailing on the continent of Europe at the time. There were, however, certain special features about this new member of the kingly order. In the great effort required to establish the electoral or royal authority over its scattered dominions it was developing an administrative machinery of unusual strength and efficiency for that age, directly dependent upon the Crown. And for the same reason it had more rigidly maintained the order of society as it emerged from the Middle Ages, with its three classes of nobles, townsfolk, and peasantry, though the clergy in this Protestant land were no longer a separate estate, but subject to the Crown like every one else. And finally the Great Elector, from his experience of the weakness of Brandenburg in the Thirty Years War, had built up the first standing army in Germany, an army which had come to be the expression of his ambition to extend his dominions, and which required both recruits and subsidies from outside his own thinly populated realm in order to maintain it. Under his successor Frederick I, a far less warlike figure who no longer led his troops in battle, this Prussian army had played its part in the final and ultimately successful struggle against the domination of Europe by Louis XIV.

The year 1713 saw both the accession of a new king, Frederick William I, to the Prussian throne and also the completion of a whole series of treaties (the Peace of Utrecht) marking the end of the long war of the Spanish Succession and of the menace from France. It might have been expected that with this threat to peace removed, and with Sweden no longer to be feared, the emphasis on the army in the Prussian state would diminish. The decision lay with the monarch, in this absolutist State, and the young Frederick William determined not merely to maintain but to enlarge the military strength of Prussia. He was equally determined, with the memory of his father's experiences in mind, to make the support of that army independent of foreign subsidies. Both of these aims he accomplished, aided by the interval of greater peace in Europe. In accomplishing them, however, he was driven, or drove himself, to an extraordinary concentration of effort, which left little room for anything else. When he died, in 1740, he left a full treasury and a large, well-drilled army. But he had done more than that. He had drilled the nation, as well as the army, into a complete acceptance of his policy and rule, filling out the sketch of the Great Elector in that regard, and giving Prussia the definitive stamp it was to retain throughout its future history. It remained for the greater genius of his successor, Frederick II, to apply the hoarded military strength for the purposes of conquest. Thus, as the final sentence of a French authority on Prussian history summed it up, [1] 'the figure of the drill-sergeant king still remains to our day as that of Prussia itself.'

In considering the work of Frederick William it would be wrong to concentrate too exclusively on his building up of his army, although that is the side of his career which is most familiar, in part from the stories of his drill-sergeant methods and his childish passion for tall soldiers. Behind that, and rendering it possible, was his work of building up and completing the absolutism of the Prussian state. Frederick William was indeed an extraordinary man. His daughter Wilhelmina, whose memoirs, if not wholly reliable, reveal ample reason why she should dislike his incredible tyranny over his family (as over his people), declared that he 'possessed all the qualities for a great man, with an elevation of spirit capable of the greatest deeds.' True, in a narrow sense he was a good man, pious, moral, with a high sense of duty. He was essentially a practical person, with a meticulous love of detail. His character had been formed rather in opposition to than in imitation of his father, whose extravagance as a newly crowned king, love of court etiquette, subjection to favourites who fleeced the realm, and to foreign allies who bought his troops, aroused his deep and lasting resentment. But his reaction carried him to preposterous lengths, making of him a mean, miserly, and tyrannical bully. He was always afraid of being 'done' in some way, and was naïvely pleased when (as he put it) he had shown that he was not the 'stupid fellow' that people thought him. He spent money freely, of course, on the army; his hunting was a royal extravagance he did not stint; and, curiously enough for so disciplined and parsimonious a ruler, he showed a complete incapacity to control his appetite for eating and drinking, ruining his health and bringing himself to a premature death. Nor could he control his temper, as his family, not least his heir, knew well from bitter experience of his tongue, fist, and stick, which he used against them as harshly as against his subjects, in fits of ungovernable anger.

To the nation, as to his family, he was a despot. He had as little doubt of his own absolute authority as he had of the existence of God, who had given him this power, and to whom alone he felt responsible. As he put it: 'We are, and remain, lord and king, and We do what We will.' His subjects had but one duty: to obey. And this despotic authority was not remote,

[1] A. Waddington, *Histoire de Prusse*, vol. ii, p. 572.

FREDERICK I OF PRUSSIA AS A BOY

PRINCE EUGENE OF SAVOY, who at the age of thirty became field marshal and commander-in-chief of imperial forces under Joseph I (1693); the most successful general ever to serve the empire, and, typically, not of German birth

Haussmann

BACH

HANDEL

but immediate, concerned with every detail of national life, swift and ruthless in its punishments, incessant in its activities. The king was at work from early morning (for he rose at the crack of dawn or soon after) busied with the incessant parading of troops which he loved, the affairs of state which he followed in multitudinous detail, the cheese-paring economy of court expenses, including the cost of the daily meals, the rigorous supervision of his family, above all of his incomprehensible eldest son and heir, so different from himself, down to the evening relaxation of the famous 'tobacco parliament.' This was no free parliament indeed, for the king still took his stick with him, and used it on occasion; yet there was a measure of freedom of discussion for the favoured few who attended and could carry their liquor in the smoke-clouded atmosphere, or perhaps provoke the royal laughter with a timely if rough jest. No patriotic German could complain of the influence of French manners or the French *salon* here.

There was small room for jesting, however, in the grim determination with which the king subordinated everything within his realm to his aims and will. This task he set about immediately on his accession, and pursued it with unremitting ardour, building on the work of his grandfather, but modifying in certain respects the methods and machinery the Great Elector had employed, and carrying further the process of centralization and the personal control of affairs by the king. Thus he made less use of the Privy Council, the main organ of administration under the Great Elector, establishing in its place more individual ministries, first of all those of justice and foreign affairs, which he made directly responsible to himself. This became a 'cabinet' government, of a kind very different from that growing up in England, however, in that it consisted of the monarch alone, receiving and commenting upon the written reports submitted to him by his ministers individually. The ministers then carried out his instructions, without discussion.

Parallel with this development, worked out over a number of years, was the series of measures which culminated in the setting up of the so-called General Directory, its full title being the General Supreme Finance War and Domains Directory (1722). Before this there had been two revenue-collecting bodies, one concerned with the income from the royal domains, tolls, monopolies, and justice for civil purposes, the other with the collection of the land, grain, and other taxes set apart for the army. Each body had its own agents and machinery, and each strove to extend its scope and its revenue, in part inevitably at the other's expense. Henceforth, although the two treasuries were kept separate, the whole machinery of collection and administration was reorganized and unified. The royal domains constituted indeed a feature of no small importance in the development of the Prussian monarchy. The weaker Frederick I had allowed some of the royal estates to slip out of his hands, but Frederick William took them back again, removed an earlier distinction between private and State domains, and made them more firmly inalienable. He then proceeded to add to them, and to render them more profitable to the point where they produced no less than

c

half of the national revenue.[1] The new system provided not merely for
finances but also concerned itself with the whole economic system and life
of the country. The Directory was divided into four compartments, each
under a ministerial head, and each responsible for a certain part of the
country and for one or more broad divisions of business. Each department
met one day a week, and reported first to the General Directory, and through
it to the king. The proceedings of the Directory were, of course, to be
secret, and an elaborate system of espionage was instituted to provide information for its use. The members themselves were subjected to rigid
control, with fines for unpunctuality and loss of salary for absences; they
were to sit until they had finished their work for the day, beginning at seven
in summer, eight in winter. Thus in thirty-five articles did the royal despot
organize his rule. The machinery was to last, with modifications, until
after the crash of the monarchy at Jena.

In furtherance of Frederick William's aim of centralizing authority, the
fiscal machinery of the various provinces was similarly unified under a single
local body (1723), a 'board of war and domains.' The former provincial
legal and other bodies remained, but there was a steady increase in the
activities and powers of the agents of the central authority, notably of the
Landrat, the official over the rural area of the Circle (*Kreis*), though the
Landrat also represented local interests, and the local *Steuerrat* (tax commissioner) in the towns. As for the local Estates, they were reduced to a
shadow of their former importance and formed no part of the royal scheme
of things. 'A fig for these Estates!' scornfully exclaimed the king. 'There
is no longer any condominium.' And the former rights of the municipalities,
undermined by the Great Elector, went down the wind in the same way.
Everywhere the royal will prevailed, the royal hand (or the royal stick) was
felt. Certainly the business of the State was carried on more smoothly and
efficiently, more economically, and (so far as revenue went) more fruitfully
under the newer system, given the tireless activity of Frederick William and
the steady growth in experience and grip of the bureaucracy. Even Frederick
William, however, in his desire to get money for the army, failed to live up
completely to his own standards in the rigid choice of certain officials (e.g.
judges), demanding a fee (for the army) from appointees. And when so
much depended on the Crown the destinies of the State and people were
subject to the chances of the royal succession.

With the age of Frederick William we are entering the age of the enlightened
or benevolent despot in European history, and Frederick William's successor
was to be an outstanding example of that type. Frederick William himself
was too narrow-minded to be termed enlightened, too tyrannical to be
benevolent. Yet he was not so far behind his greater son in any true estimation of those qualities, the title to which was far too easily claimed and lightly
bestowed. Perhaps Frederick William, despite his severity and bullying,
had in him a little more of the literal meaning of benevolence, well wishing,
towards his people than his son, as he had undoubtedly less of general

[1] O. Hintze, op. cit., p. 275.

enlightenment.   But in both men it was the State and its power, rather than the people considered benevolently, that they had in mind.   Thus, for example, with regard to the legal system Frederick William might well claim with Catherine II of Russia that he was a beginner of reform, for he issued a number of decrees designed to simplify and accelerate legal processes. But although he had the assistance of the greatest legal luminary produced in Prussia in the century, Samuel Cocceji, the decrees yielded relatively meagre results.   His own severity prevented him from softening materially the cruel criminal code of the time.   He did indeed put an end in Prussia to the shocking trials for witchcraft which still disgraced Germany; yet he accepted and sanctioned the continued use of torture to get confessions. We think of eighteenth-century Britain [1] as very backward in its criminal justice; but Prussia in the same period was more barbarous still.   Similarly, although Frederick William issued decrees abolishing serfdom on the royal domains in Prussia and Pomerania, these were not effective.   In general, the lot of the peasantry continued unchanged.   We should hardly expect so rigid a disciplinarian and autocrat as Frederick William to do aught to interfere with the stiff social structure of Prussia, and in fact he did his best, and with success, to check any change in it, regarding it as divinely appointed. Hence it might rather be said that he increased the rigidity of the system by his strict regimentation of all classes, from the highest nobility downwards.

It is true, however, that a slow change in the balance of society was taking place in this age by the steady increase of the towns.   Agriculture remained the chief industry of the State and the real basis (together with the royal economy) of the steady improvement of the national finances.   Nevertheless there was also a marked increase in industry and so of urban life.   This was partly fed by the continued French and other immigration, and was encouraged by the protective mercantilist system, to which Frederick William subscribed without question, for with its faith in regimentation it fitted his nature like a glove.   The woollen industry was specially marked out for encouragement, in part because it could clothe the growing army, and similarly the iron industry grew by the same military incentive.   Salt, beer, sugar, paper, linen, amber, and other industries likewise developed, all protected from foreign competition (often by absolute prohibition of imports, as in the case of woollens and salt) and all subject to meticulous regulation; they were mostly concentrated in the towns, and organized under corporations. Hence not merely Berlin and Koenigsberg, but also Halle, Magdeburg, Stettin, Potsdam, and the towns of the Rhineland increased in size and prosperity, though the great industrial development of this last area was still in the future.

As elsewhere and at other periods, the encouragement of industry on these terms was made at greater cost to the consumer.   And whilst internal trade expanded and was aided a little by removal of some of the old restraints, trade with the outside world could hardly grow.   Efforts were made at trade agreements with German and other states, notably with Russia by the

---

[1] English laws regarding witchcraft were reformed in 1736.

organization of a Russian company. But they failed to thrive in the
atmosphere of restriction. Of maritime activity in the Baltic or beyond
there was little trace; the remains of the Great Elector's colonial ventures
were disposed of to the Dutch, and their ships and those of the English
carried on the trade along the Baltic shores. The heart of Frederick William
was set upon other things than foreign trade or colonial expansion.

Chief amongst these other things was, of course, the army, to whose
interests and growth he was drawn by both natural inclination and policy.
'From his most tender youth,' says his daughter, 'he always showed a
penchant for *le militaire*. It was his ruling passion,' and he was early given
opportunity to develop it by being allowed to drill a company of cadets
and later a regiment of grenadiers. For policy he had the example of his
grandfather, and indeed that of his father, the latter a warning as much as
an encouragement, since Frederick I had been unable to raise men or money
for armed intervention in the Northern War. So Frederick William proceeded
to make his state an armed state, as no state in the western world had ever
been before in proportion to its size and numbers. It was for this that he
crimped and pinched to lay up treasure; on this he lavished his most ardent
and continuous thought. It was, though he would have denied it, his
religion. For the last fifteen years of his life he wore its dress and no other.
'I find pleasure,' he once declared, 'in nothing in this world save in a strong
army.' To his son he said: 'Concentrate on a good army and on money,
for in those two things lie the glory and safety of a ruler.'

So Frederick William believed, and so he acted, aided by men such as
'the old Dessauer' (Leopold of Anhalt), a soldier of three reigns, whom
Frederick the Great summed up as 'a happy warrior and a bad citizen,'
by Grumbkow and others, but bearing the main burden himself. He
gradually worked out a system of raising the larger number of men required
for the new regiments he created. Every male in the land was in theory liable
for military service though this was not enforced; the country was divided
into districts (cantons) for the different regiments, and the recruiting agent
became more than ever a regular feature of the Prussian landscape, any
irregularity in his methods being covered by the royal avidity for promising
recruits. Nor was recruiting, or these methods, confined to Prussia, for
nearly half of the army was raised elsewhere in Germany or abroad, and
adjacent states had at times much to complain of from Prussian recruiting
agents. Above all, Frederick William sought everywhere for recruits for
his 'regiment of giants,' his Potsdam grenadiers. To secure these he was
willing to spend his hoarded gold, and presents of them from his own subjects or from foreign princes delighted his heart. Peter the Great provided
him with one hundred every year, in return for an equal number of artisans.
There was no limit to length of service, and it was above all the infantry on
whom the king lavished his attention. Their training, drill, discipline, equipment, and general organization, the provision of barracks, of supplies of food
in special granaries, of uniforms of 'Prussian blue,' were tasks of absorbing
and continuous interest to him. Discipline was severe, punishment brutal,

THE ELECTOR FREDERICK WILLIAM I   FREDERICK THE GREAT

HAMBURG TOWN HALL IN THE EIGHTEENTH CENTURY

and desertion frequent. Frederick William was, more than any other Hohen-zollern prince, the creator of the Prussian army, though here as elsewhere he built on the work of his predecessors.

We see this in his establishment of the Prussian officers' corps, begun by the Great Elector, but given firm and lasting shape by Frederick William. It was recruited primarily and mainly from the territorial nobility, the *Junkers*, and by compulsion as much as choice. An academy for their free education and training was set up in Berlin (1722), and their class, or caste, became the mainspring of the whole military system. The nobility became, to a great extent, a nobility of military service. This involved some loss of individual freedom. But it had its compensations, not indeed in money, nor, in the peaceful days of Frederick William, in military glory, but in the superior prestige and importance which they came to enjoy in the State. Frederick William had at his accession shown his preference for military officers over civilians, and his taste did not change as time went on. The higher estimation of the military, a cause of offence to the future Frederick II for a time, became firmly founded in this reign, and was not to be changed so long as the Prussian monarchy lasted; was, in fact, to survive it. Thus the militarization of the Prussian state and society became the main achieve-ment of the drill-sergeant king. The army of 40,000 men left by his father was more than doubled in his reign, without any urgency of war, and Prussia, thirteenth state in Europe in population, and sixth in size, had by the time of his death become fourth in the strength of its army. That army was drilled and prepared for war as no army in Europe since Roman times, and was provided with a war chest of 8,000,000 thalers.

Yet Frederick William did not go to war, once the two wars in which his reign opened were concluded. That in the west, the War of the Spanish Succession, in which he had seen service at Malplaquet, was really over when he succeeded to the throne, although it remained to him to make peace. This he did by joining England and Holland to make a separate peace with France, gaining thereby a part of Guelders across the Meuse from the Spanish Netherlands. In the closing years of the Northern War he fished to some advantage (despite Peter the Great's jibe that he wished to fish without wetting his feet), having his eye on the crash of Charles XII and hoping to get Swedish Pomerania. He made alliance with Russia to this end, occupied Stettin, besieged and took Stralsund against the redoubtable Charles himself, and in the end (1720) secured Stettin, the mouth of the Oder, and the eastern half of Swedish Pomerania, paying Sweden com-pensation. It was a considerable accession, of importance for the future developments of Prussia in the Baltic, although Frederick William's economic policy was little calculated to make use of it.

On these achievements in the field of Mars he stood, and made no further wars. He was not without further ambitions, indeed, having a great desire to secure the succession to that part of the Rhineland territory which Branden-burg had failed to get a century earlier, and which now seemed likely to lack heirs. But he had no desire to go to war for it. There is a likeness between his policy and that enunciated by Bismarck in his last years in office, when he argued that as Germany (i.e. in Frederick William's time, Prussia) was the carp in the European fishpond, she must be strong militarily to hold the balance.   So Frederick William argued in his day, which was *par excellence* the day of the Balance of Power.   And had not the aggressive policy of his son (which he made possible) reaped such dividends, his policy might have been more highly regarded by later historians.   It is true that, as the best German historian of the Hohenzollerns agrees,[1] he had not the head for foreign policy.   He lacked subtlety, being of too simple a nature.   He was intensely suspicious and full of prejudice, whether against the Dutch 'cheese-mongers,' as he termed them, or against France, whose religion, influence, and manners he detested (he repudiated wigs, and taxed them), or even against the Hanoverian kings of England, though he grudgingly admitted that the English were men of their word.   And he was not prepared to risk his beloved army on a gamble.   'No profits, no Prussia' was his answer to proposals for alliances.   He preferred above all, like the Great Elector, to keep his hands free, and hated the idea of being obliged to divide his army.

Thus, although in the face of an alliance between Austria and Spain, he was persuaded to join with England and France in a counter alliance (1725), he quickly regretted it, and turned first towards Russia and then to Austria. The proposal for a double marriage between his eldest son and daughter and the eldest son and daughter of the English king likewise proved fruitless, despite his Hanoverian queen's repeated efforts.   His alliance with Austria satisfied him for a time, and Prussian troops shared with those of the empire in the futile campaign of 1734 on the Rhine; but although he termed himself 'a good imperialist' he had no more faith in Austria than in any foreign state.   The emperor, he grumbled, treated him like a dog; he was to be esteemed, but not trusted.   So, like other Prussian rulers before him, he swung away from Austria again, towards France, hoping to get Jülich-Berg. But although he made a treaty of alliance with France he did not live to reap any fruits therefrom.   Through all this period the question of the Polish succession brought innumerable diplomatic discussions, as did also that of the succession to the empire itself, where Frederick William pledged Prussia to respect the Pragmatic Sanction of the uneasy Charles VI for his daughter. It remained for his son to take his profit by arms from both these issues. For Frederick William, more fearful and less unscrupulous, the record of his foreign policy contained no such brilliant reputation or profit.   Yet he forged the weapon his son was to use.

It was hardly to be expected that under such a king the cultural life of Prussia should flourish.   Nor did it.   The tender beginnings of a spring under his father suffered a wintry set-back: the Berlin Academy was almost literally starved to death, the new king finding no usefulness in its activities. The idle extravagances of his father shocked his more frugal mind, and he swept them away.   There is little to record in the way of intellectual or artistic achievement in his reign, apart from the copious exposition of the rationalist

---

[1] O. Hintze, op. cit., p. 316.

philosophy of Christian Wolff, for which Wolff was driven out of the university of Halle and out of the kingdom. The Saxon Manteuffel declared in the last year of Frederick William's reign that barbarism gained ground every day. Yet some light there was, shining from Hanover into the royal palace itself; and there is something almost pathetic in the preposterous spectacle of the struggle between the burgeoning if somewhat affected growth of the genius of the Crown Prince, and the fierce and uncomprehending tyranny of the royal father.

The admixture of good and bad in Frederick William reveals itself in his attitude towards education. Here as elsewhere he had no idea of freedom, and had as low an opinion of professors as he had of women; and they were paid accordingly. He brought the universities more closely under State supervision by the appointment of a director for each, as part of his general policy of centralizing control in his own hands, and subjected them (like the churches) to frequent visitations, in order to see that both professors and students performed their appointed tasks. He was more interested in primary education, and here he left a permanent imprint on the country. He appreciated its value for inculcating the principles of the Protestant religion, sound morals, and a fitting respect for royal authority. Within a few years of his accession, in 1717, he ordered all children from five to twelve to be sent to school, under pain of severe punishment, to receive instruction in religion, and in reading, writing, and arithmetic. Later decrees and regulations showed the king's continued interest in this matter. Thus although primary education may not have become universal in Frederick William's reign, the maker of the Prussian army may also be regarded as the founder of the Prussian primary educational system.

With all his faults of temper and tyranny Frederick William remained a man of firm religious beliefs. A Calvinist, he was hardly a strict adherent of the more rigid Calvinist tenets (he did not believe in predestination), but, as we might expect, laid more stress on the application of Christian principles. Thus, although no professing Pietist, he approved and supported Pietist activities. Like his father, he wished to see a union of the two major Protestant faiths in his realm, and although he failed to secure this he managed to get them to use the same churches to some extent. Some of these churches he built himself. As head of the Protestant faith in his lands he legislated freely on religious matters. He created a Department of Ecclesiastical Affairs (under the Ministry of Justice) and used it not merely to regulate every side of church activity, including the length of sermons, but also to ensure that the pastors did their share in inculcating loyalty and obedience to himself. It was a natural corollary of his centralizing policy that in his reign the Protestant consistories of Berlin should acquire authority over the provincial consistories. Other religions, chief of them the Catholic, he tolerated, though disapproving and contemptuous, and not acknowledging any outside authority over his Catholic subjects in the Rhineland or elsewhere.

Frederick William wrote his own epitaph in the final words of counsel he

gave to his son and successor three days before he died. 'As for me,' he said,
'I have put in order the State and the army.' So indeed he had. And since
no power remained in Prussia but that of the monarch it was for the son to
decide how he would rule the State and use the army. In due course he
was to raise Prussia and himself to heights unimagined by his simpler
father. But without the preparatory work of that father, the great Frederick
would not have been able to embark on those wider seas of conquest and
glory.

II. FREDERICK THE GREAT

With the reign of Frederick II, the Great (1740–86), the evolution of Prussia
is completed. He is the third of the trinity of the makers of Prussia, with
the Great Elector and Frederick William I as the first two. In some ways
he was less constructive than the other two. He took their creation, preserving both its form and its characteristics and making no fundamental
changes in it. But he used it to achieve ends of which they were incapable,
taking risks which they would never have taken, and achieving, though at
great cost, triumphs which made his name and fame stand far above theirs.
In all this he was, of course, nearer to the Great Elector than to his father.
By combining their solid work with his own daring and successes he gave a
final stamp to the qualities which had been developing for nearly a century
and a half when he died. In the year of his death a Frenchman of genius,
the Count Riquetti de Mirabeau, visited Prussia, and had the temerity to
draw up a memorandum of advice to Frederick's successor. In it he noted,
as subjects for reform, some of the very qualities most characteristic of
Prussia: the conscription for the army; the refusal to allow Prussian citizens
to travel abroad; the feudal rights of the landlords; the refusal to allow the
bourgeoisie to buy land from the nobility; the excessive bureaucratic spirit;
the over-regulation of trade; and the too great extent of the royal domains.

Yet if Frederick thus followed the example of his predecessors in certain
fundamental respects, it was not that he resembled them in all things. Far
from it. It might have been expected that he would differ markedly from
his immediate predecessor and father, just as that father had himself differed
sharply from *his* father, Frederick I, and as the Great Elector had likewise
exhibited marked contrasts with his father, George William.[1] And Frederick
was so widely and deeply different from his father in his early years as Crown
Prince that he seemed to belong not merely to a different generation, but to
a different country, a different world. There was no throw-back to his
great ancestor, the Great Elector, although his Hanoverian grandmother
doubtless contributed, and to a lesser extent his mother. So too did his
precocious sister, Wilhelmina. But Frederick was a child of the eighteenth
century, born in 1712, just at the close of that brief heyday of the first
Frederick's reign, when the new kingdom of Prussia seemed to have set its
course for a different goal than the bleaker one pursued before, and when

[1] Similarly the last Hohenzollern to rule over Prussia (and Germany), William II, differed
markedly from *his* father, Frederick III.

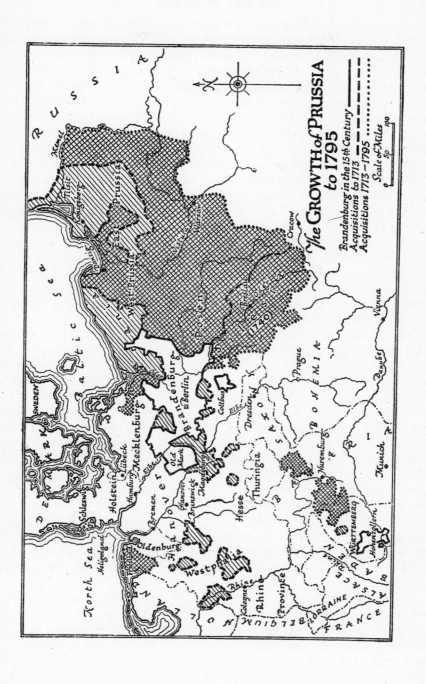

The GROWTH of PRUSSIA
to 1795

Brandenburg in the 15th Century
Acquisitions to 1713
Acquisitions 1713-1795

Scale of Miles
0   50   100

the winds seemed to blow from the south and west rather than from the north and east. And although within a year those winds changed, and under Frederick William I blew with steadily increasing rigour from the colder north, the young Crown Prince, despite all that injunctions, threats, and even beatings could do, continued for long to sigh for these softer breezes, to the intense wrath of his simpler-minded father. He was born and grew up just when the Gallic influence was at its height in Germany. Alien though it was to Prussia in many ways it was fortified there by the extensive Huguenot immigrations, so that even the French-hating Frederick William allowed his son a French nurse and appointed a French tutor for him. To this tutor, Duhan, Frederick owed his introduction to the currents of French intellectual and cultural life, with its classical foundations and standards, its assured canons of taste, its wealth of literary achievement, its highly developed critical faculty, its growing emancipation from the restraints of Christian dogma, whether Catholic or Protestant. And since all this was anathema to his father it had to be hidden, or even outwardly recanted when discovery was followed by the inevitable sudden and violent explosions of paternal wrath and disgust. Thus Frederick early learnt duplicity and secrecy. He became increasingly self-centred, and his vanity was nursed by the recollection of his sufferings. It was a bad training for a prince.

Yet the story did not end there. If Frederick would not give up his flute, his versifying, or his reading of Racine and Voltaire, his father could, and did, use force to compel him to conform at least outwardly to his own standards and ways. The great crisis came in 1730, when Frederick was eighteen, and made a hopelessly ineffective attempt to escape from his father and his country. All Prussia shook with the tempest of the royal wrath. The prince was hurled into captivity, narrowly escaped the execution which fell upon his dearest friend and confidant, Katte, and was subject for some time to the utmost rigours of imprisonment. Slowly and painfully he emerged, under a rigid regimen of military and 'practical' studies devised and super-intended by his father, with hymn singing recommended as a relaxation, to be married off to a colourless niece of the emperor, whom he made not the slightest attempt, then or later, to accept as a partner. For Frederick was not in the least repentant or converted from his flute-playing and his (in Prussian eyes) unorthodox literary tastes and ways of thought. He continued to read and write as before, to compose verses and music with undiminished zeal.

Yet to these activities he added in the decade before his father's death a steadily growing appreciation of what Frederick William had done and was trying to do for his kingdom. He drilled and redrilled in proper Prussian fashion the troops placed under his command. He took part in the profitless campaign on the Rhine in 1734 under the aged Prince Eugene, where Prussia joined the emperor against France in the War of the Polish Succession, and he found that he enjoyed it. He visited various parts of the kingdom, including East Prussia, to report on conditions and to make recommendations. And in time he found a degree of freedom in setting up his own house at

Rheinsberg in the Mark, surrounded with the French *décor* that he admired so much, classical allegory suited to ambitious young princes, pictures by Watteau for rural delight, with Horace and Voltaire as the presiding deities of the house. There he studied and wrote indefatigably, yet found time for the diversions of society. He burned to distinguish himself, whether in undying verse or (and here newer ambitions intruded) in heroic action, to win fame comparable to that of Prince Eugene or Peter the Great or the Charles XII of Sweden whose life his French mentor, Voltaire, had written. Thus by 1740, when his father at last paid the price of his uncontrollable appetite for eating and drinking, and his equally uncontrollable temper, Frederick, aged twenty-eight, was a remarkable, indeed a unique combination, of old Prussianism (minus its religious faith) and French culture nourished in an alien land. It remained to be seen which of the two strains would dominate. One omission in his education was never repaired. Neither in these years nor later did he travel abroad as he had once so ardently desired. And it is noteworthy that when later on he came to set down his ideas upon the education suitable for a future king of Prussia, he made no mention of foreign travel as aiding that process. Here at least the views of his father held him fast.

The forty-six years of the reign of Frederick II (1740–86) divide naturally into four parts, a period of war (1740–5) followed by eleven years of peace, then a second period of war (1756–63) followed by a longer period of peace, momentarily interrupted by a short final conflict with Austria over the succession to Bavaria in 1778. But the two wars and the succeeding periods of peace are all connected; the second war grows out of the first, the second period of peace continued the work of the first. Further, the sharp alternations of war and peace find curious correspondence in the contrasts of Frederick's own character and personality, between the would-be poet and philosopher, the pattern of the enlightenment of the age, and the hard realist soldier-statesman, egotistical and ambitious, unscrupulous, aggressive, and at times tyrannical. And just as the wars and the peace are connected, so do the contrasts of Frederick's character form parts of one person. Thus war and peace, philosopher-poet and autocrat-conqueror, are all linked together into the career and work of this most outstanding of all the Hohenzollern rulers of Brandenburg-Prussia.

The general expectation both in Prussia and abroad when Frederick became king was that there would be an immediate and marked change from his father's regime. Change indeed there was to be, but hardly in the expected direction. For whilst Frederick paid immediate tribute to his love of French culture by going off to Kleve to meet Voltaire within three months of his accession, he had already shown that in two all-important matters he intended to hold to the system of his father: he meant to govern Prussia himself, and to maintain the enormous army which his father had built up. True, his yoke was less openly harsh and oppressive. Torture was (almost) abolished; the philosopher Wolff was restored to his professorial chair at Halle; there was more freedom of speaking and thinking, though more on

religious than on political matters, as Lessing noted with disgust. The
regime was no less autocratic than before, and it allowed less rather than
more room for ministerial action.   And whilst Frederick got rid of his
father's absurd regiment of giants he immediately added to the army in its
place seventeen new battalions (10,000 men).   And he put himself from
civilian dress into the stiff Prussian military uniform, to wear it for the rest
of his life.   He continued to write French poetry, to play the flute, to keep
up his correspondence with Voltaire, Jordan, and later d'Alembert.   But
that was henceforth only a part of him.   The dissimulation and secrecy he
had learnt under his father's illiberal rule was to mark him always.   The
ruler must hide his thoughts and ambitions is the advice given in both his
Political Testaments.   'If my shirt knew what I was planning I would tear it
off,' he once remarked.   With no friend whom he really trusted, with no
wife (save in name), he nurtured his plans in secret, and kept counsel in
matters of state with himself alone.   And already he nourished, and quickly
revealed, ambitions other than those of writing verse to be corrected by
Voltaire.

In the peaceful days at Rheinsberg, before he became king, Frederick had
written a book against Machiavelli, *Anti-Machiavel*, to be published in 1741.
In it he had been decidedly superior in his criticism of the Italian realist,
condemning him for not seeing that a prince's first duty was to his subjects,
with justice as the guide to all his actions, with their lives as his most precious
possession.   He even went so far as to praise parliamentary government!
'If there was any constitution which should be considered as a model of
wisdom it is that of England, where the Parliament is an arbiter between
king and people, and the king has every power to do good and none to do
evil.'   It is bad policy (to put it no higher) for a prince to deceive his neighbours, and aggressive war is both wicked and unprofitable.   'True glory is
not won by usurpation. . . .   The new conquests of a prince do not enrich
or improve his existing dominions . . . a few leagues more of land will never
make a prince more illustrious.'   This was Frederick's manifesto as a prince
of the age of the Enlightenment.   His actions as king did not always
correspond.   There was always something of the *poseur* in Frederick, as he
knew very well himself.   He was indeed to continue to concern himself with
Machiavelli's teachings, but it was to be rather as a disciple than as a critic.
The prince of the age of Enlightenment becomes in practice curiously like
the prince of the age of the Renaissance, thirsting for conquests, pursuing
the art of war, showing a like absence of scruple in his diplomacy and
alliances, ruling as a complete autocrat, filled with a low opinion of mankind,
above all with a like emphasis upon the State, and with 'reason of state' as
the supreme law.   'Policy,' he put it in 1752, 'is the interest of the State,
within and without.' [1]   In all this, Frederick may be said to have followed
the precepts of the great Italian thinker, adapting him to German soil; the
most outstanding, but not the last, example of this indebtedness.

The first result of Frederick's turn from *Anti-Machiavel* to Machiavelli,

[1] R. Fester, *Friedrich der Grosse, Briefe und Schriften*, 1926–7, vol. ii, p. 133.

and the most decisive and important step he took in all his long reign, was his completely unprovoked attack on Austria and the seizure of the rich province of Silesia within six months of his accession.   Whether he had really (as he said) had this in his mind 'for a long time' we cannot tell; there is no written evidence therefor.   Prussia had had claims to lands in Silesia, but they had been formally given up.   She had better claims to put forward to lands on the Rhine, the small but valuable duchy of Jülich-Berg, and Frederick William had some reason to feel that he had been cheated by Austria in the matter of the succession there.   Here was room for action by a young ambitious prince.   But Frederick when king was never much interested in the Rhineland.   He felt none of the ambition which his ancestors had so sedulously pursued there, accepted the French conquests, and was even ready to give up the Prussian Rhenish provinces if he could get Saxony. Throughout his reign he looked rather east than west, to lands nearer home; in particular, at this moment, south-east.   He bothered himself little about formal or real claims to Silesia; he even termed the elaboration of such claims, drawn up for him, a good piece of chicanery.   He was more concerned, as he tells us in the *History of My Own Times,* written in 1745, with making a name and winning fame for himself by striking some sudden blow with the weapon his father had prepared but never used, and with the solid gain which would ensue to Prussia.   The opportunity for such a blow now presented itself with the sudden demise of the Emperor Charles VI a few months after Frederick became king, and the succession to the Austrian dominions of the young and inexperienced Maria Theresa, a woman and therefore an inferior being.   True, the King of Prussia had promised to respect her succession to all the domains of her father (the Pragmatic Sanction), but that was of no account.   Had not Austria failed to fulfil her promise about Berg?   So Frederick prepared in the utmost secrecy and haste, gave orders to ministers and generals alike, sweeping away objections, and launched his attack, notifying Vienna two days after his troops had entered Silesian territory.

The Silesian wars (for there were two, the first one closing in 1742, the second opening within two years, to close in 1745) had profound effects, not merely for Silesia and Prussia, but also for Europe.   There is no intention here to attempt any description of these wars, or of the greater one which followed in 1756.   Frederick secured his Silesian booty by the second peace of 1745, though not with the ease and speed on which he had counted, and not without set-backs, since the young queen turned out to be of tougher metal than he had thought, and war and diplomacy more difficult arts than they had seemed.   But he acquired these arts, the one at some cost of his country's blood, the other at the price of his reputation for honest dealing, when he twice left his allies in the lurch to make a separate peace with Maria Theresa.[1]   Silesia was a rich province, more developed in trade and industry than Brandenburg-Prussia, and it formed a valuable pendant to the wide-flung lands that Frederick had inherited.   About the same time he succeeded,

[1] O. Hintze, op. cit., p. 339.

by reason of earlier arrangements, to East Friesland, with the port of Emden, as the local line of princes died out. The young king had made his name and won a reputation not merely at home but all over Germany, and indeed Europe. The weapon forged by his father had been tested and found good; Prussian military discipline had been decisive in the victories over Austrian armies. Henceforth there was no question as to where would lie the strength and power of the Prussian state. In Germany, indeed, the reception was naturally somewhat mixed. There was pride in the military achievement of a German prince. But there was also apprehension and distrust of this seizer of German soil; and Catholics, both in Silesia and elsewhere, were naturally displeased at the change in the former balance between the two faiths.

Maria Theresa, however, refused to accept as final the loss of Silesia to 'the wicked man,' as she termed Frederick. Hence the diplomacy of central Europe came to be dominated by this issue between Austria and Prussia. The Empress Elizabeth of Russia could be relied upon to be hostile to Prussia, in part from general policy, the desire for westward expansion and concern over the rise of a rival power there, in part from the personal pique provoked by Frederick's expressed contempt for her as a woman ruler. Even more important, the traditional Habsburg-Bourbon rivalry between Austria and France in time gave way before the strength of this new issue, and with the aid of Louis XV's mistress, Mme de Pompadour, another feminine object of Frederick's sarcasm, the able Austrian minister Kaunitz was able to bring into being a Franco-Austrian alliance against the upstart King of Prussia, who was disliked in any case by Louis XV. This alliance was made easier by the fact that Britain, in her long struggle with France to protect Hanover, now made a treaty with Frederick, despite the dislike of George II for his nephew, whom he roundly called 'a mischievous rascal, a bad ally, a bad neighbour, and a bad relation.' Frederick had not believed that an Austro-French alliance was possible, but now, in 1756, saw himself surrounded by enemies, and decided to precipitate the inevitable war. He did not believe in waiting to be attacked,[1] and so in August 1756 suddenly opened operations against Austria by invading Saxony, much as in August 1914 Germany was to overrun Belgium to attack France. The bitter Seven Years War had begun.

The Seven Years War was to be an infinitely harder, more exhausting, and more dangerous war for Prussia than the Silesian one. While Saxony was easily overrun, the knock-out blow Frederick designed for Austria failed, and despite victories in battle, notably Rossbach and Leuthen, and the help of English subsidies and her victories over France, the war would have been lost for exhausted Prussia had Austrian and Russian forces been able to co-operate, and had not the death of Elizabeth of Russia in 1762 ended the danger from that quarter and brought the almost equally exhausted Austria to peace. Silesia remained Prussian, but as much of the Prussian kingdom

---

[1] 'If you must go to war, fall on your enemy like thunder and lightning,' he had written four years earlier. (Political Testament of 1752. *See* R. Fester, op. cit., vol. ii, p. 182.)

was wasted as in the Thirty Years War. Frederick had fame and to spare, both in Germany and Europe, and his army (even if it was now half foreign) no less. Despite her relatively small population Prussia was now a great power and the avowed and accepted rival of Austria in Germany, launched on a path which was to end a century later in the exclusion of Austria from Germany and the union of Germany under Prussia. These were to be fruits of successful war and the celebrated Prussian discipline, now master in every department of Prussian life.

These wars left an ineffaceable stamp on both Frederick and Prussia. It is Ranke's final tribute to Frederick (in his *Prussian History*) that he first freed the idea of the State from its connection with a definite religious creed. But he omits to add that in place of this Frederick identified his state with military power, an achievement of a more positive kind. As we have seen, Frederick did not begin the process. But the Great Elector succeeded to a state already involved in war, and King Frederick William I, although he built up his army to quite disproportionate heights for a small state, was careful to avoid offensive or indeed any war. It was Frederick who deliberately plunged his state into war to seize lands which belonged to others. After the Silesian wars Frederick came to recognize that further wars were likely, and in the Political Testament of 1752 warned his successor to expect them,[1] since Prussia was surrounded by powerful neighbours jealous of her rise, and had one implacable enemy, Austria. But neither then, nor after the experiences of the Seven Years War, did Frederick limit himself to the idea of merely defending either his inherited lands or his conquests. 'The first duty of a ruler,' he wrote in the 1768 Testament, 'is to maintain himself; the second is to expand.' Saxony, West Prussia, and Swedish Pomerania were the lands he wanted; and he accepted the fact that the territory he most coveted, Saxony, would hardly be won without further war. The implications of these views, policies, and actions caused the life of the Prussian ruler, State, and nation to be bound up with war, and the methods and means of making war, in a way new to the history of Europe, comparable indeed (as Frederick saw and said) to Rome in its conquering days, or (as he might have said) to Sparta. As a modern Prussian historian put it:[2] 'The first commandment of policy for Prussia remained the maintenance and improvement of its armed strength.'

This task, identified with the interest of the Prussian state, remained Frederick's main concern for the rest of his life. He quickly outgrew his early desire for military glory. By 1763 he had sounded the depths of defeat, and even momentary despair, had tasted the sweets of victory, and could rest on his fame as the greatest soldier of his day. But to keep what he had won, to defend the State against dangers from without (there were, as he once noted, none from within), and to take advantage of any opportunity for expansion, all these demanded in his view of policy the most unremitting attention to the military strength of the nation. So he steadily increased the size of the army, from 90,000 at his accession to over 200,000. And since

[1] R. Fester, op. cit., vol. ii, p. 185. [2] H. Prutz, op. cit., vol. iii, p. 231.

Prussia, despite her steady growth in population, could not supply his needs, Frederick drew recruits from outside, including prisoners in time of war, so that about half the army was made up of foreigners, with frequent desertions as a natural accompaniment. Frederick himself looked after the financing, training, organization, discipline, disposition, annual review, and preparation for war of his army, and, of course, commanded it in the field. The military, he said in 1752, must be the first estate in the realm and the first care of the ruler. 'If the ruler does not concern himself directly with the army and set an example therein, all is lost,' he wrote in 1776. His successor, he laid down, should begin early to study the art of fortification, should enter the army at fifteen, and go through all the ranks. His subjects, too, were liable to military service by the decree of Frederick William of 1733, although there was no complete conscription. Mirabeau declared that war had become the national industry of Prussia, and the Italian traveller Alfieri found Prussia 'a great barracks,' and thanked heaven he was not a slave of its ruler. It was this military despotism which made Lessing declare that Prussia was 'the most slavish country in Europe.'

For the emphasis on the army and its needs permeated and dominated the whole structure and life of Prussia.[1] The whole spirit of the administration and the whole life of the nation were coloured thereby. Autocracy must be preserved intact over every department of government, since everything, from finance down, touched the army. The social order must be preserved unchanged for military needs; as ranks and discipline were essential to the army, so it should be in society. Economic policy, whether concerned with settlement and improvement, with the regulation of trade, the building of granaries, or the increase of the state 'treasure,' was measured or affected by military and strategic considerations. Some of Frederick's concern for these considerations was legitimate enough in that age, and in view of Prussia's geographic situation, relative poverty, and lack of manpower. But much of it stemmed directly from Frederick's own character, policy, and ambitions.

Frederick was to win the name and fame of an enlightened (if not benevolent) despot, a product of the newer light bathed in reason which had begun to shine upon if not to flood the eighteenth-century landscape. Claims to this indeed he had. In education, in intellectual interests and powers, in freedom from the trammels of tradition, he rose far above contemporary rulers whether in Germany or outside. Although experience showed that he and Voltaire could not live together at Potsdam, because they were too set in their respective ways, too temperamental and jealous, too alike in possessing greater qualities of mind than of character, nevertheless Frederick never lost his admiration for the great Frenchman and continued to write to him. If Frederick was no great poet or musical performer, he was ardent in pursuit of these arts; and of his many prose writings his historical works

[1] Hintze testified to permanence of this influence in Prussian history: 'The army is an organization which penetrates and shapes the structure of the State. The navy is only a mailed fist which extends into the outside world. It cannot be employed against the internal enemies.' (Fraenkel, *The Dual State*, 1941, p. 154.)

at least have value both for their quality and for their information on contemporary events. His unceasing correspondence testifies to the activity of his literary and intellectual interests. The revival of the Prussian Academy, with a French scientist, Maupertuis, at its head, was more than a royal gesture, and his search for genius to surround him at Potsdam more than an attempt to find a chorus of acclaim. If Frederick was no philosopher, he possessed certain philosophical qualities, pagan rather than Christian, developed by the perils and chances of war, the loneliness of his later years, and the self-imposed slavery of governing an ungrateful people, into a Roman stoicism which carried him through.[1] Much of his intellectual life had very little to do with Prussia or Germany. His culture was cast in a French (and classical) mould; his friends and correspondents were French, or Italian (Algarotti), or Scottish (the brothers Keith). Germans, to Frederick, were boorish and uncivilized, and their language like unto them.

Yet some of Frederick's enlightenment was applied to his Prussian subjects, always, it is true, with an admixture of state policy. Thus in religion he displayed a tolerance unusual at the time. This arose primarily from his disbelief in the dogmas of the Christian churches, a scepticism which at times found vent in a scurrility pleasing to the anti-clericals of the day. His toleration, indeed, did not exclude anti-clericalism and opposition to papal pretensions. He claimed to be the Pope of the Lutherans, and noted with satisfaction that 'a Protestant prince is far more master in his own state than a Catholic one.' The Catholic clergy he distrusted, and if he gave asylum to French Jesuits it was partly to counteract the influence of the pro-Austrian Jesuits of Silesia. Similarly he disliked Jews, but tolerated them for their economic activity. His general attitude he summed up in the Testament of 1768: 'It matters not to the State what metaphysical opinions dominate men's minds; enough that every one behaves as a good citizen and patriot.'

As a prince of the Enlightenment Frederick declared that a ruler should love his subjects. But he was hardly capable of any such emotion. Rather he was driven by an inexorable will, partly inherited, to labour incessantly for the material improvement of his country and the betterment of its administration. Notable here, perhaps most in keeping with the enlightenment he professed, was the improvement he fostered in the administration of justice. The legal reformer, Cocceji, was given a free hand in the reform of legal procedure, delays and abuses were remedied, and law became more uniform over all Prussia, more equal and impartial for high and low alike, although cases involving the State were defined as beyond the capacity of the ordinary courts. The system of training for legal officials was improved, and Frederick kept unremitting watch over the whole system, having a profound distrust of lawyers and their ways. The *Corpus Juris Fridericanum*, the codification of Prussian law, and largely the work of Suarez, did not come into full operation until after Frederick's death, but is properly associated with him.

[1] 'We must bear the yoke laid upon us by Fâte. Our birth decides our position, and we must, for good or ill, follow the calling to which we are destined.' (Frederick to Wilhelmina, from A. Berney's *Friedrich der Grosse*, 1934, p. 366.)

Frederick's enlightenment was, however, in many respects a personal affair. His absorption in affairs of state, his static views of society, and his isolation from the intellectual life of Prussia and Germany prevented him from giving any wide encouragement to education, to German letters, or to art. He did initiate some improvement of popular education. But little came of it, or indeed could come of it, in the face of the needs of the State, and Frederick's dislike of anything which might disturb the social order. For university education he displayed little regard; his own cultural interests lay outside their halls. He had more interest in the provision of schools for the training of the sons of the nobility for the army or for training administrators for the State. Art he patronized in a more private and personal than national way, though by his building of Sans Souci and the New Palace in Potsdam, of the Opera House and other public buildings in Berlin, he set a stamp on and standards for architecture in and about the capital. Berlin took on increasingly the air of a capital in his reign, though it was not comparable to the other and greater capitals of Europe, providing as it did the sharpest contrasts between light and shadow, culture and backwardness. Yet it was beginning, and more, to take a leading part in the new age of German as distinct from French intellectual enlightenment. And if Winckelmann could find no place there, men such as Nicolai and Moses Mendelssohn and Lessing for a time were making it a centre of literary activity for the new movement in Germany. But this was rather in despite of than by any encouragement of the king, who had as little use for them as for the outpourings of the young Goethe or others in this springtime of the new German literature.

For in all Frederick's rule there is predominant not so much the enlightenment or happiness of his people—he had in fact very little idea of happiness —as the strengthening of the State and its military needs and interests. 'There is but one good, that of the State in general,' he wrote in 1777. 'The ruler is only the first servant of the State,' but: 'The Prince is to the society he governs as the head is to the body; he must see, think, and act for the whole community.' Frederick displayed no intention of lessening the autocracy of the Prussian system: indeed he increased it. We see this in his attitude to what he regarded as the three most important pillars of government: Finance, the Army, and Foreign Policy. The army, it goes without saying, was his own immediate concern, and his exercise of military leadership naturally encouraged his sense of authority. Finances he saw as 'the nerves of the human body, controlling all its members' (1776). And as the army took four-fifths of the national income, there was good reason for him to give finance his continuous attention, the more so since the Crown, as owner of more than a quarter of the land of Prussia, itself drew in from a third to a half of the national revenue. As for foreign policy, only by immediate personal direction, he argued in the Testament of 1752, could the requisite secrecy be secured, and policy and alliances modified to meet changing circumstances,[1] So Frederick exercised a continuous and all-embracing

[1] R. Fester, op. cit., vol. ii, pp 181-2,

control over all the main branches of the administration, a control that went even further than that of his father, if exercised in a less violent manner. Even the administration of justice, at first sight more independent of royal control, was subject to his close and constant scrutiny.

Thus, whilst the General Directory, Frederick William's ministerial council, was continued, it lost some of its former pre-eminence. New ministries were created, for Commerce, the Army, Silesia, Mining, and Forestry, with general rather than provincial fields of action, save, of course, that for Silesia. Frederick dealt more with the individual ministers than with the council, so that the collegiate nature of the Directory declined. And Frederick's method of dealing with his ministers curtailed what power and freedom of action they possessed. He met with them only once or twice a year. For the rest, they reported all business to him daily in brief memoranda, to which he replied by 'cabinet,' i.e. royal decisions drawn up by his secretary Eichel or other secretaries on his instructions, decisions from which no appeal was allowed. To deal with the mass of business in this way Frederick rose at three (four in winter). Only so could he keep in his own hands that incessant control of every side of the life of the State which he regarded as essential. Only he knew what the total income of the State was, and he alone determined how it should be used.

Clearly, however, even so devoted and meticulous a ruler as Frederick could not hope to run all the business of the State himself. Prussia had long been a bureaucracy, and under Frederick became more than ever a bureaucratic state. Administration by written reports and memoranda became more than ever the rule, with less and less room for the exercise of individual initiative, save by the king, who never faltered in a decision whether right or wrong. 'You have no initiative at all,' he wrote to a provincial Chamber in 1783. 'All matters must be reported directly to me. And the General Directory must do the same.' So as changes came to depend entirely on the royal will, the regime inevitably tended to be highly conservative, save when galvanized into activity by the masterful king. On the whole Frederick was faithfully served by his officials, better indeed than his suspicious and ungrateful nature deserved. If these had little or no freedom, Frederick had no hesitation in exercising his own prerogative in that regard. When in 1766 the General Directory balked at imposing more taxes, the king boldly went outside the existing system, placing an excise tax on tobacco (now coming into wider use), coffee, and salt, and putting the collection for these royal monopolies in the hands of French officials. But what he gained in money, and he gained less than he had hoped, he lost in popularity, both with the disregarded officials and with the people, and he never regained what he had lost.[1]

Although the feelings of his subjects made little difference to the king, who became more lonely as he grew older, he had been popular enough in the decade or so after the Silesian wars, when organizing his new provinces

---

[1] 'He loved no one and no one loved him' is the summary by Thomas Mann of Frederick after 1765. (*Friedrich und die Grosse Koalition*, 1924, p. 75.)

of Silesia and East Friesland, and labouring for the recovery and growth of
Prussia, which grew markedly in population and prosperity during these
years of peace. Berlin grew to well over 100,000 people, whilst the king
established himself at Potsdam, where his summer chalet of Sans Souci now
rose to grace the hillside, and to enshrine the circle of his favoured intellectuals, from Voltaire downwards. In the growing loneliness after the Seven
Years War, Frederick again took up the task of restoring and increasing
the resources of his country. 'The ruler,' as he put it in the *Duties of
Sovereigns* (1777), 'must look to the cultivation of the soil; he must secure
abundant food for his people, and encourage industry and trade.' Frederick
had well-defined views on economic matters, in accord with the mercantilist
principles followed by his predecessors, and he applied them with the zeal
he had learnt from his father. They called for, and received, infinite and
detailed regulation by the ruler, whether in the older provinces or in the new
acquisitions. The latest of these was West Prussia (1773) for whose assimilation and economic improvement Frederick took extraordinary pains. There
and elsewhere new settlers were drawn in in large numbers, new lands were
provided for them by draining and damming, as in the Oder basin, the new
crop of the potato was forced upon the unwilling peasants to reduce the risk
of famine from a failure of the cereal crop.

The new settlers found their way to the towns as well as on the land.
Frederick was concerned to build up industries in Prussia, and welcomed
new ones, such as the silk manufacture brought by French immigrants, on
behalf of which he forbade the import of foreign silks or silk goods (1756).
The protection of native industry by limiting imports was a natural and
essential part of his system, and the manufacture of cotton and wool,
porcelain and glass, sugar, and the products of mining, owed much to his
efforts. He has even been called the founder of Prussian industry. Domestic
trade grew and flourished. Foreign trade, however, was another matter,
for Frederick's determination to keep in Prussia any raw materials which
might be manufactured there, to refuse to import what might be made in
Prussia, to sell more than he bought, and in general to control all foreign
trading activities, inevitably checked the development of foreign trade.
State efforts at such trade were no more successful than earlier Hohenzollern
efforts of this nature, a Levant company (1765), and an Emden company
for a monopoly of the herring fishery having little success. No doubt
Frederick's efforts did (as they were intended to do) assist in welding the
country together, the old provinces with the new, and assist the emergence
of the firmer concept of the State.

The pursuit of this policy determined Frederick's attitude to the social
structure of his state, overruling projects or professions of enlightened
humanitarianism. If Frederick was relatively free from the purely social
regard for rank and birth, and the dynasticism still prevalent in Germany
as elsewhere, he was none the less profoundly conservative in his views as
to the organization of Prussian society. The clear-cut division of that society
into nobles, townsfolk, and peasants suited his orderly mind and purposes.

and he did all he could to preserve it intact. Believing in the superior virtues of the nobility for command, he drew his officers for the army solely from them. He also increased their numbers in the administrative machine; and since many entered this from the army, the bureaucracy took on a more military tinge. Thus, like his later contemporary Catherine II, he rather increased than diminished the caste quality of society. The townsfolk were for trade and industry, and town and country were more sharply divided. The *Junker* could not engage in trade in the towns, the burgher was forbidden to acquire *Junker* land or property rights, and could not hold the office of *Landrat*. Special organizations (*Landschaften*) were set up to provide financial aid to needy landowners.

The peasantry had to be content with their lot. For whilst Frederick cherished agriculture as the basis of national prosperity, and, as an enlightened ruler, could stigmatize serfdom as the worst of all conditions which revolted humanity, he did nothing to liberate the peasants from their burden of service to their overlords. Early and very tentative efforts towards the reduction of these burdens had aroused the opposition of the landed nobility, and Frederick's predilection for this class, and concern lest such changes might disturb the existing class system and perhaps interfere with the role of the peasantry as the main source of manpower for the army, caused him to abandon any such schemes. Not until some years after his death were the peasants on the royal domains to be freed from serfdom, in 1798, and the others even later. Similarly with popular education. Despite a law of 1763 for its encouragement, little was done to promote it, in part because too many invalided soldiers were given posts as schoolmasters. The law was added to the other Frederician projects of enlightenment, but subject, like them, to the needs and power of the State.

The Hohenzollerns were German princes, Electors indeed, and Prussia a German state, a member of the empire, represented in the Imperial Diet, with obligations to both empire and emperor. Here again the affair of Silesia was definitive and to a degree decisive, for in it Frederick more plainly and with less excuse than any of his predecessors showed himself to be concerned with the interests and aggrandisement of Prussia regardless of the empire. And as he began, so he continued. He was not above making appeals to German interest against Austria, as in 1742, but it was to serve the aims of Prussia. As he seized Silesia, so he coveted Saxony, and invaded it in 1756 without scruple, though he was unable to keep it. He saw no reason why France should not acquire Alsace-Lorraine as he had acquired Silesia, and in his Political Testament of 1752 [1] went so far as to declare that 'Silesia and Lorraine are two sisters, of whom Prussia has married the elder, France the younger. . . . Prussia could not see without concern that either Alsace or Lorraine should be taken from France.' He even agreed that France should have the Austrian Netherlands as well. The attempt of Emperor Joseph II to exchange those distant provinces for southern Bavaria in the later years of his reign aroused Frederick to strong and effective

[1] R. Fester, op. cit., vol. ii, p. 155.

opposition, in pursuance of which he formed the *Deutscher Fürstenbund* (1785), an alliance joined by Hanover, Saxony, and many other German princes. It had its significance as the first effort of German princes to reorganize themselves without foreign aid or interference. But to Frederick it was merely a diplomatic move for his own advantage. Its aim was to preserve the rights of the princes, rather than to unite Germany, and for that very reason it raised opposition in Prussia, since it might lessen the chances of further Prussian expansion in Germany. Pride in Frederick's victories there was indeed in Germany, as the triumphs of a German leader over foreigners,[1] even in part over Austria with its many non-German peoples, and ambitious to regain or increase its hold over the empire. But Frederick hardly responded to the slowly rising national sentiment, which in the last years of his reign was coming to express itself in the burgeoning literature of the day. For him French literature and French culture in general were sufficient and supreme; the German language, the new German literature and thought, like the German Pietist movement in religion, were 'barbaric.' By the time the new movement came into any prominence, indeed long before, Frederick was too set in his ways of thinking to change. His address to the Prussian Academy in 1780 was a sweeping condemnation of the German language and all the works produced in it. Although the conversion of the Duke of Saxony to Catholicism in 1697 left the way open for Prussia to become the leader of Protestant Germany, Frederick's religious views (or his lack of them) inevitably lessened any serious advantage from that side, although his toleration was of advantage to Prussia itself.

Yet if Frederick's whole attitude and way of thinking was Prussian rather than German, local rather than national (like that of most if not all German princes of the age), his rule in Prussia and his extraordinary achievements were of great significance for the whole of Germany, and for her future destinies. Although it remained for Napoleon formally to dissolve the old Holy Roman Empire, Frederick had in fact dealt it a mortal blow by his victories over it. What shreds of authority remained to the Habsburgs over the Empire after 1648 were now further weakened; what had been defiance was now defeat. The challenge of Hohenzollern to Habsburg was now so clear and strong that it created a dualism in Germany, to be resolved in the end in favour of Prussia, and by the same means and weapons with which Frederick had created it. And thereby he not merely dealt a mortal blow at the old empire, but forecast the formation of a new organization for the whole of Germany. In that new organization Prussia and the Prussian model were to be both core and master. Hence the importance for Germany of the final definition by Frederick of the principles and practice of Prussianism, with its stiff social structure, its autocratic and bureaucratic system of government, its great emphasis on military power, and the summation of all this in the Prussian state.

Frederick's achievement was, however, of significance not merely in Germany; it also profoundly affected the position of Prussia and Germany

---

[1] Goethe, *Poetry and Truth*, vol. i, pp. 58, 248.

in Europe. The Balance of Power which Frederick had lauded in the *Anti-Machiavel* as preserving the peace and tranquillity of mankind against the ambitions of any ruler, he had himself changed so decidedly that Mirabeau could declare, in the year Frederick died: 'Prussia is to-day the pivot of war and peace upon the continent of Europe.' His elevation of Prussia to be a great power had been made primarily at the expense of Austria. But in view of the interests of other powers in Germany, his wars had of necessity been European wars. And he had always had the European scene in mind, from the writing of his earliest political pamphlet, *Considerations on the present state of the body politic in Europe* (1738), which begins pompously enough: 'Never have public affairs demanded the attention of Europe more than at this moment. . . .' This attention he continued to give, as his many writings show, not least in the two Political Testaments which give more than half their space to discussing for his successor the problems of foreign policy which a Prussian ruler must face.

Of those problems the most important in the later years of his reign, beyond his relations with Austria, was that of his relations with Russia, discussion of which, significantly, he moves up to first place in the second Testament. Russia's entry against him in the Seven Years War, in part the result of his own ineptitude, had threatened to be fatal to him; her withdrawal and swift change of policy on the death of the Empress Elizabeth had proved his salvation, and he had improved the shining hour by a treaty of alliance with Russia (1764). His gain of Silesia had extended his frontiers with the Slavic world, and he had ambitions to extend his dominions still further by adding West Prussia from Poland, that 'kingdom of anarchy,' as he termed it, only kept alive because of the jealousies of its neighbours. This he accomplished, collaborating with Russia and Austria in the First Partition of Poland in 1772 'in the name of the Holy Trinity,' being indeed the prime mover in that fateful step. The gain to Prussia was considerable: a large piece of Polish territory and a stretch of Baltic coast, new subjects, East Prussia now linked solidly with Brandenburg, and possibilities opened of further gains from the enfeebled Polish state. But Frederick was aware that the picture had less pleasing features. As Poland crumbled and disappeared from the land of the living, so did Russia and Prussia approach each other. True, he had his alliance, which he defended in the Testament of 1768. Yet there was something forced in his defence; he was allied with Russia because he had no choice. He feared this *'terrible puissance,'* as he termed it in a letter to his brother of about this same date. He hoped it would break up; he envisaged an alliance to hold back this 'dangerous flood.' But he knew full well no such alliance was possible, and so joined hands with Russia to make his profit in Poland. A century later the greatest of his successors, Bismarck, was likewise to make his profit of friendship with Russia, was likewise to cling to alliance with her, but was likewise to share the same fears and the same misgivings, misgivings to be slowly but inexorably fulfilled in our own day.

It has been claimed for Frederick that he marked the progress for Prussia

and Germany from the absolute state to the state of law, the constitutional
state, with the king as the first servant of the people.   Certainly he made
little or no claim to a Divine Right to rule.   He was a most conscientious
ruler, a contemner of royal luxury and extravagance, genuinely enlightened
(up to a point), and would doubtless have done more for his people but for
his wars.   He abolished torture, practised toleration, believed in a certain
measure of freedom of opinion and speech, established equality before the
law, provided honest and efficient administration, improved the prosperity
of his land and people.   On the other hand, his scepticism could hardly
allow him to make serious claims to divine sanction for his rule.   He
declared himself the first servant not of the people but of the State, and his
devotion to the duties of government was likewise more concern for the
power of the State than for the well-being of the people.   He had no belief
whatever in popular sovereignty, the right of a people to govern itself through
an elected assembly, a written constitution, or in public (or even ministerial)
control of the national revenue, having in fact the lowest opinion of human
nature in general.   He would have thought it sheer lunacy to hand over to
any one else the conduct of Prussian diplomacy; as well hand over the
command of the army.   'The orders of the commander-in-chief are to be
strictly followed' was a military dictum of his, and he carried the same rule
into the affairs of state: he was the final arbiter of the lives and fortunes of
his people.   If, as is claimed, his wars prevented him from carrying out a
fuller programme of enlightened legislation, it was he who was responsible
for these wars.   More obvious and true than the claim that Frederick was
the founder of the State of *Law* is the claim that he was the champion and
exemplar for Germany, and indeed the world, of the State of *Power*, based
upon Machiavelli's principle of 'reason of state.'   This was the political
legacy he left to Prussia, to be inherited by Bismarck in due course.   And
hence Frederick, as one of his recent biographers [1] remarks, created a gulf
between the old cultural tradition of Germany and this new gospel of State
interest and power.   There was indeed an astonishing new birth of cultural
interest and achievement in Germany, evident in the latter part of Frederick's
reign.   But the old king was blind to it, and, despite its importance, in the
end the Prussian ideal was to be the stronger, to conquer and distort the
other vision.

[1] G. Ritter, *Friedrich der Grosse*, 1936, p. 259.

CHAPTER IV

THE INTELLECTUAL AND LITERARY REVIVAL OF THE EIGHTEENTH CENTURY

Introductory — Lessing — Herder — Goethe — Schiller — Kant

I. INTRODUCTORY

GERMANY in the middle and more especially the latter part of the eighteenth century experienced a remarkable revival of literature and thought. It was a movement comparable in importance to the Reformation, and like that was one of the great movements in German history. Hence the historian concerned with German history in general, and not merely with either politics or literature, must take cognizance of it. For whilst the movement was at first and in its own day almost purely literary and philosophical, and markedly remote from politics, in the long run it was to exert profound effects on the whole history of the German people, including that of the State. Indeed within a generation it was to contribute powerfully in creating the spirit behind the War of Liberation against Napoleon.

It is to be remembered that whereas Germany's western neighbours, France and England, had proceeded steadily and uninterruptedly in their intellectual and literary growth and achievement, despite the contrast of their political development, in Germany such development had been checked and stunted by the struggle engendered by the Reformation, reaching its climax in the Thirty Years War. But in the middle of the eighteenth century growth burst forth again with the suddenness of a belated spring (which indeed it was), releasing its pent-up energies through a decade of 'Storm and Stress,' to find maturity and fulfilment in the work of a galaxy of great writers and thinkers. To a mid nineteenth-century German musician and writer, Richard Wagner, this renewal of the German spirit first showed itself, indeed, not in literature or philosophy, but in what to him was the pre-eminently German art of music, in the work of Sebastian Bach (1685–1750). As Wagner put it in an essay of 1865 on *What is German*:

If we wish to grasp the wonderful originality, strength, and significance of the German spirit in an incomparably eloquent example, we should look closely and thoughtfully at the phenomenon, mysterious and almost inexplicable from any other point of view, of the musical genius, Sebastian Bach. He *is* the history of the innermost life of the German spirit during the terrible century which saw the complete obliteration of the German people. Look at his portrait, hidden in that absurd French periwig. Look at this master, dragging along as a wretched precentor and organist in miserably paid jobs in one little Thuringian place or another that we hardly know by name. He remained so little known that it took all of another century to rescue his works from oblivion. Even in music the art form he found awaiting him was externally the very image of the day, stiff, dry, pedantic, like wig or pigtail in musical notation. And now consider what a world the incomparable Sebastian created from these elements. I can but point to this creation, for it is impossible by comparison to express its richness, its sublimity, its universal significance. But if we wish to account for the amazing rebirth of the German spirit in the other fields of poetry and philosophy we can only clearly do so when we realize from the example of Bach what the German spirit really is, wherein it dwells, and how even when it seemed to have completely disappeared from the world, it ever re-created itself.

But granting the high achievement of German music, historical opinion will inevitably differ regarding its place as an agent of national regeneration. And the undoubted fact remains, accepted by Wagner, that Bach's work was for long little known. Esteemed, as a recent writer [1] has shown, only in small circles in Berlin and Vienna, it was not until the national revival of the early nineteenth century, associated with the Romantic movement and the struggle against Napoleon, and expressed in literature, religion, history, and music, that interest in Bach and his works began slowly to be awakened.

On the other hand, the work of the great writers and thinkers of the middle and later eighteenth century became widely known and influential almost immediately. Five of the most outstanding of these, Lessing, Herder, Goethe, Schiller, and Kant, have been given separate though brief treatment below. But before glancing at the careers and work of these men, it seems desirable to say something of the general background from which they emerged, and the characteristics and general significance of the movement which they led. They were, of course, not alone, for whilst the movement was hardly a national one in the broader, modern sense of the word, it was widely spread and had many contributors and votaries who cannot find mention here. And whilst it is fairly easy to mark its beginning, its close is by no means easy to define, for it both merged into the Romantic movement and continued into and through the storms aroused by the French Revolution, the effects of which upon Germany require separate treatment.

Political conditions in Germany during the last century of the life of the Holy Roman Empire both discouraged and fostered the new movement. The two outstanding features of the declining *Reich* were its lack of central control or unity and the prevailing autocracy of the rulers of its many independent states, large and small. The Habsburg emperors ruled over their own lands, but possessed little authority over Germany as a whole. There, notwithstanding local variations, the princely houses tended to monopolize authority. The old representative Estates (*Landstände*) still existed in many cases, but they were in decline. And although some of them (e.g. in the Rhineland) continued to assert, and even on occasion to exercise their old rights, a ruler who set his mind to it could behave in the most tyrannical fashion, as did some of the dukes of Wurtemberg in this age. There was in general little desire or freedom to discuss political problems and issues. Where some freedom of opinion existed, as in Prussia, for example, under Frederick the Great, it was decidedly limited and hedged about. So that whilst Berlin could play some part in the movement, and Frederick's victories in the Seven Years War provided a stimulus to literature, we find such men as Herder, Winckelmann, and Lessing shaking the dust of Prussia from their feet as Schiller similarly fled from Wurtemberg. For whilst the new movement was in general led by men who accepted the

[1] F. Blume, *Two Centuries of Bach* (trans.), 1950.

existing political and social system in Germany, had little interest in political questions, and found scope for their activities without trenching thereupon, nevertheless a measure of freedom of expression was essential for any creative movement, and there were great abuses in the existing political and social system to which they could hardly remain completely blind. The advent of revolution in France was to create difficulties for them as for their rulers.

On the other hand, the worst days of princely tyranny were over by the middle of the eighteenth century; absolutism was becoming more enlightened, and even Schiller's tyrannical prince, Duke Charles Eugene of Wurtemberg, underwent a conversion of sorts. And the absence of political unity allowed for a great variety of rule and situation in the various states. Mme de Staël, a little later, remarked [1] that knowledge and interest in literature were more widely spread in Germany than in France, where provincial life was more backward under the pull of Parisian attraction; and certainly Vienna, despite the virtues of Maria Theresa and the efforts of Joseph, can hardly be imagined as the leader in a broad intellectual movement at this time. Fichte claimed that in Germany 'a truth which cannot be proclaimed in one place can in another,' though as Lessing's career showed there might be some difficulty in finding that other place, and the ageing Kant could hardly be expected to uproot himself from Koenigsberg when his utterances drew upon him the displeasure of Frederick II's successor. But there did exist princes who were ready both to patronize literature and learning, and to allow it the degree of freedom it required for expression. Karl Friedrich of Baden was probably the best and most truly enlightened ruler Germany possessed in the later eighteenth century, but his South German and Catholic state (though he was a Protestant) played relatively little part in the intellectual revival. Karl August of Saxe-Weimar, the little Thuringian duchy, is, of course, the best-known princely patron of the new movement, and the long and intellectually fruitful residence in his little principality of Goethe and Schiller, Herder and Wieland, affords ample testimony to his relative liberality of mind and purse. Hanover, because of its English connection and its lack of a local court, breathed a somewhat freer air, and some of the Imperial Cities, as Hamburg and Frankfurt, could and did foster a spirit of civic freedom, a freedom limited, however, to the local mercantile oligarchy.

The economic basis of the movement was to be found in the slow revival of the material prosperity of the country after the ravages of the Thirty Years War, a revival more particularly manifested in the recovery of middle-class prosperity in the cities. It is true that this revival was interrupted by later wars. Large parts of the south-west were ravaged in the later wars of Louis XIV (1689–99 and 1702–14), and the north, from Hesse-Cassel and Saxony to East Prussia, suffered in the wars of Frederick the Great. Yet these wars were less widely calamitous in their devastations, and they were followed by more speedy, consistent, and fruitful efforts to repair their damages, as, for instance, in Prussia. Hence the eighteenth century was

[1] *De l'Allemagne*, 1813; *Œuvres*, 1871, vol. ii, p. 29.

marked by a steady if slow recuperation, with a growth of population (aided by immigration) and an increase of material well-being, although the degree of such improvement naturally varied greatly in the many separate and autocratically governed states. The pattern of rural Germany did not change drastically before the French Revolution. The system of agriculture of past centuries still prevailed. In the west indeed, and as far east as Thuringia in central Germany, serfdom slowly disappeared. It was one of the Duke of Baden's claims to enlightenment that he abolished serfdom in his dominions in 1783, whereas in eastern Prussia the trend ran rather in the other direction, save on the royal domains.

It is in the cities and towns that recuperation and growth may more easily be seen. Doubtless this was connected with agrarian revival, for the towns were still small and closely connected with the land on which the bulk of Germany's twenty millions of population lived. Yet these towns were deep-rooted, whether as state capitals such as Dresden, Berlin, and Weimar, or trading towns surviving from the old Hansa, as Hamburg, or free Imperial Cities such as Frankfurt or Augsburg. The Imperial Cities clustered in the south-west did not all recover their earlier prosperity, and the possession of the mouths of the Rhine by an independent Holland was a check to the revival of the lower Rhenish cities; nor did the Baltic cities of the Hansa win back their former importance. Hamburg, however, continued to grow in pros-perity, with its riverine trade up the Elbe and its foreign trade with England and elsewhere. Free from princely control it was to be a prime agent in the all-important literary contact with England. At the other extreme of Germany, the Swiss city of Zürich, with its republican freedom, was likewise to provide stimulus to the new movement for a time. To the west Frank-furt and towards the east Leipzig, both outstanding trading centres with connections north and south as well as east and west, were likewise to be strategic points in the revival, the one a Free City, the other under its Saxon prince, but providing in its university a focus and magnet for all Germany.

It was in these and other German cities such as Bremen or Nürnberg, Berlin or Brunswick, mostly free or becoming more free from the court influence which had predominated after 1648, that the middle class began to revive again. And the literary movement was in large measure a middle-class movement, although, as Weimar showed, it drew materially upon princely support. This 'middle class,' like all middle classes, was a composite one, resting on the traders and the masters of the handicraft industry then prevailing. Its members might be relatively poor or solid enough to main-tain a young Wolfgang Goethe. It was not yet the capitalist middle class of the nineteenth century, but it also included the professional class, the professors in the universities and the teachers in the secondary schools, the Lutheran parsons of small means but more education, and the numerous lawyers and officials required for the administration of the multitude of separate political units making up the *Reich*. The youths of this class thronged the universities, and were to provide many of the leaders in the movement, although some of these leaders, as Herder, Winckelmann, Schiller,

German court life at the beginning of the eighteenth century.   The prince and his friends
at a little shoot
(*From Hemming's 'Teutsche Jaegerei,' 1719*)

After J. M. Kraus

German court life at the end of the eighteenth century. Evening study-circle at the
Dowager Duchess Amalia's in Weimar

and Kant, for example, emerged from humbler surroundings to reach the universities. The many branches of this growing middle class provided the readers, and to a large extent the writers, of the flood of journals of mixed moral, literary, and intellectual content which appeared early in the eighteenth century, following English example, and which began, or greatly extended, that passion for books and reading which was to mark Germany henceforth.

Foreign literary influence was indeed an essential part of the background to the literary revival. To it, as helping to form the cultural basis of the movement, must be added the Pietist movement, the Enlightenment of the age, and the share of the universities and indeed the schools. The literary revival, it is important to recall, took place in northern and Protestant Germany. The Catholic south, including Vienna, had little to do with it, and the connection with Zürich was in origin a Protestant one. And whilst few if any of its leaders might be Pietists, and some, like Goethe, were hardly to be accounted members of the Protestant or any Christian Church, yet quite a number of them, as Klopstock, Herder, Kant, and Wieland, had been brought up under Pietist influence; Klopstock's *Messiah*, commonly taken as marking the start of the new era in poetry, was largely the product of Pietist influence. And many more had felt indirectly the influence of that stirring of the spirit of Protestantism in the later seventeenth and early eighteenth centuries associated with Spener and Francke at Halle, with its demand for a renewal of faith and religious feeling, and its emphasis on the application of Christian ethics to social life and problems. And from Halle the influence of the movement had spread as far as East Prussia on the one hand and Wurtemberg on the other.

But Halle, for the time the leading university of Germany, was also the centre for the teaching of the philosophy of the Enlightenment (*Aufklärung*), the rationalism which was in direct opposition to certain aspects of Pietism, but which throve there and helped to create the background for the revival. The university there also harboured for a time the liberty-loving Thomasius, notable for his insistence upon the use of German rather than the customary Latin in his lectures. His independence of mind led to his being driven out by the despotic Frederick William I, to return later. The almost official exponent of the philosophy of the Enlightenment was Professor Christian Wolff, 'the father of the *Aufklärung*,' whose writings provided the standard exposition throughout Germany of the championship of Reason as the guiding principle of human life and conduct, until Kant displaced him. Frederick the Great and the Prussian Academy likewise contributed to the spread of rationalist ideas, despite the king's divorce from German letters and thought. Without his advocacy, and the stimulus from the French immigration he fostered, Berlin would hardly have come to play its part in the movement. French influence at other courts in Germany likewise counted, if in a lesser degree, in the spread of the dominant ideas of the day. The kernel of these ideas was that of the pre-eminence of Reason. By its growth man had emerged from the earlier Dark Ages into the present Enlightenment, and by its liberating influence humanity would put an end to the still existing abuses of society and attain to the fullest knowledge of the world of nature, including man himself, irrespective of national differences or boundaries. This optimistic faith reduced the importance of revealed religion, at all events for the more educated middle and upper classes of society, and aided the secular trend characteristic of the age. The professor of theology for nearly forty years in Halle itself, Johann Semler, did much to whittle away the official dogmas of Lutheran Christianity.

Protestant universities elsewhere in Germany likewise played their parts in the revival of intellectual and literary activity. The educational system of Germany had, of course, suffered in the general decline of the seventeenth century, but the framework of the grammar schools (*Lateinschulen*), set up under the stimulus of Luther and Melanchthon at the Reformation, survived, and these now took on new life. The universities likewise revived again, strengthened by the new foundations of Halle (1694) as already mentioned, and Göttingen (1737). Göttingen was a Hanoverian foundation, and so connected with England. Its greater freedom drew to it a number of eminent teachers (as Gesner, Schlözer, Heyne) and it became increasingly important as a focus of enlightenment for all Germany. More immediately important for the new movement in literature, however, was the university of Leipzig. For it was there that Gottsched, long the leader in literary standards in Germany, had made notable if limited efforts to revive German letters. There too was Gellert, stylist, moralist, writer of both fables and hymns, and almost equally famous. For German students in the mid-eighteenth century almost all roads seemed to lead to Leipzig. Klopstock studied there, Lessing found himself there, the youthful Goethe frolicked in its lightness and freedom. Later on Goethe was to find more solid stimulus in the flourishing university of Jena, then adorned by Schiller and, for a time, Fichte. Thus, although the new literary movement was not confined to the universities, indeed can hardly be called 'academic,' it nevertheless had close and continuous connections with the Protestant universities of the empire.

English literature undoubtedly had a good deal to do with the preparation and development of the German literary movement, although the story of its working is far too large and complicated to be adequately described here. It was in part the replacement of French court influence by English middle-class influence, but it would be absurd to suggest that French influence ceased when first the ideas of the French *philosophes*, and then the broader enthusiasm and sentimentality of Rousseau, met with so evident a response in Germany, or when Goethe later turned back to French classicism for some of his dramas. Yet there was a change: whereas formerly French literary and intellectual influences had had it all their own way, now English influences became powerful, and to a certain extent prevailed. The movement began with the copying and adaptation of the English essayists, notably Swift and Addison, in the twenties and thirties of the century, bringing a marked improvement and polishing of German prose style. Then came a more pronounced turn to poetry, when the youthful Klopstock (1724–1803), fired by the translation by Bodmer in Zürich of Milton's *Paradise Lost*, began the production of his epic *The Messiah*, retailing the sufferings, death, and resurrection of Christ. The work was hailed as marking the opening of a new era, and of its debt to Milton (though not the Milton of the political pamphlets) there was no question. Klopstock was to remain a figure of importance in the new movement during a long life, but was to be much surpassed by later poets. Another long-lived character born a decade later, Christoph Martin Wieland (1733–1813), of far greater versatility than Klopstock, likewise lived through the whole movement, and illustrates the trend to the next phase, when Shakespeare became if not, like his own motley, 'the only wear,' at least the paragon of dramatic achievement.

This phase, which came with the sixties, marked the climax of English influence. It has been preceded by the vogue of Young's *Night Thoughts*, of English dramatists of lesser than Shakespearian fame, one or more of whom provided Lessing with the model for his 'middle-class tragedy,' *Miss Sara Sampson*, then a novelty in Germany, by the enthusiasm of Hamann and Herder for Ossian and the Percy Ballads, and not least by the sway of the English novelists from Defoe to Richardson, Sterne, and Fielding. Wieland is of interest here because although he was not to attain the highest rank as a German classic, he nevertheless shared in almost every side of the movement, the classical and the French as well as these English influences here recorded. A Wurtemberger like Schiller, the son of a Pietist Lutheran parson, but as impressionable as the young Goethe, he turned to literature, and displayed so versatile a mind and so facile a pen that he almost rivalled Voltaire in the volume of his literary activities. He was indeed regarded as more French than most of his contemporaries, perhaps partly because he had a gift of satire unusual in Germany. Yet Wieland responded more quickly than most to the cult for Shakespeare, translating into German in whole or part over a score of his plays in the years 1762–6. Like other and greater writers, he was to find an asylum in Weimar (1772), as tutor to the young princes there, and promptly started what was to be one of the most important of the many journals of the time, the (*New*) *German Mercury*. Meanwhile, through Hamann, Herder, Goethe, and others, Shakespeare had burst upon the German world as the culmination of this succession of English influences, and combined with other forces such as the influence of Rousseau to bring about that outburst of poetic and literary enthusiasm usually designated by the title of 'Storm and Stress' (*Sturm und Drang*).

This phase of the new movement, lasting about a decade, was ushered in by a little book entitled *Of German Style and Art* (1773), in which Herder extolled both Shakespeare and folk-songs, Goethe eulogized the Gothic art of Strassburg cathedral, and Justus Möser praised the forgotten liberties of the early Germans. In title and content the little book seemed to be primarily an expression of German national feeling, and it was in part a manifesto against the French influence which had so long prevailed, under the sway of Gottsched in Leipzig and his disciples. But though Herder and Justus Möser were to find places amongst the creators of German national feeling, Goethe was to outgrow his youthful enthusiasm for the German Gothic.   And more important than any specifically national or other quality of the work was the fact that it acted as a curtain raiser to the new enthusiasm. A surer indication of the new temper, and one which aroused more public attention, was the appearance at almost the same moment of Goethe's play *Götz von Berlichingen,* purely German in theme, but avowedly Shakespearian in its freedom of form, over-Shakespearian in fact, and with a corresponding appeal to freedom in its theme.   And Goethe proceeded to illustrate in his other writings of this period the essential qualities of this phase of the new movement, its youthful enthusiasm and demand for the unfettered expression of genius, its turning to nature, its Rousseau-like emphasis on feeling and emotion as opposed to reason.   Thus was initiated amongst this non-political people a literary revolution at the same moment that the more politically minded English colonists across the Atlantic were making their demands for liberty of another kind.

The merging of this initial phase of the movement into the broader stream illustrated by the sketches given below of Herder, Goethe, and Schiller demands, however, the addition of one essential element which was to colour and characterize its later course.   This was the new interest in and new approach to classical studies.   In certain ways Germany was, of course, already Latinized.   The medieval Church had set its ecclesiastical Latin stamp strongly upon her, and that remained in Catholic Germany.   And with the Renaissance, and Melanchthon's patterning of Protestant higher education, the Latin tradition was continued.   We are told that more Latin than German books were produced in Germany until nearly the beginning of the eighteenth century, university lectures were given in Latin, and the study of Latin and Greek grammar and texts dominated the philosophical or arts faculties in the universities.   The study was, however, pedagogical rather than human-istic, and it was utilitarian also, since education, the churches, and the legal and other civil services of Germany's hundreds of princes required and used Latin.

With the middle of the century, however, a new era in classical studies opened in Germany.   Its definition was due above all to a poor Prussian boy, Johann Joachim Winckelmann (1717–68) who with no advantage of means or social position, and no prospects in Prussia, developed a passion for classical art, Greek above all.   Leaving his remoter homeland he found inspiration first in the more artistic Dresden, and then in 1755, having accepted the faith of Rome, he departed for Italy, to find there in its ancient capital and elsewhere the examples or copies of Greek art which embodied what he sought.   He wrote two works, *Reflections on the Imitation of Greek Works in Painting and Sculpture* (1755) and a *History of Ancient Art* (1764), which together may be said to have founded the vogue of Greek art in Germany.   Doubtless the moment was propitious; the time and the man came together.   Yet that does not take away from Winckelmann's importance. For him the prime appeal was aesthetic.   Greek art was to him characterized by 'noble simplicity and serene greatness,' and was without peer in the works created by man. It remained for Lessing to make the application to Greek literature, with some criticism of Winckelmann, and so prepare the way for Goethe's conversion to the worship of the classical, with Herder and Schiller, Wieland, and others accompanying or following in varying degrees or ways. To Goethe Winckelmann was 'a literary Columbus.' Meanwhile the universities played their part in the turn to a new conception of classical and above all Greek studies, with Gesner at Göttingen and Christ (the teacher of Lessing) at Leipzig encouraging the study of Greek civilization in a more humanistic way. And at the same time Zedlitz, in charge of Prussian education, was furthering the study of Greek in the high schools or gymnasia there. Thus did Germany enter upon her Greek heritage, combining it with the other forces which were to make up her great age of literary production, the classic period of which Goethe is the centre but by no means the whole.

The whole movement had indeed so many ramifications, and spread into so many channels, that it is impossible to sum it up briefly or completely. Thus it ran directly and plainly into the Romantic movement, itself very complex, but in some essentials sufficiently different from the earlier movement. If the revival began by being radical (though not in a political sense) it quickly showed certain conservative tendencies. Whilst it marked a reaction against certain features of the Enlightenment, it yet retained some of the qualities of that earlier and broader movement. Its most important achievement no doubt was to give to Germany a medium of expression which she had so far lacked, in the form of a large body of great literature in the national language. Hence was fulfilled one of the necessities for the growth of a nation, the creation of a medium through which national consciousness could be fostered. It was little wonder that Fichte and others saw in language the prime characteristic of a nation. In this achievement the movement also helped to emancipate Germany from the earlier intellectual dependence upon France. Instead it gave to Germany a degree of cultural unity which combined with other forces to prepare her for the age of nationalism, and the conversion of cultural into political unity and nationality.

That is to look forward into and through the next century, and obviously the contribution of the literary movement to the political unification of Germany cannot be measured in any precise way. The share of Schiller in evoking patriotism, of Herder in discovering *das Volk* (the People), and in contributing to the idea of the organic historical development of societies, can perhaps most easily be recognized in this connection. But the contribution was more general, shared in by Kant, whose philosophy, if modified or added to by Fichte and Hegel, yet became a national possession, and no less by Goethe, who if no nationalist became a national possession comparable to England's Shakespeare. And this movement, it is important to note, had little or no connection with Austria, the old leader of the *Reich*, but developed largely in northern Germany, and so helped to open the way for the future predominance of the leading northern state, Prussia. On the

D

other hand, the movement was primarily neither political nor nationalist. Its divorce from public affairs, its lack of interest in either politics or the life of the people, has indeed been made a charge against it. The answer must be that in the then condition of affairs in Germany there was no room for the connection between literature and politics which obtained in England and in a different way in France, desirable though such a connection would have been. And as to its importance for the nationalist movement it is well to remember that at its highest and best the movement was far more than a merely national one. Its prime values, not merely in Goethe and Kant, but also in Herder and Schiller, possessed a more universal quality and a wider appeal, capable of outreaching and outlasting the nationalism into which they were merged from Bismarck to Hitler.

II. LESSING

Gotthold Ephraim Lessing (1729–81) was the outstanding 'Enlightener' of Germany in the eighteenth century. It was characteristic of Germany in that age that he emerged from a Lutheran parsonage, and in Saxony. For the Enlightenment in Germany developed in Protestant lands, and when Lessing was born in Kamenz, about a score of miles north-east of Dresden, Saxony still retained some of its former pre-eminence in Protestant Germany, providing from its Lutheran parsonages many of the leaders of the movement. The poverty and humble social position of the average Lutheran parson did not prevent him from securing for his children a remarkably good education, and the elder Lessing was far above the average. Young Lessing showed precocity in book-learning, received an admirable if severe classical training at one of the Electoral Saxon schools endowed from an earlier monastic establishment, and at the age of eighteen entered the university of Leipzig as a student of theology. But although he was to be deeply interested all his life in questions of religion, and indeed in theology, he was not to follow his father's footsteps. Leipzig and its university were interested in other and more secular things. Free of immediate princely or aristocratic control, long a centre for east-west trade, and now emerging as the great book mart of Germany, Leipzig had survived better than most German cities the decline which followed the Thirty Years War, and was a centre of rising middle-class activity like Hamburg, with the addition of a university as a focus for a higher intellectual life. It had indeed for a time claims to be the literary centre of Germany (if any such centre could exist in this divided land), with the indefatigable Gottsched and the simpler but more attractive Gellert as its literary leaders, both of them professors in its university. Although Lessing was to aid in the downfall of Gottsched and much that he stood for, he nevertheless owed much to Leipzig. For whilst his theological studies suffered, he found in his wide-ranging intellectual interests a special zest for literature, and particularly for the drama. To the acute distress of his family he forsook the path laid down for him, and with no financial resources, and debts which caused him to flee from Leipzig, he embarked on the career of a critic and man of letters. It was a new career in Germany, and was to be beset for Lessing with even greater difficulties than those faced in England by his older contemporary Samuel Johnson.

Yet if Lessing had more continuous economic difficulties than Johnson, with twenty-five years less of life (and no Boswell), he probably accomplished the more for German intellectual life. Outwardly he was a restless, unsettled person—the very opposite of Kant—going to Berlin from Leipzig, leaving it and returning to it more than once, but failing to find a permanent resting place there. He acted for a time as secretary to the military governor of Silesia, then as theatrical critic to an ill-fated dramatic enterprise in Hamburg, only finding a permanent home at last (in 1770) as librarian to the ducal house of Brunswick at their former capital of Wolfenbüttel. There too he found domestic happiness in marriage, but only for a brief period, since his wife died a year later. And his nature was too independent for him to be a mere guardian of books and an obedient servant of a princely house, so that he found himself involved in controversy which threatened both his freedom to write and publish, and almost his place. Yet this restlessness was no mere discontent with his lot, or inability to pursue a settled or chosen course. Rather was it a sign of his continued growth, and of his efforts to stimulate a like growth in others. It was this capacity for self-development and for teaching others both by criticism and example, which made Lessing so important in the intellectual revival in Germany. And his movements about Germany probably aided in the diffusion of this influence.

Lessing was first of all a scholar, a student on classical foundations of modern literature—his own, French, English, Italian, and even Spanish, with a special interest in the dramatic art. With that he developed a marked critical faculty, exercised in the *Literary Letters* which he began to publish in Berlin, in his more purely dramatic criticisms at Hamburg, and indeed throughout his life. His criticism could be severe, at times devastating, but it was never merely destructive. If he criticized the imitation of French drama, which as part of the general Gallic influence flooded the German stage, it was because he had found a more worthy model in Shakespeare. And he proceeded to show how a better German drama could be written, with his plays *Minna von Barnhelm* and *Emilia Galotti*. We are not here concerned with Lessing's views on the dramatic art or the technical quality of the two plays. The former play struck an anti-French, and even pro-Prussian, note which found its response in Germany. Lessing was indeed, for a time at least, an admirer of the Great Frederick, notably in his fight against the French. He had found himself, and enjoyed life, in his capital, and with the aid of F. Nicolai and Moses Mendelssohn had worked powerfully to make Berlin a centre of the Enlightenment. Yet it is doubtful whether he could have stayed there, even had he secured the position he once sought. 'Don't talk to me,' he wrote later to Nicolai, 'of your Berlin freedom of thinking and writing. It amounts simply and solely to freedom of publishing as many *sottises* as you like against religion.' And Lessing shared the cosmopolitan feelings of the men of the Enlightenment: 'I have no conception of the love of country,' he once declared, 'and it seems to me at best a heroic weakness which I am well content to lack.' The play *Emilia Galotti* had its application to German conditions in its portrayal of the tragedy wrought by the unbridled licence of a petty princeling; it won popular but hardly princely approbation.

Thus Lessing taught by both criticism and example. He could not paint pictures or carve statuary to develop a new theory of art; but in his best-known prose work, *Laokoon*, he began by criticizing the theories of Winckelmann (though with much appreciation of his work) as to the dominating serenity in Greek art, going on to discuss most fruitfully the relations between art and poetry, and the nature of poetry as action rather than, as it had become in Germany, description. It mattered less that not all his views were tenable, or that the *Laokoon* itself, like others of Lessing's works, was admittedly a fragment. More important was the stimulus he provided for the Germany of his day, a stimulus both to newer and freer ideas of poetry, and to classical and, above all, Greek studies. Winckelmann had begun to awaken Germany to the final perfection of beauty in Greek art; Lessing performed a parallel service for Greek poetry. Goethe was to testify to the effect of the stimulus on a young man like himself, twenty years younger than Lessing, of 'the beam of light which shone upon us through dark clouds from this most eminent thinker.'

Lessing's role in eighteenth-century Germany was that of a teacher, and perhaps, like Goethe himself, though under far less happy circumstances, he performed it the better outside rather than inside the walls of a university. His teaching sprang, like the finest teaching from the days of Socrates onwards, from his own desire to know the truth. And the final truth for this son of the parsonage was bound to be that of man's relation to God. Above all, how far could the Reason and the ever-growing knowledge of the century be applied to this problem; how far must the answer depend upon the unique Revelation of Scripture? Lessing had gone a long way from the parsonage, yet he never ceased to be concerned with the fundamental questions of religion, was far more religious than the average *philosophe*, and was greatly interested and very learned in ecclesiastical history. He had been drawn into religious controversy by publishing portions of a treatise criticizing parts of the Christian faith, together with his own counter-arguments. He had been attacked for this, and defended himself vigorously. Then in 1780 he published a fragment, brief but amongst the most important of his works, entitled *The Education of the Human Race*. In it he sought to reconcile Revelation and Reason within the widest historical framework. Reason, he argued, was not contrary to Revelation, but supplemented it both in the first Revelation of God to the Jewish people and likewise in the later Revelation of Christianity. And only by the exercise of human Reason could humanity hope to attain to the full enlightenment to which it was destined.

Lessing had another lesson for mankind, less theological but no less in keeping with his own convictions and with the best in eighteenth-century thought. This was the lesson of religious toleration. One of his earliest plays, *The Jews*, had attacked the disabilities under which members of that race, including his friend Mendelssohn, suffered. Now in his latest years he returned to the theme in a wider setting. His great play *Nathan the Wise*, 1779, depicts a crusading Christian knight, the great Moslem ruler Saladin, and a wise and tolerant Jew, Nathan, as drawn together in common bonds by the aid of a truly Christian friar, regardless of their differences of religion. 'Hold to the best alone, praising God who best can reconcile,' is Saladin's (and Lessing's) conclusion. And if *Nathan* was more a dramatic poem than a play suited to action on the stage, it was meant for action on that wider stage of the world which Lessing had done his best to improve.

III. HERDER

Johann Gottfried Herder (1744–1803) is properly regarded as one of the leading figures in the intellectual and literary revival in Germany. At first sight it is not entirely easy to say why. For Herder was no great poet or dramatist, he founded no new philosophy, and he attained no great position. He was the son of a sexton in a small town in distant East Prussia, and he was to spend nearly half of his life as Lutheran parson and superintendent in the little state of Weimar.

Yet these limitations did not prevent him from exercising a quite extraordinary influence over the literary and intellectual life of his day, and later. Certainly he owed much to others: to his wife Caroline, to Kant when he was a student at Koenigsberg, to Klopstock, Lessing, and Goethe, to French and still more to English literature. But he owed most to his own unflagging zeal for the enlargement and improvement of his own mind, from the childhood days when he tied himself into an apple-tree that he might safely lose himself in his book, to his dying wish for some new ideas which would quicken his soul and so revive his bodily strength. The explanation of Herder's influence lies partly in the moment at which he appeared, partly in the wide variety of his interests, but most of all in his enthusiasm and his unusual capacity for inspiring a like zeal in others. The outstanding example of this last quality is, of course, the young Goethe, who bore generous testimony to it in his autobiography.

Herder was an intellectually precocious child, who absorbed quickly and easily the education which his native town of Mohrungen had to offer. It was a testimony to Prussian (and German) education at that date that within a year after Herder as a youth left Mohrungen for Koenigsberg we find him teaching Greek, Latin, French, mathematics, philosophy, and history there, while at the same time he attended lectures from Kant and others at the university. Thence in due course he moved to Riga, in Russia, where he taught, and where he entered the Lutheran ministry. He also made acquaintance with English literature, and not content with a growing reputation as teacher and preacher, began to write *Fragments* on German literature. These fragments are important as revealing that young Herder was already alive both to the need and to the opportunity for a fuller and more original development of German literature. The visit to France, following on five years spent at the Russian outpost of German culture, confirmed and deepened these convictions. Indebted as he was, like all German writers, to the French authors of the Enlightenment, and to Rousseau, Herder now reacted against the Gallic influence, and found more kinship in Ossian and Shakespeare. And being above all a teacher, though a very different one from Lessing, he proceeded to impress his views on the Young Germany of that day. This Young Germany he was shortly to meet at Strassburg personified in the twenty-year-old and impressionable Goethe. It was a meeting significant for both, but especially to Goethe, and so through him to Germany.

Herder has been called a German nationalist, and so within certain limits he was. He laboured with all the enthusiasm characteristic of him to free German literature from what he regarded as its classical swaddling clothes, and from foreign influences. Fired by the Scottish and English balladists, he sought and found inspiration in simple ballad and folk literature. In such poetry, he believed, did the culture of a people, a *Volk*, express its identity and special character, its national genius. By his precept and example in this field he contributed to lay the foundations of later phases of German nationalism, from Romanticism to Nazism. But if Herder could gird at the harmful effects of foreign influences on German cultural development he never narrowed his view to German literature alone. He did not think of German culture as separate from the broad stream of European culture, or deny the classical and Hebrew influence upon it. Still less did he think in terms of political or racial nationalism, or the power of the nationalist state. He was always universal as well as national, both in his interest in folk literature and in his view of history. As a young man at Riga, a subject of Catherine II of Russia, he had lauded the Russian eagle, and he heartily disliked the militarism of his own Prussia. He even went so far as to declare that 'the states of the kingdom of Prussia will not be happy until they are divided up.' Further, he never felt or expressed any feeling of racial superiority, and had a particular sympathy for the Slavic peoples.

Herder, after all, was not merely a Lutheran parson by profession, but remained throughout a devout Christian. As superintendent of the Lutheran Church in Weimar for so many years he was continually occupied with his religious duties, preaching to his flock, baptizing, marrying, and burying, examining and ordaining candidates for the ministry, and generally responsible for the religious interests of the community. If on occasion he could follow Gibbon in some of his carpings at the early Christians, he never lost faith in the ethical heritage of Christianity or indeed in the Lutheran position. It is true that the unusual variety of his interests and the fertility of his pen caused him to be regarded with some suspicion by the more orthodox theologians of his day. On the other hand, it was partly his religious beliefs which caused him to remain aloof from some of the later trends of the literary revival he had helped to foster.

Herder's writings amply reflected his many-sided interests, and there was

probably some truth in his own judgment: 'I believe I write too much.'
Nor was he always consistent in the views he set forth. He began in 1766
with *Fragments*, and there was throughout a certain fragmentary or unfinished
quality about much of his writing. He followed up the *Fragments* with
other essays discussing and criticizing current literary trends and writers in
Germany. It was these writings, with Herder's own personality behind
them, which excited the young Goethe and made Herder, at twenty-six, the
father of 'Storm and Stress.' For already Herder revealed not only the
wide range of his literary interests, from ancient to modern, but his belief
in the importance of all that was individual and spontaneous in the thought
and literary expression of different peoples. Such a view made all wrong for
Germany the mere imitation of classical or French models. Herder's
appreciation of simple folk literature drove him back behind the Renaissance,
which had so profoundly affected German literary and scholastic development, to the medieval period. Thereby he evoked an interest which was to
be one of the marks of the Romantic movement.

Herder continued for a time to be active in the new movement, writing in
the journals of the time, publishing his *Popular Songs and Ballads* (1778–9),
a work on *Plastic Art*, and other writings. But he gradually dissociated
himself from some of the prevailing tendencies, going his own way, with a
continuous interest in religion and a growing feeling for the historical
approach. He wrote in defence of Spinoza (*Dialogues on God*) and against
the Deism of the century. In his latest years, and less successfully, he wrote
in criticism of the new philosophy expounded by Kant and Fichte, the latter
a neighbour at the university of Jena. Earlier than this, however, he had
written his most important mature work, his *Ideas for a Philosophy of Human
History*. He had already put his hand to the subject of general history in a
short sketch which he wrote in 1773 entitled *Another Philosophy of History*,
interesting for its defence of the Middle Ages against the depreciations of
Voltaire and others. During the years 1783–91 he proceeded to set out on
a larger canvas his conception of the place of man in the natural universe
and his development in history. Although Herder had great hopes of science
for the improvement of the world, he was hardly a scientist, and took his
scientific information from the writings of men such as Buffon, Haller, and
Linnaeus. He saw God behind the natural world, and distinguished man from
the animal world by his upright gait, his power of reasoning, and his effort
to attain 'Humanity.' Like Montesquieu, if not following Montesquieu, he
laid stress on the influence of geographical features upon history; the rivers
and coastline of Europe, he argued, had fostered the mixture of peoples.

The history of mankind to Herder was one, and it was the story of man's
progress towards an ever-greater 'Humanity,' which to Herder meant his
growth and achievement in art, religion, literature, science, and government.
We can only indicate the lines of his sketch of world history from the origins
of speech and religion among primitive peoples to the Greeks, who gave us
the first example of a fully developed culture, and left the seeds of its blossom-
ing to be scattered abroad for the modern world. Rome, despite its conquests

and greatness, was bound to fall as Montesquieu had shown, and was a bad bridge from the ancient world to our own. But despite set-backs man is bound to grow in reason and justice, and God is present in history as in nature. It was well for the future of Europe that the Germanic peoples, with their high qualities, occupied the Roman world, but this did not give them any claim to rule over other peoples; they owed their culture to classical origins and to a foreign religion, Christianity. For a time the medieval Church provided an invaluable protective covering within which society could develop. But papal power and pretensions required to be held in check by secular rulers, and out of the clash of these two great forces European society was slowly to develop its characteristic form and culture. Herder had meant to continue his survey to the French Revolution but, perhaps wisely, left it unfinished at the Renaissance.

Herder's sketch of world history appeared about midway in time between those of Voltaire and Hegel. It was less complete than either, more a sketch indeed, less masterly than Hegel's *Philosophy of History*, less a history and less skilfully written than Voltaire's *Essai sur les Mœurs*. Yet it had qualities which gave it importance. To begin with it was German—the first German work of this kind on any scale. If it was less a universal history than the work of Voltaire it nevertheless had more unity and was in some ways more historically minded. It was free of Voltairian cynicism and from Voltaire's prejudices against 'the age of faith,' the medieval period. Writing a generation later than Voltaire, Herder bore witness to a changing perspective. Here, as in his earlier literary work, he was a precursor of the coming Romanticism, with its greater emphasis on imagination and, in history, its deeper comprehension of the historical process. Indeed Herder has been credited with doing most to define and to found the historical point of view which was to pervade nineteenth-century thought. Kant might criticize the *Ideen* for its lack of logical reasoning, but Goethe, perhaps with more prevision, could declare that its influence on the development of German culture was beyond estimation.

It was Goethe also who predicted that the *Ideen* would exert its influence gradually. That indeed was true of much of Herder's work, with 'Storm and Stress' as a notable exception. 'No man,' a later critic pronounced,[1] 'ever scattered abroad a greater quantity of fruitful seed than he.' The Romantic movement, the Classical movement, the Nationalist movement, amongst Slavs as well as Germans, and the Historical movement—all these and more owed something to Herder. How much each owed will naturally be matter for dispute. Herder, with his restless enthusiasms and ardent temperament, the qualities which have rather improperly suggested the title of 'the German Rousseau,' had his critics as well as his admirers, and doubtless will continue to have. If we measure him by the touchstone of his attitude to the French Revolution, we find him at first welcoming it with all the zeal of an enthusiast, defending its sweeping changes and attacking

---

[1] K. Hillebrand, *German Thought from the Seven Years War to the Death of Goethe*, 1880, p. 114.

the counter-revolutionary forces which gathered in Germany and elsewhere. But after the execution of Louis XVI his attitude changed, and with surprising suddenness. Herder was naturally impulsive, and may have been affected by the opposition which his views aroused in Germany. He was also little acquainted with politics, and was the more disillusioned by the violence of the political passions manifested in Paris; and he hated war with a feeling akin to that of Kant. He had matured early, and his powers likewise declined relatively early. Yet he did not give up faith in the revolution as a great step forward in the emancipation of mankind, and as an advance towards that 'Humanity' which man, with his inextinguishable and godlike life-force, was destined to attain. And that faith was Herder's truest and most important legacy.

IV. GOETHE

The work of Herder and Lessing was given new strength and direction by that of the two greatest figures amongst German poets and men of letters, Goethe and Schiller. The life of Johann Wolfgang von Goethe (1749–1832), the elder by ten years and far the longer-lived, extended through the whole period of the revival in Germany, and indeed beyond it, for he was born the year after Klopstock began to publish his *Messiah,* and he outlived Hegel, the last of the immediate successors of Kant, by a year. We cannot explain the appearance at that time of these two writers of genius,[1] but for Goethe it was important that he was born and brought up in a free Imperial City of south-west Germany, Frankfurt, and that he was a product not of the Lutheran parsonage but of a comfortably off middle-class family in that ancient city, where the Holy Roman Emperors had once been elected. And Frankfurt was ever a great trading and meeting-place, midway between north and south, just off the great highway of the Rhine and open to the west winds from France. Thus it was that Goethe enjoyed from birth great advantages of economic, political, and intellectual liberty; and it was above all this *freedom,* expressed primarily in the medium of poetry, which was his greatest gift to Germany in the first and most purely creative period of his life. The service to German literature was not, of course, confined to these years, but the later picture is more complex and disturbed. In old age Goethe himself rightly defined his services to Germany as being primarily a liberating influence: 'If I were to say what I had really been to the Germans in general and to the young German poets in particular, I should say that I had been their liberator.'

This early period of Goethe's life, work, and influence, whether considered as ending with his move to Weimar at the age of twenty-six in 1775, or as continuing until he made the famous journey to Italy eleven years later, has in general been defined as the period of 'Storm and Stress' in German

[1] Cf.: 'The movements of the human spirit, its sudden flashes, its expansion and its pauses, must for ever remain a mystery to our eyes, since we can but know this or that of the forces at work, never all of them together.' (J. Burckhardt, *The Culture of the Italian Renaissance* (trans.), p. 445.)

literature, and the movement centres round Goethe, its stormy petrel.   The
years at Leipzig University (1765-8), where he studied almost everything but
the law he was supposed to be imbibing, formed a precocious adolescent
background, but it was the succeeding year and more at Strassburg which
really started off both the poet and the movement.   For there, at the age
of twenty-one, and impressionable almost to weakness, Goethe was subjected
(the influence of French culture apart) to the stimulus of Herder, the mighty
genius of Shakespeare, and the acute if short-lived passion for Friederike
Brion.   The resulting excitation of spirit, continued by other journeyings,
other contacts, and other loves in these formative years, expressed itself in
the turbulent rush of his writings of this time, the unsurpassed lyrics, the
drama of the unbridled *Götz von Berlichingen* of Luther's day, the haunting
tragedy of the original version of *Faust*, the story of the excessively emotion-
alized *Sorrows of Werther*.   Through them all breathes the rich ferment of
the young Goethe's restless, emotional, impulsive spirit, untrammelled, yet
engaged in a perpetual struggle with himself, and communicating some of that
spirit to the Germany of his time, with a vivacity and force denied both to
Lessing and to Herder, by the impress of his unique personality and the
medium of his verse and prose.

From the point of view of one seeking to describe and explain the intellectual revival of Germany in the eighteenth century it could be argued that
Goethe had already made his decisive contribution thereto by the time he
had settled in Weimar (1775) as an official of the young duke of that little
Thuringian principality with its population of slightly over half a million.
For Goethe, however, and for Germany too in a longer view, that was but
the first stage, the first of the three periods, almost three generations, into
which his life and work was to be divided.   Yet the two later stages, the
second which began in 1786 with his journey to Italy and continued to the
death of Schiller in 1805, and the third which carried the story from that
date down to Goethe's death in 1832, are, of course, bound up with the first.
Thus the *Faust* which was begun in his twenties was completed in his eighties.
But, inevitably, Goethe grew and changed, and since his writings were always
to an unusual extent self-revelatory, such changes reveal themselves in his
writings.   Without attempting to follow them and their reflection in his
work, we may indicate their general course and nature in order both to fill out
the picture of the man and to illustrate his place in the times.   Throughout
the period, Goethe remained the official of the little Duchy of Weimar,
fortunate if not always happy there, a faithful and trusted servant, friend
indeed, of its Duke Carl August, superintending the theatre, the mines, the
university of Jena, in due course ennobled, free to travel, profoundly influenced by Frau von Stein yet breaking with her in the end, disregarding
convention with a poor liaison which turned—in the end—into a poorer
marriage, going his own way throughout, unique at the end as at the
beginning.

Goethe's first period, his share in the 'Storm and Stress' movement, was to
foreshadow, indeed to help to bring on, the full flowering of the Romantic

movement in Germany. Doubtless just as Goethe would have emerged without Herder's stimulus, but owed much to it at a decisive moment, so the Romantic fervour and fever would have seized upon Germany without Goethe; but it was none the less powerfully assisted by him. Yet Goethe himself outgrew much (though not all) of his earlier romantic mood, and turned away from the enthusiasm for the Gothic which he had found at Strassburg, and from the almost over-Shakespearian freedom of *Götz*. Instead he followed Winckelmann by going to Italy. There he sought and found in the classic example and spirit, above all in Greek art and literature so far as it was revealed there, a higher and nobler ideal of beauty and life. And this view, conviction rather, once attained, was to remain with him permanently, to show itself in *Iphigenia*, to colour *Hermann und Dorothea*, to intrude into *Faust*, to turn him back to French drama as nearer to classical models, and to divorce him both from the Romantic trend now beginning to prevail in Germany, and from the nationalist emphasis which that movement was to take on. The efforts and example of Schiller and himself, conjoined in that remarkable intellectual partnership from 1794 to 1805, could not avail to stem the Romantic tide, or impose classical disciplined simplicity in its place. The Romantic northerners did not experience, as Goethe did, 'a feeling of freer life, higher existence, lightness, and grace,' in the spirit of antiquity, any more than they could feel the sunshine of Italy. Yet the inspiration which Goethe received from the Greeks, and which he expressed in drama and poem, reinforcing as it did the earlier example of Winckelmann, Lessing, and Herder, and supported by Schiller, had deep and lasting effects on German thought, and has in fact been made responsible for a 'Greek tyranny' over the German mind, as fostering in them 'a hopeless passion for the absolute'[1] to be represented above all in the poet Hölderlin.

It is tempting to see in Goethe's latest years, from Schiller's death to his own, the emergence and triumph of a kind of synthesis of the outstanding, if partly contradictory, forces at work in him during the two earlier periods. But this is, of course, to oversimplify matters. Goethe was one person throughout, even if his development did not by any means proceed, in his own oft misapplied phrase, 'without haste, but without rest' (*ohne Hast, aber ohne Rast*). His way to achievement, to self-mastery and renunciation, to the fullest development of his gifts, was by more than one channel, and never by one route alone at one time; indeed he needed to be absorbed in a number of things at the same time. 'The necessity of my nature,' he wrote about 1780, 'impels me to a manifold activity.' Yet the channels and routes were connected in the one personality. His varied literary productions, from the simplest lyrics to the dark profundities of the second part of *Faust*, were all the products of the same energy, or δαίμων, of his genius; and this cannot be reduced to a single formula, a single 'idea'; Goethe was too complex a being for that. He sought to understand nature, 'to hold fast to nature alone,' as he puts it in the *Werther*. And he did indeed spend an enormous, if not an inordinate, amount of time for a poet in the study of

[1] E. M. Butler, *The Tyranny of Greece over Germany*, 1935.

natural phenomena; botany, geology, optical physics, and anatomy in turn or together absorbed him. Nor were his researches entirely unfruitful. But the unhappy story of his strenuous and long-continued attempts to disprove the Newtonian theory of light suggests a certain weakness or gap in his quality as a scientist. Goethe was in fact both less and more than a scientist. As his biographer puts it,[1] 'his persistent endeavour was to attain a conception

of the *Kosmos* which would satisfy both his intellect and his heart.' And Goethe's mind, and still more his heart, were irreducible to scientific terms or measurements. Certainly not in the scientific knowledge of that day, or by a Goethe, could such satisfaction be found.

For Goethe's prime interest was in *human* nature, and his interest in natural science sprang partly out of the increasing interest in all natural things that was common to the time, and was related to the problem of finding a harmony between man and the universe, outside or independent of the revelation of orthodox Christianity. But it sprang above all from the need to find a philosophy of life for himself and for others, a guide to conduct, a moral basis for life. The 'pure humanity' of Herder (as of Lessing and Rousseau and the Enlightenment generally) supplied at least a partial answer, and it was one of the attractions of the Greek world, to Goethe, that he saw this ideal of humanity embodied in it, as the *Iphigenia* showed.

Goethe
*Maclise-Thackeray,
after Stieler*

In this humanity were subsumed the highest in both art and life, and the whole duty of the individual man was to strive unceasingly towards the fulfilment in himself of this highest ideal. So Wilhelm Meister rises from devotion to the theatre to the pursuit of the highest cultivation of his individuality and gifts by the harmonious combination of action and reflection. And if reflection and inner growth implied a certain withdrawal from the world, Goethe nevertheless recognized that the scene for action and the development of character was human society.

Thereby is raised the whole vexed question of the relations of Goethe to the Germany of his day, and to the overwhelming events which opened in 1789, a subject far too big to be seriously discussed here. Goethe grew up in a Free City, nominally subject only to the decayed imperial authority of Vienna. He was a poet, a man of letters, and men of letters in Germany had no place or part in the public life of the country. Yet Goethe responded for a time to Herder's evocation of national sentiment, and his own writings were a powerful stimulus to the growth of German national consciousness

[1] Hume Brown, *Goethe*, 1920, vol. i, p. 275

FREDERICK WILLIAM II

LESSING

After Kügelgen

HERDER

WIELAND

in terms of literature. Also he passed early into the service of one of the many small princes of Germany, fortunately for him one of the more enlightened of those princes. Therein, if on a small scale, he played no small part in embodying and furthering that enlightenment, whether in wise counsel to his prince or in actual administration. But he was no bold reformer. The frame of society as he knew it suited him, and provided amply for his needs both economically and intellectually.

When the French Revolution broke out Goethe was forty years of age, and had just found himself at home in classic beauty and serenity. Little wonder, then, that he saw the revolution as a disturbing 'nightmare,' and tried to withdraw into his shell as a 'private man.' As he had previously refused to be interested in the partitions of Poland, so now he displayed little concern for the issues at stake in that Paris which he had never visited. He made the campaign of 1792 into France with his ruler, attached to the army of the Prussia he so disliked, but he did it with a singular detachment, to judge from the account he wrote of the campaign. And he viewed the French invasions of Germany with a similar lack of strong national feeling. What he disliked was the threat to the established social order, and the rantings for an equality which was meaningless and could only destroy. Against that he wrote, both in dramatic pieces and in *Hermann und Dorothea*, the idyllic if stylized picture of German village contentment and happiness in contrast to a revolutionary background. For the rest, he was satisfied, for a decade, with the fruitful contact with Schiller and others at Jena, until that bond was broken with Schiller's death in 1805. The crash of Prussia in the following year brought fresh official duties, but neither then nor later was he greatly moved in opposition to French rule. He accepted the rule of Napoleon, holding to his dislike of Prussia, disbelieving in any national German cause. And when Napoleon was driven out he found refuge in the writing of his *Autobiography*, in the completion of *Faust*, in his scientific studies, and in the study of oriental literature, so remote from the upheavals of the West. If he disliked the repressive measures of Metternich, he distrusted the ebullitions in the twenties of a national feeling to which he was a stranger, and for this a later age of more active and passionate German nationalism has not forgiven him. Yet he has never lost his place in German life and thought. Successive generations of German scholars and thinkers have turned back to him for inspiration. And the call of the philosophers, 'Back to Kant,' has been rivalled by the call for a return to Goethe.[1]

V. SCHILLER

The influence of Johann Christoph Friedrich von Schiller (1759–1805) upon the revival of German literature and thought was to be no less marked than that of Goethe. And since they felt and thought alike, if not identically, on a number of matters of importance, that influence was exerted in the same

[1] So, for example, in the work of the distinguished German scholar Friedrich Meinecke after the crash of 1945. (*Die deutsche Katastrophe*, 1945.)

general direction.   Thus they were both from south-western Germany, both creative poets of the 'Storm and Stress' period; they both fell under the sway of classical Greece; and they both disliked the French Revolution and its doctrines.   But if they were alike in these and indeed other matters, they were never identical, being far too highly individual.   They differed in origin as in character and temperament; Schiller lived little over half as long as Goethe, wrote no autobiography, made no Italian journey, never left Germany indeed, and in contrast with Goethe's many emotional entanglements, was a model of conjugal virtue and happiness.   He could never have been a courtier or administrator, as Goethe would hardly have fitted the professorial chair which Schiller (through Goethe's efforts) came to occupy at Jena. And so one could go on to list what may better be illustrated by reference to Schiller's career and work.

In the year 1759 which saw the birth of Schiller, Robert Burns was born in Scotland, to endure even greater poverty and hardship, and to live an even shorter life.   But Burns was more akin to Goethe in his lyric power, a 'child of nature' in a far more literal sense than Goethe could ever claim to be.   Frederick Schiller was born well within a hundred miles of Frankfurt, on the Neckar rather than on the Main, and grew up in circumstances far less favoured than those of Goethe.   For the Schillers were humble subjects of that Karl Eugen, Duke of Wurtemberg, who, in his aping of French ways and court extravagance, illustrated the worst aspect of the infinite variety of the Holy Roman Empire in its decline.   And although the duke reformed his manners and morals during the years young Schiller was at school he remained just as arbitrary as before in his treatment of his subjects.   So that while Schiller got a fairly good grammar-school education he was forced by princely authority into a strait jacket first of legal and then of medical education, to emerge as an army surgeon in ducal service.   His early poems reflected his isolation and unhappiness; and the plays which accompanied and followed them showed plainly his violent opposition to and criticism of the society in which he had been born and brought up.

The first of these plays, *The Robbers* (1781), owed something both to Goethe and to Rousseau.   But it was above all a personal and violent protest by a completely unknown youth.   Goethe at just the same age had re-created a rebel knight in his play *Götz*.   But Götz lived and died within the framework of existing society, rebel yet loyal to the emperor, and indeed at bottom profoundly conservative.   Schiller's robber-hero, Karl Moor, is driven to be an outcast, a rebel against society, leader of a robber band.   Schiller followed this up by two other plays, *The Conspiracy of Fiesco*, which lauds the heroism of a sixteenth-century Genoese conspirator against ducal tyranny, and *Plot and Passion* (*Kabale und Liebe*) which came nearer home to depict the web of intrigue, oppression, and monstrous abuse of privilege and rank in a German princely court.   These poems and plays constituted Schiller's contribution to the 'Storm and Stress' movement, and drove him in flight from the narrow confines of Wurtemberg to look for fame and fortune first in Saxony and then in Weimar, where he was to find a wife, and, at Jena, a professorial chair. Here he enjoyed both leisure to write and the years of close contact with Goethe.

The decisive change in Schiller's life and fortunes which set in with his arrival in Leipzig in 1785 was reflected almost immediately by a change in temper and attitude to society, and in due course by the growth of fresh interests and the general maturing of his genius. A new-found happiness in life was expressed in the well-known *Hymn to Joy*, familiar through its incorporation in Beethoven's Choral Symphony. He ceased to be a rebel against society, and found first hope and then faith in the possibility of its improvement. The modifications made in his tragedy of *Don Carlos* illustrate this change; in the final form, the philosophic Marquis of Posa, in his speeches to King Philip II, expresses boundless faith in humanity and freedom. From acute pessimism Schiller came to harbour an optimistic belief in the power of reason to educate mankind, and this within the existing framework of society. These views and convictions were to have profound effects on Schiller's work for the remainder of his life. Ceasing to be a revolutionary, he was to look with disapproval at the revolution in France, like many another eighteenth-century thinker. Whilst he did not cease to be a poet and a writer of tragedies, he nevertheless became increasingly concerned with this problem of the education of humanity. Ever more of a moralist than Goethe, more abstract where Goethe was more scientific, though never strictly a philosopher, he came to see in great literature and art the moral teacher of mankind, by which even freedom is attained. 'It is through beauty that we arrive at freedom,' he declared in the *Letters on Aesthetic Education*.

Schiller's more formal connection with education came with his appointment, largely through the good offices of Goethe, to the chair of history at the flourishing university of Jena in the Duchy of Weimar. This was in the notable year 1789. But although Schiller was to devote himself largely to historical work and writing for the next few years, writing a *History of the Thirty Years War*, and continuing an uncompleted *History of the Revolt in the Netherlands*, he was not to make a final or complete transition from poet to historian. He first turned from history to lecture on aesthetics, and then, following a breakdown in health, he ceased to lecture at all after 1793. Yet his historical studies were to be valuable to him as a historical dramatist, e.g. in *Wallenstein*. Meanwhile he was finding another and more congenial approach to the work of educating his fellow countrymen, using art and poetry rather than history as the medium, in the writing of essays published in what we might term reviews, between 1793 and 1796.

These essays show the increasingly philosophical bent of Schiller's mind as he grew into middle age. The chief influence was that of Kant, mainly the Kant of the 1790 *Critique of Judgment*, in which the philosopher discusses the nature of our judgments on beauty. The *Letters upon the Aesthetical Education of Man* (1795) 'rest chiefly,' affirmed Schiller, 'upon Kantian principles,' although Schiller was by no means a complete disciple of Kant, and developed his theme in his own way to his own conclusions. These *Letters* and the other *Essays* of the period, such as that upon *Grace and Dignity* (1793) and that upon *Naive and Sentimental Poetry* (1795–6), also reveal very clearly another development of Schiller's mind in these years.

Schiller

They show that he had followed Goethe from the early enthusiasms of the 'Storm and Stress' period into the worship of the classical, and more particularly the Greeks, 'amongst whom,' as he puts it in the *Letters*, 'the perception of the beautiful attained its highest development.' Yet Schiller's conception of Greek beauty, with its serenity and grace, as of all beauty in art and literature, is far from being merely sensuous enjoyment. It is, on the contrary, closely bound up with moral development. To him beauty 'will never endanger moral truths,' but will foster moral progress and the attainment of those ideals of a loftier humanity which formed the core of his thought and teaching.

It was in great measure this community of belief in the transcendent qualities of Greek art which now began to draw Schiller and Goethe together, in opposition to the growing Romantic trend of the day, for the last decade of Schiller's life. Goethe was to acknowledge fully the debt he owed to Schiller for his 'second spring' of renewed poetic activity, and Schiller undoubtedly drew a parallel encouragement from the contact with the greater poet. They shared together the attacks of the writers of the more Romantic and national school, and together replied to them in a famous series of epigrams; and they shared also attacks on their lack of Christian faith or teaching. They joined forces in a project of ballad writing which gave an immense stimulus to Schiller's poetic production, and led to the writing of many of his best-known ballads and lyrics. Indeed Schiller became immensely active in writing and literary criticism in these years. His final energies, however, were given to the drama with which he had begun, the subjects being now mainly historical. In the last seven or eight years of his life he produced the great plays of Wallenstein's tragic end, *Mary Stuart* (Queen Mary of Scotland), *The Maid of Orleans*, the classical tragedy *The Bride of Messina*, and last and best known (at least outside his native land), *William Tell*. For this last play he was indebted to Goethe both for the subject itself and for the descriptions of Swiss scenery. Schiller was aided also by the theatre at Weimar in the production of his tragedies, to make his decisive contribution to the development of the drama in Germany.

The two poets had still another element in common, in their dislike of and opposition to the French Revolution and most if not all of what it stood for. Lover of freedom and reason as he was, Schiller, as we have seen, had passed beyond his 'revolutionary stage,' if we can call it such, before the revolution broke out, and had found within the limits of later eighteenth-century German thought and society, from which politics were almost completely excluded, both scope and satisfaction for his energies. Eighteenth-century enlightenment and cosmopolitanism, with Kantian philosophy and the worship of Greek beauty, freed him from all concern with national feeling, and the French Revolution he found wanting in the *moral* aims which to him were the core of human advancement. The State, he concluded, cannot establish perfect humanity. He even thought of writing in defence of Louis XVI. The revolution, like the Lutheran movement, hindered peaceful cultural development, as one of the Goethe-Schiller epigrams put it. So he turned his back on it, as indeed on the political and social conditions of Germany itself, and concerned himself with his poetical and intellectual pursuits. In his well-known poem, *The Song of the Bell*, as with Goethe in *Hermann und Dorothea*, he lauded the simple, solid qualities of the ordinary German folk, undisturbed by revolutionary thoughts; peace and happiness are the themes rung out by the finished bell.

Yet Schiller, far more obviously than Goethe, was to serve the cause of German freedom and nationalism. True, his greatest service was educational in a more general sense. He provided for his countrymen a large body of poetry and prose, moral and idealistic in tone, which became by its quality and expression 'classical'—a national possession second only to the contribution of Goethe himself. But whereas Goethe, living through the collapse of the old Germany before the might of Napoleon, and the liberation that followed, retained his aloofness from political life and his disbelief in either nationalism or political freedom, Schiller, dying in the year before the downfall of Prussia at Jena, became within a few years an inspirer of national effort. His drama of *William Tell*, the liberator of Switzerland, became a call to the liberation of Germany. And the tradition thus established was to remain a force in German history perhaps stronger, and certainly more widely diffused, than the influence of his longer-lived contemporary.

VI. KANT

Older by a generation than Goethe and Schiller, and a score of years older than Herder, there grew up in the remoteness of East Prussia a boy, Immanuel Kant (1724–1804), who was to be the deepest thinker Germany had produced, and who in the realm of pure thought represented the grand climacteric of this intellectual and spiritual revival of Germany in the eighteenth century. Like Herder, he was poor, the son of a strapmaker, but like Herder he managed to get a good educational foundation, first at the Frederick's College in Koenigsberg and then at the local university. But unlike Herder his way was not to be the way of the Lutheran parson, despite the Pietist influences which surrounded him in home and school. Nor was he like Herder to shake off the dust of his native Prussia to merge himself in the freer and wider German life developing in Saxony and elsewhere. Instead he was to remain in his native Koenigsberg for the eighty years of his life, save for a few years spent in the adjacent countryside as tutor in the early days after his graduation from the university in 1746.   It was not indeed that the university of Koenigsberg displayed any swift or marked desire to secure his services.   For the decade or so spent in the humble role of private tutor was followed by fifteen years (1755–70) as unpaid lecturer at the university (during which time he lived on the fees he could collect from his students).   Only in 1770, at the age of forty-six, was he appointed professor of philosophy at the university, to hold that office for the remainder of his days, until his death in 1804.   Thus for many years Kant's lot was straitened by poverty.   As he never married, his life remained undistracted by family cares, and being of somewhat delicate constitution he was free to develop into an old-maidish bachelor scholar, of so regular a habit that the time-pieces of Koenigsberg could be set by him.   Heine, with his customary irreverence, saw him, on one side, as 'the perfect type of the petty shopkeeper.'

The picture of Kant's modest environment was contained within the isolation of the remote province of East Prussia and its capital city, which he refused to leave when opportunity offered.   Yet the isolation of this university city of about fifty thousand inhabitants was relative.   It had able men, such as the well-known Hamann, connected with it; it had its outlet to the sea; it was the capital of a province with an active life of its own. And there were compensations in its relative quietude for a man whose life was devoted to philosophy, and who from such an eyrie could view the world of western thought much as Tycho Brahe had viewed the heavens from his little island in the Baltic.   And Kant had that within him which, given the sufficiency of intellectual contact which the university afforded, could by close and undistracted attention and reflection arrive at new conclusions which were to be fruitful and important from that day to this, not merely for Germany but for the whole western world.   We may perhaps attribute in part to his alleged Scottish ancestry on one side that spirit of indefatigable tenacity of inquiry which marked his genius.   Kant felt no urge to travel into foreign countries, to gain the entrée into the *salons* of Paris, or to worship pagan beauty beneath an Italian sun.   And we may admit that he was little touched by the emotional upheaval which found vent in and through the young Goethe, or by enthusiasm for the classical form, or indeed by any aspect of the purely literary movement of the later eighteenth century in Germany.   Rousseau was to stir him by his appeal to a broader interpretation of humanity than the more limited vision of the *philosophes* allowed, but not to the point of putting the natural before the civilized man, or preferring undisciplined emotion to the sober light of reason.

More important than any new current of thought wafted from France in the formation of Kant's general views was the influence of the Protestant Pietism dominant in Koenigsberg at that time.   As a child in the home, at school and university, Kant was subject to the influence of this spiritual revival in the Lutheran Church.   In part he reacted against it; as an adult, we are told, he never entered a church.   But his life and thought bear testimony to the force which Protestant evangelicalism exerted upon him. It may have strengthened the general feeling for humanity encouraged by his reading of Rousseau. It assuredly pervaded and strengthened his whole attitude to life, his emphasis on moral goodness and duty, his conviction that even if the existence of God and the immortality of the soul could not be scientifically proven they were necessary presuppositions of man's moral action and must be accepted.

Kant arrived at manhood in the middle of the eighteenth century. Indeed he and Frederick II, the two greatest citizens of Prussia in that century, both in a sense started their careers in the same year (though Frederick was twelve years older). But the one was a king, the other a penniless university graduate. They were to have little in common, and their claims to greatness were to be very different. True, they both arrived at a high sense of duty. But the conceptions were differently based, and bore different implications and different fruit, the one to the service of the State and to power, the other to the moral progress of mankind. That is to take the longer view. In their earlier years, when Frederick was burning to win fame, plunging his country into war, first to enlarge his kingdom and then to maintain his gains, Kant was struggling to complete his education and to establish himself as a scholar and a teacher. In these years he was concerned in his teaching and writing not so much with metaphysics and ethics as with natural science. This was natural enough for a budding philosopher in that age: for whilst all the scientists of the time were not philosophers, no philosopher could erect a system which did not take account of the great development of science in the modern age since Copernicus, more particularly the development of physics and mathematics from Galileo and Descartes to the culmination in Newton, who died three years after Kant was born. Only a generation later, after Hegel, did philosophy and science part company for a time, and had Kant lived then he might well have continued to follow the path of science undisturbed by its philosophical implications and problems. For Kant in the three decades before he produced his *Critique of Pure Reason* (1781) both lectured and wrote upon a variety of scientific subjects. His most original contribution was the theory that 'the starry world' originated in the nebulae, a generation before Laplace formulated this 'nebular hypothesis' more precisely. But he also wrote on tides, on winds, on the causes of earthquakes, on the races of mankind, and lectured on physical geography. Thus he both demonstrated his interest in and knowledge of natural science, and assisted in the application to the universe of the methods of experiment and observation coupled with mathematical deduction which marked the Newtonian system, and indeed modern science in general.

Kant did not stop there, however, or continue in the pursuit of scientific knowledge alone. For him natural science, however important, was but a part of the whole. Its development had opened up vast new horizons to mankind. But it had also raised momentous questions as to the nature and position of both God and man in this newly seen universe, above all, the problem of how to reconcile the scientific view of the world, and its insistence upon the universal reign of law, with the existence of man's moral sense and his freedom to choose.   The leaders of western thought from Descartes and Leibnitz to Locke and Hume had essayed to provide answers to some of these questions, but had differed in their approach, some laying more stress on the certainty of mathematical deduction, others on the necessity for the empirical approach through observation and experiment.   Both relied on reason, but the one path led to dogmatism, the other, in Hume, to scepticism. Hence, as Kant explained in the preface to his first *Critique*, the science of reason, metaphysics, had fallen into confusion and discredit.   He therefore set himself to make a new survey of the nature and limits of human thinking, which would take account both of experience and of the universal certainty of mathematical conclusions.   And since, as he put it, 'our age is an age of criticism in every sense of the word,' he cast his work into the form, and gave it the title, of a *Critique*.

The *Critique of Pure Reason*, which appeared in 1781, has been accepted as marking the opening of a new era in philosophical thought.   Kant himself believed that it brought 'a Copernican revolution' in the subject, and it did in fact furnish a more complete and convincing answer than had so far been given by the modern world to the philosophic problems created by the rise of modern science, on the then more prominent sides of mathematics, physics, and astronomy.   Kant was concerned with the methods of reasoning by which the human mind arrived at valid conclusions about the natural world.   And herein he came to the conclusion that human knowledge is of necessity limited to appearances, but that beyond these there lay an unknowable realm of what he called 'things in themselves.'   Hence the *Critique* did not and could not provide for all time a solution of the central questions posed by the meeting of science and philosophy.   And it was not to be expected that a metaphysical treatise such as this, complex, abstruse, couched in its own special terminology, and emerging from the remoteness of East Prussia, should exert any immediate effect upon the general thought of Germany or elsewhere.   But Kant followed up this first *Critique* by two later volumes, *The Critique of Practical Reason* (1788) and the final *Critique of Judgment* (1790).   These by their nature exercised a wider influence upon thought at the time, and also, as complementing and completing the argument of the first *Critique*, provided a synthesis of the new 'critical idealism' which was to make the little philosopher of Koenigsberg the most creative figure in German thought for the next generation and more.

The *Critique of Practical Reason* was concerned with the problem of human conduct.   If pure reason could not finally prove (or disprove) the existence of God, practical reason nevertheless found in Him the idea of moral perfection, after which by the aid of free will all men should strive. The 'good will' was everything, and man was led by his moral and rational nature to formulate and live by the highest concept of duty, the 'categorical imperative.'   'Act as if the maxim of thy action were to become by thy will a universal law of nature.'   'The moral law should directly determine

GOTTSCHED

GELLERT

the will,' for 'we stand under a discipline of reason,' but this discipline is based upon the freedom of the human will, for only on such a basis is the world intelligible.   Herein Kant is providing a redefinition of freedom, a freedom based upon a self-imposed, rational law, and not merely the absence of restraint of the *laisser-faire* philosophy.   And as the moral law postulates the freedom of the will so does it also postulate the existence of God and immortality.   Thus did the son of Lutheran Pietism become the ripe philosopher of the Enlightenment, yet find in his philosophy a deeper and more universal appeal to morality and duty than the great king, his ruler, who had died at Potsdam a year or two before.   In the preaching of what were so largely Christian ethics, Kant was nearer to Lessing and Herder than to Goethe and Schiller, though Lessing was no longer alive, and Herder, a former student and admirer, was to become a severe critic.   The truth was that Herder was too different in temper and outlook to agree either with Kant's method or with his conclusions.   It remained for Schiller to absorb more of the Kantian teaching, although Schiller with his devotion to classical humanistic ideals found Kant's moral code too rigid and narrow.

The third and final *Critique*, however, *The Critique of the Faculty of Judgment* (1790), offered more common ground for the two men.   For in the first part of this *Critique* Kant discussed the judgment of the ideal of beauty, its relation to both pleasure and goodness, and analysed the relation of beauty to nature and the essence of original genius, in a manner fruitful for the formulation and exposition of Schiller's own views.   And although Kant was far from being carried away by the 'noble simplicity and calm grandeur' of the Greek ideal as expounded by Winckelmann and matured by Goethe, nevertheless he aided materially, both directly and through Schiller, in the building up of the general theory of aesthetics.   In the second part of this *Critique*, and not very closely connected with the first part, Kant asks in what sense science should recognize design and purpose in nature. His conclusion is that in explaining the organic world, and accounting for the natural and moral qualities of man, the hypothesis of design and purpose is the most fruitful one to adopt.   Included therein is the conception of a Divinity which shapes our ends.

Kant's thinking was not wholly absorbed by the working out of the *Critiques*.   As there was no line of division between his studies of science and of philosophy, so none existed between his study of the nature and limits of human thought, and of the society in which men lived and exercised that thought.   The workings of reason and the 'moral law,' and humanity generally, were of abiding interest to him.   He had seen great changes in the world about him, notably the successful efforts of his own ruler to raise Prussia to be a great power, with the hazards of the Seven Years War, during which East Prussia had passed under Russian rule.   He had seen adjacent Poland partitioned, and he lived through both the American and the French Revolutions.   And we know from the evidence of others as from his own writings that Kant took an intelligent and even keen interest in these happenings.   Yet it would be wrong to make too much of Kant's direct interest in political affairs. He was primarily a moral philosopher, living the quietest of lives in a remote city and province, in a state wherein there was no encouragement for citizens to take an active or indeed any part in political life. Like other leaders of the Enlightenment he accepted the authority of the ruler, given his respect for the law, some concern for the welfare of his subjects, and a measure of freedom of thought and expression, all of which existed in Prussia under the rule of Frederick the Great. Similarly, belonging as he did to the rising, progressive, and enlightened middle class, he was able to accept as reasonable the existing gradations of society, save for such glaring injustices as the survival of serfdom. When in 1794 he fell foul of the notably *un*enlightened regime of Frederick's successor on the charge of attacking the Christian religion in his teachings, Kant (he was then seventy years of age) bowed his head in obedience to authority.

Such submission, however, hardly impaired the implication and indeed the requirement of intellectual freedom which underlay Kant's whole system and teaching. True, there was the assumption that such freedom would be used in a rational, responsible, and moral way. There was in addition the belief that the exercise and spread of reason were necessarily leading to the steady improvement of society, and this on the widest, indeed on a universal, scale. But this progress was no mere triumphal march. In a short treatise published in 1784, *The Idea of a Universal History from a Cosmopolitan Point of View*, Kant essayed to demonstrate how under Natural Law, and by the proper use of reason, mankind had advanced, and would continue to advance. Yet there were obstacles, both in human weakness and lack of experience in organizing a society based upon perfect justice, and in the animosities of nations. And whilst these conflicts of states were seen as nature's plan for furthering man's growth, only in a universal society based on justice and liberty could that plan be realized in its perfection. This was theory, elevated indeed, but with little reference to the actual course of historical development.

The opening of the French Revolution, however, brought him a concrete example. Kant had been sympathetic to the attempt of the American colonists to free themselves from arbitrary control, and now looked with a new-found sympathy for the French on their attempt to establish a state in accord with the principles of rational enlightenment. But he was now an old man, and not in any case a friend to violence, so that although he did not, as many others in Germany as elsewhere, turn against the revolution, he nevertheless was by no means swept into unmeasured enthusiasm for all its actions. His foundations were too deeply set for that. Thus to the wars which ensued he reacted by the publication in 1795 of his most important piece of political writing, *On Perpetual Peace*. In it he seeks to define the principles which should underlie the making of peace in order to prevent the recurrence of war, e.g. that states should renounce intervention in each other's affairs, the conquest of new territories, the maintenance of standing armies. For permanent peace, however, more is required. The people of each nation must have a share in its government, not only to prevent an irresponsible autocrat from plunging it into war, but also to ensure peace between like-minded nations all enjoying freedom, representative institutions, and equality under the rule of law. Further, such nations must join together into a federal union, with a common citizenship, in order to achieve the desired end.

Thus did Kant, on the very eve of a wave of Romanticism which was to foster nationalism throughout the nineteenth century and beyond, both bear testimony to the cosmopolitanism of his age, and provide a vision for a future age which was eventually to be sated with nationalism. We may see the essay as a legacy of the aged philosopher to mankind. For although some of his other later writings have their reference to political issues, they do not change the picture materially. And whilst Kant has a place in the foundation of nineteenth-century liberalism, it is hardly possible to define that place in political terms. He has been acclaimed as the first expounder of the idea of the *Rechtsstaat*, the state founded upon and limited by law, in his own land. But time was to show that this 'State of law' as exemplified in Prussia and Germany could exhibit features very different from those of the Kantian ideal. And Kant himself, for all his love of freedom, had condemned opposition which might endanger the Prussian state, forgetful that the attainment of the political liberty which he admired elsewhere had in fact implied the use of force against royal authority comparable to that which existed in Prussia. The truth is that Kant's greatness and influence are to be measured, apart from his services to metaphysics, rather in the field of ethics than of practical politics. 'A philosopher,' wrote Matthew Arnold of Spinoza, 'to be great must have something in him which can influence character, which is edifying; he must, in short, have a noble and lofty character himself.' And so it was with Kant.

CHAPTER V

THE REMAKING OF GERMANY THROUGH THE FRENCH REVOLUTION AND NAPOLEON

Introductory — The French Conquest of the Rhineland, 1789–1800 — The Conquest of Germany, 1800–10 — The German Revival and Liberation — The Settlement of 1815

I. INTRODUCTORY

THE EFFECTS of the French Revolution and the Napoleonic period upon Germany were second only to the effects upon France herself, greater than the effects upon Italy, and far greater than the effects upon Britain. In the first place it broke up the old shell of its political life. Not merely did it give the *coup de grâce* to the old and decaying Holy Roman Empire but it produced an immense simplification of the political geography of the country. The medieval map of Germany, as modified by the settlement of 1648, disappeared, and the number of political units was reduced to little more than a tenth of its former size. It did not, as many Germans hoped by 1815, give real unity to the country; particularism was still too strong for that. But its successive ploughings-up of the old territorial boundaries loosened the bonds which these had created, and so prepared the way for later reorganization and unity. The most obvious territorial change was the elimination of the numerous and large estates held by the archbishops, bishops, and abbots of the Roman Catholic Church, whose lands were absorbed by neighbouring secular rulers. A similar fate befell many of the smaller states, the hundreds of Imperial Knights, and many of the Free Cities. The process of redistribution was a complicated and shifting one, so that for a time parts of Germany, especially in the north-west, were in almost complete dissolution, reduced to shifting sands of rapid and seemingly endless change in their political shape and fortunes, until the French invaders were expelled.

The final settlement of 1815 which brought order out of the confusion of over two decades, and which was to last until overthrown by Prussia in 1866, inevitably revealed certain changes in the balance of political forces in Germany. The Catholic Church had lost its secular power both in the new federal authority set up in place of the old Diet and in its former principalities. But its adherents remained, and time was to show that it could adapt itself to the new conditions, and even exercise political influence comparable to that which it had enjoyed in the old *Reich*. The most obvious gainers through the successive upheavals were the middle-sized states of South Germany, which emerged enlarged in size and increased in status. Of the

two greatest states, Austria and Prussia, the latter took the lead in the
liberating of Germany, the former recovered ground in the Peace Congress
held in her capital, as in the successes of Metternich's diplomacy. With the
permanent presidency of the new Germanic Confederation, and the closer
alliance with the middle-sized states, her strength in Italy, and her greater
prestige in Europe after 1815, Austria appeared to have gained rather than
lost by the changes of the revolutionary period. Yet there was another side
to the picture. Austria had lost some of her allies in the old Germany, the
ecclesiastical princes, the Imperial Knights and Free Cities. And she had also
given up her territorial connection with north-western and western Germany,
the Netherlands, and her upper Rhenish possessions, to expand to the south
into Italy. In her place Prussia had become the guardian of western
Germany, and so modified that *Drang nach Osten* which had marked the
Frederician regime of the eighteenth century. Thus the settlement of 1814
helped to prepare Prussia for the role Bismarck was to mark out for her.

These political changes were to have their social and cultural accompaniments. They involved for large parts of western Germany the sweeping
away of the old social system, with its rigid class divisions and the feudal
rights of taxation, and the affirmation of equality before the law. The rule
of revolutionary France meant the confiscation of Church property, the
closing of convents, the separation of Church and State. It brought peasant
proprietorship for parts of western Germany and the Napoleonic administrative and legal systems. But whilst the French regime thus opened up new
vistas for the commercial middle class, as for the peasantry, yet the wars,
the rigidity of Napoleonic rule, and the conscription of soldiers, the abuses
of power by French agents, and the deadening effects on trade of the so-called
Continental System, all contributed to check any great development for the
time being. Yet the changes cleared the way for later growth. On the
cultural side the outstanding development of this period was that of the
Romantic movement, which was to exert such wide and deep effects on the
life of Germany through the coming century. Its immediate importance in
this period lay largely in the stimulus it provided for the emergence of a new
patriotic feeling in the later years of the French occupation, thus helping
to prepare the way for the liberation.

Romanticism apart, the great changes of this period in Germany were the
work of a foreign invader. Certainly the old regime in Germany was ripe
for change, and it would have been better had such changes been the fruit
of internal pressures or revolution, as in France and England. But neither
the old *Reich* nor its members were capable of such action, and so the changes
were imposed from without. In part this French intervention, notably the
occupation and seizure of German lands west of the Rhine, merely continued
the long process of French expansion eastwards. This process had already
taken France from the Somme and the northern tributaries of the Seine to
the Meuse and the Scheldt, from the Meuse to the Mosel, and then on to
the Rhine with the gain of Alsace. Now she proceeded to complete the
acquisition of her 'natural frontier,' thereby seizing the remainder of the

lands west of the great river from Alsace to the sea.   Nor was this the end, for Napoleonic aggression and the pressure of his unending struggle with England pushed French rule further and further into Germany until it extended clear across the whole country, to reach through Poland to the borders of Russia.

But this greatest wave of French expansion eastwards was also to be the last.   Thereafter was to come a change, and in due course the tide of invasion was to roll the other way.   And as the political tide ebbed, so also the cultural influences diminished.   Whereas French influence had been all powerful in the century and more after the Thirty Years War, the new German movement in literature and thought, running on into the Romantic movement, provided a flood of sentiments and ideas which whether original to Germany or not were expressed in the German tongue and found a new response in German minds and hearts.   Germany no longer needed to import French culture; she had her own philosophy, her own classics of literature.   She was even ready to export her philosophy to France, as the teachings of French thinkers were to show, from Cousin onwards.   And by way of reaction to the revolution which had led to this latest and greatest French invasion of Germany, the restored representatives and champions of the old order were to cherish henceforth a deep hatred of the revolution and all its works, a hatred which was to be a strong and permanent bulwark of conservatism as of nationalism in Germany.

The quarter of a century between the opening of the French Revolution and the final defeat of Napoleon was for much of Germany a period of rapid, confusing, and complicated change, of war with its campaigns, battles, and sieges, of the rapid twists and turns of diplomacy, of the ups and downs of fortune, of republican freedom turning into Directorial and Napoleonic tyranny.   But whilst it is impossible within narrow limits of space to follow the course of events, on the other hand the succession of these events cannot be ignored; the temporary and the more permanent are inextricably mixed in them.   Looking over the whole period we may see it in three stages, the first two of about a decade each, the last of less than half that number of years.   In the first stage, to about 1800, after the first reverberations in Germany of the revolution, the armies of Austria and Prussia invaded France, only to be driven out, and the aggressive, expanding republic pressed forward to the Rhine, to absorb all the German land west of that river into France, with manifold effects on the life of the people there.   In the second stage, after 1800, the French, now under Napoleon, pushed more deeply into Germany, to redistribute and consolidate its territories, put an end to the Holy Roman Empire, defeat both Austria and Prussia, and by the Peace of Tilsit (1807) to establish French domination over the whole country.   The third and final period saw the slow turning of the tide from about 1808 to the Napoleonic defeat in the Russian campaign of 1812, which opened the way for the liberation of Germany in the following years, first to the Rhine, then of the whole of the country.   In view of its importance for the future history of Germany, this final period demands closer examination

than the other two.   Over the whole period Austria was at war five times
with the French, for more than ten of the twenty-five years, Prussia three
times, for less than half that period, the lesser states in varying degree, but
fighting with and for the French as often as against them, so divided was
the country, so powerless, and so lacking in national consciousness.

II. THE FRENCH CONQUEST OF THE RHINELAND, 1789–1800

The first expressions of German opinion about the revolution which
opened in Paris in May 1789 were from the middle-class intellectuals.   The
American revolution had aroused sympathy, and this new and greater movement nearer home evoked more lively and widespread interest.   One of a
number of German visitors to Paris in the summer of 1789 saw in the
revolution 'the greatest blessing vouchsafed to mankind by Providence since
Luther,' and another, Johannes Müller, went back to see in the fall of the
Bastille 'the most wonderful day since the fall of Rome.'   The most eminent
writers of Germany, old and young, voiced their approval, as did the aged
Kant and the youthful Hegel among the philosophers.   In England a like
approval by poets and writers had also the support of voices raised in
Parliament.   But Germany lacked any such sounding board, as it lacked
any other connection between these expressions of public opinion and the
policy of its many rulers.   Of popular opinion there is no need to speak,
for it hardly existed.

Of the rulers of Germany the two whose attitude really mattered, the rulers
of Austria and Prussia, were in 1789 more concerned with eastern than with
western affairs, although the reforming Emperor Joseph II (1765–90) of
Austria had trouble on his hands in his Netherland provinces.   The days of
Viennese obscurantism had seemed over when the cautious changes sponsored
by Maria Theresa were succeeded by the bolder efforts of her eldest son to
modernize, centralize, and rationalize his polyglot dominions.   He had in
addition the problem of Poland, now almost ready for the final stages of its
dismemberment, and he was also involved as the ally of Russia in war with
Turkey.   But Joseph, ever hastening, in the great Frederick's jibing phrase,
to take the second step ere he had taken the first, passed off the stage in
1790 at the early age of forty-eight, leaving his younger brother Leopold to
face the problems raised by developments in France.   Prussia too had seen
a change of ruler, when in 1786 Frederick II was succeeded by his nephew
Frederick William II.   The defects of character, the weakness and incapacity
of the new Prussian king were both to reveal cracks in the Frederician
structure of the State and to propel Prussia down the steep slope leading to
Jena.   He too was at first more concerned with Poland than with affairs
in the west, but responded more quickly than Leopold, whose sister Marie
Antoinette was the wife of Louis XVI, to the threat to monarchy in general
resulting from events in France.

As the revolution developed the glaring contrast revealed between its
glowing radicalism and the hide-bound conservatism in Germany became

more apparent and more dangerous.   The hospitality shown by German princes to the many French aristocratic *émigrés*, their picture of a France in dissolution, and their anti-revolutionary propaganda, aroused antagonism on both sides.   Many Germans who had welcomed the revolution drew back as its violence grew.   The French abolition of feudal rights in Alsace, without indemnity, injured and further alienated the emperor and other German princes who still held lands there.   Austria and Prussia, the Turkish war over, drew closer in opposition to French maltreatment of royalty, and their famous Declaration from Pillnitz (August 1791), inviting European co-operation on Louis's behalf, naturally aroused bitterness among radicals in France.   Jacobin propaganda in the Belgian Netherlands, and Girondin intransigence, were matched by German inability to estimate the fortunes of a war with revolutionized France.   On 20th April 1792 the French Legislative Assembly declared war on Austria, the old Habsburg enemy; with the entry of Prussia shortly afterwards the long wars of the revolutionary period were begun for Germany, as they were shortly to begin, and go on even more continuously, for Britain.

The first stage of these wars, to the Treaty of Lunéville in 1801, was to see the French armies advance to complete occupation and control of Germany west of the Rhine.   The over-confident march of the Austro-Prussian forces into France in the summer of 1792 ended in failure, owing to their lack of unity and energy, their errors of judgment, and the unexpected military quality of the new revolutionary armies, once they had recovered from their first indiscipline.   Valmy marked the first check to the invaders (its significance noted by Goethe), and Fleurus in June 1794 saw their expulsion from French soil for twenty years.   The French had already overrun the Austrian Netherlands, and reached and crossed the Rhine at Mainz, the chief Rhine fortress.   Although driven out of Mainz, they were soon to return to the Rhine, this time to stay.   They won a notable success when Prussia deserted her allies to make a separate peace at Basel (1795), recognizing the Rhine as the eastern boundary of France, an example followed by other German states.   And whilst Austria and Bavaria continued the struggle for a time, further defeat, both along the Rhine and in Italy, where the new star of Bonaparte's military genius was rising, forced Austria to make peace in 1797 (Campo Formio).   She too, though secretly for the time, recognized French mastery of the lands west of the Rhine, including Belgium.   Within two years, however, the Habsburgs were again at war with France, joined with Britain and Russia.   But when the French victories at Marengo and Hohenlinden had been translated into the terms of the Treaty of Lunéville (1801) the cession of the west bank of the Rhine was openly avowed.   As in the Prussian treaty, there was to be compensation for lands thus lost to France, and the vast estates of the Catholic Church in Germany were already marked out as the obvious source from which this could be provided.

Long before the Peace of Lunéville, however, the French had occupied and begun to organize their newly acquired territories, comprising 25,000 square miles of German soil, with 3,500,000 inhabitants.   The little republic of Mainz (1792–3) set up by Custine had forecast what was to come. For in that ancient capital, where Frederick Barbarossa had held his court at the height of the medieval empire, the French had set up a republic in place of the rule of the Prince Elector, abolishing tithes and feudal dues, and seizing the property of the Church and the nobility. Thus was 'German slavery' exchanged for 'French freedom.' And there were enough 'enlightened' citizens in Mainz to welcome that exchange and so provide at least a show of popular support for the new regime. Outstanding as leader was Georg Forster, errant son of a Lutheran pastor, a convinced radical and reformer, gifted in pen and speech, and chief figure in the newly formed local club of German Friends of Liberty and Equality. When the new republic was very shortly absorbed into France, Forster went to Paris as a delegate, to be swallowed up like so many more by the revolution. Meanwhile Mainz had been retaken by the Prussians, after a siege of three months, and republican liberty disappeared with the French troops for a time.

The French returned to the Rhine, however, and after the Peace of 1797, and without awaiting the conclusions of the Congress of Rastadt, set up to work out the terms of that treaty, they proceeded to reorganize the West Rhenish area. Four departments under the Directory at Paris replaced the confusion of nearly one hundred separate rulers. The change to the Napoleonic consulate in 1799 saw the work continued after the new pattern, with prefects, sub-prefects, and mayors over departments, districts, and communes respectively. The old regime was now completely abolished. Titles of nobility and feudal rights disappeared, religious houses were suppressed, and Church property was secularized. Peasant proprietorship was established. The French legal system, first of the Directory and then of the Napoleonic Codes, was introduced, with French as the judicial language. Education was taken out of the hands of the clergy and made to conform to the new Napoleonic pattern. Similarly the system of the Napoleonic Concordat with the Papacy in due course replaced the earlier introduction of Directorial religion with its *décadis* instead of Sundays. French taxation and the French system of conscription for the army likewise became part of the new regime.

Thus Germany west of the Rhine became part of France, its four departments by decree of 1802 placed on the same footing as all the other French departments. Like them, they enjoyed the benefits of the revolutionary and Napoleonic administration, more enlightened than any they had ever experienced. But like them also they possessed not a jot of political freedom, as former Rhenish radicals found to their cost. Thus Görres, a young journalist of Coblenz, who had lauded French republican freedom and even declared that 'Nature has created the Rhine to be the frontier of France,' was completely disillusioned by a visit to Paris, and abandoned his faith both in the revolution and in France.

Görres, however, was an intellectual. The more ordinary citizen of the Rhineland, never having enjoyed political freedom before, and having done nothing to win it, could hardly be expected to miss it. True, he was ruled by a foreigner.   But this foreigner was at that time no more alien to him than many of those who spoke a variant of his own speech, and his yoke was in many ways easier to bear, more uniform, and no longer hedged about with class distinction and privilege.   He had social if not political liberty.   Inter-marriage between classes was as free as the transfer of land, the peasant could go where he would, the Jew could become a full citizen.   There must have been good Catholics who disliked the treatment of their Church; but that Church had not been so enlightened or immune from either abuses or criticism by its members.   The new access to ownership of the soil by the peasants quickly took root, to be a strong support of the new regime.   French law was long to outlive the end of French rule.   The fact that under this rule the western Rhineland enjoyed fourteen years of peace was a strong argument in its favour.   Apart from the abuses of authority by individuals, a matter not peculiar to the French regime, the solid grievances of Napoleonic rule were two: the check to trade and economic development caused by the restrictions of the Continental System, and the net of the conscription, which caught and carried off the youth of the region to fight all over Europe, often never to return.   Yet despite these very real hardships, and despite also the rise of German patriotic feeling, many of those Rhinelanders who in 1814 exchanged French for Prussian citizenship were to greet the change with sorrow rather than with joy, and the social and legal effects of the French regime were far to outlast the reunion of the area with Germany.

III. THE CONQUEST OF GERMANY, 1800–10

The second stage of the impact of the revolution (now personified in Napoleon) upon Germany saw the extension of French control over the whole country in the decade after 1800.   True, Austria was not continuously occupied, but Napoleon twice occupied Vienna, and Austrian territories in Germany, Italy, and Poland were carved up and disposed of by him in the successive peace treaties of Lunéville, Pressburg (1805), and Schönbrunn (1809) as well as in the redistribution of 1803.   And in northern Germany French control for some years stretched even beyond Germany to include Poland.   This extension of French control east of the Rhine meant far more to Germany than a military occupation.   It also brought wide and to a great extent permanent territorial changes there.   Without the consolidation it effected it is difficult to see how Germany could have been united in the nineteenth century.   Hence Napoleon, much as he disliked Prussia, made Bismarck's work possible, unwittingly preparing the way for the French defeat in 1870 and the future menace of a united Germany.   Yet this exten-sion of French control was almost inevitable, given the continued division and weakness of Germany, the growing ambitions and aggressions of Napoleon, and the continued pressure of his war with Britain.   The Rhine, great river though it is, provided no firmer frontier now than it had done in Roman times, when Romans and Germans alike had pushed across it east or west.   And French pressure, if not direct intervention, was implicit in the terms of the peace treaties of both 1797 and 1801, which provided that the losers of territory west of the Rhine should be accorded compensation east of that river.

The obvious source of such compensation lay in the vast estates of the Catholic Church. Their secularization had been begun at the time of the Reformation, but had not gone very far; the bishoprics of Bremen and Magdeburg, and the Teutonic Order, had then been the outstanding victims. The more rationalist eighteenth century had seen further proposals for secularization, and the example of France in 1789 had given further support to such proposals. The Congress of Rastadt had discussed this method of providing compensation, but clerical protests, the rivalries of the different states, and then the reopening of the war, had prevented any agreement, so that the congress was dissolved with nothing accomplished. Meanwhile the French had proceeded to secularize church lands west of the Rhine, and after the Peace of Lunéville the question of compensation to lay princes who had lost lands in that area became more urgent. Yet neither the Imperial Diet called to ratify the treaty, nor the delegation or committee appointed by it to deal with the matter, could agree upon a scheme. It became clear that only the voice of the First Consul of France, now firmly established in the saddle, could be decisive. Nor was Napoleon unwilling to seize this opportunity to interfere further in the affairs of Germany, in association with the Tsar of Russia. So the scene shifted to Paris, and there in an atmosphere of diplomacy, or more properly intrigue, was written what has been termed 'the most degrading page in the history of Germany.' [1] There was the French interest to keep Germany, and not least Austria and Prussia, divided, to hold Prussia in leash, and to favour the middle-sized states as vassals; the Russian family interest to favour Baden; the greed of Talleyrand through whom the business was carried out; and finally the competing claims, backed by bribery, of the representatives of the German states. When the sorry business was carried through, and the various German states had signed separate treaties with France, the resulting settlement was accepted by the delegation of the Imperial Diet, the Diet itself, and the emperor in turn. The people of Germany had naturally no say in the matter.

Thus was what has been called the revolution of 1803 carried through. It was hardly a revolution in the full sense; there was no sudden or violent transfer of power from one class to another, no change in the economic system. Yet it had certain revolutionary qualities. At one stroke this Recess, as the enactment was termed, redistributed no less than one-sixth of German land, and reduced the number of German states by about one half. And this change, like the Reform Act of 1832 in England, made further change easier. The bulk of the transfers were made at the expense of the ecclesiastical estates, for centuries rulers of great stretches of Germany, and pillars of the imperial structure as of the Catholic faith. Now these estates were wiped out, save for those of the heads of the Teutonic Order and the Knights of St. John, and also for lands bestowed on Archbishop Dalberg of

[1] Herbert A. L. Fisher, *Studies in Napoleonic Statesmanship, Germany*, 1903, p. 41.

Mainz, a unique episcopal survivor who had won Napoleonic favour.   Most of the Imperial or Free Cities were likewise absorbed, only six remaining. The nature of the redistribution was determined less by the extent of the land lost west of the Rhine than by the aims of French policy and the varying success of German lobbying in Paris.   Thus Prussia got a string of episcopal estates between Magdeburg and the Rhine, five times larger than her losses west of that river.   The terms for Austria had been in the main set by the Peace of Lunéville, and represented, with Italy included, more loss than gain.   The outstanding gainers were the middle-sized states which Napoleon sought to tie to himself, Bavaria (which lost most west of the Rhine), Baden, Wurtemberg, the two Hesses, and Nassau.   Saxony, no loser across the Rhine, got nothing.

   Thus the settlement marked a very considerable change in the political structure of Germany, much but not all of it permanent.   It also marked a change in the balance of forces there.   Whilst it strengthened the middle-sized states it weakened the empire, and therewith Austria, for the clerical estates and the Imperial Cities had in general been supporters of the empire. So far as the Imperial Diet was concerned the change meant that the Protestants now had a majority (52 to 30), since both the clerical Electors and many of the clerical and Catholic members of the College of Princes were eliminated. ‘This mattered less, however, since the Diet had now so little power and was soon to disappear.   More important was the blow to the general political influence and the wealth of the Catholic Church, although time was to show that part at least of this could be regained.   Catholic as well as Protestant princes had shared in the redistribution, and there was no question, as in the Reformation settlement, of the change of faith or exile of those subjects who did not share the faith of their new rulers.   It goes without saying that subjects so transferred had no voice or option in the matter of their transfer.   Nor was there any consideration of the interests of Germany as a whole; such interest was only beginning to take shape in the minds of a few thinkers and writers of these years.   And such interest, as, for example, in Stein, did not seek to undo the work of 1803 and restore the spiritual principalities of Germany.   Their day was over, and the final settlement of 1815 confirmed the fact.

   With the Recess of 1803 Germany entered upon a period of rapid fluctuation of its internal political boundaries, as Napoleonic aggression and intervention extended their range, especially in northern Germany.   Thus the connection between Hanover and his persistent enemy England provided a reason for Napoleon's intervention there, the more so as Prussia wanted Hanover, and he was determined that she should not get it.   French troops had in fact overrun Hanover in 1802 and proceeded to drain its resources. In 1804 came the monstrous seizure of the Duc d'Enghien, a Bourbon prince, from the soil of supposedly independent Baden, and of a British agent in the presumably Free City of Hamburg.   Then adjacent Holland became a kingdom under Napoleon's younger brother, and there was further aggression in Italy.   From all this came a renewal of the war in Germany in 1805,

KLOPSTOCK

THE YOUNG GOETHE

After W. Böttner

QUEEN LOUISE OF PRUSSIA

LUDWIG VAN BEETHOVEN

as Austria became a rather reluctant and ill-prepared ally of Russia and Britain, with Prussia at first neutral and then a French ally, and the South German states allied with Napoleon from the start. The disasters at Ulm and Austerlitz justified Austrian fears and broke up the coalition, and the resultant peace made at Pressburg (December 1805) reduced Austrian rule in both Italy and Germany. The rulers of Bavaria, Wurtemberg, and Baden were rewarded by a share of the lands taken from Austria, and they were elevated in rank, Bavaria and Wurtemberg to kingship, the ruler of Baden to Grand Duke. They likewise proceeded to absorb ('mediatize') the lands of the Imperial Knights lying within their borders. It was little wonder that the Emperor Francis within some months pronounced (6th August 1806) the formal and final end of the ancient Holy Roman Empire; it had in fact been dead for some time.

Much of its heritage passed immediately to France. The lands west of the Rhine were already incorporated into France; now in 1806 those lying east of the river were organized into a new union, the Confederation of the Rhine (*Rheinbund*) under Napoleonic control. The method of the making of this body was similar to that used for the Recess of 1803. It was worked out in Paris under much the same conditions, and agreed to by the representatives of the sixteen German states to be included. The new organization was given a constitution based on that of the empire, its members independent in internal affairs, with a Diet of two Chambers, and with the complaisant Dalberg as Prince Primate. But Napoleon was not interested in its constitutional aspect. 'I desire only a federation of men and money,' he declared, and so the Diet never met. More important in his eyes was the article fixing the number of soldiers each state was to provide for his armies. Yet there was some compensation for this, of importance to the future of Germany. The members of the *Bund* were allowed to 'mediatize' the lands of the lesser princes, dukes, counts, Imperial Knights, and Free Cities contained within the bounds of the Confederation. Frankfurt and Nürnberg, for example, were absorbed in this way. Thus was accomplished a further stage in the simplification of the political geography of Germany, and again by foreign agency. The actual estates mediatized were retained by their former owners, but now as subjects of local rulers. And by the military provisions of the *Rheinbund* all of those rulers themselves were subject to the all-powerful Emperor of France in a far more real way than they had ever been subject to the Habsburgs, one of whose difficulties had always been that they could never command the raising of an imperial army.

Prussia was not included in the Confederation of the Rhine. Throughout the period she had played for her own hand, too full of the old rivalry with Austria to collaborate properly in the first war against France, and doing little to earn the subsidies supplied her by Britain. It had proved much easier to gain territory from Poland than from resurgent France, and so she had made her peace with the republic in 1795, a peace which Hardenberg declared was 'safe, advantageous, and honourable.' And this peace she

E

was to maintain for eleven years, by which time it was neither safe nor advantageous; honour it could hardly claim.   The great Frederick had made similar treaties with France in his day, but had been shrewd enough to renounce them as soon as they ceased to serve his purpose.   Neither of Frederick's successors, however, was of his calibre.   Frederick William II (1786–97) was a medley of some of the worst features of the eighteenth-century German prince, and his successor, Frederick William III (1797–1840), while much superior in character, as a ruler was possessed of Prussian con-servatism without Prussian strength.   Weak himself, he preferred ministers of like quality, and under him the discipline, devotion to duty, and efficiency which had marked the Frederician regime continued to decline.   The army reflected this decline, and at a time when the French Revolution had intro-duced new methods of warfare and produced a greater military genius than Frederick II himself.   'We have ceased to be a military state and become a drilling and a scribbling one,' declared Stein in his disgust at the policy of neutrality.   The system of administration left behind by Frederick degener-ated without his firm grip, and his static conception of society became increasingly out of date in the new age.   The avoidance of war had, of course, brought its benefits, and Prussia had managed without war to add enormously to her territory, to the west as we have seen, and to the east by sharing in the latest partition of Poland.

The year 1806 was to reveal the other side of the picture, however. Whereas in the early years after the Peace of Basel Prussia had collaborators in her policy of peace and neutrality, by 1806 she stood painfully isolated and increasingly hemmed in by the French advance.   The formation of the *Rheinbund* made this clearer.   French occupation of Hanover was a blow to her ambition, and French control of the Elbe and Weser rivers and their outlets in Hamburg and Bremen worsened her economic position.   For the campaign of 1805 against Austria, French troops had marched across Prussian territory (Ansbach) without hesitation or permission, and for a moment Prussia had turned towards the allies.   But after Austerlitz she turned again, bribed by the offer of Hanover to make a definite alliance with Napoleon, only to discover that he was secretly offering to return Hanover to England in exchange for Sicily.   This was too much.   There were not lacking in Prussia critics of the royal policy—Queen Louise herself, officers in the army, reformers such as Stein and Hardenberg—enough by this time to form a war party.   Now even the king was roused and declared war on the perfidious emperor of the hated French.   But it was too late to win allies in Germany, save for Saxony and Brunswick, who had little choice, and the rusted Prussian war command proved no match for the experience, skill, and speed of Napoleon and his generals.   The two battles of Jena and Auerstadt on the same day (14th October 1806) decided the issue within two months.   Napoleon occupied Berlin, the garrison towns of Brandenburg surrendered, and only the remnants of the Prussian army escaped to join the Russians in East Prussia.   But the French victory at Friedland (June 1807) put an end to the Franco-Russian conflict, and Frederick William had perforce to accept the terms agreed upon by Alexander with Napoleon in the famous interview and Peace at Tilsit (July 1807).

This peace settlement of 1807, and the political arrangements accompanying and following it, marked the completion of the Napoleonic control of northern Germany. By it Prussia lost at both ends: on the west she was pushed back across the Elbe, thus losing not merely all her recent gains but also Magdeburg, Halle with its university, and her original home, the Altmark. To the east she likewise lost most of her gains from Poland, saving West Prussia, and by Alexander's mediation she retained Silesia. In addition, a very large indemnity was exacted, she was occupied by French troops, was drawn into the net of the Continental System against England, and in general was completely subordinated to French arms and influence. The confiscation of the states of Brunswick, Hesse-Cassel (Electoral Hesse), and Fulda (Orange) for open or suspected alliance with Prussia further increased the territory in north-western Germany now at Napoleon's disposal. Saxony, however, was more gently treated, as having taken the wrong side by compulsion. She was to be given the role of counterweight to Prussia. Drawn, with the adjacent small Saxon duchies, into the Confederation of the Rhine, her ruler was also elevated to be the head (under French guidance) of the newly created Grand Duchy of Warsaw, incorporating Polish territory taken from Prussia and later from Austria. Similarly in north-western Germany a new kingdom was created from the confiscated lands, the state of Westphalia, and placed under the rule of Napoleon's younger brother, Jerome. His kingdom was in a few years enlarged (1810) by the addition of most of Hanover.

These later territorial changes forced upon Germany by Napoleon were more arbitrary, and were to be more short-lived than the earlier ones. They broke more completely with the past, were less linked with existing conditions, and took less root; the settlement of 1815 was to wipe them out. The new King of Westphalia resembled too much the irresponsible and pleasure-loving princes of the *ancien régime*, whether in France or Germany, to adapt himself either to German needs or Napoleonic demands. He was no tyrant, however, and there was good as well as bad in the French administration of the region. But to Napoleon, apart from dynastic considerations, the general hold on Germany, and its value as a reservoir for soldiers, it was the struggle with England that defined much of his policy in northern Germany. The so-called Continental System, the effort to destroy the obstinate nation of shopkeepers by preventing Europe from buying its wares, largely determined the final form of Napoleonic aggression there. To that end he put the north-western coast of Germany under military governors, took in the northern part of Hanover and Oldenburg, and then (1810) absorbed this elongated coastal strip into France itself, together with Holland. To the same end he garrisoned the Prussian ports and Danzig, closed the northern German rivers to foreign trade, and drew the Mecklenburg duchies and other states into the Confederation of the Rhine. And the same aim was to draw him further and further round the coastline of Europe, from the

Baltic to the Adriatic, including the obdurate and, in the end, irreducible Iberian peninsula.

The Continental System had very important effects on Germany.   True, it was not completely successful in keeping out English goods.   The British navy seized the island of Heligoland, and made it a base for a vast smuggling trade in which not merely the merchants of Hamburg and elsewhere, but also French officials, took their part and their profit.   Yet such profit was small and local compared to the widespread damage and loss to trade and industry which the Berlin decrees of 1806, the later decrees, and the English counter-blockade, imposed upon Germany.   Her great rivers, from the Rhine downwards, were almost empty of ships, her harbours dead, her warehouses closed, and many of her merchants bankrupt.   Of what use was it to wipe out feudal burdens and social inequalities and introduce a more enlightened system of law and administration, or to sweep away many of the old restraints on internal trade by promoting political unity, when an iron fence was placed round much of the country to prevent the natural flow of external trade?   Despite their pursuit of philosophy Germans were not immune from the pull of economic interest, and the Continental System undoubtedly played its part in the building up of dislike and opposition to French administration, though it would be very difficult to weigh or measure that part with any precision.

IV. THE GERMAN REVIVAL AND LIBERATION

In the third and final stage of the French occupation and domination of Germany the emphasis naturally turns from French policy and action to the consideration of the forces which led up to the War of Liberation and the reorganization of Germany at the Congress of Vienna.   There was little sign of any broad or deep movement making for German liberation from the French yoke when in 1808 the vassal princes of the *Rheinbund* gathered for the famous conference between the Emperors Napoleon and Alexander at Erfurt in the heart of Germany, where Luther had studied.   Goethe, honoured by an interview with Napoleon, had no thought of it: 'The man is too big for you' was his word to his countrymen.   Yet in this same year the tide did in fact begin its slow turn, with the resistance of the Spaniards in the 'May Days,' and the British intervention in Portugal in this same year. In the next year, indeed, Austria challenged the French again, urged thereto by the patriotic efforts of Stadion and the Archduke Charles, and hoping for support from northern Germany, even from unfriendly Prussia.   Efforts at revolt in North Germany there were, in Westphalia, in Hanover, in Hesse, and in Brandenburg.   But the King of Prussia did not move, and the sporadic efforts were vain.   And although Austria managed to inflict a severe check to Napoleon at Aspern, within two months the defeat at Wagram drove her to accept terms in the Treaty of Schönbrunn, which stripped her of her holdings along the Adriatic, of Salzburg, and of part of Galicia.   Hofer's brave revolt in the Tyrol was likewise suppressed.   This third defeat put an end to Austria's pan-German efforts. Henceforth, with the growth of Metternich's influence, the Habsburgs were to fall back into the more dynastic policy they had so long pursued at the expense of their German interests. The initiative in the effort to liberate Germany three years later was to come from Prussia rather than from Austria.

What made that effort possible was, of course, the Napoleonic failure and disasters of 1812 in Russia. But behind the Prussian rising lay the events elsewhere in Europe: the continued opposition in Spain, Napoleon's 'Spanish ulcer,' with the slow but steady advance of British arms there, and in Germany the growing discontent from French financial exactions, the economic distress from the Continental System, and the insatiable demands for recruits for the French armies. To these must be added two causes calling for some description, one more particular, the other more general. The reforms associated with the names of Stein and Hardenberg, Scharnhorst and Gneisenau in Prussia formed an indispensable prelude to the role that Prussia was to play in the emancipation. No less important was the emergence of a national feeling which was to give the War of Liberation a character it would otherwise not have possessed, and to make it both memorable and influential in the coming century. That feeling arose from many sources. But a prime agent in its rise was that bundle of influences which we term the Romantic movement, and hence that movement took on a wider significance in German history than elsewhere, save perhaps in Italy.

Although the Romantic movement in Germany began, as we have seen, with Herder and the then youthful Goethe, it remained for a group of younger men to define and exemplify its characteristics. Yet this group of the two brothers Schlegel, Schleiermacher, Tieck, Novalis, and Wackenroder, who in 1798 in the capital of unromantic Prussia founded their short-lived review, the *Athenaeum*, included widely diversified gifts and special interests. Thus from the start the movement was a highly individual one, galloping off in many if not all directions at once, and so not easy to define. And it was not merely individual in its rich variety, but also highly subjective. Its prime feature was a love of poetic beauty, accompanied by a strong feeling for music, although it was not at first closely connected with the great development of music at this time in Vienna. Much of its importance lay in the fact that it marked a decided reaction against the rationalism of the earlier age. To reason it opposed imagination, feeling, intuition. Whereas Voltaire had derided the Middle Ages, the young 'Novalis' (Frederick von Hardenberg) looked back with longing to a time when a deep and common faith gave a unity to western civilization under a German emperor. This view was to carry some of the leaders of the movement into the Catholic fold. Not all, however, for Schleiermacher, while he applied Romantic feeling to religion (and also translated Plato), yet remained a Protestant preacher and theologian. Romanticism was, however, far from religious in many of its aspects, with its claim to complete freedom, its egoism, its interest in the natural world. Its mysticism was as much aesthetic as religious. From its beginnings in Berlin its leaders quickly moved to Jena, and from there were scattered and the influence of the movement diffused widely throughout Germany, finding centres as far removed from each other as Berlin, Vienna, and Heidelberg. The emergence of Vienna as a centre is to be explained by its long imperial tradition and connection, its Catholicism, and its leadership in music in this age of Haydn, Mozart, and Beethoven. And in Heidelberg the movement could link up with the rich traditions of medieval Franconia and Swabia.

For the Romantic contribution to the growth of national feeling is bound up with the interest of the Romanticists in German history. In this they owed a debt to Herder, and also to Burke, whose *Reflections on the French Revolution* (1790) had much influence upon German thought. His insistence upon the importance of tradition, of the deep roots of modern society and its growth therefrom, helped to foster the idea that such a society, a nation, was an organic growth, differentiated from its fellows. Schelling in turn defined and extended this view in his *Philosophy of Nature*, likewise influential with the Romanticists. They responded by turning away from the cosmopolitanism of the preceding age and seeking, and finding, their roots in the medieval history of their own country, Novalis in its religion, Arnim and Brentano in its early folk-songs, Adam Müller in the medieval state and society with its aristocracy and firm class gradations. Thus they both expressed and fostered a growing feeling of German patriotism. It is true that this needed time to take effect. Mme de Staël, visiting Germany in 1807, noted the lack of such a spirit, which was to be more widely manifest in and after the War of Liberation than before. Romanticism after all was primarily a literary movement, a middle-class rather than a popular one, and in origin little concerned with public affairs. Yet its enthusiasm for medieval Germany could fire a journalist such as Görres, who after his disillusionment with France returned to be the voice of patriotic and liberal Germany in his *Rhineland Mercury* in 1814. Similarly Arndt, the Swedish Pomeranian turned Prussian, first set himself to diagnose the reasons for German weakness, and then with his pamphlets and war songs aroused enthusiasm for the national cause. And Kleist, if only in part a Romantic, and though he was to put an end to his life in 1811 in despair with himself and his country, had given the strongest expression of national feeling and hatred of foreign conquerors of Germany, whether Roman or French, in his play *Die Hermannsschlacht*. Stein acknowledged that the work of the Romanticists was the complement of his own efforts for the reform and freeing of Prussia.

Other than Romantic writers also contributed to the growth of national feeling during these years. Gentz, the translator and admirer of Burke, and (after a momentary admiration) a strong and able critic of the French Revolution and Napoleon, was more concerned, like his master Metternich, to preserve or restore the old regime in Germany than to foster nationalism. The Saxon philosopher Fichte (1762–1814), on the other hand, not merely welcomed the revolution, but defended it after opinion in Germany had turned against it. Yet his was to be the strongest voice raised to foster national revival against France after the Prussian downfall in 1806. Fichte was a difficult and dogmatic person, as egoistic as the philosophy he developed after studying under Kant. He had risen by hard struggle from humble origins, was expelled from his professorial chair at Jena, and only slowly established himself in Berlin after 1800 as an independent thinker and forceful writer and lecturer. He illustrates better than any one perhaps the transition from the cosmopolitanism of the eighteenth century to the nationalism of the nineteenth. Before Jena his values were still largely those of the preceding age. But after it he stands out through his *Addresses to the German Nation* (1807–8) as the champion of German nationality. The Germans, he argued in those famous lectures, were a superior people because of their philosophy and their possession of an original and still living language. Low as their estate might be they had it in them both to regenerate themselves and to lead in the development of mankind; their leadership in the Reformation furnished proof of this. What was needed was a new system of education, national in its scope, to bring all Germans to a living faith in their Fatherland, 'a single and undying flame of patriotic feeling.' Yet, although Fichte thus vigorously espoused the Prussian and German cause, he was never wholly a nationalist. The nation to him was not so much an end in itself as a vehicle, a working medium, a necessary stage in the philosophic illumination of humanity, the triumph of liberty and the moral law. Nor was his influence for the nationalist cause so great at the time. It remained for later generations, both inside and outside Germany, to see in him the apostle of the nationalist creed.

With Fichte and his *Addresses* we are in Prussia after the debacle of 1806. 'We slumbered on the laurels of Frederick the Great,' said Queen Louise of Prussia, after the State which half a century earlier had aroused the enthusiasm of Germany by the great king's victory over the French at Rossbach had collapsed like a pricked bubble with the defeats of Jena and Auerstadt. After Tilsit (1807) most of what was left of the Prussian state was occupied by French troops, its fortresses were garrisoned by them, its cities were under French commandants, even the taxes were collected by French officials. True, by a convention of July 1807, the occupation was to end when the war indemnity was paid, but the amount of that indemnity was not fixed, its figure was constantly increased, and so the occupation continued. Prussia was surrounded by the vassal states of Napoleon, and the Tsar of Russia, if at heart no friend to his upstart brother of France, was ready to renew his alliance with him in the meeting of Erfurt in 1808. The situation of Prussia was grim indeed, and it was made worse by the failure of the monarchy, on which so much rested in this autocratic state, to realize that Jena had rung the knell of the old order, or even to overcome its traditional hostility to Austria. Nor was Frederick William III alone in this, for many of the nobility similarly refused to admit that the stiff old regime had contributed to the defeat, or to countenance any changes. Such changes, they argued, would smack of Jacobinism. 'The citizen's first duty,' ran the order issued from Berlin after the defeat at Jena, 'is to be quiet.'

Fortunately for Prussia, however, it had citizens who took a different view, who believed that the State and the monarchy could be saved, on condition that the administration, the army, and even the social order were radically reformed, and who devoted their energies to those tasks.   Although they had able Prussian-born helpers, the four men whose names stand out as leaders in this movement were non-Prussian in origin: Stein, the Imperial Knight from the Rhineland; Hardenberg, the Hanoverian; Scharnhorst, likewise from Hanover; and Gneisenau from Saxony.   The last two were to be particularly concerned with the reform and remaking of the Prussian army, Scharnhorst as the modest, scholarly, but indomitable reorganizer, Gneisenau as the co-worker, exemplifying the new military pattern and spirit in action. Hardenberg, in like manner, was to be the co-worker with Stein in the field of civil reform, more successful than Stein indeed as minister and diplomatist, but less broad in mind, less firm in principle, and lower in character.   Thus it is that although Hardenberg was to play a far longer and in some ways much more decisive part on the stage of Prussian and German politics, Stein may be said to occupy a larger place in German history and so calls for fuller mention.

Henry Frederick Charles 'of and to' Stein (1757–1831) came from Nassau in the hills north of the Main.   Drawn by the repute of Frederician Prussia, he found a career in its service rather than in the Austrian service more natural to an Imperial Knight of the old *Reich*.   But he never lost either his feeling of knightly independence or his attachment to Germany as a whole. Thus his career embodies both the efforts for the revival of Prussia to enable her to take a leading part in the liberation of Germany, and also the wider effort to reorganize the liberated country.   The loyal and enlightened servant of Prussia evolved into the patriotic German statesman who could declare in 1812: 'I have but one Fatherland, Germany, and am wholly devoted to it rather than to any portion of it. . . .   My confession of faith is unity.' [1]

Stein's active career falls into three periods.   In the first (1780–1804) he is a local administrator in Rhenish Prussia.   The second covers his two terms as Prussian minister (1804–7 and 1807–8).   The third includes his activities between his expulsion from office in 1808 and the Congress of Vienna.   Beginning his career under an able minister, Heinitz, in the Department of Mines, he was then placed in charge of mines and manufactures in part of Prussia's Rhenish provinces, and later became head of the governmental administration in all the Prussian Rhineland-Westphalian region (save East Frisia) with a tenth of all Prussian inhabitants under him. It was of importance for his development that these western lands, despite efforts at their complete absorption, still preserved a measure of self-government, with local Estates which both approved taxation and shared in local legislation.   And they were less feudal, with serfdom almost a thing of the past.   Further, they were more concerned with manufacture and trade than the rest of Prussia.   Here Stein, the landowning squire, in his over twenty years of experience, became a remarkably able administrator, combining

---

[1] Letter to Münster (from Seeley, *Stein*, vol. iii, p. 17).

energy and firmness with a growing liberality of view. This last was confirmed by local conditions, by the proximity of freer Holland, and by a
lengthy visit to Britain a few years before the French Revolution broke out,
a visit from which he returned with an abiding admiration for the freer
spirit and institutions of the island kingdom.

It was in the second of these three periods, and more particularly in the
later of the two periods of ministerial office, that Stein won the name of the
reformer of Prussia. In his first term, from 1804 to 1807, as Minister of
Trade, Industry, and (in part) Finance, he introduced certain reforms in
such matters as the salt monopoly, the State bank, and the freeing of trade.
But he quickly found, indeed he must have known already, that in the pre-
Jena system of Prussian administration there was little scope for ministerial
initiative or freedom of action. The bureaucracy was too strongly entrenched, too hide-bound and limited in its views, and it was little wonder
that the ardent and forthright Stein became and remained a severe critic and
opponent of the Prussian bureaucracy. Further, real control of affairs
rested not with the ministers, who had no access to the monarch, but with
an inner 'cabinet,' part of the heritage of Frederick the Great's system of
government. Under a weak king, such as Frederick William III, this cabinet
became a clique of royal favourites, and the system bred corruption and
inefficiency, both anathema to Stein. Finally the system of ministries was
illogical and unsound, some being responsible for particular areas, others
for particular subjects. Nor was there any ministerial solidarity. Thus, for
example, Stein had no connection with Prussian foreign policy, which was
carried on by Haugwitz, the champion of the policy of neutrality, in a way
that Stein roundly declared to be both 'cowardly and dishonest.' The result
of the whole system was that, as Stein put it in a memorandum of April 1806,
'the Prussian state has no constitution.' He went on to say that if no
measures were taken to remedy the defects exposed, 'it is to be expected
that the Prussian state will either dissolve or lose its independence,' for it is
on 'the brink of the abyss.' Stein proved only too sound a prophet, as the
collapse of the same year showed. But autocratic monarchs do not usually
enjoy being bluntly shown the defects of their methods of government, and
Frederick William III, if a weakling, was full of the consciousness of his own
supreme position. Thus when, after Jena, Stein refused to continue in office
unless radical changes were made in the system of government, the king
dismissed him as a 'refractory, stubborn, and disobedient servant of the
State.' It seemed the end of Stein's public career.

Instead it proved a breach in the old system in Prussia. For within six
months Frederick William was obliged to recall Stein, now as minister in
chief, and (in Hardenberg's words) 'the only man who can save what remains
of Prussia.' That was indeed an extraordinary tribute, and it must be
admitted that Stein was to be out of office again, and this time finally, too
soon to be able to fulfil Hardenberg's hopes. But he made a notable
contribution. He had already, whilst in retirement at Nassau, indicated the
direction his efforts would take. His main object was to create a more

active and responsible sense of citizenship among the widespread people of Prussia, as the basis for a national uprising against French domination. For this he would replace bureaucratic rule by provincial self-government (even including the Polish provinces), with a national parliament or Estates as the ultimate aim.   The central government would be reformed by getting rid of the inner cabinet, and ending the confusion amongst the ministries by making each responsible for a definite subject for the whole country.   And since serfs could hardly be expected to make good citizens, serfdom must go, as it had gone elsewhere in western Europe.

The Edict for the emancipation of all the serfs in Prussia was actually drafted by the time Stein returned to office, with men such as Schön, Schrötter, and Hardenberg behind it.   But Stein put it through (1st October 1807) and it carried his name.   The sad state of East and West Prussia after the war, and the fact that serfdom had just been abolished in Napoleonic Poland, undoubtedly aided its passing.   In the first place the decree gave the peasant personal freedom, and it also put an end to the distinction, cherished by Frederick II, between noble and burgher occupations, and between noble, burgher, and peasant lands.   Henceforth, on the one hand, the burgher could buy land belonging to the nobility; on the other, the noble could engage in trade.   The old caste system was thus seriously undermined.   So far as the peasant was concerned certain judicial rights of the lord remained (until 1891), and while the hated domestic service of the serf to the lord was abolished, his obligations in field labour remained.   Later laws (of 1811 and 1816) were to remove most of these also, but at the price of much of the peasant's land.   This, with the freedom of sale and purchase now permitted, worked out, however, to the disadvantage of the peasantry.   Instead of creating a class of free and secure peasant farmers as in France, and as Stein had intended, emancipation tended ultimately either to drive the peasant off the land or to reduce him to agricultural labour on the lands of the *Junker* (squire).   These landowners had indeed protested violently against the decree, but they survived it, and even turned it to their own advantage in the end.

More successful and complete was Stein's Municipal Ordinance of 1808. The Prussian towns had never enjoyed any freedom comparable to that of either the Hanseatic or the Imperial Cities, and the eighteenth century had seen a steady increase in royal control over them, a control codified in 1794. The crisis of 1806 had shown that neither civic nor national feeling was strong in them.   The new measure was designed to build up a spirit of citizenship.   By it all the cities and towns of Prussia were to elect both aldermanic and executive councils, the latter to share in the royal nomination of the burgomaster or mayor.   Save for justice and police, still regarded as matters for state control in this autocratic regime, the civic councils were to have charge of financial and other affairs in the local community.   Whilst some of these powers were to be lost in the reaction after 1848, in essentials the system thus established was to remain an accepted and integral part of the Prussian administration, perhaps its most enlightened and liberal part.

The new law reflected Stein's admiration for English local self-government, but it owed also a direct debt to the French legislation of the early years of the revolution.   To Stein it marked a first step towards the wider application of this principle of self-government, but for this his term of office was too short and the forces against it too strong.

The military reforms of the same period likewise aimed at the development of a greater sense of civic responsibility, in this case for the defence of the country.   Here too the example of revolutionary France, with its *levée en masse*, played its part.   While Scharnhorst and Gneisenau took the lead here, Stein gave close and indispensable support.   As with the land reform, the new system made a breach in the stiffer social structure of Frederician Prussia, by opening the rank of officer to some at least of the middle class. Flogging was abolished and promotion was to come by merit.   Old or inefficient officers were removed from the higher command and the training of officers in the royal cadet school in Berlin was rejuvenated.   Indeed the reforms may be said to have begun with Scharnhorst's work as instructor there.   The creation of a national army thus reformed, on the basis of universal military service in the active force or in the reserve of *Landwehr* (militia) or *Landsturm* (home defence force), was impeded for a time by royal fears of such radical changes, as by the terms of the treaty with France (1808) prohibiting the formation of a national militia and limiting the size of the army to 42,000 men.   This latter provision Scharnhorst overcame in part by training and replacing recruits as rapidly as possible.   The institution of universal compulsory military service was not to come until 1814, a year after Scharnhorst had died from wounds in the struggle for which he had prepared.

Long before this Stein had ended his brief second term of ministerial office. His reforming energy had naturally aroused opposition.   To the enmity of displaced bureaucrats or court officials and elements pro-French by tradition, sentiment, or interest was added the criticism of conservative nobles such as Marwitz and Yorck, who saw or professed to see in him a dangerous radical, a Jacobin, whose work would destroy the very foundations on which the Prussian state was built and had risen to greatness.   This opposition might have driven him out of office in any case.   But it was Napoleon's suddenly aroused hostility which was decisive.   Much of Stein's energies and time, from his entry into office, had of necessity been spent in the vain effort to come to some agreement with the French over the size of the indemnity demanded, and with the provision of means both for this and for the recuperation of Prussia after the war.   At the same time his patriotic and impetuous nature led him to encourage any movement of opposition to French domination, and he most rashly revealed in a letter seized by the French his hopes from the Spanish uprising against Napoleon in the 'May Days' of 1808.   Henceforth to the all-powerful emperor, who had earlier approved of him, he was a marked man, '*le nommé* Stein,' to be driven out of office and into exile to escape a worse fate, his property confiscated.   It was a misfortune for Prussia, as for Stein, although Stein was to play a part in the liberation of Germany on a wider stage.

Yet the reconstruction and revival of Prussia did not cease with his removal. The military rebuilding continued, and in 1810 Hardenberg, like Stein driven out of office by Napoleon, returned with the new office of Chancellor, minister-in-chief, an office he was to hold until his death twelve years later. Hardenberg too was a reformer, for the time at least; and aided by secret conference with Stein, he proceeded to carry through a number of reforms. He carried the emancipation settlement a stage further, made internal trade freer, raised money by partial disendowment of the churches, gave more liberty to the Jews, and went some way towards the institution of a national representative system by calling a provisional assembly of Estates, with, however, a preponderance of the nobility. Of great importance also was the work done by Wilhelm von Humboldt, called from scholarly retirement to be Minister of Education, in reforming primary and secondary education and in founding the university of Berlin (1809) to replace the loss of Halle. With men such as Fichte and Schleiermacher, the historians Niebuhr and Savigny, among its teachers, the new institution in the capital of Prussia was an embodiment of the spirit of revival now slowly spreading through the kingdom.

It was, of course, the Napoleonic disaster in Russia in 1812 that provided the opportunity for Prussia to turn against her conqueror. Before that, as the breach slowly opened between Napoleon and Alexander in 1811, she was drawn closer to France, even to the point of making a formal alliance with her (February 1812) by which she supplied troops for the French invasion of Russia. But when in December of that year the frozen remnants of the once *Grande Armée* staggered back out of Russia again, the way was open to a turn in Prussian history which was to be decisive both for her and for Germany. A Prussian general, Yorck, took the first step on his own initiative when he changed sides. Stein, who had been called to Russia in his exile, persuaded Alexander to disregard the advice of his generals who wished to make peace on Russian soil or at the border, and organized East Prussia for war. After much hesitation, Frederick William was persuaded to take the step of allying his country with Russia for a common effort to drive out the French invader. Then indeed the revival of Prussia manifested itself. The king called to arms, the nation responded in a way new in Prussian history, and the aged Blücher led the newly raised levies through the discipline of defeat to the glory of victory. And in so doing they not merely liberated their country, but wiped out the disgrace of Jena and Auerstadt and re-created for Prussia the military tradition of the Great Elector and the great Frederick, a tradition to be henceforth less identified with the Hohenzollern rulers in person, but none the less potent for the future.

The drawing into the struggle of the other states of Germany took time, however, and had accompaniments all important for the future. Austria, like Prussia, had been allied with Napoleon for the struggle with Russia, and it was not until some months after the May battles of Lützen and Bautzen in Saxony that Austria was ready to commit herself to a change of sides, so cautious was the diplomacy of Metternich. With Austria and

Prussia united against France for the first time since 1792, and joined with Russia and Britain, the last and greatest coalition against the common enemy came into being.   It took even longer, however, to draw in the lesser states of Germany.   The rulers of the middle-sized states had profited greatly from the Napoleonic conquest, as the peoples of the land west and north-east of the Rhine had benefited from the social changes introduced by the French.   There was little love for Prussia, and feeling for Austria was tinged by fear of her ambitions: Bavaria feared, for example, to lose the Tyrol.   The members of the Rhenish Confederation had supplied troops for the Napoleonic campaigns in Spain, as against Austria in 1809 and Russia three years later.   And they were still ranged on the French side through much of the fighting in Germany itself in 1813.   The allies had indeed, in the spring of 1813, appealed to the princes of the Rhenish Confederation to join them in the struggle, threatening them with the loss of their lands if they refused.   But with the French still in possession of most of Germany, and Austria still doubtful of her course, it was not surprising that there was little response.   In September, with Austria now joined to them, they took another course and promised at Teplitz 'full and unconditional independence' to the leading members of the Rhenish Confederation.

It was on these terms that Bavaria was persuaded by Metternich to join the allies just before the battle of Leipzig, by the Treaty of Ried.   The troops of Saxony and Wurtemberg changed sides during that prolonged but decisive battle, and with the ensuing French retreat to and across the Rhine, state after state made treaties with Austria, with the same guarantee of independence.   It was to be a fatal barrier to hopes of an effective union of liberated Germany.   Meanwhile the allies, having reached the Rhine (November 1813), were ready to halt there, in part because of their own dissensions, and had Napoleon been able to read the writing on the wall France might have held, for a time at least, her conquests west of that river. But since Napoleon refused to accept the allied conditions of German and Italian independence from France, war continued.   With the allied occupation of Paris, the first treaty signed there in May 1814 left only the Saar region in French hands.   And after the return of Napoleon from Elba and the Hundred Days, the second treaty, signed in Paris in November 1815, completed the liberation of Germany with the restoration of the boundaries of 1789: the score and more years of French occupation were over.

V. THE SETTLEMENT OF 1815

By the time Napoleon had been finally defeated at Waterloo, the problem of what shape the liberated Germany was to take had also been settled. The great question had been whether after the tremendous upheavals of the past twenty years she could solve the unsolved problem of the old *Reich*, and weld the remnants of the 'monster' which emerged from the last great settlement in 1648 into an organized political unit, a national state after the fashion of other western states.   We may see the issue in part in terms of the aims of two of the outstanding statesmen in Germany at this time, Stein and Metternich.   Both were Rhinelanders, but as different in temperament and character as in their views and aims.   Stein was the champion of those who wished to seize the opportunity presented by the disintegration

Germany in 1815

of the old empire, and with the aid of the enthusiasm for the national cause generated by the struggle for liberty create a new Germany, free from foreign control, its parts reduced in number by the absorption into larger units of the 'petty despotisms' fostered by Napoleon for his own ends. Stein had even declared himself ready to break up Prussia, if this could aid national unity.   And this new Germany would be dowered with an effective central authority, would possess both national and local representative assemblies, and guarantees of civic rights against princely oppression. Austria would be at the head of the new state with Prussia as second in command.

This was the gist of the proposals which Stein put forward during the war in a series of memoranda written mainly for the guidance of the tsar, whose unofficial adviser he was on German affairs. The proposals were modified somewhat as circumstances changed. And they show both the conservative and the liberal elements in Stein's views. Like Burke, he would not reform unless he could preserve. So whilst he would demote the princes and accept the abolition of the ecclesiastical estates, he would preserve the aristocracy (to which he himself belonged) as a link with the past and a pillar in the graded society of the age. His representative assemblies would also mirror these gradations. But they would reflect, too, both his belief in the right of the German people to a share in their government and his faith in their capacity for political development. In this, as in the high ethical quality of his thought, Stein stands far above Metternich, and also above Bismarck.[1]

But Stein's views and hopes for Germany were not to prevail. The settlement made at the general Congress of Vienna reflected far more the influence of a younger man, Prince Metternich, since 1809 Foreign Minister of Austria, agent of the marriage alliance of the Austrian Archduchess Marie Louise to Napoleon, a skilful and now experienced diplomatist, an enemy of the French Revolution rather than of Napoleon, concerned above all to secure the interests of Austria, whether against Russia, France, or Prussia, a courtier and man of the old regime, as full of intrigue and finesse as Stein was of moral passion. Not that Metternich had it all his own way at the Congress of Vienna, or that he alone was responsible for the very modest achievement of the congress in the matter of remaking Germany. He was the servant of Emperor Francis II, weak indeed, but still his master. There was the all-powerful Alexander, determined to have Poland as the Prussians were determined to have Saxony. And there were the lesser German states led by Bavaria and Wurtemberg, struggling to preserve their independence. That independence had been promised by treaties which Metternich had negotiated to win their support in the war, as other nations at war before and since have made similar promises to gain allies. These promises could not be completely ignored, nor was the insistence of the lesser states upon them wholly unnatural, in view of their relative weakness and the acquisitiveness shown by both Austria and Prussia in the past.

On the other hand it was obvious that *some* form of organization for all Germany was necessary, if only to protect her from France. If the treaties of 1813 had promised to maintain the sovereign independence of the separate German states, those made at Chaumont and Paris in the following year had agreed that some form of federal union should be set up there. A quarter of a century earlier, across the Atlantic, the revolted English colonies in their Articles of Confederation had laid it down that 'each state retains its sovereignty, freedom, and independence.' Yet it had proved possible to establish 'a more perfect union' in the constitution finally adopted for the United States, with a federal authority supreme in what were regarded as

[1] *See* Ricarda Huch, *Stein*, 1932, and in *Stein, Napoleon, and Bismarck.*

essentially national affairs. That in essence was what Stein and others wished to do at Vienna through the 'German Committee' set up there within the general framework of the congress, and composed of representatives of Austria, Prussia, Hanover, Bavaria, and Wurtemberg. Various proposals for union, eight in all, were presented to this body during its protracted meetings, notably by Humboldt of Prussia, which would have given Germany a federal authority covering some at least of the powers essential to such an organization, if not that 'firm and vigorous constitution' which Humboldt desired. But all these were strongly opposed by Bavaria and Wurtemberg as representatives of the smaller states, and were scarcely pressed by Prussia, still less by Austria.[1]   In the end Metternich threw the great weight of his influence on the side of the smaller states, with 'the result that the mere hasty and uncompleted sketch of a federal union emerged from the committee, to be greeted more with protest than approval in Germany. The German problem was left to be settled at a later date, and by other means than a peace conference.

The reasons for the failure are not far to seek. There was the opposition of the lesser states based on history, nurtured by fear of the two larger states, and recognized by the treaties of 1813. There was the rivalry of Austria and Prussia, difficult, if not impossible, to harmonize in any scheme of union. And both these states had interests outside Germany proper. Prussia had her Polish provinces, Austria her connections with Bohemia, Hungary, Poland, and Illyria, together with her revived interest in Italy, now extended by the gain of Venetia. Thus Austria, if German at heart, was more than ever a supranational state, and the balance between her German and non-German interests could be better preserved in a looser German union, in which she could hope for the support of the South German states, Catholic like herself. Further, the sentiment of national German unity was new, and could muster little effective force. The support of Prussia, now seeking to absorb Saxony, was not unnaturally regarded with some suspicion. And the national sentiment was associated in the minds of men such as Metternich with radical and dangerous tendencies, to be repressed rather than encouraged. Castlereagh, for England, and Alexander of Russia, were friendly to the idea of a closer union, but Talleyrand, for France, naturally used what influence he had to preserve the disunion which had in the past served French policy so well.

Two particular developments during the congress likewise worked in the same direction. The first of these was the Polish-Saxon question, the question whether the bulk of Poland was to be constituted into a kingdom under Russian control, with Prussia compensated by Saxony. But Austria refused to agree to Prussian absorption of Saxony unless she recovered part of Poland, and the issue put an end to the short-lived alliance between Austria and Prussia, and threatened to disrupt the whole congress, even to

[1] The great Prussian historian Von Sybel opined that had Austria supported the Prussian proposals for a real union, of which she would have been the head, her domination over Germany would have been so revived as to endure indefinitely. (H. von Sybel, *The Founding of the German Empire* (trans.), vol. i, p. 50.)

plunge Europe once again into war. In the end Prussia got part of Saxony, Austria part of Poland. But the bitter dispute played into the hands of the lesser German states as it did into those of France, and helped materially to frustrate the hopes of the German nationalists. Further, the return of Napoleon to France from Elba in March 1815 made it urgent to find a solution of the German problem, or at any rate to put an end to discussions which had already gone on for over a year in Vienna and elsewhere, the more so as by this time the remainder of the vast and complicated treaty was near completion. Almost inevitably the weaker proposals for unity won as arousing less opposition. A week before the battle of Waterloo an agreement was signed which did indeed set up 'a perpetual Confederation,' but which declared its objects to be not merely the security of Germany, but also 'the independence and inviolability of the confederated states.' This 'Act' was incorporated in the general treaty of the congress, and so was signed, and supposedly guaranteed, by the greater as well as the lesser European powers which signed that treaty.

By the terms of this emasculated agreement the Confederation or *Bund* was to have a federative Diet for ordinary business, composed of seventeen members for its thirty-eight (later thirty-nine) states, the eleven largest with one vote each, the remainder grouped into six units. These seventeen members were delegates only, acting on instructions from their governments. The Diet was to sit at Frankfurt, and was to be presided over by Austria, which thus to some extent retained its old role. For constitutional changes a General Assembly (*Plenum*) was called, in which all the states were directly represented by from one to four voting members, and unanimity was required for any major decision, which made change almost impossible. There were no arrangements for defence, a federal judiciary, or trade, though the treaty declared that the Diet should at once proceed to work out such arrangements. But no effective scheme of defence ever came into operation, though beginnings were made at it, and still less resulted from half-hearted attempts to set up a federal tribunal for disputes between states. The hopeful provision that representative assemblies of estates were to be set up in all the states, a sop to the demand of Stein and others, was for long to find only partial acceptance.

The territorial arrangements of the treaty, which were set out in the greatest detail, had been the subject of much controversy, and some details were left to special commissions to work out. The new boundaries between Prussia and Saxony, and of the Rhineland, were particularly complicated. The Germany that resulted was still a patchwork of states of infinitely varying size, but a relatively simple one as compared with the old empire. The many ecclesiastical states were not restored, despite their protests and that of the Pope, whilst only four of the Imperial Cities (Hamburg, Bremen, Lübeck, and Frankfurt on Main) survived, and only one of the mediatized principalities (Hesse-Homburg). Southern Germany was now consolidated into four largish states, diminishing in size from east to west, viz. Austria, Bavaria, Wurtemberg, and Baden. Austria gave up her claims to her

Netherland and Upper Rhenish possessions, but won back Salzburg and Tyrol from Bavaria, as well as Illyria and Milan, joining up these southern lands by Venice.   Thus the Habsburg possessions were more closely connected, but at the cost of Austria's northern and western German connections. Bavaria was compensated for her southern losses by the addition of Würzburg and the old Palatinate west of the Rhine.

Northern Germany was likewise more consolidated than in 1789, with Prussia the chief gainer.   In place of the divided fragments of western German territory she held before, she now received a solid block of Rhenish-Westphalian land reaching from the Netherlands and Luxemburg across to Hanover.   This was due largely to Castlereagh's desire to provide a strong bastion against French aggression, and generally to stiffen northern Germany against pressure from either west or east.   By these gains Prussia succeeded Austria as the western guardian of Germany, and acquired territory of immense strategical and economic importance, with Cologne at its centre, the Mosel and Saar valleys included to the south, that of the Ruhr to the north.   Prussia likewise broadened her central provinces by adding two-fifths of Saxony to the south and Swedish Pomerania to the north.   Of her Polish gains from the partitions she lost wide areas to Russia, but retained West Prussia, with Posen and Thorn.   Thus she now faced Russia (or Russian Poland) on an enormous frontier from Memel to Cracow.   All in all, however, the settlement swung Prussia back from the eastern trend of the eighteenth century, and made her more German in composition, a fact of importance for the future.   The remaining North German states were not greatly changed, save that Hanover, still tied to Britain, now stretched round Oldenburg to the Dutch border.   Middle Germany, from the junction of Rhine and Main across to Saxony, became now, in succession to Swabia, the centre of German particularism.   Its welter of small states reached its height in Thuringia, whose three-quarters of a million people, no more than the population of a large city, were divided amongst nine sovereign princes, five Saxon, two Schwarzburg, and two Reuss,[1] each with its own paraphernalia of government, tariffs, even of coinage and soldiery in some cases. Thus was the kernel of the old *Reich* embedded in the newer Germany.

The general significance of this period of German history has been indicated at the beginning of this chapter, and so need not be restated here. Every side of German life was affected by it, saving the religious division of the country established after the struggles of the Reformation period. Yet the wars and upheavals did not destroy the vitality of the country as did the Thirty Years War.   Indeed in some ways they stimulated it.   The French Revolution was a creative as well as a destructive force, and the movement of thought already active in Germany continued to bear fruit, in part under its influence.   If one side of it, with Goethe as the outstanding example, pursued the even tenor of its chosen way relatively little disturbed by that revolution, as in England Jane Austen's earlier novels illustrate a

---

[1] See H. Treitschke, *History of Germany in the Nineteeth Century* vol. iii, p. 20, for a graphic account of this region, and the 'ludicrous megalomania of its amiable dynasts.'

like inattention to the Napoleonic wars, another side of that movement, seen in Fichte or in part in Schiller, was stimulated to new activity thereby. Treitschke could declare [1] that 'the whole energy of luxuriant sentiment which had been accumulating throughout the classical period of our poetic literature was now streamed into political life.' There was some truth in this, as we have seen, in regard to the rise of national sentiment. But there was much less in relation to the development of new and promising political forms. For the period did not bring any marked change from the pattern of autocracy prevailing before 1789. The promise of it was there indeed. It had been defined by the Prussian minister Hardenberg, assuredly no Jacobin, in a letter to Stein in 1807:[2] 'Democratic principles in a monarchical government, such appears to me the formula fitting the spirit of the age.' But this formula found no acceptance in the settlement of 1815, nor was it represented in the political organization of the separate states, so strong were the forces marshalled against it in Vienna, Berlin, Munich, and elsewhere. And although it survived it was to fail again in its effort to find recognition a generation later in the revolution of 1848. Not until 'monarchical government' itself disappeared, seventy years later, could 'democratic principles' find free expression, and then only for a few years.

[1] op. cit., vol. i, p. 352.
[2] From Cavaignac, *La Formation de la Prusse Contemporaine*, vol. i, p. 340

CHAPTER VI

CONSERVATIVES, LIBERALS, AND NATIONALISTS, 1815–40

Introductory — The Confederation, Austria and the Lesser States — Prussia

I. INTRODUCTORY

THE PERIOD following 1815 was bound to be one of difficulty and controversy, if not internal conflict, in Germany. The land had been overrun by the Gallic flood, which had swept away old structures, wiped out old boundaries and landmarks, wasted the people's substance, and subjected them to alien rule. But it had also introduced new laws, new methods, new concepts, some of which were more liberal and enlightened than anything the old Germany had known. And it had likewise built up new interests such as those of the enlarged South German states. Germany had emerged from the flood, however, and the effort to do so had aroused a new national consciousness. Yet she had not been able to win freedom solely by her own efforts. Foreign aid had been required, above all that of Tsar Alexander I, and this had brought Russia with her great military strength into the affairs of central and western Europe in a way new in history. This was to mean the more to Germany since the buffer state of Poland no longer existed, and henceforth Germany (or rather Prussia) directly faced the vast Slav empire for many hundreds of miles along its eastern frontier, a factor of much importance for the future.

With the peace a new and immensely simplified structure of Germany appeared. Yet certain fundamentals of the old Germany of the eighteenth century survived. In the new *Bund*, as in the old *Reich*, Germany was a loosely connected union of states. As before, Austria and Prussia were predominant, the unsteady balance of their old dualism still unresolved. And below them was the scattered cluster of middle-sized states from Bavaria downwards, with a tail of quite unimportant small units. Nor was there any such marked change in the internal organization of these states, large or small. Whilst the rulers of a few states, as Brunswick and Electoral Hesse, had been driven out and now returned, the leading dynasties had lived through the storms. The same Habsburg Emperor, Francis II, ruled over Austria as when the first revolutionary war with France broke out in 1792, and he was to reign for another twenty years after 1815. And whilst the Hohenzollern Frederick William III had begun his reign five years later than Francis, he was to make up for it by outliving him by five years to 1840. Similarly the Wittelsbachs of Bavaria, the Wettins of Saxony, the Guelphs in Hanover, and most of the other ruling families of the surviving states, retained or regained their positions. And these princes, like the restored princes elsewhere in western Europe, had undergone no great change in their view of their status or powers.

There had been changes of course. There were the reforms undertaken in Prussia, so far as they had gone. Bavaria too had had her reforms, carried out by the enlightened minister Montgelas, including the seizure of monastic lands, the grant of full civic rights to Protestants, and judicial and educational reforms. Then there were the revolutionary changes brought about by the French in the Rhineland and Westphalia. And there was the clause in the Federal Act of 1815 providing for the creation of representative assemblies in all the states of the *Bund,* and the particular pledge of Frederick William of Prussia to the same effect. But the prevailing concern of the rulers and upper classes in Germany after 1815 was to preserve rather than to change. They were in general fearful of anything which suggested revolution or Jacobinism. Metternich was the prime exponent and supporter of these views, and he owed his predominating position in Germany in no small part to the fact that he represented so well the views of the great majority of the ruling princes of Germany, in opposing both political changes in the individual states and also greater national unity.

What was coming to be called (from Chateaubriand's paper *Le Conservateur*) the conservative view was, of course, based to a considerable extent on the autocratic system of pre-revolutionary days. But this was not wholly the case, for to Restoration thinkers that system had become too secular in its views, and had absorbed dangerous liberal elements from the Enlightenment, even to the point of seeing the ruler as the first servant of his subjects. The French Savoyard, de Maistre, had shown the evils of such thinking, and the way back to order and authority under the head of the Catholic Church, in his book *Du Pape.* The German Romantic writers, as we have seen, had gone back to the medieval period for inspiration and colour, and in the very year 1815 a popular writer, La Motte Fouqué, published the first of his series of medieval romances, filled with a gilded and heroic but highly unhistorical chivalry (of whom Heine was rudely to write that they possessed the strength of a hundred lions and the wit of two donkeys). More important, however, than the gilding of fiction was the support which the Romantics gave to the conservative view of society. Looking back to the German medieval empire they saw in it a stability and order which in truth it hardly possessed, and which they attributed to its Christian faith under one Church, and to its system of clearly separated but firmly conjoined classes. Some of these writers such as Frederick Schlegel, Adam Müller, and K. L. von Haller were moved to repudiate the breach made by Luther and to join the Catholic Church. Even the more sceptical Gentz came to regard the Reformation as the beginning of all revolutionary ideas. Adam Müller, who found a place in the Austrian service under Metternich, lauded the virtues of the old Estates of the Realm as giving stability and order to civil society, in opposition to the liberal individualism of Adam Smith or Wilhelm von Humboldt.

K. L. von Haller, in origin a Swiss aristocrat, envisaged the Christian state in patriarchal terms with the king responsible only to God, and a landowning and privileged aristocracy below him.   This was the 'legitimate' state, based on religion and tradition rather than on Natural Law or Contract, and legitimism, with its aura of religion to foster obedience, had a natural appeal to princes and aristocracies.   The compact of the Holy Alliance embodied its principles in the pledge that its princely members were 'to regard themselves towards their subjects and armies as fathers of families, taking as their sole guide the precepts of that Holy Religion, namely, the precepts of Justice, Christian Charity, and Peace.'   Metternich echoed the same attitude when in his Confession of Faith [1] he urged rulers 'to show themselves as they are, fathers invested with the authority belonging by right to the head of families.'

The view advanced by Schlegel, that the more conservative a nation is the more national it is, found some support in the teachings of the new Historical Law School of the Restoration period led by Savigny in Berlin. For this school saw the laws of a people as a natural and spontaneous growth, not wisely to be tampered with by the introduction of modern codes based on rational or general principles.   Philosophy similarly made its contribution to conservative views of the state in the teachings of Hegel, successor to Fichte in the university of Berlin.   True, there were both liberal and conservative elements in Hegel's teachings upon society and the state.   But whilst the emphasis upon the spirit of freedom in the development of human society might be the more elevated, the emphasis upon the all-powerful state as an end in itself and 'the embodiment of the ethical idea' was both more concrete and more easily and naturally applicable to Prussia. There, in the years after 1815, high state officials and army officers attended the lectures of the 'royal Prussian state-philosopher.'   And if, as Hegel put it, 'what is rational is actual, and what is actual is rational,' then there was little or no need for change in the system existing in Prussia, and so no need to fulfil the promise of a constitution given by Frederick William III to his people.   The greatest German historian of the Restoration period, Niebuhr (d. 1830), was as ardent in his condemnation of the French Revolution as in his efforts to elucidate the early history of Rome, and helped thereby to define conservative opinion on the revolution.

But there were many in Prussia and elsewhere in Germany who held different views.   Liberalism in Germany as elsewhere was a tree with many roots and many branches; the fragmentation of the liberal political parties in the time of Bismarck and later was only too abundantly to illustrate the latter quality.   The word itself was new, adopted from that party in the Spanish Cortes which championed the constitution of 1812 against royal absolutism.   But the roots went far back into the past of Germany, and far outside that country.   It represented in part the attachment to the old system of elected Estates existing before the inroads of princely autocracy in the seventeenth century.   It was fed by Calvinism and to a lesser extent by

[1] *Memoirs* (trans.), vol. iii, p. 471.

Lutheranism. More plainly it drew upon the Enlightenment with its encouragement to rational thinking and emancipation from earlier dogmas, not least with regard to religion. The Kantian Philosophy of Right, seeing the State as founded upon justice and law, provided a moral basis, while Stein's reforms and aims gave the stimulus of practical example. The ideas and actions of the early stages of revolutionary France (and more recently of the charter of Louis XVIII) supplied an armoury of foreign teaching and example, and hardly less influential was the example of Britain with its constitutional monarchy, its age-old parliament, its stable yet freer social organization, its local self-government, its system of trial by jury. And across the North Atlantic was rising a new state avowedly founded upon the principle of freedom. And while American free society could hardly be compared to the strait jacket of German society, nevertheless liberalism in Germany had something in common with it, since it was just the newer middle class in Germany that was championing the liberal creed.

For liberalism in Germany was primarily a middle-class faith, a product of the revival of that class already noted as taking place in the eighteenth century. This class was still small in the period after 1815, but as an educated class it could express its views. Its prime concern was for the freedom of the individual, the educated and enterprising individual, who could and would use that freedom for the benefit of society as well as of himself. Hence liberals disliked the authoritarian or 'police' state such as Prussia still was, the word 'police' having a wider significance than with us to-day. Some wished the State to be no more than an agent to secure protection and freedom for its citizens, a view expressed by Wilhelm von Humboldt in a little book written in 1795 on *The Limits of State Interference*. Liberals wanted freedom of religion, freedom of discussion and the press, freedom of trade and economic activity, equality before the law, a measure of political freedom. Such liberties, they argued, could best be attained in the constitutional legal state (the *Rechtsstaat*) in which the powers of the ruler were limited by a written constitution comparable to that of France or the United States. Herein these civic rights would be assured and guaranteed by a parliament with a separation of executive, legislative, and judicial powers. Liberals also believed in local self-government as they saw it in England. From England also they drew their theories of economic freedom. The arguments of Adam Smith in favour of free enterprise and free trade appealed strongly to many in the rising new middle class, and were to prevail until Bismarck's day. Economic liberalism was indeed quite as strong as, and more effective than, political liberalism.

Since liberalism by definition implied freedom it naturally followed that liberals held and expressed a wide variety of views. Whilst most liberals of the professional and mercantile class were men of the *juste milieu*, monarchists who would limit political rights to property owners and persons of education, there was no clear line of division between them and the holders of more radical views, believers in the sovereignty of the people, and laying more stress on equality than on liberty, even capable of harbouring republican sentiments. But such radicals were few as yet in Restoration Germany. The common people in country and even in town were still little touched by political or social unrest. Germany was still a greatly divided country, its loyalties still local, its communications of almost medieval slowness and difficulty in this pre-railway age. East and west, north and south, differed in outlook as in social and economic conditions. Lacking any political centre of its own its people were more inclined to look outwards for political inspiration, the eastern landowners towards absolutist Russia, the western liberals towards France, those of the north-west towards England. Thus Dahlmann in Kiel and then in Hanoverian Göttingen drew inspiration for his teaching and writing from English parliamentary example, whereas Rotteck and Welcker in Baden, and Görres in the Prussian Rhineland, were more directly influenced by French example.

German liberalism was inextricably connected with the wave of national feeling aroused by the struggle for freedom from Napoleonic domination. To the majority of liberals the two were conjoined, inseparable. So it was with Görres at this time and also with the fiery patriot Arndt, who while violently anti-French, and desiring greater national unity in Germany, would base that unity on political, legal, and social freedom, liberty of speech and writing. And the *Burschenschaft* with its motto of 'Liberty, Honour, Patriotism,' was to exhibit the same connection. For a time, in part conscious of the debt to the cosmopolitanism of the eighteenth century, German liberals were sympathetic with the national feeling, not merely of the Greeks in their rising against the Turks, but also nearer home to the efforts of the Poles in 1831 to free themselves from Russian rule despite the threat therein to Prussian rule over western Poland. Here the revolution of 1848 was to show a wave of anti-Slav feeling, as 1840 had shown a revival of antagonism against the French.

Liberals were, however, naturally most concerned with the problem in German lands. The settlement of 1815, with its revelation of the weakness of the confederate Diet, bitterly disappointed them. It became increasingly clear that there was no hope of attaining any real unity or political freedom from that source. And the problem of finding a focus for a united, free Germany was rendered more difficult by the lack of liberal governments in the separate states. It was futile to hope that Austria would either change her form of government or champion closer German unity. Prussia was equally illiberal and more feared as more aggressive. Yet she had her liberals, increased in number by the addition of the Rhineland. A well-known merchant of Cologne, D. Hansemann, looked for a union under a liberalized Prussia. F. von Gagern, a liberal of Hesse-Darmstadt, in a writing of 1823 argued that Prussia might unite Germany on a liberal basis, if she ceased to be a separate state, and the Wurtemberger Paul Pfizer, in his *Letters Between two Germans* (1831), recognized Prussia as the only possible centre of German unity, but likewise suggested that she should be broken up to disarm fears of Prussian domination. But that was hardly to be hoped for under Frederick William III. Another liberal, the journalist

Lindner, placed his hopes of the setting up of a 'Third Germany,' that of the south-west, the old home of German culture, and free of non-German elements. Yet the two largest states there, Bavaria and Wurtemberg, were as particularist as any states in the country, and hopes of leadership in union therefrom could but be dreams based upon a for ever departed past.

Nevertheless liberals came to believe that the most hopeful course was first to attain political freedom in the individual (and smaller) states, and then build thereon a liberal regime for the whole united country. And in this the south-west could and did take the lead. For there, in accordance with the provisions of the Federal Act of 1815, constitutions were set up and essayed their early steps. But the struggles which ensued were to make plain the difficulties in the way of attaining liberal aims, even on so limited a stage, when to local opposition was added the resistance of the two largest states in the Confederation. Hence the progress made in the fulfilment of liberal hopes in these years was meagre and disappointing. The revolutions of 1830 did indeed arouse fresh hopes and produce reverberations all over Germany. Two of the worst of the Restoration princes, those of Brunswick and Electoral Hesse, were driven out by local uprisings, and new constitutions were introduced in Electoral Hesse and Saxony. A rising radicalism found expression in the festival at Hambach in the Bavarian Palatinate (1832) where, with much windy if sincere rhetoric, the demand was raised for German unity on a popular, even a republican, basis. But this merely brought the imposition of repressive measures by the combined weight of Austria and Prussia. And already a French observer, Edgar Quinet, declared [1] that German liberalism (or democracy) was showing signs of being ready to accept the leadership of Prussia, and barter its idealism for the power which Prussian autocracy might give to the national cause.

The Restoration period in Germany was not wholly concerned with political issues. There were religious issues also, as we shall see. And already in these years we can trace the beginnings of those economic and social changes which were in due course to make of Germany a modern industrial society with great cities, with factories and mines, and with new social classes at the top and the bottom. But these changes were as yet quite limited in size, although already in this period we find some social and industrial unrest. More obvious is the survival into this period of some of the influence and some of the leaders of the great intellectual and literary movements of the later eighteenth century. Goethe and Schleiermacher, Hegel and Humboldt, were still alive in 1830, Frederick Schlegel only just deceased, many of the Romantic writers still living and writing. And below or beyond such significant movements or figures the great majority of the German people in country and town (and three-quarters of the population still lived in the country) followed the plough, worked with shuttle or hammer, bought and sold, undisturbed now by war, and seemingly little affected by impending social change or higher intellectual currents.

The next generation, looking back at this era in terms of the way of life

[1] In *Revue des Deux Mondes*, 1832.

of the ordinary folk of Germany, saw it as marked by quiet simplicity, stability, and solidity, the *Biedermeier* time.[1]   The view was partly an artificially created one, a nostalgic looking back from a more complicated, materialistic, and restless age to a simpler and more contented one.   The very title was based on a faked collection of old-fashioned poems attributed to a Swabian village schoolmaster.   Yet there was some truth in the picture. This period between the storms of the revolutionary period and the stirrings preceding the revolutions of 1848 was for the rank and file of the German people one of relative quietude.   They still had their roots in the soil or the home workshop, their local loyalties were still strong, they moved about little in this pre-railway age, they were conservative in thought and habits, still firmly established in their niche in the social order.   Most of the old towns still preserved some of their medieval appearance, even in some cases the old walls.   The ties of religion and family life were still strong, their tastes in art and literature, furniture and decoration, were simple.   In music indeed, with Beethoven, Schubert, and Weber still alive, they could make higher claims.   'In no country,' said Goethe to Eckermann in 1828, 'are the taste for and the practice of music and singing so widely spread as in Germany.'   The pictures of Spitzweg admirably reproduce the outward pattern of their life.

Yet if much of the old Germany still survived, the new one was growing up.   The real founder of Krupps was born in 1812, Bismarck in 1815, Marx in 1818.   The waves of influence sent out by the intellectual and literary revival, and by the French Revolution, had not ceased to flow. They were aided by the growth of journalism, which despite censorship steadily extended its influence.   Schooling and education were widespread, from the universities to the village schools.   If this was a time of quietude it was also a time of waiting and of preparation.   The fact that between 1830 and 1840 some 180,000 Germans, mostly from the south-west, left their country to find new homes and new opportunity in the growing United States indicates that already old roots were being pulled up.   'What the next few years will bring,' to quote Goethe talking again to Eckermann in 1824, 'I cannot predict: but I fear we shall not soon have repose.   It is not given to the world to be contented: the great are not such that there will be no abuse of power: the masses not such that they will be contented with a moderate condition.'   So Goethe spoke at seventy-five.   And if the coming of the storms and rapid changes was to be delayed a little for Germany, the prophecy was sound enough in a longer view.

II. THE CONFEDERATION, AUSTRIA, AND THE LESSER STATES

The history of Germany from 1815 to 1840 still ran as before 1789, not in one broad stream but in a number of separate channels with little unity of direction, purpose or effort, following the victory of particularism in 1815.

---

[1] 'Early Victorian' has been suggested as an English equivalent, but this can only partly be true, if only because of England's earlier economic developments.

Nor, despite the stimulus of the efforts of 1813–15, was there any strong or prevailing current of change in the quarter of a century from 1815 to 1840. Up to 1840 the conservative and particularist forces were amply strong enough to hold the liberal-nationalist forces in check, and there was an air of futility about local manifestations in favour of constitutional change or political unity.   Only after 1840, in the years leading up to the fateful events of 1848, was there a marked and increasing change, its opening conveniently marked by the death of old Frederick William III of Prussia and the accession of his very different son.   It was the apparent springtide of liberalism and unity.

Yet it would be quite untrue to represent the period between 1815 and 1840 simply or solely in terms of the triumph of conservative particularism. The period was one of general recuperation after the prolonged crises and wars of the revolutionary and Napoleonic era, although such recuperation was delayed by the floods, the failure of crops, and the resulting famine of the years 1816–17.   The political map of Germany, drawn and redrawn so drastically, needed time to settle into its new shape and boundaries.   Here Prussia had the most arduous task, and the work of consolidation she accomplished in these years was to be of the utmost importance both for the Prussian state and for Germany as a whole.   It may, therefore, best be considered separately, following some account of the Confederation, Austria, and the lesser states of the *Bund* in this period.

The Federal Diet set up by the Congress of Vienna may indeed be absolved from any effort to give an effective lead to the country in these years, and it is unnecessary to follow its proceedings in detail.   By definition, in the Treaty of Vienna, its function was to maintain 'the independence and inviolability of the confederated states,' and the requirement for a unanimous vote of its members on major issues proved an effective barrier to any far-reaching activity.   Despite a display of formal authority in its first meeting at the end of 1816 under the presidency of Count Buol of Austria, it quickly showed that it possessed neither the power nor the desire to exercise any real control.   It refused a request to interfere in an issue between the masterful Elector of Hesse and certain of his subjects.   It failed to take action to implement the article of its constitution providing for the establishment of representative assemblies in the various states.   It likewise failed to fill up the gaps in the Federal Act relating to the military defence of the country, the setting up of an effective supreme court or judicial machinery to deal with disputes between states or the removal of trade barriers between them. And this preliminary policy, or lack of policy, continued to mark its attitude and proceedings throughout this period, and indeed throughout its history. We need not be too severe upon it.   On the one hand, as the stunted child of particularism the Diet was unable to take any initiative in national affairs; on the other, it was subject to Austrian domination or Austro-Prussian domination in which Metternich of Austria took the lead.   And since Metternich believed, as firmly as he believed anything, that liberalism and nationalism were dangerous to Austrian interests, and indeed to Austrian existence, the Diet quickly degenerated into a mere agent for the repressive activities of conservative policy led by Austria and Prussia.

This role of the Diet was clearly enough defined within a few years after 1815 by its share in repressing what were alleged to be the dangerous activities in the universities. The universities of Germany, while locally controlled, had always cut across the particularism of the country. The universities of Leipzig in Saxony, Jena in Saxe-Weimar, Göttingen in Hanover, with Heidelberg in Baden, and Halle in Prussia, drew students and teachers from most if not all of Germany. They had been active in the general revival of thought in the eighteenth century and had been the homes of the so-called New Humanism with its worship of Greek culture, fostered by Gesner and Heyne at Göttingen and F. A. Wolf at Halle, as it spread through Germany from north to south. And whilst it has been a charge against this movement that it had too little concern for active citizenship, the universities had played their part in the final effort for the national cause against Napoleon. The enthusiasm thus evoked could hardly disappear after the victory, to be sunk without trace. German university students had long been organized into societies after the medieval pattern; now there appeared at Jena in 1815 a new one, the *Burschenschaft*, affiliations of which quickly arose elsewhere. Its aims were partly moral, but also liberal and nationalist. A product of north-German Protestantism, it was not surprising that in 1817 the society should join to the celebration of the fourth anniversary of the great battle of Leipzig that of the three hundredth anniversary of Luther's breach with Rome, and at the Wartburg, where Luther had taken refuge, and conveniently near to Jena.

The Wartburg gathering of some five hundred students and a number of professors was of no importance politically, despite the fact that a final burst of enthusiasm led to the burning of some conservative and anti-national literature and emblems. Yet it aroused considerable concern, if not alarm, in the authorities in both Prussia and Austria. And when eighteen months later a weak-minded theological student (who had been present at the Wartburg) proceeded to murder the well-known dramatist Kotzebue, suspected of being an agent of Russian autocracy, these governments seized the opportunity to curb such 'revolutionary activities.' A conference was called at Carlsbad of nine of the major German states, and agreed upon the suppression of the *Burschenschaften* and other similar societies, the setting up of a Central Judicial Commission at Mainz, and the censorship of the press. The Diet showed its quality (or lack of it) by a vote of unanimous approval of the decrees, thus making it clear that it was a mere puppet.

The later history and activities of the Diet did nothing to change that position or character. When the Final Act of Vienna (1820) whittled down Article XIII of the original treaty, the Diet ratified the decision without even the formality of a vote. And when the French and other revolutions of 1830 caused a fresh wave of unrest in Germany the Diet again left the initiative to Austria and Prussia. Thus when the radical 'festival' held at

Hambach went so far as to call for a national German republic, it was the two leading powers which took action and drew up the Six Articles prohibiting political associations and the holding of public festivals—the Diet merely adopted them.   Similarly it was a conference of states in Vienna which followed up these articles by further regulations, one of which was to set up a permanent federal arbitral tribunal on constitutional matters, though this, like most of the other articles, never came into effect.   So low had the reputation of the Diet sunk that it could be described about this time by F. von Gagern as 'the shame of Germany and the contempt of Europe.' There, for the time, we may leave it.

The position and policy of Austria in Germany are, of course, to a considerable extent defined by what has been said already of the settlement of 1815, and of the Federal Diet.   Her prime objects were to preserve the predominant position she had secured there in 1815, and to prevent any contagion of revolutionary feeling or activity from Germany disturbing the Habsburg dominions.   Despite her success at the Congress of Vienna, the old connection with Germany had been materially diminished by her loss of the Netherlands and her trans-Rhenane lands, while her gain of a solid block of Italian territory had added to her non-German territories, which were now larger than her Germanic lands.   The old and distracting connection with the Italian peninsula was revived, to last for half a century more.

So far as Austrian domestic affairs were concerned she was able for most of this period to avoid any dangerous contamination of revolutionary ideas, and to maintain the unrelieved torpor of Austrian public life.   This she accomplished at the cost of financial and administrative decay, under the procrastinating rule of Francis II and that of his mild but epileptic successor Ferdinand I.   But there were problems connected with Hungary, with Bohemia, Galicia, and other Slavic lands of the empire, where the disrupting influence of nationalism was beginning to show itself.   And beyond the south-eastern frontier the Balkan peoples were now entering the first stage of their efforts to emancipate themselves from Turkish rule, thereby creating difficult problems in Austrian relations with Russia and other European powers.   The Greek bid for independence in the twenties, with its wide reverberations throughout Europe, including Germany, was both an unwelcome disturbance of the peace and a harbinger of future troubles.

The safeguarding of Austrian interests throughout the irregular confusion of the Confederation was, of course, a prime concern of Prince Metternich, as Chancellor and Foreign Minister of the Austrian Empire.   And it must be admitted that in a shorter view he was remarkably successful in this, notwithstanding his limitations of character, prescience, and policy.   The harsh judgments of later Prussian historians, such as Treitschke, upon him are in part a tribute to his success.   He was aided, of course, by the weakness of the Prussian king and the Prussian lack at this period of any German policy of her own.   Thus Metternich could claim in 1819, and with some

reason, that he had Prussia in his pocket.   He was likewise helped by the
survival in Germany of the old tradition of attachment to Austria as, for
example, in Stein.   And although Austrian hegemony was by no means
universally liked or trusted, it was regarded by the princes as less dangerous
to German particularism than the more openly predatory policy of Prussia.
Community of religion also played its part in Catholic Germany, the more
so since Vienna, despite the tradition of eighteenth-century Josephism, now
became one of the centres of the Catholic revival.   Romanticism added its
influence also, as some of its leaders, such as Frederick Schlegel and Adam
Müller, found a home there.   Austria was, after all, the largest and strongest
state in the *Bund*, with a far larger population than Prussia, and Prussia
was in no mind as yet to repeat the Frederician challenge to its military
power.   So Metternich, aided by his vast European reputation, could take
the lead in the affairs of Germany in the years after 1815, either directly by
calling conferences of German states to Vienna, or through the councils of
the Diet over which Austria presided with little fear of any resolute or combined opposition.   And with his ineffable and unfailing conceit he could
preen himself on his success in checking the spread of 'the contagious
disease' of liberalism.

Yet time was to work against him and the tide of his success to turn in
Germany as elsewhere.   Whilst Austria had become less German in character in 1815 Prussia had become more so, and in due course became more
conscious of the change.   This was first manifested not, as in 1740, in any
sharp military success, but in the slower moving field of economic life,
when Prussia was able to build a commercial union of Germany which
excluded Austria.   In the long run Austria could not hope to maintain her
position in Germany when she pursued economic and political policies
both defective and weakening in themselves, and regardless of or alien to
German interests.   The policies were old, but the times had changed.
The wonder is rather that she was able to maintain her hegemony in
Germany so long.

The position and development of the thirty odd lesser states of Germany
in this period of the Restoration, from Bavaria and Hanover, the two
largest, down to the tiny Thuringian states and the six Free Cities, can only
be briefly indicated.   The rulers of these states were primarily concerned to
make good their gains, consolidate their realms, and preserve both their
territorial integrity and their princely powers.   They were the heirs of the
long particularist tradition in Germany which neither they, nor their subjects
for the most part, wished to change.   Some of them indeed were mere
echoes of the princely irresponsibility of an earlier age, as Duke Charles of
Brunswick, the Elector William, and his son Frederick, of Hesse-Cassel.
Others were more enlightened, although as the possessors of power they
were in general conservative, finding support in the revived conservative
doctrines of the day as in the survival of much of the old social order.   For
whilst that order varied a little from state to state, being freest in the
west and stiffest in the east, in general the pattern was similar; the

small class of landed nobility formed the predominant group, with a numerous peasantry still not fully freed from feudal burdens and control. And most of these lesser states, like Germany as a whole, were still largely rural.

Yet all these states had their cities and towns, some of them old Free Cities of the empire, and herein the middle class, trading and professional, was becoming increasingly active and self-conscious, more alive to its own interests, and more stirred by the liberal ideas of the age, without, of course, being universally liberal. But just as the lesser states of Germany suffered in comparison with their two greater partners, in that being so scattered and divided they could not make their weight tell, so the liberal forces in these lesser states were more divided and less effective. Hence in part arose their stronger national feeling. There was hardly a city in these lesser states which had not some champion of freedom of speech and the press, of a representative assembly, or some proponent of greater national unity. There were indeed men who in speech at all events were much more radical, especially after the revolutions of 1830 had encouraged liberal and national hopes.

There was indeed much variety between the different states. We should not expect much evidence of widespread political interest or activity in the rural and socially backward Mecklenburgs of the far north. Saxony also, victim of both the Napoleonic wars and Prussian rapacity, although beginning to be more industrial, was slow to exhibit any liberal stirrings under its strongly conservative rulers. In the welter of Middle German states west-wards from Saxony to the Rhine the prevailing trend was likewise conservative, save for the shining example of Saxe-Weimar, small in size but a light to all Germany, intellectually and also politically, with a constitution dating from before the new era. To the north, Hanover, enlarged in 1815 and elevated to a kingdom, lit no candle of political freedom despite its connection with parliamentary England. In fact it moved away from rather than towards any such constitutional growth. For, from a government in which the Crown and the nobility shared power, it degenerated after 1830 into a system in which the king absorbed almost all authority. This process was carried still further after the separation from England in 1837, and evoked a famous but ineffectual protest then made by the group of seven Göttingen professors. The best known of these, Dahlmann, Gervinus, and the two brothers Grimm, were driven out of the state.

It is to southern and in particular to south-western Germany that we must turn to find the clearest and sturdiest expressions of liberal feeling and example in this period after 1815. It was as if the cultural heart of the old *Reich* now began to beat to a new rhythm, aided as of old by its closer contacts with western Europe, notably France and republican Switzerland. There were periodic suggestions that a 'Third Germany,' purely German, should be organized there to balance the weight of Austria and Prussia with their non-German elements. Meanwhile the states there showed their difference from the two greater states by setting up representative assemblies:

Bavaria in 1817, Baden and Nassau in 1818, Wurtemberg in 1819. All of these constitutions were grants from the princes, like the French charter of 1814 on which they were based. Like their prototype they were extremely moderate, setting up two chambers but reserving most of the power to the prince and the nobility of the upper chamber. The lower chambers were composed of property owners of lesser rank in town and country, officials, and in some cases clergy. Their members were chosen by indirect election and enjoyed a quite limited range of legislative and fiscal authority. There was no suggestion of 'responsible government,' no enunciation of 'fundamental rights' of speech, press, or freedom from arbitrary arrest. Nor should we expect those in what were so patently but beginnings, made in societies still so marked by the class structure of earlier times.

Uhland
by Christiane Duttenhofer

The growth of such infant regimes into anything approaching parliamentary systems would obviously be difficult and slow. Bavarian history in these years was complicated by territorial and border disputes and by religious controversy. The absorption of the Palatinate into the kingdom presented problems, for it was separated from the rest of the kingdom, and being West Rhenish land had a different history and different economic interests. The kings of Bavaria, although liberal according to their lights or in comparison with the rulers of Austria and Prussia, took fright at any sign or breath of radicalism. Thus Maximilian Joseph (d. 1825), despite his distrust of Austria and Prussia, appealed to them for aid against such dangers within a year of granting his constitution. And his successor, Ludwig I, romantic lover of art and beautifier of his capital, became increasingly conservative as first the revolutions of 1830 and then the alarming sentiments expressed at the Hambach Festival of 1832 in his Palatinate, shook and then destroyed his faith in constitutional government. As the champion of particularism he was naturally opposed to nationalist aspirations, and under him Bavaria became and remained until 1848 a centre of reactionary, clerical, and ultramontanist influences.

Nor was the constitutional development of the neighbouring kingdom of Wurtemberg so markedly different. Whilst her rulers were superior to those of Schiller's early days, it cannot be said that much active political life developed there after the grant of a constitution, despite its possession of men such as the poet Uhland, Pfizer, with his call for national unity, and the impetuous and optimistic List. It was in the Rhenish state of Baden that

Krüger

Cornelius   Dieffenbach   Meyerbeer   Schelling   Wilh. Grimm
        Schönlein   A. von Humboldt   Rauch   Jak. Grimm
                     Tieck

TAKING THE OATH OF ALLEGIANCE TO FREDERICK WILLIAM IV

hopes of real liberal growth shone brightest. Even there the grant of a constitution led at first only to a deadlock between prince and parliament over the familiar matter of taxation, and it was not the parliament which won. But after 1830, with a new and more liberal Grand Duke, Baden became the centre of liberal Germany. On its small stage Rotteck and K. T. Welcker, Itzstein, Basserman, and Mathy, strove to set up a real parliamentary system, to establish freedom of the press, to end feudal burdens on the peasantry, to foster closer national unity. Yet it cannot be said that they brought about great changes, and some of them, as Mathy and Welcker, were persecuted for their efforts. In the forties religious issues arose to becloud the political scene, and new and more radical voices were raised to make far more alarming demands as the fateful year of 1848 approached.

III. PRUSSIA

The future destinies of Germany, however, were not to be in the hands of the Federal Diet, or Austria, or the middle and smaller states. That Prussia should unite Germany was by no means a foregone conclusion in the generation after 1815. But undoubtedly the events of 1813–15, and especially the settlement of 1815, witnessed a marked advance in Prussia's position and interest in Germany and German affairs. The new Prussia was no longer a north-eastern German state with a Frederician trend towards further expansion in that direction. She had not even regained all her former Polish lands, and the Russian colossus whom she now faced directly along all her eastern frontier stood in the way of any further expansion there. The compensation for her Polish losses in the shape of two-fifths of Saxony added valuable territory and German subjects to her central massif of Brandenburg. But her most important gains were to the west, and likewise German. There she now stood possessed of a relatively thickly populated block of Rhenish-Westphalian territory, reaching along both banks of the great western waterway, and stretching from the Weser to the borders of the Netherlands, Luxemburg, and France. Thus she now became mainly a German state, her component parts more representative of all Germany. She also became the guardian of German soil to the north-west, as she already was to the north-east. Unfortunately for Prussia this western block of land was cut off from the remainder of her territories, including the seat of government in Berlin, by the states of Hanover, tied to a foreign power, of Brunswick, and Hesse-Cassel. Further, Hanover, Mecklenburg, and Hamburg shut off her direct approach to the North Sea and the mouth of the Elbe, as did Hanover, Bremen, and Oldenburg to that of the Weser, and the Netherlands to the mouth of the Rhine. In the Baltic, however, her coastline now ran uninterruptedly from Memel to the border of Mecklenburg-Schwerin.

Hence, in addition to the problem of recuperation from the wastage and loss of the years of Napoleonic domination and war, Prussia also faced the problem of assimilating to her rule lands and populations which had never

F

been part of Prussia.   Polish Prussia was not a new problem, and the task there was rather one of subjection than of assimilation.   And while the Saxons now forcibly joined to Prussia naturally disliked the enforced change for a time, their land immediately adjoined the main block of Brandenburg-Prussian territory, save for the narrow island of Anhalt.   But the Rhenish-Westphalian area was different.   Parts of it had indeed been under Prussian rule for longer or shorter periods.   But never the Rhine area from Coblenz to Düsseldorf with the great centre of Cologne, never the Mosel valley with its vineyards and the once Roman city of Trier.   For centuries the bulk of this region had been under Church rule, either under the electoral arch-bishops of Cologne and Trier or as part of the vast bishopric of Münster. Then for twenty years much of it had been under the despotic but enlightened rule of France, which had transformed its social system and aroused its political consciousness.   Of Frankish or Lower Saxon stock, its population was more than three-quarters Catholic.   In that, as in much else, it differed from Prussian society east of the Elbe.   Thus its nobility had lost both their privileges and their lands during the French occupation, and the peasantry had gained both freedom and land.   And, whereas Prussia proper was still predominantly rural, in the Rhineland the towns were more numerous and far more wealthy than those in the east, helped by the flow of trade up and down the Rhine.   The easy contacts with Holland, France, and England had enlarged the views of its urban middle class, as Stein found in West-phalia, and they responded both to the national feeling aroused in 1813–14 and also to the liberal currents of the time.   They had in fact more feeling for Austria than for Prussia, disliking the stiffer aristocratic military and bureaucratic quality of the Prussian state and having no special attachment to the Hohenzollern monarchy.   They clung to the Napoleonic code of law and claimed that they were overtaxed in comparison with the rest of Prussia.

Yet the years after 1815 were to show that the Prussian state which now undertook to assimilate these new provinces had not changed in any essential features from its older pattern.   The reforms of Stein and his collaborators had strengthened it, but they had been checked too soon to bring about the fundamental changes he desired; the land reform was incomplete, the institutional changes had hardly begun, and the military reforms in the direction of making a people's army had no attraction for the government now that the war was over.   Frederick William III, forty-five years old in 1815, and to reign until he was seventy, had gained in experience and firmness of character during the years of adversity, his religious feelings and his sense of responsibility for his people had increased, but at bottom he was little changed.   Whilst he was ready to rebuild, he had done with anything which smacked of radical change.   He must have regretted almost as soon as he made it the rash promise of 1815 to create a national representative assembly based on the provincial Estates.   He grew steadily more adverse to fulfilling it and in fact never did so.   In his Political Testament of two years before his death he declared that such a step must have the assent of all the princes of the royal house, a typical old Prussian dynastic pronouncement.

The growing conservatism of the Prussian monarch was likewise reflected in the ministry, the administration, the military men, and the landed aristocracy still dominant in Prussian lands east of the Elbe.   There were individual exceptions, chief of them the chancellor himself, Hardenberg.   But although Hardenberg remained in office until his death in 1822, and even drew up further plans for a constitution, the tide was running against him too strongly for his views to prevail, and his own powers and influence were in fact in steady decline.   Meanwhile the influence of Wittgenstein, the Minister of Internal Affairs, the 'chief agent of reaction' and in the pay of Metternich, of Ancillon, and others, whom Stein contemptuously described as 'insects and pygmies' surrounding the king, steadily increased.   These men, from the king down, thought in terms of Prussian problems; there was little or no concern for Germany as a whole; the *Zollverein*, when it came, was designed in and for Prussia.

Thus it followed that the measures by which the Prussian state was reconstituted on this enlarged territorial basis were aimed at preserving most of the essential elements of the old Prussia, authoritarian, military, and Protestant, and with a due regard for social gradations.   In essentials Prussia succeeded in this rebuilding, thanks to the strength of the old system and the efficiency of the administration.   Thereby she created the Prussia of the nineteenth century.   At the same time the economic resources of the formerly poor Prussian state were growing steadily.   For with the coming of the industrial revolution it appeared that in the Rhineland and Silesia Prussia possessed the two areas which by reason of their wealth in coal and iron were to be the greatest centres of industrial development in all Germany. This was a notable historical accident, something of which even the great Frederick could not have dreamed.   But it meant that to Prussian superiority in military power and efficiency of administration was to be added greater economic strength.   This was to fill out Bismarck's work, so that Prussian hegemony in Germany came to be based upon the tripod of military, political, and economic power.   The process was not to be accomplished without opposition.   And the supremacy was to be an incomplete one.   For these forces could not absorb or dispose of the cultural heritage of Germany, since this embodied an element of freedom alien to the Prussian spirit.   And so the triumph of Prussia was to bring (as Nietzsche pointed out) grave dangers for the cultural life of Germany, and weaken the great heritage of the past.

That is to look far ahead.   Of immediate importance after 1815 were measures dealing with administration, the army, and the peasant lands.   The enlarged Prussia was organized into ten provinces, the number reduced to eight within a few years by the union of the Rhineland provinces and of East with West Prussia.   Each was placed under a Chief President (*Oberpräsident*) and divided into districts (twenty-eight in all), and each province developed special departments for religion, education, indirect taxes, communications, and mines.   At the centre in Berlin arose the earlier planned State Council (*Staatsrat*) composed of ministers and high officials, military and civil, and the princes of the royal house. There were now special ministries for war, police, religion, and education. The recently created office of chancellor was to disappear with Hardenberg's death. The State Council discussed but did not decide upon proposals for laws; there the king had the last word. Thus with regard to the reconstitution of the army for peace time, Frederick William, whilst accepting the continuation of the general pledge to military service, refused to accept the plan of the Minister of War, Boyen, for the preservation of the separate identity of the militia from the regular army. To the king, as to the military chiefs, this seemed a danger both to discipline and to the State, and Boyen resigned (1819). The crisis showed the growing fear of revolution in the royal mind, and also indicated that the Prussian army was to remain unchanged in spirit as in organization.

Similarly the fulfilment of the edict for the emancipation of the peasantry was now to be carried through in the interests of the conservative land-owning class. Only the peasants with larger holdings were by decree of 1816 freed from their services, and that at the expense of one-third to one-half of their holdings given up to their former lords. And the lesser peasants who wished to free themselves of services did so in the next generation (to the number of over 100,000) by the abandonment of all their holdings, to become mere day-labourers bound by long-term contracts. Thereby the landed estates were markedly enlarged, especially in Upper Silesia. The finances of the country were, after much difficulty, set on a sound footing after the expenditures of the war, and the national debt consolidated, with the limiting proviso that no new debt was to be incurred without agreement by the representatives of the Estates. Taxation was increased to balance the increased budget. The 'hunger year' of 1817 after failure of the harvest brought great hardship, but the twenties saw both recuperation and new growth aided by state efforts after the Prussian pattern. New roads were built, steamboats appeared on the Rhine and the Oder, a treaty with Holland (1831) opened the lower Rhine to Prussian trade.

The most important single step for the encouragement of Prussian trade was, however, the measure of 1818 which was to lead in due course to the formation of a tariff union (*Zollverein*) for all Germany. The Federal Act of 1815 had by Article XIX given the Federal Diet the task of regulating trade and navigation between the states. But it had done nothing in the matter, and the Prussian Edict of 1818 was concerned solely with Prussia, and not, as often suggested, with the aim of drawing the rest of Germany into a Prussian net. It was part of the general effort of these years to unite Prussia despite her geographical divisions. For within her own borders Prussia had no less than sixty-seven different tariff areas, and nearly three thousand different classes of trading goods as well as a highly complicated excise system. The enlarged State needed more revenue, the long frontiers encouraged smuggling, a feature increased by the Continental System, and Britain with her cheaper methods of production and her shipping was a strong competitor in the domestic market.

It was to meet all this that the Prussian Director of Taxes, Maassen, a Rhinelander, drew up the plan whereby all internal tariffs were abolished in Prussia and raw materials admitted free.   A low tariff was imposed on foreign manufactures, with a higher one for 'colonial products' such as sugar and coffee, and a fairly stiff tax was imposed upon goods passing through from the enclaves of Thuringia or adjacent states.   In this last matter Prussia acted somewhat after the good old fashion of the Rhenish barons who exacted tolls on goods passing up or down the river.   As she sat across most north and south German trade routes, as well as some east–west routes, she was in a strong position to do this without loss to herself, however unpopular the step might be to her neighbours or enclaved lands.   Doubtless the low tariff favoured the agrarian eastern interests more than the western provinces, though the Rhenish traders, if not the manufacturers, profited.   But the measure was an outstanding part of the policy of drawing together eastern and western Prussia, its success dependent upon the efficiency of the administration.   Yet, whilst it was a measure dictated by Prussian needs and interests, from the start it necessarily affected non-Prussian German lands, some of which were entirely surrounded by Prussia.   One such state, the tiny Thuringian enclave of Schwartzburg-Sonderhausen, surrendered within a year to the new economic weapon now wielded by Prussia and entered the Prussian customs system, receiving a share of the tariff revenue in proportion to its population.   The accession provided a model for later entries.

The extension of the Prussian system of tariffs into a national customs or tariff union (*Zollverein*) took fifteen years (1819–34) and was not accomplished without considerable difficulty.   The states of north central and southern Germany showed no particular desire to link up with Prussia, and Prussia herself was primarily concerned at first in making a success of her own system.   Austria had her own system of high tariffs, entirely separated from those of Germany.   And Metternich was opposed to the formation of the tariff unions on both economic and political grounds, as it hurt Bohemian trade with Germany, and he realized the political possibilities of such a union under Prussia.   Yet he was unable to counter it by any alternative policy.   The southern German states did indeed make efforts to create a customs union of their own to face that of Prussia.   But the divergence of economic interest between the riverine states there (Baden, Hesse-Darmstadt, and Nassau) and Bavaria and Wurtemberg, the first group more dependent upon the Rhine traffic and so more free trading, the latter more concerned to foster their industries, brought to nought three years of negotiations.   In the end Bavaria and Wurtemberg managed to form a union of their own (1828), but it was not very strong and in the same year Hesse-Darmstadt joined the Prussian union.

Similar efforts by the central and northern states to form a commercial union were not much more successful.   A Middle German Commercial Union, made up of Hanover, Saxony, and most of the other smaller central and northern states, came into existence in 1828, but it was hardly a real tariff union and was weak from the start. Within three years the strategically situated state of Hesse-Cassel surrendered to Prussian pressure, and by union with the Prussian system both joined up commercially Prussia's eastern and western provinces and broke the Middle German Union. Then Saxony and the little Thuringian states joined the union in 1833, and in the next year the southern union likewise joined, to be followed shortly by Baden, Nassau, and Frankfurt. Hanover and a few other northern states stayed out, organized in a 'tax union' of their own, which, save for the desertion of Brunswick in 1841, was to last for twenty years. But the *Zollverein* had come into existence, a union of a score of German states and over twenty-five million people, now united with Prussia in a free trade area—a new and significant phenomenon in German history.

The successive adhesions to the Prussian union by which the *Zollverein* was built up had come less from desire than from economic necessity and from the growing pressure exerted by Prussia. And dislike of Prussian power, particularism, and difference of economic interest continued to show themselves within its borders. Yet these did not prevent the union from making a marked progress, its success aided by a variety of factors. The union helped to satisfy and to promote the interests of the rising mercantile and manufacturing class, which found increasingly intolerable the existence of the endless barriers to internal trade. It was helped by the improvements in communication, first the roads which Prussia exerted herself to build, then the railways which in the forties began to be pushed across Germany. The Rhine and other rivers also began to feel the throb of steam-engines. There was the solid fact of material gain which ensued both to governments and to people as trade and manufacturing increased, though agriculture did not profit in like degree.

In Prussia at least economic progress was stimulated by the provision of scientific and technical education, as the English observer John Bowring noted in 1839. Bowring also noted [1] that by that date the *Zollverein* was breaking down the localism so marked in Germany, and encouraging a national feeling not confined to trade. 'The general feeling in Germany towards the *Zollverein* is that it is the first step in what is called the Germanization of the country. . . . By a community of interest in commercial and trading questions it has prepared the way for a political nationality.' Another English visitor to Germany at this very time, Richard Cobden, added a more specific prophecy, remarking that 'the effect of the league must inevitably be to throw the preponderating influence over thirty millions of people into the hands of the cabinet of Berlin.' That was hardly a concern of the Prussian ministers who initiated the original reforms of 1818 in the Prussian tariff, or even in the first extensions of the system. But there is no doubt that in the later stages of the formation of the *Zollverein*, and no less after its completion, such considerations were in the minds of men such as Eichhorn and Rudolf Delbrück, the able administrators of Prussian commercial and fiscal policy. One evidence of this is provided by the efforts

[1] *Report on the Prussian Commercial Union* (addressed to Palmerston), London, 1840.

made by Prussia to prevent Austria from joining the union.   For after 1848 the able and enlightened Austrian Minister of Trade, Bruck, a Rhinelander, made strenuous efforts to unite both Germany and the whole Austrian Empire in one free trade area.   But Prussia defeated his efforts both then and later in the fifties.   She drew Hanover and the tax union into the *Zollverein* (1851) on terms which strengthened the freer trading interests, so making union with Austria more difficult, and although she made a trade treaty with Austria (1853) which envisaged the possibility of a fuller union, and a monetary agreement (1857), her opposition, combined with that of other German states and Austrian internal objections or difficulties, prevented further progress.   A final attempt of Austria to utilize for her own ends the opposition which arose in Germany to the Franco-Prussian trade treaty of 1862 revealed both the strength of the Prussian hold over the *Zollverein* states and the futility of Austrian efforts to break it.

Meanwhile, on the positive side, the 'preponderating influence' of Berlin foreseen by Cobden steadily increased.   Already in 1832 Quinet had remarked on the 'intelligent, challenging, and enterprising' leadership of Prussian despotism.   Not that Prussia had it all her own way.   The organization of the union gave every member a voice, though not an equal voice, in its concerns.   Again and again Prussian proposals for tariff reductions were defeated by the veto of the more protectionist South German states. Yet Prussia was the founder, the head, and far the largest member of the union.   Her officials had most to do with the actual working of the system, including the collection and distribution of customs revenue, and she took the lead in the direction of policy.   Thus she undertook the negotiations for the entry of new German states into the *Zollverein*, and largely determined the conditions, as, for example, in the case of Hanover, where she secretly made and signed a treaty without consulting the union.   Similarly she arranged the entry of Luxemburg (1840) and negotiated commercial treaties with foreign states on behalf not merely of herself but also of the *Zollverein*, whose agreement she then secured.   Thus she made trade treaties with England, Holland, Belgium, the United States, and France.   This last treaty of August 1862 she made in the knowledge of certain opposition from some of the South German states, as well as from Austria.   But she persisted, and after a three years' struggle secured its acceptance by the *Zollverein*.   Her leadership was also shown in the move towards a common coinage for Germany, and in the adoption by the union, after long controversy, of a Code of Commercial Law based upon specifically Prussian legislation and practice.   It has been argued [1] that German particularism could comfort itself with the belief that unity in tariffs, weights and measures, and coinage would satisfy German needs, leaving local political sovereignty intact.   But it seems clearer and more certain that an economic leadership won in an age when Germany was feeling the stimulus of the industrial revolution, and was being drawn together more closely by the new means of communication, would enable Prussia not merely to end the traditional claims of Austria

[1] E. Brandenburg, *Die Reichsgründung*, vol. i, p. 117

to hegemony in Germany, but to establish there an undisputed political supremacy of her own, given the requisite force and leadership.

In the days of the Restoration, however, that lay far in the future. Bismarck was in his cradle in 1815, and Frederick William III in the years immediately following was more interested in the religious than in the economic union of his kingdom. True, he could not hope to convert to Protestantism the four million or so Roman Catholics now included in his realm. But he ardently desired to unite the two Protestant churches therein. The controversies between Lutherans and Calvinists had died down in the more rationalist atmosphere of the eighteenth century. The king himself, although Calvinist by formal profession, was also chief bishop of the Lutheran State Church (*Landeskirche*) in Prussia, and he saw no reason why the two Protestant bodies should not be united and serve as a barrier against revolutionary ideas. The Romantic movement and the events of the revolutionary years had encouraged a revival of religious feeling amongst Protestant as well as Catholic circles. Schleiermacher was its outstanding philosophical and pastoral exponent, Stein a representative in public life, Max von Schenkendorff in poetry, Arndt in fiery appeal to Luther as to patriotism. But this revival had naturally brought with it a new awareness of the differences between Lutheran and Calvinist beliefs and practices, and there were also demands for greater freedom in church affairs, as, for example, by both Stein and Schleiermacher. Frederick William, however, had as little conception of freedom in religion as in politics, and his Minister of Religion and Politics, Altenstein, was a disciple of Hegel, religiously indifferent, regarding church affairs purely in terms of the closer union of the country. State control of the Protestant Church was, in fact, to reach its height in this reign.

Hence it was by royal decree, and not in response to any wide popular demand, that in 1817, three hundred years after Luther had opened the Reformation at Wittenberg, the Lutheran and Calvinist Churches in Prussia were united in a new 'Evangelical' Christian Church. Nor did the king stop there. Keenly interested in religious ritual, and believing that the drabness and lack of colour in German Protestant services had fostered conversions to Roman Catholicism, Frederick William proceeded to elaborate and present to his Protestant subjects for their use a new prayer book, based upon the earliest Lutheran pattern, made before the Reformer had moved very far in ritual from the Roman usage. This liturgy brought back the crucifix and the altar lights, the set prayers and the choir, and reduced the place of the sermon and congregational singing. Here indeed was matter for concern for good Protestants, and the proposed imposition at clerical ordination of a pledge to support 'our wholesome monarchical form of government' caused further concern. The so-called Old Lutherans of Silesia objected to the union as a betrayal of pure doctrine, a product of the Enlightenment, and former controversies between Lutheran and Calvinist as to the manner of celebrating the communion were revived. Schleiermacher approved of union, but disapproved of one imposed from above, as also of the new ritual which most Calvinists similarly disliked.

The organization of the newly united church also aroused discontent. For the king proceeded to create a centralized constitution on an episcopal basis, with a general superintendent appointed by the Crown for each province (sometimes as bishop), functioning as an official of the State. Thereby not merely were hopes of greater freedom destroyed, but also the local self-government of the existing church synods of western Prussia. In the end some concessions were made, both as to the use of the liturgy and the completeness of the union; thus the Old Lutherans were allowed to continue. But state organization and centralized control of the Evangelical Church in Prussia (the word Protestant was distasteful to royal ears) prevailed until the old king's death. The accession of Frederick William IV indeed aroused fresh hopes of greater freedom, for the new king's religion was of a richer and more generous kind, and the freeing of the Protestant Church in Prussia was one of his avowed aims, 'dearer to him than all others' in Treitschke's view.[1] But although local synods were set up, a general synod called to Berlin was dismissed without achieving anything in the way of freedom from state control. For all his generosity of speech the new king's conception of his Divine Right left the Evangelical Church pretty much where his father had left it; it was to be a buttress of the State, like the army and the bureaucracy. The Christian State, as defined by Haller, embraced by Frederick William IV and his circle, and now being expounded in the university of Berlin by Stahl in somewhat different terms, had little more conception of religious than of political freedom.

Meanwhile the Prussian Crown had been engaged in another religious struggle, that with the Roman Catholic Church in the Rhineland, and there the result was to be somewhat different. Catholicism too had revived in the early nineteenth century, and although the secularization of 1803 had destroyed the Church's temporal power in Germany and confiscated its wealth, it was to bring it far more under the control of the Papacy. Centres of revived Catholicism arose in Cologne and Münster, as also in southern Germany. As part of the organization of its enlarged territories Prussia had to create a new ecclesiastical system for its large Catholic population, and to provide for its maintenance. It did not, like Bavaria in 1817, make a concordat with the Papacy, but after much negotiation in Rome an agreement was reached in 1821 whereby five bishoprics were set up in Polish Prussia and four in western Prussia under an archbishop of Cologne. Candidates for these offices were to be approved by the Crown, and the State reserved the right to license monastic orders, censor Catholic publications, and control both education and the relations of the Catholic Church in Prussia with the Roman See.

Thus the Prussian state, at some cost in reparation for the secularization of church property, seemed to have come to satisfactory terms with Rome

---

[1] *History of Germany in the Nineteenth Century* (trans.), vol. vi, p. 304. Treitschke, however, allows himself to say the same thing of the king's desire for the freedom of the press. Ibid., p. 525.

for the reconstituted Church, and for a short time, aided by the liberal policy of Archbishop Spiegel of Cologne, the new regime appeared to work smoothly. But within a few years difficulties appeared. Revived Catholicism looked with some alarm at the examples of state power in the Evangelical Union, and this feeling was strengthened by Rhenish local self-consciousness, as by the increasing papal authority. There was no lack of possible subjects of controversy between the Protestant Prussian State and the Roman Church, and the agreement of 1821 had perhaps wisely not been specific on every point. The actual issue which started what became known as the 'Cologne Troubles' (*Kölner Wirren*) was the question of the religious upbringing of the children of mixed Protestant and Roman Catholic marriages. The problem was not confined to Prussia, and it had not created difficulties in more rationalist days, or in Polish Prussia where the faith of the father prevailed unless otherwise agreed upon. But revived Canon Law would not accept this ruling in the Rhineland, and hence arose a conflict which steadily increased in both breadth and bitterness, despite negotiations in Rome and attempts at compromise. It reached its height in 1837 with the arrest and imprisonment without trial of Archbishop Droste zu Vischering of Cologne, the intransigent successor of the more politic Archbishop Spiegel. This brought protests and disorders in Cologne, echoes in Polish Prussia, and reverberations throughout Catholic Germany with a veritable flood of controversial writing. It was a foretaste of the *Kulturkampf* of Bismarck's day, and modified the former alignment of conservative and radical forces, putting radicals like Arndt and Heine on the side of the Prussian state. Görres, exiled for his earlier liberal opinions and now in Munich a champion of revived Catholicism, in a famous pamphlet (*Athanasius*) demanded for the Catholic Church 'the freedom of 1789,' however that might be defined.

The issue was still unsettled as the old king died. But his more romantic successor Frederick William IV took a different view of what his relations should be to his Catholic subjects, as also to the Pope. Conciliation was now the order of the day, and the excitement gradually died down as the new monarch made marked concessions and restored friendlier relations with Rome. A separate Catholic Section was established in the Ministry of Religion and Education; Catholic bishops were given the right to communicate freely with Rome; the State abandoned its former standpoint in the matter of mixed marriages; difficulties which had arisen over episcopal elections in Trier and the episcopal oath of loyalty were smoothed over; and the king shared in the ceremonial beginnings of the completion of the great unfinished Roman Catholic cathedral at Cologne, making it almost a national enterprise. It was a victory for the Catholic Church in Prussia more striking, if not more important, than that later won over Bismarck. And indeed it helped to foster that ultramontanism against which Bismarck was in due course to launch his thunderbolts.

No less important for Prussia than the religious problem, if less complicated, was the constitutional and political problem. Would the new Prussia, enlarged by its addition of western elements with freer traditions and experiences, modify her former autocratic system and thereby give a lead to liberal and national forces in Germany as a whole? There was no possibility of Austria moving in this direction. But Prussia had had her liberal leaders and impulses. Although Stein was no longer of political importance some of his colleagues and followers were still in office after 1815. The chief minister of Prussia, Chancellor Hardenberg, still believed in the idea of a representative assembly for the country, as did Wilhelm von Humboldt. The Rhineland cities had their liberals, some of them nationalists as well. Görres of Coblenz was at first one of these. And although his newspaper, *Rheinische Merkur,* was suppressed in 1816, he further published both a tractate on a future constitution for Germany and his better known *Germany and the, Revolution,* predicting the overthrow which would follow, as in France and England, unless the various opposing elements of society were drawn together in constitutional form. This last effort indeed led to his exile from Prussia. The King of Prussia himself, after agreeing to the provision in the Federal Act for the setting up of representative assemblies in all the member states, had separately and independently in 1815 given his people a pledge that 'a representation of the people shall be set up,' based on the provincial Estates. True, this was done to arouse popular support for the renewed struggle against France following Napoleon's return from Elba, but it implied that the king was well enough aware of popular feeling in favour of such a change. And the Rhinelanders in 1818 presented an address to the chancellor urging that the royal promise should be fufilled.

Without exaggerating the possibilities of such a fulfilment, it was nevertheless a tragedy for Prussia and Germany that Frederick William did not do so. Instead, with the passing of the peril he repented of his promise, as King Pharaoh of his pledge to let the Israelites depart from Egypt, and never called a national assembly. The nearest he got to it was a decree of 1823 for the organizing of provincial Estates, which in his mind meant an end rather than a beginning. Thus the general character of the Prussian monarchy remained as it had been hammered out in the eighteenth century. In Frederick William's view any change would encourage revolution and bring destruction to both the monarchy and the State. This view was shared by the majority of the ruling class in eastern Prussia, the higher officials, civil and military, and the landowners. So able and moderate a thinker as the historian Ranke could declare a little later that 'the true destiny of Prussia is to be and remain a military state. . . . It is an error of our day to assume that the happiness and welfare of societies lies in the wisdom of deliberative assemblies and written constitutions.' Looking back after 1870, Treitschke believed [1] that Prussia needed a 'monarchical dictatorship' for some years after 1815, before being 'encumbered with parliamentary forms.' But Treitschke was a Bismarckian. The outsider, and with an even longer perspective, may take a different view and see in the failure of

[1] Op. cit., vol. iv, p. 567.

Frederick William III to foster the political education of his people one of the decisive turning points of Prussian and of German history. True, such a development, were it to bear fruit, would have implied fundamental changes in the nature of the Prussian state and the structure of Prussian society. But it was in fact high time that such changes took place, as Stein had seen, and nothing in the later triumphs of Prussia and the Hohenzollerns could make good the misguided and obstinate failure of the monarchy to recognize this fact.

CHAPTER VII

THE REVOLUTION OF 1848–9

Introductory: General Influences — Frederick William IV and the Immediate Background — The Revolution in the Lesser States — Austria and Prussia — The Frankfurt Parliament — Epilogue

I. INTRODUCTORY: GENERAL INFLUENCES

THE YEAR 1840 is a convenient halting place in German history. It allows us to get a fair run up to the revolutionary year of 1848, and not merely meet it as a bolt from the blue. We cannot claim that the year marks a change or changes on all sides of German history—no one year can do that for all phases of history, particularly for cultural and social history. Yet we can seize on particular events of that year, of wide significance in themselves, such as the international crisis of 1840 and the accession of Frederick William IV to the throne of Prussia. We can also mark certain general changes as taking more positive shape about this time. Thus Engels, in his survey of the revolutionary year, written in 1851–2, dates the 'active movement' of the new capitalist class from 1840,[1] and that of the new industrial proletariat from the rising of the Silesian and Bohemian factory workers four years later. This is to be over-precise, but it is true enough that the forties saw the more positive definition of these two new classes in Germany. In a more general way still, we may note a feature of the later thirties and the forties which forms a necessary part of the background of the revolutionary year, namely that there is more evident activity of thought and expression in these years. The still years are over, the repression of the twenties and thirties is weakening, perhaps partly because Metternich and his 'System' are growing older and weaker. There is an increasing sense of movement in the air as Germany stirs with new life. This is indeed not easy to define, but may be illustrated by reference to the poetry of the time. In 1841 a young Swabian of twenty-four, Georg Herwegh, published a volume of verse entitled *Poems of a Live Man*. It was a significant title and a significant volume, for Herwegh, if his poetry was not of the highest quality, represented the spirit of the new decade and of its revolution. And he was but one of many writers, of many kinds, who burst into activity about this time.

This movement in literature and thought was not comparable to the great creative movement of the later eighteenth century. Its poetry in general was decidedly inferior to that of the earlier age. The Italian philosopher

---

[1] The economist Roscher is credited with having introduced the word socialism into Germany in the same year.

Croce has remarked [1] on the decline of intellectual power in Germany after 1830, and its lack of original thinkers, and no doubt he is right as to philosophy. Schopenhauer indeed was still in middle age and had published his chief work, *The World as Will and Idea*, as long ago as 1819. But he was living in retirement in Frankfurt, thinking and walking his poodles, and exercised little influence in these years. If pure philosophy was dormant, however, there was plenty of intellectual activity of a more specialized and limited but more concrete and 'practical' kind, more fitted to an age which saw the introduction of the steam-engine and the sugar-beet into Germany. It is indeed astonishing what a large number of works of significance appeared within a year or two of this date of 1840. Hegel was dead, but the 'Young Hegelians' were active in Berlin, applying the Master's dialectic, but to arrive at conclusions very different from and often far more radical than any he would have sponsored. The young Karl Marx, for example, was in due course to find material therein for his new and revolutionary theory of social evolution. In the realm of religion David Strauss, in his *Life of Jesus* (1835), borrowed from Hegel for his more critical and rationalist interpretations of Christianity.

Their criticism was in part an illustration of the growing turn to the historical approach, best marked by the work of Leopold von Ranke, whose *History of the Popes* and *History of the Reformation in Germany* appeared in these years. H. Leo's *Universal History*, with its strong nationalist views, likewise appeared about this time, as did also Gervinus's *History of German Poetry* as well as Karl Ritter's *Geography*. Dahlmann used the enforced leisure after his expulsion from Göttingen in 1837 to produce his *History of Denmark* (1840-3). Roscher applied the historical approach to the study of political economy in his *Elements of Political Economy* (1843), as did Frederick List in his famous *National System of National Economy* (1841). In this same year appeared another work characteristic of the changing views of the day, Feuerbach's *Nature of Christianity*, which, going further than Strauss and Bauer, found God in man himself, and so not merely reduced theology almost to a branch of anthropology, but (as Ricarda Huch points out),[2] by freeing man from divine authority, weakened the hold of human (i.e. princely) rule. With the materialist Feuerbach we are on the way to the time when natural science, no longer in the hands of gifted amateurs such as Goethe, was to assume a leading place in German intellectual activity. It was in this very year, 1840, that the chemist Liebig produced his *Chemistry Applied to Agriculture* to aid in the development of modern scientific farming in Germany and elsewhere.

We have mentioned Herwegh as exemplifying the more radical spirit of the poets of the forties. But there were radical writers before Herwegh. In the middle thirties the Federal Diet had launched an attack on a group of writers who, under the name of 'Young Germany,' had, it asserted, attacked religion, flouted existing institutions, and endangered both discipline and morality. The first name mentioned was that of Heinrich Heine, but the

[1] *Germany and Europe*, p. 62.   [2] *1848*, p. 192.

name of Ludwig Börne, likewise Jewish and an exile in Paris, might equally
have been mentioned, save perhaps that Börne was older (d. 1837).   Börne
had contributed as much as any one in the way of criticism of the political
and social conditions in Germany, writing ironical and brilliant *Letters from
Paris* which, despite the censorship, provided much of the stimulus to critical

Heine, aged thirty-two

journalism in the Fatherland.   Heine was a more complex character, too
complex for Börne indeed, and the two quarrelled, as Heine did with most
people.   And whilst Heine was unsparing in his scourging and satire of his
country, as in *Germany, a Winter Fairy Tale*, he yet presented his native
country with an incomparable gift, in lyrics second only to those of Goethe,
which only the blindest of German anti-Jewish nationalism, as in the Nazi
regime, could ignore.   It is not possible to measure the influence of Young
Germany.   If its members had followers, they also had critics; and they
hardly touched the mass, or the masses, of the German people.   Nearer to
the temper of the forties with its aspirations for freedom and national unity
were the poems of such men as August Hoffmann (of Fallersleben), the
professor turned wandering singer, dismissed from Breslau for his *Unpolitical
Songs*, the author of *Deutschland über Alles* (Germany First); or Freiligrath,
long an exile in England, both there and in Germany writing lyrics and

political poems of an increasingly radical trend; or Herwegh himself, whose Swabian muse continued to pour out stirring songs for freedom and the Fatherland in a steady stream from his exile (softened by a wealthy Jewish wife) in Zürich.

Some of the growing unrest in these years before 1848 was directly caused

by the economic and social changes which now begin to emerge more plainly. The old social order had consisted of a privileged landed aristocracy, an under-privileged and still in many parts an unprivileged peasantry, and an urban middle class in part professional or official, but mainly concerned with trade and manufacture on a small and local scale, including many craftsmen who were potential rather than actual members of that class, and some lower than that. But with the coming of the industrial revolution with its machines and steam-power, its larger scale of operations in factories, its wider connections by railway and steamboat for raw materials and markets, its greater financial needs and opportunities, two social changes of importance took place. On the one hand there was emerging a class of larger scale manufacturer, trader, and financier, a new upper stratum of the old middle class: on the other, a class of factory workers, an urban proletariat. The change was aided by the increase in the rural population of Germany in the years of peace after 1815, which overflowed into the towns, as well as overseas to America. At the beginning of the century Germany was four-fifths rural and agricultural in population; by 1848 this was slowly changing in favour of the towns.

August Campe, partner in the firm of Hoffmann & Campe, Hamburg. Heine's publisher and a major influence in the literary world of Germany, 1810–35

The new developments first became clearly apparent in the Rhineland-Westphalian area of Prussia and in Saxony. In Rhenish Prussia there was coal and iron ready to be used and a long-established textile industry. The Engels family, for example, were old-established textile manufacturers there. There too was the river highway with its feeding tributaries, the easy access abroad, the contact with foreign countries, the wider political and social experience, the established urban centres. It was natural enough that larger enterprises should arise out of the smallish manufactures there. Thus Frederick Harkort, scion of an old-established iron foundry family, set off immediately the Napoleonic wars were over to bring back skilled mechanics from England, and by their aid built the first steam-engines applied to textiles in Germany. Frederick Krupp began to cast steel in Essen about the same time. Camphausen of Aachen found his opportunity in the old cathedral city of Cologne, combining the leather industry with a growing interest in rail and water transportation from that strategically placed centre, becoming one of the leading citizens there by about 1840, a champion of mercantile and Rhenish interests in Prussia, and by 1848 important enough to be called to head a Prussian ministry.

Two more of these enterprising leaders of the new upper middle class from the Rhineland, Hansemann of Elberfeld and Aachen, and Mevissen of Cologne, also call for mention. The former was perhaps the best representative of the way in which a hard-headed manufacturer could develop into a capitalist with wide-branching trading and financial interests, and champion the interests of his class and its activities against the hindrances and (to him) shortsightedness of the government in Berlin. He too was to reach office in Berlin in 1848, first as Minister of Finance, in which office he set up a Ministry of Trade and Commerce for Prussia, then as successor to Camphausen. Mevissen was no less successful as a business man, but was also a man of unusually wide culture, and appreciated, partly from the reading of Saint-Simon, that the new age could (and did in the middle forties) bring hardship for the worker as well as opportunity and wealth for the capitalist, and that it lay in the interest as well as the duty of the employer to concern himself with the condition of the new working class. In general the business men of the Rhineland were liberal, seeking greater German unity, with political and economic freedom, though varying in their attitude to tariffs. And though they were loyal enough to Prussia, they naturally disliked the predominance of its eastern agrarian interests. The Swabian, Frederick List, while unsuccessful in business affairs, and before his time in his advocacy of protection, nevertheless was a brilliant champion of their views on the need for greater economic unity and the building of railways.

The factory worker was just emerging as a recognizable figure in the Rhineland-Westphalia towns, and also in Berlin, whose population had more than doubled in the generation before 1848 (180,000 to 400,000), and there the workers, such as those from Borsig's steam-engine factory, were to play a notable part in the rising of March 1848. The number of factory or mine workers was still far exceeded by that of the handicrafts or guild workers, whether in small shops or working at home under the putting-out system; and the factories themselves were small, the textile factories the largest. But already there existed the conditions familiar in industrial England, as bad if not worse in Germany: the crowded and bad living quarters, the long hours of work (the twelve-hour day was regarded as unusually short), child labour from the age of four upwards, the truck system of payment, an increase in the drinking of spirits, and crises of unemployment. The middle forties brought the first of such major crises, when work and wages fell rapidly, and there was much misery. The handicraft workers were likewise suffering, for they were less and less able to compete with the factories or with the factory-made goods imported from England. The linen-weavers of Silesia were cruelly hit by these changes,[1] and their efforts at protest in 1844 were harshly repressed by the Prussian authorities.

[1] Hauptmann's play *The Weavers* gives a picture of their hardships, and Legge, in *Rhyme and Revolution in Germany*, 1918, p. 185, a translation of their bitter song *The Bloody Assize*. Their sufferings inspired some of the more striking lithographs of Kaethe Kollwitz.

Yet voices were raised on their behalf and in protest against the whole economic system now taking shape. Heine and others had helped to make French Saint-Simonist socialism known in Germany, and Lorenz Stein enlightened Germans still further with his book on *Socialism and Communism in Present-day France* (1842). German writers took up the discussion, but it was a journeyman tailor from Magdeburg, William Weitling, who first began to preach a revolutionary doctrine of 'Christian Communism' against the ruling classes, protesting against the new machines and calling for a new Messiah to save society. His teachings caused rather alarm than serious disturbance. Weitling was a member of the German exiles' 'League of the Righteous' in Paris, which in these years was a sort of headquarters for radical and revolutionary German thought, though exiles in Zürich and Brussels, London, and even New York, contributed their share.

The Rhineland-Westphalia area, as it supplied the best examples of the new industrial growth, likewise naturally produced radical critics of the system. Karl Grün was one of these, and a trenchant one, but his name was to be obscured by those of two others from the same region, Frederick Engels and Karl Marx. In 1841 young Marx (aged twenty-three) became editor of a Cologne newspaper, the *Rheinische Zeitung*, but he and his paper were too radical for the Prussian government (though Mevissen was a contributor) and the paper died within two years. Marx then went to Paris, to Brussels, to London, and joined forces with Engels, who had already found his feet as a critic of the industrial system in England (by which he nevertheless lived, profited, and was to support Marx). Marx began to work out the theories of social development and class struggle, leading to the ultimate triumph of the proletariat, which were to make him a prophet of future revolution, though not, as he and Engels firmly believed, revolution in the immediate future in Germany, England, and France. For Germany, despite an increasing amount of radical and even revolutionary agitation and writing, was by no means ready for a social revolution. The *Communist Manifesto*, when it came in 1848, played no part in the German revolution of 1848. There were plenty of theoretical republicans about: even a *Junker* such as Bismarck could on occasion call himself a republican. But when the Baden radicals led by Struve and Hecker drew up their programme of reforms at Offenburg in the autumn of 1847, the nearest they got to a programme of social revolution was a demand for the protection of labour and the right to work. The rest was simple democracy, political and social, and did not even include a demand for a German (or Badenese) republic.

II. FREDERICK WILLIAM IV AND THE IMMEDIATE BACKGROUND

Democracy of any kind seemed, and was, a long way off when Frederick William IV at the age of forty-five succeeded his father on the throne of Prussia in 1840. That strong national feeling existed was shown in the international crisis of that same year at the threat that the French, in chagrin at the defeat of their policy of supporting Mehemet Ali against Turkey, might make a thrust towards the Rhine.   The poets went into a fine frenzy over 'the free German Rhine': Germany would keep 'the watch on the Rhine,' and so forth.   The French, wrote Leo, were a race of monkeys and Paris the abode of Satan.   This was what Quinet called 'Teutomania,' and we shall see it again in 1848.   But although the crisis showed how Germany looked to Prussia for protection, it was fortunate that it passed without war, for the new King of Prussia was no warrior, but (as Treitschke remarks in his notable sketch of him) the most peaceful of all the Hohenzollerns, short-sighted, who disliked riding and had no love of military parades.   While his accession aroused hopes comparable to those evoked just a century earlier when the young Frederick II became king, he bore little or no resemblance to his great ancestor.   As a man he had many admirable qualities.   He was warm-hearted and affectionate, deeply religious, cultured, and artistic, a belated Romanticist, gifted with an eloquence which carried him away.[1]   He might have made a fine public orator to a university.   But he was narrow and pedantic, chaotic and contradictory in his thinking, though with a fixed belief in his own Divine Right, weak, but obstinate and conceited, not always honest, lacking in judgment of both men and events.   These qualities gravely marred his capacity as a ruler, particularly in days which though free of foreign war were to be agitated and stormy within Germany.   He survived (if he did not ride) the storms.   But as 'the man of destiny' for Germany and Prussia in these fateful years he was to be singularly weak and ineffective, and from the enthusiasms of his early years was to sink finally into the tragedy of insanity.

That finale lay far in the future when Frederick William ascended the throne in an enthusiasm reflected far beyond the bounds of Prussia.   And for a brief time, as with Pope Pius IX on his accession a few years later, it seemed as though the new king might fulfil at least part of the aspirations of liberals (if not radicals) in the Rhineland, Berlin, and East Prussia, the three centres of such hopes in the kingdom.   He freed or restored to office some of the victims of his father's severity, including such well-known figures as Arndt, Jahn, and the brothers Grimm.   There was some relaxation of the censorship of the press, which gave young Marx his chance to edit his paper in Cologne.   He took pains to conciliate his Roman Catholic subjects, as earlier described.   The provincial Prussian assemblies, which had not met for several years, were now called together again.   And he displayed a warm and seemingly open-hearted sympathy for his people, and indeed for Germany as a whole, as was shown, for example, by his efforts for the completion of the great unfinished cathedral at Cologne, an enterprise which took on a national as well as a religious significance.   But these were rather gestures than acts of clear liberal intent.

In the first months of his reign the Provincial Assembly of East Prussia, which had fought hard for its rights two hundred years earlier, asked for the fulfilment of the pledge of 1815 to set up a national Prussian assembly,

[1] The phrase applied by Disraeli to Gladstone, 'inebriated with the exuberance of his own verbosity,' fits him well.

and the request was reinforced by pamphlets, memoranda, and newspaper articles. The king was not entirely opposed to such a step, but he held firmly to the conviction that any move in this direction must come from himself, as a grace. He took fright at any suggestion of radical change in the Prussian state and society, and proffered only the calling to Berlin of delegates or committees of the provincial assemblies, a poor substitute which achieved nothing and pleased nobody. His circle of royal friends, headed by the brothers Gerlach, combined stout conservatism with the evangelical pietism strong in upper Prussian society, save for the gifted but somewhat impractical Catholic Radowitz and the less influential Bunsen. His chosen Minister of Religion and Education, Eichhorn, was notoriously and actively hostile to freedom of thought or discussion, and the Council of State, headed by that staunch conservative, his brother, Prince William (nicknamed 'the Russ'), was opposed to any constitutional change, largely because it would weaken the army he loved.

The result was that within a short time enthusiasm turned to disillusion- ment and discontent. The criticism which the king disliked so much sharpened, and the brief period of journalistic freedom came to an end. The discontent was much increased by the growing economic crisis of the middle forties. The harvests of 1846 and 1847 failed, bringing hardship to agricultural as well as to industrial workers, and not merely in Prussia. The government did something to help, but with little effect. Of more general significance was the appointment in 1845 (to Metternich's disgust) of a com- mission to consider how a system of national representation based on the Estates could be worked out, a slow and cautious process, but resulting, early in 1847, in a scheme to call all the provincial Diets or *Landtage* together in a United Diet, to be divided, however, into an upper and a lower House. There was a particular occasion for this decision. The old king had pro- mised in 1820 that no further government loan would be raised except by agreement of the Estates of the kingdom. But this was the railway age, and the Crown greatly desired to unite East Prussia with the rest of the kingdom by an Eastern Railway.

It was to approve a loan for this project, and to modify the banking system for the new age, that the United Diet was to be called together. But there was no pledge of any periodical or regular meetings, no grant of legislative rights, or rights over taxation in general. And the creation of a separate House of Lords (*Herrenhaus*), a feature the king had greatly admired in the English Parliament, sharing equal rights with the lower House, although, of course, representing a far smaller class, made it clear that the framework of the old Prussia was to be preserved. Even more plainly was that true of the Crown, which, while claiming to have conceded much, in reality kept power in its own hands. The king made that clearer (if that were needed) in his famous opening speech to the United Diet in April 1847, when with all his wonted warmth—and length—of oratory he proclaimed that whereas other countries might have their 'scraps of paper' constitutions, Prussia, made great by the sword of war and internal discipline, must continue to be ruled by its king.   He was bound to his people by a bond which 'no power on earth will ever persuade me to change into a one defined by a written constitution.'   It was a chilling warmth for liberal hopes.

'Every beginning is difficult,' says the old German proverb, and certainly this attempt to set up a national parliament in Prussia was no exception. In France, sixty years earlier, the calling of a national assembly had precipitated a revolution: in Russia, sixty years later, the attempt was to be followed by convulsions no less tremendous.   Prussia's effort lay half-way between in time, as Prussia herself lay half-way between in space; her western provinces looked more to freer France, her eastern provinces (save for the little group of Koenigsberg liberals) more to autocratic Russia.   Actually the widespread revolutions of 1848 were shortly to alter the whole situation in Prussia and in the end allow but a meagre development of parliamentary life there.   But even without the failure of 1848 it is hard to see how there could have been much hope for growth when the king, the powerful landed aristocracy, the army chiefs, and the bureaucracy were in general so opposed to it.

The three months of life of this first United Diet (*Vereinigter Landtag*) revealed the gap between the royal (and conservative) attitude and that of the liberals, but did nothing to close it, or provide straw for the bricks of a parliamentary edifice.   The king made one notable concession: he promised to recall the United Diet (and not merely the delegates therefrom) within four years.   And the liberal majority in the lower House stood firm in their refusal to approve the desired railway loan, on the grounds that this Diet was not the competent 'Estates of the Realm' as defined in the royal pledge of 1820.   A host of petitions to the Crown was presented in the lower House, dealing with the claims of the Diet in meeting, legislation, and finance; the freedom of the press, or particular grievances such as those of the Poles of Posen and Silesia.   But most of these petitions perished in the upper House, since they required a two-thirds majority in both houses before being sent on to the Crown.   Of laws drafted and sent on for royal approval there were very few, because of the acute differences of opinion: one of these laws ameliorated the position of the Jews in Prussia, and was duly authorized by the king, with but slight alteration.

The real importance of the United Diet lay in the precedent it established, and in the opportunity it presented for free and public discussion by its members of the affairs of the kingdom.   Of this they took full advantage, and the ministers of the Crown, such as Bodelschwingh and Canitz, unused to open discussion of national affairs, were often worsted in debate if not shaken in position.   Inevitably there was much futile wrangling, much wandering from the point at issue, much wordy or windy eloquence.   But there was also strong and clear presentation of the rights claimed by the deputies, warm and even heated debate.   Vincke, a noble from Westphalia but a champion of parliamentary rights, was an outstanding figure.   But some of the leaders of the new upper middle class, Beckerath, Hansemann, Mevissen, and Camphausen, proved able supporters of a system which for the first time gave them a chance to play a part on the national stage, and to express their views on the economic and financial questions which so concerned them. The king's brother, Prince William, left no doubt as to his opposition to any constitutional change, and a thirty-two-year-old squire named Otto von Bismarck made a name for himself by the energy and ready tongue with which he countered the liberal claims. Thus the United Diet, if it did not achieve great things, provided a sounding board for public opinion in Prussia, from Rhine to Vistula, as never before. And all Germany watched and listened, stirred by the unprecedented spectacle, and stirred also by the growing murmur of the even greater events which were shortly to engulf Germany as Europe.

Elsewhere in Germany nothing of such moment as the developments in Prussia occurred in the years immediately preceding 1848. The general influences already mentioned were active there, not least the economic distress in both country and town. There were the rumblings of civil strife in some of the smaller states, e.g. in the two Hesses, and also in Saxony, where the radical bookseller Robert Blum was making a name as a popular orator to be reckoned with. The German Catholic movement, a protest against ultramontanism, was causing a good deal of excitement in Saxony and the Rhineland. And there were a number of serious efforts by members of the ruling class to find remedies for the obvious weakness and generally unsatisfactory character of the existing confederate system. Radowitz, the confidant of Frederick William, drew up a lengthy memorandum on the subject, demanding an enlargement of federal authority, and Prince Karl Leiningen, half-brother to the English queen, proposed to solve the problem by making Prussia supreme over the *Reich*.

There was most movement in Baden and Bavaria. In Baden the liberals were strong and active, with Itzstein as leader, Bassermann, a merchant of Mannheim, Mathy, equally able, and others. But after an election to the local chamber there in 1846-7 a group of more radical men became very vocal in the chamber, led by the impetuous Hecker and the cooler, more doctrinaire Russo-German Struve. These men were scornful of the bourgeois half-way reform, demanding a social revolution, but more radical than socialist in any clearly defined way. Baden, open to both French and Swiss radical propaganda, was obviously the possible home of a movement which might stir all Germany. And it was very properly in Baden that there took place what has been called the first step in the German revolution of 1848, when on 12th February 1848 Bassermann proposed in the Baden chamber that a national German parliament should be called. Bavaria, on the other hand, had long been under the control of the conservative ministry of Abel, backed by the all-powerful and ultramontanist Catholic Church. Early in 1847, however, this came to a sudden end, when the temperamental King Ludwig I threw out the ministry because they refused to grant Bavarian citizenship to the (allegedly) Spanish dancer Lola Montez, whom the impressionable king wished to favour with a title of nobility. But this storm in a beer mug quickly developed into an Alpine tempest, loosing feelings held in check for many years, and strong enough in the general tumult of the spring of 1848 to drive Ludwig off his throne.

The headship of the *Bund* still lay in Vienna, and whether through the Federal Diet slumbering in Frankfurt, or directly through the governments of the various states, Metternich could and did still exercise a considerable influence throughout Germany. Yet in general there was a decline of grip and vital force in the government in Vienna, as Metternich grew older (he was seventy-five by 1848), as the epileptic Emperor Ferdinand I (of Austria) was no more able to rule, and the financial position there worsened. In German Austria there was little overt movement as yet, but growing discontent, most clearly expressed by Austrian exiles living in Germany. Beyond German Austria, however, the Magyars, the various Slav peoples, and the Italians were becoming markedly restless. In Hungary there was a strong revival of national feeling, together with a disturbing liberal movement led by Kossuth and Deák. In Italy the people of Lombardy and Venetia were no longer the docile subjects of a generation ago. And whilst the southern Slav peoples in the empire were not yet a threat, to the north the Czechs were being reawakened to the memory of their earlier freedom, and the Poles of Galicia had a particular grievance against the Austrian occupation in 1835 of the tiny free republic of Cracow. Mieroslawski had indeed planned a general Polish rising, to begin in Galicia and Posen and spread to Russian Poland. But there was no chance of success. In Galicia the peasants were encouraged to rise against their landlords, and the rising merely confirmed the Austrian hold on Cracow, which was now annexed. The rising in Posen failed completely. Yet it added a cause of unrest in Germany, where there was much sympathy for the Poles and Polish exiles on both liberal and national grounds, until it was swamped by the upsurge of German nationalism in 1848.

The Polish question was part German, part foreign, but nevertheless forms part of the background (and on occasion the foreground) of the German revolution of 1848. Similarly some of the developments in the Austrian Empire were more foreign than German, yet influenced events in Germany. The re-emergence of Czech national consciousness touched Germany even more closely, since Bohemia was included within the Confederation, and contained Germans as well as Czechs. The duchies of Schleswig and Holstein presented a parallel problem, which was now coming to a crisis of importance for Germany and demands brief explanation. The Duchy of Holstein, with its German population, was a member of the *Bund*, but was closely joined to Schleswig, which was not, and whose inhabitants were part German, part Danish. Both duchies were under the Danish Crown, but with local rights, and not subject to the Danish law of succession to the throne. As national feeling developed in Denmark, demands arose there for the more complete incorporation of the duchies in that kingdom, arousing strong counter-feeling both in the duchies and in Germany. At the very beginning of 1848 the death of the Danish king brought a crisis in the vexed question, since the new king immediately issued a draft constitution which threatened to merge the duchies in the kingdom, to the loss of their special position and ancient rights.　The issue was to have serious effects on the whole fortunes of the revolution in Germany.

The most immediate and decisive stimulus to revolution in Germany came, however, from foreign lands.　For whilst she had her sum of internal discontents, revolution there was not and could not be the 'spontaneous manifestation' which Engels termed it.　Indeed it is quite doubtful whether there would have been any revolution without that stimulus, so strong were the old forces, so relatively weak the new.　The Swiss influence must not be omitted.　For Switzerland, small as it was, lay immediately adjacent; it was partly German, in speech at any rate; and a portion of it, Neufchâtel, belonged to the Prussian Crown, though that hold was shortly to be broken. Further, republican Switzerland had long served both as an asylum and a stimulus for liberal-radical ideas in Germany, as it did for Piedmont in the case of Cavour.　And in 1847 the tension which had existed for some time in Switzerland between the more democratic elements which sought to enlarge the central federal authority, and the seven Catholic and Jesuit-controlled cantons which had formed a separate league (*Sonderbund*) in opposition, burst into open conflict.　The victory of the liberal and federal forces in the three weeks' war echoed down the Rhine and through the forests of south-west Germany, a seeming augur of a like triumph in the *Reich*. Actually, as has often been remarked, the Swiss revolution was to be the only successful revolution of 1848.　Yet Swiss example was too local and limited to start a revolution in Germany.　An upheaval in France, however, was another matter.　When the mother of continental revolution, the pattern of national unity, the nursemaid of radical and socialist ideas, living since 1830 under a regime which despite its limitations was far more liberal than any obtaining in Germany, was so bold as to overthrow that regime in the last days of February 1848, to proclaim a republic, and engage in radical social experiments, the effects in central Europe were both immediate and overwhelming.　The fall of Louis Philippe at once threatened monarchy and all it stood for from the Rhine to the borders of Russia.

III. THE REVOLUTION IN THE LESSER STATES

The revolution of 1848–9 in Germany presents a picture of extreme complexity and confusion, and cannot be followed through its course here. For there was not one revolution, but as many, or almost as many, as there were states in the *Bund*, nearly two score, with a national effort (at Frankfurt) thrown in.　From Karlsruhe to Koenigsberg, Cologne to Vienna, and beyond far into non-German Austria, the month of March 1848 saw uprisings of greater or lesser intensity, like a series of firework displays set off by the master-display in Paris.　And each one had its own special circumstances and fortunes, although the course of events in Berlin and Vienna was to prove all important and even decisive both for the revolutions in the lesser states and for the attempt made in Frankfurt by the National Parliament to create a

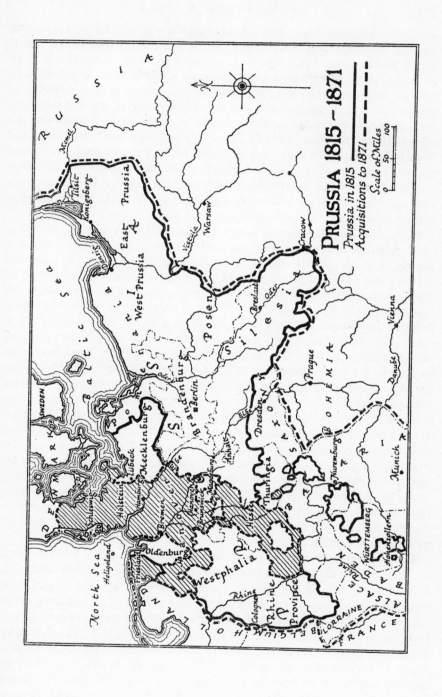

PRUSSIA 1815 ~ 1871

Prussia in 1815
Acquisitions to 1871

Scale of Miles
0   50   100

new union for Germany. This attempt was the product of the main driving force of the revolution in Germany proper, the liberal-national movement of the middle class. In addition there were two other major forces to be reckoned with. There were the conservatives, the princes and their supporters, in power when the revolution opened and in general opposed to political or social change; and the radicals and social revolutionaries of every shade, from the democrat who might or might not be a republican, as Robert Blum, the bookseller of Leipzig, to the doctrinaire 'socialist' of the French Saint-Simonist type such as Struve of Baden, and the newer 'communist' represented by Marx and Engels. The *Junker* Otto von Bismarck and the baptized Jew Karl Marx were to be outstanding examples of the extreme opposing views, both of an age, both active in the revolution, but neither as yet exercising great influence on events.

While it is not possible to follow through the story of the revolution some reference must be made to its development in the various states and centres, first the smaller states, then the two largest ones, Austria and Prussia, and finally some account must be given of the effort and failure of the Frankfurt Parliament. To the major historian of the revolution, the late Professor Veit Valentin, the revolution was 'the great historical turning point of the Germans in the nineteenth century,' dividing their history by a great gulf. So in fact it was, with the reminder that the revolution ended in failure and tragedy, so that, as has been wittily remarked of the revolution in general, it was a revolution in which Germany failed to turn. But whilst the main reason for the failure lay in the strength of the old regime, and its possession and use of armed force, both liberals and radicals must share some of the responsibility for the failure. The radicals and revolutionaries of the Left tried to go too fast and too far, and by their attempts at violent upheaval so frightened the middle-class liberals as to drive them towards the Right, to accept or seek support from the regime they were trying to supersede. And although the liberals were right in believing that Germany was not ready for extreme change, and faced an almost insoluble problem in their effort to unify Germany on a parliamentary basis, under a head responsible thereto, nevertheless they wasted precious time and showed a lack of political sense, which contributed materially to their failure.

These things were hidden when the revolution broke out from one end of Germany to the other, beginning naturally enough in Baden where on 27th February liberals and radicals united in the drawing up of a petition to the local Diet, demanding wide reforms. The prevailing spirit among those who responded to the stimulus from Paris was one of spring-like optimism, and the moderate rather than the extremist took the lead. In the many smaller states the picture naturally is one of considerable local variety. There is an almost comic-opera quality about the March revolution in Munich where the well-meaning and artistic King Ludwig lost his throne in attempting to defend the court favourite, Lola Montez. And Thomas Mann, in his greatest novel, *Buddenbrooks*, has portrayed the bloodless unreality of the revolution in the little city state of Lübeck. In general, however, there is a likeness between the demands put forward in state after state, and these are rather reforming than revolutionary in character. They include freedom of the press, an amnesty for political offenders, more power to local assemblies and a wider franchise, new ministers, to be responsible to the assemblies, the removal of feudal burdens and tithes on the peasantry, the merging of the incomes from princely Estates with the general revenue of the state, trial by jury, in some cases (e.g. Baden) a citizens' army in place of the princely one, and the calling of a national parliament. In Hanover, somewhat surprisingly, there were demands for universal free education, improved working conditions, and guarantees of work for all.

'Freedom' was the general cry, and Schiller's youthful *Song of the Robbers*, with such lines as 'A life of freedom we enjoy,' echoed from one end of Germany to the other. For the moment most of these demands met with remarkably little opposition. Former autocracy was pliant, if not converted, and while these demands clipped the princely powers they left them their thrones, and more. Even that tough old despot, the King of Hanover, bent to the storm, whose force was, however, moderated by the wisdom of Stüve, the new chief minister there. In Saxony some of the force of the movement was deflected by the strong rivalry between courtly Dresden and trading and academic Leipzig, where the more radical Blum was content for the moment to accept the liberal lead.

Thus within a month from the opening of the movement most of the smaller states of Germany had secured the promise and even the partial fulfilment of changes which seemed to put an end to the illiberal regime prevailing through most of the Restoration era. And by mid March Metternich had fallen—it was as if the skies had fallen—and Vienna was plunging into revolution, whilst in Berlin Frederick William IV on 18th March (but too late to stop the rising of that day) issued his patent calling the United Diet to meet again, presumably to draw up a new constitution for Prussia, and emphasizing the need for reorganization and greater union of the *Reich*.

While middle-class liberal hopes thus seemed on the way to speedy fulfilment, other and more truly revolutionary aspirations likewise found voice, helped by the confusion which inevitably set in all over the country. True, there was as yet no clear line of division between liberals and radicals, as events in Berlin and Vienna were to show. But radical divergence from the liberal demands showed itself immediately in south-western Germany and elsewhere. In Baden Hecker and Struve sought to force the pace, threatening the proclamation of a Badenese republic, demanding the separation of Church and State, taxation of the rich, and purging of the Assembly. The peasants in the over-populated Black Forest and the more northerly Odenwald rose in a way reminiscent of the great revolt of 1525, attacking local officials, agents of the large landowners, and money-lenders. The disturbances spread all over south-western Germany, reaching their height in Nassau, where the peasants demanded the end of landlordism and the distribution of the estates among themselves, accompanying the demand with wide destruction of the property they coveted. Whilst these risings of the forgotten class, suffering from the depression of the time, were local and unorganized in any wide sense, they added to the growing unrest, as to the alarm of the landowners and the authorities. And the peasants swarmed into the towns, adding to the excitement and unrest there. The urban workers too were restless and excited, in the south-west as elsewhere. They were beginning to be organized into clubs and associations (which sprang up mushroom-like in these hectic days), but were far from corresponding to the class-conscious proletariat envisaged by Marx and Engels. This was true not merely of the south-west, but also of Rhineland-Westphalian Prussia. Even in Berlin, which presented the greatest single conglomeration of factory workers in one city, and where Marxian agents such as Stephan Born were active, the mobs which fought the soldiers and surged into the palace yard on 18th March were made up not merely of factory hands, artisans, and apprentices, but also of students, shopkeepers, and all sorts of men of the middle class, together, of course, with the combustible elements to be found in all large cities. And the like was true of Vienna.

Agitations and efforts to bring about more rapid and far-reaching political and social changes than the slow-moving whig-liberals would countenance were to continue throughout the whole period of the revolution and may be briefly referred to here. They were encouraged by the new freedom to meet and write, as by the earth-shaking collapse in March of autocracy in Vienna and Berlin. Thus in June 1848 Marx was able to set up his *Neue Rheinische Zeitung* in Cologne, and with Engels direct the work of their new Communist League, recently formed in Paris. The league on 1st April set out a programme for Germany, demanding a united republic with a people's army, the ending of all feudal rights and the nationalization of all large estates, as of banking and transportation, separation of Church and State, the establishment of national workshops, the recognition of the right to work or State support for the worker, universal and compulsory education, and family allowances. In Paris and in Switzerland bands of exiles were formed to assist in the establishment of the German republic. The contingent from Paris was led by the poet Herwegh, whose leadership proved, however, not to extend to military affairs, and the 'invasion' petered out miserably enough. Nor indeed did Hecker in Baden fare better in an attempt to raise the country.

Yet agitation continued, grew indeed during the summer, fed by events in the two chief capitals. In May a clash at Mainz between the newly formed citizens' guard and the Prussian federal garrison there illustrated the civilian dislike of the Prussian military. Meanwhile in Cologne, Berlin, Hamburg, Leipzig, Frankfurt, and elsewhere representatives of diverse radical, socialist, and the newer communist views were active in writing, speech, and organization. Apart from Berlin and Vienna, Frankfurt, where the National Parliament was now sitting, was a natural centre of attraction for such efforts. Workers' congresses of various kinds met there, proving an embarrassment to the labours of the Parliament. Then a fateful day in September saw a mob invade the Assembly in a way reminiscent of Paris in 1792, determined to sweep away what they termed the 'betrayers of the people.' The red flag appeared over the black-red-gold standard of the Parliament, there was much tumult and street fighting, with the murder of two leading members of the Right-Centre party. The Assembly was only saved by Prussian and other troops, an omen of the future. A few days later Struve 'invaded' Baden from Switzerland to set up the red republic (Hecker had emigrated to America) and was ignominiously defeated and captured.

The 'September crisis' of 1848 did not see the end of popular disturbances, republican or socialist efforts, in the many smaller states of Germany. There was rioting in Munich and Weimar in October, an uprising in Saxony in November (after the execution of Blum in Vienna), and a whole crop of outbursts in the spring and early summer of 1849, the most serious of which occurred in Baden where the Grand Duke had to flee and the republic had a momentary existence. But the autumn of 1848 did in fact mark a turn in the fortunes of the revolution which was to be decisive, defining and sharpening the opposition between liberals and radicals, revealing the helplessness of the moderates in the face of force, and their dependence on military support in case of need. Paris had by this time passed through the agony of the 'June Days'; all hope of the red republic and the rule of the people was gone, and a general, Cavaignac, was in control, backed by the bourgeoisie. In Germany the fortunes of the revolution in the smaller states, and indeed in the National Assembly, in the end depended upon the course of events in the two largest states. And there too by this time the tide was turning, and was shortly to run in the opposite direction.

IV. AUSTRIA AND PRUSSIA

The revolution in the Austrian Empire, with its mixture of races and peoples, was an immensely complicated affair, far more complicated than that in Germany proper. Less than half of the Habsburg Empire was included in the German Confederation, but the spirit of revolution recognized no dividing line either at the river Leitha or the Alps, upward on the Danube or downward on the Elbe. The Emperor of Austria was titular head of the *Bund*, and from the Ballhausplatz in Vienna his ageing chancellor exercised his wide influence over Germany. But now the hand of Metternich was to be removed, and the Habsburg realm was to be plunged into the most frightful confusion from end to end, its central authority destroyed, its emperor in flight from his capital, while the many provinces which had been gathered and husbanded over hundreds of years threatened to break away. The once 'fortunate Austria,' *Austria felix*, seemed for a time only to survive, as the poet Grillparzer put it, in the camp of its octogenarian general Radetzky in Italy.

Whilst there were, of course, stirrings in German, Magyar, Slav, and Italian Austria before the revolution in Paris in February 1848, it was the French example which provided the immediate stimulus, above all in Vienna. There the pot boiled over with astonishing suddenness on 13th–14th March. A popular rising caused the downfall and flight of Metternich, an event received with wild jubilation, the old autocratic regime collapsed almost without a blow, and a new regime of moderate liberalism appeared to succeed it.   The State Council disappeared and a new ministry headed by Pillersdorff, an official of known liberal views, was set up.   There was to be a new constitution on the Belgian model, with a two-chamber parliament, there was freedom of the press, a civic guard, the promise of far-reaching reform, and wide concessions to both Magyars and Slavs.   But the jubilation of the Viennese was to be short-lived.   The problems of the Austrian Empire were too complex to be so quickly or so lightly solved: the revolution had in fact hardly begun, and what had been done had raised more problems than it solved.   The economic and financial situation was already bad, and got steadily worse in the general and growing unrest.   Freedom, whether of the press or of assembly, was heady stuff to those so unused to it, and Vienna became increasingly unsettled.   Many of those who had shared in the first stage of the revolution, including many of the students of the university who had played a notable part in it, were dissatisfied with the proposed new constitution as being not sufficiently democratic.   The workers in the industrial suburbs of Vienna began to find voice and present their views and claims.

Meantime, outside the capital, in the Austrian provinces the peasants were demanding the end of serfdom.   And further afield Magyar national feeling was rising against Viennese German domination, while their own nationalist policy was alienating their South Slav subjects.   There the Croats held their own Diet at Zagreb (then Agram) in May, and found a leader in Ban Jellačić. Parts of Galicia were in revolt, and in Bohemia the Czechs, if loyal to Austria, were increasingly hostile to the Germans in their midst.   Their rising Slav consciousness found vent in the calling of a Slav Congress in Prague.   And beyond the Alps in Italy the war went badly, and Venice and Milan were temporarily lost.   The new April constitution might declare that the union of all the Habsburg lands was indivisible, but the facts seemed to challenge the claim.   A rising in Vienna on 15th May destroyed the new-born constitution and affirmed the principle of democratic control.   But the emperor fled, the solid burghers were alarmed by talk of a Viennese republic, the powerful Catholic interests were alienated by a cry of 'Free from Rome,' and the Committee of Security set up was unable to keep order in the capital, much less solve the problems of empire.   The one solid and permanent achievement of these summer months was the passing of a law by which serfdom was ended for the Austrian lands.

While Vienna thus fell into deeper confusion the counter-revolution in Austria was beginning to emerge and to rally its forces.   It was but a legend that Austria had been built by marriage alliances rather than by the sword, and now the army was to save the empire again.   The fortunes of its leaders, the nobility, were bound up with the old regime, and although the Magyars were in revolt and some of the German troops unreliable, the South Slavs under Jellačić could be trusted to oppose the Magyars, and the Czechs and other northern Slavs could be used against revolutionary Vienna.   Divide and rule was no legend, but solid fact in Austrian history.   Stadion had long ago put down the rising in Galicia, Windischgrätz in June put an end to the Slav Congress in Prague and reduced Bohemia to obedience, and Radetzky in the next month redeemed the Austrian name and turned the tide in Italy by the victory at Custozza. In Vienna a final rising on 6th October marked the height of the confusion there, driving away the emperor for a second time, but causing Windischgrätz to decide that the time had come to restore order and authority in the capital. There was bitter fighting as he bombarded his way in, and heavy loss to the revolutionaries, but despite vain attempts by the Hungarians to relieve the city, by the end of October all was over save the hanging. Among those executed was Robert Blum, an emissary from Frankfurt, and the death of this outstanding figure in the German movement was a signal as well as a blow to the German national effort. Meanwhile the almost eliminated Diet or *Reichstag* was called to meet at Kremsier in Moravia to devise a new constitution, and Vienna could once again be her carefree self for those of its citizens who thus preferred her, and they were many.

The reduction of Vienna did not end the revolution in the Austrian Empire, since Hungary and Italy had still to be reduced, the former only after a long struggle and by Russian aid. A new emperor, the youthful Francis Joseph, was to succeed the aged and feeble Ferdinand at the end of 1848, and the following spring was to see at Kremsier the issue from above of a new constitution, which was, however, to be swept away in due course by the hand that gave it. But for Germany events had gone far enough with the fall of Vienna: in fact, too far. For just as the March revolution in Vienna had done much to precipitate the like movement in Berlin, so the success of the counter-revolution in Austria gave a decided encouragement to the same movement in Germany, above all and quickly in Prussia. And since Schwarzenberg, now all powerful in Austria, reiterated the thesis of the indivisibility of the Austrian dominions and the centralization of control over them, a blow was thereby dealt to hopes of the inclusion of German Austria in any new and more effective German federation. Further, the hopes of creating any such new union at all were imperilled, since Schwarzenberg already talked of a restoration of the old *Bund*, which he was later to bring about.

Prussia had indeed gone through deep waters between the first meeting of the United Prussian Diet in 1847 and the victory of the counter-revolution in Vienna in October 1848. The revolution proper there may be said to have lasted about eight months, from early March 1848 to early November, with its height in June, when the royal arsenal in Berlin was stormed by the mob. In some ways it was the most clear cut of all the movements in Germany, far more so than that in Austria, though it had its Polish and Danish as well as its German complications. But it was in the main a struggle between the old Prussia with its absolute king, supported by a landed aristocracy which was tied in with the officer class of the army and the bureaucracy, and the new Prussia represented by the rising middle class, trading, manufacturing, and financial, and the growing urban working class.

The struggle centred largely in Berlin, which was now not merely a court and social capital, the centre of government and administration, with a big garrison of some 15,000 men, but also a growing mercantile and industrial centre. Further, since Berlin 'grew up' so to speak, in the later eighteenth century, it had come to house elements which were very different from the characteristic 'Prussian' features, freer and more cosmopolitan influences, musical and artistic, owing something to Jewish blood, and more open to new ideas. The university combined elements of both the old and the new. And since Berlin was now a large city there was also the drifting mob element, the larger in these days because of the economic crisis, and reinforced by Poles and other aliens, many of them very recent additions to the population, and sharing in (but not causing, as Frederick William insisted) the revolution there. To a considerable extent the king made the revolution himself. Had he been a more determined upholder of his authority he could have prevented its outbreak or crushed it by force at the start. Or had he been a more prescient and liberal-minded statesman (perhaps any kind of statesman), he could have forestalled it by moderate concessions. As it was, he held out until the revolution was upon him, then surrendered too late to stop it, cutting a pathetic and ignominious figure in the apparent plenitude of his surrender, but changing his convictions of his Divine Right not one whit, and profiting in his turn from the errors of the Prussian National Assembly to win back the prerogative he had lost. All in all, the Prussian revolution is a sorry story.

Until the revolution struck in Berlin, and indeed after, Frederick William seemed to be more interested in schemes of federal than of Prussian reform. He was a better German than his forefathers, and responded almost eagerly to the idea of making a more real union of the German states. And he shared a commonly held belief that Prussia was in a position to give a lead in this task. But such a lead was for him conditioned by two things. There was first his belief in the Divine Rights of the German princes: only through them and with their assent could such a closer union be achieved. And second was his belief in the prior and historic right of Austria to the headship of the reconstituted *Reich*, with himself as commander of its armed forces. The Austrians (with memories of Prussian history) never trusted his good faith, and the German reformers who set about reconstituting the *Reich* at Frankfurt inevitably fell foul of his monarchical convictions. So indeed did the would-be reformers in Prussia.

For by early March 1848 there was in Prussia a considerable and widespread demand for reform of a kind going far beyond anything Frederick William envisaged. A petition of 3rd March from Cologne would indeed have destroyed the whole basis of the Prussian monarchy, abolishing the standing army in favour of a citizen force with elected officers. But this was a communist effort, and a more moderate civic address to the king at the same time contented itself with requests for parliamentary rule, freedom of the press and religion, demands echoed all over the Rhineland-Westphalian area, as in Prussian Saxony, Silesia (where in Breslau there was a clash with

SCHILLER AT CARLSBAD

E. T. A. HOFFMANN   *Self-portrait*

E. M. ARNDT

DUKE CHARLES AUGUSTUS OF WEIMAR

the soldiers), at Koenigsberg, and in Berlin. There, in the capital, where the king resided, was the place to apply pressure, and it was sufficiently apparent for all who had eyes to see that Frederick William, with so much in himself and his immediate environment to hold him back, needed pushing if he was to go forward. He had refused to accept even the periodic meeting of the United Diet, but conceded it on 6th March, though with no pledge of when the next meeting would be. Even his ministers, or Bodelschwingh at least, saw the need to go further. Meanwhile, helped by the growing unemployment and distress resulting from the economic crisis, popular gatherings were taking place in the *Tiergarten* (Zoological Gardens) near the centre of the city, with much discussion, and even the drawing up of an address to the king. These gatherings grew in size and momentum, formulating more radical demands, until on 13th–14th March came clashes between people and soldiers, antagonizing both, and foretelling worse to come. The royal promise that the United Diet should meet at the end of April made far less impression than the overwhelming news of the downfall of Metternich and the outbreak of revolution in Vienna. There was a moment of calm, and then on 18th March the full tide of revolution struck the capital.

The 'March Days' (18th–22nd) in Berlin saw events entirely unprecedented in Prussian history. The unarmed crowd which on 18th March surged towards the royal palace and heard (or more likely could not hear) the reading of a new royal decree dealing mainly with proposed federal reform, but promising constitutional changes in Prussia itself, was composed not merely of the lower populace but of citizens of all sorts, including many students. The prevailing cry was for the removal of the hated troops. And when these, obeying but going beyond royal orders, drove back the crowd with horse and foot, sabre and shot, the people responded with the building of barricades and street fighting. But the Berlin populace was less prepared and experienced than the Parisians in such activities, and lost both men and ground in the confused night that followed. The king, however, had no stomach for bloodshed, and spent half the night composing his famous 'address to my dear Berliners,' with its mingling of sentiment and perversion of the truth as to the shooting and the alleged foreign agitators. More important (and risky) he ordered most of the troops to withdraw from the city, and since in error they were all withdrawn, he had to face alone the full sweep of the bitter resentment of his 'dear Berliners,' and had to see and salute their dead as they were borne before him in the palace courtyard. Then, in token of reconciliation, he rode in procession through the streets of his capital, wearing the new national black-red-gold colours, and in speeches and a proclamation expressing his devotion to the national cause. 'Prussia,' ended the proclamation, 'is henceforth merged in Germany,' a vague and misleading phrase.

Thus the 'March Days' had ended in a seemingly complete victory for the people over the army, the king, and the conservative forces in general; the new Prussia (or Berlin) had defeated the old. The motley uniforms of the civic guard superseded the splendour of the royal bodyguard at the palace.

G

There was a febrile excitement in the capital, an excitement reflected in rioting in some of the other larger cities of the kingdom. The king had not merely been defeated, he had been discredited; there was even talk of replacing him on the throne. Yet he had by no means been converted, and when, after a time, he withdrew to Potsdam, the royal circle of the Gerlachs and others helped to confirm him in his opposition to all that was implied in the popular victory. The aristocracy and the army leaders were by no means ready to accept defeat, and they still had their hold in rural Prussia. The situation was further complicated by a national rising in Prussian Poland, which was only repressed with great difficulty, and another in Schleswig-Holstein where Frederick William had committed himself to support the duchies against the King of Denmark. In both cases Prussian policy was to arouse the ire of the all-powerful Tsar Nicholas. But obviously the most important issue was whether the victors of the 'March Days' could translate their triumph into legal form, could create and secure acceptance for a new and liberal parliamentary system of government in Prussia, before the opposition could organize itself sufficiently to prevent them.

It was something to secure a new ministry headed by a middle-class liberal, Camphausen of Cologne, with Hansemann, another liberal and mercantile Rhinelander, as Minister of Finance. Then the United Diet met (2nd April), much earlier than the king had intended, with the specific object of arranging for the calling of a Prussian National Assembly to draw up a new constitution. There was much lively skirmishing in the meeting, with a *Junker*, Otto von Bismarck, acting as cornet of horse for the opposition, but an electoral law with universal suffrage (though with indirect election) was duly passed, and on 22nd May the first really popularly elected body in the history of Prussia met in Berlin to frame a new form of government for the country. It was indeed a remarkable assembly, some four hundred in all, with practically no representatives either of the aristocratic landowning class, or, more surprisingly, of the urban factory worker class. The land was represented by middle-class owners and by peasant farmers, even illiterate labourers. There were nobles, mostly of liberal views, many lawyers and officials of all grades, some professors and more teachers, and many clerics. It was a strange hodge-podge for Prussia, with able men such as Jacoby, Waldeck, Rodbertus the economist, Unruh, and Jung, but rather overweighted on the intellectual side, and on the Left Centre and Left than on the Right Centre; the real Right of Prussia was hardly represented at all. The Assembly was thus more radically minded than the liberal ministry, in part because some of the more moderate Prussian reformers had preferred election to the Frankfurt Parliament. And it was, of course, infinitely more radical in view than the king, though less so than the workers (or more often in these disturbed days the workless) ranging the streets of Berlin.

The Assembly was to sit for nearly six months. It must be admitted that its proceedings were not wisely conducted. Whilst it had reason to reject as too illiberal the draft constitution put before it by the ministry at its opening, it was politically foolish to allow weeks and even months to go by without producing anything in place of that, whilst debating on capital punishment, the behaviour of the army, the abolition of titles of nobility, or whether or not the king reigned 'by the Grace of God.' The Camphausen ministry resigned, and its successor proved little more able to cope with the situation. Berlin became increasingly restless and disorderly, with demands for a democratic republic, and in June the storming by a mob of the royal arsenal. Neither Assembly nor civic guard could control the capital. Meanwhile, as time went on, the conservative forces in the country took heart and began to organize themselves for action. The king, more and more antagonized by the Assembly, was moved at last to appoint a definitely conservative ministry (Brandenburg-Manteuffel), and then (9th November) to prorogue the Assembly, with orders to meet later at Brandenburg. The next day Wrangel entered the capital with troops, and though the Assembly protested, its meeting-place was closed, the radical press was muzzled, and further efforts to meet in Berlin prevented. Berlin was declared to be in a state of siege, the civic guard was dissolved, and by a mixture of firmness and moderation the Berliners were made to understand that the king (or the king's men) once more ruled in the capital; for many of the more solid burghers a matter of profound relief.

The revolution in Prussia was in fact over, and the final dissolution of the Assembly (or that remnant of it which met at Brandenburg) followed within a few days. With that dissolution was joined the issue by the Crown of a new constitution. There were some attempts at protest against the forcible closing of the Assembly—in Saxony, Silesia, and Westphalia—but these were easily put down. Since Berlin, which had asserted its leadership so clearly in March, was now reduced by the army to the impotence of Vienna (with far less effort and bloodshed), it was hardly to be expected that the provinces would make any serious stand. The swift collapse of Berlin and the National Assembly is at first sight surprising. It was in large part due to the divisions between the parties, above all that between the more moderate and more radical wings of the liberals themselves, and the failure to get on with the job of constitution making whilst the times were favourable. But it was more than that. The 'March Days' had too much of the fortuitous and accidental in them to form a solid basis for a national revolution. Berlin was not Paris. The new Prussia had not defeated the old, still less absorbed or destroyed it. It had merely, thanks to Frederick William's weakness, driven it out of the capital to the rural Prussia where it belonged, and where it recruited its forces. The Assembly had not secured control of the Crown, the ministry, the army, the administration. The majority there continued to accept a king who, for all his fine words, held and continued to hold views diametrically opposed to theirs. 'The Assembly wished to take from me my Divine Right,' Frederick William angrily replied to a deputation therefrom bearing good wishes on his birthday. 'Tell them that no power on earth is strong enough to do that. I shall hold it as I have inherited it from my ancestors.' For by this time (15th October) he felt safe at Potsdam, the reaction was well under way, and he could say what he thought.   The Left in the Assembly might rage, but only a small minority there and in the capital wanted a real revolution, and they had no force to carry it out.

The constitution granted (*octroyé*) on 5th December 1848 was surprisingly liberal, too liberal indeed for the king and the reactionaries.   It did not really emanate from the king but from the Brandenburg-Manteuffel ministry, using both the earlier draft placed before the National Assembly and the work of that body's constitutional committee.   By it civil rights were assured to all, with freedom of religion and the press.   A parliamentary system was instituted, with an upper House composed of elected and nominated members and a lower chamber elected by universal suffrage, though indirectly.   There was no precise mention of ministerial responsibility to parliament, but this body could originate legislation and must agree on taxation.   The constitution was, however, to be subject to revision at the first meeting of the new Assembly (February 1849), and when agreement on this failed the Assembly was dissolved and the electoral system for the lower House radically altered from universal suffrage to a three-class system favouring the upper and wealthier class.   Aided by this change the constitution was further amended in a later Assembly (August 1849) in accord with royal and conservative views, to reach its final form early in the fifties.   In this form the king once more ruled as well as reigned, with a ministry unmistakably responsible to him.   There was a House of Lords made up of hereditary members (nobles and princes), officials of Church and State, and life members nominated by the Crown; and a lower House or House of Deputies (*Abgeordnetenhaus*) elected on the three-class system, and with limited control over either legislation or finance.   Thus did the old Prussia defeat the dragon of revolution, and although liberalism was not dead, it was seriously weakened.   Hence Bismarck could ride roughshod over it to the accomplishment of his ends, and the constitution was to remain unchanged as long as the Hohenzollern monarchy survived.   Yet in the longer view, by repudiating the idea of a liberal Prussia Frederick William had prepared the way for the ultimate downfall of the Divine Right monarchy to which he was so devoted.

V. THE FRANKFURT PARLIAMENT

The fortunes of the Prussian revolution were intimately connected with those of the attempt made at Frankfurt to create a real union of Germany with a national parliament.   In fact, looking back, it is clear that the national effort could not succeed unless a liberalized Prussia supported it.   With such support it might have faced the inevitable Austrian opposition, to say nothing of that of the lesser princes.   For a time there seemed some hope of this, since Frederick William appeared so full of zeal for the national cause. But as his fundamental conservatism and attachment to Austria emerged more plainly the chances of a successful issue to the deliberations in Frankfurt steadily declined, and with the collapse of the revolution in Berlin the fate of the Frankfurt Parliament was in effect decided.   But that does not deny the importance of the Frankfurt effort.   While the men who met there were not to succeed in their aims, they nevertheless wrote a chapter of considerable historical significance, the effects of which were to survive in Germany despite their failure.

In the spring of 1848, however, the predominant feeling among the men who were to meet at Frankfurt was one of hope, even of confidence, that with the ice of the old regime cracking so plainly through all the lands of the *Bund*, the time had come for the realization of the aims voiced a generation ago for unity and political liberty.   These were to be represented at Frankfurt by the octogenarian Arndt, and Jahn.   But by 1848 new aspirations and new interests had appeared, the fruit of the economic and social changes already referred to.   In addition to the middle-class liberal-national movement which was to take the lead at Frankfurt there was also the more popular movement, more democratic and even in part republican and 'socialist.'   Two meetings held late in 1847 in south-west Germany had gone some way to define the respective programmes of these two groups. At a popular meeting held at Offenburg in Baden in September a programme inspired by Hecker and Struve demanded a citizens' army with elected officers, a popularly elected German parliament, freedom of press, speech, and religion, taxation proportionate to income, trial by jury, the abolition of all privileges, education for all, and 'the protection of labour against capital, and the right to work.'   In October liberals from Baden, Wurtemberg, and Hesse, including Gagern, Hansemann, Itzstein, Bassermann, and Mathy, at Heppenheim made similar demands for the freedom of the press, trial by jury, the removal of feudal burdens, the revision of taxation, and better educational facilities, but said nothing about labour.   And whilst they too wanted a national parliament, some preferred to see the *Zollverein* extend its functions to serve that purpose, a proposal which would have excluded Austria.   Bassermann, among the first of the mercantile class to play a part in political life, proposed early in February 1848 that representatives of the local parliaments should meet alongside the *Bundestag*, and Gagern a little later demanded a national parliament, and a new (provisional) head of the State, with responsible ministers.

With the revolution in France and the growing excitement in Germany, such demands acquired both reality and momentum.   The *Bundestag* was rudely awakened from its long slumbers and began hurriedly to evince a zeal for reform, lest a worse befall.   Thus it now recognized the red-black-gold national flag, the use of which it had prosecuted for years.   But neither such belated concessions, nor Austro-Prussian proposals for a conference of princes, could keep up with the pace of events.   Liberal and radical members of South German parliaments gathered at Heidelberg (5th March) took a decisive step when they agreed upon the calling together of a national assembly.   Their committee in due course invited all 'former or present members of German legislative assemblies' to meet at Frankfurt to arrange this, and hence there met at the end of March in the ancient capital of the *Reich* a body of some five hundred men, which was to go down in history

as the Pre-parliament (*Vorparlament*).   This body had, of course, no lega[l]
status whatever, was in fact revolutionary, though in that law-abiding Germa[n]
way which Heine so derided.   But it was emboldened by the stupendou[s]
events of March in Vienna and Berlin, as by the enthusiastic welcom[e]
received in Frankfurt, to set itself down cheek by jowl with the exalte[d]
Bundestag and to take immediate steps for the calling of a national parliament
Therein this *Vorparlament* exhibited one great virtue: it struck whilst the iro[n]
was hot, completing its sessions within a week from 30th March to 5th April, i[n]
marked contrast to its successor and the Berlin Assembly.   It was not tha[t]
its voice was unanimous: the radical minority led by Struve put forwar[d]
most sweeping proposals for the reorganization of Germany into district[s]
(*Reichskreise*) under a president, proposals which were naturally rejecte[d]
by the monarchist majority.   Yet there was agreement that the nationa[l]
parliament should be elected on the widest suffrage, and that it alon[e]
should decide upon the future constitution.   A committee of fifty was lef[t]
to arrange this, but allowed itself to be distracted by various issues so tha[t]
it was not until 18th May that the Frankfurt Parliament met.   There wa[s]
some excuse for delay in the confusion of the times, and more particularl[y]
in the Prussian pressure to postpone the elections to suit themselves.   An[d]
these elections were more confused and less universally democratic than wa[s]
intended.

   The Frankfurt Parliament, whose members marched four abreast throug[h]
the streets to fill the pews of the circular St. Paul's Church, its big gallerie[s]
crowded with spectators, was a fairly representative gathering of those wh[o]
wished to build a new roof for their country and had faith that they coul[d]
accomplish the task.   Yet the nearly six hundred members who ultimatel[y]
appeared there revealed not merely the desire for unity but also the wid[e]
and deeply rooted diversity, if not divergence, of the German people thu[s]
for the first time gathered together in this way.   And the Parliament wa[s]
not a complete representation of the population, since there were no lan[d]
or factory workers.   Three-quarters or more of the members were product[s]
of the German universities, lawyers and officials of many grades, professor[s]
and teachers, some doctors, parsons of both faiths, a number of writers
The remainder was made up of nobles, property owners large and small[,]
business men of various kinds and degree, and a few army officers.   It coul[d]
claim to include many of the ablest men Germany could produce, men o[f]
the highest ideals, many gifted speakers.   But it lacked, inevitably, men o[f]
much political experience, and whilst it was not, as sometimes asserted, [a]
'gathering of professors,' it tended to be too doctrinaire, and displayed to[o]
little appreciation of politics as the art of the possible in a given time.   Th[e]
omens were not unfavourable when they began.   The general situation wa[s]
fluid as never before, the *Bundestag* gave its blessing, the states, even th[e]
two greatest of them, had allowed the elections and were too absorbed i[n]
their local problems to hinder proceedings.   Of foreign countries, Britai[n]
and France were not unfriendly, and although Nicholas of Russia termed th[e]
effort 'madness' and looked on with a baleful eye, he could not interfere.

But the Parliament was late in starting, and its slowness in getting on with its task of constitution making contributed to its ultimate failure.

The members of the Frankfurt Parliament were divided by their political views into three main groups, a Right, a Centre, and a Left. But these groups took time to form and were never rigid; men moved from one to the other on particular issues, even major ones. Thus a religious question saw Catholics of varying political opinions standing together, anticipating the later Catholic Centre Party of the Bismarckian Empire. And both the central and left groups or parties were themselves divided into right and left wings, or rather shaded off from right to left, so that the whole picture was decidedly confusing. A foreigner, coming to Frankfurt, would have found the members meeting for private discussion as 'clubs' in no less than a dozen different hotels or inns. Even the Right was not wholly united, for while its general attitude favoured a minimum of change, and that by agreement with the princes, it also was in part an Austrian party, led by the able Schmerling, out to defend the rights of the Habsburgs and Greater Germany. Radowitz and Vincke were outstanding men on this side of the chamber. On the other side were the democrats, a minority like the Right, but divided into moderates, such as Blum and Vogt, who favoured a republic but were ready to compromise if need be, and the extremists, who were more rigidly republican and more concerned for social change, with A. Ruge, Brentano, L. Simon, and others as outstanding exponents. As in the *Vorparlament*, the middle-class liberals of the Centre were most numerous, but they too varied in opinion. They were monarchist and parliamentary, but differed in their interpretation of the role of a national parliament and of the executive, as of the degree of centralization desirable. The older whig-liberals fought shy of 'the sovereignty of the people,' preferring Gagern's 'sovereignty of the nation,' and wished to compromise with the old regime even to the acceptance of an hereditary emperor. The newer representatives of the rising bourgeoisie thought more in terms of the need for greater unity for economic progress, and trusted the princes less and the promise of parliamentary control more. Yet it was the Right Centre which provided the outstanding leaders and helped to give the Assembly its over-academic flavour; men such as Dahlmann, Bassermann, Mathy, Beckerath, Welcker, Simson, and Heckscher.

The man who was elected to preside over the Assembly, Heinrich Gagern, although belonging to the Right Centre, was, however, no professor, but one of the many sons of a Hessian squire who had been a friend of Stein. Gagern was not a great or original thinker, but had made a name for himself in Hesse and outside as a liberal and as an impressive, statesmanlike leader, and he was to give dignity and worth to his office as to the Parliament over which he presided. He believed with Dahlmann[1] that, although unlimited monarchy was out of date, the world was still 'permeated with the monarchical order,' and that the Frankfurt Parliament could establish a new constitution and select a head for it. His difficulty, as that of the party to which he

[1] Dahlmann, *Two Revolutions*, published shortly before the revolution.

belonged, was that he sought the unattainable: a liberal prince of Prussia to head a united and parliamentary Germany. But Frederick William, as time showed, would have none of it. 'Remember,' he was to tell members of the Parliament at a festival at Cologne, 'that there are princes in Germany and that I am one of them.' And again, later: 'What right have these men of Frankfurt to justify their setting up a king or an emperor over the legal authority to which they have sworn obedience?' The dilemma was to prove insoluble in Gagern's terms.

No such shadow of failure, or insoluble dilemma, darkened the opening of the Parliament, though there was inevitably some delay and confusion before it settled down to its work. Gagern was elected president, various other officials elected, and a number of committees (later increased) were set up to prepare material for discussion. Chief of these was, of course, the constitutional committee, presided over by Bassermann, but there were others for dealing with the flood of petitions which poured in upon the Assembly, for economic matters, for international affairs, defence, legal questions, and so forth, as well as special committees. Such a committee was appointed to deal with one of the earliest major problems which presented itself, that of providing this legislative body with a provisional executive head. Here the Right wanted a prince (of whom indeed there was no lack), the Left a directory of three, elected by and perhaps drawn from the Assembly. Gagern settled the matter in late June by a 'bold stroke,' getting the Parliament to elect the elderly Archduke John of Austria as administrator (*Reichsverweser*), a high prince indeed, but one who had married a humble commoner, and was credited with both ability and goodwill to the national and popular cause. Actually he was rather a schemer, with an eye on the Habsburg throne. He was to be irresponsible, but with a ministry responsible to the Parliament. His appointment made it easier for the old Federal Parliament (*Bundestag*) to hand over its powers and withdraw from the scene (though the *Bund* itself survived).

Thus strengthened, and with a first ministry under the mediatized Prince Karl Leiningen, the Parliament proceeded during the summer to build up its authority as the now supreme legislature for Germany, somewhat to the neglect of its prime function, the making of a constitution. Its members were, of course, encouraged in this course by the 'vacancy of power' (to borrow Thier's phrase about France after 1870) in Vienna and Berlin, as by the surrender of authority from the old Federal Diet. So they began to take over some of the functions of this latter body in relation to the states of the *Bund*; they asserted their right to legislate on national affairs, they sought to secure authority over the military forces of the *Reich*, naturally with limited success in the case of Prussia and none in that of Austria, they sought to exchange ambassadors with foreign countries, they adopted a flag (the black-red-gold with the double eagle of the old *Reich*) for trade and war, and discussed at length the issue of national defence and the merits of 'standing' as against citizens' armies.

In all this the members of the Frankfurt Parliament manifested the strong national feeling which had created that body. And they manifested it more plainly in two particular matters which came before them for discussion, the matter of Prussian Poland and that of Schleswig-Holstein. The Prussian-Polish question was also related to the general question of German-Slav relations, notably in Bohemia, where the Czechs had not merely refused the invitation to send representatives to Frankfurt, but in their Pan-Slav Congress had raised a rival of sorts to the Frankfurt Parliament, in what one speaker in the Parliament called 'this original German land.' Behind the Prussian-Polish trouble lay a long record of liberal German sympathy for the Poles, which had found expression in the vote of the *Vorparlament* that the German people should restore Polish independence, even at the cost of war with Russia. Meanwhile Poles and Germans in Prussian Poland were in conflict, and in Frankfurt the Polish representatives were urging the Assembly to declare for the revival of Polish freedom.

Out of this arose a great debate (24th to 27th July) in which a newer German nationalism, more exclusive, more racial, and more aggressive, triumphed over the earlier more tolerant and more liberal nationality. The East Prussian Jordan, of the Left, split with his party on the issue, championing the Prussian right of conquest and the expansion of German culture in Prussian Poland, and found wide support for his views. Yet a hundred members of the Left (against well over three times that number of the Right and Centre) voted that 'the partition of Poland was a shameful wrong' and that the Assembly should support the re-establishment of a free Polish state. The division was significant of the changing relationship between liberalism and nationalism as they grew up together, a change not confined to Germany. It did not destroy German liberalism, but it weakened it at a time when the crystallization of German political thought was taking place, and when the enemies of liberalism were beginning to gather together their forces.

The affairs of Schleswig-Holstein, where there was a rising against the effort to incorporate Schleswig more completely into Denmark, had more immediate repercussions on the fortunes of the Frankfurt Parliament. From its opening voices had been raised there, notably that of Dahlmann, on behalf of the Germans in the duchies. Hence arose in part the demand for a German navy, and the Assembly followed with the greatest interest the complicated diplomatic moves involving Russia, Sweden, Britain, and France, as also the fortunes and misfortunes of the Prussian troops now engaged there on behalf of the *Bund*. But Prussia, despite a partial recognition of the authority of the new national provisional government, proceeded to come to terms with Denmark (Truce of Malmo, 26th August 1848) without any reference to the Frankfurt Parliament. This was a bad blow for the repute of Prussia but an even more serious one for the Frankfurt Parliament, which had made the issue its own. There were stormy and prolonged debates on the subject, bringing the fall of the ministry, and threats from the Left of a 'second revolution,' before by a small majority the Parliament agreed to accept the armistice. The day of this acceptance (16th September) has been called 'the black day of the Frankfurt Parliament,' and there is some truth in the appellation. For there followed immediately the popular rising in Frankfurt which threatened the very existence of the Assembly, forcing it to call for protection on the Prussian and Austrian troops from the adjacent federal fortress of Mainz. A few days later came Struve's futile 'invasion' from Switzerland and the proclamation of a German republic. A clear breach appeared between the majority in the Parliament and radical opinion in the country, and the fear of social revolution now pushed the moderates in the Parliament more plainly to the Right. No less significant was the revelation that the Parliament could neither defend itself, nor engage in the defence of what it regarded as German interests abroad, without the military aid which one or both of the two great German powers might (or might not) provide.

The Frankfurt Parliament had not entirely neglected its task of constitution making during these summer months. Its constitutional committee had decided, however, that it must first of all lay firm foundations, and so produced at the beginning of July a draft of Fundamental Rights (*Grundrechte*) on which the new constitution was to be erected. This modern Magna Charta for the German people overrode all local boundaries and assured to all equality of civil rights and the abolition of privilege, freedom of speech, the press, and religion, the ending of all surviving feudal rights, and trial by jury. There was to be local self-government, democratic and responsible government in all the states, and cultural freedom for non-German citizens. This was all very fine, excellent in fact. But Jacob Grimm had remarked: 'We Germans, it must be admitted, have a great tendency to learned discussion,' and the *Grundrechte* afforded such admirable material for the exercise of this quality that six months elapsed before the Parliament completed its discussion thereupon and the Fundamental Rights were published as a law of the *Reich*. The discussion on religious freedom and the relations of Church and State had naturally evoked ardent debate.

Meanwhile, although not until its hundredth sitting, on 19th October, the Parliament had opened its discussion of the draft constitution itself. Here it ran immediately into the two related questions of whether Austria was to be included, and how the headship of the State was to be organized. The constitutional committee indeed proposed that Austria should be included, but on condition that she separated the rule of her German and non-German lands. For a time these questions were left unsettled, and the Parliament proceeded to define the powers which the new central authority was to possess. The states of the *Bund* of 1815 were to survive, but were to lose the sovereign right of diplomatic representation abroad (won in 1648), and much of their legislative, fiscal, economic, and military authority. It was agreed that there was to be a national Parliament of two houses, the upper or State House being half nominated by the State governments, half elected by the State legislatures. The lower or People's House was (by later decision) to be elected by universal suffrage, with secret voting; it was to have prior rights in finance. The head of the *Reich* (when constituted) was to have a suspensive veto, but his ministers were to be responsible to the Parliament.

By Prussian instance this scheme was submitted to the individual states for consideration, and a large number of the smaller states voiced their objections to the proposed clipping of their powers, and demanded an absolute veto for the head of the new State, in their fear of what a national popular Assembly might do. The Parliament, however, refused to compromise.

The all-important attitude and response would be, however, those of Austria and Prussia. Austria had now not merely a new emperor, but a strong man as chief minister. Prince Schwarzenberg for a time seemed ready to accept exclusion from a new German union headed by Prussia. But as the new regime in Austria came to sit more firmly in the saddle, while Frederick William still oscillated uncertainly in his German policy, he took a firmer stand. The Kremsier constitution of March 1849 proclaimed the indivisibility of the Austrian state, and Schwarzenberg announced that only on these terms, and with no menace to internal peace in the shape of a national German parliament, would Austria unite with Germany. The Frankfurt Parliament met the challenge by trying to create the new *Reich* without Austria, and on 28th March offered the hereditary headship (*Reichsoberhaupt*) to the King of Prussia. But Frederick William, thus forced at length to declare himself openly, refused the proffered crown, despite much persuasion to the contrary. 'It would be,' he declared to Bunsen, 'a dog-collar fastened round my neck by the sovereign German people.' He could not have done otherwise and remained himself.

The refusal, however inevitable, was fatal both to the Frankfurt Parliament and to the revolution. The Parliament strove to secure the acceptance of its headless constitution, and even arranged for elections to the new *Reichstag* in the coming summer. But whilst some of the smaller states accepted the constitution, Austria withdrew her representatives from Frankfurt, and Prussia followed suit, refusing acceptance, as did Bavaria, Saxony, and Hanover. The great Assembly began to break up. Gagern resigned office, and he and many other men of moderate views withdrew, leaving a Rump of mainly South German radicals which strove to carry on first in Frankfurt, then in Stuttgart, only to be dispersed and the Parliament thus brought to an end in the most ignominious fashion. Meanwhile, as might be expected, popular discontent at the threatened end of so many hopes led to ferment in many parts of Germany, and in May there were uprisings in Saxony, the Bavarian Palatinate, and Baden. The King of Saxony was temporarily driven from his throne, and such oddly assorted partners as Richard Wagner and Michael Bakunin fought together against the Prussian troops who had resumed their role as protectors of princely authority. The Prussians likewise assisted in the putting down of the revolt in the Bavarian Palatinate, and rounded out their task by sharing in the suppression of the most serious of these risings, that in Baden. There the army mutinied and Brentano led in the attempt to set up a republic, aided by the irrepressible and able Polish general, Mieroslawski. But although the Grand Duke had to flee, the insurrection could not hope to withstand the military power raised against it from all sides, and with its collapse the revolution may be said to have ended in the same south-western corner of Germany where it began.   There was still much to clear up, much to repair or rebuild.   But power was back in the hands of the princes, above all Prussia and Austria.   It remained to see what use they made of it.

The failure of the Frankfurt Parliament and the revolution of 1848–9 in Germany has been attributed to a variety of related causes, and much contumely has been heaped upon the heads of the men of Frankfurt.   To Engels they were an 'assembly of old women,' though he is just as severe upon the democrats as upon the men of the middle class for their lack of vigour.   But Engels wanted a real social revolution which would arm and enthrone the urban proletariat of Germany, cost what it might.   The majority in the Assembly, however, desired no such revolution, but rather an evolution towards greater national unity and a parliamentary monarchy.   It was a misfortune for them that by the time they were ready to make their effort, views and aims far more radical than theirs had begun to permeate parts of German society.   Yet it would be absurd to claim that the mass of the German people in 1848 wished for a social revolution of the kind envisaged by either the communists or the less extreme social and republican revolutionaries of the day.   True, revolutions are made by minorities, but there must be a sufficiently strong and united nucleus, with a gospel and leaders capable of attracting sufficient support; the Marxian gospel had only just taken shape, and there were no real leaders for it available.   The majority of the German people were not even republican, hardly democratic in any real sense.   They had grievances, such as the remnants of the feudal burdens and the hardships of the economic crisis, but they were still largely enmeshed in the bonds of the old local societies, political and social.   A Bavarian peasant told his king that he wanted a republic.   'And me?' queried the king.   'Oh, we will have you too,' was the reply.   True, the Bavarian peasant, like the peasant of eastern Prussia, was more backward than his fellow of the west and north.   But Germany was still more than two-thirds agrarian, and some of the old rural distrust of the towns (and even more of the bigger cities) still survived.   Even the middle class was by no means united in either its nationalism or its liberalism, for there were still many local attachments and interests, many contented holders of local office under the princes.   Both dynasticism and particularism were still strong, and were long to survive.   The love of titles and social precedence was still strong in the German heart.   Börne had suggested that to cure it every German child should be given a title at birth, but Börne was a Jewish scoffer writing from that sink of iniquity, Paris, and little regarded by respectable folk in Germany.   Further, there was no foreign threat or great pressure to drive home any urgent need for closer national unity.

The Frankfurt Parliament (or its majority) was certainly too theoretically minded, and treated political problems too much as problems of philosophy and ethics, in the tradition established from Kant to Hegel.   Thereby they lost precious time, failing to seize the moment when conditions in Germany made political change more possible.   The choice of the Archduke John as provisional head was a mistake, though not a decisive one. They allowed themselves to be drawn by the aroused perfervid national feeling into areas and problems (Schleswig-Holstein and Poland) where they had no solid bottom to stand upon. They had an active economic committee, which strove to go faster and further in the direction of the economic unity of the country than the Parliament would go, but was less constructive in dealing with the flood of petitions sent in demanding the reform of social grievances or the alleviation of distress arising from the economic crisis. Hence the Parliament achieved little on this side, though the *Grundrechte* abolished serfdom and judicial and hunting rights of the landlords, and a law of March 1849 provided for supervision of the growing emigration. Their constitution was in many respects an admirable piece of work, and in general well designed to serve its purpose; all later constitutions for Germany (including that of Bismarck) have drawn upon it. It required, however, not merely the exclusion of Austria, but also some reduction in the weight of Prussia to give it a fair chance of success. Gagern and others would have liked to merge Prussia into the new union by abolishing the Prussian National Assembly and letting her provinces send representatives to the National Parliament, like the other states of Germany. Had this merging (vaguely pledged by Frederick William himself in the March crisis) been possible, and had Frederick William been a different person, there might have been some chance of Germany securing a real start on the road to political self-government without making the sharp break with her still strong monarchical traditions.

Such a break-up of Prussia (though earlier proposed) had to wait for another hundred years for its fulfilment, and given the character and views of Frederick William, with the triumph of the reaction there and in Austria, the forces against the Frankfurt Parliament and its constitution were too strong to be overcome. The Prussian Parliament showed little enthusiasm for being merged in Germany. Bavaria and the other middle-sized states had liked neither their proposed subjection to a powerful central authority nor the predominant position given to the King of Prussia, and the lesser states naturally followed this lead when the tide turned so swiftly and disastrously against the Frankfurt Parliament. And since the counter-revolution triumphed, it stamped history with its version of the errors of the effort of 1848, and of the political incapacity of its leaders. It stigmatized parliamentary liberalism and democracy as foreign doctrines, alien to the true German mind and spirit; an interpretation which was to reach its climacteric in the Nazi doctrines.

Yet whilst the national feeling evoked at Frankfurt was to be largely merged in Bismarck's work, the revolution of 1848 also had other less equivocal if less marked or immediately important results. The old autocracy could not be completely restored. Some of the legal constitutional rights for which the rising middle class stood survived, and this class won henceforth a larger place in the life of Germany. The revolution helped to remove the remnants of the feudal regime in Germany, and gave freedom to the Jewish population. It stirred up interest in political and social-economic questions. In addition to the flood of newspaper, pamphlet, and broadsheet material poured out through a free press, the publication of the complete proceedings and debates of the Frankfurt Parliament as they went along was a notable advance for a country formerly so little politically conscious as Germany. Nor were the effects of this short-lived effort in political education entirely lost in the days that followed, despite the reaction (and the efforts of Bismarck). The revolution also helped to define the position and aims of the new urban working class, or rather of its leaders, of whom Lassalle was to remain in Germany to become the organizer of German socialism. And whilst the efforts of the revolution were for long to be almost obliterated by the successes and glory of Bismarck's work, they were to be recalled, and bear fruit when that glory had departed, in both the first and the second German republics.

VI. EPILOGUE

Whilst the revolution was in fact over when the Frankfurt Parliament was scattered to the four winds of heaven, the fertile brain of Frederick William IV continued to spin its gossamer threads of schemes to bind together Prussia and Germany in a closer union (and Austria in a wider one), but free of what to him were the errors of the Frankfurt constitution. And since his ministers were too narrowly Prussian to aid him in this effort he turned to his friend Radowitz, Catholic, non-Prussian, a member of the Frankfurt Parliament, but as devoted to the cause as the king himself, and ready to support the royal efforts even when he realized their futility.[1] Briefly their plan was to build a German *Reich* headed by Prussia, with a constitution based on that of Frankfurt but modifying its elements of centralized and popular control, and hence more agreeable to the princes for whose adhesion they hoped. Beyond this there was to be a wider union including the whole Austrian Empire, with freedom of trade, and, it was hoped, a common foreign policy. This wider union was to be headed by a Directory in which Prussia would represent the narrower union, with two votes for Austria and two exercised by Prussia.

The efforts to implement this grandiose scheme continued for a year and a half, with continuous and complicated negotiations, until they were finally and completely destroyed by Austria at Olmütz (Olomouc) in November 1850. There was in reality little hope of success, given the division of opinion in Prussia, the endless hesitations of the king, the fear and dislike of Prussian domination by the lesser German princes, and the opposition of Austria. For some time, however, since Austria was absorbed with more domestic issues, the scheme of Prussian union gained a measure of support. A conference at Potsdam in May 1849 brought the adhesion (with reservations) of Saxony and Hanover; and in June a number of former members of the

[1] Bismarck in his *Reflections and Reminiscences* (trans., vol. i, p. 70) is highly critical of Radowitz, doubting his motives and terming him 'a skilful keeper of the medieval wardrobe in which the king dressed up his fancies.'

Frankfurt Parliament, gathered at Gotha under the lead of Gagern and others of like mind, accepted the proposals as salvaging something at least of their own work.   By August most of the other states had likewise accepted the scheme (as they had earlier accepted that of Frankfurt), with the significant exception, however, of Bavaria and Wurtemberg.   But by the time a parliament representative of the new union met at Erfurt in the spring of 1850 Saxony and Hanover, with some of the smaller states, had withdrawn their support.   And Frederick William himself had so far lost his enthusiasm for the plan that he refused to accept the constitution drawn up by the Erfurt Parliament, which was left to follow its Frankfurt predecessor into collapse and oblivion.

The initiative which Prussia had lost passed to Austria, now freed from both the Italian and the Hungarian wars.   Schwarzenberg, although limited in his views, had none of the hesitation of the Prussian king.   The Austrian historian, Friedjung, compares him to a bold and tough sea-captain, capable of commanding his ship through a storm, though he might not be able to read his charts correctly.   Schwarzenberg heartily detested the Prussian scheme of union, as he did that of Frankfurt, and was determined to preserve if not increase Austrian influence in Germany.   He had the backing of the Emperor of Russia, the support of Bavaria and Wurtemberg, and some at least of the Prussian ministers were ready to deal with him, rather than follow the plans of Radowitz and the king.   Following an interim arrangement between Austria and Prussia, by which these two states agreed to exercise temporary control of German affairs in the absence of other authority, he proceeded to invite delegates from all the German states to Frankfurt. And there, without Prussia's presence or assent, was set up what turned out within a few months to be the old Diet, incomplete as yet but unmistakable, and naturally headed by Austria.

This step by Austria was a direct challenge to the Prussian attempt to create a new Little German Union, and evoked a crisis between the two powers reminiscent of Frederick the Great's day.   There was a rustle of arms in both countries, and a natural turn to the all-powerful Nicholas of Russia, brother-in-law indeed of Frederick William, but the upholder of legitimacy and the deadly foe of all change which could be suspected of democratic or revolutionary qualities.   His attitude was to be important in two crises which arose at this time, and in both instances worked to the detriment of Prussia, and so to the advantage of Austria.   The first of these was the familiar Schleswig-Holstein trouble, wherein in the spring of 1849 war had broken out again, with Prussia again in command of the German federal troops.   But the tsar was wholly on the side of the Danish king, and as Frederick William likewise disliked the idea of supporting rebels against royal authority (even Danish), he abandoned the cause of the duchies and made first a truce in July 1849, and then a year later, a peace which abandoned the duchies to Denmark.   The prestige of Prussia in Germany inevitably suffered as a result, and Austrian policy received corresponding encouragement.

Worse was to follow, from a crisis in the affairs of the Electorate of Hesse-Cassel. There the Elector had by no means reconciled himself to the changes brought by the revolution in his state, and seized the first opportunity to recall his hated minister Hassenpflug and repudiate the constitution conceded in 1848. Declaring a state of siege, he then appealed against his recalcitrant subjects, not to the Prussian Union which he had joined but to the re-emerging Federal Diet, where Austria naturally welcomed an opportunity to take action on behalf of the old regime. Here was another challenge to Prussia, the more vital since Hesse-Cassel divided the two parts of her kingdom, and two Prussian military roads ran across it. When Prussia sent troops into the Electorate to safeguard her interests Austria replied by inviting the South German states to join her in counter-military action. War threatened, and a minor clash actually occurred before Prussia gave way in the face of an Austrian ultimatum. There was a severe crisis in Prussia, but Manteuffel had all along been in favour of compromise, and at Olmütz he and Schwarzenberg in November 1850 came to an agreement which preserved peace indeed, but at further cost to Prussia. Whilst she was in the end able to defeat Schwarzenberg's plan for the inclusion of the whole of the Austrian dominions in a reorganized Germany, she had to give way in the matter of the military occupation of Hesse-Cassel, she had to demobilize before Austria, she had to abandon the Prussian Union, and in default of any other arrangement to accept the revival of the old *Bund* with Austria at its head. For the time being the Prussian bid for leadership in Germany had suffered a decided set-back, and the way was open to the free flow of the tide of reaction which had already set in.

This reaction was most obvious and, indeed, went furthest in Austria itself. There, with the withdrawal at the end of 1851 of the constitution granted in March 1849 (though never put into effect), an absolutist regime returned. The new absolutism differed, however, in several respects from the old. It was based less on the support and share in government of the aristocracy. The peasants remained free of feudal burdens as of seignorial justice. And, more markedly after Schwarzenberg's sudden death in 1852, men of the middle class rather than of the landed aristocracy remained in charge of the administration, such men as Alexander Bach, a Viennese lawyer, and for a time the Rhenish merchant Bruck. Thus the administration became less feudal and more bureaucratic in character. It also became more openly centralistic, so that the rights or claims of the various units of the empire, above all those of defeated Hungary, were more openly disregarded. As a recent writer [1] put it: 'The Austrian Empire became, for the first and last time, a fully unitary state.' Further, one marked change came in the position of the Church, formerly controlled by the State in the Josephist tradition, but now with imperial favour given by the Concordat of 1855 a remarkable degree of freedom and power, and enlisted in the support of the new regime. Of popular freedom, in assembly or press, there was now no question; the days of popular control in Vienna seemed incredibly remote.

[1] A. J. P. Taylor, *The Habsburg Monarchy, 1809–1918*, 1948, p. 85.

In one respect, indeed, there was little change; the financial affairs of the empire were in no better state than in the days of Metternich, despite the efforts of Bruck.

The spirit dominant in Austria was also manifested in Germany from one end to the other. The reaction in Prussia did not go quite so far as in Austria, but it went far enough. As we have seen, the constitution fought for, promised, and seemingly won was markedly changed in a conservative direction before the king would sign it. And even after so doing he proceeded to refashion the upper chamber after the pattern he so. greatly admired, that of the English House of Lords, and in his Political Testament advised his successors not to take any oath to a constitution. The revival of the power of the landed class was seen in their recovery of the right of entail of their estates, and of their police rights over their estates. Indeed the new constitution, as revised, provided a stronger bulwark of their position and interests whether against popular or even royal demands. The freedom of the press disappeared, and the promised local self-government failed to materialize. The use of trial by jury was reduced, the judges were no longer irremovable, liberal officials were expelled from office, leaders in the revolution were brought to trial, State control over education and religion was increased. In all this the worst features of the pre-1848 police system in Prussia were revived, indeed for a time Prussia seemed to be back in the days not merely before 1848 but before 1740. Credit—or discredit—for all this must go primarily to the king and the court *camarilla* surrounding him, led by the brothers Gerlach. Yet Manteuffel, head of the ministry to 1858, must bear his share of the responsibility, since although he did not approve of much of the reaction, he neither openly protested nor resigned.

The restored confederate authority at Frankfurt naturally reflected the views of its re-creator, Schwarzenberg. A committee of the *Bundestag* with the ominous title of Reaction Committee was set up in August 1851 to see that the work of what Frederick William now called 'the year of shame' was undone all over Germany. Under Austrian leadership the *Bundestag* now displayed a greater readiness to interfere in the internal affairs of the various states than it had shown before 1848. The Fundamental Rights of the Frankfurt constitution were declared abolished, and the political changes of the revolution attacked and largely destroyed from one end of Germany to the other, save where, as in Bavaria, they had been relatively limited. A new King of Hanover recovered the right of his ancestors. In Hesse-Darmstadt the old upper chamber was restored. In the adjacent Hessian Electorate it was proposed to restore princely absolutism almost intact, and the conflict between Elector and people was to continue through the next decade. In general, however, the atmosphere was less one of strife than of repression, with prosecution and punishment of those champions of radical change in the revolutionary years who could not escape abroad. A 'still time' ensued after the storms, but it was less the quiet of content than of sullen embitterment. Intellectual life, creative activity in thought and letters, suffered. The day was approaching for the recognition and acceptance of the pessimistic philosophy of the elderly sage of Frankfurt, Schopenhauer, centring on the undying activity of the human will, and the inescapable tragedy of human life and history. One side of German life did indeed continue to develop during these years of reaction: the economic changes and industrial growth begun before the revolution went on like the machines which had aided its emergence, though there was little attempt to meet the social problems created by such changes.

One method of relief from both political persecution and economic distress there was which became a marked feature of German life during this period, namely emigration, above all to America. Emigration was, of course, no new thing for Germans. A *Drang nach Osten* had been an element in German history since the tenth century, when the *Nordmark* (the future Prussia) began to push out from its eastern boundary on the Elbe, and the *Ostmark* (the future Austria) faced the harder task of pushing down the Danube from about Vienna. This eastern push sent German colonists as far as the Volga in the eighteenth century, and had not ceased with the new age. In the years immediately after 1815 many Germans (with Russian encouragement) found their way to the Black Sea and the Caucasus, and more still, perhaps a quarter of a million, went to Russian Poland, where they helped to build up textile cities such as Lodz. But the main direction of the emigration in this century was to be not east but west, and out beyond the bounds of Europe to America, above all to the United States, now beginning its giant strides westwards towards the Pacific.

The motives for this movement were as usual mixed. Much has been made of what we may term the political reasons, the discontent deepening to despair with the illiberal conditions in the Fatherland after 1815, disillusionment after the enthusiasm aroused by the War of Liberation, flight from the era of repression which set in with the Carlsbad decrees, repeated after the failure of hopes aroused in 1830, and reaching its height in the reaction which set in with the failure of the national-liberal effort in 1849. Certainly such discontents and fears, such escapes from trial or prison, sent many men across the ocean, a List, a Herwegh, a Kinkel, among names well known, together with younger men such as Karl Schurz, who were to win fame in the New World. Religion played a part also, sending out groups or individuals who found princely orthodoxy too cramping for their particular tenets or ways of worship. Thus did many Old Lutherans of Prussia, and the Saxon followers of Martin Stephan, the mystic of Dresden, seek religious freedom for themselves in North America in the late thirties. There was no federal or state effort to found colonies in the New World in this period, although there was talk in Prussia of reviving old schemes for such colonies, with an eye on Mexico or Oregon. Private efforts to establish German colonies in the Middle West likewise came to naught.

As with England and Ireland, however, so with Germany, it was most obviously economic and social causes which sent first a trickle and then, in the fifties, a stream of families across the Atlantic. There was a steady and marked increase in German population in the years after 1815, an increase greater than the country could absorb at home. For whilst the old partly feudal society was breaking up, a new industrialized society had not yet emerged. The small scale hand industry could not compete with the products of the factory, whether imported from England or beginning to be made at home. The peasant farmer might be freed, but he sometimes lost his land in the process; redemption of feudal rights imposed financial burdens, and peasant holdings, especially in south-west Germany, tended to be cut up into units too small to maintain families. There were the 'hunger year' of 1817, the Rhine floods of 1824–5, the hard winter of 1828–9, the drought of 1842, the growing economic crisis of the middle forties, the general unrest and the dislocation of normal life during 1848–9. 'Things are better in America' even Goethe had said in the last year of his life, and many Germans of humbler place believed and found it so, despite the hardships inevitable in the uprooting, ocean and land travel, and settlement in the new environment. The improvement and greater freedom of travel in Germany itself by road, river, and finally railway aided the movement, as did the establishment of regular trade with America from Bremen and Hamburg, and the growth of shipping. The reports of travellers and successful emigrants were widely publicized and read.

All the emigration was not to North America, but that was the commonest goal, combining as it did economic opportunity with political freedom. The number of emigrants was not so large until the middle forties, but the economic crisis which then emerged gave a sudden lift to the numbers, which rose to and passed 100,000 in 1847. With the revolution year came a slight drop, but after 1850 there was a sharp rise again for the next few years, so that between 1849 and 1854 some 1,100,000 Germans left their native land to find homes abroad, the vast majority in the United States. It is impossible to separate, or define the relative strength, of economic and political motives in this great movement of the German people, which was to be of considerable moment in the building up of the United States. But undoubtedly it had a direct connection with the failure of the revolution, and it took from Germany men who, if the revolution had had a happier issue, could have contributed to the building up of a liberal-democratic state at home, instead of in a foreign state four thousand miles away.

CHAPTER VIII

THE UNIFICATION OF GERMANY

*From Olmütz to the Italian War of 1859 — The New Era in Prussia
and the Constitutional Crisis — The Entry of Bismarck, 1862–4 —
The Seizure of Schleswig-Holstein — The Extrusion of Austria — The
Completion of Unity*

I. FROM OLMÜTZ TO THE ITALIAN WAR OF 1859

WHILST AN appreciable amount of German youth and strength was thus
establishing itself in the New World just in time to play a part in the great
struggle there for national unity on the issue of free and slave, in Germany
itself the scene was likewise being set for the decisive effort for the attainment
of national unity. In both cases the North was to impose its will for national
unity upon the South through victory in war. Without forcing the parallel
too far, and not forgetting the shortcomings of the Reconstruction Era in
the United States, time was to show that Lincoln's 'new birth of freedom,'
however imperfectly realized, was a sounder principle on which to erect a
state than the 'blood and iron' of Bismarck, despite the glory and acclaim
that policy was to win.

The situation in Germany at the end of 1850 (Olmütz, November 1850)
did not seem to presage any early domination of Prussia over Germany.
True, the Frankfurt Parliament had offered Frederick William an imperial
crown, which represented a certain enlargement of Prussian prestige, and
behind that were the recognition of Prussia's military power and the economic
bond of the *Zollverein*. But the imperial crown had been refused, and the
succeeding efforts of 1849–50 to form a Little German Union under Prussia
were likewise to come to naught. Feeling in Germany was far from unanimous in desiring to accept Prussian leadership, and the reaction in Prussia
alienated German liberal-national opinion. More significant seemed the
revival of Austrian influence expressed most plainly in the restoration of the
old *Bund* machinery over which she presided as before, but with more energy.
And as the Austrian star blazed forth again so did that of Prussia under her
weak king appear to decline. Had Schwarzenberg lived indeed the revived
Austrian ascendancy would probably have lasted longer than it did. But
with his death (April 1852) the control fell into weaker hands, whilst the
problems the new ministers, Bach and Buol, had to face under the new
emperor were more urgent and difficult than anything Metternich had had
to face after 1815, while the new men lacked the ability of the old prince.
The domestic issues were serious enough, with the finances as bad as ever,
the Magyars and other non-German nationalities chafing at the restored

German-Austrian hegemony and the reaction, widespread social disturbance, no settled constitution, and a new and untried emperor. And the foreign issues were to be more threatening still. For the long years of peace in Europe following the removal of the Napoleonic menace were over, and the middle and late fifties were to see two major European wars, in both of which Austria had a direct and immediate interest. One of them, the Italian War of 1859, was indeed an Austrian war; and both of them, in the result, were to weaken her position in Germany and her relations with her Prussian rival there.

The first of these wars, the Crimean War, deeply and permanently affected Austrian relations with her great neighbour to the east, Russia. For Austria, more swayed by fears of the forward policy of Nicholas I along the lower Danube and towards Constantinople than by memory of benefits received in the suppression of the Hungarian bid for independence in 1849, joined with France and Britain not indeed in war, but in strong diplomatic pressure not far short of war to thwart the Russian effort. She even occupied the Danubian principalities for a time. And Russia (as Bismarck discovered to his delight when he went there as ambassador in 1861) neither forgave nor forgot her ingratitude. Nor did Austria improve her position in Germany by her policy. True, on Frederick William's initiative, she secured in April 1854 a treaty of alliance with Prussia which even covered her Italian possessions. Nevertheless, neither Prussia nor the German states of the *Bund* showed any serious disposition to support her anti-Russian policy, although liberal opinion in Prussia was hostile to the tyrant of 1848. The Prussian Government held to a neutral policy, the April treaty notwithstanding. It stood aloof from Austria's negotiations with the western powers, including the preliminary conferences at Vienna on the terms of peace, and so naturally enough (if to her annoyance) Prussia was given little say in the final peace conference at Paris in 1856.

Thus in the immediate and shorter view Prussia appeared to have lost ground at the close of the Crimean War, whilst Austria was secure for a time at least from the menace of a Russian advance southwards. On the other hand, Austrian relations with Russia had permanently worsened, whilst those of Prussia had by comparison improved. And Austria had not won allies in the west by her policy, and so was left isolated, as she was to learn to her cost in 1859. The lesser states of Germany, if not more drawn to Prussia than before, had at all events followed a like policy in their fear of the costs and perils of war, refusing to give Austria the support for which she hoped. Relations between Austria and Prussia were cooler, as Prussia refused to renew the full treaty of 1854, and they would have been cooler still had the views of Prussia's ambassador at Frankfurt, the *Junker* Otto von Bismarck, prevailed.

'Great crises,' Bismarck had written during the Crimean War, 'provide the weather which favours Prussia's rise, in so far as we use them fearlessly, perhaps even ruthlessly.' And when the Italian War of 1859 broke out he was prepared to use the crisis in just that way, by a swift campaign of the

Prussian army to seize part of central and southern Germany for Prussia whilst Austria was engaged in Italy against Franco-Italian forces. But Bismarck was not yet in power, and Prince William, now Regent of Prussia, was not ready for such a policy. He had indeed his grievances against Austria, which wanted Prussian support, but was not prepared to pay for it by conceding Prussian command of the federal German forces should Napoleon attack on the Rhine. William went so far as to mobilize first part and then the whole of the Prussian army, partly to protect Germany, partly with the idea of offering armed mediation, perhaps even to attack France. But with the two Austrian defeats of Magenta and Solferino in June 1859 the prospect of an armed Prussia thus taking the lead in Germany was too much for Francis Joseph, and the thought of a Prussian attack was equally disagreeable to Napoleon. So the two emperors hastily patched up a peace at Villafranca (11th July 1859), to the disgust of the Prussian regent, who had thus wasted good money and effort, and risked alienating his western neighbour, with nothing to show for it. Yet the war had weakened Austria, leaving her isolated as before and with growing discontent at home, and was to aid the steady turning of the balance in Germany in favour of Prussia.

The Italian gains by the war of 1859, to be followed by the further successes of the national effort led by Cavour in the following year, caused widespread stirrings in Germany which signified the end of the decade of reaction and the opening of a New Era not merely in Prussia but far more widely. Indeed the decade had not been all reaction. The economic life of the country had profited by the more stable conditions. Agriculture improved, with better markets and the completion of peasant emancipation, e.g. in Bavaria. The commercial and industrial middle class continued its growth, aided by the railways, and the extension of the *Zollverein* by the entry of Hanover and Oldenburg in the early fifties, a growth interrupted but not broken by the worldwide economic crisis of 1857.

More directly connected with the stimulus from Italy and of more immediate political importance was the stirring in the academic and professional middle class, now led not by philosophers but by historians such as Sybel and Droysen, Häusser and Mommsen, concerned for the future as well as the past of their country. The 'men of '48' had mostly disappeared from the scene, some dead or exiled, others no longer active. But new leaders were arising, mostly liberals from northern Germany, and if not Prussian, believing in and urging Prussian leadership for the achievement of the more effective unity of Germany on a parliamentary basis. True this urge was by no means universal. The rulers of the two leading states of the south, Bavaria and Wurtemberg, were still primarily concerned to preserve their own sovereignty, and so preferred the older and looser connection, with Austria at the head. From his middle position in the Saxon kingdom the able though vain chief minister Beust continued to put forward compromise schemes for federal reorganization, which found, however, little response. In Baden, however, the accession of a new Grand Duke, Frederick I, married to a Prussian princess, brought a decided change there in favour of both liberalism and closer union under the Prussian monarchy.

The new spirit found most definite expression in the foundation in 1859 of a National Association (*Nationalverein*) based in part on the Italian National Society of a few years earlier. It was led by Rudolf von Bennigsen, a landed noble of Hanover and leader of the liberal opposition there, who was in due course to find a larger field of political activity in Bismarck's Germany. The new society was mainly an upper middle class one, though men such as Schulze-Delitzsch were interested in working-class problems. Its programme was in essence that of 1849, first a reorganization of the *Bund* to provide effective central government under the leadership of Prussia, with a real national parliament to which Prussia, like all the other German states, would be subject, and later a union with Austria on terms to be worked out. This society found wide, if not very large, membership, naturally more in the north than in the south, and its activities undoubtedly did much both to foster and to define the demand for closer and stronger national unity. Nor was it the only body now making such demands. The lack of such things as a common coinage for all Germany, or a common system of mercantile regulation, brought into being at this time an economic organization to promote in this field closer union than the *Zollverein* had achieved. About the same time many of the jurists of the country put forward proposals for a common legal system and practices. And whilst the rulers of southern Germany and the smaller states, the 'princekins,' might view with alarm changes which were bound to affect their cherished sovereignty, the crisis and war of 1859 had plainly shown their inability to defend their status, and the limitations of Austrian power to do so. It was the Prussian army which had marched to defend the western frontier against any threat from France. By 1860 the gaze of the politically conscious in Germany was turned, with a new intensity of hope or fear, upon the northern kingdom.

II. THE NEW ERA IN PRUSSIA AND THE CONSTITUTIONAL CRISIS

Prussia indeed was approaching one of the great crises in her history, perhaps the greatest. During the middle fifties she was a prey to internal divisions and intrigues, as the physical and mental powers of Frederick William IV steadily declined. The reaction continued, with the actual power shared between Manteuffel, the man of Olmütz, as head of the ministry, and the even more conservative court *camarilla*, led by the two brothers Gerlach. The Prussian Parliament played little part, but a new group was forming in the capital, more liberal and more national, led by a Bethmann-Hollweg, and called, after its journal, the *Wochenblatt* party. Off stage Prince William, the king's brother and heir, marked time at Coblenz, being out of favour, and at Frankfurt Bismarck, Prussian ambassador to the Federal Diet, continued to develop for his own and Manteuffel's benefit his views on what lines Prussian policy should follow.

With the final breakdown of the king's health and powers in 1857, and the establishment of Prince William's regency, the scene in Prussia began to change, at first slowly and uncertainly, then more rapidly and dramatically. The significance of the succession of William, first as regent and then in 1861, on the death of his brother, as king, was hidden for a time. For William, although on becoming regent he defined his policy as resting on 'a sound conservative basis,' disliked both the court *camarilla* and the existing ministry. He dropped Manteuffel, and took some moderate liberals, e.g. Bethmann-Hollweg, into the new ministry. He also ended the government habit of putting pressure on the elections to the House of Deputies. Liberal opinion took heart at the change, and the elections to the lower House in 1858 saw the return of a majority of men of liberal or whig-liberal views, though by no means united in one firm party. A New Era of liberal character seemed to have opened in the history of Prussia.

This belief was, however, a delusion. For William, now sixty years of age, was neither capable nor desirous of inaugurating anything of the kind. Born in the last years of the eighteenth century, and only two years younger than his brother, he had begun a career in the Prussian army at the age of ten, had smelt powder in the latest fighting against Napoleon, and had become a major-general at the age of twenty. Thus his character and opinions were formed within the rigid and narrow limits of the high army officer class, with no thought that he would ever succeed to the throne, and were not to change materially. There was an attractive simplicity about him, but his firmness was in part sheer obstinacy, and he could generally be led by a stronger and less scrupulous (or more subtle) character such as Bismarck. He stood for and prized above all the old Prussian qualities: loyalty to the Crown, the State, and the Protestant religion, discipline and obedience, Prussian honour, belief in a firmly graded and stable society. Thus he was a conservative, not precisely a *Junker*, but sharing many of their views. He had little understanding of the social and economic changes taking place in Prussia, and thoroughly detested the Berlin revolution of 1848, from which he had to flee. He was sincerely religious, and although without any of the flamboyancy of his brother he shared his belief in the sacredness and Divine Right of the Crown which he now inherited. Thus whilst he was ready to accept and take oath to the constitution granted by his brother, he was unable or unwilling to see it as seriously reducing the prerogative of the Crown. This applied particularly to the army. For although he was no sabre-rattler like his grandson William II, or a would-be conqueror like the youthful Frederick II, he was a soldier, and now war lord (*Kriegsherr*) of Prussia, as well as king. He possessed an unshakable belief in the military character of the Prussian monarchy, and in his duty and right to maintain that quality, which had declined under the unmilitary regime of Frederick William IV. It was from this issue that there arose the great constitutional crisis in the kingdom which led to the calling of Bismarck to office, and so to many other things.

For William the military problem and its solution were simple enough. The Prussian army was too small, and it was inefficient. The regular army was still based on the universal military service law of 1814, but its numbers had not been increased proportionately to the growth of the population from ten to over seventeen millions by 1860, nor was the original three years of regular service maintained. And the second line, the militia (*Landwehr*), though highly regarded by the people as having played the major part in the War of Liberation, was looked down upon by the higher command as inadequately trained for active service, and the mobilization of 1859 appeared to prove this. So the net of compulsory service must be flung more widely, three years of service must be enforced, and part of the *Landwehr* merged with the regular army, with the remainder reduced in importance. Thereby Prussia would secure a considerably larger regular army, with fifty-three new regiments, and be better prepared for any new emergency that might arise, whether outside the country or (as in 1848) within. This, in essentials, was the scheme which the new Minister of War, Roon, put before the Prussian Parliament early in 1860. Roon was a soldier, a conservative of the *Kreuzzeitung* stamp, with a low opinion of parliamentary assemblies and written constitutions. Yet the proposed changes would cost large sums of money every year, and by the constitution the budget therefor would have to be passed by the Prussian Parliament. It was out of the refusal of the House of Deputies to provide the necessary moneys that the constitutional issue came to a head.

Like all such matters the issue was complicated. At bottom it was the issue fought out and settled for England in the revolution of the seventeenth century, the question whether the king or a representative parliament was to rule. And as in England there were 'rights' on both sides. But whereas in England the Parliament had had centuries of development before the decisive struggle took place, in Prussia the Parliament was a mere infant, the child of the revolution of 1848 (though the spirit if not the tradition of the old rights of local Estates survived in East Prussia). Before 1848 the Prussian Crown had ruled unfettered, but as a result of the revolution had made certain concessions embodied in the constitution of 1850–2, setting up a parliament of two houses, both of which (and not merely the House of Deputies) had to pass the budget. There was an awkward article (No. 108) which suggested that in case of disagreement over a new budget the government might continue to use the last one agreed to, but this was generally admitted (save by William) to be a merely temporary provision. The larger question of responsible government (ministerial responsibility to parliament) was left unclear, and supporters of the Crown developed a convenient theory, adopted by William and Bismarck, that there existed a 'gap' in the constitution, so that when disputes arose this must be filled from the reservoir of unused royal prerogative, a specious but entirely one-sided and untenable argument. No less unsound was William's conviction that he alone could decide on the military needs of the country, for which the Parliament must supply the necessary moneys. The House of Deputies (or its majority) unquestionably possessed the right to scrutinize, amend, or even reject the budget presented to it by the ministry. But as liberals of the nineteenth century, and looking much, as they did, to English example, they naturally thought in wider terms of a ministry (and so a Crown) responsible to the votes of an elected majority in parliament. In this they represented the growing change in the balance of forces in Prussia, primarily the rise of a new middle class.

The struggle was thus one between the old and a new Prussia, and Bismarck was right when, in a famous speech in January 1863, he declared that if compromise failed the question of power came in. 'Since the life of the State cannot stand still, whoever has the power will advance in his own way. Might goes before Right.' (*Macht geht vor Recht.*) Bismarck later denied having used this last phrase, but it expresses his view plainly enough. In an appeal to force the scales were undoubtedly weighted against the champions of the new Prussia. For not merely had they against them the Crown, ministry, army, aristocracy, and conservatives generally, but they were divided amongst themselves and were too exclusively a middle-class party. The ties of the old social order in Prussia were still strong enough to make it doubtful whether the peasantry would support them, and the new proletariat was beginning under Lassalle's inspiration to define and pursue its own class ends. There were without question, as in 1848, gifted and wholly sincere liberal leaders, such as Virchow, Twesten, Lasker, Unruh, Waldeck, Schulze-Delitzsch, and others. But they lacked the combination of Puritan religious zeal with parliamentary experience, strategy, and opportunism which their predecessors in seventeenth-century England (if we may so call them) possessed. Being German they were inclined to be more doctrinaire and less empirical. They were, in a word, not prepared to be revolutionary. Further, they were to have against them a singularly gifted and ruthless opponent in Bismarck, who was to outflank and defeat them on the side on which they were most vulnerable to attack, their German and Prussian patriotism. They laid claim to be a German national party, were zealous for the Fatherland, its unity under Prussia, its defence from outside. In the event the clash between liberal and national loyalties and aspirations was to be fatal for them. Already before the end of 1863 so ardent a champion of liberalism as Twesten could declare in the House of Deputies, apropos of the revived Schleswig-Holstein question: 'I would rather suffer the Bismarck ministry for some years longer than allow a German land to be lost to us.' Thus did nationalism weaken and betray the cause of liberalism.

The liberals made a serious mistake at the very beginning of the struggle, in 1860, when the regent, realizing that the House of Deputies would reject his (or Roon's) budget proposals for army reorganization, changed tactics, like a good soldier, and requested the necessary moneys as a 'provisional grant.' The liberal majority led by Vincke, still believing in William's liberalism, loyal to the Crown, and unwilling to precipitate a crisis, gave 'provisional' assent, somehow persuading themselves that they could still control military expenditure. But William and Roon promptly went ahead with the creation of new regiments, and in the next year William, now king, repeated the procedure and again secured (though by a very small majority) an 'extraordinary' grant which they used for the same purpose. It was a grave, even a fatal, mistake by the House of Deputies.

Belatedly the House, and the country, awoke to the perils of such a course. From East Prussia, the champion of constitutional liberties in the seventeenth century, there sounded a call for an end to this policy of concession, and therefrom the formation of a new and more truly liberal party, the German Progressive party of Prussia. Their programme called for a more active German policy in accord with the aims of the *Nationalverein*, full adhesion in Prussia to the constitution with the recognition of the responsibility of ministers to parliament and reform of the upper House, more local self-government, and the reduction of the rights of landowners and officials. For the army it demanded the retention of both the *Landwehr* and the two years' service. The response in the elections of December 1861 was remarkable. For despite the three-class electoral system the new party won over a hundred seats, the 'moderate' or old liberals lost heavily, and the conservatives were reduced to a mere handful.

The issue now became clearer, the struggle sharper. As the king refused to give up the three years' service, the House of Deputies refused the aid demanded, and itemized the budget (as in modern practice) to prevent diversion to army purposes of funds provided for other needs. To this the king replied by dissolving Parliament (March 1862). The New Era was over, and the more liberal ministers resigned, to be replaced by conservatives. But despite governmental efforts to influence the elections in May the progressives increased their strength in the new House of Deputies, which proceeded to cut out from the budget all increases for military reorganization. Matters had reached a deadlock, since the king refused, even against the advice of his ministers, to compromise on the three years' service. More ministers resigned, and the king himself was not far from abdication in favour of his more liberal-minded son. It was at this moment that Roon produced Bismarck, whom he had recalled from France by a famous message: 'Danger in delay. Hurry,' and William on 22nd September 1862 appointed him President of the Ministry and Minister of Foreign Affairs, despite a promise to the Crown Prince that he would not do so. It was the most fateful step William ever took.

III. THE ENTRY OF BISMARCK, 1862–4

Otto von Bismarck-Schönhausen, now in his forty-eighth year, came on his father's side of a family which had been settled as landowners in Brandenburg for centuries, far longer than the Hohenzollerns, as Bismarck recalled on occasion. They had indeed shared in the struggle of the landed nobility against the rising tide of Hohenzollern autocracy, but in the eighteenth century had been won like their fellows to loyalty to the Prussian Crown, while preserving for a time much of their feudal rights over the peasantry. This was the conservative *Junker* side of Bismarck, ever present in him: as he once remarked: 'I am a *Junker*, and must profit from it.' And by the control he won over William I he was to provide a modern example of the old *Junker* motto: 'Absolute the king may reign, if our will he doth maintain.' [1]   This squirearchy was not in general wealthy, and Bismarck himself had to assist in recuperating the family fortunes by managing the Pomeranian family estate of Kniephof for some years after 1848.   And although after a time he found this rustic life both boring and cramping he never lost his pride in his landed connection.   Later, when his desire for power had been realized, he was to satisfy his land hunger by acquiring as reward for his political triumphs the two estates of Varzin and Friedrichsruh, thereby to rise from a *Junker* to a *grand seigneur* of sorts.   Bismarck further strengthened his *Junker* ties by his marriage to Maria von Puttkamer, the daughter of an old Pomeranian landed family noted for its strong evangelical piety.   Bismarck compromised with such all-compelling faith: 'I love pietism in women,' he wrote shortly after his marriage.   For himself he preserved enough religious belief to feel sure of divine support in case of need, but was careful not to allow it to interfere with his political activities, or with the immeasurable hatred he cherished against those who opposed him.

The *Junker* was only one side of Bismarck, however.   His mother came from the German middle class as it revived after the Thirty Years War, and this Mencken family had provided both university professors and in the person of his grandfather, a Prussian privy councillor to Frederick the Great and his immediate successors.   Bismarck in his *Memoirs* makes little of this influence, but it was probably from this side that he inherited his unusual intellectual gifts, his readiness of speech and pen, his wide reading habits as a young man, and also his freedom from conservative ideas in such matters as foreign policy.   To this side too he owed a connection with the influential Gerlach family, and also with Frederick William IV, which eased the path to a recognition of his qualities.   Such recognition, which came in the turmoil of 1848 in Berlin, did not necessarily mean approval of the fire-breathing violence of his conservative views.   The king indeed marked him down as 'only to be used when the bayonet rules supreme.'   Yet he realized the force and ability which Bismarck displayed for the royal cause in the *Landtag* and outside, and it was to this that Bismarck, no professional diplomat, owed his appointment as Prussian ambassador to the Federal Diet in Frankfurt in 1851, a post he was to hold for eight years.   He had already tried and rejected what he contemptuously called the 'pen pushing' required for apprenticeship to a post in the administration, and the alternative of an army career was no more tempting.   He preferred, as he put it, 'to make his own music.'

These Frankfurt years were of great importance for the clarifying and maturing of Bismarck's views.   The world round about was changing and, like the *Junker* he was, Bismarck sought profits for Prussia therefrom, since, as he had already declared, 'the only sure foundation for a great State is state egoism.'   The defeat of Russia in the Crimean War and her breach

---

[1] 'Unser König absolut
Wenn er unser'n Willen tut.'

with Austria, the rise of Napoleon III, the Italian struggle for independence and unity—all these were discussed at length in his letters and memoranda. In Frankfurt itself came the revelation of the weakness of the *Bund* and its lesser states, and above all the realization that the great obstacle to any enlargement of Prussian power was the pre-eminence Austria enjoyed there. He had approved of the settlement at Olmütz in 1850, but now took umbrage at the attitude of superiority adopted by the Austrian President of the *Bund*, wrongly assuming that this was a new and unprecedented claim. He opposed alliance with Austria because in what he termed her 'pampered egoism' she merely made use of Prussia for her own ends. There was some truth in this, but Bismarck excelled in building up a grievance to cover an aggression. The truth was, he argued, there was not room for both of them in Germany, and sooner or later the issue must be settled by war. He admits that the lesser German states do not and cannot trust Prussia, since they realize that they stand in the way of her expansion. But that is no reason for Prussia to change her age-old policy, rather must she take advantage of Austria's difficulties and the unsettled state of Europe. She must preserve the old friendship with Russia, and cultivate good relations with Napoleon III undisturbed by his revolutionary origins or the sinister memories his name arouses for Prussia.

This was political realism, the new *Realpolitik*, of which Bismarck was to be the great and most successful exponent in the nineteenth century. The word *Realpolitik* had recently been coined by a liberal writer anxious to convert his fellows from mere theorizing to political realities. With Bismarck, however, it came to be applied to the use of power, free of any moral considerations, to attain political ends for the State. This was no new doctrine, for Machiavelli had preached it in *The Prince*, and Frederick the Great had both practised and preached it in his day. Hegel had provided some support for it, and after 1870 Treitschke was to give it weighty professorial approval from his chair in Berlin. For Bismarck it involved a breach with his old mentor Leopold Gerlach, who stood by the struggle against the revolution and all its works, whereas his protégé thought in terms of the increase of the power and greatness of the Prussian state, and sought allies in so far and for so long as they were useful to that end. As an Austrian minister of the day complained, Bismarck could be revolutionary abroad while conservative at home.

Thereby, and with the aid of boldness, cunning, and the Prussian army, he was to achieve his triumphs over Denmark and Germany, Austria, and France, and therewith the attainment by Prussia and Germany of a position and prestige undreamed of even a mere generation earlier. But such swiftly and ruthlessly acquired power had its dangers, not merely for Germany's neighbours, but for Germany herself. In the second quarter of the eighteenth century Montesquieu had set himself to inquire why the Roman Empire fell from the great height it had attained. He concluded that its power had been built up too quickly (though it rose far more slowly than modern Germany) and too exclusively by military force. 'An empire created by arms must maintain itself by arms.' Both criticisms apply to Bismarck's work and creation. Further, had Bismarck been less impatient, less prone to rely on force and trickery, he would have served Prussia better. For with her superiority in size and weight, the economic advantages both of the leadership of the *Zollverein* and the possession of the growing industrial areas of the Rhineland and Silesia, Prussia was bound to win the hegemony in Germany, the more so since Austria was growing steadily weaker, a house divided against herself, lacking in both policy and statesmanship. In his egoism for Prussia Bismarck furthered Austria's decline, and thereby, despite his later alliance with her, weakened the cause of Germanism against Slavism in eastern Europe. He had no understanding for the belief voiced by the greatest Slav statesman of our own day, Masaryk, that 'no state, no society, can be governed without general recognition of the ethical bases of the State and society.'

In the spring of 1859 Bismarck was moved from Frankfurt to St. Petersburg, rather against his will. Yet the three years as Prussian ambassador to Russia were of great value to him as giving him a first-hand acquaintance with that land and its rulers, and he showed himself an active, shrewd, and able representative of Prussian interests there. Tsarist absolutism naturally appealed to Bismarck, and Alexander II seemed to approve of him, talking to him of the 'sacred legacy' and the bond of blood which bound him to the ruling house in Prussia. Thirty years later the next Tsar Alexander was to modify his appreciation of Bismarck's genius by the remark that he 'was always afraid of being deceived by him.' Bismarck's relations with Gortschakoff, minister in charge of foreign affairs, were somewhat cool. Both were highly opinionated and ambitious men. Gortschakoff, conscious of Russia's greater power, was inclined to be superior, Bismarck was touchy both for himself and for his country. They were indeed natural rivals, as later events were to show. The St. Petersburg period was followed by a few months as ambassador to France in the summer of 1862, but this was rather one of impatient waiting for ministerial office than of diplomatic activity. Napoleon III he found friendly, as on a previous visit to Paris, but his support of closer relations with the French emperor found little favour in Berlin. He visited England and holidayed at Biarritz, but mainly he waited for the call which finally came from Roon in September of that year.

Bismarck entered office pledged to support William's plans for military reorganization, in direct opposition, therefore, to the voice and vote of the majority in the House of Deputies. We need not take seriously his proffer of an olive twig, a sign of peace, from Avignon. He had no thought of compromise, rather it seemed that he preferred to embitter relations between ministry and chamber. He began with arguments as to the constitution and the alleged 'gap' in it, but as this had no effect he and Roon tried to ride down the opposition in cavalry fashion, to bully them into submission, refusing to attend the Budget Commission, and denying the authority of the presiding officer in the chamber to call them to order. This last was to encourage the king, who was drawing gloomy pictures of himself and his minister ending on the scaffold, like Charles I and Strafford in England. Bismarck then began to put pressure on government officials, first to discipline those who needed it, then to dismiss those who proved obdurate to ministerial direction. By 1866 some thousand such officials had lost their positions. In May 1863 he prorogued the *Landtag* and immediately issued a stringent press decree to stifle the criticism which, as always, irked him almost beyond endurance. But the criticism continued outside (and so across) the borders of Prussia, and the restraints on the press in Prussia could only last until the *Landtag* met again. So he dissolved the recalcitrant Parliament (September 1863), hoping for better results with a new one. He had serious thoughts of abandoning the three-class restrictions on the franchise, believing that he would get more popular support thereby. He even approached the revolutionary socialist Lassalle, who shared his hatred of middle-class liberalism, and approved a strong State, though a very different one from that of Bismarck. But Bismarck was to postpone his experiment in universal suffrage for a wider field than Prussia alone. Meanwhile, despite all efforts to sway the election, the new House of Deputies which met in November 1863 proved no more complaisant than the old, the deadlock remained unbroken, and early in the next year the session was closed. It remained for the minister so ambitious of office to find a new and different road to his ends.

Bismarck's claim to greatness lies in no small degree on his success in finding such a road, which led into Denmark, through Frankfurt, to the gates of Vienna, and along the Champs-Élysées into Paris. Thereby he did much more than defeat the liberal opposition in the Prussian House of Deputies, though that must be counted among his achievements. He likewise decisively defeated Prussian, and therewith German, liberalism, which never recovered from the blow in his lifetime or to our own day. On the particular and narrower ground on which the struggle had been mainly fought, the issue of the budget and the provision of funds for the reorganization and enlargement of the Prussian army, he won out by doing without a budget and without a State loan until after the victory of 1866. He was able to do this thanks to the Prussian State treasure or war chest, but also to the increased revenue to be drawn from the State domains, from forests and mines, posts and telegraphs, from railway concessions. Thus paradoxically did the economic activity of the rising liberal middle class contribute to its own defeat. There was indeed talk of refusing to pay taxes, but the traditional obedience to the State in Prussia, to say nothing of the force available to the government, dispelled any hope of this. And it was, of course, the enlarged and reorganized army which achieved victory in the succession of campaigns and battles from Düppel in Denmark to Sedan.

Behind these, however, were the brain and hand of Bismarck himself, now turning from the unprofitable field of domestic parliamentary strife to the one most suited to his genius, that of foreign policy. Therein he was but following the advice put by Shakespeare into the mouth of the dying Henry IV for his more famous son to 'busy giddy minds with foreign quarrels,' and thereby distract them from domestic discontents. Long before he took office Bismarck had offered to bring on a war within a month if desired, and within a few months of taking office he frankly warned Austria that since Prussia needed more elbow room in Germany war would threaten unless the Habsburgs bowed themselves out of the *Reich* and turned eastwards. He was, of course, no mere hothead or lover of war for its own sake. But he was filled with ambition for Prussia, and ready to make war to satisfy that ambition. In almost the first speech he made after taking office Bismarck, in arguing for his budget, defined his aims: 'Germany does not look to the liberalism but to the power of Prussia. Bavaria, Wurtemberg, Baden, may indulge in liberalism, but Prussia must strengthen and maintain her forces for the favourable moment, which has more than once been missed. Her boundaries by the Congress of Vienna are ill-suited for a sound political life. The great issues of to-day will be settled not by speeches and majority votes —that was the great error of 1848-9—but by iron and blood.'

The range of Bismarck's activities in the field of German and foreign policy between 1862 and 1870, and therewith the creation of the Bismarckian German Empire, expands like the ever-widening circles created by the throwing of a stone into a pond. It begins with the mere local matter of a squabble in Hesse-Cassel, extends from there into federal affairs of Germany, takes in the surrounding countries of Poland, Denmark, and Austria, and finally spreads across the Rhine to envelop France. There is a unity, an air of inevitability about the process and its results, almost an appearance of long foresighted planning. That is indeed too much. The ageing king might have died before Bismarck was well in the saddle, or sufficiently successful to overcome the dislike and distrust of the Crown Prince for him. But there was a marked and unusual admixture of immediate expedient and long-range purpose in him as there was in Cavour, though the bases of his thought were narrower, as his policies were more forceful and his strength greater.

Bismarck may be said to have fired the first gun in his conduct of Prussian foreign policy by sending a rough note to the Elector of the adjacent little state of Hesse-Cassel within a few weeks of taking office. There the Elector had been making a general nuisance of himself by his efforts to get rid of the constitution and return to absolute rule, and Bismarck's predecessor as Foreign Minister, Bernstorff, had already taken steps to call him to order, backing up the efforts of the Federal Diet. Bismarck's blunter methods had their effect. They also served notice to other lesser states of the temper and methods of the new Prussian minister. More important were other issues, likewise alive before Bismarck took office, concerning trade relations, and therewith general relations with Austria. The first issue was a double one. On the one hand Austria in 1860 had raised again, as she was entitled to do by the expiring trade treaty of 1853, the question of her entry into the *Zollverein*. At the same time Napoleon III, having made his free trade treaty with England, made overtures for a similar treaty with Prussia. There in the prevailing freer trade temper both ministers and *Landtag*

BISMARCK

LUDWIG II (standing), with the actor, Joseph Kainz

G GEORGE V OF HANOVER as a boy at the court of England

approved of the treaty. Elsewhere in Germany opinion was divided, yet the treaty would need approval by all the *Zollverein* members. And Austria, with her more protective trade system, could hardly accept such a treaty. Prussia, however, went her own way, signed the treaty, and then put pressure on the South German states by threatening to end the Customs Union unless it were accepted. At this point Bismarck entered the scene and, as with Hesse-Cassel, continued the previous policy with more force, threatening not to renew the *Zollverein* treaty when it ran out in 1865. The struggle was to continue through the next two years, but in the end Bismarck had his way and the *Zollverein* treaty was duly renewed in 1865. Thereby, although certain concessions were made to Austria, in fact the door was firmly and finally shut against her entry into the Customs Union, and the Prussian economic hegemony in Germany was both endorsed and increased.

Long before this economic issue was settled another of more political character affecting Austro-Prussian relations had emerged. This was the matter of federal reorganization, wherein the Little Germans, looking to Prussia, were active. If Austria wished to keep the initiative, and her head-ship in any new scheme, it was high time she took action, and the internal crisis in Prussia seemed to play into her hands. A former revolutionary of 1848, Fröbel, now converted to the Greater Germany faith, produced in 1861 a very conservative scheme for the reorganization of the *Bund*, one feature of which, a meeting in Frankfurt of all the German princes, to be presided over by the emperor, appealed to Francis Joseph. Further plans were worked out in Vienna for a Federal Directory of five members, a Federal Council of princes, and a lower House of delegates from the local State Assemblies. To these proposals Bismarck replied by the revolutionary demand for a real National Assembly elected directly on a wide franchise. Yet Francis Joseph called his conference of the thirty German princes, a *Fürstentag*, to meet at Frankfurt in August 1863, and all attended save only the one most essential to any agreement, the King of Prussia. William would have accepted the invitation, presented through the King of Saxony in person, but Bismarck saw such participation as a serious, perhaps a fatal, obstacle to his ambitions for Prussia, and after a dramatic struggle with his ruler prevented him from attending. It was a significant victory for the new minister, both over the king he had sworn to obey and over Austria. The *Fürstentag* did indeed take place, and resulted in the draft of a new constitution which continued Austrian headship with the other features of her plan. But the scheme was stillborn, and Bismarck now openly demanded for his state equal rights with Austria in the headship of the Federation. There was deadlock in Frankfurt, as in Berlin, and Austria had made her last effort for federal reorganization. The next and more successful attempt was to be made by Bismarck himself.

Before this crisis at Frankfurt had been surmounted, Bismarck had taken a first step in the wider field of European diplomacy in relation to Poland. He had looked at Poland from both west and east, with the interest of the Prussian state with its Polish land and many Polish subjects in mind. He

H

had no thought that a Polish state, if an uncomfortable neighbour, might be a useful buffer against Russian power, and did not share in the least the sympathy felt in Germany, even in Prussia, for the divided and subject nation. 'Every success of the Polish nationalist movement,' he had written from St. Petersburg in 1861, 'is a defeat for Prussia. . . . Polonism cannot be looked at by us humanely and impartially, but only with hostility. No peace is possible between us and any revival of Poland.' His hostility to the Poles was more pronounced than that prevailing in Russia, where opinion was greatly divided before the revolt of 1863. The Poles, he declared, should be 'rooted out' like wild beasts.

Hence it was natural enough that when the Poles rose in January 1863 at Warsaw and elsewhere in Russian (but not in Prussian) Poland, Bismarck should be concerned for the speedy suppression of the revolt. He went rather further indeed than was required on military grounds or even desired by Russia, in immediately proposing a military convention with Russia for mutual aid, and preparing the eastern Prussian forces for action. Liberal feeling in Prussia was aroused and there were angry scenes in the Prussian House of Deputies. In Catholic Austria there was more sympathy for the Poles, whilst the interest of Napoleon III (and still more that of Eugénie) added to that of England, created an international crisis, with notes of protest against Russian treatment of the Poles from the western powers, proposals and counter-proposals for alliance of a kind reminiscent of a decade earlier, with the sudden proposal of Napoleon for a general European conference thrown in. The notes and other diplomatic activities were barren of results, save to show up the differences existing between the views of the powers. Yet the crisis had served to define Bismarck's attitude both to the Polish question and to Russia, from the latter of whom he hoped for cheaply bought gratitude, even though the proffered convention was not in the end ratified.

IV. THE SEIZURE OF SCHLESWIG-HOLSTEIN

The next stage in Bismarck's progress in foreign policy yielded more definite results, and was more revealing as to his aims and methods. This was the affair of Schleswig-Holstein, which he pronounced the hardest struggle he had to wage. But the difficulties were of his own making, arising from the fact that he set himself the task of securing for Prussia territory to which she had no claim. He tells us in his memoirs how once the crisis had arisen he kept the annexation of the duchies steadily before his eyes, and how he reminded William of his duty to extend the borders of Prussia as his ancestors had done. The opportunity arose out of the clash of Danish and German nationalism in relation to the two duchies, both under Danish rule, but largely German in population (Holstein almost wholly so, Schleswig more than half) and possessed of ancient rights of self-government. And although they were united, one of them, Holstein, was a member of the German *Bund*. The national problem had created a serious crisis in 1848, as we have seen, but a settlement appeared to have been reached by an international conference in London in 1852. This conference had asserted the integrity of the Danish monarchy, with due recognition of the special rights of the duchies, and had decided the vexed question of the succession to the throne. In this the duchies, unlike Denmark, were under the German (Salic) law of male succession only, but the potential claimant on those grounds, the Duke of Augustenburg, was bought off in the same year, for himself and his family.

The success of this settlement in an age of rising national feeling depended very much upon the wisdom and moderation of the Danes, and unfortunately these were lacking. The government in Copenhagen, pushed by the nationalists there and provoked by rising nationalism in Germany, carried through measures denying the ancient rights of the duchies. Agitation steadily increased through 1863 both in the duchies and in Germany, and rose to a height on the death of the old King of Denmark, Frederick VII, in November of that year. For the new king, Christian IX, although a German prince, found himself forced to sign a new constitution which separated Schleswig from Holstein, and incorporated it more completely in the kingdom. At the same time the eldest son of the Duke of Augustenburg raised a claim to the duchies, on the ground that his father's renunciation did not apply to him, and his claim was immediately accepted in the duchies and received much support in Germany. There the Federal Diet had already threatened to interfere on behalf of Holstein, and now (7th December 1863) voted for immediate federal military occupation of that duchy. Both Austria and Prussia supported this, and as signatories to the treaty of 1852 demanded the immediate revocation of the offending Danish constitution.

This treaty of 1852 had, however, been made and signed by other powers as well, by Britain, Russia, Sweden, and France. The first three had a common interest in preserving the integrity of Denmark, with its strategic position guarding the gate to and from the Baltic, and Britain, or rather her aged but ebullient Prime Minister, Palmerston, had rashly encouraged Denmark to think that she might count on British aid in case of need. Russia, alienated from the west over Poland, did not go so far, and Napoleon III as the champion of nationalities was inclined to favour the duchies. Hence there was little chance of agreement by outside powers for any common action in the crisis, and their differences were to aid the tortuous path of Bismarck's diplomacy. Yet he had obstacles enough. King William was friendly to the claims of Augustenburg, and embarrassed his minister by avowing even after the war with Denmark that he had no claim to the duchies: but William could be drawn along by the bait of military success for the Prussian army. The Crown Prince and the Prussian House of Deputies likewise favoured Augustenburg, and were less tractable than the king. Similarly all over Germany the rising patriotic tide now ran strongly in the same direction. Augustenburg himself, ardent if inexperienced in statecraft, was likewise an obstacle. And while the duchies themselves were mere pawns in the game, Denmark was determined to defend her rights.

This, however, was an attitude Bismarck rather encouraged, since he wanted the Prussian army to win both glory and a commanding position.

Last of all, but most important, there was Austria, the hated rival in Germany, but a necessary accomplice in what Morier was to term Bismarck's 'successful villainy'; for Bismarck and Prussia were not ready as yet to act alone. The greatest triumph of Bismarck's diplomacy was his use of Austria for Prussian ends. Events were to show that Austria had nothing to gain by joining hands with Prussia to defeat Denmark and seize Schleswig-Holstein. She went in, as Francis Joseph later admitted, 'blindly.' At the time it seemed desirable that she should not let Prussia act alone in a German matter, and perhaps win profit therefrom. But her venture represented in fact a reversal of the roles against which Bismarck had protested so strongly at Frankfurt. In fact it provides an illustration of that reversal of roles and fortunes which a modern historian, A. J. Toynbee, has depicted as marking on a larger scale one of the features and causes of the breakdown of a civilization, a 'failure of self-determination.' For it was to lead directly to the final struggle of 1866, to Austria's exclusion from Germany, and more. The military defeat of 1866 was, of course, the result of Prussia's superiority in military leadership and power. But this was preceded and in part prepared for by the diplomatic and political defeat in the Danish affair. Much of the immediate responsibility for this must be borne by Rechberg, the Austrian Foreign Minister, who, whilst defining Bismarck (in 1862) as 'the enemy of Austria,' nevertheless in his fear of democracy, revolution, and Napoleon III, clung to a policy of working with Prussia. In a wider way, however, the defeat reflected the growing weakness of the whole Austrian system, wherein, as Schmerling, an abler minister than Rechberg, put it, 'every one works against everybody else,' whilst Francis Joseph insisted on maintaining the lead, without knowing very well where he was going.

Bismarck, on the other hand, had the goal in what he later termed his 'drama of intrigue' clearly in view. Toward its attainment he displayed an infinite amount of resource and dexterity, shrewdness in judging of men and events, the alternation of procrastination and speed of action, the use of guile, suasion, lies, or force where each would help, a readiness to compromise for the moment without losing sight of the desired end. One issue, the constitutional struggle in Prussia, he quickly pushed into the background, in effect eliminated. He had already told the troublesome House of Deputies that only the government could carry on foreign policy, and that 'if we need to go to war we will do so, whether you consent or not.' Now he proceeded to close their sessions for a year, by the end of which time the fate of the duchies was sealed. The Federal Diet, however, and the claims of Augustenburg, could not be disposed of in so speedy or high-handed a fashion; there he had to compromise for a time, until a military success could clear a path. That meant an invasion of Denmark, and, with much effort, by the beginning of 1864 he managed to bring both his king and Austria to the point of demanding the immediate revocation of the new Danish constitution, with the assurance that this would bring war. As

Denmark refused to give way, the two powers invaded Schleswig, since Holstein was already occupied by German federal forces. With the capture of the Düppel forts by the Prussians in April the way was open for a wider invasion of Jutland, which Denmark could not hope to withstand alone.

Therewith Bismarck was in a better position to deal with the attempt at mediation by outside powers, chiefly by Britain, out of which emerged an international conference held in London (April to June 1864). But although the conference secured a six weeks' armistice it entirely failed to reach a solution of the problem of the duchies, in part from its own disagreements, but also through Bismarck's efforts. And since no one was prepared to fight for the integrity of Denmark, within a month from the reopening of hostilities the Danes were compelled to sue for terms. Meanwhile the federal forces in Holstein were elbowed out of the way, and thereby it became clearer that the *Bund* was to have no say in determining the fate of the duchies. Likewise the Duke of Augustenburg, whose chances of succession to the duchies had for a time seemed so bright, with even Bismarck in unwilling agreement, could now be pushed aside like (in Bismarck's rustic metaphor) the ox that had set the plough in motion. The duchies naturally were not allowed to decide their own fate. That was to be settled at the peace conference held in the late summer of 1864 at Vienna. There Denmark gave up the duchies (together with the adjoining smaller Duchy of Lauenburg) to Austria and Prussia jointly. It remained to be seen how they would dispose of what Bismarck later on truthfully if somewhat boastfully described as the bag of their joint hunt.

V. THE EXTRUSION OF AUSTRIA

In the meantime Bismarck could preen himself on having achieved something positive. He could no longer be regarded merely as an uncompromising champion of the claims of the Crown and the bitter opponent of Prussian liberalism. True, he was losing the goodwill of thorough-going conservatives such as Gerlach, and had as yet won no general popularity. But that mattered little to him in comparison with the fact that he had won the confidence of the old king, and was becoming so successful in managing him that soon an acute if disrespectful observer could report that he had William in his pocket.[1] For he had given him a measure of military success and prestige, and the prospect of territorial gain. Within a year he had secured for him personally (by a cash payment to Austria) the little Duchy of Lauenburg, adjacent to Holstein. And such gains, whether material or immaterial, meant loss to his opponents, ever a heartening thing for a fighter like Bismarck, now elevated to Count in reward for his work. The liberals had been unable to prevent him from raising money to carry on a war, and were in danger of being undermined by the potent weapons of military

[1] Cf. Roon's remark to Bismarck apropos Emperor William's dislike of Bismarck's policy in the *Kulturkampf*. Bismarck was grumbling that he tried but could not please the emperor. 'I am a *Junker*, a soldier, and I wish to obey him.' 'Yes,' replied Roon, 'you want to, but you don't.' (M. Morier, *Memoirs*, vol. ii, 1911, p. 259.)

and political success. The *Bund*, ignored by Prussia and left in the lurch by Austria, was more than ever conscious of its impotence. And to Austria herself the victory in Denmark had brought embarrassment rather than gain, since she did not want a new Austrian Netherlands, and by her co-operation with Prussia she had lost influence and prestige in Germany, with no compensation elsewhere. True, Bismarck during the crisis had spoken of his alliance with Austria as 'a pillar of his political faith,' but it was in fact merely a piece of temporary scaffolding, to be discarded when it had served its turn.

Yet Austria was still a great power, in the eyes of Europe in general still stronger than Prussia. And although she might have no use for the duchies herself, it was inconceivable that having helped to win them she would allow Prussia to seize them for herself without opposition, even to war. Such a war, however, Bismarck had long foreseen, and proposed to use not merely as a means of securing the duchies but also to extrude Austria from Germany, and if possible to round out and extend Prussian territory and power. Therewith the whole of Germany, and its organization in the *Bund* of 1815, were involved. In view of Bismarck's later achievement of the closer unity of Germany under Prussia, with all that was to mean in terms of prestige and power, it was not unnatural perhaps that Germans, and Prusso-German historians, should see the work of Bismarck from 1864 (if not from 1862 or before) in terms of a considered and continuing policy to bring about that wider union. But the truth is that at this stage, as to a large extent throughout, Bismarck was concerned with Prussia, seeking *her* extension, *her* power, and *her* prestige. The German problem comes in as part of the Prussian problem, rather than as an end in itself. 'For myself,' he said in June 1866 to the Italian ambassador in discussing possible concessions to France for Napoleon's benevolent neutrality in the coming war with Austria, 'I am much less German than Prussian, and would agree without difficulty to the cession of the whole area between the Rhine and the Mosel.' (Most of this area was Bavarian, but a goodish slice was Prussian, and Bismarck knew, and admitted, that the king would never agree to give this up; he later denied the whole story.) His policy during the years 1864–6 is one of opposition to, and indeed contempt for, the *Bundestag* and the national interests it represented. He pushed its troops out of Holstein, denied it any claim to a share in the settlement of the duchies, and finally, in June 1866, withdrew from it to ease his path to war on *Bund* members and the seizure of *Bund* territory.

To the preparation for the struggle with Austria Bismarck bent his main energies during the next two years. War, he knew well enough, was a risky business. For the military arrangements and plan of campaign he relied upon the labours of Roon, as Minister of War, and Moltke, Chief of the General Staff, and it was largely through their efforts that when the test came the new Prussian army showed itself superior to the Austrian in speed of mobilization and action, organization, discipline, and quality of command. Moltke, while no field commander, was a military genius of the highest order, and the Prussian army was now equipped with its bolt-action, breech-loading rifle, the Dreyse 'needle gun,' the use of which had been gradually extended since 1841. The fire-power which it conferred was to outweigh the Austrian superiority in artillery and cavalry. On the domestic political side Bismarck failed to carry the liberal majority of the Prussian House of Deputies with him, although there were attempts at compromise from their side which the king rather than Bismarck refused to meet. So he fell back on his former methods of crushing or outwitting them, and when he failed to get from them either a war loan or a budget, he closed and then dissolved the *Landtag* after a short session early in 1866, and carried on the war without aid from them. More important than the approval or support of the *Landtag* was it to carry the king with him, and this could only be done step by step, until he could bring William to the point where he was prepared to break with so long and strong a tradition of friendship with Habsburg rulers as to be ready to war against Francis Joseph.

To achieve this Bismarck had to make it appear that Austria was injuring Prussia in some way. No one could be more skilled at this than Bismarck, more capable of 'making the worse appear the better part,' and to help it there flowed from Berlin to Vienna a stream of complaints of Austria's sins of omission or commission in relation to their joint possession of the duchies, which both influenced the king and provided excuse for such actions as the Prussian seizure of Kiel as a naval base. In the summer of 1865 an effort was made to deal with the growing differences between the two powers by the compromise of Gastein (14th August 1865), whereby the indivisible duchies were divided, provisionally at least, Holstein going to Austria, Schleswig to Prussia. This suited Bismarck well enough for the time, since Prussia could now 'dig herself in' in Schleswig, and prepare for the next stage, the gaining of Holstein; meanwhile Gastein had, in Bismarck's well-known phrase, 'papered over the cracks' appearing between the former allies. The wide criticism of the settlement, which the English statesman Clarendon compared to the partition of Poland, moved him not at all. Rather did he intensify his complaints in what to-day would be termed his 'cold war' against Austria, until her patience began to be exhausted, and she began to protest more firmly against such treatment.

Meanwhile Bismarck was increasingly concerned with preparing the diplomatic background for the coming struggle. After years of telling others what Prussian foreign policy should be he was now master of it, and a master he proved to be of such 'high policy' for the next quarter of a century. It can hardly be said that he raised its level; rather is the reverse true. The only criterion was success, and even his admirer Treitschke could note with regret about this time the absence in Bismarck of any conception of moral forces in the world. It was not, of course, that all his fellow and rival actors on this stage were in a position to throw stones at him in this regard, least of all the man whose attitude at this moment gave him most concern, Napoleon III. And there was nothing new in his admixture of bullying and deceit, nothing that had not been practised by other rulers or ministers at times. But Bismarck's tenure of office was so long, and his success and power so outstanding, that his influence could not but be both great and lasting. This was above all, of course, the case in Germany itself, where Bismarck worship was to become not merely a fashion but a faith drawing not merely the crowd, but the instructed, the champions of intellectual freedom, with ill results on the national thinking. And inevitably this faith accepted not merely Bismarckian diplomacy, but also to a greater or lesser extent his methods of government, with results no less serious for German political development or lack of it.

Closest to hand, although not most important, in Bismarck's consideration of the attitude of other states to a struggle over the headship of Germany, must necessarily be the lesser states of the *Bund*. He was well aware of the preference for Austria and the dislike of Prussia in the southern German states (though the government of Baden was friendly), but rightly took little account of any military power they might bring against Prussia, save for Bavaria. He clung to his view that the proffer of universal and direct suffrage for a German parliament was a good card to play for general support. Contemptuous of the governments of these lesser states, he was rough and threatening with most of them, notably with Saxony, but tried to detach Bavaria from the Austrian side by suggesting that she might succeed to the Austrian hegemony in the south. In Bavaria the philosopher-king, Maximilian II, was now (1864) succeeded by his young son Ludwig II, aged nineteen, little prepared for ruling, and already a confirmed Romantic, more concerned to establish his hero Wagner in Munich than with political issues. Yet Ludwig was by no means lacking in either intelligence or concern for his own and Bavarian independence. His chief minister, Pfordten, was jealous of Austria, but neither he nor Ludwig could be brought to join forces with Prussia. In the end Bismarck broke with the *Bund*, with its pro-Austrian sympathies, and went his way, leaving the South German states to join Austria and share in her defeat.

In the broader field of European diplomacy Bismarck could feel pretty sure that neither Russia nor Britain would interfere directly or immediately if a civil war opened in Germany, and he had every hope of a short conflict. But the French emperor was another matter. As a Napoleon he was almost an interferer by definition. He had intruded into France and made himself emperor. He had interfered against Austria in Italy, and had been rewarded for his efforts on behalf of Italian independence and unity by Nice and Savoy. True, by the middle sixties his star was declining; his interference in Mexico was going badly, his health was poor, and criticism was developing in France. But he could by no means be disregarded, and a war in Germany might afford him an admirable way of reviving his prestige.

Bismarck had cultivated Napoleon's acquaintance, had indeed favoured an alliance with him, and knew that he was not unfriendly to Prussia or, within limits, to the cause of German nationality. But he would certainly object (and all France with him) to the complete unification of Germany under Prussia, as to any great disturbance of the balance of power in central

Europe. And with equal certainty he would expect to receive for any material extension of Prussian territory or power some compensation (a tip —*Trinkgeld*—as Bismarck contemptuously called it), some expansion of French territory towards the Rhine. One all-important service Napoleon did render to Bismarck, by encouraging the new kingdom of Italy to ally with Prussia; Bismarck needed this alliance to divide the Austrian forces, while the Italians wanted Venice. There was little trust on either side, but after much haggling a treaty of alliance was finally signed (8th April 1866) by which Bismarck had to produce his war against Austria within three months. But although the question of reward for Napoleon's goodwill was discussed, as at Biarritz between the emperor and Bismarck, in October 1865, Napoleon was a little diffident in naming the specific Belgian, Luxemburg, or German Rhenish territory he had in mind. And although all these were mentioned then or later, it suited Bismarck very well to leave the matter vague. Each party hoped to outwit the other and do better for himself at a more critical moment, Napoleon hoping to interfere or mediate in a protracted or indecisive war, Bismarck hoping that there would be no opportunity for Napoleon to interfere with any dangerous effect.

After infinite scheming and provocation, designed so as to make Austria appear the aggressor, Bismarck at length got his war, which opened on 14th June 1866. But instead of Prussia finding herself in need of mediation, or of a prolonged and indecisive conflict, the Prussian victory at Königgrätz (Sadowa) on the Elbe in north-western Bohemia on 3rd July brought a swift and overwhelming decision.[1] Austria sued for peace, and with the signing of the peace preliminaries at Nikolsburg (Mikulov) in Moravia on 26th July the Six Weeks War came to an end. Nor had Austria alone been defeated. The North German states of Hesse-Cassel, Hanover, and Saxony had been overrun with but one momentary check, in Hanover. The South German states which had taken the side of Austria had shared in her defeat in a series of lesser engagements. Bavaria indeed, after mobilizing, had refused to leave her own borders when she might have aided Hanover, or perhaps even have turned the scale in Bohemia, but she too shared in the defeat. The Austrian success in Italy at the battle of Custozza (24th June) whilst it destroyed the Italian hope of liberating Venice, availed Austria nothing in the north, and in her extremity she ceded Venice (via Napoleon III) to Italy, thus losing there also. It might seem indeed that with such swift and complete success all Bismarck had to do was to allow the fruits of victory to fall into his lap. The truth was very different. Never did he work so hard and under so much pressure of time. It was the first clear revelation of his diplomatic genius, the astonishing combination in him of ruthless and

[1] The *Roman Journals* of the eminent German historian, Gregorovius, long a resident there, give us some idea of the overwhelming effect on opinion of the Prussian victory at Königgrätz: 'Rome, 8th July. The entire Prussian campaign has no parallel in the history of the world. Its rapidity, magnificent as a thunderstorm, excites universal admiration. . . . Deeds that took Frederick the Great seven years to accomplish, his grandson accomplishes in seven days . . . 'Rome, 14th July. The battle of Sadowa turns out to be one of the most terrible in history, and will prove also to be one of the most important. The consequences of the battle of Sadowa are at least as follows: the unification of Germany through Prussia, the consummation of Italian independence, the fall of the temporal power of the Papacy, the deposition of France from the dominion she has usurped over Europe . . .'

unresting energy, adaptability to every change in the wind, yet firm grasp of what he wanted, and pursuance of those ends by every means available.

The making of peace was indeed a very complicated affair, involving many different parties and issues. There was the settlement of northern Germany, the making of peace with both Austria and the South German states. And in all these Prussia's neighbours to east and west, but particularly Napoleon III, took a lively and active interest. For on the eve of Königgrätz Francis Joseph had invited French aid in negotiating an armistice with Italy, and immediately after that decisive day Napoleon had offered his mediation between Austria and Prussia, an offer which Bismarck unwillingly accepted. The settlement of the extent of Prussian gains in northern Germany presented its own problems. William would have liked to salve his conscience by leaving the former rulers of the states absorbed by Prussia some small fragments over which they could play at ruling, but Bismarck would have none of this. Both Austria and France refused to agree to the desired Prussian annexation of Saxony, and the Tsar of Russia's relationship to the Grand Duke of Hesse-Darmstadt prevented the seizure of most of the northern part of his duchy. Napoleon likewise insisted upon the provision for a plebiscite by the Danes in northern Schleswig, to decide whether they desired to return to Danish rule; but this clause had to wait fifty years for fulfilment. In the end Prussia took over the two Danish duchies, Hanover, Hesse-Cassel, Nassau, and the Free City of Frankfurt (which was very severely treated by the Prussians), in all some four million new subjects. There was no question, as in Cavour's annexations in Italy, of plebiscites, and many of Prussia's new citizens, particularly in Hanover and Frankfurt, became so unwillingly and long retained their dislike of their new condition. Nevertheless, Prussia now consolidated her territory from west to east, and secured far freer access to both the Baltic and the North Seas, with the important harbour of Kiel. Thereby, continuing the settlement of 1815, the balance between east and west in Prussia was further modified in favour of the west, though the *Junkers*, with Bismarck and the monarchy behind them, were still strongly entrenched beyond the Elbe.

The settlement with Austria herself presented even larger issues. Bismarck was determined to exclude Austria from Germany, and had not hesitated to try to stir up the Magyars, and even the Czechs, against Vienna. But he did not wish to destroy Austria, since, as he remarked, 'we shall need her support later.' He had first of all to curb the desire of the king and the army leaders, flushed with success, to march triumphantly into Vienna, and to take Austrian territory. Only after stormy scenes, and with the help of his former opponent the Crown Prince, did he prevail upon William to be content with peace terms moderate enough for Austria to accept them without long delay. For to Bismarck speed in agreeing upon peace terms was of the utmost importance, in order to forestall interference from outside, whether from Russia or France. The Tsar of Russia was naturally concerned at the sudden and violent overthrow of the great settlement of 1815 in central Europe, as with the unseating of legitimate rulers in northern Germany, and proposed a European congress to regulate matters. To this Bismarck replied by the rather absurd threat to raise Poland against Russia, but later (when he had got his peace) made some amends by offering to support Russian demands for the removal of the clause in the peace terms of 1856 which barred her warships from the Black Sea. The suggestion of a European congress was still-born.

The effects of the Napoleonic mediation were diminished by the speed with which Bismarck carried through his negotiations for the peace preliminaries at Nikolsburg. Napoleon agreed to the Austrian exclusion from Germany, and in the final treaty signed at Prague (23rd August 1866) Austria lost no territory, paid a moderate indemnity, and agreed both to the dissolution of the old *Bund* and that Prussia should form a new one for northern Germany. Napoleon was insistent that the states of South Germany should set up an independent *Bund* of their own, and a clause to this effect was duly included in the Prague treaty. But although Bismarck agreed to this, he took steps to nullify it in advance. He softened the terms of the peace treaties with the South German states on condition that they signed secret defensive and offensive alliances with Prussia, giving her command of their forces in case of war; Wurtemberg and Baden were opposed to a southern union headed by Bavaria in any case.

Bismarck was no less successful in countering the inevitable demand by France for 'compensation' in view of the large gains secured by Prussia. For Napoleon had failed to take the one step which could exert real pressure on Bismarck and Prussia, the movement of troops to the unguarded Rhine. Hence when the French ambassador, Benedetti, sounded Bismarck on some secret arrangements which would restore the French boundaries of 1814 and give her Luxemburg, or West Rhenish lands of Bavaria and Hesse-Darmstadt, together with Mainz, Bismarck at first temporized, but hastened his final peace negotiations with both Austria and the South German states. These secured he took a stiffer stand, and France got nothing, whilst he emerged with the draft of a French treaty embodying such suggestions, which he was able to use with great effect in 1870. Napoleon had, of course, no real claims to Belgian, Luxemburg, or German Rhenish land, yet to emerge from the crisis with empty hands when Prussia secured so much was a serious blow to the weakening empire, as to France. To an observer such as Quinet it was a 'monstrous error' thus to have aided the unification of Germany, since a united Germany would inevitably be a threat, and more, to France. In fact, the victory of Prussia, and the resulting reorganization of Germany, was to mark the close of a French ascendancy in Europe which had lasted, with temporary set-backs, since France destroyed the Spanish ascendancy in the days of Richelieu. Thus Bismarck's mixture of daring and moderation in war and diplomacy, a real 'Bismarck touch,' had yielded spectacular results in record time, and at amazingly small cost to Prussia in men and money. True, he was neither king nor army commander. But neither William nor Moltke would or could have embarked on any such bold courses, much less have secured such amazing results, without him.

And the achievements of Frederick II, great as they were, had been incomparably more expensive and long drawn out, and they had not yielded such immediately significant returns.

Nor did all this comprise the whole of Bismarck's achievements. He had left Berlin for the campaign at odds with the House of Deputies, and in general mistrusted and disliked rather than popular, as was shown in the lack of sympathy when someone tried to kill him. He returned little over a month later to be received with jubilation. He promptly showed his political wisdom and shrewdness by his insistence, against the royal will, in requesting from the newly elected *Landtag* an Act of Indemnity for the government's previous illegalities with regard to the budget, with a pledge to respect parliamentary rights therein in the future. This was indeed a master stroke. The Act appeared to be a real olive branch of peace, and the House of Deputies, moved like the whole country by his dazzling achievements, voted three to one for its acceptance. In fact, it was rather an apple of discord, for it split the liberal-radical opposition; half the progressive party voted for it, half against. Thereby the cause of liberalism in Prussia, and so in Germany, was seriously weakened, and Bismarck was on the way, in his own words, 'to defeat parliamentarism by parliamentarism.' He and the king, in the face of parliamentary opposition, had created the army they wanted, and used it with conspicuous success. They had no intention of surrendering control over it, and the king, at least, declared that he would act again in the same way if necessary. Hence the Indemnity Act was little more than a skilfully concocted sop, with little significance in terms of the hoped for evolution towards a real parliamentary regime in Prussia, or a Germany to be ruled by Prussia, so long as Bismarck and the old king ruled and reigned respectively. Its passing may be said to mark the effective end of the great constitutional struggle in Prussia and the turn to a new epoch, for though the issues continued to be alive and debated, they had in fact been settled in favour of the Crown and the royal ministers.

Thus, much of the significance of the victory of 1866 lay in the triumph of the old Prussia, of Crown and army, linked up with the landed aristocracy and gentry and the loyal conservative officials. As the liberal Twesten sadly remarked in 1867: '*Junker* rule and military absolutism will outlast our day.' This meant more than the stultification of liberal political hopes; it had social and indeed cultural implications as well. The old Prussian three-class society had been slowly breaking down under the impact of the growing industrialism and liberal-democratic ideas, with some contribution, slight as yet, from revolutionary socialism. But the victory of 1866, confirmed in 1870, gave new life to the old system, though with certain changes. Under the new more universal system of military service the military quality of the Prussian state became more marked again. It continued to permeate Prussia, and to spread in varying degrees through Germany, so that the last Minister for War of the Weimar Republic, General Groener, could still describe the army as 'the rock upon which the State is built.' This military state was also a class state, wherein a few gave orders and most obeyed, wherein discipline, order, and obedience were esteemed as the highest virtues. Civil liberty and equality could not thrive in it, and the old ideal of a 'people's army' survived only in the programmes of the emerging socialist party. The jurists might claim that Germany was a *Rechtsstaat*, but it could never be that in the fullest sense of the word. Bismarck, no professional soldier, wore a military uniform when he appeared in parliament since (to parody the Shakespearian phrase of the Forest of Arden) 'military was the only wear,' and the army took ninety per cent or more of the budget.

This helped to preserve the position of the Crown as the war lord and the old class divisions, since the aristocracy and the officer class were so closely connected. The system likewise found support from intellectuals such as Treitschke and a host of followers, who now, so differently from Kant or Goethe, saw the German spirit and genius expressed in this way. The trend did not prevent the economic development of the country; it could even stimulate this by the state paternalism which was part of the Prussian tradition. But the social stratification continued there too. The rising upper middle class of industrialists and financiers, at first jealous of aristocratic privilege, later came to terms with the landed class east of the Elbe on the basis of mutual advantage from tariffs for both agriculture and industry. At the other extreme, however, urban labour likewise developed in a strongly class-conscious way, and in the absence of a robust and fruitful liberal-democratic tradition drew supporters of democratic development, as Bebel, for example, into the discipleship of Marx and Lassalle, to build up the great social democratic party of Germany.

More immediately visible than the foregoing results was the effect of the victory of 1866 on the political parties in Prussia and the new organization of northern Germany. The change in parties was indicated in the Prussian *Landtag* elected on the day of Königgrätz, which accepted the Indemnity Act, but it was more plainly manifest in that elected in the following year. The conservatives were offended by Bismarck's readiness to ally with revolutionary Italy, his disregard of legitimism, and his concession to liberalism in the Indemnity Act, and the breach thus made was to last for some time. An important minority of them, however, calling themselves 'free' conservatives, and composed chiefly of higher nobility and officials, declared their intention of supporting the government. A middle Catholic group, naturally opposed to the war with Catholic Austria, now disappeared. The most important change, however, resulted from the split already referred to in the liberal-progressive ranks. The suddenly opened prospect of the speedy achievement of national unity brought much heart-searching there as to the wisdom of continued opposition to the man who had made that possible. 'Liberals must rid themselves of their old illusions,' wrote the liberal Baumgarten. 'The day of Ideals is over,' cried the Hanoverian liberal Miquel. First a small group, then a larger one, declared its intention to accept the Indemnity Act as closing the old struggle, to support the government's foreign policy (and therewith the new military system), the annexations, above all the closer union of Germany. At the same time the new party reaffirmed its faith in liberal principles, and its intention to work for the rights of parliament over legislation and finance, for full freedom of speech and the press, local self-government, and the reduction of taxation.

There was an obvious inconsistency between the two parts of this programme, and the leaders of these national liberals, as they called themselves, Twesten, Forckenbeck, Lasker, Unruh, with Bennigsen from Hanover and others, realized the difficulty of working with Bismarck and the old king. Time was to show that their fears were fully justified. The party title they adopted, however, indicated precisely enough the precedence which their national feeling took over their liberalism, and the triumph of the one was to mean the defeat of the other. Their great achievement was to aid in the organization first of the North German Confederation, then of united Germany, in ten years of fruitful effort. They had a strong backing of public opinion in Prussia, as was shown by the fact that in 1867 they won a hundred seats in the House of Deputies; and they were to constitute the largest party in the *Reichstag* of the North German *Bund* and then in that of the completed *Reich*. Yet all the former liberals did not follow them. A minority of the left wing of the progressives still held to their liberal-democratic principles, including such men as Virchow, Hoverbeck, Schulze-Delitzsch, and Waldeck, but they were not strong enough to be a serious obstacle to the support on which Bismarck could now hope to count.

How far Bismarck was from any thought of real concession to liberal ideas was shown by the draft of the constitution which he and his advisers drew up at the end of 1866 for the new North German *Bund*, to be composed of twenty-two states. In this draft Bismarck was concerned to secure the predominance of Prussia; to preserve its identity, which meant that he favoured a looser rather than a closer union; and to prevent the parliament of the new *Bund* from exercising any undue control. Indeed the draft gave the new assembly little or no power over the executive and little room to legislate. As for the budget, over nine-tenths of it was for the army, and this was to be set at so much per head of the population, and revisable only every ten years. Since the customs duties were set by the *Zollverein* there remained little financial work for the *Reichstag* to do. On this basis Bismarck could better afford to allow the election of this body by universal and direct male suffrage, the more so as he intended that voting should be open, whereby the government and landowners could exercise due influence over the voters. He had long meditated such a franchise, believing that he would thereby tap a reservoir of sound conservative (and amenable) support. So, like Disraeli in England in this same year 1867, he made his 'leap in the dark' and in the end with somewhat the same disillusioning result. The upper chamber or Federal Council (*Bundesrat*) was based largely upon the old *Bundestag*, made up of delegates from the various states, with the significant difference that as Prussia had now absorbed the votes held in the older body by the states she had annexed, she had a solid block of seventeen out of forty-three votes, and so in practice could sway enough votes to secure a majority. Prussia was also to hold the presidency (*Präsidium*) over the *Bund*, with the right of deciding on war and peace; her king was the head of its army and navy, its diplomatic and certain other services. In theory executive power was shared with the Federal Council, but in fact this was exercised by the King of Prussia's chief minister, Bismarck, whose position and powers needed no definition.

It was the first and perhaps the most notable achievement of the national liberals that in the Constituent Assembly to which the draft constitution was submitted in the spring of 1867, after approval with slight alteration by the various states, they managed to amend the illiberal draft of Bismarck very materially. Whilst they did not possess a majority in the Assembly, they comprised the largest party there, some eighty strong, and were able to draw support from both right and left of their central position, sufficient to force Bismarck to accept many (though not all) of their amendments. They were concerned primarily to extend the limited authority of the *Bund* over its members, and to enlarge (one might almost say create) the power of the elected *Reichstag*. They were able to extend the competence of the *Bund's* central authority in a variety of matters such as taxation, police, communications, even railways. And some of this added authority came to the *Reichstag* itself. Thus the *Reichstag* was to share with the *Bundesrat* the control over the annual budget, though that for the army was to run unchanged until 1871. Important also for the *Reichstag* were provisions for the regular recalling of a prorogued *Reichstag*, as for the election of a new one within a limited time after a dissolution; for secret instead of open voting in elections; for permission for officials to be elected as members; for the privilege of free speech for its members; and for the publication of debates. Payment of members they could not secure; Bismarck had too great a fear of encouraging professional law-makers or critics. They likewise failed to secure a ministry responsible to the *Reichstag*; the best they could gain was a provision that one minister, the chancellor, i.e. Bismarck, should countersign the acts of the presidency, and so assume a certain responsibility for such acts before the *Reichstag*, though it was not clear as to whom he should be responsible.

Yet these were considerable achievements, only obtained by dint of unremitting effort. And Bismarck only conceded them because he feared to jeopardize the union and lose the support of his new-found allies. But accept them he did (though he was later to evade some of them), and as the lesser states also accepted them the new North German *Bund* of thirty million people came officially into being on 1st July 1867. In its constitution it represented a compromise between the autocratic views of Bismarck and the parliamentary pattern spreading over western Europe, with even France now moving in that direction. The King of Prussia still held control of the army, which one observer, Camphausen, defined as the essence of the new union. The *Reichstag* had managed to get some control of the purse strings, and it had a possible lever in the weak financial basis of the *Bund*, though only the future could show how far this would enable it to control the ministry. In terms of territory the new Confederation united all northern

The Unifica

SWEDEN

BALTIC SEA

Memel

POMERANIA

Danzig

WEST
PRUSSIA

Königsberg

EAST
PRUSSIA

Stettin

ENBURG

erlin

POSEN

R. Vistula

Warsaw

RUSSIAN
POLAND

Dresden

ONY

SILESIA

Breslau

plitz

HEMIA

ad

Prague

Sadowa

Königgrätz

MORAVIA

Troppau

Olmütz

GALICIA

Nikolsburg

AUSTRIA

R. Danube

Vienna

Pressburg

zburg

HUNGARY

Buda Pesth

stein

Germany as far as the river Main, thus leaving out only the four South German states of Bavaria, Wurtemberg, Baden, and Hesse-Darmstadt. And these four were joined with Prussia by military treaties, and with the north by the economic ties of the *Zollverein*, shortly to be developed into a national Customs Parliament. Complete union was bound to come, though it was widely agreed that this might take a generation to achieve. Such a view was expressed by Bismarck himself, and King William declared in 1868 that he did not expect to see the union completed, although his son might do so.

VI. THE COMPLETION OF UNITY

The North German Confederation was to last in its existing boundaries and some of its forms only four years. But then it was to be enlarged into the German Empire, with but little change, continuing thereafter for nearly half a century. Hence its structure, and the nature of its development in what were to be formative years, were of considerable significance, since they were to condition much later history. It was a unique constitutional creation, above all in the fact that one out of the twenty-two states composing it contained five-sixths of the total population, and so, on the basis of universal suffrage, the vast majority of the members of the *Reichstag*. This body met in Berlin, the capital of the largest state, alongside the Prussian *Landtag* to which many of its members had belonged and continued to belong. True, the *Reichstag* of the new *Bund* now came to occupy the centre of the political stage. But the Prussian *Landtag* was still important, as was also the fact that its House of Deputies continued to be elected on the old three-class franchise, and so with its conservative House of Lords and its imperfectly developed political life provided for Bismarck a useful brake on the *Reichstag*. And both the headship and the executive of the new *Bund* were Prussian, as was the control over the army and foreign affairs, with much of the administration and economic life of the new structure.

Prussia had her own problem in these years immediately after 1866 in the integration of Hanover and the other new provinces she had acquired by conquest. As in the Rhineland after 1815 Prussian officials and military men were stiff and high-handed, so that anti-Prussian feeling in Hanover, Schleswig-Holstein, and Frankfurt persisted. The old and blind King George V of Hanover, although he made terms with Prussia, refused to abandon hope for the recovery of his kingdom, and a small 'Guelph Legion' was formed for this purpose. Bismarck revenged himself by seizing a considerable part of the ousted king's wealth, theoretically to fight the 'reptile' Guelphs. In fact the money provided a most useful fund, free of any control, which Bismarck used throughout his term of office to buy support for his policies, whether in the press or elsewhere, and which by an apt inversion of his original term became known as the 'reptile fund.'

The first *Reichstag* of the new *Bund* was elected in August 1867, and naturally reflected the colouring of both the Prussian *Landtag* and the recent Constituent Assembly. The national liberals were the strongest party, and with other middle groups could command a majority. To the Prussian leaders Forckenbeck, Twesten, and Lasker were now added Bennigsen and Miquel from Hanover. As they were now less a purely Prussian party they were the more concerned to build up the new *Bund* and to complete the union of the whole country. Their neighbours on the left, the progressives, though they had won all the six Berlin seats, were too weak with only thirty members to fight the battle for democracy alone, but could be of importance in a crisis or a fight with their old antagonist, now the chancellor. At the extreme left, of little or no seeming significance as yet, 'a cloud no bigger than a man's hand,' were half a dozen members representing Germany's working class, W. Liebknecht and Bebel from the Saxon group, Schweitzer and Reinke from the followers of Lassalle, the forerunners of the social democratic party. On the right a strong conservative party, nearly all Prussians from east of the Elbe, was mainly concerned to preserve the rights of old Prussia, distrustful of Bismarck and his new union, yet not prepared to oppose outright a creation headed by their king. Their neighbours the independent conservatives, smaller in number, contained a sprinkling of the new capitalist class, were less particularist, and more ready to co-operate with the new regime. Finally, whilst there was no Catholic party as such, there were a number of opponents of the results of 1866 from Hanover and elsewhere, who found a leader in the gifted Hanoverian Catholic, Windthorst.

The outstanding achievement of this new body was the building up of the new union. The extension of the Prussian military system through the newly annexed lands and the *Bund* states, with the new units officered (save for Saxony) by Prussians, and all under the Prussian king, lay outside their scope, and was efficiently carried through under Roon and Moltke. But in the less well-marked social, economic, and legal fields the *Reichstag* did a notable work in the three years following its creation. Here Bismarck was wisely content to leave governmental activity in the able hands of Rudolf Delbrück, head of the *Bund* Chancery, long experienced in such matters, free trading in opinion, nationally minded, and so the more ready to work with the predominantly middle-class national liberals in changes which not merely united the states of the *Bund*, but helped to modernize their economic life. Together they carried through the *Reichstag* measures providing for freedom of movement within the states of the *Bund* and the lessening of police controls; for greater freedom of trade and industry; to aid in the abolition of the old stiff guild organization of industry; for liberty to both employers and workers to combine; for a common system of weights, measures, and postal services. They gave more freedom for the formation of joint stock companies, encouraged the development of banking and credit institutions, revised commercial law and provided for a common criminal law code, increased religious equality, removed river tolls, made provision for a *Bund* consular service, and the use of the black-white-red *Bund* flag. In all this the government and the majority in the *Reichstag* managed to work together to the advantage of the new state and the growing middle-class interests. The workers too benefited by changes which their associations (*Arbeitervereine*) had been demanding for the past decade.

But these harmonious relations between government and *Reichstag* did not extend to the field of finance, or to the general question of the responsibility of the ministry to the parliament. There the old issue of the Prussian House of Deputies was carried over into the new *Reichstag*. By the constitution of the new *Bund* the charges for the army, which took most of its budget, were fixed for four years. But the limited financial resources of the *Bund* proved inadequate for the vast army expenditure, and the little states found themselves faced with an intolerable burden of additional so-called 'matricular contributions.' Prussia too felt the strain. Bismarck proposed to raise more money by increasing the existing indirect taxes on brandy, beer, sugar, and other commodities, taxes which could be manipulated without reference to the *Reichstag*. The national liberals and their allies, however, proposed an income tax, a direct tax which Bismarck disliked, partly because it would be subject to parliamentary control. In the end the so-called matricular contributions remained, but the *Reichstag* won the right to set the amount of these each year, which was a material gain, but did not make for easier relations between parliament and chancellor. On a similar attempt by the *Reichstag* to interfere in the matter of a loan for the development of a *Bund* navy and coastal defences, however, the liberals were defeated, as they were also in their effort to make the ministry more responsible to the *Reichstag*. Thus the difference remained, dependent for its solution upon forces not available to a representative assembly, or a party which had sold part of its birthright, but capable of being mobilized by a bold and defiant statesman such as Bismarck.

Meanwhile the four South German states looked with mingled feelings at the erection of the new *Bund* formed by their compatriots north of the Main. There was sympathy for the national cause, especially among the educated middle class, with hope for the speedy completion of national unity. There was likewise recognition of the solid benefits conferred by the *Zollverein*, as of Prussian military achievements and power. The Grand Duke of Baden was strongly pro-Prussian, as were individuals and groups throughout the south, and all four of the southern states had signed military treaties with Prussia. On the other hand the south was still noticeably different from the north, particularly from Prussia, the more so as one got further away from the great south-north highway of the Rhine valley, through old Swabia with its claims to leadership in German culture, and eastwards into Bavaria, with its five million people, pattern and pillar of German particularism, an original *Stammesherzogtum* (tribal duchy), predominantly Catholic and with a strong ultramontanist strain, open to Italian as to Austrian influences, as Baden was to French and Swiss. Backward in some ways as compared to the north, the southern Germans enjoyed more political freedom than the people of Prussia, life was less regimented, the old middle class of the 'little man' survived better there, they disliked the militarism and bureaucratic quality of Prussia, and feared its expansionist thrust. Austria had been an easier overlord, likewise Catholic and more akin, and their defeat and humiliation in the war of 1866, the fate of Hanover and other northern states, the harsh treatment of Frankfurt, were not calculated to relieve fears of Prussia.

The Treaty of Prague had envisaged a South German union, but this proved impossible of attainment. Bavaria, it is true, had from 1867 to 1870 a statesman-like chief minister in Prince Hohenlohe, liberal, friendly to Prussia as to German unity. He played a part in the reorganization of the *Zollverein*, and made efforts for the closer union of the South German states, hoping then to form an alliance between this union and the North German *Bund*, with Austria also brought into the alliance. But he was disliked by the Bavarian ultramontanists, who were growing in power and who ultimately drove him out of office. King Ludwig supported him, but was withdrawing more and more from both the tasks of government and humanity in general into the solitude of the Bavarian Alps, pursuing his fantastic schemes of building and decoration at enormous expense. In Wurtemberg the king and the chief minister Varnbüler were anti-Prussian and jealous of Bavaria, in Baden the Grand Duke pursued a pro-Prussian policy, whilst both Wurtemberg and Baden were opposed to any southern union which would give Bavaria the hegemony in South Germany, in part from fear of the revival of old Bavarian schemes for expansion at their expense.

It was clear that as things were there was little hope of any overt move by the southern states to join the northern *Bund*, save for Baden, whose ruler did in fact request the entry of his state. The Luxemburg crisis of 1867 showed the feeling of the north in favour of the speedy completion of union. But the initiative lay not with the northern *Reichstag*, but with the master of northern policy, Bismarck, and he was not, for the moment, in any hurry. There were the enlarged Prussia and the northern union to set firmly on their feet. As a Prussian, a *Junker*, and a Protestant, he had never been an admirer of southern Germany. As late as 1869 he told the British ambassador that he did not care whether the southern states made a separate *Bund* or not: they were unreliable folk, and he was ready to give up both the military alliances and the Customs Union. Doubtless this was in large measure the familiar Bismarckian grumbling of the moment and intended for foreign ears. At home he was working with the national liberals, who were strongly for the completion of unity, and it was sound policy to use rather than to discourage them. Unity was bound to come, and Bismarck was fully alive to the potentialities of a united Germany under Prussia. It was his object to canalize the rising tide of national feeling (somewhat as King William had once announced his intention of canalizing the constitution of Prussia) in terms of the two primary articles of his faith as a *Realpolitiker*, Prussia and power. His great wisdom lay in not trying to force the pace in the achievement of this end until he considered the time ripe for decisive action.

This did not mean that he stood still or rested on his oars, though he had formed the habit of disappearing for lengthy periods to his newly acquired estate of Varzin in Pomerania, his health was not too good ('He eats too much, drinks too much, and works too hard,' was Gortschakoff's later comment) and his temper was somewhat uncertain. He took a decided step forward in the translation of the Customs Union (*Zollverein*) into a Customs Parliament (*Zollparlament*). The war of 1866 had broken the old ties, and the old machinery with its requirement for unanimity of voting by the member states for any change (a *liberum veto*) created difficulties for Prussia. So Bismarck decided to make a fresh start, and placed before a conference of all the members of the Customs Union a plan for a Tariff Parliament, using the *Bundesrat* and the *Reichstag* of the North German Confederation as the basis, and adding representatives of the South German states. The new Customs Parliament would take over the functions and power of the old *Zollverein* in the making of trade treaties and the regulation of tariffs, with control over certain indirect taxes (salt and tobacco). But instead of unanimity, a majority vote would suffice for action, though any overriding of Prussia was guarded against.

It was hardly to be expected that the South German states would accept the scheme without objection. Nor did they; both the Bavarian and Wurtemberg parliaments raised difficulties. At the same time these bodies were called upon to approve of the secret defence treaties made in 1866, and now published by Bismarck, a matter which likewise raised objections. But Bismarck could and did threaten to repudiate the common tariff system unless the two arrangements went through together. As he put it, 'economic partnership and military partnership go hand in hand,' and the southern states had no option but finally to accept them both. Therewith they took an important step towards fuller union with the north, since the pattern thus set of participation in an enlarged German *Bund* clearly made it more difficult for them to bring forward any alternative scheme of political relationship. True, the functions of the new Customs Parliament were limited; but they were not unimportant in their results, and the contacts made therein doubtless had some effect in accustoming south and north to work together. And in accord with the military defence treaties, the southern states now began to work more closely with Prussia in military reorganization. Yet there was still plenty of particularist and anti-Prussian feeling in the south. There was talk again of a South German union, and in Bavaria the elections of 1869 resulted in a clerical, anti-Prussian victory. It remained for Bismarck to assert his genius in another field, that of foreign policy, in order to complete the unification of the Fatherland.

The central consideration in Prussian foreign policy in the years immediately following the victory over Austria was of necessity its relations with France. Bismarck might continue to speak (as at the end of 1866) of Franco-Prussian friendship as 'the natural expression of the lasting agreement of their common interest,' but that was a mere manner of speaking. Even before 1866, whilst there had been professions of friendliness, there had never been the trust on which an alliance could be based. How could there be between two such men as Napoleon III and Bismarck? And the events of 1866 had left Bismarck conscious of his own success, of Prussian military prowess and power, well aware that Napoleon expected 'compensation,' but annoyed with the emperor's intervention and out to evade rather than support any claims on him. And Napoleon was conscious of having failed to take advantage of the situation during its course, of the decline in his prestige at home and abroad, of the change in the balance in central Europe, and of the possibility that not merely the north but the whole of Germany might be united under Prussia. Relations were inevitably cooler and were to deteriorate.

The trend showed itself in 1867 when Napoleon, as some substitute for the greater things earlier hoped for, proposed to buy the Grand Duchy of Luxemburg from the King of Holland. With the dissolution of the old German *Bund* Luxemburg was no longer politically tied to Germany, yet it was still a member of the *Zollverein*, and Prussian troops still occupied the former federal fortress at its capital. Its people, though they spoke a German dialect, had ceased to think of themselves as German, and Bismarck did not wish to include the duchy in the North German Confederation. Napoleon took the precaution secretly to sound out Britain, Austria, and Russia, who showed no opposition to his plan. Bismarck also was at first encouraging, and agreed to remove the Prussian garrison. But although the Dutch king, who needed money, was ready to sell the duchy, he refused to do so without definite Prussian approval, and to this Bismarck would not commit himself. Instead, seeing which way the wind was now blowing in Germany, he first published the secret treaties with the South German states, a rude shock to French hopes of an independent South German *Bund*, and then allowed and probably instigated a discussion in the North German *Reichstag* in which national feeling expressed itself strongly against the cession of 'this old German land.' Indeed he struck a national note himself with a declaration of German power to defend the right of German states and peoples.

The result was that the Dutch king refused at the last moment to sign the treaty of sale, and relations between France and Prussia immediately took a sharp turn for the worse. There was even talk of war, which Moltke at least would have welcomed, believing Prussia more ready for it than France. The other European powers were drawn into the crisis, and at a conference in London agreed upon a collective guarantee of the neutrality of Luxemburg and its continued possession by the Dutch royal house. Napoleon secured an agreement that Prussia should withdraw her garrison, but that was all. The blow was severely felt in France, with the fresh revelation of Bismarckian diplomacy, and marked the end of any serious pretence of good relations between the two powers. A final attempt of Napoleon to secure some economic influence over Belgium by the French purchase of Belgian railway lines in 1868–9 not merely aroused national opposition in Belgium, but saw Bismarck active in arousing European and especially British concern, and this French effort likewise ended in failure.

Thus Franco-Prussian relations worsened. We cannot say that the war which came in 1870 was inevitable, for we do not know what would have happened had the ruling powers in the two countries suddenly been changed.

But this did not happen, and Bismarck testified in his *Memoirs* to his belief 'that a Franco-German war must take place before the construction of a united Germany could be realized.' Napoleon did not want war, but French criticism of his regime and its failures was mounting and finding freer expression as his grip weakened, and he essayed the dangerous transition from an autocratic regime towards a 'liberal empire.' He could even say to the British ambassador in October 1868 that 'if Bismarck draws the South German states into the Northern Confederation our guns will go off of themselves.' And meanwhile in Germany, especially in the north, feeling was rising in favour of just that consummation, and against France, especially Napoleonic France, as the ancient enemy of Germany and German interests. Further, Bismarck was now identifying himself more openly with the national German cause, speaking rather of 'German hearts' than of 'Prussian honour' or 'Prussian power.' He was likewise concerned with the growing demands of the *Reichstag* for power, with the attitude of the South German states, with thoughts of making the King of Prussia into an emperor, which would certainly annoy France, above all with the prospect of war with France and the attitude of the other powers of Europe to such a development.

There was indeed both military and diplomatic activity on both sides. The French, with the more need of the former, enlarged their army and rearmed it with a new breech-loading rifle, the chassepot. Across the Rhine Roon and Moltke continued their methodical preparations for war. On the diplomatic side Napoleon turned to Austria and Italy, with hopes of forming a triple alliance. But with Italy he ran into the difficulty of papal Rome, so ardently desired as a capital by the Italians, yet protected by French troops which Napoleon dared not remove because of French Catholic opinion; and this proved an insurmountable obstacle to anything more than assurances of friendship. With Austria-Hungary there seemed for a time more hope of success, since both Beust, now Foreign Minister in Austria, and Francis Joseph were friendly. But Austria was by no means prepared for a possible war, and the Hungarian minister, Andrassy, was more concerned with Russian and Balkan issues than with the west. Hence in the end all that Napoleon secured was an exchange of friendly letters between the two emperors in September 1869, with no pledge of support in case of war. Meanwhile Bismarck, with no intention of allowing France an indefinite period for military preparations, had likewise been active, making lavish use of the Guelph fund to influence opinion in South Germany, but finding little response from the hostile Beust in Austria, and being met by what must have seemed to him absurd proposals for disarmament from England. From Russia, however, he secured not indeed general approval or a treaty, but an invaluable pledge to hold Austria in check should Prussia and France go to war.

Further, Bismarck early in 1869 discovered an issue which might with skilful handling either inflict a severe diplomatic defeat upon France, one perhaps fatal to the declining empire, or cause her to declare war and so appear the aggressor. This was the candidature of a Hohenzollern prince,

Leopold of Hohenzollern-Sigmaringen, for the Spanish throne, now vacant by the deposition of Queen Isabella following the revolution of 1868. The story of this Hohenzollern candidature is complicated, tortuous indeed, largely owing to Bismarck's underground activities. For, despite his denials, then and later in his *Memoirs*, there seems no doubt that he bent every effort to secure both an offer of the Crown from Spain and its acceptance by the German prince, working on King William, the head of the family, and sending secret agents, well equipped with bribes, to Spain. He had used similar means some years earlier to secure the throne of Rumania for another prince of this family, but the Spanish royal crown was a far more important prize. It was also far more serious in its implications. A Hohenzollern on the throne of Spain might, as Bismarck claimed, be worth two army corps to Prussia in a war, but to France, in addition to the blow to imperial prestige, it would mark a revival of the old Habsburg encirclement of the sixteenth century. Such a development she could not tolerate, as her government early made clear. England too warned against it, and the Hohenzollern prince himself, his father, and the old King of Prussia were reluctant to engage in the dubious and risky venture, which Bismarck's agent in Spain, Bucher, later described as 'a trap for Napoleon.'

Yet Bismarck persisted in his efforts and won them over, until a premature revelation in Madrid in July 1870, of the arrangement which Bismarck had intended should emerge as an accomplished fact, brought a veritable explosion of feeling in France. Even at this moment, however, the affair threatened to boomerang against Bismarck, since King William, left to himself whilst taking the waters at Ems near Coblenz, withdrew his previous royal approval of the candidature in response to a French protest. Bismarck's scheming was only saved by the stupidity of the French in demanding that the king would never again allow the candidature to be raised. William refused to go so far, and it was his telegram reporting this to Bismarck, now in Berlin, which the latter by skilful editing and prompt publication turned from a simple account of events into a seeming rebuff and challenge to the over-excited French, and so led to their decision for war on 15th July 1870. Prince Hohenlohe a few years later wrote [1] that after the publication 'war was inevitable.'

Thus with the 'Ems' telegram (which should really be the 'Berlin' telegram) Bismarck had successfully played again his old game of appearing to be the injured party rather than the aggressor. He strengthened this impression by publishing, as if of recent date, the unfortunate Benedetti's draft of 1866 of a treaty of alliance between France and Prussia by which France might secure Rhenish or adjacent territory, and this had an immediate effect upon both German and foreign opinion. The southern German states, after a brief attempt by Bavaria to take a stand of armed neutrality, and with decided reluctance by the King of Wurtemberg, fell into line, and therewith the path was opened which was to lead across the bloody battle-fields of France to the proclamation of German unity in the great hall at Versailles.

[1] *Memoirs*, vol. ii, p. 107.

Bavarian and Prussian joined in a common war against a common enemy, and so, as Bismarck had foreseen, could be welded together in a common political mould.

The war which thus opened in July 1870 was to last for over seven months, until the signing of an armistice in February 1871, with peace finally signed at Frankfurt on 10th May 1871. From the first, despite an outburst of French confidence, the Prusso-German army showed its superiority. It was decidedly larger, was better organized both for mobilization and for fighting, the planning and execution of operations under Moltke's direction was incomparably better; its artillery was likewise superior. The French suffered from a lack of efficient preparation and organization, above all from a divided and inadequate leadership, whether from Napoleon himself, sick and weak, his generals in the field such as Bazaine, or the War Council in Paris. Out of this confusion and weakness came the calamitous surrender of emperor and army at Sedan (2nd September), the succeeding surrender of Bazaine and his even larger army in Metz (27th October), the German advance to and siege of the French capital. Zola could rightly call his great novel of the war *La Débâcle*. Yet despite the German successes they did not achieve as in 1866 the knock-out blow on which Moltke had counted. The people of Paris swept away the discredited empire, and Gambetta proceeded, as only his fiery enthusiasm could, to build new French armies to fight further south. And although neither this nor the heroism of the Parisians in their four months' siege could avert the final defeat, yet they enabled Frenchmen to lift their heads again, and drew English and other foreign sympathy for the calamities of so great a nation.

The peace which the republican Favre tried unsuccessfully to negotiate, and which shrewd old Thiers finally concluded, involved the payment of an enormous war indemnity, with German military occupation until it was paid, and the loss of Alsace-Lorraine, excluding Belfort, but including the great north-eastern fortress of Metz, which the German generals insisted upon. Bismarck indeed, with his clearer political vision, would have taken only Alsace, dismantling Metz. He even admitted that, in addition to the French feeling of Lorraine, 'the Alsatians have become French and wish to remain so.' But as a good Prussian he shared some of the desire for conquest which national feeling in Germany, whipped up by patriots such as Treitschke, coloured with the demand for the recovery of territory once part of the old *Reich*, and agreed to the larger annexation. Therewith, however, he provided a focus for French antagonism stronger and more permanent than the memory of the defeat or the payment of the indemnity. This last indeed was paid off with quite unexpected speed.

It was characteristic of Bismarck that he accompanied his king and the high military command on campaign through northern France, to establish himself with them in Versailles during the long siege of Paris. He had done the like in 1866. Then the military men had disliked his interference with their operations, and now they excluded him from their councils as much as they could, which caused bad feeling between him and Moltke. Yet

Bismarck was busy enough. In addition to his considerable activities in connection with both war and the making of peace, and the ever watchful eye for the reaction of the European powers to the unexpectedly rapid and great German successes, he managed to carry through on French soil and whilst the war continued the all-important matter of the completion of German unity. Thereby he avoided the interference he might have met in Berlin after the war or the possibility of having to call a new constituent assembly. And he was able to make use of the general enthusiasm aroused by the successful co-operation in victory of North and South German soldiers, now at the gates of Paris.

Despite this enthusiasm, however, the task was a difficult one, the more so as it was bound up with the question of the title of the head of the new state. Whilst the agreement of Baden and little Hesse-Darmstadt to union could be assured, the hatred of the ruler of Wurtemberg for Prussia made him pro-French, and the King of Bavaria possessed a fanatical sense of his own royal importance. Further, the old King of Prussia feared the possible infection of Prussia with South German radicalism. Like his brother in 1849 he would not accept an imperial crown with any popular flavour about it, and was so deeply impregnated with loyalty to his Prussian crown that he feared to see it, as he protested, 'pushed into the background.' The Crown Prince, flushed with the success of his armies, was all for the speedy proclamation of the empire, and would have liked to use more haste and pressure than Bismarck was ready to employ on the southern states to bring it about. But he wanted for it a real House of Lords and a parliamentary ministry as in England, whereas Bismarck found the existing North German *Bundesrat* a very convenient vehicle for getting his own way, and was unalterably opposed to making his ministry responsible to the *Reichstag*. And Bavarian opinion still opposed entry into the North German *Bund*, preferring the creation of a new and looser union outside it.

Bismarck, however, went on his way with his own admixture of forthrightness and subtlety. He had one clear advantage in the disunion of the southern states, above all the jealousy between Bavaria and Wurtemberg which made it impossible for them to trust each other and so secure the strength of a common stand against so masterly a bargainer. Hence Bismarck was able to deal with each of the four states separately, calling their representatives to Versailles, and playing off the two more difficult ones against each other. Under these conditions the idea of any wider union disappeared, and it became simply a question of the terms on which the southern states would enter the North German *Bund*, to make of it a German *Reich*. This involved indeed lengthy and tedious negotiation, complicated by King Ludwig of Bavaria's refusal to commit himself to any decisions, and the King of Wurtemberg's justifiable fears that Bavaria was securing greater concessions than those being offered to himself.

Yet by the end of November 1870 all four states had signed separate treaties agreeing to the enlargement of the North German *Bund* into a German *Reich*, with the King of Prussia as emperor, so that Bismarck could joyfully announce 'German unity is achieved, and the emperorship likewise.' Over the latter indeed he still had considerable difficulty with the old king, who preferred to be Emperor of Germany, rather than German Emperor, the title Bismarck had agreed upon as less offensive to southern susceptibilities. Bismarck got his way, but at the cost of royal disfavour. And to secure the union he had made certain concessions to Bavaria, with regard to her control of her army in peace time, control of her own railways and posts, with certain excise duties. Bavaria was also to hold the chairmanship of a *Bundesrat* committee for foreign affairs, but this was to prove of little importance. Wurtemberg likewise secured rights similar to Bavaria regarding railways, posts, and certain excise duties; Baden secured the last of these. There was also a secret and long hidden arrangement by which Bavaria, or rather her king, was to receive a large annual sum from the Guelph Fund which Bismarck controlled. Thereby the loss to his royal dignity was solaced by the king's freedom to indulge his expensive tastes in building, without the difficulty of recourse to public funds.

Thus the terms of union were drawn up. They had to be accepted by the various parliaments involved, and were so agreed to, though not without criticism, the Bavarian Parliament attacking the concessions to them as too small, northern opinion feeling that they were too large. But Bismarck was right in thinking that these concessions would not seriously disturb the working out of union, and could rejoice that the North German *Reichstag* in a short special session accepted them without difficulty. But how little the *Reichstag* counted in the whole operation was illustrated by William's insistence that the imperial crown should be offered him by the princes, grudgingly led by the King of Bavaria, without any reference to his own or any other parliament. And although the northern *Reichstag* sent a somewhat belated delegation to congratulate the new emperor, the historic ceremony of the proclamation of the empire at Versailles on 18th January 1871, the anniversary of the founding not of the *Reich* but of the Prussian kingdom, was reserved for princes (though King Ludwig refused to attend), generals, and officers of state. That was indeed symbolic of both the new emperor's and the new imperial chancellor's views. For the victory in war had not merely defeated France, raised a united Germany to a predominant position in central Europe, and given cause for concern to the other powers of Europe. It meant also the triumph of the Prusso-German army, and of all Bismarck's policy which had led directly to so magnificent and unexpected a culmination. It thereby both confirmed his power and appeared to justify his political principles and methods. Hence it was to destroy the possibility of making the new *Reich* a liberal, much less a democratic state in accord with the hopes raised in 1848 and cherished during the succeeding generation. But for the moment all was joy and jubilation, and the new *Reichstag* elected in the spring of 1871 for the whole nation, with a national liberal and allied majority drawn from both north and south, adopted the new constitution framed in the Bismarckian treaties, conscious above all that the long-sought unity had at last been attained.

CHAPTER IX

ECONOMIC, SOCIAL, AND CULTURAL TRENDS IN THE MIDDLE OF THE NINETEENTH CENTURY

Introductory: Railways — Industrial Growth — The Rise of Socialism: Lassalle — Agriculture — Natural Science — History — Literature — Religion

I. INTRODUCTORY: RAILWAYS

IN THE necessary concentration upon the major theme of the political unification of Germany, and the bold and successful policy of Bismarck towards that end, there is a danger of losing sight of other aspects of German history in and through the middle years of the century, once the crisis of 1848–9 has been safely overpassed. Yet the new empire was not built on political efforts and achievements alone. Economic forces also helped, indeed economic historians have claimed that the empire of 1871 was largely based on such developments, typified in the building of the railways and the coming of the industrial revolution. Similarly the cultural and social life of the country forms a necessary part of the background, affecting and being affected by political and economic trends. But economic, social, and cultural developments had likewise their own paths, halting places, phases, and ends, which did not necessarily coincide either with each other or with a dominant political pattern, although they could not but be affected thereby. In this chapter it is proposed to indicate what the main trends in these aspects of national life were through the middle years of the century, roughly from the forties to the middle years of the seventies, a generation which saw not merely the creation of political unity but also the binding of Germany together by the railways, the firm establishment of the new system of industry, the triumph of ultramontanism in the Catholic Church in Germany, the emergence of socialism, as of realism in literature, the turn from the domination of philosophy to natural science and history.

Without attempting to decide upon the relative weight of political and economic factors, there is no doubt as to the importance of the economic developments of the middle years of the century, especially those made between 1850 and 1870, when, as the economic historian of modern Germany puts it,[1] 'Germany made the first decided steps towards becoming a modern industrial state.' One of the most striking features in this development was the creation of a national railway system, which the sociologist Riehl declared at the time 'was creating not merely a new land but also a new people.'

It was indeed a remarkable coincidence that Bismarck, who at this

[1] Sartorius, *Deutsche Wirtschaftsgeschichte, 1815–1914*, 1923, p. 135.

period had as little immediate interest in the economic life of the country as he had in the Hegelian philosophy, should have achieved the political unification of the country just as the railways were knitting it together. Its main line system was completed just in time for the Prussian Guard to be moved partly by rail in the war with Austria. And by 1870 the speedy mobilization of the army against France was notably assisted by the full use of the new transportation. Railways were in fact indispensable for German unity; without them Berlin, so remote from western and southern Germany, seems almost unthinkable as the capital of the new *Reich*. The poetic imagination at their beginning saw the railways as 'bridal bracelets' uniting the age-long divided country, and so in fact they were. For Germany, by European measurements at least, was a large country, and nowhere else in that continent, save in Russia, were these new bonds so vital politically. Germany's rivers, splendid as they were for communication, had their limitations; thus none of them connected Bavaria with the north. And her roads were in general bad. Pre-railway travel was extremely slow; six German miles, equal to twenty-eight English ones, was the average daily run for the post-coach. When a Prussian official, the novelist Spielhagen's father, was moved from Magdeburg to Stralsund in 1835, just before the railway age, the family took over a fortnight for a journey later covered by rail in a few hours.

The father of the German railways was Frederick List. As an exile in America, 'in the midst of the Blue Mountains,' he wrote, 'I dreamt of a German railway system.' After his return to Germany in 1831 he moved to Leipzig, the old trading centre for eastern Germany, and strove to promote therefrom a scheme of railway building which would not only serve Saxony but would radiate to all Germany. He did in fact forecast the plan of the German railway system, and integrated his arguments therefor with his later *National System of Political Economy*, as with his efforts for the *Zollverein*. Meanwhile the Westphalian industrialist, Harkort, and Motz of *Zollverein* fame, were likewise interested. But it was in the more backward Bavaria, and characteristically by royal effort, that the first German railway was opened in 1835, spanning the five miles from Nürnberg to Fürth. List's Saxon line from Leipzig to Dresden came four years later, to be extended to Prussian Magdeburg in the following year. The forties saw a fairly rapid emergence of local lines in various states, so that by 1850 Germany (apart from Austria) had over three thousand miles of lines, half as much again as France. The fifties and early sixties brought the extension of these to make a main-line system, though the building of connections and branch lines was to continue for another generation.

The German railways were built partly by the various states, partly by private effort. The Prussian Government was at first rather hostile than friendly. 'I can see no great pleasure in reaching Potsdam from Berlin an hour earlier or later,' remarked the old Frederick William III. His successor was more interested, but the real push came mostly from the Rhenish industrialists; the Prussian state was for long concerned primarily to check indiscriminate promotion and the speculative fever which in Germany as elsewhere accompanied the building of the lines. In other parts of Germany, however, State effort was more prominent. Thus all the lines in Hanover, Baden, and Wurtemberg were State lines, and most of those in Bavaria. Yet with the annexation of Hanover and Cassel the Prussian State became the owner of railways on a considerable scale, and from the late seventies on Prussia began to acquire private lines, so that by the end of the century less than a tenth of German railways remained in private hands. In this military state strategic reasons played no small part in aiding the process, though the railways also proved a source of revenue, and their operators a loyal and obedient part of the Prussian and imperial bureaucracy.

As in other lands the newer and speedier form of communication stimulated trade, both domestic and foreign, and the growth of industry and its concentration in the growing urban centres. For a time it hurt the older river transport, as on the Rhine, but later the greater cheapness of water transport for bulky materials as coal or grain, and the increased use of steam barges, with state aid for the improvement of river navigation, redressed the balance; before the end of the century the Rhine valley carried the traffic of two railways, as well as of river and roads, in a steady stream. And the growth of trade and industry brought new wealth, so that whereas the earlier railways had been built in part by foreign capital (as they had used foreign-built engines and rolling stock), it was German capital, public or private, which financed the later ones, though the French indemnity helped in the seventies. The social and political effects of the new transportation, to which must be added the new telegraphs, inaugurated just before 1848, are not so easy to define, yet were undoubtedly important. The railways did not wipe out local differences; these were too deep-rooted for that. Thus a Bavarian novelist, Ludwig Thoma, at the end of the century, could not abide the atmosphere of Berlin. Yet to be able to travel from Munich to Berlin in ten hours instead of ten days was obviously of importance in drawing the two major states of Germany together, and made easier their incorporation in a common empire. It also helped to make more effective the predominance of Prussia in that empire, and this did not always make for better feeling. Similarly the greater connection established through the railways between Germany and her neighbours, whilst it could give support to her claims to be 'the heart of Europe,' and of course greatly stimulated trading and other intercourse, did not necessarily improve political relations between her and her neighbours. Bismarck saw a danger to Germany in the growth of the Russian railways. The development of German shipping, notably of ocean-going steamships, was slower, partly owing to the predominant position of British shipping on the high seas. Not until after 1870 did the now united *Reich* begin to expand her mercantile marine comparably to her earlier development in railways.

II. INDUSTRIAL GROWTH

It is natural that in looking at the industrial growth of Germany up to our own day attention should be primarily focused on the great expansion which set in *after* 1870, or indeed more exactly in the era of William II, which saw Germany attain an outstanding position among the great industrial nations of the world. But, as already suggested, the real 'foundation time' came earlier, most markedly in the fifties, aided by the flow of gold and silver from the New World and Australia. This movement continued through the sixties, was given a feverish burst of activity by the gold from France after the war of 1870, but was checked for more than a decade by the financial and economic crash of the middle seventies. Not the railways alone but the whole economic framework of modern Germany arose during the period *before* 1870: the industrial centres, the use of the new power and the new machines of the steam age, the technical skill, the industrialists to direct and the men and women to work in the new undertakings, and, no less important, the financiers, the banks and joint stock companies.

Before this time Germany had been not merely a divided but also a poor country, backward in her economic as in her social and political life, hampered by her class structure, as also by the remnants of feudalism and of the guild system in industry. She had, however, large natural resources, coal, iron, and most other minerals, and valuable chemicals such as potash; she had a steadily growing population, rising, despite the large emigration, from twenty-five millions in 1815 to over thirty-five millions in 1850 and nearly forty-one millions in 1870; and her people were in general hard-working, docile, and content with a simple standard of living. She had, especially in Prussia, an efficient and loyal if rather conservative bureaucracy. Her educational system, while primarily geared for higher education in her many universities, was capable of being developed to provide technical training for the new age, whilst its strong tradition of academic research could be extended from philosophy or philology to natural science. The emancipation of the Jews in 1848, whilst not complete to the point of allowing them to enter government service (in Prussia at least), added their long experience as traders, and above all as bankers and financiers, for the development of the new era. One must not exaggerate the growth of industry and trade before 1870. The *Zollverein*, important as it was, could not remove all the obstacles—e.g. the endless varieties of coinage, etc.—to internal or international trade. The newer factory worker did not in this period supersede the local handicraft or domestic worker. Indeed he was never to do that entirely, for the small shop-worker and the domestic worker (e.g. in wood or weaving) were to survive throughout.

Yet in the so-called heavy industry of coal, iron, machinery, and to a more limited extent in some branches of the textile industry, this period before 1870 (or perhaps more exactly before 1875) did see a partial transition to the modern form. The raw materials, coal and iron, wool and flax (cotton was, of course, imported from America), were already there, the main centres of industry for the most part already established, in Rhineland-Westphalia, Saxony, and Silesia, i.e. roughly in three Prussian regions stretching across from Aachen in the west to Breslau in the east, with Berlin as an increasingly important northern centre. Growth was naturally uneven, with the greatest development so far in the Rhineland-Westphalian area. Most of the German coal-fields lay in Prussia; in the west the great coal-field of the Ruhr valley, with those of Westphalia, Aachen, and the Saar; in the south-east that of Upper Silesia; and in between the lignite or brown coal-field of Prussian Saxony, less important at this stage (like the Silesian coal) but steadily increasing in production. And Germany's iron, though less abundant, lay likewise mainly in Prussia and in fairly close proximity to the coal, so that already in the thirties it was superseding wood for smelting.

This proximity of coal and iron was to make the Ruhr area an almost unique treasure house of wealth and power: the great resources of the Lorraine iron Germany was to win in 1870. With the growing demand in this period for iron to make and coal to drive the new steam-engines, whether locomotive or stationary, the production in these two industries grew steadily, with Dortmund the chief coal centre. The Prussian coal output increased tenfold from 1840 to 1870, to 30 million tons, though, of course, the great expansion was to come later, to over 100 million tons in 1900. The demand for iron was indeed greater than Germany could supply, so that she imported raw iron from abroad. In coming later into the field she could take advantage more quickly of earlier foreign experiments, mistakes, and progress. Thus in the earlier stages of her industrial revolution she imported foreign capital, foreign skilled labour, foreign machinery, from England, Belgium, France. Her first railway engines and rails, her first textile (spinning) machinery, came from abroad, mainly from England, and she profited by the scientific and technical advances made by Bessemer and others in the smelting and refining of iron and steel.

Germans were, however, already taking a steadily increasing part in their industrial revolution. We have already mentioned Harkort and Krupp of the Rhineland as pioneers. Alfred Krupp was left as a boy of fourteen in 1826 to carry on the recently established iron foundry in Essen, with seven workers. By the fifties he was making steel for the new railways, and above all guns for the coming wars of Bismarck, with a thousand workers. As the 'Cannon King' he was to have 16,000 workers in 1873, and 70,000 before he died in 1887. Johann Borsig, the 'Locomotive King,' founder of the great Berlin engineering works named after him, a penniless boy from Breslau, was fired by the success of Stephenson's railway engines to set up as an iron founder in the Prussian capital. He produced his first engine in 1841, and had built five hundred before his early death at the age of fifty. He had also secured the friendship of the great scientist, Alexander Humboldt, and with his men played a momentary role in the Berlin revolution of 1848, when for a time he commanded the Civic Guard.

One of the best examples of the connection between science and industry, which was to be of such great moment for Germany, is provided by the

I

record of the Siemens brothers, sons of a fairly well-to-do Hanoverian farming family. Werner Siemens (1816–92) remarks in his autobiography on the gulf which existed between these two when in his early days he tried to combine soldiering with scientific invention. Yet just as a generation or more earlier the five sons of Meyer Amschel (Rothschild), the Jewish banker of Frankfurt, spread their banking activities through the capitals of Europe, so did Werner Siemens and his four brothers combine to apply science and technology to industry even more widely. William Siemens settled in England and won high honour there as a scientist, combining with another brother to invent the regenerative furnace for the making of steel, whilst Werner, after some success with explosives, returned in the fifties to apply electricity to communications, and with his other brothers spread telegraphs and then submarine cables further and further afield, until the firm of Siemens & Halske became one of the great industrial organizations of the world.

The application of the new power and the new machinery to the many branches of the textile industry came less quickly and more unevenly than to coal and iron. The linen industry of Silesia was in fact on the decline after the hard times of the forties, partly from the increased use of cotton fabrics, partly from foreign competition and the failure to adapt itself to the new methods. These developed most quickly in cotton spinning, which was strongest in Saxony, but long established also in the Rhineland. With the aid of the new machinery it also grew steadily in South Germany in these years. Thereby Germany's earlier dependence on England for cotton yarn was lessened, though as in England the industry suffered for a time from the cutting off of cotton supplies owing to the American Civil War. In weaving, machinery came into use more slowly, and hand-loom weaving was to survive better in all branches of the industry, notably in Bavaria and Baden, as a natural side industry in rural parts. The transition to machinery was aided in these years by the establishment of trade schools and polytechnic institutes and was, of course, manifested in varying degrees in other established industries. There were in addition examples already of new industries resulting directly from the growth of science and industry, such as the machine-making industry, the chemical industry, and the even younger electrical industry, all of which were to attain such great importance later.

The full effects of the industrialization of Germany were, of course, to come in the next generation and more, but already by the early seventies they were marked enough. As production increased so did trade, both domestic and foreign; the latter trebled in value per head of the population between 1850 and 1870. Paralleling the growth of industry came that of the financial machinery needed for it. 'The whole banking system of Germany,' says the historian of German capitalism, Sombart, 'was erected in the sixties.' In addition to the big banks such as the Darmstaedter Bank, the Discontogesellschaft, the Deutsche Bank, and the Reichsbank, successor to the Prussian State Bank, many smaller banks appeared, nearly a score of new ones in Prussia between 1850 and 1870. And these German banks not merely provided money for industry, they also shared in its control, a special feature of German industrial and banking history. And as wealth grew, more and more joint stock companies appeared to aid industrial and trade expansion.

The centres of industry and business grew mightily as sons and daughters, or whole families, left the land or the rural towns to congregate there in a Germany which in 1815 was only one quarter urban. By 1860 this had grown to over a third. And whilst Germany as a whole was not to see her urban population overbalance her rural population until the middle nineties, Prussia had already reached that stage by 1867. Berlin more than doubled her population (to 800,000) in the sixties. By the time she became the political capital of the new empire she was likewise a considerable manufacturing and financial centre. Housing conditions for the many workers there were notoriously bad. Her many multi-family 'barrack houses,' product of the wild land speculation in this sprawling city, were a poor substitute for rural space and light: and the death-rate was for long correspondingly high there as in many of the other similarly overcrowded centres of machine industry. Few employers as yet concerned themselves with the living conditions of their workers, as Krupp began to do in the sixties. The new capitalist class, the *Grossbürgertum*, were in general still supporters of the *laissez-faire* attitude, which was, in fact, attaining its maximum influence during these years. Their growing wealth was modifying the old predominance of the landed class, though not, as we have seen, to the extent of securing political control of the Prussian state. Yet they were on the way to the partial making good of this failure indirectly by their growing wealth, intruding by intermarriage, the purchase of land, and the gaining of titles, into the former preserves of the aristocracy.

The growth of industry and wealth was not without its set-backs. The capitalist world and age had its cycles and crises, and these could be sharper than those of earlier and simpler times, and were more directly and immediately affected by conditions elsewhere. Thus the panic of 1857 in the United States, marking the end of the gold fever, and fruit of excessive land and railway speculation, hit Germany as it did England, giving a decided check for a time to industrial development. Agriculture was less affected. More serious still was the crisis of the middle seventies. The glorious success of 1870–1, followed by the golden rain of the French indemnity and its use (in part) to pay off German state loans, thus providing large funds for other uses, induced an unparalleled furore of investment and speculation in both domestic and foreign concerns, in which all sense of restraint on the one hand, and often of honesty on the other, were completely lost, a *Gründungs* mania, spreading outwards from Berlin. With the American panic of 1873 this ended, as it was bound to end, in a crash which involved successively or together finance, production markets, prices, wages, and employment, bringing a general shrinking of values and a loss of German credit abroad. The crisis continued for several years (to 1879) and gave a set-back to the country's economic progress which was not completely made good

until the middle of the nineties.   And this time the crisis was intensified by
the threat from 1877 on to German agriculture by the competition of cheaper
American-grown wheat.

III. THE RISE OF SOCIALISM: LASSALLE

Of more permanent importance than the economic crisis of the middle
seventies was the first clear definition at this same time of another result of
the industrial revolution in Germany, the formation in 1875 of a German
Socialist party.   The growth of German socialism to this point was of course
connected with the revolutionary effort and propaganda in 1848, led by
Marx and Engels, and this remarkable pair had continued their activities in
England, where in 1864 they had founded the first socialist international,
and where Marx had produced the first-fruits of his vast economic researches,
Capital, three years later.   During most of this period, however, their
activities had little direct influence upon the growing industrial proletariat
in Germany, from which they were in fact remote.   The man who stands
out as the leader in the growth of German labour to political and economic
consciousness as a class, and the formation of both socialist doctrine and
party, was Ferdinand Lassalle (1825–64), one of the most colourful figures
in the history of Germany in the nineteenth century.

This astonishing and contradictory genius possessed to the full the
precocity of his race.   The son of a Jewish merchant of Silesia, and so of the
newer German Jewry (whereas the Marx family had been in West Germany
for centuries), he disliked both trade and Jews, changed his name from its
earlier form of Lassal, was drawn to the Hegelian philosophy, as also to the
nationalism and radicalism of Fichte, and wrote on ancient philosophy
(Heracleitus of Ephesus), as well as a considerable work of a philosophical
legal character on *The System of Acquired Rights*.   Further, no sooner had
he reached manhood than he plunged into an eight-year struggle to secure
justice and a share of her husband's patrimony for Countess Sophie Hatzfeldt,
a woman twenty years older than himself, with whom the rest of his short life
is inextricably connected.   Distracting as the effort seemed, and was, for the
social revolutionary in the making, he secured from his no less than thirty-six
appearances before the courts on her behalf an experience in pleading which
was invaluable for his own frequent legal trials, he gained an entrance into
Berlin society through her, and with the winning of the case he won as reward
a measure of financial independence.   In any case the effort was characteristic
of him.   And it was hardly less characteristic of him that he should meet a
tragic end, at the age of thirty-nine, in a duel over another woman whom
he wished to marry.

Shortly after he began his crusade for the countess, however, Lassalle had
been drawn into another crusade and a more historically important one,
which he pursued with no less energy, that for the German worker.   Lassalle
never worked with his hands and knew little of working conditions first hand;
like Marx he drew more on English and French conditions than on those in

Germany, though he dealt far more directly with the German workman than did Marx. Lassalle was caught by the growing radicalism of the forties, aided by a visit to Paris, where Heine acclaimed him as a new Mirabeau, and he entered the lists in the fateful year of 1848 in the Rhineland, an avowed disciple of the new Marxian creed. He played little part in the revolution, spending most of the time in jail, but helped to organize the workers of Düsseldorff, was arrested for inciting disorder, and made a name for himself by the brilliance of his defence at his trial in May 1849. There he showed his astonishing oratorical and argumentative powers, his courage, passionate force, and quickness of apprehension, qualities which both carried away his hearers and, on occasion, favourably affected the verdict. And he escaped the fate of exile which fell upon Marx, Engels, and many other advocates of revolution, so that he was able, although under difficulties, to continue his development and work on German and even Prussian soil. This fact was of great moment, for it enabled Lassalle to keep in touch with developments and people in Germany, and gave his views a national and even a Prussian stamp which was to have permanent effects on German socialism. Thereby, however, was to come a breach between Lassalle and Marx. For Marx with his internationalism and distrust of the State was a jealous leader, brooking no rival or divergence from his gospel. Hence Lassalle was to become for him an outcast, an enemy, even 'a Jewish nigger.'

Whilst the reaction of the fifties in Germany gave little room for widespread or open agitation the advent of the more liberal New Era in Prussia, and the growth of industry, provided more opportunity for Lassalle to spread his now more developed views. For these he drew on Hegel and Fichte for his philosophical and historical foundations, on Rodbertus, Marx, and Saint Simon for his economics, but on himself for the brilliance, force, and effect with which he put his case. The 'law of historical development,' he argued, led inevitably to the triumph of the workers, who in effect constituted the modern state, both by their numbers, as also because they provided the labour for production. But under the capitalist bourgeois regime with its free competition the 'iron law of wages' prevented the worker from receiving his fair share of the product of his labour. To remedy this the State must cease to be the mere 'night-watchman' State approved by the liberal bourgeoisie. Its basis must be broadened by the introduction of universal suffrage, and with this lever its power and resources could and must be applied to aid in the reorganization of industry by the workers in 'productive associations.' This would come about slowly, and perhaps peaceably, but to attain it the workers must organize and agitate.

This, in barest summary, was the gospel of state socialism which Lassalle preached and fought for in the early sixties, whether in election addresses to the workers of Berlin in 1862, in attacks on the 'bourgeois' co-operative associations of Schulze-Delitzsch, in the famous open letter of early 1863 to the Leipzig Workers' Association, or in speeches to the industrial workers of the Rhineland, ever his most ready listeners. Out of these efforts came (together with prosecutions by the Prussian authorities) the formation in the spring of 1863 of the General Union of German Workers, with Lassalle at its head, armed with almost dictatorial powers, powers which he exercised somewhat spasmodically until his death some fifteen months later. It was in this short period that Lassalle had his fleeting connection with Bismarck.

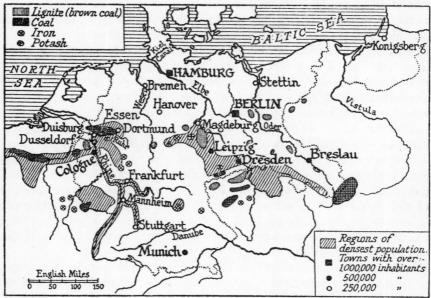

Courtesy of J. A. Stembridge and Messrs. Christophers

Industry in Germany

At that moment, despite their fundamental differences, the two men could find common ground in their detestation of Prussia's bourgeois liberalism. Lassalle was enough of a Prussian nationalist to support the annexation of Schleswig-Holstein, and he approved the strong State, while Bismarck was already considering the adoption of the universal suffrage called for by Lassalle, and was not alarmed at the idea of state aid for the workers. Of any recurring connection there could be no question, but Bismarck many years later was to pay tribute in the *Reichstag* to Lassalle as 'one of the most gifted men I ever met.'

Yet, despite his gifts, Lassalle, 'thinker and fighter,' as his tombstone fittingly defined him, was no organizer, and though a realist in appreciation of the power of the (Prussian) State, he exaggerated the role of the new industrial workers in the Germany of that day. Nor did he win all such workers. He had not captured those of Berlin, and those of Saxony were greatly divided. There the existing workers' educational associations in which August Bebel, a turner by trade, was coming to occupy a leading place, were only partly won for Lassalle's programme and leadership, and South Germany was as yet little affected. And within a month of Lassalle's death there was founded in London the (First) International Working Men's

Association, with its Marxian programme, opposed to Lassalle's ideas of state and nation.

Hence the decade following Lassalle's death was for the emerging German socialist movement a period of controversy and rivalry, the more so since Lassalle left no adequate successor.   Schweitzer came nearest to this, but with all his ability this Frankfurt mercantile intellectual lacked the magnetic force of Lassalle.   More important for the future of the movement as a whole was the emergence of Wilhelm Liebknecht, likewise a bourgeois intellectual in origin, but a victim of 1848–9 and long in exile in England, as poor as his friend and admirer, Bebel. A sincere (if little esteemed) disciple of Marx, Liebknecht was now in Leipzig and from there worked for the International.   The first programme his group produced at Chemnitz in Saxony in 1866 was purely democratic.   But by 1869 Liebknecht had carried both Bebel and the Saxon unions, with some Lassalleans, into the International, and at Eisenach formed a new social democratic

Bebel

workers' party which came out more definitely for economic as well as social and political changes, including the abolition of the capitalist system.   Yet the Lassalleans were still the more numerous, and the disunion and rivalry continued through the disturbing days of the Franco-Prussian war, during which both Liebknecht and Bebel were sentenced to prison terms for opposing both the war and the annexation of Alsace-Lorraine.   Such persecution, however, in which both socialist groups suffered, and which was followed by the economic hardships setting in in 1873, drew the rival parties together, and led to their union at the Gotha Congress of 1875.

. The programme of the now united 'socialistic workers' party' reflected the Lassallean superiority in numbers.   For whilst it drew from the two previous programmes of the Liebknecht-Bebel group, and recognized the international character of the labour movement, it drew heavily on Lassallean phraseology for its statement of general principles (e.g. the iron law of wages), and as its prime demand put forward 'the setting up of socialistic productive associations with State help.'   Both Marx and Engels criticized it severely, but Bebel and Liebknecht defended it as 'the utmost that could be attained,' and no doubt they were right.   The programme was to remain until superseded by that adopted at Erfurt in 1891, which was to be more

Marxist in the formulation of its general principles. But whilst German socialism was thus to give priority to Marxist leadership in doctrine, in the matter of practice the history of the social democratic party was to show plainly the influence of the more realist views of its prime founder, Lassalle.

Courtesy of J. A. Stembridge and Messrs. Christophers
Agriculture in Germany

IV. AGRICULTURE

Whilst industry in the narrower sense was thus taking on new forms, agriculture, the main industry of the country, was likewise developing, though in a slower, more uneven, and less spectacular way. Yet the changes in agriculture were no less fundamental than those in industry, for they marked the completion of the transition from the system which had obtained for so many centuries, based on serfdom and the common field system, so that they have been adjudged as being in fact greater than those in any other sphere of the national economy. In some respects indeed there was little change. Germany continued during these middle years, despite its growth of population, to produce from the soil more than she needed to feed herself; she was still a grain-exporting country down to about this same year of 1875 which we have specified as marking a stage in industrial development. And the general pattern of the distribution of land was not radically changed, although it was somewhat modified at the two extremes of the largest and smallest holdings. After 1815, and indeed throughout the nineteenth century, north-eastern Germany was a land of large estates, largest in Prussian Poland, Pomerania, and Mecklenburg (where over half of the area was in estates of more than 500 acres) but large also in the rest of eastern Prussia, including Silesia. What we may call north-central Germany, in and round Hanover, had more medium-sized farms of 50 to 250 acres. The south and west, including the Rhineland, where, as we have seen, the French Revolution had left its mark on land tenure, was mostly cut up into small holdings, though, of course, there were larger estates as well.

Two changes were needed before Germany could develop a system of modern agriculture and a modern rural society, viz. the completion of the emancipation of the peasantry from the remnants of feudal tenure and burdens, and the break-up of the old common (usually three-field) system of farming. Both of these were carried through or completed in these years. The emancipation begun by the impact of the French Revolution and the work of Stein and Hardenberg was completed by the revolution of 1848: in that year by Bavaria and Wurtemberg; in 1850 by Prussia. Meanwhile the change from the more rigid open-field system was largely carried through in the thirties and forties. Thereby, with the emancipation, the way was opened to the introduction of new and more varied crops and methods, but the growth of population encouraged in the upper Rhineland the division into ever smaller holdings, in many cases too small for subsistence. In eastern Prussia, however, the trend was rather the other way, as many of the smaller peasant holdings were absorbed by the large landowners there. For these owners were now beginning to pay more attention to the profit-making possibilities of their estates, some of which, as the century wore on, passed into the hands of wealthy burgher families with more commercial traditions. And whilst much of the soil there was sandy and poor, with rye as the main crop, there was a domestic as well as for long a growing foreign market for the grain produced.

After the bad years of the forties, the fifties and sixties were indeed a profitable period for German agriculture, paralleling the growth of industry, with rising prices and a steadily increasing market. And like industry again, agriculture, with its freer conditions and with improved communications, began to profit in these years from the applications of natural science. Thaer of Celle (d. 1828) had led the way with his *Foundations of Rational Agriculture*, but it was the great chemist Justus Liebig (1803–73) who firmly established the scientific principles of modern agriculture. Determined to be a chemist, and finding no facilities for experimental chemistry in the German universities, he went to Paris (as Alexander Humboldt before him), returning to become Professor of Chemistry at Giessen and later at Munich. For agriculture his great service was to show from his studies of plant life, first that the farmer must return to the soil the minerals which the growing plants drew from it, in order to restore its fertility, and second that these could be provided to a large degree from chemicals, such as the potash which Germany possessed in vast amounts, above all near Stassfurt in central Germany. Such lessons would not easily or quickly change the slow pace of farming ways, but some aid was given (as in other industries) by technical schools, as by agricultural loan banks, better communications, and the stimulus of growing markets. Improvements in fodder brought improved cattle, which with pigs increased in numbers, though those of sheep declined. The potato was now widely grown, especially in the north, despite the failures of the forties, and the growing of beets for sugar and the sugar-making industry developed in this period, chiefly in Saxony and other parts of central Germany. Bavaria grew the hops for her beer, as well as wheat, and the south-facing slopes of the Middle Rhine and the adjacent valleys ripened their grapes for the important wine industry.

V. NATURAL SCIENCE

The name of Justus Liebig is associated with something even bigger than the improvement of agriculture, since he was one of the pioneers in the great advance of science in general in Germany which marked these middle years of the century. This advance was to have profound effects on German life, in some ways greater than those in other western European countries. With it Germany partially succeeded France as the leader in scientific progress as she did in military and political power. There was indeed a connection between the two factors, since German science was to prove a great supporter of the growing German power, and all the world was to pay tribute to its achievements by sending students there for scientific training in the years before 1914. German industry benefited greatly from its scientific discoveries (e.g. the dyeing industry), and German thought, both secular and religious, was deeply affected by the same development.

During the early years of the nineteenth century Germany was still the land of philosophy, and the names of Kant and Fichte, Hegel and Schelling, were still supreme in her many universities. True, the classical revival and the vigour of the philologists led by F. A. Wolf at Halle had built a system of higher education, almost a philosophy, round the study of classical philology, broadening that term to include the study of classical, and especially Greek, culture in general. But the towering figure of Hegel, in Berlin from 1818 to his death in 1831, had seemed to establish the supremacy of philosophy for all time, as he proceeded to combine all knowledge—of methods of thought, of the natural world, of human psychology, ethics, aesthetics, religion, and finally history—into one grand and comprehensive system. Therein everything was subject to the absolute Idea, the Philosophy of Spirit, and development occurred through the working of the dialectical process, in which thesis was opposed by antithesis, leading thence to a synthesis comprehending both.

The influence of Hegel and the idealist philosophy was to endure. And the tendency to think in universals, to seek and to find general ideas, even systems, of philosophy, had become too deeply ingrained in German ways of thought for it to be lost. Yet we have seen how within two decades of Hegel's death Marx had turned the Hegelian dialectic to serve his own ends.

And the two channels in which the thought of nineteenth-century Germany was now beginning to flow, natural science and history, were both to rebel against Hegel's domination. Thus in science the *Philosophy of Nature* of Hegel and Schelling was early to prove vulnerable. For Hegel not merely attacked the great Newton but (to give a minor example) insisted that there could only be seven planets round the sun in the very year 1800 in which an eighth was discovered. Exact observation and measurement, detailed research and experiment, were on the way to replace for a time the speculations of the metaphysicians.

Science in the eighteenth century had been predominantly concerned with mathematics, physics, and astronomy. And it was in this field that one of the earliest of modern German scientists, Friedrich Carl Gauss (1777–1855), a poor boy from the little state of Brunswick, emerged to be 'the prince of mathematics,' by some compared to Newton and Archimedes, showing his mathematical precocity at less than three years of age by correcting some calculations made by his father, and then by providing proofs, corrections, and additions to mathematical formulae whilst, by help of a ducal scholarship, he was still a student at Göttingen. In this famous university town Gauss was to spend the rest of his life as director of the observatory, with some teaching duties in the university. In addition to his important work in higher mathematics he furthered the study of geometry and geodesy. Much of his work was hardly known at the time, for he was little interested in either fame or the practical applications of his discoveries. Yet one of these, that of the electro-magnetic telegraph, was soon to be of importance.[1] A younger contemporary, C. G. F. Jacobi, was likewise to further the progress of mathematics, and to aid in the setting up of the mathematical schools in the universities of Berlin and Koenigsberg.

A more romantic and widely known figure of great importance for scientific development in Germany was that of Alexander Humboldt (1769–1859), younger brother of the great William Humboldt. He won fame from his four years of exploration through the almost unknown forests of northern South America and over the Andes, then extended his knowledge of many branches of science in Paris, where he lived for many years before returning to Berlin. Goethe paid tribute to his genius,[2] of which the final flowering was to be 'the effort to comprehend the phenomena of nature as a whole,' as he described his famous *Cosmos*, begun at the age of seventy-six. Humboldt thus belonged to the encyclopaedic age; Hegel and other philosophers had used this approach in teaching. But long before Humboldt died the study of science was dividing into its many channels, beyond the possibility of following here. Liebig was the leader in one of these channels, that of

---

[1] During the war of 1939–45 Gauss's name and fame were to be made widely known when British scientists discovered how to meet the threat of the Nazi magnetic mines by 'degaussing' their ships.

[2] Eckermann, *Conversations*, 11th December 1826, quoting Goethe: 'Alexander von Humboldt has been with me for some hours this morning. What a man he is! Long as I have known him he ever surprises me anew. He has no equal in knowledge and living wisdom. He has a many-sidedness such as I have found in no one else. On whatever point you approach him, he is at home, and lavishes upon us his intellectual treasures. He is like a fountain with many pipes, under which you need only hold a vessel; refreshing and inexhaustible streams are ever flowing.'

chemistry, more particularly of organic chemistry, in half a century of teaching, research, and writing.   Another chemist, Wöhler, broke new ground in 1828 by making an organic substance from inorganic matter, and he and Liebig, separately or together, developed the modern system of analysis for organic compounds.

The most outstanding development of the nineteenth century in science was to come in the realm of biology and during this period; and the greatest name in this broad field was to be that of the Englishman, Charles Darwin, whose *Origin of Species* appeared after long labour in 1859.   Yet before that epoch-making book appeared German scientists had begun to make a contribution to physiology which was to give her a leading position in that subject.   Johannes Müller (1801–58), the first great name in this development, while preserving much of the philosophic breadth of the age in which he grew up, contributed both by his own researches on nervous reaction and also as the founder of the Berlin school of medicine.   Then the botanist Schleiden in 1838 put forward the cellular theory of plant life and growth; his friend the anatomist Schwann then extended the theory to include animals; and the great Rudolf Virchow of Berlin (1821–1902), pathologist, anthropologist, social reformer, liberal politician, and opponent of Bismarck, established in the fifties the application of the theory to diseases of the human body.   Thus by the work of these men, and others such as E. W. Weber, Helmholtz, and the two Dubois Raymond brothers, the various branches of modern biological and medical science were firmly established. Helmholtz indeed was eminent in both physics and biology, defining the principle of the conservation of energy in the year before the revolution of 1849 (though rivalled in this by R. Mayer), and inventing the ophthalmoscope a little later.   He likewise became a most notable exponent and champion of natural science and its methods against the earlier claims of the metaphysicians, above all Hegel.

The developments of natural science in Germany, thus summarily referred to, and which continued with an ever-widening range of application, were to have wide reverberations on thought there as elsewhere.   By 1865 Prince Hohenlohe, writing to Queen Victoria, spoke of the scientists who believed nothing that was not visible in the microscope, and of the danger therefrom to religion in a land where the voice of the professors was so potent and where science was becoming so popular.   Büchner's *Force and Matter* and Karl Vogt's *Science and Superstition* showed the trend of the scientists in the fifties towards a materialistic interpretation of life.   The views of Darwin's *Origin of Species* found acceptance above all by Haeckel (1834–1919), professor of zoology at Jena for over forty years, who was to become the outstanding champion of *Darwinismus* in Germany, and who already in the sixties in his *Natural History of Creation* sought to apply the theory of evolution in the widest terms.   Thus did science attempt to provide a philosophy of its own, and build up its empire in the same years in which Bismarck was performing a like task in political life.   And whilst there was, of course, no such thing as 'German' science, any more than there could be

'French,' 'British,' or 'American' science, nevertheless the great German contribution thereto naturally assisted the growth of national self-consciousness.

VI. HISTORY

The second marked development of thought during this period, the turn from philosophical to historical writing, above all to the history of Germany itself, provided a more obvious stimulus to national feeling. The turn to history owed its rise indeed very largely to the upsurge of national feeling in the final struggle with Napoleon. Hence it was bound up with the Romantic movement, and much of its earliest activity was concerned with the medieval period, beloved of the Romantics. Thus Stein and others founded in 1819 a society which in the volumes of the *Monumenta Germaniae Historica* began and long continued the publication of the original sources for early German history. Herein the labours of Pertz, Waitz, Giesebrecht, and others re-created for Germans the history of the great days of their medieval empire. In its own field, the Historical Law School of Eichhorn and Savigny likewise encouraged the historical approach. Hegel himself contributed thereto by his *Philosophy of History*, seeing in the great sweep of world history 'the realization of the Idea of Spirit,' which culminated in the Germanic world and the modern State. But Hegel's more historically minded colleague in Berlin, Ranke, repudiated this abstract and too schematic representation of history as the product of a 'sophistic and empty philosophy,' which did not allow for the infinitely varying course of human development. It was Niebuhr, Prussian patriot and reorganizer of her finances after the crash of 1806, who inaugurated the new method of exact historical research in his work on the development of Roman institutions, and the pattern thus set was to be the model for the development which followed in this period.

The leading figure in that development, and by general consent the greatest historian Germany produced in the nineteenth century, was Leopold Ranke (1795–1886). Some of that reputation he owed to the great length of his active career, for he produced his first book in 1824, and the volumes of his *World History* were appearing over sixty years later. In between he had written a series of masterpieces on the modern history of most of the great states of Europe, including his own, as well as a history of the Papacy in the Reformation Era and beyond. Most of these were written in the period with which we are here concerned. Ranke saw history largely in terms of the development of the modern national states, their character and individuality moulded by their rivalries and struggles with each other. He also believed that by critical examination and comparison of the original sources the past could be revealed 'as it actually happened,' free of bias, given the imagination of the historian. Later historians have questioned this faith in the achievement of such complete impartiality. But no one doubts the importance of the influence of Ranke in his famous historical seminar in Berlin in inculcating 'scientific' methods in the study of history, or that of his example in writing it, despite the attack which Nietzsche was to make on such works.

It was above all the Prussian historians who were to set the dominant stamp on German historical writing of this age and later. But although Ranke was a good Prussian, and wrote Prussian history, the members of the 'Prussian school' proper differed from him in their more active concern with political issues, above all in the zeal they displayed for the unification of Germany by and under Prussia. Thus Sybel, Ranke's greatest pupil, played some part in the revolution of 1848, and a more active one in the sixties, liberal and national, and then in 1867 national liberal, and strongly Protestant. His political views were reflected in his large historical works, both that on the French revolutionary period, and later as the almost official historian of the founding of the Bismarckian Empire. Meanwhile the Pomeranian Prussian, Droysen, spent thirty years on a vast history of earlier Prussian policy, depicting the rulers of Prussia as the conscious and enlightened workers for German unity. Yet the services of these two historians to Prussia were to be surpassed by those of the even more striking figure of Treitschke, whose historical achievements and influence belong more, however, to the period of the empire itself.

There were, of course, other German historians of eminence in this period, and with other interests and views. Thus Gervinus in South Germany cut a wider swath than the Prussian political historians, with his interest in literary and intellectual history, and was far more democratic in his nationalism. The Schleswiger Mommsen was the successor of Niebuhr in Roman history, as fine a writer as he was a scholar, who despite his admiration for Julius Caesar as 'the complete and perfect man' was a true and active liberal, both before and after 1870. There was Gregorovius, the learned historian of Rome in the middle ages; Döllinger, the Bavarian ecclesiastical historian, far removed in his loyalties from the Prussian school; and across the Swiss border Burckhardt, the wise historian of art and civilization, preferring his mountain eyrie to the honour of succeeding Ranke in Berlin University; and many others who helped to make Germany almost as renowned for historical as for scientific research and achievement.

VII. LITERATURE

It was a testimony to the strength of the historical current flowing in Germany during this period that not merely did it fan the growing national sentiment but it also overflowed into the literature of the time. Thus one of the outstanding novelists of the day, the Silesian Freytag, liberal and nationalist journalist, novelist, and dramatist, turned to history to write in the fifties and sixties five volumes of popular 'Pictures' from German history, and later *The Ancestors* was to provide a series of romances from the same source. Similarly the South German Scheffel produced in the fifties his fine historical novel, *Ekkehard*, a story of the famous monastery of St. Gall in the tenth century. Both Fontane in Brandenburg, and C. F. Meyer the

Swiss writer, were to follow in a like strain, whilst the Austrian Stifter re-created the twelfth century in Bohemia in his fine if inordinately lengthy novel *Witiko*.   Yet the turn to history for material for fiction, or even the dominant position which the novel and the *Novelle* or short story came to occupy in literature in this period in Germany, may be seen as marking a decline of literary creative power.

Certainly there was such a decline in the fifties and sixties, not merely from the heights of the later eighteenth century and the succeeding Romantic Age, but also in poetry from the days of Young Germany and the lyrical excitation of the forties.   It may be that the years after the failure of the revolution of 1848–9 were less favourable for the emergence of literary genius. On the one hand the failure of the movement which had absorbed so much of the national feeling and energy was bound to be followed by some years of disillusionment, if not despair.   While many of the most ardent spirits before or in 1848 were in prison or exile, the way was open for the philosophy of Schopenhauer, after long waiting, to come into its own.   And Schopenhauer's philosophy, despite its origin in Kant and the skill with which it was presented, was essentially uncreative, and strongly pessimistic. For the *Will* which Schopenhauer declared to be the prevailing force in all nature, including man, availed man nothing in the struggle with the inevitable tragedy of life.   The only solution lay in the denial of Will, and the acceptance of a gospel of renunciation, whether in Christianity or Buddhism. This pessimism was to be represented by other thinkers, such as Hartmann in his *Philosophy of the Unconscious* (1869), and more widely by the tragedies of Richard Wagner.   Heine's latest writings reveal a similar state of mind.   At the same time, with the opening of the New Era in Prussia, and the activities of the *Nationalverein*, more of the national interest and energy began to be absorbed in political issues.   The increasing concern with material interests, as manifested in the growth of industry and trade, and the growing claims of science, were likewise less friendly to pure literature.   Finally the decline of many of the little states which, like Weimar in the eighteenth century, with all their faults had provided centres and nurseries for poetic and dramatic talent, may have contributed to the general trend.

This is not to say, of course, that Germany did not produce much literature in this middle period of the century.   Germany had long been a bookish land, and with the increase of the educated middle class and of material well-being the demand for books and periodicals grew steadily, and with it the supply.   And if the quality did not reach the Olympian heights only attained by Goethe, Schiller, and a few more, yet the sight of these peaks was never entirely lost, just as men never ceased to be influenced by the work of the great philosophers.   Schopenhauer had gone back, in part, to Kant, and the 'return to Kant' was to be preached by others later in this period, though the development of natural science and psychology inevitably affected any such movement.   In a different field also, that of verse, above all lyric poetry, the tradition was maintained.   For while the novel came to be the more characteristic form of literary activity during this period, many, if not

most, of the writers of fiction wrote verse as well.   So it was with Storm,
with Keller, Raabe, Fontane, and others.   And whilst the group of poets and
writers who made up the Munich group, 'The Crocodile' as they called
themselves, drawn to the Bavarian capital in the early fifties by the efforts of
King Maximilian II, was not wholly one of lyric singers, or indeed of poets,
the lyric strain was the dominant one.   It was to be best expressed in the
many poems of the Lübecker Geibel.

Germany was still a land of many states and wide local differences, and
the peasant farmer was still the dominant figure in its varied landscapes,
despite the growth of industry.   The Romanticists (and Herder before them)
had discovered *Das Volk*, the common people, and it was in part from
Romantic influence that in this period there appeared a whole series of
stories of village or peasant life (*Dorfgeschichten*).   To the Munich sociologist
W. H. Riehl, writing *The Natural History of the German People* shortly after
1848, the conservative peasant farmer, as a type peculiar to Germany, had
saved the country from revolution, and was 'the true kernel of the German
being,' both past and future.   A Swiss pastor, Gotthelf (Bitzius), set the
fashion in the forties, to be followed by Auerbach in his many stories of the
Black Forest village folk, as by Stifter (and later Rosegger) for Austria,
M. Meyr for Swabia, and many others, above all Gottfried Keller for his
Swiss countryside.   Of local interest too are many of the short stories
which from the fifties onwards became a sufficiently distinct literary form to
have a special designation in Germany as *Novelle*, little novels, in which
Stifter, Theodor Storm of Schleswig, Otto Ludwig the Thuringian, Keller,
and Heyse the Berliner who found a home in Munich and was a most prolific
writer in this form, all excelled.   Novels proper likewise form an important
part of the literature of these days.   Keller, a leader here, was Swiss, but
wrote in German and had lived there before and after 1848 and even written
there his masterpiece *The Youthful Henry* (*Der Grüne Heinrich*) (1854), with
its touching picture of much of his own early life.   Fritz Reuter, an innocent
victim of Austro-Prussian repressive measures after 1830, emerged from
prison to take a place as one of the foremost novelists of the day, despite the
fact that he wrote in Low German.   For he showed in his stories of Mecklenburg life a masterly capacity for the depiction of character, with an unequalled
fount of gentle humour.   The novels (and many *Novelle*) which the prolific
Wilhelm Raabe of Brunswick wrote in this period, the most outstanding
perhaps the *Hungerpastor* (1864), likewise show a Dickensian humour, but
combined with a realism which is at times akin to pessimism.

This period in the literary history of Germany stands between the earlier
Romantic age, which markedly influenced it, and the later vogue of Natural-
istic Realism owing so much to French example.   It has been called, or
called itself, the age of Poetic Realism, and the title has some value as
marking the increasingly more realistic approach to life found in many of
the writers of the period.   But the phrase hardly indicated the social changes
taking place at this time and the emergence of a more definitely middle-class
point of view.   This was expressed in literature by praise of the solid virtues

of the good, simple burgher, with his diligence and devotion to his work, and his growing resentment at the social claims and privileges of the aristocracy to whom he felt himself to be superior in both mind and character. Immermann (d. 1840), a local magistrate in Düsseldorff, is usually regarded as opening this attack on the aristocracy in two novels he wrote in the thirties, but Immermann was half a Romantic, and not so ardent a champion of the changes he foresaw. The 'Young German' Gutzkow, of proletarian origin but rising to the middle class, was more sharply critical in his attempt to depict in novel form the reaction in Prussia after 1848. Then Freytag in his best-known novel *Debit and Credit* sets the steadfast and virtuous (and successful) pursuits of the honest trader in Breslau against the socially superior but weaker and less capable noble, who is brought to ruin by a wily Jew. Finally, Spielhagen in more than one of the widely read novels which he wrote in the sixties and seventies, after a hard apprenticeship to letters, was a bitter critic of the life and ways of the landed nobility of Pomerania, where he grew up, though (like Freytag) he makes the rare exception. This expression of middle-class self-consciousness never possessed the hard core of class hatred, and was to decline as wealth began to count more than rank later in the century and the line between burgher and noble was less clearly defined. Then indeed a new phase in literary history, the era of Naturalism, could find a place for the so far almost neglected proletariat.

Whilst many of the men of letters of this middle period wrote plays, in general the drama was in low water during these years. Hebbel, a Holsteiner who found a home in Vienna, was an outstanding exception. Hebbel went his own way throughout, writing between 1840 and 1860 tragedies of considerable power, mostly on classical or biblical subjects. Yet Hebbel's services to the drama were only to receive due recognition at a later date. Born in the same year, 1813, as Hebbel, however, was another figure likewise interested in drama, but as connected with its musical setting in opera. Richard Wagner was the youngest of nine children of a city official in Leipzig, and his father's early death brought an acquaintance with hardship which, thanks partly to his own improvidence and extravagance, was to recur periodically. A complete egotist and a rebel against authority, whether political or musical, Wagner began to make a name for himself in the forties with his operas *Rienzi*, *The Flying Dutchman*, and *Tannhäuser*, and had attained to the position of director of the Royal Opera in Dresden when he was caught by the revolutionary fever in 1848–9. After the street fighting in Dresden in the spring of 1849 he only saved himself from arrest by flight. The succeeding period of his exile in Switzerland was to see the more precise formulation of his theories of the union of poetry and music in opera, and his stupendous attempt at the realization of that union in the four operas of *The Ring of the Niebelungs*. Wagner was hardly to realize his full aim. For his genius was primarily musical, and it was as a musician that he was to take his unique place in the long line of great musicians Germany produced, of whom Beethoven, Schubert, and Weber were still alive as he grew up, and Mendelssohn, Schumann, and Brahms were active in his maturer years.

Wagner, however, was to occupy a wider if not a higher place in German history of the modern age. He was indeed, like Bismarck and Lassalle, a phenomenon, a product of the national genius, more original perhaps than they, but remarkably like them for his force, which resembled that of the Swiss mountain torrents near which he long lived. This restless energy

Wagner

gushed forth not merely in his operas but also in a constant stream of other writing, whether upon his theories of the music drama or upon himself, or in pamphlets such as the attack on the Jewish contribution to German music in *Judaism and Music*, on *The State and Religion*, on *What is German?* And his writings were like himself, full of change and counter-change, as he passed from the materialism of Feuerbach to the pessimism of Schopenhauer, from anti-Christian or anti-Catholic views to the 're-generation' of his last opera, *Parsifal*. In much of this he represented the variations in what was more than usually a period of transition, in politics, in economics, in thought. But in it all he was representative of his age and country, above all perhaps in the Romanticism which made him turn to German legends for so much of his work, and in the concomitant national feeling. For Wagner shared Fichte's belief in the greater virtues and originality of the German tongue, together with a belief in the supreme capacity of the Germans for music. Therefrom was to come his share in the creation of an intolerant German nationalism and racialism, which was to help to build up the creed of national socialism.

VIII. RELIGION

The religious life of Germany ran during this period as before in its two main channels of Protestantism and Roman Catholicism, Protestantism with its minor sectarian channels still persisting, despite the union of Lutheranism and Calvinism in Prussia and elsewhere. Only in a few of the smallest Protestant states, such as Mecklenburg, Brunswick, and Saxe-Weimar, did the political and religious boundaries coincide, although Saxony under its Catholic rulers was nearly ninety-eight per cent Protestant, and these northern Protestant states, together with the adjacent Protestant portion of Prussia, formed a united block in religious faith.   But Prussia as a whole was one-third Catholic, as was likewise Wurtemberg.   Baden, on the other hand, was one-third Protestant and was ruled over by a Protestant dynasty; Bavaria was nearly three-quarters Catholic.   Whilst in Germany proper the Protestants outnumbered the Catholics by about two to one, the presence of Austria in the *Bund* for long maintained an almost even balance in numbers. Thus her exclusion in 1866, and the subsequent unification under Prussia, had religious as well as political implications.

Similarly the social, economic, and intellectual changes outlined in this chapter were bound to affect the religious life of the country.   Yet it is not easy to assess simply and briefly the results of these changes on so deep-seated a matter as religion, the more so as such changes take time to produce their full effects.   In general the economic changes affected the Protestant north, in Saxony and Prussia, earlier and more than the Catholic south. But if Saxony was Protestant, Rhenish Prussia was largely Catholic, which meant that both faiths were involved.   And the growth of the industrial cities, with the freer movement of population, tended to mingle the two faiths more than before.   Hence both Churches had to face the problems created by the early industrial revolution and the rise of a new urban proletariat. The new socialist creed might declare in its programme that 'religion was a private matter,' but in so far as socialism was Marxian it was in theory hostile to 'bourgeois' Christianity, as identified with the capitalist or possessing class and the capitalist state.   The increasing preoccupation with economic progress was reflected in the growth of what Schopenhauer scathingly defined as 'the crude materialism which has been served up again under the ignorant delusion that it is original.'   Therein philosophic-scientific writers, from Feuerbach to Haeckel, were to be caught.   Yet if Schopenhauer's pessimistic philosophy was anti-materialist, it was hardly Christian. The growing Realism of the age was more secular-minded than the earlier Romanticism with its religious and medieval colouring, and the literature of the time mirrored the change.   It is not surprising to find that novelists such as Storm and Spielhagen, though of Protestant stock, were unorthodox in religion.

Protestantism was indeed by its nature and history more open to the influence of the new intellectual trends.   For Protestantism had always contained radical as well as conservative elements, both within its official bounds as also outside in the free churches.   Thus Pietism, its most characteristic expression, had striven on one side to come to terms with the rationalism of the eighteenth century.   Protestantism was closely connected with the idealist philosophy, though that philosophy was critical rather than Christian: yet to Hegel the Reformation was 'Christian freedom made actual'; to Fichte it was a proof of German superiority.   In this new age Protestant thought made efforts to harmonize its faith with the prevailing scientific and historical spirit, at times with danger and loss.   Thus the Protestant theologian David Strauss, after shocking orthodoxy with his critical *Life of Jesus* in the thirties, was to end his days proclaiming in *The*

Old Faith and the New (1872) the gospel of natural science, with Darwin as its high priest. Thereby he was to bring upon himself the wrath of a new prophet, Frederick Nietzsche, who saw in him merely an example of the cultural philistinism prevailing in Germany at the time. Liberalism with its doctrines of freedom and progress, without being a monopoly of Protestantism, had an obvious affinity with that faith for many, though more on its Calvinist than its Lutheran side. And with its centre in Prussia, German Protestantism naturally responded the more readily to the aim of uniting Germany round that state and could approve the results, if not all the methods, of Bismarck's achievement.

This connection with the Prussian state, however, reveals the more conservative side of German Protestantism, best illustrated there. Orthodox Lutheranism, as we have seen, accepted this union of Church and State as an integral part of the Lutheran tradition. And although in the revival of religion early in the nineteenth century there were some, such as Schleiermacher, who protested against the subordination of religion which it brought, the regime of Frederick William III showed the Church harnessed to the reaction after 1815, and Lutherans and Calvinists united by royal command in the Evangelical Church of Prussia. In the reign of Frederick William IV, the conception of the Christian State as preached by Stahl conflicted with liberal demands for the freedom of the Church. But although the king in 1848 decreed the freedom of religious associations to manage their own affairs, then set up an Evangelical Supreme Council to look after the Protestant Church in Prussia, and made tentative beginnings at the setting up of representative synods after the Calvinist pattern, he went no further; the synods had to wait for twenty years before they were established.

The truth was that neither the Crown nor the more conservative Lutherans favoured real freedom from State control for the Protestant establishment. For this connection was part of the old Prussian system, surviving like so much else in modern Prussia: the Crown protecting and supporting the Church, the Church through the pulpit and its influence in the primary schools preaching loyalty to the Crown, acting as a bulwark against revolutionary ideas, and forming part of the patriarchal social system in rural Prussia. This connection, however useful as it had been to the Church, brought obvious disadvantages and limitations for it, and these increased as the State became more secular, military, and power-seeking in Bismarck's day. It also limited the capacity of the established Church to adapt itself to the changing social and economic conditions, and it tended to encourage sectarianism and even religious indifferentism.

The Prussian Evangelical Church, although the largest and strongest, was only one of many Protestant State Churches in Germany, whose situation and development, though varying from state to state, were not so markedly different from that of the Prussian Church as to call for separate mention. And of course there were other Protestant bodies, old and newer, enjoying varying degrees of freedom outside the State Churches, some of them related to similar bodies in England or elsewhere. One might have expected that the growth and achievement of national unity in the political sphere would be accompanied by the formation of a national Protestant Church. Schleiermacher had proposed this, and some efforts in that direction did indeed take place in these years. The King of Wurtemberg opened the matter in 1846, and the enthusiasm for the national cause in 1848 led to the calling in that year of a congress in Luther's city of Wittenberg to further this end. The congress drew up a programme for a Confederation of all German Protestant Churches which, while preserving their existing state allegiances, organizations, and doctrinal differences, would seek to protect the position and interests of Protestantism, end internal strife, foster relations with Protestant Churches outside Germany, and further common Christian social aims and the missionary work of the so-called 'Home Mission' in Germany. But although the congress was to meet at intervals down to 1872, and the effort was to be supported by an Evangelical Church Conference meeting at Eisenach, it failed to overcome both State localism and doctrinal fears. Not until after two revolutions, those of 1919 and 1933, was a united German Evangelical Church to come into existence, and then it was created by and subject to a regime which was more dangerous to its faith than ever the Prussian monarchs had been.

We have seen in an earlier chapter how the Catholic Church in Germany, although threatened by the rationalism of the eighteenth century and the radicalism of the French revolutionary period, subject to Josephist theories of State domination, and despoiled of its temporal possessions, nevertheless revived after 1815, aided by a renewal of its faith and by the legitimist and conservative triumph. Whilst Catholicism like Protestantism lacked a national organization, it had the support of the two mainly Catholic states, Austria and Bavaria, to balance the power of Prussian Protestantism, it had its connection with Rome and its greater unity of faith, its episcopal and hierarchical system. It also possessed in Protestant Prussia itself two Catholic strongholds, that of Prussian Poland, where Catholicism was identified with Polish national feeling, and the Rhineland, with its strong local feeling. Largely through the strength and efforts of Rhenish Catholicism, it had gained in the early forties a notable series of concessions from the Prussian state, including the setting up of a Catholic section in the Ministry of Religion and Education, and freedom of communication with Rome, a matter of great importance for the future. From the position thus secured the Catholic Church in both Prussia and the rest of Germany was to grow in strength during the next thirty years and thereby prove strong enough in the seventies to withstand the thunderbolts launched at it by Bismarck.

The revolution of 1848 marked a decisive stage in this growth. The Frankfurt Assembly's declaration in favour of general religious freedom was indeed to share the fate of the rest of its Fundamental Rights. But the new Prussian constitution, despite its amendment in 1850, gave to the Catholic Church there more freedom than it enjoyed elsewhere in Germany, more indeed than was given to the Protestant establishment. It was, as a Catholic bishop put it, a charter for Catholicism. The year 1848 saw also a congress of the Catholic bishops of Germany at Würzburg which had some significance, though it revealed the divergence of opinion between those who, like Döllinger, hoped for a National Catholic Church, and others, such as Archbishop Geissel of Cologne, who looked more to Rome since, as he once put it, 'From Rome we get our strength and our freedom from the State.'

It was Cardinal Geissel (d. 1864), as he now became, who as head of the Catholic Church in Prussia proceeded with statesmanlike ability to use the new freedom in building up his Church in Prussia and indeed elsewhere in Germany. No less important in this task was Bishop Ketteler of Mainz, an Imperial Knight of the empire, a man of wisdom and moderation, though later a strong supporter of ultramontanism, more alive than most ecclesiastics to the new social problems of the day, even to the point of offering support to Lassalle's project of state associations of workers. The revolution of 1848 had one other result of some importance to the Catholic Church, since it opened the way to the return of the Jesuits to Germany. And their efforts for the faith (and for Rome) were supported by those of other religious orders, old and new, which now began again to spread through Prussia and Germany, active in preaching, in educational and social work. There was also a rapid growth of Catholic associations in town and country, and an active Catholic press appeared, led by the *National Gazette* (*Volkszeitung*) of Cologne.

In keeping with this new freedom and consciousness, and of great significance for the future, was the emergence in the early fifties of a Catholic group in the Prussian House of Deputies. The Catholic bishops declined an invitation from Frederick William IV to enter the upper House, fearing to compromise their newly won freedom, but in the lower House the numerous Catholic members were drawn together in defence of their liberties against conservative attempts to change the constitution. Hence for a time they could co-operate with the liberals there. With seventy members in the fifties, and led by the two brothers Reichensperger and Mallinckrodt, they constituted a strong body representing Catholic interests, although on other than religious issues they were naturally less united. In 1859 they adopted the name of Centre party, which gave a fair indication of their position. With the rise of the constitutional struggle in the early sixties, however, and the sharper definition of a more radical liberalism in the Progressive party, there was less room for a middle party opposed both to Lutheran conservatism and to radicalism. Their numbers dropped in the successive elections of 1862 and 1863, until they practically disappeared as a party. Yet the precedent of political action had been established, and the formation of the empire was to see a revival leading to the permanent establishment in the imperial *Reichstag* of a political party on a confessional basis.

The growth of these years was not achieved without struggle, and conflict both internal and external. Like Protestantism, the Catholic Church had to contend with the growing materialism and secularism of the age. The appeal of liberalism and philosophies based on the discoveries of natural science was, however, naturally less strong to a faith which was now turning back more to the teachings of the medieval religious thinkers.   Pope Gregory XVI in 1832 had formally condemned the 'pseudo-science' of the age, and his successor Pius IX in the famous Syllabus of 1864 denounced liberalism, materialism, and secularism, together with nationalism, as 'leading errors of our day.'   Yet it took time to eradicate rational or liberal tendencies inherited from an earlier age, attempts such as that of Professor Hermes of the university of Bonn to harmonize Kantian philosophy with the Catholic faith, or efforts such as that of Bishop Wessenberg of Constance in and after 1815, and of the so-called German-Catholics in the forties, to set up a National Catholic Church in Germany.

The South German states had their share of religious-political troubles. In Baden Catholicism was engaged, during the two decades after 1848, in almost continual strife with the government, which under its Protestant dynasty with its Josephist tradition was slow to concede the freedom claimed by the energetic Catholic Bishop Vicari of Freiburg.   And although a concordat with Rome was signed there in 1859, the predominantly liberal chamber opposed its passing, and the struggle continued over such matters as education, civil marriage, the position of the religious houses, the attitude to Rome, the claims to freedom of the Protestant Church.   This Baden struggle indeed foreshadowed the wider struggle to come after 1870.   In Wurtemberg, where a concordat had similarly been signed, there was likewise controversy, in part the old antagonism between the two faiths, mixed with liberalism, and nationalist protests against the growing claims of Rome. Bavaria, before 1848 the stronghold of ultramontanism, ceased to be so with the accession of the more liberal-minded King Maximilian.   Nor was his successor, Ludwig II, so different in this regard, choosing as chief minister in 1866 Prince Hohenlohe who, although a Catholic, was a decided enemy to ultramontanism and friendly to Prussia.   Hence there was much strife in the southern kingdom.

The concurrence of the rise of papal ultramontanism with that of German nationalism was indeed a crucial matter for both.   German Protestantism, mindful of its original struggle for existence, naturally viewed with alarm the growing claims of papal absolutism.   There were also nationally minded German Catholics who shared at least some of that feeling, who were proud of the achievement of German thought, Catholic or Protestant, and disliked the idea of being ruled by Italians less cultured than themselves.   And there were great Catholic scholars led by Döllinger of Munich, who, while admitting the primacy of Rome, contested its claims to spiritual infallibility over the Church.   Yet the claims for the promulgation of that doctrine were growing in the sixties, encouraged by the Jesuits, and the Vatican Council which met in 1869 presented grave problems for the German Catholic bishops.   Some approved of the dogma, others were dubious, and more, like Bishop Ketteler, questioned the wisdom of the pronouncement at this time.   In the end, after stormy scenes in St. Peter's, the German bishops were to bow before the determination of the aged Pius IX and the largely Italian majority of the council.   But a small minority of German Catholics was to follow Döllinger, who had consistently opposed the decision, into what became known as the Old Catholic Church.   The issue formed a grave crisis for German Catholicism, and, combined with the completion at the same time of German political unity under Prussia, was to be followed by a storm which shook Germany from end to end.

CHAPTER X

THE BISMARCKIAN EMPIRE:
I. THE RULE OF BISMARCK, 1871-90

The Formative Period of the Seventies — The Maturity of the Eighties

I. THE FORMATIVE PERIOD OF THE SEVENTIES

THE BISMARCKIAN Empire, an extension of the North German Confederation, came into existence on 18th January 1871, although the Bavarian Parliament only agreed to enter some weeks later, and the new constitution was not passed by the *Reichstag* until April. The empire was to last until November 1918, nearly forty-eight years, a generation and a half of human life. As it rose on the crest of victorious war, so it collapsed with military defeat. The political unity Bismarck gave to Germany was not destroyed in 1918, but the imperial system proved unable to stand the shock of a great defeat, partly from the weakness and political mistakes of its latest ruler and his advisers, partly from more fundamental faults, for which Bismarck must bear much of the blame. There is thus a unity about the history of the empire, and yet it breaks naturally into two parts, one from its foundation in 1871 to Bismarck's fall in 1890, the other from that date to the downfall. The first of these periods again divides naturally into two. The decade of the seventies was the formative period in which Bismarck gave the empire its decisive shape both internally and in relation to the outside world; that of the eighties saw the ripening and maturity of this system. The last two decades and more were to reveal the weaknesses of the regime, and the development of animosities both within and without, from whose combined influence the empire was to crash beyond recall.

The period of youth and establishment, covering roughly the first decade after the founding of the empire, saw the elaboration and working out of the new unity in its many spheres and the definition of the domestic and foreign policies of the regime. Thus in the domestic sphere it witnessed first the collaboration of Bismarck with the national liberals, then the turn against them in the late seventies and the decline of their influence. Bound up therewith was the rise and crisis of the great struggle with the Catholic Church, which was likewise on its way to a close by the end of the first decade. The turn from free trade to protection in 1879, and the decisive attempt to crush the rising socialist movement by the legislation of 1878, similarly form essential parts of this period of definition. In the sphere of foreign policy the same years saw the formulation of policy with regard to the new French republic, and the more difficult problem of relations with the two great empires of eastern Europe, Austria-Hungary and Russia. This was to lead through the crisis of 1877–8 and the 'honest brokerage' of the Congress of Berlin to the fateful alliance with Austria in 1879, which was to be of fundamental importance for foreign policy henceforward. Although there were to be modifications of both domestic and foreign policy in the years that followed, the main lines were to remain unchanged. The empire was to remain fundamentally conservative and anti-socialist, protectionist in commercial policy, alienated from France, allied with Austria-Hungary, and armed against France and Russia.

The constitution of the New Empire [1] was that of 1867 modified in certain details by the entry of the southern states. There were no 'Fundamental Rights' of the kind included in the constitution of 1849. The empire was a federal state, its power and functions divided between the *Reich* and the twenty-five states of which it was now composed. It could not have been otherwise, nor did Bismarck, with his strong Prussian particularism, wish a closer union. The states, whilst no longer sovereign or free to secede, preserved their own constitutions, rulers, parliamentary and administrative systems. All the larger states possessed two chambers, with limited and varying franchises. Thus conservative Mecklenburg had a medieval Estate system, Prussia its three-class system for the House of Deputies, the little Thuringian states their familiar multiformity. The South German states were already more democratically organized than Prussia, and were to be more so as time went on. These states were free to legislate for a wide variety of local matters, carried out federal laws, and collected federal taxes as well as their own. But subject to the reserved rights (*Sonderrechte*) conceded to the South German states, and the right of Prussia to the headship of the *Reich*, the empire controlled relations with other states, treaties, war and peace, the army and navy, rights of citizenship, civil and criminal law, foreign trade and tariffs, banking and coinage, railways and posts, regulations for the press and associations, and taxation for imperial purposes. As with the North German *Bund*, some of these federal rights were exercised by the Crown (e.g. the headship of the army and the appointment of the chancellor), others were shared with the Federal Council (e.g. the declaration of war and the dissolution of the *Reichstag*). And similarly imperial legislation was to be the joint work of the Federal Council and the *Reichstag*. A lengthy section of thirteen articles on the army imposed universal military service, and provided for the immediate introduction throughout the empire of 'the entire Prussian military legislation.'

A summary of the constitution, however, gives an inadequate idea of its special features or its working. Outstanding was, of course, the superior position of Prussia, whose king was to be hereditary head of the empire, and which possessed seventeen out of fifty-eight votes in the Federal Council, as against Bavaria, the next highest, with six. Since no less than seventeen small states in this body possessed but one vote each, Prussia could almost

[1] Given in English in B. E. Howard's *The German Empire*, 1906.

always count on securing a majority there. The Prussian predominance is clearly defined by Treitschke in an essay of 1886 on *Our Empire*:

> However carefully the wording of the constitution may conceal the fact, Prussia occupies both in reality and law a position altogether different from that of the other states of the empire. Prussia alone remains a true state, and cannot be forced by an executive decree to carry out her imperial duties. For only the emperor can enforce such decrees, and the emperor is King of Prussia. Prussia has the determining voice in all matters of decisive importance, and the sound sense of the nation has long agreed that this responds to the distribution of power, as to justice itself. Prussia alone in the empire retains the right to take up arms, since its king, as emperor, is the war lord of the empire. . . .

Just as it was impossible to separate the position of the Prussian king from that of the German emperor, so also the functions of the Prussian Minister-President and Foreign Minister, Bismarck, were intertwined (though less formally) with his functions as chancellor of the *Reich*. There is indeed almost as little mention of the chancellor in the imperial constitution as of the communist party in the constitution of Soviet Russia. Yet both were all important, Bismarck more obviously so as he exercised many of the powers ascribed to the Crown in the constitution. He presided over the Federal Council, and this small body, which met privately and continuously, although more a collection of state delegates than an upper chamber, possessed certain executive and judicial powers, regulating disputes between states, preparing legislation for the *Reichstag*, and possessing the right, with imperial consent, to dissolve that body. It was in fact under Bismarck a most important part of the constitutional machinery. The general position of the *Reichstag*, which also had the power to propose legislation, and was now enlarged by eighty-five new members from the South German states, was not changed by the new constitution: it remained to be seen whether or how it would develop. Alsace-Lorraine was not mentioned in the constitution, since it was not yet formally annexed.

The first years of the new empire were bound to be difficult, despite the enthusiasm with which its creation was greeted. In the domestic field the long tradition of separatism, the force and speed with which union was accomplished, the religious division and the triumph of the leading Protestant state in making what Bennigsen called a 'Protestant empire,' created problems. To these must be added the unsettled issue between autocracy and parliamentarism, the rising tide of socialism, the influence of the nationalist triumph in stirring like feelings in the minorities included in the empire—Polish, Danish, and now French—the economic and social transitions (with an economic crash just round the corner), to say nothing of the emergence of new intellectual and literary trends. And abroad there was France, in confusion, defeated and militarily occupied, but by no means reconciled to her defeat; Italy whose sudden seizure of Rome created a contradiction between the papal loss of temporal power and its claim to spiritual infallibility; Austria with her memories of recent defeat; Russia looking with concern at the sudden emergence of a great military power on her western flank. Figures so different as Marx, Renan, and Burckhardt alike prophesied that the Prussian victory over France would inevitably lead to war between Germany and Russia. The chancellor's position was no bed or path of roses, and his combative nature found ample scope for expression in the issues that presented themselves. In some ways his terrific energy of the past eight years had appreciably aged him, and whilst his grasp was as firm as ever, firmer indeed since his position was now so assured, it was at times less constant, partly because of his growing habit of disappearing for long intervals to the remoteness of his Pomeranian estate of Varzin.

These first years of the empire revealed indeed that the achievement of political unity, so far from bringing complete internal harmony, could engender strife in the important sphere of religion. From what has been said in the preceding chapter it is evident enough that there would be danger of friction between ultramontanist Catholicism and German Protestantism, opposed to ultramontanism both for its spiritual aims and for its particularist attitude to the State which Protestant effort had done most to bring into being. And Catholicism, concerned for its position in this State, now proceeded to organize itself for political activity, led as before by the Rhineland. Catholics won more than fifty seats in the election to the Prussian House of Deputies in November 1870, and fifty-seven seats in the first *Reichstag* of the new empire elected early in the following year. The revived Centre party found allies in the Polish Catholic members, a leader, Windthorst, and some supporters in the Hanoverian Guelphs, and backing from the Bavarian 'patriots.' It showed its attitude immediately by proposing in the *Reichstag* first that the empire should assist the Pope to regain his temporal power, and next that the articles in the Prussian constitution of 1850 which assured their position should be incorporated in the constitution of the empire. Whilst these proposals were heavily defeated, Protestant feeling was also aroused by episcopal action against Catholics who refused to accept the decree of papal infallibility, such as the excommunication of Döllinger, the dismissal of professors in the university of Bonn, the dismissal and excommunication of a teacher of religion in Prussian Poland. It was from such beginnings that there arose what Virchow first and many others after him were to call the *Kulturkampf*, the struggle for civilization, a struggle waged primarily in Prussia, but also in the empire.

Bismarck was to declare in his *Memoirs* that 'the beginning of the *Kulturkampf* was decided for me preponderantly by its Polish side,' and indeed Bismarck was always susceptible there. But the whole intrusion into politics of a confessional party was bound to be annoying to him. For it not merely complicated the political party picture and issues in both Prussia and the new empire, but the Centre party with its loyalty to an external, supra-national authority challenged Bismarck's whole conception of the supremacy and power of the national state, whether Prussian or German. There were also foreign implications, which as always weighed so much with him. Whereas the Catholics wanted his intervention in Italy on behalf of the Pope, he was concerned to be on good terms with the Italian national state. And his relations with France were made more difficult by the sympathy of French Catholics for the papal cause. Whilst his own religious sympathies were naturally on the Protestant side, at bottom the issue was to him a question of political power. As he declared in the Prussian House of Deputies in March 1873: 'The issue is essentially a political one, concerned with the age-old struggle for power between king and priesthood, the struggle which dominated German history through the Middle Ages down to the fall of the medieval empire, when the last emperor perished on the scaffold, with a French conqueror allied to the then Pope.' But long before this speech he had declared for a policy of 'meeting aggression with aggression, both within and without,' applying the power of the Prussian state, and in part that of the *Reich*, to that end.

The first blow (in 1871) was the abolition of the Catholic section in the Prussian Ministry of Religion and Education, to be followed in the next year by a law taking away the Catholic rights of supervision of Catholic schools. The imperial *Reichstag* co-operated to the extent of expelling Jesuits from the empire. The three succeeding years (1873–5) saw the passing of the so-called 'May laws' in Prussia, under the direction of Falk, now Minister of Religion and Education, an able and conscientious jurist, but lacking Bismarck's political suppleness. By these laws the State now imposed its own standards of education for both Catholic and Protestant candidates for clerical office, and ratified (or vetoed) their appointment. A special court was set up, with power to dismiss recalcitrant clergy from office. Marriage by civil authorities was made compulsory, first for Prussia, then for the empire. All religious orders in Prussia, save those engaged in nursing the sick, were dissolved, and State financial support for the Catholic Church was withdrawn by the 'Bread Basket' Act. The clause in the Prussian constitution guaranteeing rights to Catholics was repealed.

Such laws, whilst supported by the national liberals, naturally did not pass without protest from the Pope, the Catholic bishops and clergy, the Centre party, and also from both Protestant conservatives who disliked the more complete subjection of their own Church to the State, and likewise progressives who supported religious freedom on general grounds. Their execution brought the dismissal and deportation of many clergy, the deposition and even imprisonment of bishops all across Prussia from Posen to the Rhine, and much discontent of Catholics all over Germany. Passions were aroused on both sides, and the chancellor was shot at and slightly wounded by a fanatical Catholic youth. Bismarck meanwhile welcomed approaches from the Old Catholics of Germany. 'I will do everything I can,' he said in 1873, 'to further a cause which is in the interests of society and the State.' But the movement was too limited to exercise much influence.

Despite the severity of Bismarck's measures, and the Prussian thoroughness in their execution, the Catholic opposition was not broken, for Bismarck, as the British Ambassador Odo Russell noted, failed to appreciate the Catholic clergy's capacity for passive resistance. In fact, elections showed the Catholics increasing their strength: in the election of November 1873, to the Prussian chamber, they increased their numbers by a half to eighty-eight, whilst in the *Reichstag* election of January 1874 the Centre party doubled its vote, and increased its membership to over ninety (one-third of these Bavarians) which, with Guelphs, Poles, and the ten new members now added from Alsace-Lorraine, made them a formidable party there. The losers in both Prussia and the *Reich* were the conservatives. This was disturbing to the old emperor, whilst the empress, to Bismarck's great wrath, was a consistent opponent of his clerical policy, as were also the Crown Prince and his wife, though on somewhat different grounds. Bismarck himself had neither liking for nor trust in the national liberals by whose aid he carried through his anti-Catholic laws, and was concerned over the rise of socialism. The war scare of 1875, to be followed by the troubles in the Balkans and the crisis of 1877–8, provided further reason for modifying a policy which weakened the unity of the new empire.

Hence the chancellor, shrewdest of political tacticians, began a slow retreat from his most forward positions, getting rid of Falk and trying to dissociate himself from some of the May laws, whilst holding on to others, seeking a way to reconciliation at the smallest cost, alive to the possibility of winning over the Centre party, but looking even more to Rome itself. There indeed he was helped by the death of the intransigent Pius IX in 1878 and the succession of the more moderate Leo XIII. But Leo was firm as well as moderate, and if in the negotiations of the next few years Bismarck did not, like Henry IV eight hundred years earlier, go as far as Canossa, he had at least to set his face in that direction ere the breach between the Prussian State and the Catholic Church was healed. The process of dismantling the edifice of the May laws was begun in 1880, and was continued to 1887 when Pope Leo could announce that the *Kulturkampf* in Germany was ended. By this time the State control of priestly education and appointment had been relaxed, the functions of the special court for ecclesiastical affairs reduced, bishops and parish priests were restored or replaced, the religious orders were back (save for the Jesuits, expelled by a *Reich* law), the confiscated funds of the Catholic Church in Prussia were restored, a Prussian ambassador was again accredited to the papal court, and Pope and emperor had exchanged friendly letters on the perils of socialism. On the other hand, the articles in the constitution of 1850 guaranteeing the Church's freedom were not restored, while the State inspection of schools, and civil marriage, remained.

Yet there was no doubt of a considerable victory for the Church. And although Bismarck, with great skill, had been able to carry the national liberals with him in his change of policy, thereby completing their breach with the radicals and so weakening liberalism, his hopes that the Centre party would lose its *raison d'être* and wither away were disappointed; it was to remain a party of about one hundred strong, available but not certain supporters, neither trusted nor trusting. Some of their strength they owed to their gifted leader, the Hanoverian Windthorst, small in stature, short-sighted, and insignificant in appearance, but as shrewd a politician as Bismarck himself, and one of the ablest debaters Bismarck had to meet; probably only Lasker compared with him there. Bismarck recognized his quality and hated him accordingly,[1] calling him (to Busch) 'a lying rascal,' which did not prevent him from approaching him for support in the crisis of 1890.

The empire had been built on two compromises, one between unity and State particularism, the other between autocracy and parliamentarism. Bismarck approved of the first, but accepted the second only so far as he had to, and because he could not get along without the support he drew from it for his ends. The nationally minded liberals too had compromised for the sake of securing national unity, and the alliance thus struck in the full and exciting years of the later sixties was to last through the next decade. For in the elections to the first *Reichstag* of the empire in 1871 the national liberals emerged with twice as many seats as any other party (125 out of 382), and with the help of the forty-six progressives (radicals), and a section of the conservatives which had as 'free' conservatives declared for support of Bismarck and the empire, could secure a majority against the old conservatives and the new Centre with its allies. Thus the work done in the organization of the North German *Bund* was continued under the same auspices in building up the structure of the empire in such matters as the extension to all Germany of a common coinage, the employment of the French war indemnity (which, among other things, aided the establishment of a gold standard), the change of the Prussian State Bank into the *Reichsbank*. In the complicated task of securing legal uniformity a common Criminal Code was worked out, and beginnings made with a Civil Code (not completed until 1896), a Supreme Court was set up, though at Leipzig rather than Berlin, a rare example of a direct overriding of Prussia. The difficult problem of what to do with Alsace-Lorraine was also worked out. The Federal Council was ready to hand it over to Prussia, but Bismarck, realizing the jealousies this would arouse in the South German states, and the strength of the old tie with France there, wisely preferred that it should remain an imperial territory (*Reichsland*) and that was finally agreed to. Bismarck also approved of a degree of local self-government for the *Reichsland*, but despite the large emigration therefrom of those loyal to France, the assimilation of the provinces to Germany was to prove beyond either this policy or the alternative of strong bureaucratic or military pressure. Thus Alsace-Lorraine was to remain a problem both to Germany and to the peace of Europe.

The working alliance between Bismarck and the national liberals was an indispensable condition for the carrying on of the struggle with the Catholic Church, and it was the more important because of Bismarck's more open break with the Prussian conservatives at the same time. This party of the landowning nobility and squirearchy had disliked Bismarck's policy of opposition to Austria, his additions of new territory to Prussia, his compromise

---

[1] 'Hatred,' said Bismarck to Tiedemann in 1875, 'is as much an incentive in life as love. Two things maintain and adorn my life, my wife and Windthorst; the one for love, the other for hate.' Vincke, an old opponent of Bismarck, summed up the three able Hanoverian parliamentarians of this period as follows: 'Bennigsen is an able man; Miquel is even abler; but Windthorst is as able as the other two put together.'

with the liberals, and his merging of Prussia in a wider unity. They likewise now took objection to some of the anti-Catholic legislation of the *Kulturkampf*, notably the School Inspection Act of 1872, which threatened the long-standing tie between themselves, the Lutheran parsonage, and the village school, and indeed (in their eyes) the Protestant religion. At the same time the liberals were endeavouring to increase local self-government in eastern Prussia in order to diminish the overwhelming *Junker* influence there. Bismarck meanwhile talked of sweeping changes in the structure of the Prussian upper House to reduce it to obedience, though nothing was to come of this, partly because the king was opposed to any such change. As so often with Bismarck, personal animosities came in, in this case hatred of Count Arnim, now German ambassador in Paris, whom the conservatives thought of as his successor, and whom Bismarck for this and other reasons pursued with his usual relentless energy.

Yet though the conservatives lost votes and seats in the elections of 1873–4 for both the Prussian and imperial parliaments, with their deep roots in the soil of eastern Prussia they managed to evade to a great extent the blows aimed at their influence. And they counter-attacked with vigour through their organ the *Kreuzzeitung*, accusing Bismarck and two of his ministers of using their inside knowledge for private profit, which further angered Bismarck, though his own use of the press, as revealed by his faithful lackey Busch, was little, if any, better.[1] Yet as with the Centre party, the breach was not to be permanent. The conservatives came to realize that the *Reich* had come to stay, and in 1876 reorganized their party as the *German* conservative party, emphasizing not merely their political conservatism, but also their agrarian economic interests, including their opposition both to socialism and to 'big business.'

This change coincided with the growing and decisive alteration in Bismarck's attitude to and relations with the national liberal party. The year 1874 saw a sharp clash over the old issue of the budget for the army, which was nine-tenths or more of the whole federal budget. This issue had been postponed in 1867 by agreement that the government's proposals should run for four years, and in 1871 this agreement was extended for a further three years. Now the government proposed that the peace strength of the army should be included in the annual budget law, but permanently fixed (at 400,000), which would have made any annual debate thereon (and so on most of the budget) a mere mockery. Bismarck had hopes of splitting the

[1] Prince Hohenlohe, in his diary (*Memoirs*, vol. ii, p. 258), exemplifies Bismarck's use of the press in February 1880, when he was trying to get the Army Septennate renewed. 'The article in the *Norddeutsche Allgemeine Zeitung* which speaks of the aggressive attitude of Russia and France has made a great sensation, and is commented on with alarm. Afterwards I learnt at the chancellor's that he had only written the article to produce an effect on the deputies, so that they might vote for the Army Bill. He laughed when I told him of the result.'
As for Moritz Busch, who wrote and 'placed' newspaper articles for Bismarck, and was the author of *Bismarck: Some Secret Pages of his History*, Hans Delbrück, one of the ablest historians of the later empire, reviewing Busch's three volumes, calls him a *canaille*, and adds of the revelations: 'The statesman Bismarck remains as high as ever, but the man Bismarck has immensely lost. . . . The weightiest thing in Busch's book is the fact that Bismarck could establish a connection with such a man, after finding him out and dismissing him from his service, but then using him to attack and belittle the royal family and army leaders on false grounds.' (*Preussische Jahrbücher*, vol. xcvi, 1901, p. 461 seq.).

national liberal party which was now, after the elections of this year, at its height with half the seats in the *Reichstag*. Its left wing, led by Lasker, was strongly opposed to the plan: Lasker justly termed the army question 'the real kernel of the "budget-right." ' But Bennigsen and Miquel, largely out of concern for the religious struggle then raging, were for compromise.

Finally, after Bismarck had threatened to resign and dissolve the *Reichstag*, it was agreed that the strength of the army (and so its budget) should be settled for seven years, the so-called Septennate. Thereby, although a breach in the national liberal party was avoided, all hope that the achievement of political unity was to be followed by the triumph of parliamentary government was destroyed, and the military quality of the Prussian state was more firmly embodied in the structure of the empire. Bennigsen with his diplomatic skill, powers of reasoned speech, and high-minded devotion to the *Reich*, managed for a time to bridge the gulf between the perfervid Prussianism of a Treitschke on the Right of his party, and the clear-sighted appreciation of the issues at stake for liberalism of a Lasker on its Left. But the real gainer in the struggle was Bismarck. And it was the high cost of the army which largely determined Bismarck to turn from free trade to protection, and so dissolve his 'marriage of convenience' with the liberals, and ally himself with the conservatives and the Catholics.

So considerable a change could not be made in a day. It was the fruit in part of the chancellor's meditations during a long period of leave (April 1877 to February 1878) spent largely on his remote Varzin estate. There by the end of that time he had made up his mind to certain ministerial and administrative changes, to nationalization of the railways, to changes in economic policy in order to secure greater revenue for the empire, perhaps even to protective duties for agriculture and industry. He must certainly have weighed up his anti-clerical policy, and found it wanting in the desired results. Bismarck, authoritarian though he was, was no doctrinaire in the narrower sense, but far more an opportunist than his contemporary Gambetta, to whom the epithet was applied. He was not bound to any economic system or political party, but was concerned to secure in his own way the safety and prosperity of the empire he had made, and was bold and decisive in action. He had worked with the liberals for ten years, with success in many things, but was increasingly exasperated at their refusal to be a kind of chancellor's party, ready to follow him, as he put it, like obedient soldiers. He tried, whilst at Varzin, to draw their leader Bennigsen into his ministry, 'to jump into my boat and help me steer.' But Bennigsen, knowing Bismarck, refused to come in without others from his party, and as the emperor protested against his entry the effort came to naught.

Nor was Bismarck, when back in harness early in 1878, more successful in persuading the liberals to support his efforts to increase the inadequate federal revenue. He wished to replace the direct tax of the 'matricular' contribution of the states to imperial revenue, which was admittedly unjust because it was based only on population, by indirect taxes on beer, tobacco, sugar, etc. But the liberals were afraid of losing parliamentary control over

K

such indirect taxes, and so rejected most of them. And as champions of free enterprise they were even more hostile to Bismarck's suggestion of a state monopoly of tobacco. Finally, when, after the first of the two attempts made in this year on the life of the emperor by men accused of socialist connections, Bismarck introduced a very hastily drafted anti-socialist law with wide restrictions on the press and associations, they rejected that also, although after the second attempt on William's life they supported a revised measure.

This socialist or anti-socialist law may likewise be regarded as a part of the definition of Bismarck's system. Despite his slight connection with Lassalle Bismarck was fundamentally opposed to the socialist creed as it came to be defined, and the attitude of the socialist leaders to the war of 1870, the annexation of Alsace-Lorraine, and the Paris Commune had naturally hardened his opposition to what he called in 1878 'the menacing band of robbers with whom we share our largest towns.' The Commune indeed was to him 'a flash of light; from that moment I saw the social democratic elements as an enemy against whom State and society must arm themselves.' He took action in three ways against them. In 1871 he proposed an international conference to concert measures against them, and although this was rather a gesture than seriously meant, the Three Emperors' League of the next year was in part a lining-up of conservative rulers against revolutionary dangers, like the old Holy Alliance. More specific was the severe police action of the seventies against socialist agitators and leaders in Prussia, which sent many of them to prison. And finally he made attempts to restrict freedom of the press (1874), and to alter the Penal Code of the Empire (1876), to punish incitement to violence and the threat to existing institutions. But neither liberals nor Catholics (the latter themselves suffering from persecution) would support such limitations of fundamental liberties, and these attempts failed.

In 1878, however, with the attacks on the life of the emperor, and the growing evidence of the anarchism which was to take the life of Alexander II three years later, Bismarck was able to secure legislation which though not so severe as he would have liked, and limited to two and a half years, was nevertheless severe enough for Lasker to call the act 'a political and juridical monstrosity.' It swept away workers' associations, publications, and rights of meeting, and gave the government the right to expel socialists from their places of residence, as was later done in Berlin, Breslau, and Leipzig. It was carried out with much police harshness and persecution, partially held in check, it is true, by the courts. Yet the law did not fulfil Bismarck's hope of destroying the socialist movement, though it played its part in increasing emigration in the years immediately following the law, to reach a peak of over 200,000 in the early eighties. The social democrats lost three of their twelve seats in the elections of 1878, but regained these three years later, and doubled the number in 1884. And their leaders in the *Reichstag*, Liebknecht and Bebel, were active and courageous as before, though stressing the reforming character of their aims, and repudiating revolution by force as 'madness.' It was indeed a misfortune for them, a profound error of judgment, that they were, in theory at all events, 'cabined, cribbed, confined' within the inflexible theories of Marx. Meanwhile they set up a journal in Zürich, distributed that and other literature secretly in Germany, held their conferences in Switzerland or Denmark, and despite the periodical renewal of the law down to 1890 were far stronger when the persecution ended than when it began.

That is to look some way ahead. So far as the liberals were concerned the cup of *their* offences and shortcomings in Bismarck's eyes had overflowed by 1878, and there now followed a dramatic and decisive turn. The regular elections to the *Reichstag* in 1877 had seen an appreciable swing towards the Right, and after the second attempt on the emperor's life in June 1878 (ten days before the great Congress of Berlin opened) Bismarck had dissolved the *Reichstag* with the deliberate aim of using the aroused popular feeling against both liberals and socialists. The results partially justified his hopes, for the liberals suffered further losses, whilst both sections of the conservatives gained, and the Centre was nearly as strong as the national liberals. A combination of conservatives and Centre would have a majority. The delicate matter of a reconciliation with the Catholic Church was already in train now that Pius IX was dead, and the industrialists were protesting against the triumph of free trade, blaming it for the economic crisis which had hit both industry and agriculture, and demanding the restoration of protective duties. The conservative landowners were shortly to follow with demands for the protection of agriculture. Bismarck was primarily concerned for revenue duties for the federal treasury, but was now prepared to aid industry, provided that agriculture also received help. The Federal Council supported the changes, but there was a lengthy and embittered debate in the *Reichstag* during the early summer of 1879 over the proposed revenue and protective duties, with Bennigsen still striving for compromise. In the end the main body of the national liberals stood by their economic faith, but some of the right wing joined conservatives and Centre to give Bismarck his majority. His recent enemies were now his allies, Falk and O. Camphausen resigned as ministers, and he was free to denounce national liberals, progressives, and socialists together as enemies of the *Reich*.

The victory was a political and personal one for Bismarck, for which the emperor duly thanked him: 'The Fatherland will bless you.' But it was more than that. Tariffs had come to stay, to be an integral part of the system of the Bismarckian Empire. Their coming marked the triumph of economic nationalism, thus wedded to the political unity. The member states of the *Reich* welcomed the additions which the system promised to their treasuries, and so were the better disposed towards the empire. Internationally, however, the effect was rather to sharpen rivalries, since other nations (save for free-trading Britain) responded to the German tariffs by raising their own. The new system represented a gain for the more conservative elements in the country, notably the larger landowners through the duty on grain and the industrialists now enjoying their varying degrees of protection. And the passing of the anti-socialist law at the same time tended to draw these vested interests together in the common struggle against revolutionary dangers. The threat to the agrarian interest by the growth of industry was lessened by the protection they now received, which further helped to maintain their position, especially in eastern Germany. The effects on the people in general are less easy to define briefly. The economic growth of Germany continued, but it is impossible to say how far the recovery from the depression of the middle seventies was due to the new system or to world conditions. The cost of living rose, the workers' bread cost more than it would have done, but employment increased and wages rose, though more slowly than prices; and emigration increased also for a time. The consolidation of capitalist interest, coupled with the anti-socialist law, increased the gap between capital and labour, and the definition of the interest of the workers likewise increased, despite the efforts Bismarck was shortly to make to win them over.

Within a few years Bismarck was to regret the loss of his former allies. But in fact the day of the national liberals was over. They had lost members from the Right, and they were shortly to lose others from the Left also. In the elections of 1881 their numbers shrank to less than a third of what they had been at their height, and save for one occasion (1887) they were never again to rise appreciably above that. They had achieved much for their country, both in furthering the cause of national unity and in incorporating into its framework far more of liberalism than Bismarck would have done. But in their overwhelming desire for unity they had accepted so much of the monarchical-military Prussian State system (and Bismarck's autocratic methods) that so far as true liberalism was concerned they had bartered much of the substance for the shadow, like the dog in Aesop's fable. They had lost, or were to lose, the fight with the Centre, which with its permanently larger membership in the *Reichstag* was to outbid them in support of Bismarck's new policies. And as too exclusively a middle-class party they were to fail to compete with socialism for the allegiance of the growing mass of the industrial workers. Bennigsen's continued efforts at compromise with Bismarck had failed, and in 1883, though a decade younger than the chancellor, he withdrew from the *Reichstag* for a time, and the party under Miquel was to abandon its free-trading principles and become the representatives of big business and imperialism, with South German leadership.

Bennigsen had represented the height not merely of the party, but also of the prestige of the *Reichstag*. He was indeed the finest parliamentary leader and speaker Germany produced, nearer than any one else to the pattern of the great English parliamentarians. With his going, and the removal by death or otherwise of men such as Lasker, Hoverbeck, Forckenbeck, and others, the prestige of the *Reichstag* was to suffer a permanent decline. Eugen Richter remained, but with all his qualities as a Bismarck critic, he lacked the breadth and depth of his predecessors. Henceforth big business rather than the political scene was to draw Germany's ablest men, and not merely was the political life of Germany to be the poorer, but the victory of the Bismarckian State over liberalism was to stultify the hopes of the continuing political education of the German people. On the eve of the war of 1914 Bülow in his book on *Imperial Germany* [1] could repeat the old tag that 'political talent has been denied the German people. We are not a political people,' when in fact it was the Bismarckian Prussian system, rather than any natural incapacity, which had hindered their education in the necessarily slow development of that quality.

A further turn towards protection of a different kind was provided in external affairs, when Bismarck now established Germany's foreign relations on lines that were to endure throughout the empire by the alliance with Austria-Hungary. There is no need to emphasize Bismarck's continuous concern with Prussian and then German relations with neighbouring states. It was not merely an integral, but the foremost part of his policy, the metal out of which he had forged German unity, and raised her to heights comparable to those of the great days of the Hohenstauffen emperors. As a result of his efforts and successes there grew up in Germany a theory that nationality expressed itself primarily through struggle with other nationalities, a theory based in part on the special position of Germany in the centre of Europe, with her frontiers marching with those of other great states. The theory implied a primacy of foreign over domestic policy, and this had been true of Bismarck's efforts from 1862 to 1870. The very success of those efforts, however, bound him to unceasing activity and anxiety in foreign policy during the remainder of his career. For if Germany was now the strongest military power in Europe, second only to Russia in population, and of rapidly increasing economic strength, her achievement of that position had constituted a revolution in the former State system and balance of power on the continent. It also raised fears that she (or Bismarck, as the acknowledged author of this change) might wish to go further. Thus Ódo Russell, the British Ambassador to Germany, not unfriendly to Bismarck, and indeed the foreign ambassador with whom Bismarck got on best, wrote [2] to his colleague in France in 1873 that 'the two great objects of Bismarck's policy are the supremacy of Germany in Europe and of the German race in the world, and the neutralization of the influence and power of the Latin race in France and elsewhere.'

This reads like a judgment on post-Bismarckian German policy, and may have been provoked by Bismarck's unpeaceful methods of trying to secure the peace which he declared he wanted, since Germany was now 'a satiated power,' and which common sense dictated in order to organize the new empire and digest the gains of the war. His immediate concern was France, defeated and occupied by German troops, momentarily in turmoil in 1871. Yet the ink was hardly dry on the peace treaty (signed 10th May 1871) before, with the Paris Commune bloodily suppressed, she began under Thiers's provisional government to exhibit her extraordinary powers of recuperation. In 1872 she set about the reorganization of her army, and by anticipating the payments due on her indemnity she got rid of the occupying German

[1] p. 103.   [2] Newton, *Lord Lyons*, 1913, vol. ii, p. 41.

troops before the end of the following year. It was abundantly clear to Bismarck as to all the world that she was quite unreconciled to the loss of Alsace-Lorraine. Her bishops angered him by speaking against his attacks on the Papacy, and the threat of a royalist restoration, when Thiers was succeeded by McMahon in 1873, was a further source of concern, since he believed that a republican France would be weaker and so less dangerous. His dislike and distrust of Arnim, his own (or rather the emperor's) ambassador to Paris was another cause of irritation.

The result was that German relations with France in these early years were decidedly uneasy, punctuated by crises when Bismarck, sometimes for internal reasons such as the fight with the Church or the issue over the army budget, set himself to arouse German fears of a French war of revenge. It was out of this unease that the war scare of 1875 arose. 'Bismarck is at his old tricks again,' wrote Odo Russell from Berlin, 'alarming the German people through the semi-official press,' as the Berlin *Post*, a free conservative paper, close to the Foreign Office, asked *Is War in Sight?* And although Bismarck denied all thought of a preventive war (which Moltke frankly favoured), and the crisis passed, it was not forgotten on either side of the frontier, or indeed elsewhere.

For this crisis was like a lightning flash which lit up the whole European sky. While France was not as yet dangerous alone, she would be so if she could find allies: so she must be kept isolated. And if her gaze could be turned from the Rhine and Europe to colonial enterprise in Africa or elsewhere, so much the better. There were, counting France, five great powers in Europe, for Italy was too weak as yet to count as such. This being so, the all-important thing, as Bismarck later explained to the Russian ambassador, was to be *à trois*, to be allied with two, 'that is the true security against coalitions.' He had angled for British friendship, but found them suspicious and unresponsive. Their rivalry with Russia was a difficulty, and their parliamentary system, with its changes of government and policy (as in 1874 from Gladstone to Disraeli) made them in Bismarck's eyes unreliable as allies. In any case Germany's long frontiers with Austria and Russia made relations with these two powers more immediately important. Despite Austria's recent defeat by Prussia Bismarck saw no reason why the two powers should not be on good terms. Further, whilst Austro-Russian unfriendliness since the Crimean War, and their rivalry in the Balkans, created problems, it at any rate prevented their allying against Germany and gave her a freer hand; and Austria was hardly to be feared alone.

Russia was the major problem. There was the old Russo-Prussian alliance, fortified by the bond of blood relationship between William I and his nephew Alexander II, and the mutual goodwill shown in the recent wars and crises. 'Prussia will never forget,' wrote William to the tsar in February 1871, 'that she owes it to you that the war did not take the widest dimensions.' In the past, however, Russia had always been the superior partner, protective, at times patronizing. Now conditions had changed, not wholly to Russian satisfaction. As there was always a fund of anti-Russian feeling in German liberal circles, so there was likewise anti-German feeling in Russia. And just as German national feeling was now stronger, so in Russia a more conscious Slav feeling was arising, nationalist in Russia, but with a wider aura of Panslavism preached by writers such as Danilevsky. Bismarck may have been thinking of an alliance with Austria in 1872, when Francis Joseph visited Berlin, but Alexander got himself invited as well, and the resulting Three Emperors' League was more colourfully spectacular than politically binding. Bismarck was annoyed when Alexander suggested he should fulfil the pledge given to hold a plebiscite in North Schleswig, and the crisis of 1875 brought more serious annoyance. For not merely did Britain protest, but the tsar visited Berlin, and the eighty-year-old Gortschakoff, who had previously reassured the French, more or less openly took credit to Russia and himself for holding Germany in check and preserving peace. It was an insult Bismarck never forgave. Thus the crisis revealed a coolness in German-Russian relations, and a Russian sympathy for the revival of France which might develop into something warmer and closer.

Hard on the heels of this crisis came the revolt against Turkish rule in Bosnia-Herzgovina, which marked the beginning of a steadily rising crisis in the Balkans and Near East and between the powers primarily interested there. Russia had her Slav sympathies and ambitions towards Constantinople and the Straits, Britain her opposition to Russian advance there or in Asia, Austria her anti-Russian interests and her own Balkan ambitions. Bismarck was not much concerned with the local issues in the Balkans themselves; they were not, he said in a speech of December 1876, 'worth the bones of a Pomeranian grenadier.' And he could even see advantages for Germany in the 'eastern ulcer' being kept open, as the powers involved there were less likely to move against Germany. But as he *was* closely interested in the relations of these powers in so far as they affected Germany, he was inevitably drawn into the complicated series of negotiations before, during, and after the local wars between Turkey and the Balkan peoples, the Russo-Turkish war of 1877, and the Russian triumph in the Treaty of San Stefano of March 1878.

Russia had claimed that in view of her goodwill to Prussia in 1870 and earlier, Germany should give open support to her policy, even suggesting an alliance. But with the threat of an Austro-Russian war Bismarck was not prepared either to ally with Russia or to see the balance of power in eastern Europe upset by an Austrian defeat. Such a war, he argued, 'would create an extremely difficult and dangerous dilemma for us.' It was with some unwillingness that he presided over the famous congress which met in Berlin in June 1878 to revise the terms of the Russian treaty in response to the demands of Britain and Austria. And although some of the most contentious issues (such as those over the 'Big Bulgaria' created by the San Stefano Treaty, and the Austrian occupation of Bosnia) had already been agreed upon, it was a great tribute to Bismarck's mixture of diplomatic skill and drive that within a month he had secured a settlement which, if defective in many respects, at any rate was accepted for the time being.

From this crisis, however, emerged Bismarck's determination to make a definite alliance with Austria, as a partial insurance against the 'nightmare of coalitions' from which, as he admitted to Schouvaloff, he now suffered. For opinion in Russia, disappointed with the results of the congress, concluded that he had taken sides against her there, and that the 'honest broker,' as he had described himself in a pre-congress speech to the *Reichstag*, had taken more than his due commission through a private treaty with Austria by which his promise of a North Schleswig plebiscite was wiped out. The new German protective duties hit Russian trade, the press on both sides was aroused and bitter, the tsar wrote a disturbed letter to William, and Bismarck and Gortschakoff continued their personal antagonism.

It was from this background that Bismarck approached Andrassy, the Austrian Foreign Minister, who 'jumped for joy,' says Hohenlohe, at the prospect, with the proposal for a treaty of alliance between the two powers. The treaty provided that the two powers were to aid each other if either were attacked by Russia. Andrassy firmly refused more than 'benevolent neutrality' in case of a French attack on Germany, but agreed that Austria would support Germany should Russia join France. Bismarck drafted this treaty entirely on his own, and it required a torrent of reiterated argument to secure his emperor's agreement to so violent a turn in his policy, one which went against both William's feelings of loyalty towards his nephew in Russia and his common sense, which forewarned him that it would drive Russia into the arms of France. Hohenlohe also believed this, and doubted both the good faith of Austria and Bismarck's declaration that Russia meditated attack on Germany. Yet he allowed himself (he says) to be convinced by the imperious chancellor. The treaty was signed on 7th October 1879, and the news of the alliance (though the terms were not published till long after) was received with joy in Germany, especially in South German and Catholic circles.

With this Austrian alliance Bismarck may be said to have completed the main structure of the empire. He had thought of trying also to draw in Britain as a third ally but quickly gave up the idea, to turn again to the renewal of the Three Emperors' League in 1881, though what value this had was necessarily reduced by the German-Austrian alliance. The alliance with Austria was to last, and Germany's fate to be bound up with that of the polyglot Austro-Hungarian Empire (less than one-quarter German), until both empires succumbed in a common fate in 1918. Seen in this longer perspective, or even in the shorter one of the Franco-Russian treaty of the early nineties, the alliance turned out to be a mistake of the first magnitude, a continuation of the error of 1871 in seizing Alsace-Lorraine. Bismarck concluded it in haste, and came himself to admit, in his *Memoirs* [1] as elsewhere, that it might have its drawbacks. In the hands of his weaker successors it was to draw Germany into a dangerous and in the end fatal support of Austrian ambitions in the Balkans, and to assist in drawing not merely France and Russia but also Britain and Russia together. Thus it was the

---

[1] *Reflections and Reminiscences* (trans.), vol. ii, p. 280.

foundation document in that system which was to divide the continent into two armed camps, and which a German diplomatist before 1914 described as 'the curse of Europe.' Friedrich Naumann, writing in 1915 in celebration of the hundredth anniversary of Bismarck's birth, calls the alliance of the two empires, the creation of *Mitteleuropa*, 'Bismarck's Political Testament,' and adds: 'As he signed in 1879 the Dual Alliance Treaty with Count Andrassy he thereby laid the foundations of this war and united *Mitteleuropa* against East and West.'[1] Earlier, as we have seen, it had been the kings of Prussia who had left Political Testaments. Now (as in old Merovingian days) it was the all-powerful 'Mayor of the Palace,' as Morier and others described Bismarck, who performed this task.

This alliance of 1879 crowned not only Bismarck's foreign policy but also his power, which was now manifested not only in the way in which he over-bore the emperor, but in his attitude to the *Bundesrat* and the *Reichstag*, as in the complete subordination he demanded from both ministers and officials. It was this which caused Schweinitz, German Ambassador to Russia, to refer to his 'dictatorship.' Eugen Richter complains in his memoirs at the way in which, in the Prussian elections of 1879, all the government machinery was employed to sway the voters. And the appointment of Puttkamer, a relative of Bismarck by marriage, to the post of Minister of the Interior in 1881 was the signal for a regular campaign to see that all officials should 'represent the policy of the government,' especially in elections, with bad effects on the quality of the bureaucracy. Lucius, the free conservative and devoted friend, had remarked[2] some years before on Bismarck's 'pathological irritability,' which made working with him very difficult. 'How much more he could achieve if he were less irritable. But it is his temperament, from which both he and others suffer.' And it did not diminish with the years. Bebel, a fighter himself, describes in his memoirs[3] how Bismarck met opposition in the *Reichstag* (on this occasion from the Frankfurt deputy Sonnemann, whom he hated almost more than Eugen Richter) during the debate over the socialist law of 1878:

Bismarck, when once in fighting spirit—and he was that day—was little wont to keep to the subject under discussion. To give his feelings free play, he jumped from one topic to another in his attack on the opponent who stood in his way. This habit was often the despair of the President [of the *Reichstag*], who did not dare to interrupt him, but then also could not prevent the man attacked from defending himself, and so arose an argument which developed far beyond the limits of the subject under discussion. So it was on this occasion.

II. THE MATURITY OF THE EIGHTIES

The autocratic quality of Bismarck's rule was partly personal, but partly inherent in the character of the empire he had created, and which was now, in the eighties, attaining its maturity. With the emperor a few years older than the century, and becoming a little forgetful (as Hohenlohe noted in his diary), and with the chancellor now in the later sixties, the empire solidified

[1] *Gestalten und Gestalter*, p. 8.
[2] Lucius von Ballhausen, *Bismarck-Erinnerungen*, 1921, p. 28.
[3] *Aus Meinem Leben*, 1930, vol. iii, p. 12.

rather than changed in these years. This state was now to find its outstanding expositor and champion in the person of the great historian of the university of Berlin, Heinrich Treitschke. Treitschke was a Saxon officer's son, prevented by early deafness from following a military career, but a most doughty fighter with his pen during the sixties for the union of Germany under Prussia. Treitschke was at first liberal, but was won to national liberalism, and became more conservative as time went on. Called to Berlin in 1874 (to stay there until his death in 1896) he was now a member of the *Reichstag*, busy with his great *History of Nineteenth-Century Germany* (to 1848), the most eloquent product of German historical scholarship, and also with the delivery of his famous lectures on *Politik* [1] defining the new state for the benefit of future leaders of opinion.

To Treitschke the State was power: 'its highest moral law' was to maintain itself and its power, and for this supreme end it might transgress the moral law itself. 'We must distinguish between public and private morality.' Warfare is 'the second most important function of the State,' the army 'is the basis of political freedom,' and 'in the conflict of states lies the beauty of history.' The ideal state was monarchical, like the Prussian, with 'all power united in a single hand.' (There is a curious blindness to the actual influence of the all-powerful chancellor, who, says Treitschke, 'has but to execute the decrees of the Federal Council'!) Treitschke's state was a class state, wherein the landed aristocracy should control local government. The middle class was certainly important, but too great wealth in their hands was dangerous; the lower classes must content themselves (outside their work) with religion and the love of military heroism. He had naturally no place for a parliamentary system such as existed in England (which he hated), and disapproved of universal suffrage; as for woman suffrage, it was mere 'flippancy.' Thus did Treitschke, in so far as he was of influence, and a recent German writer terms him 'the most widely influential political publicist for centuries,' [2] contribute to support the militarist and autocratic Prussian qualities of the Bismarckian Empire, blind to other views and trends whether in Germany or without. [3] With his narrow intolerance it is not surprising to find him an active supporter of the anti-Semitism which now began to take shape in Germany, or to hear him claiming that Luther (who

---

[1] These are partly translated by A. L. Gowans, 1914, and are discussed in H. W. C. Davis's *The Political Thought of Heinrich von Treitschke*, 1914.

[2] G. Ritter, *Europa und die deutsche Frage*, 1948, p. 105.

[3] Gerhart Hauptmann, who was a schoolboy in Breslau after 1870, describes in his autobiography (*Das Abenteuer meiner Jugend*, 1937, vol. i, p. 261) how the victory of Prussianism affected education: 'The German victory [of 1871] by means of the Prussian-Potsdam principle caused this to be regarded as the sole way of salvation, and so led to its general strengthening as much as possible. The schools, with their reserve officers as teachers, felt the first results of this, and the pupils had to adapt themselves thereto. Thus when the teacher entered the classroom the boys sprang from their seats and stood stiff and tense until the command "Sit" rang out in cutting tones. The manner in which instruction was handed down from the teacher's desk exactly resembled the teaching methods in the army. Thus did Jurich [the teacher] bellow forth religious instruction, asking questions from the New Testament, such as "What did St. Paul say?" "How did the disciple John put it?" "What did Christ teach in the Sermon on the Mount?" At the same time, if a boy was slow to answer he would haul him up by the tip of the ear as far as he could, short of tearing off his ear. Simple terms, good nature, friendly encouragement of the pupil, were ruled out as sentimentality: they were regarded as soft, effeminate. For behind the teacher as his driving force stood not Lessing or Herder, Goethe or Socrates, but the Prussian non-commissioned officer.'

was also anti-Semitic) 'incorporated the inner nature of the German people,' unmindful of the Catholic faith of millions of his fellow countrymen.

Bismarckian policy in the eighties was for the most part concerned with the maintenance and consolidation of the recent changes, with one important new development, that in the colonial field. The social legislation of the eighties, striking though it was, is bound up with both the general turn from *laissez-faire* and more particularly with the socialist law of 1878. For Bismarck was not content with repression alone in dealing with the socialist danger. He can hardly be called a social reformer in any full sense, but he had some realization of the hardships of the new working class, he was 'a man of infinite resource,' and, as we have seen, not frightened by the idea of State action in social matters. So with his customary boldness he proceeded to try and destroy socialism with State socialism, as he had earlier tried to destroy parliamentarism by universal suffrage. Some voices, such as those of the so-called 'Socialists of the Lecture Room,' Schmoller, Brentano, A. Wagner, and others, not socialists but economists with consciences, had already been raised on behalf of the workers, and beginnings made in Prussia with factory legislation by an act of 1874, extended to the *Reich* four years later, which greatly restricted child labour. Bismarck now launched upon a bolder policy, of significance not merely for Germany but for most modern states.

This began with an imperial message to the *Reichstag* in November 1881, declaring that the removal of social ills was not to be sought merely in the repression of social democratic excesses, but also in the positive furtherance of the well-being of the worker, and foreshadowing the coming legislation. First came a bill for accident insurance in certain more dangerous industries, originally on a contributory basis, but modified before its passing in 1884 to make the employer alone responsible for its charges, and soon extended to most industries. State insurance against sickness, paid for by both employer and worker, came in the same year, and in 1889 a measure providing for old age pensions and permanent incapacity for work, this by contributions from worker, employer, and State. This labour code, for long unique, had to meet much opposition before being passed through the *Reichstag*, both from the free-enterprise radicals as also from the little group of social democrats who saw it as an attempt to win the workers away from them. Combined with the socialist law it was to them a policy of 'whips and sugar-plums'; and a liberal such as Weber, looking back from the 1914–18 war period, could call Bismarck's policy herein 'demagogy, and bad demagogy, however valuable in fact,' since it was the work of an authoritarian state. Yet the workers, and socialists too in time, accepted the laws with their solid benefit, and by 1905 nearly nineteen million German workers were insured against accident, twelve million against sickness, fourteen million against old age and incapacity. The benefits were indeed not large: the average annual old age pension at that date was under £8 ($38 or so), but this had its value in those days.

More plainly continuing the policy of the preceding years was the further development of protection, bound up as before with the problem of imperial finance. The eighties was a period of uneven economic recovery from the great crash of the seventies, with labour unrest and strikes, but preparing for the great forward spring to come in the nineties. Overall, industry and trade increased considerably, with coal production growing by one half, steel output more than doubled, the great General Electrical Company founded by Emil Rathenau in 1883, foreign trade increasing, steam tonnage more than trebled. The big cities grew despite the large emigration. The position of agriculture was complicated by the general fall of world prices of grain, and also by the fact that Germany was no longer raising enough grain to feed her growing population. And Bismarck was concerned for agriculture more than for industry, not merely as a landowner, but because, as he put it, 'I see in the decline of agriculture one of the gravest dangers to our existence as a state.' Industry, where combinations (cartels) were already arising as the protectionist interest grew, was, as always, better able to look after itself. As the inevitable demand for more protection increased Bismarck responded, in 1885, by trebling the duty on wheat, rye, and barley, with a smaller increase in other agricultural products, and likewise raised (though far less) the duties on manufactured goods. As agricultural prices continued to fall, a further increase was given in 1887, so that Germany now had the highest grain duties in Europe,[1] which meant that the price of the workers' bread was likewise higher.

Since Germany was a federal state, whose members possessed and used taxing powers, the problem of imperial revenue was always a difficult one. The gain by the 1879 duties was lessened by a clause called after its Centre party proposer, Franckenstein, whereby any future surplus therefrom should be given to the states. Hence, as federal expenses increased (e.g. by the social legislation) new revenue was needed, and the *Reich* slowly began to incur a national debt by loans. Bismarck stood by his refusal to impose federal income taxes (partly because these were already collected by states and towns), and made in these years a succession of attempts to raise money by stamp duties, increased taxes on beer (especially unpopular in beer-drinking Bavaria), and above all by creating a federal monopoly of tobacco or brandy. There was in fact room for higher taxes on both of these: German tobacco bore only a fraction of the tax imposed in other countries. But despite his efforts in 1882 for a tobacco monopoly, and three years later for brandy, both special commissions and the *Reichstag* refused to agree, and the best he could do was to increase the taxes on these products, in 1887, and thus, with the increased customs duties, secure some relief for federal finances.

Bismarck's difficulty with the *Reichstag* after the break up of the national liberal party was the lack of what he termed a 'phalanx of trusty supporters' strong enough to give him a firm majority there. In a *Reichstag* of nearly four hundred members the Centre remained the strongest single party, about a hundred strong, with allies in the Poles, Guelphs, Danes, and Alsace-

[1] W. H. Dawson, *Protection in Germany*, 1910, p. 95.

Lorrainers, but it was not yet reconciled after the *Kulturkampf*. The two groups of conservatives numbered less than eighty in 1881, though they were slowly to increase in the elections of 1884 and 1887. The national liberals were now a party of about fifty only, and when the radicals (progressives and secessionists of 1881) managed to join forces in 1883, with the somewhat inept title of Freeminded (*Freisinnige*) party, their programme of parliamentary government, freer trade, and opposition to State socialism was one of open hostility to the chancellor. Their leader, in succession to Lasker (d. 1884), was Eugen Richter, an able if somewhat doctrinaire financial critic, and one of Bismarck's chief bugbears.

Yet it was with these parties that the increasingly autocratic chancellor had to deal through the eighties in the *Reichstag* as he carried forward his legislative programme, fought for the renewal of the anti-socialist law and of the seven-year army budget, reversed his anti-clerical legislation, and faced the likelihood that the old emperor would die and leave him to deal with a liberal successor. He tried to get a two-year budget (and so a biennial meeting of the *Reichstag*), thought of abolishing the secret ballot, or even the universal suffrage, and openly abused the party system whilst manœuvring with it for his ends. 'The parties,' he declared in the *Reichstag* in 1884, 'are the ruin of our constitution and our future,' and to the trusty Bucher he confided that the best training for an imperial chancellor would be as a juggler in a circus, learning to throw balls (parties) into the air and catch them again. But it was largely his own fault if the parties behaved in ways he considered irresponsible, for he ever refused to share responsibility with them. Everything must depend upon him. 'There are occasions when one can rule liberally, and others when one must rule dictatorially,' he told the *Reichstag* in 1880; but it lay solely with him to decide which. 'He goes his own way,' a friend had earlier written to Bennigsen; 'whoso goes with him is his friend; whoever opposes him is his enemy, to be trampled upon': 'personal policy,' as Bennigsen succinctly noted.

For his social legislation and tariff changes Bismarck was able to secure a majority from the conservatives, national liberals, and Centre. The anti-socialist law was renewed four times, though for shorter periods than he wanted, and with increasing difficulty as its failure to stamp out socialism became manifest. More difficult still was the renewal of the Army Septennate, first in 1880 and then again in 1886-7. On the first occasion he secured renewal of the seven years' grant, with some increase in the army's peace strength, by dint of heavy press propaganda and the abstention from voting of the Centre. But the second occasion brought a greater crisis, complicated by the presence of foreign issues. In France the defeat of Ferry's policy of colonial expansion and of better relations with Germany favoured the meteoric rise of General Boulanger, now Minister of War, busy with the reorganization of the army, and momentarily a national hero. There was talk of a *coup d'état*, perhaps with a royalist restoration. And in the Balkans there was trouble over Bulgaria's attempt to unite with Eastern Roumelia, which caused reverberations and jealousies between the great powers again, with a wave of anti-German feeling in Russia, and demands for a Russo-French alliance.

Out of this situation Bismarck secured what was to be his last outstanding political success. In a great two-hour speech of 11th January 1887, intended for Russia and France as well as for its hearers in the *Reichstag*, he stressed the good relations existing with Russia and reiterated that Germany had no warlike needs or designs. 'We belong to what old Prince Metternich called the satiated states. . . . If the French will keep the peace, then peace is assured. . . . But we still have to fear an attack, whether in ten days or ten years . . .' since Boulanger was a menace to peace. True, the German ambassador in Paris, Münster, had just reported that there was no fear of a ,French attack. But Bismarck refused to accept the report, since, as he told Münster: 'If His Majesty and the German states shared these views the government would hardly be able to put forward and support its military proposals in the *Reichstag*.' Despite his efforts the *Reichstag*, or rather the Centre with its allies and the radicals, refused to renew the Septennate, though they were ready to vote an increased grant for three years. Bismarck immediately dissolved the *Reichstag* and turned to the task of getting a majority in the ensuing elections. There was heavy press propaganda, the calling up of reservists, frightening the Stock Exchange, getting Bennigsen to stand again, above all, the formation of a cartel or bloc arrangement between the two conservative parties and the national liberals not to stand against each other. By these means, although the Centre remained as strong as before, radicals and social democrats suffered heavy losses, to the gain of the three parties of the Right, so that these now had a majority. The Septennate was passed, and Bismarck's power assured, the more so as the term of the *Reichstag* was now lengthened to five years. It was a famous victory.

This crisis of 1886-7 illustrates the problems and issues of Bismarck's foreign policy during the later years of his rule. In general this filled out rather than changed the policy of the earlier decade, continuing to be defensive save in the new colonial issues, resting primarily on the alliance with Austria, but seeking good relations with Russia, and indeed with France so long as she was isolated and was content to find distraction away from the Rhine, as, for example, in North Africa by the seizure of Tunis. 'The pear is ripe and it is time for you to gather it,' he had told the French in 1879. Two years later the French did so, to the anger of Italy, who had ambitions there herself. But this was grist to Bismarck's mill, for it caused Italy to turn to Germany and come to terms with the Dual Alliance in 1882, despite her irredentist feeling against Austria. The Treaty of Alliance was for five years and it was to be successively renewed. Thus the Dual Alliance became a Triple Alliance, and Bülow was later to acclaim it as 'a mighty fortification dividing the Continent into two.' Yet the Italian partnership was never whole-hearted, and Bülow himself was to see it change to open hostility. The network of the Bismarckian alliances was to be extended even more widely, for his ally Austria made in 1881 an alliance with Serbia, and two years later Germany adhered to a treaty between Austria and Rumania. This complicated structure of alliances, with its centre in the chancellor's brain in Berlin, was certainly a triumph of diplomatic genius. It was a work of art, indeed of artifice, for, as with the original alliance with Austria, time was to reveal both weaknesses and dangers in the system.

The hub of such dangers was Russia, and the fear that she might ally with France. Yet Russia, at odds with both Austria and Britain, was ready for the time at least to draw more closely to Germany, despite the change in 1881 from the second to the third Alexander, with his Danish empress. Bismarck still thought of an alliance à trois, and so drew in the somewhat unwilling Austria in 1881 to revive the Three Emperors' League of the early seventies. The alliance provided for 'benevolent neutrality' of the other two powers in case one of the three were attacked by a fourth state, and defined their attitude to Balkan issues. The treaty was secret and ran for three years, but at Russia's instance was renewed in 1884 for another three years. And when this ran out, and the worsening of Austro-Russian relations prevented its further renewal, Bismarck replaced it with his famous 'Reinsurance' treaty with Russia alone. In his speech of 11th January 1887 to the Reichstag he had declared: 'We will allow no one to lead us by the nose and embroil us with Russia,' a warning to Austria, and in the treaty he recognized 'Russia's historic rights' in the Balkans. The provision for 'benevolent neutrality' did not cover a Russian attack on Austria or a German attack on France. But the treaty was kept secret from Austria (at the tsar's request), though Bismarck revealed to Russia the terms of his alliance of 1879, and the new treaty represented a modification of that alliance.

The Reinsurance Treaty did not, however, prevent a certain deterioration of Russo-German relations in the last years of Bismarck's rule. The newspapers in both countries were increasingly unfriendly, and there was even talk in German military circles of a 'preventive' war against Russia. Bismarck deplored the turn, and protested against it in his last great speech to the Reichstag on foreign affairs, perhaps his greatest, on 6th February 1888, which he closed with the famous assertion: 'We Germans fear God and naught else in the world.' But that speech was in support of a further increase in the imperial army caused by concern over Russian troop concentrations along her western border. And he had already taken certain anti-Russian steps, such as making the Reichsbank refuse loans to Russia; he approved an Anglo-Italian and Austrian agreement for the Mediterranean which partly contradicted his Russian treaty; and he threw out feelers for an alliance with Russia's rival, Britain, which Salisbury, however, did not take up. Meanwhile France had begun to supply arms to Russia in 1887, and in the following year began to loan money. The basis of the feared coalition was being laid.

The one markedly new turn in Bismarckian policy in these later years was that to overseas expansion. He had refused to consider the seizure of French colonies in 1871, and on various occasions up to 1882 expressed himself plainly as opposed to German efforts at colonial expansion, being in fact a continentalist like Clemenceau in France, and disliking emigration which lessened German manpower. 'I am no friend to emigration in general. A German who has cast off his Fatherland like an old coat is for me no more a German.' In 1881 he declared flatly: 'So long as I am chancellor we shall pursue no colonial policy. We have no fleet for it, and we want no vulnerable points far away from Germany which can fall to the French immediately they attack us.' Certainly Germany was less favourably situated for colonial expansion than either Russia to the east, with only the low hills of the Urals separating her from advance into Asia, or Britain, France, and Holland, with their open sea roads to west and south, or round Africa (after 1869 through the Suez Canal) to the east. Further, Britain in possession of Heligoland barred the exit from the Elbe and the Weser, and the western exit from the Kiel Canal when that might be completed.

Yet the Germans had long been colonizers on land to the east, as we have seen; the rulers of Prussia in the seventeenth century had made unsuccessful attempts to found overseas colonies, the wandering habit was still traditional in Germany, reflected in Goethe's *Wilhelm Meister* and practised by university students and journeymen artisans such as Bebel in his youth, and there was a very large flow of Germans overseas reaching its height just at this time. The Hansa cities of Hamburg and Bremen, which now, after sharp controversy, agreed to join the Imperial Customs Union, had long sent out traders down the African coast and to the Pacific, there were German traders and missionaries scattered abroad, and German explorers contributed materially to the exploration of the 'Dark Continent' of Africa. German science, as with Humboldt, was insatiably curious about the world. Germany was now politically and economically united, with expanding industry and trade, and her national consciousness was aroused as never before. And she had before her eyes the spectacle of Britain and France, and even little states such as Portugal and Belgium, carving out large areas of the vast African continent into colonies or protectorates.

Thus it was quite natural that there should arise in Germany a demand for colonial expansion. Books were written on the subject, Treitschke then and later lending his powerful pen and voice in its favour; societies appeared to further the cause: the German African Society (1878), the German Colonial Association (1881), and in 1884 the Society for German Colonization. By this date indeed the movement was under way, and Bismarck now so far modified his attitude as to commit himself to limited support, though less, it would seem, from a change of conviction than to win support in Germany and to further his diplomatic aims in Europe, perhaps to win Heligoland from England. Since Germany was so late in entering the field, Africa and the western Pacific islands were the only obvious areas available and these not without friction with states already established there, notably Britain. It was a Bremen merchant, Lüderitz, who opened the new era by requesting protection for lands acquired or to be acquired along the south-west coast of Africa, immediately north of the Orange River, which was then, save for Walfish Bay, the effective northern boundary of Britain's Cape Colony. Bismarck agreed to give support, subject to British rights there, and after undue delay Britain recognized the German claim to found this first African colony. But when Lüderitz then tried to establish a similar base on the south-east African coast Britain had reason to fear that German ambitions looked, as Treitschke and others had suggested, to the formation in union with the discontented Boers of an empire stretching right across southern Africa, and she took steps to prevent it by extending her own dominion there. Thus German efforts inevitably speeded up the process of African partition.

Therewith began a short period of Anglo-German rivalry in the 'scramble for Africa,' and also in the Pacific. In Africa it now centred round what were to be the German colonies of the Cameroons and Togoland, again in an area where the British had long been established but had failed to define their position as they could have done, and Germany with some Bismarckian guile intruded herself in 1885. Similarly in East Africa, though with less friction, the efforts of the ambitious but unscrupulous Karl Peters brought the establishment of German East Africa, reaching from the Zanzibar coast inland to Lake Tanganyika. In the western Pacific, where there was a grievance against British treatment of Hansa merchants' claims to the possession of land in Fiji, by 1880 schemes for acquisition of parts of both New Guinea and Borneo had been put forward. Now (1883) a New Guinea Company was formed, and definite attempts made to acquire territory, which caused the Australian colonies to make vigorous protest. Bismarck used the issue for election purposes in 1884, and criticized Britain in the *Reichstag* and through the press. He turned to cultivate better relations with France, where Ferry was pushing colonial expansion, and with her co-operation called the Berlin Congress of 1884–5 of colonial powers, which set up the Congo Free State under Leopold of Belgium, provided for free trade along the Congo River, and showed to the world that Germany could now play a leading part in colonial as well as in purely European affairs. Britain, facing grave trouble in Egypt and the Russian advance to the borders of Afghanistan, proved more accommodating to German claims in the Pacific, and Germany secured both the northern part of eastern New Guinea (Kaiser Wilhelmsland) and the adjacent islands of what became the Bismarck Archipelago.

Bismarck was by no means carried away by enthusiasm for colonial expansion. The brief period of good relations with France came to a sudden end when Ferry fell in March 1885, and the French once more turned their eyes from Tonking to the Rhine. He had, in any case, strictly limited ideas of any overseas expansion. Unlike List, who had thought of colonies to settle Germans in, he favoured chartered companies for trade, after the early English pattern, companies which should run their own affairs with little more than external protection from the State, a pattern which for various reasons was not to prove satisfactory. And whilst he defended the colonial efforts against critics such as Bamberger, Richter, or Windthorst in the *Reichstag*, he was not in the least prepared to divert to colonial enterprise strength which he considered was needed for the home front. Yet the German colonial adventure of the middle eighties was an astonishing achievement. In two years Bismarck by diplomatic pressure had acquired for Germany an overseas empire of enormous extent, a 'sandbox' perhaps, as Richter contemptuously called it, in South-West Africa, but elsewhere capable of exploitation, though, save for East Africa, of quite limited value for settlement. It remained to be seen what Germany would make of this gift, whose acquisition marked in some ways the crown of Bismarck's power and work. The achievement was made, however, at some cost to the future of good relations with England. For Germans had been encouraged to feel that Britain grudged them a modest share in the vast spaces of Africa or the Pacific, despite assertions such as that of Gladstone to the contrary, whilst British statesmen were left with a decided suspicion of Bismarck's methods of securing his ends.

Among the continuing problems the Bismarckian Empire had to face were those created by the national minorities included in the *Reich*: the Poles, Alsace-Lorrainers, and Danes. As for the last and smallest of these, the treaty of 1878 with Austria, abrogating the provision of 1864 for a plebiscite in North Schleswig, led to expulsions of recalcitrant Danes there, but this was not important enough to create a major issue. The three million Poles in Prussian Poland constituted a more serious problem, especially since the *Kulturkampf* had stirred animosities on both sides, and the rise of the Centre party both in the *Reichstag* and the Prussian House of Deputies gave the Polish members there strong allies. There had been efforts in the seventies both to suppress the use of the Polish tongue in education, law courts, etc. (contrary to the promise of Frederick William III in 1815), and to settle Germans on lands bought from Polish nobles. Now in the middle eighties Bismarck made more decided efforts in this latter direction, to which the Poles responded by raising funds to buy German lands there to settle with Poles, and with greater success. The Polish population increased more rapidly than the German, so that Poles began to flow into the towns, formerly more German, and to compete successfully in trade and industry. They likewise began to migrate in considerable numbers both to the industrial Rhineland and to Silesia, but neither there nor at home did they abandon their passionate faith in the ultimate revival of Polish freedom, so that the problem remained, unchanged in essentials, until the arbitrament of war decided it in favour of the Poles.

The problem of Alsace-Lorraine (the *Westmark* as certain German writers liked to call it) was partly akin, partly different. The *Reichsland* was not Prussian, though largely under Prussian control from Berlin; its population was four-fifths Catholic and discontented. True, Alsace was mainly German in race and speech, and patriotic Germans felt that this province, and even Lorraine, as former parts of the Holy Roman Empire, rightfully belonged to the *Reich*. But the French proximity and feeling, the national kinship of Lorraine in particular to France, and the now lengthy connection of both provinces with France, had no exact parallel in Prussian Poland. The German administration of the *Reichsland* was efficient, and increased its material prosperity, but despite certain concessions to feeling there made in 1879, and the efforts of General Manteuffel as governor from 1879 to 1885, it failed to win the hearts of the people. Their representatives in the *Reichstag* (since 1874) were 'Protesters,' save for a short period when local autonomists shared their seats. Nor was Prince Hohenlohe, despite his diplomatic gifts and the fact that he was a South German Catholic, markedly more successful as governor from 1885 to 1894. This was in part due to the crisis of 1886–7, with the harsh measures then taken to cut off communication with France, and such incidents as the Schnaebelé affair of 1887, when a French official was lured across the border into Alsace and wrongfully arrested. As with Polish Prussia the issue remained to be settled (for a time at least) by war, in the same way.

Despite Bismarck's many-sided achievement, and his success in 1887 in securing his cartel majority in the *Reichstag*, time was working against him in the three years of power that remained to him after that date. He had overpassed the biblical span of three score years and ten, though his health had much improved by the restraints upon his gargantuan appetite for food and drink imposed upon him by his new doctor, Schweninger. But the old emperor was ninety, and died in March 1888, fittingly mourned by all, despite his limitations, and by no one more than his 'true German servant,' as Bismarck defined himself shortly afterwards in writing an epitaph for his own tombstone. True, the long anticipated and feared liberal regime did not set in, for the new emperor, Frederick III, was already mortally ill, and in his short reign of three months could not make any appreciable changes, though he got rid of Puttkamer, Bismarck's unscrupulous ministerial agent in the exertion of administrative and electoral pressure. With Frederick's son and successor, however, it was a different matter. Bismarck had taken steps to secure, as he thought, sufficient influence over the young William II, both for himself and his son Herbert whom he designed as his successor. But it quickly became clear that William had no desire or intention to be kept in leading strings. And although the final breach was to be delayed for a time, it was foreshadowed. Bismarck's long absences from Berlin were a mistake if he wished to remain in power, the more so since his son proved no effective substitute, possessed of his father's overbearing qualities, but lacking his genius, and disliked by many.

With 1890 the *Reichstag* elections swept away the majority of the cartel parties, to the profit of the Centre, the radicals, and the social democrats; the last of these nearly trebled their seats. Bismarck's efforts for the further renewal of the socialist law were opposed by the *Reichstag*, so that the law now lapsed, with its policy exposed as a failure. The issue also brought the final break with the emperor, who to Bismarck's infinite disgust wished to kill socialism by kindness. There were influential elements in the conservative party and round the emperor ranged against the old chancellor: Hammerstein and the *Kreuzzeitung*; Waldersee, the successor to Moltke as Chief of the General Staff; and lower down the scale Stoecker, anti-Semitic leader and court chaplain. These men were moved in varying degree by the old distrust of Bismarck, by jealousy, or the desire to worship the rising sun. It became clear that relations between Bismarck and William II were impossible, and after a series of rather unedifying manœuvres on Bismarck's side to retain power, and growing anger on the other, ending in a great storm, Bismarck accepted at any rate momentary defeat and in March 1890 was forced to resign, as he had so often threatened to do before. But this time there was no William I to say 'Never.'

Bismarck's fall brought that of his dynasty also, but he hardly needed that to increase his anger, which he proceeded to vent for the next few years through the press and in interviews, attacking persons and policies, domestic and foreign, despite a partial reconciliation with the emperor in 1894. The height was reached with his revelation in 1896 of his secret treaty of 1887 with Russia, which had not been renewed by the new regime. With the help of the faithful and able Bucher he also compiled his *Memoirs*, a magnificent apologia, filled with Bismarckian wisdom, illustrating both the strength and weakness of the ageing giant. 'He will not,' complained Bucher,[1] 'admit his own share in anything that failed, and will admit no one to be of any consequence compared to himself, save perhaps the old emperor.' But if the purely historical value of the *Memoirs* suffered somewhat thereby, as is common enough in memoirs, the part played by Bismarck in German history was so big that for him there could be no clear dividing line between auto-biography and history.

For no one could deny the greatness of his achievement in uniting the age-long divided Germany, or his possession of great qualities, his boldness, solidity of mind, clear-sightedness (to a certain point), capacity for decision and action, powers of concentration, political and diplomatic skill, social charm when he chose to exert it, a clarity of thought and expression rare in Germany, even a mastery of literary style, as shown by his ambassadorial dispatches, his letters to his wife, and various of his speeches. And his loyalty to Prussia and (though less) to Germany was undoubted. But he had the defects of his qualities, and more, a growing love of power for himself and for the Prusso-German state, a narrowness and rigidity of view which made him incapable of seeing value in other men's views, thus making his own opinions, as someone noted, a kind of categorical imperative in a perversion of Kant's term. And this was the more dangerous since he was both ruthless and unscrupulous.

In his domestic policy he did more than any one to destroy the liberal-democratic ideal of 1848, and in an age in which social, political, and economic developments in the western world were working towards a more egalitarian society and a fulfilment of the medieval English maxim that 'what concerns all should be approved by all,' he both helped to prevent such a development in Germany, and by his military and political successes educated his countrymen to believe that his way, the old way in Prussian history, was still the best for them. Thus, as one of the greatest Bismarck scholars in Germany put it: 'Bismarck became the German idea.'[2] And his conservatism was social as well as political. Whilst he contemned the narrowness of the

---

[1] Busch, *Bismarck, Secret Pages*, vol. iii, p. 377.
[2] Erich Marcks, *Otto von Bismarck, Ein Lebensbild*, 1919, p. 215.

Prussian *Junkers*, at bottom he shared much of their social outlook. Thus his hatred of the *Engländerin*, as he called the wife of the Crown Prince Frederick, the daughter of Queen Victoria, was due not merely to her liberal political views, but also to her more emancipated social attitude as a woman (e.g. her friendship with Henrietta Schrader, the advocate of wider education for girls). He preferred the model of the old German *Hausfrau*, akin to his own wife, an excellent but narrow-minded woman, uninterested in his political activities, save for a blind faith in the rightness of everything he did. The liberal sociologist, Max Weber, asking himself [1] in 1917 'What then was Bismarck's heritage?' gave the answer that Bismarck

left behind him a nation lacking in all and every political education, far below the level they had reached in this respect twenty years earlier. Above all, a nation without all and every political will, accustomed to the idea that the great statesman at their head should alone control their political life.

In his foreign policy he was similarly limited, believing only in the rivalry of nations, never in their honest working together for the common good, with no other idea of peace than that of the strong man armed more than his neighbour, with no advance on the military tradition or the diplomatic methods of Frederick the Great, the admixture of force and cunning as the common coinage of intercourse between nations. His most glaring mistake was the seizure of both Alsace and Lorraine from France in 1871, thereby preventing hope of peaceful relations with his western neighbour. He partly admitted error in this, but excused himself by putting the blame on the army leaders. Yet it is difficult to believe that the man who had so success-fully withstood the insistence of his king four years earlier for the seizure of Austrian territory could not now, when he was so much stronger, have withstood Moltke had he wished to do so. His alliance with Austria was likewise a mistake. For though *he* could hold Austria in check, his weaker successors neither could nor tried to do so. That indeed was the final rub. He kept peace in his time, but he left a heritage of troubles, and by the very nature of his rule, his intense jealousy of power and ruthless elimination of any possible rivals, he neither trained nor left any successors adequate to deal with these troubles. That was not merely his tragedy, but Germany's also.

The fight for an attainment of political unity, and the great political issues of the seventies and the eighties, were bound to affect the cultural and literary life of the country. Pride in the achievement was perhaps better expressed in the historical than in the purely literary field. For the absorption of so much of the national energy in military life and effort, in political issues, in the growing economic activity, in the new sciences, was hardly favourable to creative literary work. Thus the first decade and more of the empire saw no marked change there from the so-called 'poetic realism' and even the localism of the earlier age. A new generation of writers was indeed growing up, of young men born in the late fifties (as Sudermann) or the early sixties (as Hauptmann, Dehmel, Wedekind, and others) and new winds were blowing

[1] *Gesammelte politische Schriften*, 1921, p. 138.

from outside, from France, across the plains from Russia, over the narrow seas from Norway, above all the current of a newer realism, that of naturalism. The achievement and triumph of this movement was, however, to manifest itself as Bismarck passed off the stage, and so belongs to the later empire. Yet there was one considerable thinker and writer whose work belongs to the Bismarck period of the empire, though his influence was to come later. This was Friedrich Nietzsche, whose active literary career was to be ended by an apoplectic fit a little over a year before Bismarck retired.

Friedrich Nietzsche (1844–1900) was the son of a Lutheran parson in Prussian Saxony who (like Wagner's father) died early. Yet despite poverty Nietzsche managed to get his schooling in the famous Pforta college not far away, as Fichte and other great Germans had done, and afterwards at the universities of Bonn and Leipzig. He was a decidedly precocious genius, and thanks thereto found himself at the age of twenty-four a professor of classics at Basel University, alongside the great Burckhardt, many years his senior. His stay at Basel was important, as seeing his first writing, but was relatively short. Within little more than a decade, plagued already by ill health and mental unease, he found his way to Italy. There after another decade of amazing and often fevered intellectual activity, during which most of his greater works were written, he fell into that final decade of completely broken health and mind which lasted to his death at the close of the century.

Nietzsche was first and foremost a critic, equipped with a magnificent sweep of language, great independence of mind, an unswerving devotion to Greek ideals and achievement in art and literature, and an appreciation of music which brought an early devotion to Wagner. This was, however, to be broken, in part because they were both too egotistical, and they went different ways. Another important early influence on Nietzsche was that of Schopenhauer, admired by him for his freedom from pedantry, his courage and honesty. This too was to be repudiated, but not before Nietzsche had taken from the philosopher of pessimism his admiration for eastern religions and his central conception of the supreme place of the Will. But with Nietzsche the Will to Live was to be transformed into the Will to Power.

Nietzsche's criticism was first aroused by the triumph of 1871, partly against the victory of the national State, but even more (as in the attack on Strauss) against pride in the superiority of German culture, both its science and what he saw as the 'malady' of history in aping that science. To him true German culture was rather endangered than fostered by the military, political, and economic success. Popular education, he declared, was too purely utilitarian, as were the universities, which, subject to the State, and with their hidebound and pedantic professors, did little to guard or encourage real culture. From such beginnings Nietzsche broadened his attack to include the age and German society in general, its bourgeois philistinism and respectability, its desire for wealth, its liberal belief in progress, its hypocrisy, as well as socialism, nationalism, racialism, and the Jews in so far as they contributed to these evils. Above all, however, he attacked the Christian tradition, priestcraft, the 'slave morality' which the Christian ascetic ideal had imposed upon the western world, and this came to be and remained the focus of his criticism. From *Human, All too Human* (1878) to *The Twilight of the Idols* and *The Antichrist*, both of ten years later, this attack was to grow in definiteness and intensity.

In the eighties, however, Nietzsche also turned to positive efforts to provide a new faith and a new philosophy, based on new values, or as he put

Nietzsche

Bust by Max Klinger

it, 'the transvaluation of all values.' Seeing himself as 'the first Immoralist' he would sweep away the Herd or Slave morality of Christianity, with its doctrine of the equality of men, and put in place of it a Master morality of aristocrats to usher in a new age. 'God is dead'; 'I teach you the Super-man' is the opening message of *Thus Spake Zarathustra* (the Persian Zoro-aster), 1883–91. The new aristocracy is to be inspired by the *Will to Power*, filled with high courage and fighting qualities, and dedicated to establish not the Kingdom of Heaven, but the Kingdom of Earth. This, with Nietzsche's doctrine of 'eternal recurrence,' a new-old cyclical theory never fully worked out, in which 'all things eternally return,' constitute the essence of the Nietzschean 'revelation' or revaluation of values, to be reiterated again and again in his later writings, together with most of his other ideas.

This new faith was less novel and less intellectually satisfying as a philosophy than Nietzsche claimed and believed. It was fragmentary, and lacked the clarity of Schopenhauer and the French writers he admired. It was at times illogical and inconsistent to ordinary thinking; to many it was the disordered product of a diseased mind. Yet it was at least significant as evidence of the growing unsettlement of the thought of the time, when, as he put it in *Zarathustra*: 'To-day everything is tottering, the whole earth shakes.' And whilst Nietzsche's works received little attention as they appeared, before his death in 1900 and increasingly afterwards they were to exercise a growing influence in literary circles, above all upon the younger generation. To these, or many of them, Nietzsche became a teacher and prophet, if not a philosopher in the stricter classical sense. Nietzsche lends himself to a variety of interpretations, and there has been endless argument as to his meaning and his influence for good or evil. Some German nationalists, such as the Pan-Germans of the early twentieth century, repudiated him for his strictures on Germany and Germans. Yet other critics, outside Germany at any rate, have seen in his *Supermen* the personification of narrow German nationalism and racialism, and found in the Nazis the 'blond beasts' of his *Genealogy of Morals*.

CHAPTER XI

THE BISMARCKIAN EMPIRE:
II. THE ERA OF WILLIAM II

*Introductory: Credit and Debit — 'The Gay Nineties' — The Bitter
Fruit, 1900–18*

I. INTRODUCTORY: CREDIT AND DEBIT

THE GERMAN EMPIRE stood in 1890 at a height never reached since the
days of Frederick Barbarossa in the twelfth century, to whose memory
William II, arrayed in white and gold Lohengrin uniform, was shortly to
dedicate a great monument on the Thuringian heights of Kyffhäuser.
According to legend Frederick and his knights slept in a hidden cave beneath,
awaiting the moment for Germany's revival. Now the day seemed to have
come, with Germany united far more effectively under Hohenzollern than
under Hohenstauffen rule. With a population of nearly fifty millions it
possessed a peace-time army of half a million, the strongest in the world.
Germany was no longer the 'Poor Michael' of two generations ago, but was
getting richer every day as its mines, its factories, its fields, poured forth
their stream of products to be carried by river, canal, or railway, or from
Hamburg and Bremen, by German ships to every part of the world. It had
large, if as yet undeveloped, colonial possessions. Its cities reflected this
growth not merely in their size but in their new public buildings, as in the
growing comfort and indeed, in cities such as Berlin, Hamburg, Frankfurt,
a rising and somewhat brash luxury. Many (though not all) of her cities
and towns were shining examples of efficient and widespreading local
administration, concerned not merely with health and welfare, but with art
and music.[1] Her score of universities, her fine secondary schools (*Gymnasia*),
classical or modern, her technical and elementary schools, with compulsory
education for all, her achievement in liberal scholarship as in science, her vast
production of books and newspapers—all testified to her wide concern for
culture. Illiteracy in Germany was far less than in the other great states of
Europe.[2] If Freytag was still her outstanding novelist, a new era was
opening in drama, with Ibsen behind it. Hauptmann's *Before Sunrise* and
Sudermann's *Honour* were both produced in Berlin in 1889.

The material progress of Germany in the two succeeding decades or so
before the war of 1914 was certainly spectacular. The population grew to
65,000,000 in 1911, though the increase was due more to a decline in
the death-rate than to a rise in the birth-rate, which declined by nearly 25 per

[1] *See* R. H. Dawson, *Municipal Life and Government in Germany*, 1914.
[2] Sartorius, *Deutsche Wirtschaftsgeschichte, 1815–1914*, p.384, gives four per thousand of population, as compared with thirty in France, over three hundred in Italy.

cent between 1875 and 1909, following more slowly the example of other western nations. Emigration likewise declined from a height of 200,000 about 1880 to one-tenth that number thirty years later, no more than that from France, and more than offset by immigration, largely of Poles. The increase swelled the industrial cities and helped to turn the balance of population from rural to urban about the middle nineties; by 1910 three-fifths of the population was urban. Berlin doubled its population between 1890 and the war, though in density and size it did not approach London or New York.

This urban growth reflected the great industrial development which at alternating pace, slow or swift, continued during these years in the centres already established. Thus it was most marked in the Prussian industrial areas: west, central (Berlin), and south-east (Silesia), together with Saxony, though it was by no means confined thereto. The Ruhr area increased steadily in size, as it did in its production of coal (70 to 190 million tons a year) and of steel, which quadrupled, now surpassing that of Britain. The electrical, chemical, machine, armament, textile, shipbuilding, and other industries similarly grew with varying but in general outstanding speed and success, thanks to the energy of German labour, the improvements in German manufactures, the ability of German scientists, and last but not least the enterprise and leadership of German industrialists. To these was due in addition a marked concentration of control over the major German industries into cartels (trusts) both for production and for marketing. The biggest of these during this period, e.g. the Rhenish-Westphalian Coal Syndicate (1897) and the Steel Works Association (1904), were in the hands of such barons of industry as Stumm, Kirdorf, Krupp, Thyssen, and Stinnes. There were also the A.E.G. (*Allgemeine Elektrische Gesellschaft*—General Electric), the great electrical combine, and the I.G. Dye Works controlling the chemical industry. As already mentioned, the great banks were closely and directly connected with these and other industries, and were likewise being amalgamated into bigger units.

Corresponding to the growth of industry was that of foreign trade, for the carriage of which the German mercantile fleet expanded over fifty-fold in tonnage from 1870 to 1914, to three times as large as that of France. Exports, increasingly of manufactured articles, nearly trebled between 1890 and the war, imports increased two and a half times, mostly raw materials and food-stuffs, with German ships trading to all ports of the world, helping to pay for the excess of imports over exports. Another aid to this, an evidence of the rapidly accumulating wealth of the industrialists and traders, was the growing investment of German capital abroad, drawing interest therein and increasing Germany's economic power. Whereas until shortly before this period Germany had borrowed foreign capital to develop her economy, now in addition to financing her own vast industry she began to export capital, establishing German banks abroad, and this process increased during these latest years before the war of 1914. Some of this represented the attempt to get control of French Lorraine iron for the Ruhr industry, and was later to foster war demands for annexation there and in Belgium. More went to Austria-Hungary, Rumania and the Balkans, to Morocco, and through the *Deutsche Bank* into the Turkish Empire, on the way to Bagdad. The colonies also took some, though far less than North and South America. But the total of such foreign investment was far less than that of France or Britain, and was subject to more government control (e.g. against Russian loans). And with her enormous industrial development at home there was less temptation to send capital abroad.

Agriculture could not hope to compare with industry in growth. Germany could no longer produce enough food for her growing millions, and imported increasing quantities of grain. Yet German agriculture did not decline in the way it did in England. Bismarck had given it a measure of tariff protection, not merely as a landowner himself, but also concerned for national safety. And although his immediate successor, Caprivi, was more concerned to secure markets for manufactures, and world prices of grain continued to fall till the middle nineties, the following years down to 1914 saw rising prices, some increase of protection under Bülow's chancellorship, and hence a general improvement in the position of agriculture. The big landowners aided this by following the example of the big industrialists, forming their Agrarian League in 1893 to demand greater protection, and working through the conservative party. They also further developed 'side' industries, such as distilleries and sugar-beet factories. Agricultural production increased steadily in the years before 1914, especially in wheat, rye (where Germany was self-sufficient), pigs, and potatoes. Thanks to the continued aid of science and technical education, farming improved in its methods and its yield per acre. And whilst the big increase in production was with the large landowners, the smaller farmers had the assistance of a growing co-operative movement, with landbanks for credit, and common marketing to some extent. All in all, German agriculture, and no less German forestry, adapted itself well to the new economic situation. Rural Germany had its labour difficulties, largely caused by the drift to the towns, but these were partly solved by immigration from the east, both seasonal and permanent. The perennial rivalry between eastern *Junker* agriculturalist and Rhineland industrialist, quieted for the time by Bismarck, was revived by Caprivi's freer trade policy, and not entirely removed by Bülow's more agrarian policy. And the urban workers were well aware that the agrarian tariffs increased the cost of their bread and meat.

The great and swift industrial development had indeed its darker side, its shadows. The mere aggregation of millions of workers and their families in crowded areas such as the Ruhr or swollen Berlin brought terrible problems of housing, health, and working conditions. The gulf between capital and labour was too wide and deep. It need hardly be said that the ideas of the employers and the workers on such matters as wages, hours, and conditions of work did not agree. To a great employer such as Kirdorf, director of the Westphalian Coal and Iron Syndicate, it was 'regrettable' that a worker should even be free to move from one job to another: rather he should be like a soldier, a conscript in the army of workers. But if the employers could organize themselves into trusts so the workers were organized into trade unions, though the employers strove to ignore them. Chief of these, were the 'free' unions affiliated with the social democratic party. These with the freedom won in 1890 grew to a strength of two and a half million members before 1914, five-sixths of the whole trade union membership. Next came the 'Christian' or Catholic unions, and below these again the older 'liberal' or non-socialist Hirsch-Duncker unions. By the Social Democratic Programme of Erfurt, 1891, the 'free' or socialist unions were opposed to the whole large-scale capitalist system, and made specific demands for the eight-hour day, no night or Sunday work, no employment of children, effective factory inspection, and union recognition. True, reforms of 1890–1 set up industrial courts for employer-labour disputes in Prussia, limited child and woman work, gave Sunday rest, and provided for better factory inspection. But issues enough remained, above all, those of wages and union recognition. Hence strikes and lockouts punctuated the economic growth, from the big Westphalian miners' strike of 1889 onwards, with over eleven thousand between 1890 and 1905, over two thousand a year between 1902–6.

Actually German labour did in fact make slow gains of better wages, working hours, and conditions during these years, although these were still far from fulfilling their aims, and they were still far behind their fellow workers in England. Socialists were better off in South Germany, in Bavaria, Baden, and Hesse, than in Prussia and Saxony, since in the southern states there was more compromise on both sides, and more possibility of politically constructive activity for socialists. The leading socialist in Bavaria, Vollmar, a noble and former cavalry officer, embodied this more practical attitude. More widely than this, there was emerging a reformist or 'revisionist' attitude to the Marxian view, expressed in Bernstein's book on *Evolutionary Socialism* (1899) and showing English and French influence, though Bernstein was more theorist than politician. Hence came a division in socialist opinion, the radicals, such as Mehring, Kautsky, and Rosa Luxemburg, holding to Marx's doctrine of the increasing misery of the workers, leading to revolution (as seemed to be happening in Russia in 1905) whilst others repudiated revolution. Bebel, the survivor of the Old Guard and the leader of the party in the *Reichstag*, professed the old creed to his death in 1913, but stood also for unity and for a practical approach to issues, which did in fact encourage compromise in action. Thus although an internationalist he declared that the socialists would fight to defend their country. In fact, as Bülow and others recognized, the social democratic party was a reforming rather than a revolutionary party [1] and later events were fully to confirm this view. Yet Prussia was still a class state to a considerable degree, and in the contrast between her social and political backwardness and her amazing economic development lay one of the weaknesses and dangers for the empire. Down to 1903 the social democrats had refused to take any part in the three-class

[1] F. Naumann, in *Demokratie und Kaisertum*, 1900, dismissed their revolutionary doctrines as 'merely a manner of speaking.'

system of election to the Prussian House of Deputies. And although in the *Reichstag* they increased their votes to over four million in 1912, and won 110 seats, more than any other party, they had not the slightest chance of being called to office and the responsibility of political power, under the existing system.

The political system of the empire was indeed increasingly unsuited to a great modern industrial state. We have seen how Bismarck made and acted in it, and what William I thought of it may be seen from a decree of 1882 which pronounced that 'no doubt shall exist as to the constitutional right of myself and my successors to conduct personally the policy of my government.' The garment might be that of the empire, but the voice was that of the King of Prussia. And his successor repeated this in much the same words in an Order of 1895: 'It is My wish to uphold undiminished the Right and fulness of Power founded on history and the constitution'—though he later (1908) boasted that he had never read the constitution and did not know it. The Prussian system rested on the Crown in alliance with the conservative landowners, the bureaucracy, and the officer class of the army. This system was represented politically in both the Prussian House of Lords and the House of Deputies, elected on a three-class system, which secured conservative predominance, with ministers appointed by the Crown or by his nominee, the Minister-President, who was usually chancellor of the empire. Prussian domination of the empire was bound up with this system, which was social as well as political, and hence growing demands for reform of the Prussian House were steadily refused. There was not even a redistribution of seats there (or in the *Reichstag*) despite the great movement of population since 1870. To Walter Rathenau, a leading industrialist, Jewish, and one of the ablest thinkers of the day, the system was absurd:

How can we justify the fact that Germany is ruled in a more absolutist fashion than almost any other civilized country? . . . It will be difficult to show—especially to foreigners who are asked to respect us—why the German is allowed by the constitution so much less influence in affairs of state than the Swiss, the Italian, the Rumanian. The continental barometer stands to-day at self-government, and we cannot for ever continue to live in a climate of our own . . . [1]

And to a great French historian, looking back from 1930:

There was indeed something paradoxical in the structure of the German Empire. Here was a highly industrialized country, the most highly industrialized of all the nations of the European continent, subjected to a political regime of feudalism and absolutism. Here was an empire founded upon the basis of universal suffrage, but in which Prussia, the leading state within its boundaries, was condemned to an electoral system that was a mere travesty of democratic institutions; in which ministers were responsible not to the elective assembly but to the hereditary sovereign; in which a minister was not regarded as even having a right to resign, but must wait until it pleased the king and emperor to dismiss him. [2]

Thus the fortunes and welfare of Germany rested to an enormous extent upon the emperor and his advisers, above all the chancellor. And the task was the harder after 1890 because Bismarck had absorbed so much power in his own hands, suffering only subordinates, and leaving no adequate

[1] In an article, *The New Era*, of 1909 (from H. K. V. Kessler, *Walther Rathenau*, 1928, p. 123).

[2] É. Halévy, *The World Crisis of 1914–18*, 1930, p. 13.

successors. When in retirement he made the work more difficult by attacks on his successor Caprivi, or in speeches such as that at Jena (1892) wherein with a complete disregard of his own practice he now preached the dangers of absolutism and (too late) the need for a stronger *Reichstag*. There was indeed some foundation for this bold criticism of his ruler, for William II was already revealing qualities which augured ill for the future. The Imperial Chief of Staff, Waldersee, who before William's accession had been (as his *Journal* shows) an ardent admirer of the young prince, looking forward to 'happy days' for Germany under him, by 1890 was already alarmed by the emperor's lack of firm opinions, his impulsive temper, his growing vanity.

Certainly this last emperor of the Bismarckian *Reich* possessed considerable natural abilities, quickness of apprehension, wide if not deep interests, the gift of easy speech, personal charm; at times more good sense than his advisers. But he lacked steadfastness of character. His early education, though well intended, had been unfortunate, and in the conflict of influences between a conservative grandfather and a dominating chancellor, a liberal father and an English mother, he had found refuge and companionship largely in the highly aristocratic, military, and conservative circle of the Potsdam Guards, who naturally flattered him. He loved uniforms and military trappings, and deferred more to military than to civilian opinion. Sensitive, even timorous at bottom, perhaps in part from his physical defect of an undeveloped arm, he covered this with an assurance bordering on arrogance and a growing self-conceit of his person and his opinions which, ludicrous in a Shakespearian Malvolio, was tragic in a modern emperor. This demanded and bred a servility which increased his incapacity for sound judgment of men, and of other views than his own. He was ambitious to play a great part in the world, but lacked consistency of thought and action in the broader field of statesmanship. He was ever restless, for ever seeking change, capable of spending more than half the year in travel. A good man in a limited sense, he was not a reliable one, but capable of sudden and even violent turns of temper. Thus Chancellor Bülow, 'dear Bernhard,' becomes 'scoundrel' after his resignation. His gift of speech was a snare to him and a danger to his people, as many examples were to show. Yet the Bismarckian system, based on and bound up with the Prussian monarchical traditions, had given enormous power to this still immature character, and this at a time when the highest qualities of leadership were required if Germany was to attain to and maintain the place to which her power, growing wealth, and prestige entitled her, not merely in Europe, but in the world.

For to the shadows, or more, within, were added the problems of relations with the outside world. Bismarck's policy, amazingly successful as it had been, had left a legacy of unresolved bad feeling with France over Alsace-Lorraine, and more generally of suspicion and distrust with his (and his son's) mixture of unscrupulousness and bullying, what the British Foreign Secretary, Grey, was to term 'the rough side of German policy.' As he trusted no one, so no one trusted him. His peace was too openly an armed peace, and his great army bred counter-armies. His alliances similarly encouraged counter-alliances, and were in themselves to prove less valuable than he had hoped as time went on. Nor could the much-vaunted 'wire to St. Petersburg' last; it was half rusted through by the time he retired, and the tie between France and Russia was already in the making. The colonial acquisitions of the eighties were of unknown quality, both in themselves and in their international significance. It remained to be seen whether Germany, a 'satiated' power on the Continent, would be satisfied with her position there, with a growing economy and a growing share in world trade, a world power indeed, but pursuing policies which would allow her to maintain good relations with her neighbours and the United States. That would depend to a considerable measure on the new emperor himself, but also upon the already awakened interest in colonial expansion, backed by the steady growth of population, of an expanding industry demanding both raw materials and markets, of the new wealth seeking profitable or seemingly profitable opportunities for investment outside Germany.

The intellectual and literary life of Germany during the later Bismarckian Empire reflected both the great achievement and the dissonances of the age. The universities, despite the chidings of Nietzsche for their pedantry and their dependence upon the State, were at a peak of their activity and of their reputation both at home and abroad. Devoted to the pursuit of knowledge, whether scientific or humanistic, they were in general middle class and conservative (with Treitschke living to the middle nineties), but playing little part in political life. And the growing claims, if not 'idolatry,' of natural science, represented, for example, in Haeckel's materialist interpretation of the universe as popularized in *The Riddle of the Universe*, 1899, conflicted with the older idealistic philosophic tradition, and led to attempts by such thinkers as Dilthey to redefine humanist knowledge in other terms than those of natural science.

Literature, similarly, in its own way, reflected the changing and at times opposing currents of the age. The main issue was that between the new Realism or Naturalism which emerged about the beginning of the reign of William II, and the succeeding revival of the older Romanticism which had never lost its hold upon Germany. But the two were not distinct or separable; many writers illustrated both trends. This Naturalist movement was not original in or confined to Germany. Flaubert and then Zola in France had helped to define Realism there. Tolstoy in Russia was mingling Realism and Mysticism, Ibsen in Norway was creating the Realist drama, the form in which the new turn best found expression in Germany. Similarly later writers, such as Stefan George, drew some of their inspiration from the succeeding French Symbolist movement. Thus these new literary developments overcame the growing nationalism of the age, as Nietzsche proclaimed culture should and must. And its writers, or the more important of them, such as Nietzsche (who may be included here so far as his influence was concerned) and Gerhart Hauptmann, Sudermann and Stefan George, Rilke and Thomas Mann, different as they were in their genius, were slowly to win a European significance in the republic of letters, in a way their predecessors of an earlier generation had failed to do.

The new Naturalism began with a 'revolt' of the younger generation, a *Sturm und Drang* on a limited scale, both in Berlin and Munich. It found opportunity in the new theatres now opening in the capital, wherein Sudermann (1857–1928) from East Prussia and Hauptmann (1862–1946) from Silesia found a stage for their plays. The new trend demanded a more truthful representation of life, as it existed, for example, in sprawling Berlin, or (for Hauptmann) in the mines or the textile industry of Silesia, a representation free of restraints as of heroics. Yet there was in it an underlying sympathy for the life of the common people with their hardships and tragedy, a criticism of the existing form of society, in some a sympathy with the cause of social reform or even socialism. And it reflected the influence of Darwinian science, seeing life as determined by heredity and environment, and was in part materialistic and anti-Christian. Hauptmann's *The Weavers* (1892), depicting the sufferings of the Silesian weavers of the forties, was perhaps the most outstanding naturalist play.

Yet Hauptmann illustrates the difficulty of confining literary creativeness within a single movement. In the year following *The Weavers* he produced a play, *Hannele's Assumption*, in which the starkness of Realism is mingled with mysticism and religion, and his later work showed a similar mingling of influences. There was indeed a partial turning away from the plainness and prose of Naturalism, to seek greater freedom and colour in what became known as Neo-Romanticism. But this, like all such developments, carried within it some of the qualities of its predecessor, which to some writers meant the pursuit of the darker sides of human life into all their depths. More fruitfully it meant a return to the beauty of lyric verse, mystical and remote in the work of the ever restless and wandering Rilke of Prague (1875–1926), more colourful and passionate in that of Dehmel (1863–1920). The influence of Nietzsche, whether as poet, critic, or prophet of the coming *élite*, likewise made itself felt. A notable woman writer, Ricarda Huch (1864–1947), a mixture of romantic and realist, found scope for her genius in the romantic-historical. There was also a revival of that earlier zest to portray the richness of local colour found in the varied regions of Germany, a *Heimatkunst*, expressed by Frenssen for Schleswig-Holstein, Stehr for Silesia, Polenz in Prussian Saxony, in part by Thomas Mann for Lübeck in his first great novel, *Buddenbrooks*. In the person and circle of Stefan George (1868–1933) poetry took on a more aristocratic quality, its verse bounded by the strictest attention to form. George's circle felt itself called upon to regenerate German poetry, even the German soul, but was too limited in its austere appeal to gain wide acceptance. And if, like Nietzsche, he may be regarded as in part an anticipator of Nazism, he found no place in Nazi Germany, and passed into exile, as did Thomas Mann, and as Nietzsche himself would probably have done had he survived so long. German literature, like literature elsewhere, inevitably suffered from the stress and strain of the war of 1914–18, and it

EMPEROR FREDERICK III

FREDERICK WILLIAM III AS CROWN PRINCE

shared in the immense and general confusion of the years that followed, until Nazism arrived with its efforts to make it serve its own ends.

II. 'THE GAY NINETIES'

Despite the enthusiasm, good intentions, and the order 'Full Steam Ahead' of the young emperor, the disappearance of Bismarck from the scene left a gap which was not to be filled. Henceforth there was a lack of overall control, of unity and consistency in both domestic and foreign policy. The emperor intended to rule himself, and did so in part, but with frequent and unpredictable changes of mind, and often without consulting or even informing his chancellor. The powers of the chancellor were thus invaded from above, while at the same time his control over the other ministers was likewise diminished. He was no longer Foreign Minister, the army and navy were under the emperor, not the chancellor, and a naval minister such as Tirpitz, sure of William's support, could act with an independence inconceivable under Bismarck's stronger grasp. One of the most sinister developments was the great influence now acquired in the Foreign Office by Holstein,

William II

an experienced permanent official, earlier favoured by Bismarck, but used by him to collect evidence in his feud against Arnim, and so a marked man henceforth. Holstein became embittered against both the Bismarcks and the world in general, a dark and mysterious figure, but with his wide knowledge, immense industry, and the lack of effective control, he came secretly to pull the strings of German foreign policy, from 1890 down to the Moroccan fiasco of 1906. Herein, obsessed by his hatreds and prejudices, and steeped in Bismarckian methods, he was to do serious damage to Germany's relations with other countries. He also used his inside knowledge of affairs to speculate on the Stock Exchange. Another unfortunate feature of the new era was the influence exerted on the weak emperor by both the military men he esteemed so highly, and friends such as Philipp Eulenberg, who was later to suffer for his enjoyment of imperial favour.

William's first chancellor after Bismarck, the man with whom he set out

L

to inaugurate his 'New Course,' and solve the social problem, was General Caprivi, a soldier with a fine military record and experience in the War Office, but no politician, although he had no mere 'military' mind. Caprivi's ablest collaborator was Miquel, as Prussian Finance Minister, whilst his Foreign Secretary was Marschall von Bieberstein, whose inexperience there favoured Holstein's power. It was in this field that the first important decision of the New Course had to be taken, since the secret Reinsurance Treaty with Russia now ran out, and the Russian Government proposed its renewal. At first the emperor approved, but then, advised by Caprivi and Holstein of its contradiction with the Austrian alliance, and of the danger to that alliance should Russia reveal the treaty, it was decided not to renew it. There followed the more open turn of Russia to France, which brought in addition to French loans the visit of the French fleet to Kronstadt in 1891, military conversations between the two powers, and finally (1893) a military agreement. The days of the French isolation were over, and the chances were that if war came, it would be a two-front war for the central European powers, who in 1891 renewed the Triple Alliance.

Given that alliance, however, a breach with Russia was inevitable sooner or later, and Caprivi was right in claiming that Russia and France were drawing together 'before my entry into office.' Yet greater efforts might have been made to preserve good relations with Germany's eastern neighbour. And in view of the turn on the Continent it became more important to secure and maintain good relations with Britain. William did indeed about this time stress in a speech the value of Anglo-German friendship, and shortly after the rejection of the Russian treaty an Anglo-German treaty was signed which gave Germany the invaluable gage of Heligoland, at the cost of delimiting German claims in East Africa. The German champions of colonial expansion were angered, but Caprivi was no colonial man, and the bargain was worth while. The good relations with Britain were, however, not to last, and the responsibility for the failure was to lie with the ambitious German emperor and his later advisers.

In domestic affairs Caprivi, though far from radical, made an honest attempt to carry through some of the reforms implied by the New Course which William had proclaimed. The labour legislation of 1890–1 has already been mentioned. Although the Prussian electoral system withstood attempts at reform, something was done to reduce *Junker* power in local government in rural areas east of the Elbe, whilst Miquel carried through a reform of the income and property taxes. A proposal for a new Prussian elementary school law which would have given the clergy (Protestant and Roman Catholic) rights of religious instruction therein, brought a crisis, however, in which the emperor used his influence against such a concession to the Centre party, where Windthorst's long leadership was now ended by his death in 1891. Yet Caprivi needed support in the *Reichstag* from the Centre (or the radicals) for his two major efforts in legislation, those concerning the army and foreign trade treaties. In the latter Caprivi, responding to the need for export markets for manufactures, made a series of trade treaties which involved reducing to some extent the high protection given by Bismarck. But whilst the Left and most of the Centre approved, the more agrarian conservatives strongly opposed the freer import of Russian grain now permitted, and in 1893 formed an Agrarian League to protect their interests.

For the army, which William desired to enlarge, Caprivi secured some addition of strength in 1890, but two years later, with the consciousness of Russo-French *rapprochement*, he brought forward proposals for a much larger increase (84,000 men) with the offer of the long-demanded reduction from three to two years' service and a five-year term in place of Bismarck's Septennate. This time, however, Centre and Left opposed, Richter being adamant in his opposition to the new financial burden the increase would impose. The upshot was, however, calamitous for the radicals, since Caprivi dissolved the *Reichstag*, and in the new elections they lost nearly half their strength, and split into the bargain. It was a final blow to the liberal-progressivism of 1861, since the national liberals were now a big industry and imperial party. Caprivi got his army law, but he had alienated the conservatives by his freer trade policy, he had further offended them by trying to conciliate the Poles as a possible aid against Russia, and he found the impetuous emperor increasingly difficult to get on with. Bismarck's unsparing criticism, too, made his task harder. He therefore resigned in 1894. He had been, as he knew, a stop-gap chancellor after Bismarck, no political genius indeed, but his reputation stands perhaps highest among William's chancellors after Bismarck's departure.

His successor, Prince Hohenlohe, Governor of Alsace-Lorraine, the uncle of the emperor, was likewise a stop-gap, if only on account of his age—seventy-five. Widely experienced, scholarly, diplomatic, a liberal Catholic and South German, he was able enough, but a poor speaker, and hardly strong enough for the office. With Caprivi's departure the New Course, so far as domestic policy was concerned, had come to an end. Indeed it was over an imperial call, in a speech at Koenigsberg, September 1894, for 'the fight for Religion, Morality, and Order, and against the Parties of Revolution' (i.e. the social democrats) that Caprivi had resigned, for he knew that the *Reichstag* would oppose any revival of the anti-socialist legislation. Yet the call found ready response in conservative and big business circles, drew the blessing of Bismarck, and legislation was duly proposed in the *Reichstag*. There was even talk of a *coup d'état* to change the constitution and get rid of the hateful universal suffrage. But William was not prepared to use force, his new chancellor saw only too well the danger to the empire in such a policy, and the *Reichstag* finally (May 1893) voted down the proposals. Yet the bitterness remained, and talk of using the army as in 1848; William had already told army recruits that at his command they must be ready to fire on their own families, an injunction which provided good ammunition for the socialists. A later attempt at a 'little socialist law' in the Prussian chamber was likewise defeated after a bitter struggle. Thus in the domestic field the scene was far from peaceful, Hohenlohe scarcely effective in the *Reichstag*, the emperor troubling the waters outside, as when he referred in one of his speeches (2nd March 1897) to Bismarck and Moltke as mere 'henchmen' to William I.

Far more significant for the future, however, was William's attempt to act as his own chancellor and foreign minister in the domain of foreign affairs. 'Why,' wailed Holstein in 1895, 'will the emperor meddle in foreign affairs?' The answer lay in William's growing ambition and belief in his own powers to conduct such matters more ably than his ministers, in the weakness of Hohenlohe, the widening breach between William and the Foreign Secretary, Marschall, whom William came to hate, partly because he was a South German, and the resulting confusion and lack of responsibility. Behind it lay the rapid growth of German industry, trade, and wealth, and the feeling of power engendered therefrom. And out of all this came a series of developments which were to determine Germany's relations with her neighbours and the world down to and including the coming of the war of 1914.

For it was in these years that Germany began openly to pursue a world policy, to feel and to proclaim herself a world power. Her emperor indeed went further, and in a speech of 18th January 1896, celebrating the twenty-fifth anniversary of the founding of the empire, announced that: [1]

Germany from a *German* Empire has become a *World* Empire. Everywhere in distant parts of the earth dwell thousands of our fellow countrymen. German products, German knowledge, German activity, spread over the ocean. Yours, gentlemen, is the task of helping me to bind this greater German Empire firmly to our homeland.

In view of the small numbers of Germans abroad living under the German flag (nine-tenths of the German emigrants in 1900 went to the U.S.A.) this was somewhat of an exaggeration, and scarcely tactful. Certainly it was inevitable and proper that Germany should now pursue a 'world policy' since her trade was now a world trade, her industry on a world basis. The question was how she would conceive that world policy, and in what manner conduct it, for on these would depend her relations with the other nations similarly engaged. And she had from her position and her past conditions, legacies, commitments, and perils, to some of which her ardent and temperamental ruler and some of his advisers were to show themselves blind.

The new trend was to show itself in a number of directions, in Asia, Africa, the Pacific, and on the seas. Perhaps its most novel feature was illustrated in the Far East, following China's defeat by Japan in the war of 1894, with the revelation of Japanese strength and Chinese weakness. The emperor, at first friendly to Japan, suddenly changed to act in support of Russia and France against the 'Yellow Peril' which he now denounced in violent terms as a menace to Europe. He supported Russian claims in Manchuria and to Port Arthur, and secured a Chinese port, Kiao Chau (1897), as a naval and trade base. The encouragement to Russia in the Far East and refusal of a British proposal for an international conference was partly designed to diminish danger from Russia nearer home, but it alarmed Austria, permanently alienated Japan, and made relations cooler with Britain.

[1] From J. Hohlfeld, *Die Reichsgeschichte in Dokumenten, 1849–1926*, 1927, vol. i, p. 308.

And although Britain and Germany were to work together in China at the time of the 'Boxer' Rebellion in 1900, and agree in the same year over the 'open door' in the Yangtse valley, their views on policy in the Far East could hardly be harmonious so long as Germany sided more with Russia, while Britain was drawing towards her alliance with Japan.

Meanwhile other and more serious causes of difference had arisen to change the earlier policy of the original New Course of 1890 of friendship with Britain. The first of these concerned Africa, where there was a slight clash in 1894 over Congo boundaries, but a more serious one in regard to southern Africa, where President Kruger of the Transvaal now looked to Germany for aid against the northern push of the British. When Jameson made his rash raid into the Transvaal at the end of 1895 William was all for steps which would have led to war, and had to be partially calmed down. Yet the famous telegram of congratulation sent in haste to Kruger (despite the British Government's repudiation of the raid), to say nothing of William's approaches to France and Russia, gave a dangerous jar to Anglo-German feeling and relations. Here, as in relation to China, the end of the century when Britain was in bad odour in Europe generally over the South African War, were marked by improved official relations (not reflected, however, in William's private letters to the tsar). They saw the repeated efforts of Chamberlain, concerned over the revelation of Britain's isolated position in Europe, to make a definite alliance with Germany. The efforts were to fail, and indeed it is difficult to see how they could have met with lasting success in view of the German naval building, the absence of trust on both sides, the rash expressions of the emperor, with what has been called his 'love-hate complex' regarding England, the press attacks at this time and later, stronger (as even Bülow admitted) in Germany than in England.

These feelings were further aroused by German activity in another field in the closing years of the century, the Near East. The Turkish Empire was still declining, still misgoverned, and still liable to outbursts of fanatical and ruthless treatment of its Christian subjects. Yet the divisions between the European powers who had signed the Treaty of Berlin prevented any joint action to check the frightful Armenian massacres of the middle nineties, despite British efforts. Britain and Russia, notwithstanding their rivalry, did manage to co-operate sufficiently in 1897 to save Greece from the full effects of her defeat in the war with Turkey over Crete in that year, and to free Crete from Turkish rule. But Germany refused to join in this effort. For the emperor envisaged for Germany a more independent, ambitious, and profitable role as the friend rather than the critic and enemy of the much-maligned Sultan Abdul Hamid II. A German general, Colmar von der Goltz, had already at the Sultan's request reorganized the Turkish army, the *Deutsche Bank* was firmly established in Constantinople, and in 1897 the former Foreign Secretary, Marschall, became the able and active German ambassador there. German expansionist writers (such as Sprenger, A. Wirth, and Naumann) had long urged the possibilities of German colonization in Asia Minor, and with more practical wisdom German financiers had already won by loans to the Sultan the right to run and extend railways there: to Angora, then to Konia, and now in 1899 (further developed by later agreements, 1903 above all) to Bagdad, earlier a British project. This last concession was in part the fruit of a spectacular tour through the Sultan's dominions made by the emperor in 1898, with his inexhaustible *Wanderlust* and flair for drama. In it, at Damascus, he assured the Sultan and his subjects that he was [1]

deeply moved by the thought of standing where the great Saladin, that knight without fear or reproach, had once sojourned. The Sultan and the three hundred million Mohammedans who reverenced him as Caliph may be assured that the German emperor will ever be their friend.

It was a pronouncement which gave thought to Russia, Britain, and France, with their many Mohammedan subjects and their interests in the Moslem world.

This same year of 1898 saw another example of the almost feverish German expansionist activity at the close of the century, this time in relation to the overseas domains of another declining empire, that of Spain. But here Germany had to contend with another emerging imperial power, the United States. Germany hoped to share in the liquidation of the Spanish power in the Pacific, notably in the Philippines. But with the outbreak of the Spanish-American War over Cuba in 1898, and American action against the Philippines, much ill feeling was aroused in the United States as a German naval squadron sent there showed a disposition to interfere with the American conquest of the islands. Disappointed there, Germany was able to purchase from Spain the Caroline and Marianne islands further east. The issue of German rights in Samoa, shared with both Britain and the United States, likewise caused friction about this time, in particular with Britain. The matter was only settled after much haggling by an agreement which gave Germany part of the island group, thanks to Britain's involvement in South African troubles, and the issue rather worsened than improved Anglo-German relations.

Further, before the old century closed Germany had embarked on a course which was finally to destroy hope of good relations with Britain, the building of a great navy. Germany certainly needed warships to protect her coastline, her trade, and interests abroad. But the emperor, master of what was admittedly the finest army in Europe, was fascinated by the vision of himself as possessor of a fleet comparable to his army, regardless of the cost. 'I will never rest until I have raised my navy to the same level as my army' (1897). 'Our future lies upon the water' (1898). In his irresponsible way he saw no reason why Britain or any other nation should object to such a policy. Whereas Britain, with her far greater extra-European interest and her far greater dependence on sea-power for her food supply, was bound to see in any such addition to German strength a menace to her very existence. For while German trade was four-fifths with Europe, Britain's was two-thirds outside the Continent, and both were increasing in these same directions. In

[1] J. Hohlfeld, op. cit., p. 341.

1897 William had appointed Bülow as Foreign Minister and Tirpitz as Navy Minister. And whilst Bülow was clever rather than strong, Tirpitz was a man of strength, obsessed with the idea of building a fleet based on battle-ships, a fleet large and strong enough to challenge Britain's naval superiority. Backed by the emperor he promptly brought forward his first naval bill in 1897, and against radical and socialist opposition finally secured a six-year naval budget, to include twelve battleships. This was to be followed three years later by a programme of far greater size, this time with open reference by Bülow to rivalry with Britain. The naval race was on, and was to continue.

Less specific than the naval building, but no less real, was the widening opinion by the turn of the century in favour of German expansion whether on land or overseas. It is worthy of note that this demand rose to a height just as Germans were in fact ceasing to emigrate in any numbers as they found more employment at home, and when there was a rising tide of immi-gration into Germany from neighbouring countries to aid in swelling the great increase of her population, some 800,000 a year in the early years of the new century. The urge to expansion was naturally stimulated by the example of other nations, Britain, Russia, France, even Italy, and backed by the consciousness of economic achievement and power. As a great industrial power Germany's economic need was for markets, raw materials, and oppor-tunities for trade and capital investment, and no colonial acquisitions in Africa or elsewhere could hope to satisfy these. Expansion eastwards was an old story in Prussian history, and in Bismarck's day Constantin Franz, widely travelled and an able writer and critic of the chancellor, had urged the formation of a federation of central Europe with Germany as its heart, to include Holland (and its colonies), Russian Poland, and Lithuania. Similarly Botticher (writing as 'Lagarde'), a biblical and oriental scholar, had looked eastwards for expansion, to seize all Poland and push down the Danube, though Treitschke had looked rather to the open sea and overseas colonies.

Now, however, the German fondness for general theories, for a world view (*Weltanschauung*), began to promulgate theories of German racial and cultural superiority whose roots go back to Fichte, and which found support in the mid-nineteenth-century views of Gobineau, a Frenchman, on the superiority of the 'Aryan' race. Darwinian theories of the selection and survival of the fittest in the struggle for existence also appeared to find application in Germany's great military and economic power. Such views and their expression were not confined to German thinkers: French, British, Russian, and even American writers could and did give expression in varying degree to views not so different. But Germans expressed them more sweepingly and took them more seriously. The relative suddenness of the industrial and commercial growth, added to the similarly sudden achievement of political unity, bred not merely a wholly legitimate pride, but also with some an overweening and overbearing conceit. The result was that German nationalism and imperialism became impregnated with conceptions of

German racial superiority, and of her destiny to cultural, political, and economic leadership. Historians such as Lamprecht and Wirth, economists such as Sombart and Hasse, anthropologists such as Woltmann, writers like Langbehn and others, gave the backing of the intellectuals. The renegade Englishman, H. S. Chamberlain, son-in-law of Wagner, and much admired by William II, added his support in his book, *The Foundations of the Nine-teenth Century* (1899), with its thesis of the all-embracing German cultural achievement. 'All European civilization,' wrote Woltmann,[1] 'even in the Slavonic and Latin countries, has been brought about by the German race.' 'God has created us,' echoed the emperor, with his customary disregard of other people's feelings, 'in order to civilize the world' (1905, Tangier). To such views the 'Latin' peoples, not least the French, were decadent, worn out, the Slavs too backward to count, the English mere shopkeepers who had somehow come to possess half the world and now stood in the way of the destined German expansion.

It is not possible to measure closely the influence of these ideas upon German opinion or policy as the new century opened, but they cannot be dismissed as idle and unimportant vapourings. Societies were formed to foster Germanism (*Deutschtum*) both in Germany and among Germans living abroad, the *Auslanddeutsche*, and to further both colonial expansion and the building up of the navy. Chief of these was the Pan-German League, organized by E. Hasse in 1893, and intensely active in propaganda from then on, coming to have many subsidiary or affiliated organizations (a recent authority counts over eighty of these in existence before 1914).[2] Its members belonged in the main to the upper middle class, and it could be and was used by big business to further its own ends. It had political connections and could make its voice heard in government circles and offices. It proved a most valuable ally in the campaign for the big navy, and equally, of course, for the big army, tied in with the Prusso-German military and officer-caste spirit. To a writer such as F. Lange 'Pure Germanism' (*Reines Deutschtum*, 1904) was embodied in the German warrior spirit actuated by the sentiment of an exclusively German 'honour,' whilst other writers such as the respon-sible jurist K. Wagner and E. Hasse of the Pan-German League glorified war as 'the only equitable judgment,' which Germany must employ in a world made soft by peace. There was a fresh outburst of the anti-Semitism sponsored earlier by Treitschke and Stoecker, and proposals for making a more national religion out of German Catholicism. But other nations, large and small, having their own cultural traditions, looked less with admiration at German culture than with alarm at German might, ambition, and lack of responsible government. They felt that it was above all *power* which Germany sought, following the Bismarckian pattern, but with a vastly extended range, a new fanaticism, and lacking Bismarck's sense of realism in politics.

[1] See C. Andler's volumes on Pan-Germanism for this and similar expressions of German racialism.
[2] H. W. Gatzke, *Germany's Drive to the West*, 1950, p. 25.

III. THE BITTER FRUIT, 1900–18

In May 1900 there were great celebrations in the German capital as the Crown Prince, heir to a crown he was never to wear, came of age, with a great assemblage of German and foreign princes.   Towards the close of the year the old and worn-out Hohenlohe was succeeded as chancellor by the brilliant Foreign Secretary, Bernhard von Bülow.   He had long been marked out for the office, which he was to hold for nearly nine fateful years, and the emperor was delighted, exclaiming: 'He shall be my Bismarck.'   The foreign scene seemed momentarily brighter as William behaved with circumspection during the South African War, and gained good opinions in England when he hastened to the bedside of his grandmother as the old queen died in January 1901.   Similarly he could write to the tsar of the 'firm bond of friendship' which united the two imperial dynasties.   Indeed, 'at no time during the reign of William II,' wrote one of the greatest authorities on this period,[1] 'had German influence stood relatively higher to that of the other great powers.'

This proud position was not to endure, despite the continued growth of German wealth and power.   By 1913 Rathenau could write [2] that 'the voice of Germany, which was more powerful than any other in Europe thirty years ago, has now ceased to matter, or at least matters less than that of France.'   This was far overstating the case, but there was undoubtedly a marked change in the international scene to the disadvantage of Germany. For Bülow turned out to be no Bismarck either in strength or capacity. And Germany owed her outstanding position not merely to her strength, her partial success in empire building, and her somewhat aggressive diplomacy, but to a great extent to the divisions of her neighbours, above all (now that France and Russia were allied) to Britain's rivalry with both France and Russia, and the isolation which had caused her fruitless approaches to Germany.   The British rivalry with Russia was an old story, bound up with the steady Russian advance into Asia, both to the Pacific and the borders of India, and also with her ambitions towards Constantinople ('Who controls Constantinople controls the world') and the Near East in general.   British rivalry with France had risen markedly in the nineties, with a sharp crisis (1893–6) over the boundaries between French Indo-China and Siam, and more continuous rivalry in Africa, as the partition of the great continent entered on its final stages.   The French resented the British occupation of Egypt and her push southwards up the Nile into the Sudan, and the British took alarm as the French, despite warnings, pushed eastwards towards the same goal.   The height of the crisis came in 1898 when Kitchener and Marchand met at Fashoda on the Upper Nile.   The French perforce had to withdraw, with some compensation in western Africa, but feeling rose high on both sides, and was not improved as Britain became involved in the South African War.

[1] G. P. Gooch, *History of Modern Europe, 1878–1919*, 1922, p. 323.
[2] From Kessler, *Walter Rathenau*, 1928, p. 155.

Yet it proved possible for the French and British governments to settle their differences within a few years, and it was largely German policy (or impolicy) which made this possible. For Bülow, Holstein, and the emperor assumed that the differences between Britain and France, as also those between Britain and Russia, were too strong to be overcome, and hence gave Germany 'a free hand,' with time on their side, to play off one against the other. They tried approaches to France, but with Alsace-Lorraine in mind the French declared against such an 'unnatural alliance.' William in his famous letters to Nicholas II (the 'Willy-Nicky' letters which were partly written in the German Foreign Office) did all he could to sow distrust between him and his ally France, and against Britain, whilst Tirpitz had worked out a 'theory of risk' counting on European support in case German naval building provoked a war with Britain. Meanwhile isolated Britain was to be subject to what Joseph Chamberlain called 'a policy of pressure' to gain concessions and perhaps force her into the Triple Alliance. But before the successive attempts made by Chamberlain to arrive at an alliance with Germany between 1898 and 1901 had ended with some sharp speaking on both sides, the British minister had warned Germany that failing such an alliance Britain would seek to compose her differences with both France and Russia, and the first of these all-important changes now occurred.

Actually Britain's change from the old policy of 'splendid isolation' was to be first marked by the alliance with Japan in 1902, but this was followed in the next year by the turn to France for which Frenchmen such as Paul Cambon had been hoping. State visits were exchanged, and Lansdowne and Delcassé as Foreign Ministers worked out a series of agreements signed in April 1904 covering matters in dispute all over the world, above all in North Africa. There France recognized the existing position in Egypt, and Britain accepted the French intervention in Morocco, subject to the open door for trade and to prior agreement with Spain. Thereby the so-called Entente cordiale came into existence. Although it could not dissipate all differences or suspicions between the two countries it marked a decided change, almost a diplomatic revolution, in the general European situation, and one unfavourable to Germany. Further, whilst the Central Powers had renewed their Triple Alliance in 1902, before doing so Italy had made up her long-standing differences with France, making a trade treaty and securing French recognition of her position in and hopes for Tripoli, in exchange for acceptance of French interests in Morocco. Bülow tried to pass this off with a phrase as merely an Italian 'extra dance' with a rival, but in fact it represented a real weakening of the Triple Alliance. And the events of the next few years continued the change, culminating in the Anglo-Russian agreement of 1907 which settled their differences outside Europe much as those between Britain and France had been settled a few years earlier, and which likewise worked to the disadvantage of Germany's position.

German policy in these years (as revealed in the Kaiser's letters to the tsar) had encouraged Russia in opposition to Japan, and when the Russo-Japanese War of 1904–5 broke out professed to see in her the champion of

Christian Europe against the Yellow Race, with Germany 'guarding her rear'; William even added advice on how to conduct the war. But behind this friendliness lay a certain satisfaction at Russian involvement so far away from German borders, and with the growing evidence of her military and naval weakness. Germany managed to secure a very favourable trade treaty as the price of her goodwill, and William likewise seized the opportunity to try and make a secret treaty of alliance with Nicholas. For some time the tsar refused to sign this without informing his ally, France. But after the final defeat which destroyed the Russian fleet at Tsushima he allowed himself, at a meeting of the two emperors at Björkoe, in July 1905, to be persuaded to set his hand to such an alliance, without informing either his ministers or his ally. The Kaiser was delighted with 'our treaty,' which provided for mutual aid 'in Europe' against attack by another European state, and talked of it as the basis of a general continental league against Britain. But Bülow, though he had some share in its making, was dubious as to its value since it was confined to Europe, and the tsar's ministers repudiated it as contrary to the French alliance. Hence despite William's angry expostulations the treaty was to be still-born, and in fact it marked the decline rather than the improvement of more friendly German relations with Russia.

This was to be revealed at the international conference held early in 1906 at Algeciras in Spain to deal with the crisis aroused over Morocco. France, with some excuse from the difficulties caused in Algeria by the growing disorders in adjacent Morocco, early in 1905 made proposals for French intervention there, to bring order and needed reforms. Germany had both treaty rights and some economic interests in Morocco, but Bülow had quite recently declared that her interests there were negligible (minimal), and France might have been wiser to try and assure German agreement in advance. For Bülow and Holstein now decided to take advantage of the Russian defeat and the opening of revolution there, and also to challenge the newly formed and still weak Entente between France and Britain, by a strong assertion of German claims. Hence the emperor on a March cruise through the Mediterranean was persuaded somewhat against his will to stage a spectacular landing at Tangier, and to pronounce for Moroccan independence and equality of foreign opportunity there. This, followed by a German demand for an international conference on Moroccan reforms and foreign interests, caused a severe Franco-German crisis and talk of war. Under German pressure the French Government repudiated Delcassé and his forward policy, and accepted the proposal for a conference. Thus far German policy appeared to have scored a success. But at this conference in January 1906 German demands for a share in Moroccan control (e.g. in police and finance) found practically no support save from Austria. France, Russia, Britain, Spain, and even Italy in the main were ranged against her, and the United States, at first friendly, now found her demands 'exorbitant.'

The Bülow-Holstein policy had thus met with a severe defeat, and Holstein's resignation balanced that of Delcassé. Bülow claimed to have won a success. But he admitted (to William) that 'the Austrian Empire is now our only dependable ally,' and Austria was soon to exploit this closer relationship in a dangerous way in the Balkans. German relations with both France and Britain were worsened, and the Anglo-French Entente instead of being broken had been strengthened. It was now that Clemenceau, pro-English, continentalist, and anti-German, came into office in France. Russia, despite all William's efforts, had stood by her ally, and it was little wonder that the emperor was enraged, though as usual he turned his rage on France and England rather than against German unwisdom. He had more reason for concern in the year following Algeciras, when after long and tedious negotiation Britain and Russia managed to reach an agreement over the issues outstanding between them in Asia, notably with regard to Afghanistan, Tibet, and Persia. The agreement was far from perfect, and the difference between liberal-democratic Britain and tsarist Russia (despite the coming of the Duma there) made close understanding difficult. Yet it was of great importance internationally, as welcome to France as it was unwelcome to Germany, marking the failure of German efforts at alliance with Russia and more. 'It is aimed at us,' was William's comment on the agreement, and whilst this was an overstatement, Britain's Entente with Russia was certainly connected with the growing estrangement between Germany and Britain.

The root cause of this was not, as Tirpitz and others asserted, British jealousy at the growth of German trade; there was more room for British concern over American than German success there. It lay in the steady increase of the German navy. To William, 'Admiral of the Atlantic' as he called himself in writing to Nicholas of Russia in 1903, 'My Navy' had become an obsession, as untouchable as the imperial prerogative. And the bigger the ships, the greater his pride in them; of their cost in either money or international goodwill he recked not at all. Yet his ambassadors in Britain, Metternich from 1901 to 1912, and then Lichnowsky, in their reports repeatedly stressed this as the prime cause of British estrangement and distrust, denying Tirpitz's arguments about trade, reports on which William's marginal comments were 'Bosh,' 'Rot,' and the like. As Metternich put it in a dispatch of 1908: 'A defeat in the North Sea means the end of the British Empire. A lost battle on the Continent is a long way from the defeat of Germany.' 'Do you wish,' asked the Rumanian minister, Ionescu, of his friend the German Foreign Minister, Kiderlen-Wächter, in 1911, 'to be both the leading naval and the leading military power? That would mean world domination. . . . You are heading straight for war with England.'

The British liberal government which came into office at the end of 1905 was intent upon social reforms, peaceful, and opposed to naval expansion, but found itself driven into a naval race which swallowed ever larger sums as Britain tried to hold the 'two power' ratio of naval strength to Germany. All their efforts to halt the race, whether through repeated discussions, the Hague Peace Conference of 1907, Foreign Minister Grey's efforts for the exchange of information on naval building, Churchill's proposal for 'a naval holiday,' visits such as that of the 'pro-German' Haldane to Germany in 1912, all broke upon the rock of William's refusal to realize the danger to peace involved and Tirpitz's open militarism.   Grey's reasoning [1] was lost upon them.   William's efforts to improve relations, by writing personally to the head of the British Admiralty in 1907, or the even more famous interview to the British newspaper, the *Daily Telegraph*, in the following year, protesting his friendship for Britain and the innocuousness of the German naval building, merely made matters worse.   The chancellor, Bülow, bore some of the responsibility, for although he made tentative suggestions in 1908–9 to Tirpitz for a modification of naval policy until Germany was 'through the danger zone' (a typically Bülow approach), he gave way in face of opposition.   Both he and his successor, Bethmann-Hollweg, an honester if less skilful diplomat, tried to use the issue to get Britain to pledge neutrality in a Franco-German war, which only tended to draw Britain and France closer together.   So the naval issue continued progressively to poison Anglo-German relations down to 1914.

Before this tragic consummation, however, other issues had arisen to worsen or endanger Germany's relations with her neighbours.   Bülow towards the close of 1906 referred in the *Reichstag* to the danger to peace of 'a policy aimed at the encirclement of Germany and her isolation.'   His concern was at bottom a repetition of Bismarck's 'nightmare of coalitions,' and like that had its origins rather in German policy.   Nor was Germany isolated, since she had her Triple Alliance, which Bülow himself a few years later described [2] as 'a mighty fortification dividing the continent into two. Europe has seldom, if ever, seen an alliance of such strength and durability.' This was to overestimate the strength of the Italian adhesion to the *Dreibund*. The German bond with Austria, however, now stood out in stronger relief. Unfortunately for Germany, however, behind its imposing façade the Austro-Hungarian Empire was exposed to grave dangers as its emperor Francis Joseph grew old.   The ancient maxim of 'Divide and Rule' was nearly worn out: the empire could divide, but could no longer effectively rule the discordant elements that threatened her very existence, the social and political discords, the national and racial antipathies of German, Magyar, and Slav.   True, she had enjoyed before 1908 a decade of what has been called [3] her 'Indian summer,' at all events in her relations with Russia, by reason of an agreement for the maintenance of the *status quo* in the

---

[1] 'There is no comparison between the importance of the German navy to Germany and the importance of our navy to us.   Our navy to us is what their army is to them.   To have a strong navy would increase their prestige, their diplomatic influence, their power of protecting their commerce; but as regards us—it is not a matter of life and death to them as it is to us.   No superiority of the British navy over the German navy could ever put us in a position to affect the independence or integrity of Germany, because our army is not maintained on a scale which, unaided, could do anything on German territory.   But if the German navy were superior to ours, they maintaining the army which they do, for us it would not be a question of defeat. Our independence, our very existence, would be at stake.'   (Speech in the House of Commons, 29th March 1909.)
'The true root of English hostility towards us,' wrote the German historian Professor J. Haller (*Die Ära Bülow*, 1922, p. 49), 'lay in nothing more or less than the building of the German battle-fleet.   This it was, and only this, which pushed England unwillingly enough, into the entangling alliances with France and Russia.'   Professor Veit Valentin (*The German People*, 1946, p. 537) comes to the same conclusion, writing from a longer perspective.
[2] *Imperial Germany*, pp. 54–5.
[3] By A. J. P. Taylor, *The Habsburg Monarchy, 1809–1918*, 1948, ch. xvi.

Balkans. But Macedonia was still in confusion there, Austro-Serbian relations were disturbed by a tariff war (the 'Pig War'), and the Young Turk Revolution broke out in the Ottoman Empire in July 1908.

It was at this moment that the Austrian Foreign Minister, Aehrenthal, ambitious and somewhat unscrupulous, decided upon a bold stroke which he intended should revive the declining Austrian reputation, and create his own. At Buchlau in September 1908 he secretly arranged with the Russian Foreign Minister, Izvolsky, not so dissimilar in character if less bold than himself, that Austria should change her occupation of the provinces of Bosnia and Herzegovina into annexation, whilst Russia at the same time should secure the right to send her warships through the Dardanelles. Both steps violated European treaties, were bound to meet opposition from other signatories thereto,' and both were blows against the Turkish Empire. Yet Aehrenthal only belatedly informed his German ally, the friend of Turkey, of his intentions, and then, whilst Izvolsky vainly sought Franco-British approval for his part of the bargain, the Austrian minister jumped ahead and announced the annexation, whilst by his connivance Bulgaria at the same time declared her final independence from Turkey.

There followed a six months' European crisis, which Lichnowsky, and not he alone, later saw as 'the real prelude to the world war.' Russia, Izvolsky in particular, felt deceived and injured. Italy likewise felt injured at the extension of Austrian territory down the Adriatic. The Turks were naturally angered, though time was to show that they could be bought off. Britain was ready to join Russia in demanding a European Congress to discuss the breach in the Berlin Treaty of 1878, but was opposed to the Russian demand for freedom for Russian warships to use the Straits, unless similar rights were given to other nations. Most bitterly resentful were the Serbs, since the Austrian step put an end to the rising hopes, encouraged by a secret agreement made with the Croats, for the union of all the Serbo-Croats in one independent state. Austro-Serb antagonism rose to a dangerous height, and the military party in Austria, led by Conrad, the Chief of Staff, were all for making a final settlement with their ambitious little neighbour.

The outcome of the crisis turned on the attitude taken by Germany and Russia. How far would Germany support her ally? Would Russia accept the Austrian coup and see Serbia humiliated and perhaps crushed? The Kaiser was at first incensed at 'Aehrenthal's frightful stupidity' in injuring the Turks, and so destroying his carefully nursed friendship with them. But Bülow did not hesitate to back Aehrenthal in the widest terms, guaranteeing German support and refusing to consider proposals for an international conference. Then in March 1909 he took a more decisive step, demanding of Russia that she should accept the Austrian annexation of the provinces. Whether this was, as often stated, an ultimatum, is in part 'a question of terminology.' [1] Kiderlen-Wächter, who drew it up, at any rate meant it to be decisive, a penultimatum, if the word be allowed. Since Russia was insufficiently recovered from her war with Japan to be able to fight, she agreed

[1] Eyck's phrase.

to the German demand, and Serbia was forced to follow suit and cease her shrill protests. The other powers accepted the result and no conference was held.

Thus the German-Austrian alliance had shown new life and strength and had scored a decided success, whilst the bonds between Russia, France, and Britain appeared shaken as the two western powers showed their desire for peace. Yet the success had been won not by peaceful discussion of the merits of Austria's case but by the threat of force. 'The German sword was thrown into the scale,' as Bülow put it; his emperor was to declare, that he had stood by his ally 'in shining armour.' It was a rash and short-sighted policy. Austria was not really strengthened, but merely encouraged to think that she was, and that she could call on German aid again. The Austro-Serb issue was not settled, but merely driven underground, there to gather fresh energy until it burst out again with fatal results. The alliance with Italy was further weakened; within six months the tsar was visiting the King of Italy and discussing their common interest in Balkan questions. And this drawing of Germany into Balkan issues, contrary to Bismarck's wiser policy, was a danger to the *Reich*, as the re-emergence of such issues into the centre of European politics was a danger to European peace. Above all, German-Russian relations were decidedly worsened. Feeling in Russia, as the German ambassador there reported, was embittered by their obvious humiliation, seeing the issue in terms of Slav against German, and convinced that war would come, and that in no long time.

The 'Bülow Era' was to end with his resignation from the chancellorship within a few months after the Bosnian crisis. His foreign policy had not been fortunate for Germany. He had refused the alliance with England, and supported the German fleet policy; he blundered into the Morocco affair which affirmed the Anglo-French Entente; and a few years later he pledged his country 'in Niebelung troth' as he grandiloquently put it, to full support of Austria in the Bosnian affair, which was likewise to draw the Triple Entente together against Germany. In short, he succeeded in alienating Britain, France, and Russia, and so must bear a considerable share of responsibility for the coming of the war in 1914. The four lengthy volumes of *Memoirs* which he wrote after that war in his retirement in Italy as his apologia, to be published after his death in 1929, confirm rather than modify this judgment. For, despite their cleverness and their undoubted interest as the record of the man who after Bismarck played the most out-standing and longest role as chief minister in the empire, they reveal only too plainly his shortcomings both as minister and man. True, Bülow served an almost impossible master. Yet the continuous and bitter criticism of the emperor which runs through the *Memoirs* like a *leit-motif* comes badly from the man who when in office was so fulsome in flattery and so generally subservient. And his criticism of colleagues, even of one-time friends, above all of his successor, Bethmann-Hollweg, is similarly less convincing, since it was so marked by meanness, jealousy, and a self-conceit which almost rivalled that of William himself. To Kiderlen-Wächter, the forthright

Swabian, who saw him at close quarters, he was 'the eel,' and later, when he learnt how Bülow had betrayed his unflattering comments on William to his master, he became the '*Schweinehund.*' Yet he thought himself indispensable, and believed that he would be recalled to office. Bismarck had been dishonest and unscrupulous, but he had a statesman's grasp of political aims and means. Bülow was no less unscrupulous, if in a smaller way, but lacked Bismarck's solidity of mind, so that his policy was weak, uncertain, and at times irresponsible.

Whilst Bülow, trained as a diplomatist, was ever more interested in foreign affairs, yet as chancellor for nearly nine years (1900–9) he was also responsible for the conduct of domestic matters. Belonging to one of the old Prussian landed families, he was naturally a good conservative and monarchist, but he was no strong party man, and indeed was to be driven out of office partly by conservative opposition. As chancellor, he proved to be a fluent and skilful parliamentary speaker, if rather showy than deep, with an excellent memory and an inexhaustible capacity for quotation; more of an orator indeed than Bismarck, but without the bite and telling force of the old master. Married to an Italian Catholic he did not share William's dislike of the Centre party, which had come to exercise most influence in the *Reichstag* during Hohenlohe's term of office, when 'the Centre rules' became a slogan. The Centre held its place not merely because it was the largest single party and had Polish and other allies, but because it could and did combine either with the conservatives of the Right or the radicals of the Left to get a majority. Bülow began with a concession to them, the repeal of the law of *Kulturkampf* days which made a foreign-born Jesuit subject to deportation, and they were to remain the dominant party until 1906. Bülow also favoured the conservative landowners in 1902 by raising the customs' duties on grain, claiming to be, like Bismarck, an agrarian chancellor. Yet as the Caprivi trade treaties ran out he strove for their renewal, and ultimately secured it.

The *Reichstag* elections of 1903 brought no major change in the balance of parties, but the social democrats markedly increased both their vote and their seats, the latter from fifty-six to eighty-one. Bülow was naturally no friend to socialism, and he and Bebel often clashed in the *Reichstag*. He was, however, no advocate of exceptional laws against them, and claimed in his *Memoirs* that had he stayed in office his aim would have been 'to give to the workers their rightful place in the State,' whatever (if anything) that might mean. It did not mean cheap food, for according to one authority [1] by his tariff policy 'henceforth the German people paid the highest price in the world for the necessities of life.' And the social democrats naturally opposed the extensions of the navy, whose budget was enlarged in 1906, and again in 1908, at the cost of a considerable increase in the national debt, and also at the expense of the army, which secured only a small increase in 1905. In the following year the social democrats were able to show their importance and the instability of the party system by combining with the Centre (the

[1] W. H. Dawson, *Protection in Germany*, 1904.

'Blacks' and the 'Reds'), and with other groups defeat government proposals regarding the colonies, so that Bülow dissolved the *Reichstag*.

For the elections of early 1907 which followed Bülow strove to follow Bismarck's example of twenty years earlier and form a cartel or *bloc*, this time of conservatives and liberal-radicals. Thanks to heavy press propaganda, he succeeded, for although the Centre remained the strongest single party the social democrats suffered a sharp set-back, losing nearly half their seats. Thereby Bülow was able to get his grant for aid in repressing the revolt of the native Hereros in German South-West Africa. More important was the appointment to the newly created Secretaryship for the Colonies of the liberal-radical banker Dernburg. For Dernburg turned out to be, what was badly needed, a colonial reformer. Borrowing from British experience in the administration of backward peoples, he put an end to the over-bureaucratic and military methods used in Africa, and the sometimes brutal exploitation practised there by men such as Karl Peters in East Africa, or colonial officials such as Puttkamer. He realized that apart from humanitarian motives the reduction of the native Hereros to one quarter of their number was stupid on economic grounds, since they alone could supply the labour needed if the colony was to develop. Dernburg ushered in a new and better period of colonial administration, but as a progressive or radical he naturally met with conservative opposition, which drove him out after four years of office.

For Bülow's *bloc*, whilst it worked for a time, was vulnerable because of the divergence between conservative and radical views, and the possibility that either side might combine with the Centre, ambitious to return to power. The radicals demanded a reform of the Prussian three-class electoral system, with a redistribution of seats to meet the vast urban growth, and Bülow referred in the Speech from the Throne opening a new Prussian Diet in October 1908 to 'an organic development' of the Prussian system as 'one of the weightiest tasks of the day.' But nothing came of this, since the conservative majority there naturally opposed any change. The conservatives in the *Reichstag* likewise opposed Bülow's efforts in the same year to raise new imperial revenue for army and navy purposes by the levy of an inheritance tax, which would have hit the so-far privileged landowners. Bülow's position in 1908–9 was further complicated by social scandals in high places resulting from Maximilian Harden's press attacks (with the sinister figure of Holstein in the background), by the Naval Law and naval issue with Britain, by the Bosnian crisis, the emperor's excursions into journalism (the *Daily Telegraph* affair), and his growing disgust with Bülow for failing, as he believed, to defend him adequately from attacks in the *Reichstag*. For William felt deeply insulted at being forced to promise that henceforth he would 'preserve the stability of imperial policy by observing constitutional responsibility.' Hence, when the conservatives joined hands with the Centre to defeat the government's tax proposals, Bülow, conscious of the loss of imperial favour, resigned (14th July 1909).

It would be a mistake to attribute Bülow's fall to a parliamentary defeat, and see therein a sign of the coming of truer responsible government: the emperor's ill will had more to do with it.   Yet it has been argued [1] that these years 1907–9 in which Bülow was working with the middle-class liberal-radicals, and which saw a seeming check on the royal irresponsibility, might have been used to produce a real change in that direction, and so in the end save the monarchy from the fate of 1918.   But William had not in reality renounced his personal rule, and Bülow was no reformer in any real sense. There was a kind of rough justice in the fact that it was the Polish votes that gave the majority against him.   For Bülow had followed Bismarck rather than Caprivi in his policy towards the Poles in Prussia, striving to settle German settlers on land acquired from Polish landowners through a Settlement Commission, to prevent Polish settlers from acquiring land, and to enforce the use of the German language instead of Polish in education, including religious education.   In this policy he had not merely German radicals and social democrats against him, but also the powerful Catholic Church in Poland.   The settlement policy raised the price of land enormously; the Poles had a higher birth-rate than the German settlers, and the economic development aided the growth of a Polish middle class, whilst the general rise of national feeling revived Polish hopes of independence.   So the Prussian Polish problem remained unsolved, leaving the problem of Germany's eastern Marches, as Bülow admitted in his book *Imperial Germany* (1913), one of the most difficult and important faced by the empire.   An able Prussian commentator of the same time, Hans Delbrück, concluded a survey of German Polish policy with the acknowledgment that [2] 'it is in no small degree our mistaken policy towards our foreign nationalities which has made us so universally hated.'

Bülow's successor, suggested by him, was the fifty-three-year-old Bethmann-Hollweg, scion of a Frankfurt banking family which had become Brandenburg landowners.   He had had a solid and successful career as a Prussian official in local government, then as Minister for Home Affairs, first (1905) for Prussia and then two years later for the empire.   He was an able, loyal, and honest servant of the Prussian system and so by definition conservative at bottom.   But more than this was needed for the office of chancellor at such a time of tensions within and dangers without.   Bethmann-Hollweg's very virtues handicapped him in standing up to the emperor and the army and navy men, and in any case he lacked the decision and strength of character required in the chancellor by the Bismarckian system.   Nor did he possess Bülow's tactical and oratorical skill with the *Reichstag*, despite his superiority of character.   Above all he had no experience in the conduct of foreign policy, no flair for diplomacy, and hence was forced to rely on Foreign Secretaries such as Kiderlen-Wächter, able and knowledgeable, but at times over bold, rash indeed.   It can be argued that the situation he inherited, both within and without, was beyond remedy save by internal reforms which would sweep away the old system and replace it by one in

[1] Arthur Rosenberg, in *The Rise of the German Republic*, 1928.
[2] *Government and the Will of the People*, 1923, p. 140.

which power and responsibility would be shared by both middle and lower classes. But for this Bethmann-Hollweg was as little ready as the emperor and the conservatives. How little William's concept of his position had changed is shown by his comment when Grey tried to deal direct with Bethmann-Hollweg, whom he felt was a man of trust, over the naval issue. 'Clearly,' wrote William, 'Grey has no idea who is master here, and that it is I who rule.' And it must be admitted that despite his defects as a ruler William was still popular enough in the country.

Since Bethmann-Hollweg was a 'domestic' or Home Office chancellor, as Bülow had been primarily a 'Foreign Office' one, he was at least more aware of the need for some attempt at conciliation, if not wide reform, in the domestic field. To meet the demand for electoral reform in Prussia he proposed to enlarge the small first class of voters (numbering less than four per cent of the whole, yet electing one-third of the deputies), and to abolish the system of indirect voting. But he retained both the three-class system and the long outdated distribution of seats [1] by which, in 1908, the social democrats with 600,000 votes secured six seats, the conservatives with 420,000 votes two hundred and twelve seats! Even so, his effort was defeated by conservatives and clericals in the Prussian House of Deputies, and disappeared into the limbo. The gift of the vote for the *Reichstag* elections to such citizens as were in receipt of State aid, previously withheld, was but a poor substitute for real electoral reform. Of more value was legislation of 1911 to improve the position of the domestic worker, so far unprotected, in terms of hours, living, and working conditions. At the same time the laws governing workers' insurance of various kinds were consolidated into an Imperial Code, and slightly extended.

Such measures, however, did little to satisfy the growing demands for more real and drastic change in the existing system, with the radicals laying more stress on political reform, the social democrats on social and economic change. These demands were sharpened by the now steadily rising cost of living, and by the similarly increasing costs of the army and navy. In 1911 the five-year Army Bill was renewed, with provision for a gradual increase in its strength. In the next year the rate of increase was quickened, and in 1913 (centennial of the great year 1813) a further and larger increase was proposed and passed to give a peace-time army of the unheard-of size of nearly 900,000 men. To this France replied by reintroducing the three-year military service, previously reduced to two, whilst Russia and Austria also pressed on with enlargements of their armies. Meanwhile the German navy was further enlarged in 1912. Since the existing imperial revenues were quite unable to provide for these increases, new taxation was required, and after much debate it was agreed to raise a direct National Defence Tax on property.

The *Reichstag* elections of 1912 were remarkable for the great increase in the vote and number of seats gained by the social democrats, who with 110 seats were now the strongest party there; the conservatives and Centre both

[1] See p. 184.

lost seats. Bebel, now in the last year of his life, was nearly elected as president, and Scheidemann was elected as first vice-president, but resigned. Social unrest had been growing in the past few years, with workers' Sunday demonstrations for reform in the large cities, and the tramp of soldiers heard in the streets of Berlin. There were strikes and lockouts, and demands for a general strike as a demonstration. There was, of course, no hope of the socialists winning a majority in the *Reichstag*, still less of their being called to ministerial office, but the result of the election revealed the inner conflict in the empire on the eve of its greatest trial. Yet so far as the *Reichstag* and the *Reich* were concerned the danger from the socialist victory at the polls was less than it might seem. The victory had been gained by compromising with the radicals for the election, and whilst the socialists voted against the army and navy increases they supported the financial measures to provide the money therefor. In theory they were opposed to nationalism and imperialism, but in practice they were loyal to the empire, ready to compromise with the bourgeoisie in the hope of reform, 'revisionist' in a larger degree than they were ready to admit. At the same time there was a small but vigorous minority which opposed any such compromise, radicals led by Rosa Luxemburg (a gifted Russian Pole married to a German), Clara Zetkin, the younger (Karl) Liebknecht, and (for a time only) Kautsky. This left wing held fast to the Marxian faith, encouraged by the revolutionary movement in Russia, and looked to the overthrow by violence of the existing class regime. They advocated a republic and raised 'the war-cry against militarism, navalism, colonialism, imperialism, junkerdom, and the Prussianization of Germany,' as Rosa Luxemburg put it about this time. It remained for the testing time of war and defeat to show what path German socialism would follow. How little a vote against the government counted before 1914 was shown when the *Reichstag* by an overwhelming majority passed a vote of no confidence in the chancellor and demanded his resignation. Bethmann-Hollweg replied that the vote was merely 'an internal affair of the *Reichstag*,' and of no concern to him as the emperor's nominee.

This vote was in connection with the affairs of Alsace-Lorraine, where Bethmann-Hollweg had honestly tried to find a solution to the problem and lessen French hopes of *revanche*. By a law of 1911 the two provinces, now containing many German immigrants, were given a partial approximation to the position of a federal state, with representation in the Federal Council and a local Diet of two chambers, the lower one elected by universal suffrage. The executive authority remained, however, with the emperor, who appointed a local governor. And when the local Chamber of Deputies tried to assert its powers William promptly threatened to 'smash your constitution to atoms and reduce you to a Prussian province.' Then in 1913 in the little Alsatian town of Zabern (Saverne) the military authorities misused their power in a way which aroused general indignation, both there and in the *Reichstag*, out of which came the above-mentioned vote against the chancellor. Thus on the eve of the war, and despite the anti-clerical policy pursued in France which naturally affected Alsatian Catholic opinion, the problem of the annexed provinces was little further solved than forty years earlier.

The failure of any attempt at fundamental change in the domestic system left the control of and responsibility for the conduct of foreign affairs in the same hands as before, under conditions of increasing difficulty and gravity. The long threatened break-up of the Turkish Empire appeared now to be imminent, and the Bosnian crisis had seen Austro-Germany ranged against Russia in Balkan issues in a way Bismarck had been careful to avoid. Bethmann-Hollweg became chancellor under the aura of the success in 1909 of the Central Powers. Yet that success had been won at the expense of good relations with Russia, and since Alsace-Lorraine was a barrier to any great improvement in relations with France it would have been wise for Germany to improve her relations with Britain. The new chancellor had some realization of this, as had Schoen, Foreign Secretary from 1907 to 1910, but William was inflexible on the vital navy question, and the chancellor weakly gave way. His efforts in 1909–10 to get Britain to agree to pledge her neutrality should Germany be forced into war with France or Russia, in return for some small abatement of German naval building, were bound to fail, and did so, and the issue remained a fatal obstacle to any marked or permanent betterment of Anglo-German relations.

The re-emergence of the Moroccan issue in 1911 illustrated the dangerous significance of this failure, when the more cautious Schoen had been succeeded by the bolder but more irresponsible Kiderlen-Wächter as Foreign Secretary. Under the pressure of the Bosnian crisis Germany had made an agreement with France early in 1909 to try and harmonize the superior political interests of France with German economic interests, which were growing with the activities of the Mannesmann mining group there. But the rivalry of French and German firms continued, and disorders in the country provoked increasing French interference. A tribal revolt round Fez, the capital, in the spring of 1911 brought an appeal to France for military aid, and a French occupation which Germany saw as likely to be permanent. She had some right to be concerned, but as in 1905 showed that concern in an unfortunate and even dangerous manner. For with William's and the chancellor's agreement Kiderlen-Wächter sent a gunboat to the West Moroccan port of Agadir, rashly arousing Pan-German hopes of a German occupation there, though in fact he intended the move as a means of putting pressure on France, in order to get compensation elsewhere in Africa.

The result was a first-class international crisis, more severe than that of 1905 because the general international situation had worsened. France was forced to make approaches to buy off Germany, the more so since Russia was still not ready to face the explosion of war. And since Kiderlen-Wächter at first demanded no less than the whole of the French Congo (French Equatorial Africa) these negotiations were both difficult and prolonged. In the end Germany received a considerable slice of French Congo, at the price of a small rectification of frontier south-east of Lake Chad. She retained her commercial interests in Morocco, but gave fuller recognition to French predominance there.

It was, however, the wider ramifications of the dispute that were most disquieting. Austria showed what to Germans was singular ingratitude for their aid two years earlier, refusing to interest herself in the Moroccan question, whilst Italy took advantage of the crisis to invade Tripoli, despite German protests. On the other hand, Britain, alarmed at both the danger of a German attack on France and the prospect of a German naval station being set up at a strategic position on the West African coast, took the French side more strongly, and announced through a speech of Lloyd George that her 'vital interests' could not be attacked without danger of war. Thereby the French stand was strengthened, but feeling in Germany, aroused by Pan-German demands for 'West Morocco to be German,' was further embittered. And Anglo-French naval discussions now, in effect, committed Britain to defend the northern French coast, in case of a Franco-German war. The general agitation declined as Franco-German agreement neared, but it left scars. While French opinion disliked the surrender of French Congo territory, opinion in Germany was even more disappointed at what seemed to be (save in square miles) the meagre result of so much shouting and effort. There was bitter speaking in the *Reichstag* and outside, despite the chancellor's effort, reminiscent of Bülow in 1906, to claim a success. German diplomacy of what Lloyd George later described as the 'blundering and blustering kind' had in fact guided the country badly, nearly brought war, and sharpened the lines of division between the two groups of powers.

The Italian invasion of Tripolitania in September 1911 was like a stepping-stone (half-way along the Mediterranean) between the Moroccan crisis and the Balkan wars of 1912–13. That this last African possession of Turkey should fall to Italy in due course had been agreed to by France ten years earlier, almost generally accepted by the other European powers, and prepared by Italian activity there. But the Italian attack was embarrassing to Germany, since she was the friend of Turkey, yet allied to Italy. Italo-Austrian relations were also strained as Italy turned to naval action, and Austria forbade this in the Adriatic as contrary to agreement. In the end it was the threat of attack by the Balkan League which forced Turkey to make peace in October 1912 and surrender Tripoli.

This Balkan League of Serbia, Bulgaria, Greece, and later Montenegro, formed in the spring of 1912 by the encouragement and aid of Russia, constituted a threat not merely to the declining Ottoman Empire, but also to the peace of Europe. For whilst their prime ambition was to drive the Turks out of Europe, not merely did their aims conflict in Macedonia, but those of Greece extended far into the Mediterranean, those of Serbia to the Adriatic coast and deep into the Austrian Empire. And whilst Rumania was not a member of the league she too had ambitions only realizable at the cost of the Habsburg Empire. The danger to European peace was recognized by the great powers, and efforts made, even by Russia, to hold the Balkan League in check. And when, almost of itself, war broke out in

October 1912, and to the general surprise the Turks were driven back in a few weeks towards Constantinople, there was more active effort to mediate, as now requested by Turkey. For Russia had as little desire to see Bulgaria ensconced in Constantinople as Austria had to see the Greeks in Salonica or the Serbs on the Adriatic. Germany and Britain showed that for the moment they could work together for peace. By Grey's efforts a Peace Conference met in London, and despite the renewal of the war after a Young Turk *coup d'état* in Constantinople, a peace was signed in May 1913.

But this peace by no means satisfied the ambitions of the Balkan states. Serbia, despite large gains, found herself still cut off from the Adriatic since Austrian and Italian influence had led to the creation of a separate Albania. Bulgaria had failed to secure Salonica and her share of Macedonia. But her sudden attack (June 1913) on Serbia and Greece to gain these was disastrous to her, for it brought Turkey in again, and also Rumania. Bulgaria was forced to accept the loss of Macedonia, restore Edirne (Adrianople) to the Turks, and lose part of the Dobrudja to Rumania. Thus the Turks were more firmly re-established in Constantinople, which restored something, a vital part indeed, of the *status quo*. But Turkish rule elsewhere in the Balkans had gone at last, with Serbia and Greece the greatest gainers. Yet though Serbia was almost doubled in size she still lacked the desired window on the Adriatic, and union with her South Slav compatriots was still but a hope. And it was not to be expected that Bulgaria, though crushed, would remain satisfied with her fate. The peace, as Grey predicted, 'stored up inevitable trouble for the time to come.'

This applied not merely to the Balkans but to Europe. For as the Balkan crisis of 1908–9 had favoured Austria (and the Central Powers) this one favoured Russia (and so the Entente Powers). Both Austria and Russia had been partly mobilized during the crisis, and Austria felt directly injured by the result of the wars. The Greek gain of Salonica was a blow, but the Serbian success was worse. Yet Austrian policy was more confused than ever. Conrad, earlier demoted but now Chief of Staff again, was all for immediate action against Serbia, to destroy her or incorporate her in Austria as Bavaria was incorporated in Germany. Berchtold, Foreign Minister after Aehrenthal's death, was a more nervous and less resolute man. The old emperor was weaker, his heir, Franz Ferdinand, had little control on policy as yet, and was in any case filled with contradictory ideas as to the empire.

Hence German policy and influence on Austria were all important. For a time these were exercised to check any rash action by Austria which might cause a general explosion, so that Austria complained of lack of support. Bethmann-Hollweg felt called upon to reassure her of German fidelity, in words which the social democrat Ledebour declared gave Austria 'a blank cheque.' With the death of Kiderlen-Wächter at the end of 1912 the Foreign Office passed to Jagow, a weaker man, and this, with the Chancellor's lack of control there, enlarged the emperor's role in foreign affairs. This had its dangers, for despite his desire for peace William's judgment was still deficient, his changes of opinion as frequent and unpredictable as ever, the expression of his views no more fortunate. Thus at first, in opposition to Austria, he saw no reason why Serbia should not have a port on the Adriatic; he was friendly towards both Greece and Rumania; he accepted the final peace made with Bulgaria while Austria demanded its revision. Yet within a few weeks of this last step he was supporting Conrad's views as to how to deal with Serbia; he approved an Austrian ultimatum to Serbia, presented without reference to Germany, to remove Serb troops from Albania. And then on a visit to Vienna shortly afterwards he told Berchtold that: 'You can be assured that I stand behind you and am ready to draw the sword whenever your measures require it . . . whatever comes from the Viennese Foreign Office is an order for me.' He was now full of the inevitability of the war between West and East, German and Slav: Slavs were born to serve and must be taught their place. It was all a far cry from Bismarck's 'The whole Eastern Question is no matter of war for us. We will allow no one to lead us by the nose and embroil us with Russia' (11th January 1887). To this later policy must be added the appointment of Liman von Sanders to command a Turkish army corps with headquarters in Constantinople, a step much resented by Russia, ever sensitive about that capital.

This year of the Balkan crisis, 1913, marked for Germany not merely the centenary of the War of Liberation, but also the twenty-fifth anniversary of William II's accession to the throne, both of which were duly celebrated. Germany had now enjoyed over forty years of peace, with unprecedented growth of material prosperity. Yet throughout this period the peace had been an armed peace, with preparation for war one of the greatest industries in the country; the emperor himself was one of the largest shareholders in the great munitions firm of Krupps. Now, Germany bristled with arms as never before, and there was a growing feeling of the imminence of war. Inevitably, especially in Prussia with its long military tradition, its large body of officers, active and retired, with their recollection or knowledge of the swift triumphs of 1866 and 1870, there was a proud belief in the invincibility of the German army, and of the as yet untried (and so unbeaten) navy, a military spirit which looked to such a war to provide a final settlement with France, to remove the menace of the Slavic hordes, destroy the effete British world empire, and give Germany her rightful 'place in the sun.' The teachings of the racialists and expansionists mentioned earlier were bearing their fruits. 'The university professors,' adjudged Baron Beyens, the Belgian ambassador in Germany, 'taken as a whole, constituted one of the most fiery elements of the nation.'[1] To the activities of the Pan-German League must be added those of Tirpitz's Navy League, the newer Defence League of 1912, and the veterans' War Leagues.

It was under the impress of the diplomatic defeat of 1911 that a General Bernhardi wrote his book *Germany and the Next War* (1912). Therein, adopting the views of the racialists, and confident of Germany's superior culture and strength in the struggle for existence, he argued that 'the crucial

[1] *Germany Before the War*, 1916, p. 184.

point is to put aside all other considerations and to prepare ourselves with the utmost energy for the war which appears to be imminent, and which will decide the whole future of our political life and our culture.' The great issue was 'World Power or Downfall.' Moltke, Chief of the great General Staff, the nephew of the greater Moltke, talked in November 1913 of the need for seizing the right moment for the inevitable struggle with France: 'This time we must finish with them.' The emperor echoed the sentiment as to the inevitability of war with France. As for Russia: 'We have become enemies.' Warlike feeling was not confined to Germany: there was chauvinism in France and Russia as well, dislike of Germany in Britain. Popular feeling could be excited in Paris as in Berlin. But as the American Colonel House, friend and confidant of President Wilson, noted on his visit to Paris in the early summer of 1914,[1] the war spirit there was held in check by the responsible statesmen. The trouble with Germany, where he noted the 'militarism run mad,' was that the government was *not* responsible. And the theoretically responsible chancellor, Bethmann-Hollweg, did not in fact 'command in Berlin' any more than the *Reichstag*. When the critical moment came, the emperor, and still more the army and navy leaders, were to speak the deciding words.

This did not mean that the majority of the German people were consciously militaristic. The big industrial and trading interests were alive to the possibilities which speedy victory in war, as in 1870, might bring, in terms of colonies, markets for German industry, opportunities for expanded trade and profitable investment; and a strongly armed country had a correspondingly strong armament industry and interest. But some at least of the commercial leaders saw the dangers and cost of a modern war to the profitable enterprise they had so successfully carried on in time of peace. The mass of the people had no desire for war, in which they would have to bear the brunt. But despite the spread of socialism they were still a highly disciplined people, trained to obedience in the army, ready to accept the word of authority, too easily persuaded that the existence of the empire was in danger, above all from the uncivilized Russians, but hardly less from their old foes the French, or from the British, jealous of Germany's growing prosperity. Georges Blondel, French student of German affairs and very appreciative of German qualities and achievement, writing in 1913 [2] on the subject after recent travel in Germany, found there *un sentiment de malaise*, fruit of the conflict between the great material growth and the decline of the older intellectual and religious ideals, the confusion of political parties and the lack of political leadership, the excessive survival of conservative interest and power, the lack of balance between the new rich and the worker, the clash with the subject nationalities, between the peace-loving majority and the militarists, the breakdown of the old strong family ties, the rising cost of living at which everybody grumbled, and finally concern over the uneasy foreign situation, as revealed in the Moroccan and Balkan crises.

[1] *The Intimate Papers of Colonel House*, 1926, vol. i, p. 249.
[2] *Les Embarras de l'Allemagne*, 1913.

Bethmann-Hollweg must indeed be given credit for desiring better relations with Britain, and the British Government, despite the failure to reach any accord over the navy, was ready to try and deal with more limited objects of friction.   Metternich's successor in London, Lichnowsky, was an ardent supporter of better relations (far more so than his superiors in Berlin indeed), and after much negotiation agreement was in fact reached on two matters still in dispute. The earlier agreement of 1898 for the partition or the African colonies of Portugal should they come into the market was revised in favour of Germany, but failed of ratification because Grey insisted and Germany refused that this treaty should be made public, together with the old British - Portuguese treaty of alliance.   Of wider moment was an agreement over the Bagdad railway, long a bone of contention as Germany on the basis of her 1903 agreement with Turkey sought to push south-east to Mesopotamia, whilst Britain was concerned for her position on the Persian Gulf and the route to India, and so failed (as did Russia until 1909) to come to terms with German plans.   Efforts in 1907 likewise failed, primarily

Bernhardi

from Bülow's opposition, and the vain efforts to secure a naval agreement delayed attempts at a settlement until this year 1913.   The matter was complicated, involving France as well, and it was not until June 1914 that a satisfactory agreement was finally arrived at, giving Germany a free hand for the railway as far as Bagdad, and even on to Basra near the head of the Persian Gulf.   Thereby was secured for her a wide field of activity in Asiatic Turkey.   But it was too late: the B.B.B. (Berlin–Byzantium–Bagdad) railway, like so much else, fell victim to the renewed Balkan crisis and the general war.

This crisis of 1914 opened with the murder of the heir to the Austrian throne, the Archduke Franz Ferdinand, together with his wife, on 28th June, whilst on an official visit to Serajevo, the capital of the Austrian province of Bosnia.   It was to lead within little over a month to a general European war, a world war indeed, which in view of its stupendous results has been the subject of closer study, and greater controversy, than almost any other event in history. It cannot here be followed in detail, but since it was to lead directly to the downfall of the Bismarckian Empire after four years of war, its general course, and German policy therein, cannot be omitted.

The crime had taken place on Austrian soil, but with indications that the plot was hatched in Serbia, possibly involving the Serbian Government, certainly a product of South Slav agitation and ambitions against Austria-Hungary. There was general sympathy with Austria and with the aged emperor, whose wife and first heir had already met with tragic ends. It remained to be seen what Austria, or rather Berchtold, Foreign Minister, and Conrad, Army Chief of Staff, with Francis Joseph, and Tisza, Minister-President of Hungary, in the background, would decide to do. They decided for a final settlement with Serbia, to cut off the head of the South Slav dragon, and this regardless of the wider reactions such a course might bring, above all from Russia, champion of Slav nationalism, who had already been humiliated once in relation to Serbia, in 1908–9. It was a decision fatal for the weakening Austrian Empire, whose last Foreign Minister, Czernin, was later to admit: 'We were doomed to die, but we were free to choose how, and we chose the most terrible way.' Austria could not even act with the necessary dispatch, for the army was not ready, Tisza was all for caution, and Berchtold, unwillingly in office and cast by fate for the role of executioner, was not very efficient at the job. He proposed a march on Serbia, and her reduction by partitions of her territory to Bulgaria, Greece, Albania, Rumania, and Austria herself, so to render her harmless. But not until twenty-five days after the murder was his list of demands made to Serbia, involving the most humble attitude and action by the little Slav kingdom within two days. They were not intended to be met, but were to provide the excuse for war. Serbia met them, however, almost completely, yet Austria began to mobilize (25th July) and declared war on her on 28th July, though still unready to march on Belgrade.

Rash as were these proceedings, the Austrian Government had not ventured upon them without some reference to the ally who had stood by her six years before, and whose emperor had been friendly to the murdered archduke. And it was to the German emperor that Berchtold appealed, through a letter from Francis Joseph delivered a week after the crime. William, on the verge of a Norwegian cruise, rose to the appeal, and before consulting his chancellor promised full support to Austria, urging speed in whatever measures they might take against Serbia even if (which he did not believe) such measures might bring war with Russia. And Bethmann-Hollweg, when advised rather than consulted on this same 5th July, approved this attitude, preferring indeed for the moment to allow Austria to decide what steps to take. Thus was Germany committed by her irresponsibly 'responsible' masters. Her ambassador in Vienna, Tschirschky, had already been rapped over the knuckles for advising caution there, and so fell into line, as did the Foreign Secretary, Jagow. There was no question, of course, of discussion in the *Reichstag*, though William called in the chiefs of the army and navy before departing on his cruise. Seen in the light of all that happened, and all that we now know of Austrian policy and the inevitable reaction it was bound to bring in a Europe bound together by alliances, this hasty German decision was a cardinal and decisive mistake. As the days and weeks went on Bethmann-Hollweg did, indeed, come to feel (what was true enough) that Berchtold was concealing his designs from him, and was embarking on dangerous courses. But he was more concerned that Germany should not appear the aggressor than to take any effective steps to prevent a general war.

For through the month of July tension was rising in Europe as governments waited to see what Austria would do, a tension which increased sharply as the harsh note to Serbia was revealed. 'You are setting fire to Europe,' exclaimed Sazonov to the Austrian ambassador when he saw this ultimatum. Russia, with strikes and other internal troubles, was not in fact ready for the war to which men like Izvolsky looked. But that did not mean that she would surrender the Slav cause in the Balkans and be humiliated again. And her ally France, despite revelations as to her military unpreparedness, was committed to support her ally; Poincaré, her president, was in Russia at this time cementing the alliance. Britain's commitments to France were less formal, but they existed. She undoubtedly wanted peace, and faced the prospect of an Ulster revolt against the introduction of Home Rule in Ireland. But there was the naval issue, the question of the European balance, and Haldane and Grey had given warning that she could not stand aside and see France crushed. Lichnowsky said the same thing to Berlin. Grey strove hard for peace, and had Germany co-operated in time, and not held to the impossible view that such a crisis could be 'localized,' the war might have been prevented, at least for the time. On the side of the Central Powers Italy early made it clear that she was not prepared to go with Austria in a venture from which she would lose rather than gain, and Berchtold refused to buy her off with the Trentino as Jagow suggested.

We need not go into the details of the last few days at the end of July 1914, before the First World War broke out. The endless discussion thereon cannot alter the verdict that the action of the Austrian Government against Serbia was the direct cause of the war, since it inevitably brought in Russia. Germany, with which we are concerned, was likewise responsible, firstly in that although she was the senior partner in the alliance, she promised Austria support without conditions; secondly in supposing that *her* alliance could operate, without bringing in the rival alliance (counting on Russian unreadiness for war); thirdly in refusing to co-operate with Britain in efforts for mediation; and fourthly in allowing her military authorities to take control at the critical moment. For Moltke, after declaring the situation 'extraordinarily favourable' for Germany to face a war, and when Russia, following Austria, had ordered only partial mobilization, urged Austria (on 30th July) to full mobilization, with the pledge that 'Germany will mobilize,' although William and Bethmann-Hollweg had so far refused to take steps towards this. His message provoked the historic question from Berchtold: 'Who gives orders in Berlin, Moltke or Bethmann-Hollweg?' Yet Austria took the advice, and Russia followed, after hesitation. Moltke got his way

in Germany, which sent ultimatums to Russia and France, and on 1st
August declared war on Russia (before Austria did so), and on France two
days later. Britain hesitated. But her bond with France made it inevitable
that she should come in sooner or later, and better early than too late. The
famous Schlieffen plan dictating German attack across Belgium assumed that
she would intervene, and eased her entry, since she was a guarantor of Belgian
neutrality. The world war was on.

The war which now opened and was to last for over four years was to be
a testing time more severe than any Bismarck imagined for every side of the
empire, military, political, social, and economic; and in the end it broke
under the strain. The defeat was primarily military, not, as the military
leaders later argued, caused by a 'stab in the back' from enemies at home.
But undoubtedly there were, as we have seen, inner weaknesses which contributed to the final result. The war was a two-front war, though in it
Germany was to escape the invasion she feared and which she was to inflict
upon both France and Russia. She was, of course, far outnumbered in
population and resources by her foes, above all when the United States
entered the war in 1917. Italy refused to join her allies, claiming that this
was not a defensive war, and Rumania followed suit: within nine months
Italy was to be ranged against her former allies, drawn by the hope of winning
from Austria her 'unredeemed' lands. Yet Germany and Austria-Hungary
together formed an enormous block of 114 millions, free to operate on
'interior lines,' east or west, over their fine railway system, and the gain of
Turkey as an ally in 1914, and then of Bulgaria (1915), opened the way to
the south-east, as the Baltic was open to the north. But this did not com-
pensate for the loss of grain from Russia, or the shutting off of the seaways
to the west for a world trading nation by the British blockade, and when
modern warfare demanded the use of products from all over the world (e.g.
oil and rubber). And the much-prized German navy, at least its most
treasured part, the battle fleet, was to be of little use here or indeed elsewhere,
after helping to bring Britain into the war. Yet Germany had the finest
army in the world, and its leaders were confident that, as in 1866 and 1870,
it would speedily bring victory.

The long-prepared plans for this called, rightly or wrongly, first for a
swift invasion of France through Belgium, with the encirclement and destruction of the main French army, to be followed by the turn eastwards against
the slower-moving Russians. There was a magnificent sweep of over a
million men through Belgium and northern France. But there were some
mistakes by Moltke, whilst the tenacity of the French with the small British
army, and Joffre's outstanding generalship, brought the advance first to a
halt and then to a turn. The battle of the Marne (6th–12th September
1914) which brought this turn, sent the German armies back on a race
with the Franco-British forces to reach the North Sea border. Therewith it led to the formation of a fortified French line between the invading
Germans and the French, British, and Belgian armies, a line which quickly
became fixed from Alsace to the sea. And although this line might be bent

or stretched by attacks from east or west, usually at enormous cost in lives, it was to remain unbroken for most of the war. Thus the battle of the Marne was a decisive defeat of the German hope for a knock-out blow to the French, and so, in a sense, for the whole German effort. Falkenhayn, succeeding the ailing Moltke within a month, turned to a policy of wearing down French resistance, as in the great stroke against Verdun (February–June 1916), only to meet indomitable French resistance, and to find that the frightful loss of life was exhausting his own forces as well. Western allied efforts in 1915, 1916 (the Somme), and 1917 (Flanders and elsewhere) had little more success, save that the growing forces of the western Allies could now better sustain both the effort and the losses. It remained for Ludendorff to return to the earlier strategy in his great offensive of March to July 1918.

In addition to the decisive western front there were other 'fronts' which played their part in bringing the final result: the eastern front in which Germany and Austria faced Russia; the southern and south-eastern front, stretching from the Italian frontier through the Balkans and Gallipoli to Mesopotamia; the sea and overseas front; and finally the home front.

On the eastern front with its vastly wider range the German military genius and training were to find more ample scope for strategy of the type attempted but defeated in the west. This genius was exemplified above all in the extraordinary partnership of Generals Hindenburg and Ludendorff, called in to check an early Russian advance, turning danger to victory at Tannenberg in East Prussia (26th–31st August 1914) and going on in the next year to the great successes which drove the Russians back from invaded Galicia, and out of Russian Poland, Courland, and Lithuania. Here, as in the west, however, the enemy armies were not destroyed. The more cautious Falkenhayn refused to risk the wider sweep into Russia which the eastern twin brethren wanted. The Russians were to show, through Brusiloff's success in 1916 against Austria in Bukowina and Galicia, that despite their growing domestic difficulties they still had the energy to stage an offensive. Indeed the successes on the eastern front (as on the southern and south-eastern fronts) were almost entirely German. Austria had twice failed to reduce little Serbia, twice been driven back by the Russians with great losses, greatest of all in this latest Brusiloff offensive. Similarly she had failed in an attack, made against German advice, on the Italian front, in 1916. It was felt in Germany that Austria, having dragged her ally into the war, was more of a liability than an asset, and bad feeling existed and increased both between the military commanders and more widely.

On the south-eastern and southern front German military efficiency brought magnificent results between 1914 and 1917. The securing of Turkey as an ally, when Italy and Rumania fell away 'like rotten apples from the tree,' as William lamented, was of great importance since it prevented contact between Russia and her allies through the Mediterranean. British efforts to break through the Straits, or seize the peninsula of Gallipoli in 1915, were to fail disastrously. Nor could the Allies save Serbia when Bulgaria joined the Central Powers in September 1915. Greece repudiated her treaty with Serbia, and Mackensen directed a German-Austrian-Bulgarian drive which swept through Serbia, Montenegro, and northern Albania almost but not quite to Salonica and the Aegean.   When in 1916 Rumania finally joined the western Allies, she too was defeated by Mackensen, and most of her land occupied by the end of that year, giving Germany the all-important oil-fields there.   Finally in 1917, with Ludendorff now in charge of military operations, Germany proceeded to organize a campaign against her renegade ally, Italy, and at Caporetto (October 1917) Austro-German troops struck a terrific series of blows which drove the Italians back to the Piave with enormous losses and for a time endangered their whole front and fortunes. Yet here too the German victory was not decisive, and with help from outside the Italian armies withstood the storm, until in their turn they were able to strike back.

Thus on land, after three years of war, Germany had gained enormous successes.   Her own territories were nowhere touched, those of Austria were redeemed from invasion, and the German armies stood firmly far within enemy territory to east and west.   The expansionists indeed argued that Germany had claims to such lands.   The military men demanded safer frontiers in the west, further from the invaluable Rhineland; the agrarians east of the Elbe looked eastward to enlarged grain-growing areas; the industrialists wanted the Belgian coal and the French iron of Longwy-Briey in Lorraine, and looked south-eastwards towards Bagdad and the Persian Gulf.   On the other hand there was the growing weakness of Austria, where the old emperor had died in November 1916 and the new emperor, Karl, was both demanding peace for his distressed peoples and beginning to make efforts on his own account to obtain it.   There was the failure of the Verdun effort in the west, and the increasing Allied pressure there as the British armies grew in size.   And there was the grinding weight of the British blockade, bringing hardships and discontent at home.   For the British held command of the seas, denying supplies from overseas to Germany.   German oceanic shipping had disappeared from the seas, German raiders were captured or destroyed, the English Channel was kept open for British troops and supplies to the western front, the German colonies were lost.   There had been an encounter between German and British battleships at Jutland (Skagerrak) on 31st May 1916.   But although the German ships inflicted greater damage than they received, and so could claim a victory, it had no effect on the blockade.   Henceforth the great ships, the emperor's pride, lay reduced to the useful but inglorious role of auxiliary coastal defence.

There remained, however, another naval weapon, the submarine.   The unrestricted use of this against enemy (or neutral) vessels had been tried in 1915, but had been given up largely because of American protests.   Early in 1917 it was begun again, with the official assurance from the naval leaders that it would bring Britain to her knees in five months, and that even if, as Bethmann-Hollweg and others feared, it brought the United States into the war, it would prevent her bringing troops to Europe.   German submarines did indeed inflict frightful losses upon British, other enemy, and neutral shipping.   But the effort failed of its main purpose; it brought America into the war and it failed to prevent her troops reaching Europe; and it alienated neutrals.   There was bitter disillusionment in informed circles in Germany, demands for the cessation of the ruthless submarine activity, and an increased demand for peace, even at the cost of the hoped-for annexations.   But the real masters of Germany, by this time Ludendorff and Hindenburg, were far from such views, and conditions on the eastern front by the end of 1917 appeared to provide an alternative road to final victory.

The Russian Revolution of 1917, bringing the collapse of her military effort, the disintegration of her armies, and the victory of a party needing and desiring peace, opened to German military leaders not merely new vistas of conquest and food supplies, but also the seeming opportunity to return to the grand strategy of 1914, and strike a destructive and decisive blow in the west before the American armies could arrive.   So peace negotiations with the Soviets were opened, broken off, resumed, and finally settled at Brest-Litovsk (signed 3rd March 1918), while German troops pushed into the fertile Ukraine in search of grain, into the Donetz basin for coal, and as far as the Caucasus in search of oil.   Meanwhile Ludendorff, 'organizer of victory' like Carnot in the French revolutionary wars, prepared for the final blow in the west, by a concentration there of three and a half million men, with more to come from the east as the attack developed from its opening on 21st March 1918.   But although he had great local successes in his series of attacks from March to July, the allied line bent rather than broke.   And by July the German energies and manpower were exhausted. There followed the allied turn and counter-attacks, with fresh British and increasing numbers of American troops now coming into the picture, leading to German retreat from the 'Blackest Day' of 8th August onwards, until by the end of September, with the south-eastern front crumbling, Ludendorff abandoned all hope of stemming the tide, and demanded that an armistice be asked for.   By the time that came on 11th November Turkey had been defeated and driven back from the south to make peace, Bulgaria had given up the struggle, and Austria-Hungary had collapsed, the Habsburg Empire breaking up into its various elements, whilst the Italians pushed in over its southern border.   The war was over.

The defeat in the war was to bring immediately the downfall of the Bismarckian Empire and system.   This was in part due to the defeat itself, but also to the defects in the structure already mentioned as existing before 1914, and which made it unable to stand the strain of the war and the defeat. The home front at first showed a remarkable unity.   On 4th August the *Reichstag* unanimously approved the war credits asked for, though some 14 of the 110 socialist members only did so to preserve party unity, and the government made the most of the widespread fear of Russian invasion.   Henceforth, declared the emperor, he recognized no parties, but only Germans.   But with this party truce the *Reichstag* almost passed out of the picture for the next two years, leaving policy, control, and management in the hands of the civil and military leaders.   The stupendous

HAMBURG WAREHOUSES, END OF THE NINETEENTH CENTURY

E.N.A

INDUSTRIAL SCENE IN UPPER SILESIA. Pitheads and iron works of Königshütte (now Krolewska Huta in Polish territory)

organization and efforts of the army were backed by the comparable industrial effort at home as the nation girded itself for the struggle, with Rathenau organizing the supply and distribution of raw materials. And these efforts increased as the promised victory failed to come either in 1914 or the next year. Inevitably, when everything was organized for the war, the power of the military leaders increased. The emperor receded into the background, his authority and prestige steadily declining, and even the chancellor's influence diminished.

This process reached its climax in the appointment, after Falkenhayn's dismissal in August 1916, of Hindenburg as Chief of the General Staff and Ludendorff as his Quartermaster-General, with the latter as the driving force in the unique combination. Therewith there ensued two years of what was in effect a military dictatorship in Germany, in which not merely the conduct of the war but an ever widening range of political and even economic questions related thereto were decided by the pair, or by Ludendorff. Ludendorff was indeed an admirable, even a great soldier, but he shared the conservative and Prussian views of his class in political matters (e.g. in opposition to Prussian electoral reform), and used what he termed his 'responsibility' to subordinate

Hindenburg

every one and everything to his conceptions of how the war was to be won, threatening, à la Bismarck, to resign unless his views were accepted. He gave the push which drove Bethmann-Hollweg out in 1917, disliking his views and his attempts to conciliate the parties of the Left, putting in his place first Michaelis, a government official, and then the Bavarian leader, the seventy-four-year-old Hertling, with little regard in this as in other matters for the emperor's views. He similarly extruded Kuhlmann from the Foreign Office in 1918 for the expression of views of which he disapproved. He supported the demand for unrestricted submarine warfare in 1917, and dominated in the matter of a severe peace with Russia at Brest-Litovsk, as in policy with regard to Poland and the eastern conquests of Germany. Representing and sharing the views of the expansionists he held out also for the acquisition of Belgium and north-eastern France, refusing to consider

M

peace without annexations. And he supported the restraints on freedom within Germany, whether in the severe censorship, the restrictions to workers' organizations, the wide powers of the local military commanders, who largely superseded the civil administration, the forced mobilization of industrial workers by the 'Hindenburg Programme' law of December 1916, the forcible transfer of Belgian workers to Germany, and the ruthless suppression of strikes or other popular manifestations. In all this he had strong support from the conservatives, the army, the industrialists, the Pan-Germanists, in part from the Centre, and indeed from a large part of the population, so long as his successes in the field continued. The question 'Who rules in Berlin?' received a firm answer for the moment. But the Bismarckian monarchy and state received a severe jolt, being weakened by the very men who professed to be its main supporters.

Yet as the war dragged on, bringing its terrible toll in death and wounds, as food became dearer and scarcer, so that not merely comfort but health suffered, as the restraints on life and freedom not merely continued but increased, and all without bringing the hoped-for victory and the longed-for peace, there were reactions against this military despotism, which in combination with the military defeat of 1918 were to bring revolution. The cost of the war was enormous, and despite the fact that much (too much) was covered by loans, taxes were necessarily increased, the issue of more paper currency by the *Reichsbank* led to the beginnings of inflation; beer and brandy, which had been cheap so far in Germany, became dearer and scarcer; a bad harvest in 1916 was followed by the 'turnip winter'; coal was short since war industry took so much; bureaucratic and military control over every side of life increased. To the popular mind, uninformed as to the true situation because of the rigid censorship of news, the fact that Germany was in possession of so much enemy territory implied that she could make peace on favourable terms, and encouraged the view that it was the military men and industrialists who prevented the making of peace. And by 1916–17 there was a growing popular opinion in favour of peace, even at the cost of giving up these fruits of victory.

It was out of this growing demand for peace that on the motion of Erzberger, a leading figure of the Centre, the *Reichstag* in July 1917 passed a resolution in favour of a peace of 'understanding' and without indemnities; of 'reconciliation' and against 'forced annexations.' But this vague declaration had no force behind it. Bethmann-Hollweg opposed it, and his successor, Michaelis, merely accepted it 'as I understand it,' which meant that he too was against it. It did indeed help to build up and maintain a *Reichstag* majority of Centre, radicals (progressives), and social democrats, but this majority proved quite unable to enforce its will, either in this matter or in another urgent matter, that of Prussian electoral reform. This weakness was in part due to their own divisions, notably those emerging in the socialist party. There the left wing which had shown itself at the beginning of the war became more definite as time went on in its opposition to the granting of the war credits and the war in general. By 1917 they were organized as a separate group, the independent socialist party of Germany (U.S.P.D.), led by Haase, Kautsky, and Dittmann, more definitely socialistic than the 'majority' socialists, and more openly for peace, without annexations. The Russian Revolution naturally stirred them, although save for a few extremists they did not, like the small internationalist 'Spartacist' group, work for or expect a social revolution of the Russian type in Germany. Yet the Russian Revolution, as it developed, inevitably affected opinion in Germany, and ironically enough it was the army leaders who gave the greatest aid to that revolution by shipping Lenin across Germany from Switzerland to Russia in 1917 to serve their own ends against Russia.

The November Revolution of 1918 in Germany came, however, not from the *Reichstag* or even from the social democrats outside that body. It came in part as a 'revolution from above,' after the great offensive of 1918 in the west had failed, and German military defeat was clear. Ludendorff, in order to meet what he knew would be allied (or American) conditions for an armistice, and perhaps to avoid military responsibility for the crash, demanded that the *Reichstag* should now take over responsibility, under a new chancellor, the liberal Prince Max of Baden. So the *Reichstag* hurriedly amended the fifty-year-old constitution to make the chancellor fully responsible to itself, and the emperor and *Bundesrat* accepted the changes. The army, peace and war, now became subject to the sovereign parliament; and on the demand of the chancellor, Ludendorff resigned on the day (26th October 1918) on which these changes were carried. But the *Reichstag* showed its unpreparedness for the responsibilities its members (or those of the Left) had for so long demanded by immediately adjourning. It had not met during most of the critical days of October, and now after four hectic days it immediately adjourned for the next fortnight!

It was in this interval that the working class, sailors, and soldiers proceeded by 'direct action' to complete the downfall of the Bismarckian Empire and the Prussian and other German thrones. There had been protests, popular manifestations or strikes, long before this. In June 1916, 50,000 Berlin workers had struck work in protest against the arrest of Karl Liebknecht for an anti-war demonstration, and many times that number had risen nine months later both in the capital and elsewhere to demand better food conditions, a governmental peace declaration, the ending of restrictions on the press and labour organizations, and the freeing of political prisoners: democratic but not socialist demands. More radical were the demands formulated by some of the sailors of the High Seas fleet, who in their close quarters, with continued inaction and short rations, were good material for socialist agitation. In July 1917 these came out with a manifesto declaring their adhesion to the U.S.P.D. programme and for the success of the international peace conference called to Stockholm by the Russian revolutionaries in this summer. This action was severely punished, with death sentences for the leaders, as approaching mutiny. In January 1918, following news of wide strikes in Austria, and more openly instigated by left-wing agitators of the U.S.P.D. such as R. Müller, with eyes on Russia and the negotiations at

Brest-Litovsk, came a big strike demonstration of working men in Berlin, with much the same demands as in the preceding year, if more forcefully expressed. This was also accompanied by the organization of a 'Workers' Council,' since the trade unions refused to take the lead. Yet both the majority socialists and the U.S.P.D. sent delegates to this body, to the anger of the Spartacists. But although the strike spread through most of the centres of industry in Germany, the hand of the military dictatorship was still strong enough to deal with it firmly. Within a week or so it was all over, and conquest in the east, with preparations for the great western offensive, went on unhindered; the socialist parties and the peace campaign seemed to have lost.

When, however, the western offensive failed, the south-eastern front collapsed, and the imminence of general defeat became manifest, the tide of popular discontent burst forth with a strength no longer to be withstood. An order of the naval chiefs, to prepare for a final bold stroke by the High Seas fleet, brought a naval mutiny. This spread rapidly through the whole fleet, with the seizure of the naval port of Kiel (4th November), the setting up of Soldiers' and Workers' Councils, involving 100,000 men, and the formulation of demands for the ending of the war as of the strict naval discipline and officers' privileges. Reserve or returned soldiers, many of these deserters, began to follow the naval example, first in cities such as Bremen, Lübeck, and Hamburg. In Munich, sensitive to the crash of Austria, the upsurge first became politically revolutionary when on 7th–8th November, under the leadership of Kurt Eisner, Bavarian U.S.P.D. leader, the soldiers mutinied, and with the populace proclaimed a republic, demanding freedom from Berlin, peace, and setting up of Soldiers' and Workers' Councils.

The effect of this example was felt immediately all over Germany. Crowns elsewhere fell of their own weight, in growing confusion, but without bloodshed. It remained to see what Berlin, and the ruler of the empire, would do, as power fell into the hands of the majority socialists, Ebert their leader, with Scheidemann, Braun, and Noske, though the U.S.P.D. led by Haase and Dittmann shared it locally. The Spartacists had little influence despite their efforts, save in the momentary adoption of the Soviet 'Councils.' But if the disorders continued and grew, more opportunity might come their way. The emperor had left Berlin for army headquarters in Spa before the end of October. His day was over, yet the monarchy might be saved for the *Reich* if he abdicated, leaving a regency for his grandson; the Crown Prince had no backers to speak of. But despite appeals William clung to his title, or grasped at the absurd suggestion that he should remain King of Prussia, abandoning the imperial title, whilst in Berlin tension and confusion increased, until on 9th November revolution broke out. The chancellor on his own authority announced William's abdication, but it was too late to save the monarchy: the republic was proclaimed, Prince Max resigned, and the same day the erstwhile emperor fled to Holland. It was a poor ending after so much imperial flamboyancy.

The Bismarckian Empire, which the liberal Professor Hans Delbrück of

Berlin had in 1913 declared to be the monarchy best able in Europe to with-stand a crisis, had come to an end. With it the rule of the Hohenzollerns in Prussia, the Wittelsbachs in Bavaria, and the many other royal and ducal houses good, bad, and indifferent, likewise disappeared. Two days later the war came to an end for Germany with the signing of an armistice. The revolution had been almost bloodless, though the war which occasioned it had cost Germany nearly six million casualties, and vast other losses. Yet the revolution meant much more than the end of the monarchy. How much more, how much of a revolution it would be, would depend upon what use the victors made of it. The unity of the *Reich* remained, not seriously endangered by the upsurge of Bavarian particularism. And much of the predominance of Prussia was bound to remain, unless she were broken up, which was unlikely. Yet the old ruling class had lost its place, the flower of its sons lost on the battle-field, the antiquated Prussian constitution was at long last doomed to disappear, the military class was temporarily if not permanently discredited, the way seemed open to the organization of a political and social democracy. Whether that was to be organized along socialist lines or not was open to question. Over all hung the shadow of the military defeat and the peace to be worked out, and that too would greatly affect the fortunes of the new republic.

CHAPTER XII

THE WEIMAR REPUBLIC AND THE NAZI DICTATORSHIP, 1918–39

The Setting up of the Weimar Republic — The Struggle for Stability, 1920–8 — The Decline and Fall, 1929–33 — The Nazi Dictatorship

I. THE SETTING UP OF THE WEIMAR REPUBLIC

AT THE end of 1918 Germany was a country militarily exhausted, greatly weakened economically, and desirous above all of peace. The military dictatorship and the old semi-autocratic rule had gone, and she was free to set up a democratic form of government. Yet within fifteen years she had abandoned that form of government, and handed herself over to a new, less responsible, and far more tyrannous form of autocracy. And within six years more she had again plunged into a longer and more terrible war than that of 1914–18, which was to bring upon her calamities far greater than any Bismarckian nightmare could imagine. Since these developments are so near to us, and have involved us all so closely, it is impossible for the historian to deal with them with an adequate perspective of time, or with that so-called 'scientific' impartiality which, despite striving, has never been reached even by the German writers from Ranke onwards who claimed and honestly believed in its attainment. Yet the historian must face this problem, and give what answer he can from the material available. Of that indeed there is no lack. In fact the volume of it is so great as to be beyond the possibility of human absorption; and most of it is inevitably controversial to a greater or lesser degree, which also makes the task more difficult.

It is to be remembered that there was not, and could not be, an entirely new start in 1918. Germany still lay in the centre of Europe, open to winds from east and west.[1] With her acceptance of parliamentary democracy she appeared to have turned to the west. But one of her ablest liberal thinkers of this time, Troeltsch (d. 1923), argued that she could never be fully western in thought. And just as the attractive hero of Fontane's earlier novel, the Brandenburg squire Stechlin, avowed that he preferred the Russians (meaning the old aristocracy there) so now German proletarians such as Karl Liebknecht looked to sovietized Russia for precept and example. The roots of German life were deep, their products lasting. As thinkers they still had the old urge to see things in terms of general systems. Politically and socially the Prussian habit of obedience and discipline, the weakness for titles, great and small, the feeling of class distinctions, were still present despite the claims and growth of socialism and democracy. The turn to republicanism, even to democracy, was too sudden to be universally accepted, and it might have

See map, pp. 356–7.

346

been better had some of the princes remained, stripped of political power, but as local stabilizing foci and ties with the old Germany. Prussia was, as before, a major problem, and Preuss was right in proposing that it should be broken up. As it was, its greater weight in the *Reich*, the influence of writers such as Spengler in his *Prussian Socialism*, 1919 (which had nothing to do with socialism though much with Prussia), and similarly Moeller van den Bruck in *The Prussian Style*, 1915, helped to keep alive the old Prussian spirit. The Bismarckian tradition of the non-responsibility of the political parties could not be replaced by a feeling of responsibility in a moment. A German liberal critic [1] of the day noted that the Germans were less ready to defend their new liberty because they had not obtained it by fighting. The religious differences still survived, and political life was still complicated by the separate Catholic representation in the *Reichstag*. The State was still a federal state, with particularism weakening indeed, but still vocal and active in Bavaria.

To these lasting issues thus barely indicated were added the immediate issues created by the defeat and the 'vacancy of power' resulting from the revolution of November 1918. There were the questions of establishing order, of arriving at peace terms, and of embodying the changes of October and November in a new constitutional framework. These three issues reacted upon each other. The question of order was the most urgent, for Germany in November 1918 was almost literally a powder magazine, full of soldiers and arms, food was short and feeling bitter, with a hastily organized and inexperienced ministry of social democrats under Ebert divided between majority socialists and independent socialists. The Spartacist extremists demanded a real proletarian revolution, and the Soldiers' and Workers' Councils in Berlin deliberated as to whether they should go with the government or the communists. Berlin was to escape a Paris Commune of 1871, but not without a series of threats to public order. Both in the capital and elsewhere, the cumulative effects of the unprecedented war losses and suffering, overwork and under-nourishment, added their toll of death and disease. In his fear of a social revolution Ebert, who admitted that he 'hated revolution like sin,' secretly took a fateful step. He asked for help from Groener, Ludendorff's successor at army headquarters, to put down disorders, thereby striking an alliance with the military men his party had so long attacked. And a little later he encouraged the enlistment of volunteers into what became the famous (or infamous) Free Corps, which embodied the strongest opposition to the democratic and republican cause. Noske, social democratic Minister of War, collaborated actively in this alliance with the army. Yet although the bond was effective in putting down disorders from the Left in the next year or so, it broke the tenuous alliance between the majority socialists and the 'independent,' more real socialists of the U.S.P.D., so weakening the republican-democratic cause, whilst it gave back to the military leaders some of the influence which they seemed to have lost. Demands for a 'people's army' remained as far from fulfilment as the like

[1] Rudolf Olden, *The History of Liberty in Germany*, 1946, p. 164.

demands of 1848–9. The left-wing semi-military organization of the *Reichs-banner*, formed in 1924 to match the *Stahlhelm* of the nationalists, the Free Corps, and the S.A. of the Nazis, was not able to save the republic.

The threat of a social overthrow was in fact smaller than Ebert feared; then as throughout the Weimar Republic, it was hunger which created communists, save for the relatively few. The Congress of Workers' and Soldiers' Councils meeting in Berlin in mid December 1918 voted by far more than three to one against the Soviet system and for the existing Ebert-Scheidemann government. True, disorders existed: in late December sailors of the 'People's Naval Division' rose in Berlin, without any clear-cut demands, but were dealt with by the regular army. Early in January 1919 the Sparta-cists, now renaming themselves the German communist party (K.P.D.), demonstrated against the government in Berlin, calling for a general strike. Karl Liebknecht was for an immediate *putsch*, the cooler-headed Rosa Luxemburg against, since the effort was bound to fail; the workers were divided, but peaceful. The government called in military aid, which restored order with more harshness than was required; officers of the Free Corps murdered the two communist leaders, and many more after all danger was over. This marked the end of any danger from the extreme Left, despite minor efforts at risings in cities of central and western Germany, and a final effort in Berlin in March 1919, likewise put down with a firm hand at the cost of over a thousand civilian lives. Munich staged its own variant of the issue in the spring of 1919. Feeling there was sharpened by the communist revolution of March 1919 in Hungary, and by the divergence of aim between the Munich intellectuals and urban workers, and the Catholic and funda-mentally conservative farmers. The able radical leader, Eisner, had been murdered by a youthful reactionary in February, and after an uneasy interval radical writers and convinced communists attempted early in April to set up a Bavarian Soviet state. But after a brief regime of wild confusion, armed forces of the *Reich*, regulars and Free Corps from the north, entered the Bavarian capital and ruthlessly crushed all opposition. Munich ceased to be a centre of radicalism, and after the attempted Kapp *putsch* of March 1920 political power fell into the hands of the bourgeois-farmer Catholic Bavarian people's party. Munich's next leading role was to be as the nursery of national socialism.

The Kapp *putsch*, led by a Prussian official, a founder of the Fatherland party of 1917, with military aid from General Lüttwitz in Berlin, and encouragement from Ludendorff, was an indication that the 'old gang,' as we might call them, of officers and Prussian conservatives, was reviving, thanks to the weakness of the government and the pressure of the peace terms as they took shape, most immediately the demand for German army reduction. It had a momentary success as Berlin was seized and the govern-ment fled to Saxony. But it was defeated by the response of labour to the government appeal to stage a general strike. In this they were backed by both the Centre and all the parties of the Left, while the right-wing parties refused to give open support to the *putsch*. So the revolt fizzled out, Kapp dying in prison, others fleeing. Labour made a gallant effort to capitalize on its victory by insisting on the carrying through of the social changes promised in November 1918, including the democratization of the Civil Service, the disbanding of the Free Corps in favour of loyal republican forces, and the socialization of the coal and potash industries. The government agreed—but failed to carry out its promises. And though Noske was forced to retire, his Democratic Party successor, Gessler, proved equally amenable to the views of the army men in the years that followed.

The task of the new regime in Germany was inevitably complicated and made more difficult by the peace-making in the seven and a half months between the signing of the armistice with the Allies on 11th November 1918 and the final signing of peace terms at Versailles on 28th June 1919. The armistice terms were a shock, demanding as they did the immediate evacuation of France, Belgium, Alsace-Lorraine, Luxemburg; the withdrawal from the Rhine, with allied occupation of Cologne, Coblenz, and Mainz; the wiping out of the treaties with Russia and Rumania and the withdrawal in the east to the 1914 frontiers; the freeing of allied prisoners of war; the giving up of war material (including all submarines) and much transport material; and the continuation of the blockade. This last blow was in part due to Germany's destruction of allied and neutral shipping, and her reluctance to provide ships for the import of food, but was none the less severely felt. The fact was that Germany was completely unprepared to face defeat. She had undertaxed herself during the war, counting on victory as in 1871, or at worst (as time went on) a compromise peace; in the first case the enemy would pay, as Russia had paid at Brest-Litovsk; in the second she would escape without loss, perhaps come off even better. She had the more hope of this because of President Wilson's statements of principles in the Fourteen Points and later (some of them made without consulting his French and British allies who had sustained the main burden of the struggle), and because of her own change of government. Her people failed to appreciate the allied view that Germany was mainly responsible for the war, its havoc and sufferings. The fair land of the *Reich* was practically untouched by the war, whereas large areas in Belgium and France were devastated, towns and villages pulverized in some cases, agricultural areas out of cultivation, mines and industries ruined. Who was to pay for this? If Germany's loss of life was frightful, France had suffered even more in proportion. Germans forgot the terms which they had imposed upon Russia and Rumania, their pronouncements as to the attainment of world power, the ruthlessness of the U-boat campaign, the introduction of gas warfare, the harshness and cruelty inflicted in Belgium and elsewhere.

All in all it would have been better if the Allies had marched into Berlin, to make the defeat clearer, and if they had made their preliminary terms with the responsible German army chiefs rather than with the civilian Erzberger as head of the armistice commission. Nor was the allied peace-making, either in method or in its terms, free from unwisdom. Since by the end of the war Germany had no less than thirty-three nations lined up

against her from all over the world, peace-making was exceedingly complicated for the conference, which met in January 1919, in Paris.[1]   There was
an immense impatience for a settlement, much popular allied pressure on
negotiators to 'get on with the job,' and for a severe peace, infinite lobbying,
much confusion, controversy, and divergence of opinion on innumerable
points large and small.   The actual procedure of the conference itself as
between the Allies and Germany, whether the terms were preliminary or
final, was unclear to many of the allied delegates.   The Germans protested
vigorously, too vigorously at times, and then and later made much of the fact
that the Treaty of Versailles was a 'dictated' peace.   But the truth was that
any possible treaty was bound to contain a considerable element of dictation,
since Germany refused, for example, to accept the claims of the French to
Alsace-Lorraine and of the Poles to reconstitution as a free nation.   It
would probably have been wiser to leave Germany some of her colonies,
though the reasons she gave for keeping them (markets, raw materials,
German emigration thereto) were demonstrably invalid, and there was a
natural fear of leaving Germany with overseas naval bases.   The War Guilt
clauses (Parts VII and VIII) 'arraigning' for trial the emperor and 'violators
of the laws and customs of war' were never to be carried out, and that
declaring Germany's responsibility with her allies for all the loss and damage
suffered by the Allies was in the end probably to serve more for German
propaganda purposes than for the reparations based upon it.   Germany
did indeed pay over the years large sums or deliveries in kind in reparations,
a matter which remained a constant source of difficulty and irritation for a
decade.   But it turned out that in the same period she actually borrowed
from the Allies to rebuild her economic life more than she paid out in
reparations.   The army naturally resented the enforced reduction from
universal military service to a small professional army of 100,000 men; but
that too was to be evaded in the end.   And although the big ships of her
navy were to be surrendered, she managed to destroy them rather than give
them up.   There were restrictions on German trade which bore hardly upon
her for a time.

The territorial losses were severe, but more justified than Germany was
ready to admit.   The loss of Alsace-Lorraine again to France was inevitable
and proper; and the temporary loss of the Saar with its coal was justified by
her destruction of the French coal-mines.   The small losses to Belgium,
with the plebiscite there and in Northern Schleswig, did not constitute major
problems.   The loss of Posen and more especially West Prussia to a resusci-
tated Poland were to be bitterly resented in Prussia, not least because of the
separation of East Prussia by the Polish Corridor.   But a revived Poland
had rights to a sea approach, as even Hitler publicly admitted right down
to 1939, and Prussian policy to the Poles, whilst it had helped economic
development, had not justified itself by winning their loyalty.   Further,
plebiscites in East Prussia enabled her to keep some of the territory at stake.
The loss of Danzig (though not to Poland) and of Memel was likewise a

[1] The final treaty was in fifteen parts, with no less than 440 articles.

hard blow, but Hitler was to treat his east Baltic compatriots with far less concern at a later date.   The proposal to give the Poles Upper Silesia, where German energy and skill had developed the mines, while the labour and the majority of the rural population was Polish, was also a bitter blow.   The Allies conceded a plebiscite, but the interpretation made of it by the League of Nations gave Germany a fresh grievance.   The refusal to allow the union of German Austria with Germany was natural enough, and not unjustified in view of the fear of Germany's still large population and size.   But the refusal to admit Germany straightway to the League of Nations seems of dubious wisdom.

The provision of a constitution for the new Germany was a much more difficult task than Bismarck had had to face.   Then he could say (after victorious war): 'Put the *Reich* in the saddle and it will ride.'   Now, with defeat, revolution, disorder, the crash of the old system, things were very different.   Actually Germany underwent a variety of constitutional changes between 26th October 1918, when the break with the Bismarckian constitution took place, and 11th August 1919, when the Weimar constitution came into effect.   The parliamentary regime set up under the emperor in October 1918 was followed in November by a republic in which Soldiers' and Workers' Councils, headed by a Central Committee, and with a ministry of 'People's Commissars' claimed sovereign power.   Then came, in February 1919, a provisional government set up by the newly elected National Constituent Assembly, to which the Central Committee of the Soldiers' and Workers' Councils formally surrendered its powers.   Finally, in August came the Weimarian constitution, although even then the National Assembly continued to sit for over nine months longer.   The majority social democrats, led by Ebert, Scheidemann, Bauer, Noske, and others, held uneasy power during most of this period, resting upon their large party in the *Reichstag*, their hold over the workers, and their alliance with the army, some common ground with Centre and progressives, and despite the withdrawal of the independent socialists from the ministry at the end of December 1918.

The downfall of the old regime brought a certain revamping and renaming of some of the old parties, which revealed itself in the elections to the National Constituent Assembly on 19th January 1919.   Whilst the majority social democrats and the Centre remained unchanged, there emerged out of the progressives and the left wing of the national liberals in November 1918 a 'democratic' party, middle class but liberal, including Haussmann, Preuss, and Rathenau, and backed by distinguished thinkers such as Troeltsch and Max Weber.   They were to join with Centre and social democrats to form the 'Weimar Coalition.'   To their right emerged in place of the old national liberal party a German 'people's' party, led by Stresemann, representing big business and free enterprise, anti-socialist, accepting the republic although preferring the monarchy.   The old conservatives reappeared as the German 'National' people's party, more openly monarchist and in general reactionary, with much the same character and composition as before.   For the election the franchise was extended to both men and women over the age of twenty, and was exercised through a system of proportional representation. In the result the social democrats received far the largest number of votes and seats (163 seats out of 421) but not a majority as they had hoped. The Centre received 89 seats, the democrats 74, the nationalists 42, the people's party and the independent socialists 22 each. Thirty-five women were elected, nearly half of them majority socialists. The Assembly wisely met not in Berlin, but in more peaceful Weimar, hallowed by memories of Goethe, Schiller, and other great men.

The National Assembly had not merely to make a constitution, but also to govern for the time being, to make what peace terms they could with the Allies, and to face both the urgent and difficult economic situation and the social unrest. They set up a provisional government, electing Ebert as president, and a ministry headed by Scheidemann, but composed from the three parties of social democrats, democrats, and Centre. The constitution which emerged from the deliberations of the Assembly was democratic indeed, but not socialistic. It was a compromise between the views of the three parties of the coalition, in which the two non-socialist parties exactly balanced the majority socialist party, and it was opposed by most of the nationalists, the people's party, and (from the Left) the independent socialists. The eminent Berlin lawyer Preuss had prepared the draft, which was subjected to lengthy discussion, both by a special commission and in the Assembly. On some points Preuss's draft was changed, notably in his proposal to create a unitary *Reich*, breaking up Prussia to form roughly equally sized provinces. Yet if Prussia remained, the central authority was made decidedly stronger. The *Sonderrechte* of 1871 disappeared; the *Reich* was given clear superiority over the states in legislation, and greater taxing powers. The old *Bundesrat*, champion of states rights, was replaced by a *Reichsrat* of quite limited powers, and the states themselves now became 'territories' (*Laender*). The seven pocket-sized states of Thuringia were now joined into one. Whilst the disappearance of the king-emperor reduced the role of Prussia, the fact that over half of the total population of Germany lived in Prussia did much to preserve her preponderance.

The new *Reich* and the states, or *Laender*, were by the constitution not merely republican, but also democratic. 'Political authority is derived from the people,' declared the first article of the constitution. Hence all over the age of twenty, male and female, elected the *Reichstag* by proportional representation, in order that with German thoroughness public opinion should be accurately mirrored. This law-making body was elected for four years, its members paid and protected by law, the chancellor and ministers responsible to it. Reference to the sovereign people was provided for in certain cases by referendum. The chancellor, however, was appointed by the president, and was to choose his ministers, a remainder of the Bismarckian pattern. The president was not intended to be a mere figurehead. With the monarchical tradition, and the unquiet times, it was agreed that more was needed. He was to be chosen by the whole people, for seven years, and was re-eligible, but could be removed by combined parliamentary and popular vote.   Yet he not merely represented the *Reich* 'in matters of international law,' but had the command over the army, he appointed officials unless otherwise provided, he could compel the *Laender* to fulfil their federal obligations, and by Article 48 could, 'if public safety and order were endangered,' temporarily suspend civil liberties, subject to the approval of the *Reichstag*.   President Ebert was to make use of this clause, and under Hindenburg its employment, or rather misuse, was to assist in the downfall of the republic.   Civil liberties were defined, with a good deal of the spirit of 1848, in Part II of the constitution, entitled 'The Fundamental Rights and Duties of Germans,' and dealing with the individual, community life, religion, education, and economic life.   Here were laid down and in part defined the equality and liberty of the citizen; the importance of the family; the freedom of association and meeting; the duties of citizenship; the rights of private property; liberty of religion, without any State Church; the nature of the State educational system, though without mention of the controversial question of religious instruction.

Associated with this part of the constitution was a lengthy section on economic life.   Here the most important issue was that of the attitude to be taken towards the socialization for which not merely communists and independent socialists but also majority socialists were supposed to stand. It was not merely a question of economic organization, but also of power, which in the old authoritarian State had been shared by the industrialists and large landowners.   But the truth was that the favourable moment for any attempt at fundamental economic change had gone by.   In their desire to save the Fatherland from chaos such as existed in Russia, their feeling for order and the discipline bred in them, the contradiction between their middle-class interest and the Marxian views they professed, the majority socialists and the trade unions behind them had shrunk from seizing the opportunity presented by the November Revolution, despite the urgings of the independent socialists.   Ebert's provisional government had set up a Socialization Commission in December 1918 to consider which industries were ripe for nationalization, but it was hardly to be expected that the coalition government of the Constituent Assembly would carry through sweeping changes in the economic system.   It did in March–April 1919 pass laws which allowed the *Reich* to take over (with compensation) enterprises considered suitable for socialization; it transferred the coal and potash industries to commissioners of owners, workers, and consumers; and later in the year approved the socialization of the electrical industry, a step never carried out.

The Assembly also grappled with the syndicalist demand for the regulation of industry by factory workers' councils, in co-operation with the employers. Article 165 of the constitution provided for the establishment of local, district, and national Workers' Councils, the last to form with employers and others a National Economic Council, to sit alongside the *Reichstag* and consider economic matters.   This Central Economic Council (or parliament) duly came into existence in 1920.   But the complete conciliar machinery never came into existence, partly from trade union objections.   More important was the fact that the employers refused to co-operate on the terms laid down, so that the proposals for nationalization and for the sharing of control never came into effect.   Hence the economic revolution which seemed on the way in November 1918 failed to materialize, neither land nor industry passed into public control, and economic power was left largely in the same hands as before.   And these hands became fewer as the cartelization of industry developed still further after 1918, with men such as Hugo Stinnes securing control over perhaps one-fifth of the whole of German industry, to be followed after his death in 1924 by others of like kind and grasp, such as Thyssen, the steel magnate.   This was the more serious since, in addition, so many of the old judicial and administrative officials, naturally conservative for the most part, were likewise left in office.   In judicial action taken against those accused of disorders in these years decisions tended to bear far more hardly on offenders from the Left than on those from the Right.   Similarly the new army, the *Reichswehr*, as rebuilt by Seeckt, represented the old rather than the new Germany.   Thus the question arose as to whether the political revolution in favour of republican democracy could hope to maintain itself when so many of the forces in the State opposed rather than supported it.

The Weimar Constitution must not, however, be made responsible for the failure of the social democrats to bring about the social revolution.   That constitution was a finely wrought document, a fair enough compromise between the views and wishes of the parties who made it.   It might seem that the hopes of the men of 1848–9 had at long last been fulfilled.   Yet the constitution had its weak points.   Like the work of the Frankfurt Assembly it was wordy and over-long in its attempt to define Fundamental Rights and Duties; within a few years many of its statements here were to prove mere wishful thinking.   Its adoption of proportional representation, with the whole country divided into only thirty-five large multi-member electoral districts, was to encourage the evil, from which Germany already suffered, of the confusion of many parties.   By 1931 there were no less than twenty-seven of these competing for votes.   The party was everything; the individual member had no local ties or responsibility as in single member constituencies.   The direct election of the president as well as the parliament by the whole nation repeated the error of the French Republic of 1848, which had led to the dictatorship of Napoleon III.   Coupled with the emergency powers given to him, this could be, and was to prove, a danger to the democratic State.

The real problem in 1919, however, was not so much that of the actual machinery of the republic, as whether it could work successfully, and overcome or circumvent the obstacles facing it.   And the chief of these was the irreconcilable divergence of political opinion and aim, the legacy of the past, which was in the end to stultify the work of the Fathers of Weimar.   The constitution was backed by parties representing 23,000,000 votes, and although the final vote for it was not quite in proportion, since there were many abstentions, it was amply large enough (262 to 75) to indicate that the majority of the German people supported it. Yet how quickly opinion could change in these disturbed days was shown in the first election held under the new constitution in June 1920. For in it the nationalist and people's parties of the Right markedly increased the number of their seats, whilst the democrats and the majority socialists lost seats, the latter party losing heavily to the independent socialists. The communist party now entered the *Reichstag* (with two seats) and the Centre lost the control over the Bavarian Catholics, who now became partly independent as the Bavarian people's party. A swing from the middle parties (counting the majority socialists as one of these) towards the extremes had already set in.

II. THE STRUGGLE FOR STABILITY, 1920–8

The early years of the Weimar Republic were full of troubles and tribulation for the German people. Much of this was the inevitable effect of the war, some the result of the hardships of the peace treaty and allied policy, some again the product of the continuing inner strife of groups and parties in the country. It is not possible to separate and measure individually or comparatively the impact of these several forces, which interacted to bedevil the efforts of the successive governments of the *Reich* to secure and maintain stability under the new regime. A more generous and sympathetic policy by the Allies in these years might have strengthened the infant republic, but in the divided state of opinion in Germany would have likewise given encouragement to the forces opposed to that republic. All the Allies had their own serious domestic problems in these years, and were no longer so closely joined. The United States Senate had refused to ratify the peace treaty, or to join the League of Nations which it had helped to make, and which it was believed would draw the nations, Germany included, together in harmony, and to that end might even rectify injustices in the peace treaties. France and its leaders, such as Foch, Clemenceau, and Poincaré, were concerned for security against the enemy which had twice invaded their country and which was still stronger than she was. And since the United States refused to honour the pledge Wilson had given France of immediate aid in case of future German attack, for which France had surrendered her demand for a permanent separation of the Rhineland from Germany, she was the more determined to assert her full rights under the treaty. Britain's similar promise to France fell with that of the United States, perhaps unwisely, and whilst Britain stood for her claims under the treaty, she was also more concerned for the establishment of peaceful relations with the new Germany, not least the restoration of the trade which had been so important for both countries before 1914.

Whilst the problem of the division of Upper Silesia, with its inextricable tangle of Pole and German living above its wealth of coal and iron, provided a tragic example of the difficulty of arriving at a solution just to both sides, the most continuously acrimonious issue during these years was that of the reparations Germany was to pay for damage done during the war. Because

Central Europe, showing new boundaries established 1918–21. Terri
lost to Germany by plebiscite or outright cession in this period—n

hlesvig, Memelland, the Polish corridor, Upper Silesia, Alsace-Lorraine,
d the Saar—is shown shaded inside the frontier of 1914 (dotted)

of the difficulty of drawing up a total bill the matter was left to be worked out by a reparations commission, although certain large amounts were by the treaty to be paid straightway.   The sum, when set, proved impossibly high, and there was protest and evasion from Germany, divisions among the Allies, and numerous conferences, with the Allies temporarily occupying certain Ruhr cities in March 1921, as Germany fell short in payments. After another crisis a few months later Germany, with Wirth (Left Centre) now as chancellor, and Rathenau as Minister of Reconstruction, decided upon a 'policy of fulfilment.'   But in 1922 Rathenau was assassinated, like Erzberger the preceding year a victim of the Right, and as German economic conditions worsened she requested a moratorium in payments, which Britain was ready to grant.   The French, however, were determined to take a strong line, and in January 1923 with Belgium occupied the Ruhr, the Achilles heel of German industry, as Germany again defaulted.   The French could claim that they had spent enormous sums in restoring their devastated areas, and looked to Germany to pay the cost.   Britain opposed the action as unjustified and unlikely to aid reparations payments.   It looked as if France now designed to carry through her earlier hope of separating the Rhineland from Germany, working on local sentiment there, the more so as she extended her activities up the Rhine towards Alsace.

The results on Germany were disastrous, threatening both her economic and her political structure.   Chancellor Cuno, a business man, called to office when Wirth resigned for lack of support, decided to meet the occupation by passive resistance.   But although this largely defeated the French attempt to exact German reparations from the Ruhr, it failed to make them withdraw as Cuno hoped.   There was trouble and disorder in the Ruhr itself, with military and police clashes, terrorism, and a flurry of separatist activity as the region was cut off from the *Reich*.   No less serious were the reverberations in many other parts of the country.   The communists were active and strong in Saxony, Thuringia, and Hamburg, protesting against the reactionary nature of the government and hoping to use the opportunity to strike a blow for a real social revolution.   Even more threatening was the development in Bavaria, where on the one hand local particularism raised its head again against Berlin, on the other the new national socialism headed by Hitler first attacked socialists and planned a march on Berlin to seize power, and then in November 1923 enlisted the support of Ludendorff in a more serious attempt towards the same end.   The attempt failed, Hitler fled, to be caught, tried, and condemned for high treason, though only to be imprisoned for eight months.

And whilst these and other disorders continued through this fateful year the weakness of the republic was shown even more plainly and poignantly in the continued and increasingly precipitous decline in the value of the currency.   This had begun during the war, and continued as Germany failed to balance her budget.   The mark, once worth about one shilling or twenty-five cents, had fallen to two cents by January 1921, to one-tenth of that by July 1922, and with ever-increasing issues of paper money it was already at

50,000 to the dollar in January 1923 and on the way to astronomical figures and complete worthlessness during the course of this disturbed year. For this fall the government's financial advisers and the *Reichsbank* must bear most of the responsibility. The effects were felt most by the workers, whose wages entirely failed to keep pace with the rising cost of living, by the small trader and industrialist, often driven into bankruptcy, and by the salaried middle class, notably by that formerly solid section of this class whose savings, investments in war loans, pensions, and the like now shrank to nothing. Here indeed was a social revolution for part at least of the once so firmly graded German community. The gainers were the owners of real property, the industrialists with loans to pay off and wages to pay, the speculators who realized what was happening, the financiers and merchants, Gentile and Jewish, who could get hold of foreign currency. An appreciable part of the middle class was plunged into poverty, proletarianized, with the choice of going socialist, or of adopting the newer faith of national socialism, as many of them, or their sons and daughters, were in fact to do, especially when the general depression of 1929 set in. The loss of values was not confined to economics. Coming on top of the shattering experiences of the war, the destruction of the value of the mark encouraged a weakening of other previously held values, moral and religious, as well as political, inducing the attitude of fatalism or nihilism which opened the way to the victory of Nazism.

It took time for the full effects of the inflation to work out. Meanwhile, before the end of this frightful year 1923, in which hunger again stalked through the land, a slow improvement began to set in, hardly discernible at first, and punctuated by crises such as the Nazi attempt in November at a rising in Munich. The middle and left parties began to pull themselves, and each other, together. The social democrats had been demanding a stronger government, and in August 1923 the man who was to be the outstanding figure among the statesmen of the Weimar period, Gustav Stresemann, creator and leader of the people's party, a business man, the son of a Berlin retailer of beer, an industrialist, a monarchist, an annexationist during the war, took over the chancellorship from Cuno. Stresemann was a realist with a touch of the Bismarckian in him. He disapproved of Cuno's policy in the Ruhr and believed that Germany and France, or at least German and French industrialists, should pull together, that only by agreement with the Allies could Germany be pulled out of the hole and set on her feet. The social democrats, alarmed at the dangers to the republic, co-operated for a time, to give the new government full powers. And although the alliance did not last, and both nationalists and some of Stresemann's own party were hostile to his policy, yet a beginning was made. Hence when Stresemann, on defeat, resigned the chancellorship after three months, the work could go on under Marx (of the Centre), with Stresemann as Foreign Secretary and Luther for Finance. Passive resistance in the Ruhr was given up, the inflation of currency was stopped, and in place of the now worthless mark a new *Rentenmark* was set up, a hard but necessary blow. Through British and American efforts the reparations question was taken in hand, and the report of the commission headed by the American Dawes, taking a more realistic view of what Germany could pay and providing for a foreign loan to tide her over the next year's payments, was accepted both by the Allies and, after a bitter struggle in the *Reichstag*, by Germany. The change of government in France from Poincaré to the radical-socialist Herriot in May 1924 likewise opened the possibility of better relations between the two neighbours.

The turn became clearer before the end of 1924. It showed itself in a comparison of the results of the two elections to the *Reichstag* held in this year. Lacking a safe majority, Chancellor Marx in the spring demanded a dissolution. In the May elections which followed, before the healing process had produced its effects, the extremists and enemies of the republic gained, nationalists at one end increasing their seats by a half (to 96) whilst at the other end the communists shot up even more spectacularly to 62; similarly the new party of the Nazis won 32 seats. The social democrats, and still more the democrats and the people's party, lost votes and seats, making government very difficult for the central parties. The acceptance of the Dawes scheme was only secured by a pledge to give the nationalists a place in the government, and in December another election took place. This time, however, whilst the nationalists made slight further gains, the communists and Nazis lost materially, to the profit of the social democrats, the people's party, and the democrats. The Catholic parties changed little in both elections. Yet although the makers and supporters of the Weimar Republic thus regained much of the ground lost, the election of this year revealed the weakness of their creation. Its fortunes, and indeed its very existence, depended too much upon the hap of circumstance, above all upon economic conditions. It never won a wide enough allegiance to stand the storms of economic adversity, partly through its own failure to establish its foundations deeply enough, partly from the irreconcilable attitude both of its older enemies (the nationalists and communists) and of its newer foes (the Nazis). This was dangerous, above all when these foes proved capable of uniting against it, despite their fundamental differences.

For a time indeed, following the crisis of 1923–4, the republic was stronger, though not so much stronger as it seemed. The government was more stable as Marx was succeeded (24th December) by the non-party but conservatively inclined Luther, and Luther by Marx again in May 1926 to last until after the 1928 elections. Stresemann continued throughout as Foreign Secretary and leading spirit, and the Centre, with its familiar capacity for turning right or left in a coalition, was the main support. That had its drawbacks, but also its advantages, as the Centre was a kind of shock-absorber for some of the irreconcilable differences between Right and Left. The republic now (April 1925) after Ebert's death in his early fifties, elected its first president under the new constitution. But for the ineffable stupidity of the communists in persisting in running a hopeless candidature, Chancellor Marx, Rhinelander, former judge, Catholic, member of the *Reichstag* since

1910, would probably have been chosen, an honour he merited by his services to the republic. Had this happened the fortunes of the republic might have been different. As it was, a national military hero, Field-Marshal Hindenburg, aged seventy-seven, and so too old, was elected in the second vote needed for the required majority, and was to retain the office until his death nine years later. As with the inflation the full ill effects of the choice, at which the nationalists naturally rejoiced and the parties of the Left took alarm, were only to be felt after a time; for some years the new president accepted his position in the parliamentary and republican system faithfully enough.

Of more immediate importance was the economic up-swing, first illustrated by the 'Miracle of the *Rentenmark*' at the end of 1923, testifying to the faith of the German people in its economic recovery and future. It was furthered by the evacuation of the treasure-house of German industry, the Ruhr, by the French in 1924, and its reincorporation in German economic life. But what really made the recovery effective was the inflow of a flood of foreign capital, mainly from the United States, for the *Reich*, the local municipalities, and industry, tempted by high interest rates. Between 1924 and 1929 this inflow reached a total half as large again as the whole amount paid out by Germany in reparations, and allowing a reconstruction of Germany's industry far greater than occurred in any other country during this post-war period. And this reorganization largely continued the concentration of control in a few hands, a process aided by the influence of men such as Rathenau, and blessed by the word 'rationalization,' as by the German genius for organization. As before, the coal and iron, electrical and chemical industries, were primarily affected, with the vast United Steel Works (1926) headed by Vögler, Thyssen, the Stinnes and O. Wolff groups; the I.G. Farben (1925) enlarging its grip over the chemical industry and spreading its tentacles far outside Germany. The electrical engineering industry continued largely in the hands of the A.E.G. and the Siemens concern. With the wheels turning again, and ever faster, and a stable currency, production enormously increased, living conditions improved for tradesmen and workers, the transportation system was restored, new shipping replaced that lost to the Allies, the trade unions revived even if the old middle class did not. The year 1927 saw the introduction of a scheme of unemployment insurance, with contributions by employer and worker, and also of new and more effective arbitration machinery for industrial disputes. A promise of land settlement in eastern Prussia for soldiers made by Hindenburg was, however, unfulfilled, largely because its opponents converted the president to their view by presenting him on his eightieth birthday with the landed estate of Neudeck there, which had once belonged to his family. And while there was prosperity, it was rather fevered and garish than solid and stable, being based in fact on the stream of gold from America rather than on earnings by restored foreign trade.

The revival was, however, shown in other ways as well. The Allies had done their best to disarm Germany, by limitation of her army to 100,000 long-term soldiers with limited armaments, restriction of her navy, destruction or removal of war material, the forbidding of an air force, all of which was to be supervised by an Inter-Allied Military Commission. But it proved difficult, in fact impossible, completely to carry out this supervision in a country where the military spirit was so strong, and in the disorderly times after 1918, so that it was never fully carried out. Nor did the Allies succeed in carrying through the pledge enshrined in Article VIII of the Covenant of the League of Nations for general disarmament. More important for the future than any evasion of the treaty terms by Germany was the way in which Seeckt, army commander-in-chief from 1920 to 1926, organized and trained the new army. Seeckt, Pomeranian-Prussian and general staff officer under Mackensen during the war, was no narrow military man or even a conservative, but rather of the national liberal tradition, devoted to the *Reich*, ready to accept the republic providing it were strong, and alive to the lessons of the war in terms of technical progress. He determined to build up his small army to a perfection impossible in a larger force, by careful selection from the large numbers available, and by training not merely of body but of mind, to preserve the old Prussian military spirit among them in the long service term. Largely through his efforts this force could and did become the nucleus of the national army, when in due course that was revived by Hitler. Seeckt's work was done by 1926 when Hindenburg, now presidential Commander-in-Chief and jealous of Seeckt's authority, got rid of him. He had been sufficiently supported by Gessler, Minister of War from 1920 to 1928, despite his social democratic affiliations. And he had used his influence not merely in military but also in diplomatic arrangements. As an eastern Prussian he was naturally opposed to the settlement of the treaty there and the creation of a Polish state partly at Prussian expense. And although utterly hostile to Bolshevism, he saw the advantages of alliance with Russia, both against Poland and on military grounds. Germany could give Russia technical military guidance and aid, and in return Russia could supply both the proving ground for the use of tanks and aeroplanes, forbidden in Germany, and become a reservoir for war material for Germany. It was in part from these arguments that with Rathenau's aid Germany made the famous Rapallo alliance with Russia in 1922, to western allied annoyance. By it Germany renounced the Treaty of Brest-Litovsk, Russia any idea of reparations. Germany drew military profit from the treaty, as did Russia, perhaps in the end even more. And it marked for Germany the reopening of foreign relations, free of the humiliations of her dealings with the Allies, which won it support at home despite the lack of any widespread community of view. It thus forecast the more fateful alliance of 1939.

With the revival of the middle twenties, and associated above all with Stresemann, came diplomatic developments of wider scope. Stresemann was no less ardent a nationalist than Seeckt, naturally repudiating Germany's war guilt, desiring to regain Polish Prussia, looking to a union with Austria, objecting to reparations and German one-sided disarmament, desiring the allied evacuation of the Rhineland, and in general the restoration of Germany to the proud and prosperous position she had held as he grew up: he was forty in 1918.   But he was also an admirable parliamentarian, a skilful diplomatist and bargainer.   Since he died in 1929 we do not know how he would have reacted to later developments.   But despite his monarchism and war-time annexationist views, he appeared to have accepted the republic, parliamentary rule, and the way of peace.   And though an industrialist he was no Kirdorf or Stinnes, and as time went on turned rather Left than Right.   Having got the French out of the Ruhr, he sought to free the Rhine from allied occupation, to get rid of allied controls within Germany, and to end or reduce reparations.   For this he was prepared to make concessions, presumably to accept the loss of Alsace-Lorraine, and to reassure the French by pledging the security of their eastern frontier.   Hence after long negotiation emerged the treaty signed at Locarno (16th October 1925) by Germany, France, Britain, Belgium, and Italy, which guaranteed the frontiers of 1919 between France, Belgium, and Germany, with the demilitarized Rhine zone, and provided for arbitration in disputes.   It was also agreed that part of the Rhineland zone (Cologne) was to be evacuated by the Allies, and that Germany should enter the League of Nations.   Germany further signed arbitration treaties with both Poland and Czechoslovakia.   The Cologne zone was duly evacuated (January 1926), and Germany duly entered the League of Nations with a permanent seat on the council (September 1926), although only after delay and difficulty from rival claimants to that honour.

Through all this negotiation Stresemann's efforts were harassed by the bitter criticism of the nationalists, and he was only saved in the *Reichstag* by the support of the social democrats.   But saved he was, and despite opposition Germany profited greatly from his efforts.   One fruit of this was the withdrawal from Germany in January 1927 of the Allied Military Control Commission.   France and Germany, or Stresemann and Briand at least, seemed to be coming closer together politically, as the industrialists of the two countries were now making economic agreements, and the common signature to the Pact of Paris (the so-called Kellogg Pact) in August 1928 appeared to confirm this.   Yet Stresemann did not omit Russia from his considerations, and Russian discontent at the Locarno Pact was soothed by a treaty of April 1926 (Treaty of Berlin) which amounted almost if not quite to an old-time alliance.   Thus the Rapallo policy was continued with wide German approval, and the treaty of 1926 was to be renewed five years later.   All in all, Stresemann had deserved well of his country and it was fitting enough that, despite the change of chancellor from Marx to the social democrat Müller when the *Reichstag* elections of 1928 had shown a decided swing to the Left, he should retain his position in the new government. Therein he was able to tackle the reparations question again and that of the Rhineland occupation, the former now linked in French and British minds with their own debts to America.   After long and tedious negotiation a compromise was reached in June 1929, called the 'Young Plan' after its American architect, arranging a scale of payments for fifty-nine years, but subject to reduction if the United States reduced *her* claims on the Allies, or if Germany ran into serious economic difficulties. The plan had to run the gauntlet of domestic approval, and this roused a great storm in Germany despite the allied promise to free the Rhineland by June 1930. Stresemann, a sick man but a fighter for it to the end, died in October 1929 before the fight with the nationalist right wing led by Hugenberg, as also with the communists and the Nazis, was won; the nationalists split in the process. Not until March 1930 was the coalition of social democrats, Centre, and people's party able to secure the plan's acceptance; and by that time Germany was facing new and more serious troubles resulting from the severe economic depression which set in in October 1929, and which brought loss and hardship to most if not all the countries of the world.

III. THE DECLINE AND FALL, 1929–33

Unfortunately for Germany her economy was weak when the depression came, so that she was less able than the other major western states to withstand the economic hurricane. True, her industrial production had increased steadily since 1924 (save in one year) to reach a height in 1928–9 greater than in 1913. But in the next three years it dropped sharply as markets declined, the foreign investors sought to withdraw their capital, American protection reached its height in the Smoot-Hawley tariff, and a *sauve qui peut* policy ruled amongst the nations. Wages, which had risen during the good years, fell by a third by 1932, and worse still was the rise in unemployment, which increased steadily, to over three millions in 1930, five millions in the next year, six millions the year after. The recent unemployment insurance scheme had not had time to build up a large reserve, so that it was quite inadequate to meet the situation, and the question of provision for large supplementary sums from the *Reich's* declining finances was hotly disputed in the *Reichstag*. The middle classes likewise suffered, not least the overcrowded professional classes, swollen by the unprecedented increase in the numbers of students at the universities in these years who now found their diplomas valueless and no future open to them. Although agriculture suffered it was less catastrophically affected by the economic crash. It was aided in 1930 by higher tariffs, while landowners east of the Elbe received a special subvention, the *Osthilfe*, both before and after the crisis opened, thanks in part to the support of the president.

Other countries than Germany faced similar economic problems in these years, if less acute. What made the whole situation more serious in Germany was the way in which political life deteriorated *pari passu* with the decline of the national economy, and in the end more fatally. Whereas Chancellor Müller could over-optimistically declare in June 1928 that the foundations of the Weimar Republic were 'firm and unshakeable,' within two years they were to be shaken and see President Hindenburg's reversion to semiautocratic rule. Within three further years, when the worst of the economic crisis was over, the parliamentary republic was to be replaced by a dictatorship compared to which the yoke of the Hohenzollern kings of Prussia at its sternest seemed both light and liberal. And most serious of all, this was the result of popular vote. The first stage of this unhappy progression came in March 1930 when the Centre and the people's party refused to support Chancellor Müller's proposals, backed by the social democrats, to help out the inadequate unemployment insurance funds, and so broke up the coalition. Müller resigned, and Hindenburg, in his eighties falling more and more under the influence of what was in effect a court camarilla, appointed as chancellor Brüning, a Westphalian Catholic and Centre deputy, able and honest, but like Bethmann-Hollweg, not strong or skilful enough for the post in such difficult times. He was unable to stand up against demands, backed by the president, for the *Osthilfe*, which the country could not afford, and for higher tariffs on agricultural products. Further, his support by Centre, people's party, and part of the nationalists was not enough to ensure a safe majority against the opposition of the social democrats, as well as of Nazis and communists. Within three months he had fallen back on the use of the presidential emergency powers, and when the *Reichstag* voted against this he invoked the presidential authority to dissolve it.

The election of September 1930, which followed, was marked above all by the spectacular rise of the national socialist party (N.S.D.A.P.: *National-sozialistische Deutsche Arbeiterpartei*). It was to some extent comparable to the elections of 1874, when the national liberal party rose to its height, and that of 1912, when the socialists won over a hundred seats. Yet the success of the Nazis in 1930, a rise from 13 to 107 seats, to increase to 230 seats in July 1932, and 288 in March 1933, was to be greater and more significant than either of the two other ascensions. In its beginnings the Nazi movement represented in part and in theory an attempt at a synthesis of those two forces of the nineteenth century, nationalism and socialism, which had triumphed in 1874 and 1912 respectively. Friedrich Naumann had envisaged such a synthesis before 1914, but had failed to do more than propound the idea. Now, under different circumstances, and under the leadership of a very different figure, Nazism was to rise by this lever to supreme power in Germany, and for a time to threaten to impose its rule over Europe and even beyond. It is true that in this election of 1930 the communists likewise greatly increased their vote, to win seventy-seven seats, and were to reach the hundred mark of seats in 1932. But this was a simpler reflection of the economic hardships of the day. The social democrats lost votes, though still remaining the strongest single party in the *Reichstag*; the nationalists suffered heavy losses, nearly half their seats, and the democrats and people's party lost also; the attempt to revive the democrats by fusion with some of the people's party in a new 'State' party had little or no effect in the election.

The success of the Nazi party was, of course, like that of the communists, due in no small measure to economic depression, as in 1923 when the Nazi party first emerged as a force, or would-be force. Its origins were, however, to be found further back, in the immediate post-war conditions, when in

Munich a tiny group of ex-soldiers calling themselves the *German Workers'*
Party emerged, depressed from the defeat and the sad state of the Fatherland,
humble folk filled with vague social discontent, but neither socialists nor
communists.   That was to be all important, if only because they were to be
joined by a man who was already irreconcilably hostile to Marxism, whether of
the Russian or the German type, partly because he identified it with Jewry,
and to him Jewry was a menace to Germany and the world.   This discovery
Adolf Hitler (b. 1889) had made in Vienna, as he tells us in the all-important
account of himself and his views which he wrote in large part whilst in prison
after the failure of November 1923, and which he entitled *Mein Kampf* ('My
Struggle').   The struggle was a real one, for he was poor, and his efforts
to find a career as painter or architect in Vienna had little success.   Although
Austrian born he came to hate his country, and rejoiced to find himself in
Munich (1912) and to be allowed to join the Bavarian forces in 1914; German
citizenship he only acquired many years later.   The war, and still more the
incredible fact of the defeat of the unbeatable German army, left ineffaceable
effects on his thinking, making him an easy convert to the view that Germany
had been 'stabbed in the back' by the 'grave diggers' within the country.
These to him were, above all, the socialists and Jews, though he also found
causes of inner decay in pre-1914 Germany, in its democratic trend, the
liberal press, the *Reichstag* and parliamentarism, which he blamed for the
errors of German policy before the war, the weakening of the peasant class
and the internationalization of German big business and industry, making
all in all a moral decline, hardly redeemed by the monarchy, with the army
and the fine official class as the outstanding exceptions.   For Hitler the
army was the school of virtue and devotion to the *Reich*, fostering discipline,
obedience, and leadership.   And for 'true Germanic democracy,' responsible
leadership by 'free choice' was what was needed, to convert the masses from
the poison of socialism.

National socialism was to provide the 'fundamental idea' for a new
commonweal or community of the people (*Volksgemeinschaft*) in which
'common interest' would replace 'individual' or sectional interest, *Gemein-*
nutz vor Eigennutz as the programme succinctly put it.   Hitler and his
co-workers, above all, Hitler himself, were to provide the drive, by ceaseless
propaganda.   On the need and nature of this Hitler expatiated at length in
his book, and he was indeed to become an outstanding practitioner of it,
an orator of great and telling power.   He had profound faith in the power
of the spoken word, and made wide and effective use of the new and
enlarged opportunities presented by the aeroplane and the radio.

Hitler is indeed better at defining the role of propaganda than in
expounding the new 'inner spiritual idea' of Nazism.   For this turns out to
be not a new religious revelation such as Mahomet provided for his people,
but to a considerable extent a hotch-potch of the familiar racial theories of
H. S. Chamberlain and others.   Thus whilst he appreciates the power of
the Catholic Church, and repudiates religious persecution, his new People's
(*Völkisch*) State is to be based on 'racially innate elements,' which 'correspond

to the innermost will of nature,' defined by purity of blood. On this the new *Reich*, aristocratic rather than democratic, is to be built, its citizens trained physically and mentally to acquire a due sense of their racial superiority. This education is to culminate in universal military training: 'the army is the last and highest school of patriotic education.' For the People's State will have to fight for its existence against its enemies both within and without, chief of them Jewry with its vast and widespread influence. No longer, however, is Britain to be an antagonist and rival, rather is she to be an ally, together with Italy. France, increasingly Judaized and nigrified, is and remains the enemy, to be dealt with in due course. But for the land to which Germany is entitled, her *Lebensraum* as it came to be called, she must look not overseas but eastwards in Europe, to the broad lands of Russia and her border states, where the German sword must win the soil for the German plough to draw its furrows.

Thus far Hitler's *Mein Kampf*. But Corporal Hitler, as already remarked, was but one of many discontented figures in Germany after 1918, and the official programme of the new party was drawn up in 1920 by Feder, a man more interested in social problems and needs, a bitter critic of the big financiers and their ways. Its twenty-five articles were partly racial and national (e.g. for restriction of citizenship to blood Germans, a Pan-German State, the repudiation of the Treaty of Versailles). More of them, however, were social: against unearned increment, for confiscation of war profits, the taking over of industrial cartels, the break-up of the big department stores and the punishment of usurers, land for the people. Others demanded religious freedom and a 'positive Christianity,' which could mean almost anything. And finally came the demand for a strong central authority and parliament to carry out these reforms. This programme was declared to be official and permanent, but its social programme was largely disregarded. For Hitler was a remarkable, if not unique, combination of fanatic and astute politician. And as the party grew up, and his ideas developed in the direction of the seizure of power, he turned for aid in this to men to whom Feder's social radicalism was anathema.

This divergence, if not disparity, of views helped rather than hindered the growth of the movement. For it drew in from the start men of varying types, capacities, and interests, many of course ex-soldiers, some of them founders of small movements which it absorbed. There were Anton Drexler; the poet Dietrich Eckart; the bold bad Roehm, head of the Bavarian 'Iron Fist'; the dashing aviator Goering; Frick; the unbalanced Hess, who was to become Hitler's closest friend; the Balt Alfred Rosenberg, journalist and later author of the would-be mystical interpretation of the age, *The Myth of the Twentieth Century*; Streicher, the notorious anti-Semite; Gregor and Otto Strasser; social radicals like Feder; Ley of the later 'Labour Front'; and last, but second only to Hitler as a propagandist for the movement, the Rhinelander Goebbels. Not all of these were drawn in at once or were to stay with the movement, and Hitler had to fight for leadership, e.g. with Streicher for a time. Gregor Strasser was a leading dissident on grounds of policy later on, and was to withdraw; Roehm, after an early breach with Hitler, was to be eliminated in the purge of 1934.

The movement was at first local in character, in Munich, but soon pushed out more widely, to establish local branches through the country. Berlin, with the energetic Goebbels in charge, naturally came to play a leading part, though control was centralized, with headquarters in the 'Brown House' in the Bavarian capital. Like other movements of the day it was semi-military, and it owed more than it acknowledged to the successful Fascist movement in Italy. It came to have its flag, with the alleged 'Aryan' swastika, its newspaper, the Munich *Völkische Beobachter*, its protective Storm Troops (*Sturmabteilungen* or S.A.) with their brown shirts, and later its Protective Unit (*Schutzstaffel* or S.S.) for the leader, with their black tunics. It tried out its tactics, with the accompaniment of force, at meetings, in parades, on marches, then in the attempted coup or *putsch* of 1923. In May 1924 it entered federal politics as a party, and in the prevailing economic distress won unexpected success with thirty-two seats, to lose more than half of these, however, in the December elections of the same year when times had improved. The party fared no better in 1928, but now in 1930, as the economic barometer fell, it shot up to be the second strongest party in the *Reichstag*.

The movement drew support from four main things, not really separable, but overlapping. There was the reiterated promise of relief from the economic hardship; the national-racial and military appeal with its condemnation of the 'Diktat' of Versailles; the fear of communism, and with it the stirring up of the sediment of anti-Jewish feeling ever present in Germany; and lastly the patent weakness of the Weimarian regime, the seeming futility of the *Reichstag* with its many rival parties and lack of strong leadership. Thus Nazism appealed primarily to the numerous lower-middle class, unorganized and badly hit by the depression, reinforced by that section of the middle class whose position had been destroyed beyond recall by the great inflation, especially their younger generation, in part products of the youth movement which had begun in Germany before the war and revived after it. Like Fascism in Italy it naturally drew 'front-line comrades,' who, like Hitler himself, had failed to readjust themselves to civilian life. It could not hope to win fanatical communists, or the bulk of the members of the trade unions and the social democratic party, though it tried to, and made some converts. It sought to appeal to the peasantry and farmers, but was primarily, like Germany as a whole, urban in general character. With some success from its untiring propaganda on the one hand, and the deepening economic crisis on the other, it drew increasing support. But it is by no means certain that it would have attained to power had it not received both financial and political help from other sources.

This was forthcoming during Brüning's chancellorship, from March 1930 to May 1932. Brüning has been variously judged. But if his record is damaged by the way in which he yielded to presidential demands, and the weakening of the republic by the use of emergency powers, no one could deny the difficulties he had to face, or the probity of his intentions.   For the economic crisis rose to its height during these years, with grave banking failures such as that of the Darmstadt Bank in 1931, the threat of national bankruptcy, immense unemployment, and hardship.   His efforts to secure a Customs Union with Austria failed through French and other opposition, as did his efforts to put an end to reparations, although he secured a moratorium which did in fact mark the end.   Nor was he able to secure recognition of German equality in armaments at the Geneva Conference on Disarmament which opened in February 1932.   His support by Centre and social democrats in the *Reichstag* was shaken as the latter party sought to prevent cuts in wages or security benefits, and outside in the country there were threats to public order by Nazi and other groups.

Actually it was the nationalists, or certain elements and leaders therein, who bore the major responsibility for undermining the republic and bringing the Nazis to power, on the one hand by abusing the influence they acquired over the aged president, now fast losing his grip on affairs, and on the other by approaches to and support of Hitler and his party.   The chief actors in this tragedy were a trio, Hugenberg, Schleicher, and Papen, all three of them almost as unscrupulous as Hitler himself.   Hugenberg was a strong nationalist and expansionist who had risen to become a Rhenish industrialist, the owner of newspapers and film companies, and in 1929 official leader of the nationalist party, driving out both Count Westarp, long its parliamentary leader, and also a left-wing group of the party.   He approached Hitler in 1929 and assured him funds from big industry as an aid against Marxism. The alliance thus struck was given more formal and wider approval in 1931 at a meeting in Harzburg, with men such as Thyssen and Schacht present. Schleicher, an army man, an 'office' general who had gained Hindenburg's ear through friendship with his son, a subtle and successful intriguer, likewise turned to the Nazis, hoping to build up a strong anti-socialist group.   To this end in 1932 he turned against Brüning, whom he had previously backed for chancellor, and used his influence to get him dismissed, proposing in his place Papen, a Westphalian Catholic aristocrat and ex-diplomat, possessed of much self-confidence, but no political experience or capacity, and with no firm party support.   For even the Catholic Centre refused to back him and his ministry, which was largely drawn from his aristocratic friends of the Berlin *Herrenklub*.

Meanwhile the Nazis had risen to new heights in the spring and summer of 1932, scoring a triple success.   First in the presidential election their leader not merely ran against the revered figure of the old marshal, but secured over eleven million votes (against over eighteen million for Hindenburg) in the first indecisive election, and then added two million more in the final one, though still far behind Hindenburg.   Next, in the Prussian state elections of April 1932 they won far the largest number of votes and seats, though not enough to give them a majority.   And finally when Papen, unable to get a majority, secured a dissolution and a *Reichstag* election in July, they rose there to 230 seats, far over-topping the social democrats, who, like the nationalists, lost seats, though the communists gained markedly. The Nazis now demanded the office of chancellor for Hitler, which Hindenburg refused, although a share of ministerial office was offered, and Goering was elected presiding officer of the *Reichstag*. Papen, with only forty supporters, had nothing to offer acceptable to the new *Reichstag*, and was shortly driven to ask the president, who approved of him, for a new dissolution and election. The Nazis were furious, as there were signs that they had reached, and perhaps passed, their peak, and Papen managed to cut off their support from big business. They did in fact lose two million votes and thirty-four seats in the ensuing election of November 1932, to be followed by further losses in local elections, which caused severe heart-searching and talk of a *putsch*. But Hitler, mindful of the failure of 1923, refused to agree. Papen, however, still lacked party support in the *Reichstag*, and Schleicher now turned against him as earlier against Brüning, to take office himself as chancellor. Under such conditions the sands of the republic's life were rapidly running out. Few people really trusted Schleicher, so that despite his efforts to win support, he lasted only two months in office. For now Papen, in revenge, played *his* turn, making a deal with Hitler (who had so recently turned the vials of his wrath upon him, but in his falling market was ready to bargain) and persuaded the mentally enfeebled president to turn out Schleicher and accept Hitler as chancellor in a Nazi-nationalist government. On 30th January 1933 Hitler took office, taking oath to maintain that constitution to which shortly he was to administer the final blow. The nationalist leaders had fatally misjudged the character of the ally with whom they had joined hands. For they were shortly to be swept away almost as if they had never been, and instead of the black-white-red of the Bismarckian Empire which they wished to see restored, or the black-red-gold of the Weimar Republic, the Nazi swastika was to wave and rule throughout the *Reich*.

IV. THE NAZI DICTATORSHIP

The Nazi regime was to last for twelve years, very far from the 'Thousand-Year *Reich*' its leader predicted for it. It had six years of peace, six of war, at the end of which Germany was in ruins, infinitely more so than after the Thirty Years War, a 'burnt-out crater,' with a large part of her land and people under the heel of the despised Russian Slav, her great army defeated and broken, her magnificent industrial machine smashed. And in addition to the material loss, there was the loss of much of the spiritual and moral heritage of the past, whether German, Western, or Christian, a loss not easily to be measured, or made good by the survivors of those who had refused to bow the knee to the Nazi gods. Whatever doubts there might be as to the reality of the so-called revolution of November 1918 there is no question as to the reality of the Nazi revolution, of its effect at a 'transvaluation of all values' in the Nietzschean phrase, although, like other German 'revolutions,' it was made from above rather than from below. Whilst many of its features derive from earlier German patterns, e.g. its autocracy and its militarism, it possessed and developed when in power features which broke with much of the German tradition, religious, moral, and intellectual.   And some of these went back not, as Rosenberg and other Nazi racialists claimed, to German medieval mystics such as Meister Eckart, or to the Germans of early historical times, but to mere primitive ruthlessness, reflecting the misuse of the power available in the modern industrialized state, aided by the triumphs of modern science, when it fell into the hands of irresponsible and amoral men.   It was also revolutionary on its social side.   For whilst it professed to establish a people's commonwealth in fact it set up a new ruling class, the Nazi *élite*, resembling in this the Russian example with its dictatorship of the communist party.

The first steps of the new regime were directed towards the destruction of the Weimar Republic and the acquisition of absolute power.   The first of these objects was accomplished with singular ease within less than two months after Hitler became chancellor, and at once set up a ministry of Nazis such as Goering, Goebbels, and Frick, with nationalists such as Papen, Hugenberg, and Neurath.   Since the Nazi-nationalist coalition did not possess a majority in the *Reichstag* Hitler secured from Hindenburg power to dissolve it.   The succeeding election (5th March 1933) was preceded by heavy Nazi propaganda, as by the burning of the *Reichstag* building, a symbolic act ascribed to the communists, although it was almost certainly Nazi work.   Hitler also secured the presidential suspension of those articles in the Weimar Constitution guaranteeing personal liberty, which enabled him to exclude the communists from the new *Reichstag*, despite their nearly five million votes.   With 288 Nazi seats and 52 for the nationalist allies (against 120 social democrats and over 70 Centre) the Nazis had indeed a majority, but not the two-thirds majority required for amendment of the constitution. By the aid of the Centre, however, Hitler was able to secure an 'Enabling Act' which, although euphemistically described as an Act to end the distress of people and State, in effect gave absolute power to Hitler to legislate, and so destroyed the very marrow of the Weimar Constitution.   Henceforth the *Reichstag* was reduced to the role of a chorus, which role it continued to play to the end of the Nazi period.   Its elections became a farce, since only those on the Nazi 'ticket' could be elected, and it met only when called together for a few hours to pass Nazi decrees, or listen to and applaud Hitler's expositions of his policy.

The powers thus summarily obtained were used to destroy not merely the republican constitution, but all opposition to the new regime.   All rival political parties were now destroyed.   First the communist party was outlawed, its property seized, its members hunted.   Then the social democratic party was attacked, its offices and all its property confiscated, its newspapers prohibited, its meetings forbidden, its members put out of all offices.   Then the nationalists, whose fatal error in thinking they could control their allies, or even share power, was now revealed, were eliminated, as was the people's party.   The Catholic Centre and the Bavarian people's party dissolved themselves.   A law of July 1933 forbade any other party than that of the Nazis to exist, and by the end of the year that party was identified with the State, as 'the bearer of the State idea,' and identified also with Hitler himself; 'the Nazi party is Hitler, and Hitler is the party.' Similarly all possible rival organizations to the Nazi brown-shirted and black-tunicked forces, such as the conservative *Stahlhelm* and the socialist *Reichsbanner*, were abolished or absorbed. In this, as in the terrible persecution of the Jews which now began, the newly established political police, the *Gestapo*, played an active part, exercising a ruthlessness which became a recognized characteristic of the new regime. The concentration camps appeared as a feature of the Nazi landscape, to engulf and often destroy communists, socialists, Jews, and any one who could be classed as hostile to the regime. The regular army, the *Reichswehr*, took longer to absorb. But when on Hindenburg's death in August 1934 Hitler became president as well as chancellor, he likewise became commander-in-chief of the army, and henceforth, the more so after the re-establishment of compulsory military service in 1935, the army too was identified with the new regime.

No less important was the establishment of the supreme power of the Nazi *Reich* over all the former states, whereby Germany ceased to be a federal state and became for the first time in its history a unitary one. The Weimar Republic had eased the path there, and the one outstanding achievement of Papen as chancellor had been the destruction in July 1932 of the long-standing social democrat-Centre control of Prussia, and the dismissal of the Braun-Severing government there. This *coup d'état* had given him the control of the all-important Prussian police force, and the social democrats had failed to oppose it by more than legal protests, an ominous sign of their weakness. The Nazis displayed no such hesitation. Within a week of taking office Hitler secured a presidential decree which dissolved the Prussian *Landtag*, and put the Prussian state directly under *Reich* control, a reversal of much Prusso-German history. A month later Bavaria was likewise placed under a *Reich* commissioner, and within a few weeks more every one of the former states or *Laender* had been brought under centralized control, exercised through a regent or governor (*Statthalter*). In due course the local Diets and most of the local ministries were abolished, their federal representatives in the *Reichsrat* likewise disappeared, and a *Reich* 'Reconstruction Law' of 30th January 1934, just a year after Hitler's entry into office, affirmed the unitary nature of the *Reich*. Thus did the 'Third *Reich*,' the successor of the Holy Roman Empire and the Bismarckian Empire, come into existence, although it was never given a formal constitution. To Nazi would-be mystics such as Rosenberg or Stapel, as to the earlier Moeller van den Bruck, this 'Third *Reich*' represented the age-long dream of the Germans, an eternal goal only to be grasped by the Germans themselves, fundamentally different from western state systems. To Stapel[1] this *Reich* was destined to rule the world: 'Only a Germanized Europe can be a peaceful Europe. . . . We demand the *imperium* because we are not merely equal to other peoples: we are Germans.'

[1] *Der Christliche Staatsmann*, 1932, pp. 255 and *passim*.

This new 'commonwealth' (*Volksgemeinschaft*) turned out to be not merely unitary, but also totalitarian, with absolute power vested in Hitler and the Nazi party. There was supposed to be something mystical in the bond between the *Volk* and the *Führer*, who by the official Nazi Order Book of 1940 'is always right,' and who to a good Nazi, such as Ley, was 'a gift from God.' Hitler spoke of his 'selection' and 'trusteeship,' and even lauded Germany as a true democracy, in contrast with the false democracies of the West. But after a few years of power we find him talking of 'My people,' in quite an old-fashioned German or Prussian way, and much of the talk of the union of leader, party, and people seems mere flummery to cover a very real and often harsh dictatorship. The new regime was never defined in a new constitution; law and justice were what Hitler made them. 'The law and the will of the *Führer* are one,' declared Goering.[1] Legislation was largely by decree, save for the few acts (seven in all) passed by the obedient *Reichstag*. *Führer* and party were above ordinary law, and absolute power was exercised by Hitler or through the Nazi ministers or agents, chief of these Goering, who collected offices as he did medals or property, Goebbels, Frick (interior), Hess (deputy party leader), Ley (labour), Kerrl (church affairs), Darré (agriculture), Himmler (police and S.S.). The system of governmental and party control was most thorough and far-reaching, so that although Hitler pledged himself to reduce bureaucratic control, actually this increased, and of a sterner type than before. In this totalitarian state everything was regimented, 'co-ordinated' (*gleichgeschaltet*) to the Nazi 'world view' (*Weltanschauung*). Freedom of individual speech and action, of the press, of publication of books, disappeared as Germany under her new masters drew away from western lines of development and, paradoxically enough, approached more to the pattern followed by its avowed and deadly enemy, the Bolshevist regime in Russia.

It is not easy to explain why the German people not merely suffered but supported this regime, giving it vote after vote of overwhelming confidence. They were, as Lamprecht had proudly insisted a few years earlier, the most literate people in Europe, producing and reading more books than any other nation. But reading, as Francis Bacon long ago pointed out, makes a full rather than a wise man. And Mme de Staël had remarked the contrast between German boldness in philosophical speculation and their meekness before authority. This long tradition of obedience to authority, and the retarded development of political and civil freedom, undoubtedly played their part. So also did the divided state of the political parties under Weimar, not least that of organized labour, wherein the communists continued for a time to delude themselves with the idea that the Nazi triumph was but a brief prelude to the proletarian revolution, whose advent it would hasten. The effects of the war in destroying the old leadership, leaving a vacancy of power which the democratic leaders were not ready to fill, likewise contributed.

Above all must be counted the economic hardships of the inflation period

[1] From N. H. Baynes, *Hitler's Speeches*, vol. i, p. 518.

N

of the early twenties and the later depression.   For these not merely hit the
workers and made them more open to propaganda which promised relief,
but also dealt heavy blows to the independence of the middle class, save the
newer, richer middle class.   Nazism offered, if not a career in the old sense,
at any rate an occupation for some of the 'proletarianized' middle class,
and promise for more, with its pledges of economic improvement and what
we might now call a 'welfare state,' for a united in place of a divided people.
The nationalist appeal naturally caught many, whether former soldiers
thrown out of their normal life, or the wider public which responded to the
protest against a peace which they believed unjust, and the accusation of
German 'war guilt.'   Hitler came into power just in time to gain advantage
from the slow lightening of the economic sky, and the positive achievements
of Nazism in creating employment and restoring confidence naturally drew
support to the new regime.   And while neither workers nor middle class
in toto succumbed to the allurements of Nazi propaganda or achievement,
the power available to and ruthlessly employed by the new regime effectively
disposed of opposition.   The 'purge' of 30th June 1934 provided example
of the way in which official Nazism was prepared to deal with opposition,
even within its own ranks.   Roehm, head of the S.A., and other Nazis,
some of them too radical socially for Nazism once it was in the saddle,
disliked the policy being followed.   Hitler promptly used the opportunity
to kill off, without formality of trial, not merely Roehm, Gregor Strasser,
and other disgruntled S.A. leaders, but also Schleicher and other nationalists,
certain hostile Catholic leaders, and an unnumbered crowd of lesser figures.

The picture of the emerging totalitarian state is more complicated on the
economic side.   There was the urgent need for State action to remedy the
acute economic situation, with (in February 1933) over six million, more
than a third of the entire labour force, unemployed, and immediate relief
promised.   On the other hand, Nazism was opposed to state socialism, as
to class antagonisms.   It believed in private initiative and had received
financial aid from, and given pledges to, the masters of big industry.   Yet
totalitarianism implied control of economic life, if not ownership of the
means of production.   And as time went on and rearmament became a
major aim, and with it the desire to overcome the blockade problem of
1914–18 by making Germany self-sufficient economically, State intervention
and control of economic life was steadily to grow.   Hence agriculture,
industry, big and little, and foreign trade, were increasingly regimented, in
preparation for the struggle which loomed nearer every year until it finally
came in 1939.

The immediate task in 1933 was to relieve the economic distress.   'There
is only one problem which absorbs all my attention: How to reduce unemployment,' said Hitler at this time.   This he proposed to accomplish by a Four-
Year Plan for both agriculture and industry, and although the methods were
in the main not new, they were carried through with a boldness and strength
which produced results.   Following Weimarian example the Nazis encouraged public works, buildings, or the new motor roads, by large State credits

and subsidies. They put pressure on employers to use more labour, they continued and in 1935 made compulsory the Labour Service, by which young men served six months in camps with only subsistence pay. The reintroduction of universal military service in the same year, and the re-armament programme, likewise changed the situation. Unemployment declined steadily, and by the end of 1935 was below the figure at the opening of the depression. Thus the unemployment problem was solved. The worker had his regular work, in factory or on the land, at about the same wages as before, and the social code for labour was continued. It was even extended in certain ways, such as the provision of holidays with pay, loans to encourage marriage, tax rebates and allowances for children to encourage the birth-rate. This did in fact increase, though not nearly to the pre-1914 level.[1] But despite the improvement, the general position of the worker had sadly deteriorated. For Nazism had swept away not merely the trade unions, socialist or other, but the whole structure built up by labour in the past half-century to defend its position against the employer. By a series of decrees from 1933 onwards the worker was forbidden to strike, to bargain with the employer, to move from one position to another, assemble, organize himself, much less aspire to play any part in political life. Many of his former leaders were in concentration camps; his precious eight-hour day came to be extended to ten, without extra pay.

In place of all his lost rights the worker found himself enrolled in a German Workers' Front, first founded in 1933, but reorganized in the following year. This 'front,' which was affiliated to the Nazi party, and was headed by Dr. Ley, became the German counterpart of the Italian corporative system. It was made up of both employers and workers, organized into 'estates' (agriculture, trade and industry, handicrafts, and transportation) as also up from the local factory or other unit to the whole 'estate.' In it employers and workers were to work together in harmony for the commonweal, but special Nazi agents or trustees (*Treuhänder der Arbeit*) were appointed for each of the regions into which Germany was divided for economic purposes, to deal with wage disputes. Recreation and popular education were provided through the 'Strength through Joy' subsidiary organization, which, active though it was, was in part a sop to disguise the lost freedom of association and other rights.

Nazism had not merely given pledges to big industry but it needed its aid for the economic recovery, and above all for the rearmament programme which was an essential part of its policy. It continued and hastened the concentration of industry, especially of heavy industry, in fewer hands, continuing the earlier trend. It handed over to the big concerns the con-fiscated Jewish property, thus preparing them for the larger gains of the immediate pre-war and war period, when the hopes of the 1914–18 expan-sionists were to be more than fulfilled, for a season. Yet in what may be called a 'pre-war economy' the degree of State control over industry inevitably

[1] C. W. Guillebaud, in *The Economic Recovery of Germany, 1933–1938*, 1939, p. 275, gives the figures: in 1913 the net increase was 12·4 per thousand, in 1937 7·1 per thousand.

increased. Whilst industrial production, especially in heavy industry, grew steadily, doubling between 1933 and 1935, reaching and then surpassing the high level of 1928, profits were restricted, the State taking by tax or loan all over a certain per cent, so that an industrial magnate such as Fritz Thyssen came to regret his earlier support of the Nazis. By the law for the Regulation of National Labour of 20th January 1934 the employer became in the labour front the 'leader' over his employee 'followers,' yet both were subject to the Nazi State, whose end was power. For Nazi economy, as has been well said,[1] 'cannot be defined in terms of socialism or capitalism, because its basic social and political assumptions are different from those of either.'

The Nazis ever made much of the German peasantry and farmers, 'the essential pillar on which all German political life must rest,' as Hitler put it in a speech of February 1933, and agriculture was in low water at that time from the low prices of its products. The official programme had specified land reform for national needs, which to the simple-minded might imply the breaking up of the *Junker* estates, many of them bankrupt or only kept going by the expensive subsidy of the *Osthilfe*. But Nazism in power continued the subsidy, leaving it to the Russians in due course to eliminate the landlords of eastern Prussia. They rather consolidated than broke up the land, seeing in the middle-sized farm the ideal security for the virtues of *Blut und Boden* (race and soil). The Hereditary Farm Act of September 1933 established the *Erbhof*, the entailed farm of up to 300 acres, for 'Aryan' farmers, and small-holdings actually diminished in the following years. With the war experiences of 1914–18 and future wars in mind the Nazis were greatly concerned to make Germany as self-sufficing in food as possible. To this end, with Darré as Minister of Agriculture, they organized in 1933 the Food Estate (*Reichsnährstand*) which steadily increased its control over every side of agriculture, the selection and growing of crops and stock, their marketing and prices, with an infinity of detail, in the effort to balance production and consumption. In this they were not wholly successful, despite great efforts. For although agricultural conditions markedly improved, they were caught, so far as self-sufficiency was concerned, between the dilemma of providing fodder to raise enough stock for fats and meat, or enough grain for food for human beings, and Germany remained only about four-fifths sufficient in food, until conquests filled the gap in 1939–40.

Nor, despite the undoubted economic recovery, the 'miracle' as Hitler liked to call it, were they wholly successful in dealing with the considerable difficulties of foreign trade and finance. The German economy was weak after the depression, and although reparations payments came to an end after the Lausanne Conference of June 1932, she still owed large sums abroad, she needed foreign raw materials for her industry, and foreign markets for her manufactured goods. And other countries likewise had their economic troubles, which were being met in part by currency devaluation and trade restrictions. Mindful of the inflation of 1923, Germany avoided formal devaluation. But to protect her shrinking gold resources Schacht, the able

---

[1] W. Ebenstein, *The Nazi State*, 1943, p. 239.

and fertile-minded head of the *Reichsbank*, was driven to all sorts of expedients, most obviously the restriction of imports, which inevitably checked exports. Herein he had official Nazi support, for they wished to make Germany independent of foreign imports not merely in food but in the essentials of war. This policy of *Autarkie* was officially announced in the second Four-Year Plan of 1936, wherein Hitler announced that Germany was to be made economically independent within four years 'in regard to all those materials which German industry and science can produce at home.' And German science and technology did, in fact, produce such needed articles as oil from coal, synthetic (buna) rubber, artificial fibre in textiles, though at far greater cost than the imported products. Germany also used her difficulties over foreign trade and exchange both to evade payments on her foreign debts and to tie weaker countries, such as those of south-eastern Europe, to her own economy by separate and complicated trade agreements, partly in terms of barter and by strict control of foreign exchange.

Yet her national finances were inevitably strained when in 1935 (after the recovery of the Saar from France by plebiscite) she openly embarked upon a vast rearmament programme, with universal military service and a greatly increased army, as well as a navy by the agreement with Britain of that year. Since she could not finance all this from revenue her national debt increased yearly, although as she ceased to publish any budget, much less to have it approved by the *Reichstag*, her financial position remained largely unknown both to the German people and to the world. The truth was that just as with its capital-labour policy Nazism did not measure its success (or failure) by any budget-balancing measure. Its economy was dictated by political-military aims, and that far more completely than in the Bismarckian Empire. It was an economy of war (*Wehrwirtschaft*) or war preparation, not without its corruption in high places, as, for example, in the enormous fortune Goering built up out of the immense Hermann Goering Works covering mining, armament, and shipping activities. And as the Nazi regime was a totalitarian one, so the war, when it came, would be a 'total' war, as Ludendorff prophesied in his book of 1935, *The Total War*. By this means Germany was to wipe out the defeat and losses of 1918. Another military writer of this time, E. Banse, the successor of Bernhardi, added his voice and pen to proclaim in a number of books that Germany must bend every effort, material and spiritual, to prepare for a future war by which to establish the whole German people in a solid State extending far beyond its boundaries of 1914.

Total war was in fact to mean almost total tragedy for Germany. But there was tragedy enough in the Nazi regime before that, with its persecutions of Jews and others, and its ruthless treatment of its opponents. And not least among its tragedies for the German people were its efforts to regiment cultural life, education in school and out, high and low, literature and art, even religion to a certain extent. For neither the Nazi leaders nor their ideals and methods were capable of furthering true German culture; on the contrary. Hence, at the very moment when the masters of Germany were advancing the highest claims for the superiority of German culture, that culture was in a state of rapid decline, as if attacked by a virus, as indeed it was. Intellectual Germany had always prided itself, with some exaggeration indeed, on its 'freedom to learn and freedom to teach.' Now they had neither. For in March 1933 Hitler had announced in a *Reichstag* speech that the 'social organism,' including every side of education, must be completely cleansed, like the political system, so that 'blood and race will again become the basis of artistic intuition.' 'The spiritual-cultural life of the nation,' said a Nazi directive, 'revealed in religion, myths, and art, must receive definite direction, ideas, and rules.' And who was better fitted to direct this than the versatile and glib Minister of Propaganda, Goebbels? So in September of the same year Goebbels became the director of a new *Reich* Chamber of Culture, highly organized after the Nazi pattern to include all branches of art and their practitioners, whilst Alfred Rosenberg was licensed to propagate his *Myth of the Twentieth Century* to his heart's content. There were bonfires of anti-Nazi or disapproved literature, heavy censorship of books and the press, much encouragement of would-be Nazi writing and art, the misuse of such writers as Goethe and Schiller, Lessing and Herder, the cutting off of contacts with the outside intellectual world. The result was an inevitable decline of standards and creative work, and a steady flow of highly cultured *emigrés*, Einstein, Karl Barth, Thomas Mann, Brüning, Gropius, among them, to Germany's loss and the gain of the outside world.

Education suffered in like measure as it was 'co-ordinated' to Nazi views, with private and church schools eliminated. Teaching, from primary school to university, had to adapt itself to the new faith in race, with Hitler's *Mein Kampf* as a gospel, inculcating extreme nationalism, militarism, the preparation for the coming struggle, at the expense of the older values. All education suffered, most obviously secondary education, where the *Gymnasia* decreased in numbers and quality, and the universities, which had recently, under the Weimar Republic, opened their doors more widely to both sexes. Now the universities were brought more closely under governmental control, professors of Jewish blood or unsuitable views were dismissed, the number of students cut down (to a half in five years), especially of women since the *Führer* did not believe in higher education for women. All students must belong to the Nazi Students' Association, poorer students were, in effect, again excluded since labour service and military service postponed their earning days too long, foreign contacts were largely cut off, and as with the schools the curriculum and professorial work and research activities were 'co-ordinated' to Nazi views. Knowledge, 'science' (*Wissenschaft*), became German, racial, military; natural science and even philosophy were drawn into the service of the Nazi State. It was a deplorable degradation of the once proud tradition of the honoured German universities, losing them their prestige abroad, as in the eyes of these scholars in Germany who retained something of the old standards. And outside the older educational system Nazism set up special schools to train future leaders, Adolf Hitler schools, higher political institutes, and even for the *élite* of the *élite* 'castles' (*Ordensburgen*) modelled on the old Teutonic Order. The generality of boys and girls were inducted into the faith in the Hitler Youth, begun in 1926 but now extended, and in 1936 made universal under Baldur von Schirach as Youth leader, to provide future members for the party, and inculcating Nazi ideals, to the loss of older and better tried ones.

Some of these older ideals were Christian, taught by the churches, and there was at bottom a contradiction between Nazism and Christianity, whether Protestant or Catholic, despite the assertion of the official programme that 'the party represents the standpoint of positive Christianity.' Its racial doctrines were unchristian, its end was too plainly power, at any cost, and some of its leaders, such as Rosenberg, were definitely antichristian. This contradiction was not so clear at first, and both Churches made attempts at compromise with the new regime. The Catholic Church in July 1933 made a concordat with the new *Reich*, which promised to Catholics in Germany freedom of worship, of communication with Rome, of its appointments, publications, protection of church property, of educational rights, and of Catholic associations of various kinds, of which there were many. But although Catholics approved of the struggle against communism they soon found that not merely were the terms of the concordat not observed, but that the whole Nazi totalitarian regime was incompatible with the beliefs and practices of their faith. The Nazis accused them, in Goering's words, of 'invoking God against the State.' Catholics, both through men such as Cardinal Faulhaber of Munich, and then in 1937 from Rome, condemned both the wide violation of the concordat, e.g. in closing Catholic schools and associations, and also Nazi antichristian writings. Whilst Hitler, for political reasons, exercised care in his treatment of Catholicism, his lieutenants such as Goebbels, and those Nazis who were trying to set up a 'German' religion, were more open in their condemnation, and were by 1937 in Germany, and then after 1938 in Austria, engaged in a *Kulturkampf* reminiscent of Bismarck's day.

Although the Protestant Church in Germany was larger it was more vulnerable to Nazism. For although by the Weimar constitution separated from the State it had a long tradition of subjection thereto. And, as we have earlier seen, it was in general more compromising, more penetrated by modern rationalism and science; and it had no outside champion like the Pope. It was also more unitary (as the Roman Catholic Church was more federal), more Prussian and more appealed to by the nationalism of Nazism. In 1933 Ludwig Müller, close friend of Hitler, was made supreme Bishop of German Protestant Churches, and sought to harmonize their faith with Nazi beliefs in race, including its anti-Semitism, even attempting to revise the Bible, leaving out the Old Testament as Jewish. This 'German Christian Church' gained a measure of support from certain of the Lutheran pastorate and from a larger but indeterminate number of Protestant laymen, drawn more by national than religious feelings. But a larger number of pastors refused to compromise with their faith in this way, and led what became known as the 'Confessional' Evangelical Church.   Hence arose both division within the Protestant Church and a severe struggle between the 'Confessional' body and the State.   This Church protested against State interference, its efforts at the dechristianization of religion, attacks on Christian standards of morality (e.g. by the notorious Streicher), the placing of Hitler's picture on church altars, and so forth.   The State replied by pressure and persecution, driving into exile the great Protestant theologian, Karl Barth, threatening to confiscate church property, excluding pastors from their churches, and interning in concentration camps such men as Pastor Niemöller, the sturdy ex-U-boat captain turned parson, and many others.   The war of 1939 was to bring some compromise, but the essential differences remained unhealed.

These issues were revealed more plainly by Nazi efforts to build up a definitely 'German' faith, following earlier attacks on Christianity, whether by racial scientists, supporters of Nietzsche's attacks on the 'slave morality' of Christianity, contemners of its Jewish elements, as of the ties with Rome forged by Charlemagne.   'The German has his own religion, rooted in his species,' began the 'Twenty-five Theses of the German Religion' put forth by Professor Bergmann in 1934.   This religion 'rests,' say theses 20–21, 'on three ancient German virtues: courage, chivalry, and fidelity, all of which spring from honour . . . Christianity is in our sense no longer a religion.' So the Nordic Wotan was to replace the Christian God, and various attempts were made by such men as W. Hauer and others to breath new life into the paganism of the pre-historical German world by celebration of Nordic festivals and the like.   These efforts were the work of a few and never gained wide support, but they form a necessary part of the general picture of Nazism in power.

Looking back at that general picture from the perspective of the events of 1938 onwards, it seems clear enough that Nazism was or would be a menace to world peace.   For it was the child of opposition to the defeat of 1918 and the humiliation of the Treaty of Versailles, grasping at the stab-in-the-back theory to explain why the unbeatable German army had not been victorious.   Its racial and national doctrines not merely refused to accept the loss of German land by the treaty and the loss of Polish or even French subjects, but looked to the union within the new *Reich* of German people outside the *Reich*, such as the German Austrians, the over three million *Sudeten* Germans in Czechoslovakia, and the nearly one million Germans in the new Poland.   Nor did it lose sight of Germans as far east as the Volga and Transylvania, as far west as the United States.   Concern for Germans abroad, the *Auslanddeutsche*, was fostered by government-sponsored societies, making use of the law of 1913 (now extended) which allowed Germans abroad to retain their German citizenship for themselves and their children, and working to ensure that the 'dominant allegiance' should be to the Fatherland, even including the liability to military service in Germany. For the Nazi view, as expounded by its leading legal authority, Professor E. R. Huber, was that 'citizenship is a bond from which a man cannot withdraw by his own free will.'   Hence Germans in the United States and elsewhere were listed, subjected to Nazi propaganda, and used to further the Nazi cause, both through German officials abroad and by the active Foreign Organization of the party, headed by Bohle. The affiliated societies, the German Foreign Institute and the League for Germandom Abroad, both of them in existence before 1933, became increasingly active, as the 'trustees' of the thirty million Germans in foreign countries, their aim defined as 'the unity of the hundred million Germans into one great community destined to be a nation.'

The Nazi greed for power and its belief in the superiority of the German 'race' caused it to envisage conquests over 'inferior' peoples, and it took over and gave new life to older dreams of expansion at the expense of Russia, and through the Near East, as well as over France and into Africa. This received support from the new science of geopolitics as interpreted by Haushofer, formerly a soldier, now a professor, and his disciples in Munich, theories which go back to the geographers Ratzel and Mackinder. Haushofer defined geopolitics as 'aimed not merely to prepare for the realization of political power in the world of space, but to present its results for immediate use,' and produced in the thirties an incessant rain of studies of world geography in terms of fields for German activity or conquest. Nazism also took over the earlier demand for 'living space' for Germans, although as an industrialized country Germany was now importing manpower. Nazism's denunciation of Jews and Marxism, as of countries under their influence, including Russia, France, and Britain, its repudiation of western liberalism and individualism, likewise constituted a challenge, and in due course a threat, to western democracy. The virtues it lauded were military virtues. It idealized force, strength of action, leadership in action. And as time went on, and its power within Germany seemed, and was, firmly established, it proceeded, 'as the night the day,' to conquest outside.

Yet implicit though this was from the start, as Hitler's *Mein Kampf* reveals, and as German exiles abroad such as Thomas Mann [1] saw, there was the internal revival and reorganization to take care of first, the army to get hold of and to build up, internal obstacles to dispose of, conversion of the mass of the people to be won by propaganda or force, or both. Rome was not built in a day, and the makers of the infamous *Diktat* of Versailles were for some years stronger than Germany. So for a time the Nazis adopted a peaceful policy, or spoke words of peace, though not without demands for equality in disarmament, and for revision of the Treaty of Versailles. Indeed, right down to the opening of the war in 1939 Hitler reiterated his desire for peace, although by that time the terms on which he accepted peace had changed, and the number of those outside Germany who believed him had noticeably shrunk. Yet it was a tribute to his and

---

[1] 'The meaning and purpose of the National Socialist State is this alone and can be only this: to put the German people in readiness for the "coming war" by ruthless repression, elimination, extirpation of every stirring of opposition; to make of them an instrument of war, infinitely compliant, without a single critical thought, driven by a blind and fanatical ignorance.' (Quoted from Thomas Mann's reply to the Dean of the Philosophical Faculty of the university of Bonn when advised in 1936 that his name had been removed from its list of honorary doctors— *Friends of Europe*, No. 52, 1937, p. 12.

Goebbels's success in propaganda that the German people, the mass of whom desired peace, were yet ready to accept his version of the situation and in the end to follow him into war.

He was aided in his policy by the divisions and weakness of the former enemies of Germany. The withdrawal and isolationism of the United States both from European affairs and from the League of Nations was a major calamity. Fascist Italy under Mussolini harboured designs directly contrary to that of the League and to peace. Britain and France drew apart, with mistakes on both sides, France looking eastwards to Poland and the Little Entente to uphold her position in Europe, Britain concerned with her domestic problems, and with the growth of nationalism in the British Dominions, as in Asia and Africa. To many the British Empire seemed to be breaking up. In Europe itself an actual break-up of another kind, that of the old Habsburg and Romanoff Empires, had left middle-east Europe in a welter of nine states, from Finland to Rumania, with a tail of divided Balkan states beyond, most of them politically and economically weak, backward, divided, and distrustful, despite the somewhat tenuous bond of the Little Entente joining Czechoslovakia, Rumania, and Yugoslavia. True, there was another and wider bond between the nations in the League of Nations. But this body, despite well-meaning efforts, had failed to grow as its founders and sponsors had hoped. One of its central demands had been for general disarmament to promote peace, and long-continued efforts herein culminated in the Disarmament Conference of 1932 at Geneva. Germany, member of the League since 1926, demanded equality of treatment as (in Brüning's words) her 'legal and moral right.' But by the time a formula for this had been evolved Germany was going her own way in rearmament, and in October 1933 withdrew first from the Disarmament Conference and then from the League of Nations, a severe blow to both disarmament and the League. Yet a plebiscite of the German people on this issue gave Hitler a vote of 93 per cent in its favour, a sign of his growing hold over them.

Thereby Nazism was freer to go its own way, untrammelled by pledges to such peace-loving and (to it) quite absurd and untenable doctrines as were enshrined in the Covenant of the League of Nations. It still professed peace, and in January of the next year, 1934, signed a non-aggression pact with Poland (followed by a trade treaty) which seemed to inaugurate a period of better relations, though without settling the differences between them over Danzig and the Corridor. Yet in the same year Austrian Nazis, mobilized and encouraged from Germany, invaded and attacked the existing government in Vienna, murdered the Christian Socialist chancellor, Dollfuss, and vainly attempted to set up a Nazi regime there. Meanwhile Nazi propaganda was active among the *Sudeten* Germans of Czechoslovakia, and Nazism under Henlein there organized itself to become, by 1935, the second strongest party in the Czech parliament. By this time Hitler was stronger in Germany, after the death of Hindenburg in August 1934 and the general acceptance of his fusion of the offices of president and chancellor. The Saar plebiscite of January 1935, with its great majority vote for return to Germany, was another triumph. This was followed by the restoration of universal military service, and in June the naval agreement was signed with Britain, which accepted German naval rebuilding to 35 per cent of the British. The resultant cooling of Franco-British relations was all to Germany's advantage.

The year 1936 was marked by further Nazi success and German revival, both economic at home and in her general position in relation to the outside world. March brought the repudiation of the Locarno Treaties and the military reoccupation of the demilitarized Rhineland, contrary to treaties signed by Germany. Doubtless Germany was bound some day to regain full control over this German territory. But the reoccupation without any prior attempt at negotiation was the greatest shock Hitler had so far given to Europe, and had wide reverberations. Yet neither France, Britain, nor the League of Nations proved ready to do more than make formal protest, so that their position was weakened whilst that of Hitler was correspondingly enhanced. This latter fact was amply revealed by the plebiscite taken in Germany after the reoccupation, when 99 per cent of the voters went to the polls and gave him their almost unanimous approval. July of this year brought the opening of the Spanish Civil War, which Germany used both to express her antipathy to communism and to try out on a small scale some of her new military methods, as was seen in the ruthless air attack on Guernica (April 1937). In October 1936 she built the Rome-Berlin Axis to Fascist Italy, which had now seemingly justified her claims to regeneration by the completion of the conquest of Abyssinia (Ethiopia). Next month came the Anti-Comintern Pact with Japan for common defensive policy against subversive communist activities. In this year also German penetration of middle-eastern and south-eastern Europe showed itself more plainly both in terms of trade and in Nazi activity, i.e. both economic and political, with a considerable measure of success in both. Military service was increased from one year to two in August 1936.

Thus by the end of this year Germany's internal and external situation had changed enormously to her advantage. Within she had completed her first 'Four-Year Plan,' and was embarked on a second, economic recovery was widespread, rearmament whilst not completed was well on the way. Germany was no longer isolated, but had two great power allies. It is true that this had not been accomplished without arousing alarm abroad, not least by German support of Franco in the Spanish Civil War. Hitler complained (February 1937) 'They [meaning foreign opinion] do not believe that I want peace,' and reiterated, as so often, his need of and desire therefor. Soviet Russia had perhaps most reason to doubt his peaceful intentions towards her, since not merely had Germany made a treaty (1934) with Poland and the Anti-Comintern Pact with Japan, but Hitler and Nazism, despite German treaties with Russia, had harped with increasing bitterness on the dangers of Bolshevism, combining this with attacks on the Franco-Russian and Czechoslovak-Russian treaties of 1935, as on Russian aid to Spanish communists. This last meant that Germans and Russians were fighting on opposing sides in Spain, and the Russian purges of this summer swept many Germans into prison, though not to death.   Yet although the Bolshevist leaders turned to the pursuit of collective security for a time, they still held to the hope of maintaining peaceful relations with Nazism, regarding western imperialism embodied in Britain as the greater enemy, whereas Hitler's Germany was in fact a far more deadly danger.   Thus the rulers of Russia courted Germany, fearing she might turn westwards to ally with Britain, whilst those of Germany, though maintaining 'correct' diplomatic relations, made no concealment of their opposition to the Bolshevist regime.

With the year 1937 we find a new tone of confidence and assertiveness in Hitlerian pronouncements, beginning with the new year proclamation to the party: [1] 'In all spheres of our national life, in the domestic sphere, in foreign affairs, in the spheres of culture and of economics, we have lived through the onrush of the greatest revolution in our German history. . . .'   At the end of January he solemnly repudiated to the *Reichstag* the German admission in the Versailles Treaty of its 'war guilt,' and at the September party conference announced that the Treaty of Versailles was dead, and a new era in German history begun, with German freedom guaranteed by the German army.   He began to repeat more insistently that Germany should have her colonies restored: 'We shall voice our demand for living room in colonies more and more loudly till the world cannot but admit our claim.' The general demand for 'living space' was also given more prominence. Germany, he continued to assert, was still peaceful, but whereas in 1934 he had said: 'Believe me we shall never fight again save in self-defence,' and in 1936 added honour and freedom as conditions, now he allowed himself to say (6th June 1937): 'Before us there stands a single purpose, and this purpose has cast its spell upon us.   Under the spell of this purpose we march.   He who sets himself in our path must not complain if sooner or later the march of a nation pursues its way over his body.'   And next day: 'No power within or without the *Reich* will keep us from going our way to our future.' [2]   In November 1937 Hitler held a secret conference with his generals and Foreign Secretary Neurath (shortly to be succeeded by the more daring Ribbentrop) to discuss how and when Germany could proceed to offensive steps to win living space: 'The question for Germany ran: where could she achieve the greatest gain at the lowest cost . . .   Germany's problem could only be solved by means of force. . . .' [3]   Hitler specifically referred to the necessity of conquering Austria and Czechoslovakia, in order to remove any threat to Germany's flanks, should he decide first to attack westwards rather than against Poland and Russia, and discussed how this could be executed.

Thus the programme of offensive action was sketched out, and the years 1938–9 were to see it put into execution.   For the army was now stronger, and at the very beginning of 1938 Hitler took over its command himself, ousting Blomberg, the War Minister, Fritsch, the commander-in-chief,

---

[1] *Speeches*, ed. Baynes, vol. ii, p. 1333.
[2] *Speeches*, ed. Baynes, vol. ii, pp. 1151, 1350, 1352.
[3] *International Military Tribunal* (Nürnberg), *Documents in Evidence*, vol. xxiv, p. 52 seq., and also the *Judgment* of the same body, pp. 15–17.   These deal with the statement of Hitler's military adjutant, Captain Hossbach, the so-called 'Hitler's Testament' in which the Führer expressed his 'fundamental ideas.'

and a dozen other high army officers, who had shown themselves critical of his policies both at home and abroad, and too independent and conservative for his liking. He reiterated to the *Reichstag* in a long speech on 20th February the 'hopeless inadequacy' of Germany's living space and natural resources, and then reminded them that 'over ten million Germans live in two of the states (Austria and Czechoslovakia) adjoining our borders.' This was the opening shot.

It was obvious strategy to begin with Austria where there was sentiment in favour of union with Germany (*Anschluss*) if only as a way out of her economic difficulties. And the Nazis were already strongly entrenched and active there, thanks to the pressure put upon its chancellor, Schuschnigg, in 1936 when, as in the previous year, Hitler pledged himself to the recognition and preservation of Austrian independence. The preparations were in fact already made when Hitler spoke to the *Reichstag*. Then, in a way reminiscent of Frederick the Great in 1740 and Bismarck in 1866, Hitler on 12th March sent a German army, 200,000 strong, roaring over the borders to seize both capital and country. The next day saw Hitler himself in Austria announcing [1] that it had always been his 'mission' to 'restore my dear homeland to the German *Reich*,' and the Nazi *Reich* enthusiastically approved, regardless of the method and the broken pledges. There were solid advantages in the conquest. The large Austrian gold treasure was removed to Berlin to bolster *Reich* finances; the Austrian economy, with its iron and timber, was welded to that of Germany; Germany gained nearly seven million more citizens, providing an appreciable addition to her army; she secured direct access to Hungary and Yugoslavia, and through them to the Balkans. Last, but of most immediate strategic importance, she now encircled on three sides the Czech bastion of Bohemia-Moravia. Hitler might well (as he did) seek to reassure Mussolini, with his Tyrolese German subjects, his Brenner frontier now with Germany, and his concern over the Adriatic.

The next victim was obviously Czechoslovakia with its over three and a quarter million *Sudeten* Germans, an old problem in Bohemian and German history. As in Austria, Nazism there had been active under Henlein, and encouraged from Germany for years, and this agitation now burst out with fresh force. For the masters of Germany, despite assurances that they had no intention of attacking their Czech neighbour, it was simply a question of choosing the most favourable moment for action. But Czechoslovakia had alliances with both France and Russia; Britain was committed to prevent aggression by the League of Nations Covenant, as were all its members; and it was clear that a German conquest, on top of that of Austria, would enormously and dangerously enhance Germany's position and power in Europe. Yet the French and British were unready for war, materially and mentally; the alliances with Russia, whether for Czechs or French, were of uncertain value; the League of Nations, if not the mere 'joke' of Hitler's contemptuous estimate, was quite unready to act. The internal difficulties and divisions of the multi-national Czechoslovakian state (45 per cent

[1] *Speeches*, ed. Baynes, vol. ii, p. 1422.

German, Slovak, Magyar, Ruthenian, and Pole, out of its total of over fourteen millions), and her wide separation from any possible military aid, including that from Russia, likewise contributed to strengthen Germany's hand, and to weaken those who opposed her policy and military actions.

The elaborate, and in the end futile, negotiations during the summer and autumn of 1938, ending at the Munich Conference (29th September 1938) of Britain, France, Germany, and Italy (Hitler refusing to admit Russia), need no recounting. Czechoslovakia lost to the Nazi *Reich* both her German citizens and the land they inhabited, while Poland and Hungary seized the opportunity to demand their share also. Whatever chances Czechoslovakia might have had before of defending herself against German attack behind her mountain barrier were now gone, and an international guarantee of her new boundaries added little or nothing to her safety. As with Austria, German Nazism had gained a great triumph and was correspondingly encouraged and strengthened. The western powers had preserved peace at a price, and could hasten their rearmament, but whether (as with Russia in the next year, when she went even further and allied with Germany) this gain was worth the loss, is open to question. Chamberlain, and many with him, honestly believed that the supreme effort to escape the calamities of war, by negotiation and even concession, was justified. But this implied *some* faith at least in Hitler's word, when he again repeated that this was 'the last territorial claim which I have to make in Europe.' The critics of the 'policy of appeasement,' and they were also many, disbelieved Hitler, and events proved them right.

For what Hitler after Munich defined for his people (on Czechoslovakian soil) as 'the beginning of your march into the great German future'[1] was continued with growing aggressiveness in the following year. In March 1939 came the annexation of the remainder of Czechoslovakia, defended on the ground of its age-long membership in the old *Reich*, continued disorders there, and German need for 'self-preservation.' In the same month came the regaining of Memel and thereby control over Lithuania, as well as demands for the return of Danzig, and for a free German corridor to East Prussia. The recovery of Alsace-Lorraine and the former German colonies also found public mention this spring as Nazi aims. It became increasingly likely that Poland was to be the next victim, and Britain at the end of March, its eyes now opened to the common danger, with French agreement promised aid to the Poles in case of a German attack, to the intense anger of the now megalomaniacal Hitler. Britain also extended her pledge of aid to Turkey, and with France pledged aid to Rumania and Greece if required. She also, in April 1939, approached Russia. In view of Hitler's often expressed hatred of Communism and his demand for eastern 'living space,' Russia might have been expected to be ready to join a defensive pact against him. Serious talks began in June. But although negotiations dragged on during the summer, they were hampered by mutual distrust. There was also the western alliance with Poland, and Poland's refusal (for which there were good grounds) to

[1] *Speeches*, ed. Baynes, vol. ii., p. 1527; ibid., p. 1586, for the final seizure.

concede Russia the right to march through her territory against Germany. And meanwhile Hitler, seeking to avoid a two-front war, and urged on by his Foreign Minister, Ribbentrop, likewise approached Russia, with offers of other peoples' territory in the shape of Polish and Baltic lands. On 23rd August Ribbentrop scored a great diplomatic success with the conclusion of a ten-year non-aggression pact with the Soviet Union which was to come into effect as soon as signed. A secret protocol provided for the virtual partition of Poland, and declared Lithuania to be in the German sphere of interest, Finland, Esthonia, and Latvia in the Russian. To avoid the danger of a two-front war Hitler was prepared to play a frivolous game which was to end in the destruction of Bismarckian Germany and make possible the expansion of Russia into central Europe.

The Nazi-Soviet Pact was a diplomatic bombshell. The burying of the Nazi-Communist hatchet was a bitter, though hardly unexpected, blow for Britain and France. It made war inevitable, as Hitler now saw no obstacle in the way of his attack on Poland. The feverish diplomacy which was pursued to the end could not deflect the course of events. In the face of the clearly stated British resolve to stand by Poland, Mussolini told Hitler that Italy was not prepared for war. This double blow caused Hitler to waver momentarily, and to postpone the attack scheduled for 26th August. That day the Nazis took over in Danzig, and redoubled their agitation in the Corridor. The British Government made a last-minute attempt to secure diplomatic negotiations between Poland and Germany as equals. But Hitler wanted surrender, not negotiation. Late on 31st August he stated his final—and not unreasonable—grounds for a settlement. But even before this attempt to justify his position, at a few minutes after noon, he had signed the final order for the attack on Poland to begin at dawn the next morning. He knew that he was risking a world war, but nourished to the last the hope that 'the little worms' whom he had worsted at Munich would remain either neutral or passive. At O.K.W. headquarters in Berlin, Admiral Canaris, the chief of the *Abwehr* (Intelligence), greeted the news with the words, 'This means the end of Germany.' Two days after the German armies drove over the Polish frontier, Britain and France declared war on Germany. It was Hitler's first defeat. The conflict which he had willed and which he hoped to localize had now become a European war.

CHAPTER XIII

TRIUMPH AND CATASTROPHE, 1939–45

THE OUTBREAK of war evoked among the German people nothing of the delirious, patriotic enthusiasm of August 1914. Foreign observers reported that the Germans appeared dazed, unbelieving, fearful. The *Wehrmacht* leadership, which had opposed Hitler's every step towards war, was riddled with pessimism, and many senior officers were actually plotting the downfall of the regime, while others were cognizant of if not actually participants in disloyal schemes. The war began as, and remained, peculiarly 'Hitler's war.' Yet there was no military *coup*, no general strike, no spontaneous uprising, as the disciplined German army moved smoothly into battle, backed by efficiently organized and maintained supply lines. And the German people sustained the war for four and a half years to the point of exhaustion of their last resources.

By the time the war broke out the concentration of power in the hands of the Nazi Party was virtually complete. A new 'Ministerial Council for the Defence of the *Reich*,' created two days before the attack on Poland, and conceived as a form of war cabinet, rarely met and soon withered away. From 1940 onwards, where power was not exercised personally by Hitler himself, it was concentrated in the hands not of *Reich* ministers, but of a small group of technicians, bureaucrats, and Party 'strong men.' Goering, in 1939 at the height of his power, was named Hitler's successor on 1st September. Himmler, with primary responsibility for internal security in the dual role of *Reichsführer S.S.* and Chief of the German Police, Goebbels as *Reich* Propaganda Minister and Gauleiter of Berlin, Hess as the *Führer*'s Deputy and the main link between Party and State, were the other principal stars in the Nazi firmament as the war began. There had been no preparations for 'war in depth,' no general mobilization of the *Reich*'s labour resources, no conscription of women. Hitler continued to believe in war along the lines of a political *coup* by military means, carried out before British or French intervention could be effective.

The war in Poland was conceived to fit this pattern, a *Blitzkrieg* employing novel weapons and tactics. Concentric attacks by columns of massed armour penetrated swiftly, while the *Luftwaffe* largely destroyed the Polish air force on the ground, disrupted communications, and terrorized the towns. The fighting was almost over when, on 17th September, the Russians, alarmed at the speed of the German advance, moved rapidly westward to Brest Litovsk, extinguishing the Polish state. Capitalizing on Hitler's uncertainty about the reaction of the western powers, Stalin won a definitive partition of Poland, the transfer of Lithuania to the Russian sphere of interest, and an agreement for the exchange of Russian raw materials for German industrial goods.   On 5th October Hitler delivered his victory speech in Warsaw.   The way was now open for him to impose his solution of the Polish problem.

By cutting Germany off from the outside world the war facilitated both the tightening up of the Nazi dictatorship and the opportunity for the first large-scale attempts to implement racist doctrines upon foreigners.   In a decree dated 1st September 1939 Hitler inaugurated the notorious euthanasia policy. At the same time he authorized Himmler to take the extraordinary measures in Bohemia and Moravia 'for the security of public order' which led to the imprisonment of thousands of prominent Czechs and the stamping out of the last vestiges of Bohemian autonomy.   Poland, however, was the prime target of Himmler's racial offensive.   Poles and Jews were cleared from the territories annexed to the *Reich* into the area around Warsaw known as the Government General under Hans Frank and Artur Seyss-Inquart, while S.S. *Einsatzgruppen* (Special Commandos) were charged with 'house-cleaning': the liquidation of Jews and the Polish upper classes to produce a leaderless subject population.   Economic resources were to be exploited for the benefit of the *Reich*.   'This extermination of a whole race, including women and children, is possible only for subhumans . . . ,' a German officer wrote to his wife from Warsaw on 21st September. '*It shames me to be a German !*'

The unexpected victory in Poland turned the fatalism of the German people into confident optimism.   'So long as things went well and without major sacrifices,' a German historian has written, 'the hearts of the majority were tolerably satisfied.' [1]   In the east the generals had produced lightning victory; in the west the French had stood passively behind the Maginot Line while Poland was erased from the map.   Hitler's gamble had paid off, and the generals' confidence in his 'intuition' had been enhanced.   The controlled German press harped on the theme that now was the time for peace with the West, and in his *Reichstag* speech of 6th October Hitler appeared at his most reasonable, declaring that Germany had no claims against either Britain or France.   His peace offer, with its demand for recognition of the new order in the east, was rejected without hesitation, and seemed aimed only at carrying the German people with him by demonstrating that, if the war were prolonged, it was through no fault of Hitler's.   A week earlier he had informed the *Wehrmacht* that he planned to attack in the west as soon as possible, and plans were now speeded up.   Even before Warsaw fell large-scale troop movements were made to the west, and by mid October seven armies were lined up along the western frontier.   Hitler's plans were vehe-mently opposed by the army leadership, and the civilian resistance leaders— Goerdeler, ex-mayor of Leipzig; Beck, former Chief of the General Staff; Popitz, former Prussian Minister of Finance; and von Hassell, former Ambassador to Rome—renewed their efforts to persuade the army to eliminate Hitler and end the war before it engulfed western Europe.   But Hitler outfaced his opponents, secured a shattering victory over the army,

[1] Golo Mann, *Deutsche Geschichte, 1919–1945* (Frankfurt am Main, 1958), p. 165.

and the conspiracy vanished.   Bad weather repeatedly delayed the offensive until, with the compromising of its plans when a staff officer crashed on a flight over Belgium, it was postponed to the spring.

By this time Anglo-French preparations to aid Finland against Russia by sending help through northern Scandinavia suggested to German intelligence the danger of their occupying Norway and cutting off the supply of Swedish iron ore.   A proposal advanced jointly by Grand Admiral Raeder and Alfred Rosenberg, the one for strategic, the other for ideological, reasons, for the seizure of Norway attracted Hitler once his winter offensive in the west was postponed.   The campaign, launched on 9th April 1940, after the end of the Russo-Finnish war, was a striking instance of careful planning and bold leadership, of technical and tactical skill.   Denmark was seized in a single morning.   Early the same day German naval forces moved from assembly positions off the coast to deposit troops in the important harbours from Oslo to Narvik.   Norwegian resistance was overcome and, closely supported by the *Luftwaffe*, the Germans drove northward to crush the retreating Norwegians and the British forces which had been landed north and south of Trondheim.   Narvik, far to the north, was recaptured by French forces, but by this time the breakthrough in France had revolutionized the situation and Allied forces were withdrawn.   The apparent success of a fifth column boring from within terrified opinion in other threatened countries; but in fact surprise was a more important factor in the German triumph, and there was no evidence of betrayal.

By this dazzling success in an operation involving sea power the Western powers were dealt a severe blow.   It greatly strengthened Hitler's position vis-à-vis the army leadership, added enormously to his prestige among the German people, and brought immediate and substantial benefits.   It extended German power northward to the Arctic and helped to strengthen the German position against the Soviet Union in an area where Hitler had made extensive concessions to secure the short-run advantage of immunity from Russian pressure.   Yet the loss of nearly half the German strength in cruisers and destroyers, so soon after the scuttling of the *Graf Spee* off Montevideo on 17th December, limited the range of strategic alternatives when the Battle of France was won.   And the need to garrison Scandinavia was, as the years passed, to impose a profitless burden on the *Wehrmacht*.

The Scandinavian operation had not been allowed to interfere with preparations for the offensive in the west.   The plan eventually agreed upon has been described as 'one of the most shrewdly and skilfully contrived plans in the annals of modern warfare.' [1]   In essence it was simplicity itself.   Holland was to be occupied in what was virtually a separate operation, to acquire and to deny to the British important air and sea bases, and to please Goering. Farther south a major blow at Liège and Brussels was to draw the western Allies across the Belgian border.   But the major thrust with the bulk of the armour was to strike through the rugged Ardennes, cross the Meuse near

[1] Telford Taylor, *The March of Conquest: The German Victories in Western Europe, 1940* (New York, 1958), pp. 179–80.

Sedan, and cut off the Allied forces in Belgium and northern France. Seventy-five divisions backed by 3,500 aircraft were concentrated on a 165-mile front for von Bock's drawing and von Rundstedt's breakthrough attack. The final plan presupposed unprovoked attacks on what Hitler referred to as 'the so-called neutrals' who were, after the pattern traced out in Scandinavia, treated as declared enemies.

With the advent of good weather, with the army strengthened and proved, the generals were reconciled to or even optimistic about the long-postponed offensive which they had so stubbornly opposed in the autumn. In despair at the fresh revelation of Hitler's intuitive leadership in Scandinavia, the conspirators found that they could secure no support for a *Putsch* from the army. Resigned to the inevitability of the western offensive which they had hoped to prevent, they could only try to ensure that the neutrals were not taken by surprise. Once again, as in the previous November and January, Major General Hans Oster, the chief of counter-intelligence, was driven by his deeply felt hate of Hitler and his aggressive plans to warn the Dutch military attaché of the precise hour of the attack. On the evening of 9th May Colonel Sas was able to telephone to The Hague the meaningful words: 'To-morrow at dawn. Hold tight.'

The masterful German plans were brilliantly executed and succeeded beyond the wildest hopes of their progenitors. In Holland it was subsequently asserted that espionage and sabotage, especially by thousands of *Reichsdeutsche*, had betrayed the country into German hands. But in fact the decisive part was played by airborne troops who seized airfields north and south of Rotterdam and the Rhine crossing. Early on 14th May, shortly before the Dutch commander capitulated, German bombers suddenly appeared and levelled the heart of Rotterdam, killing over 800 and rendering some 78,000 homeless. It was a foretaste of the blows which were later to bring terror to German cities.

Farther south the Germans pushed swiftly through the Maastricht appendix to assault the forts which barred the way to Liège, Louvain, and Brussels. According to their agreed plan, the British and French crossed the Belgian frontier and within forty-eight hours were deployed with the retreating Belgians on the Dyle, ready to meet what they imagined was the main German thrust. The essential conditions for the breakthrough on the Meuse of Rundstedt's Army Group A had thus been established. Pushing through the Ardennes, German tanks and infantry crossed the Meuse on 13th May, and shattered the French line all the way from Namur to Sedan. While Hitler and the high command wrangled over the threat to the southern flank of the breakthrough, the *Panzers* rolled on, and by the evening of 20th May Guderian was in Abbeville. Allied efforts to break through the steadily tightening encircling bonds from north and south proved fruitless. After two weeks of heroic resistance the entire Belgian front began to disintegrate. On 27th May King Leopold agreed to unconditional surrender—the only terms Hitler would concede. One day earlier orders had been issued for the evacuation of British and French forces through the sole port remaining in

Allied hands north of the Somme, Dunkirk. Here a desperate rearguard stand on the Dunkirk perimeter and the evacuation of 350,000 Allied troops were assisted by the decision—the product of initiative by both Hitler and Rundstedt—to halt German armour and leave the pocket to the infantry and Goering's *Luftwaffe*.

On 5th June, less than twenty-four hours after Dunkirk fell, the whole of the German army stood poised along the Somme and the Aisne, ready to crush the new defences manned by the weakened and demoralized French. Relentlessly the German flood surged from the Somme to the Seine, from the Aisne to the Marne. The French government fled Paris for Tours on 10th June, the same day Mussolini made his belated intervention against a stricken foe. On 14th June German troops marched into an abandoned Paris, and as German forces fanned out towards Brittany, the Loire, and the Rhône, trapping the remnants of the French forces still in the Maginot Line, the new government at Bordeaux requested an armistice. 'I've really done it! And how remarkably easy it has all been!'—so Hitler exulted when the news reached him. In a final theatrical gesture he confronted the delegates of the aged Marshal Pétain in Foch's 1918 railway carriage, which had been hastily rolled from its museum into a sun-drenched clearing in the Forest of Compiègne. The armistice concluded on 22nd June provided for German occupation of a broad belt of northern France, including Paris, and the coast to the Spanish frontier. In a device skilfully designed to link defeated France with the Third Reich, French administration was to continue in both parts. Two million French prisoners were to remain as virtual hostages in German hands, and the French fleet and army were to be demobilized under German supervision (*Kontrolle*).

With the French armistice Hitler consolidated a stunning victory which has no parallel in European history. In little more than two months he had made himself master of western Europe from the North Cape to the Pyrenees. The price had been extraordinarily light. The Battle of France cost but 156,492 casualties (of which 27,074 were fatal)—about 1,150 per division engaged. In the more difficult, costly, and complex phase of the war ahead Hitler had to decide how to exploit the dazzling tactical victory his generals had won. But to the question '*Was nun?*' German leadership could provide no coherent answer, and, 'victorious in battle but planless,' the Germans staggered into a new phase of the war.

So long as England remained undefeated, victory in the west was incomplete. But for this phase of the war the Germans had neither plans nor preparations, and in the weeks after Dunkirk the entire resources of the *Wehrmacht* had been marshalled needlessly for the final blow at a tottering enemy. Hitler hoped, not unreasonably, that in the face of disaster on the Continent Britain would either collapse or capitulate. But British resistance since 10th May had stiffened under the incomparable leadership of Winston Churchill. Gradually it became clear that, as the Prime Minister had stated on 4th June, the day the Germans entered Dunkirk, the British meant 'to ride out the storm of war, and to outlive the menace of tyranny, if necessary for years, if necessary alone.' 'The *Führer* is greatly puzzled by Britain's unwillingness to make peace,' Fritz Halder, the German Chief of Staff, confided to his diary. In the *Reichstag* on 19th July Hitler made a last appeal 'to reason and common sense.' 'I can see no reason why this war must go on,' he said. As a propaganda device to rally the German people for the fight against Britain the manœuvre was brilliantly successful. But it contained no concrete suggestions for peace terms, no answer to the problem of German conquests, and it was rejected without hesitation. Britain's 'No,' as Golo Mann has written, was the decisive event of the year.[1]

Hitler's continued reluctance to contemplate so hazardous and, for the *Wehrmacht*, so novel an operation, was indicated by the statement in his directive of 16th July that he had 'decided to prepare, and if necessary to carry out, a landing operation against Great Britain.' Intensified air and sea warfare might, he hoped, avert the necessity of invasion. At any rate defeat of the R.A.F. was the essential preliminary to a large-scale landing. The air offensive began on 13th August, and victory seemed within German grasp as British losses mounted. A sharp but probably accidental attack on London's residential quarters caused the British to retaliate with the first bombing raid on Berlin. This did negligible damage but shook German morale and led Hitler to promise devastating reprisals. On 7th September massive German bomber fleets shifted their attack to London itself and saved the British fighter force from acute peril. London suffered terribly; but a series of battles culminating on 15th September revealed the R.A.F.'s revival. Two days later Hitler admitted that the requisite conditions for Operation *Sea Lion* had not been met. And while on 4th September he had publicly pledged himself to invasion, and preparations were far advanced, the operation was postponed 'until further notice.' The fact that it was not finally abandoned until March 1942 shows Hitler's realization of the importance of ending the war in the west before embarking on his great adventure in the east. British resistance had administered a severe strategic defeat.

By this time Hitler had already taken the fateful decision to attack the Soviet Union before the conquest of England was completed. It is not difficult to find an explanation for this 'irrepressible conflict' in Nazi ideology. 'To guarantee the German nation the soil and territory to which it is entitled on this earth . . . we are bound to think first of Russia and her border states,' Hitler had written in *Mein Kampf*. Besides acquiring *Lebensraum* at the expense of an 'inferior race,' victory in the east would eliminate once and for all the 'eastern menace' of Bolshevism by 'building a dike against the Russian flood.' However, despite the emphasis which the Goebbels propaganda machine later placed on 'anti-communism,' ideological factors played little or no part in the decision. Nor was Hitler moved primarily by the fact that Stalin had followed up the advantages seized in Finland at the conclusion of the Winter War by incorporating the Baltic states into the Soviet Union while Germany was involved in the west, and at the very moment of the fall of France had taken the first steps towards strengthening his southern flank by

[1] Mann, *Deutsche Geschichte*, p. 170.

annexing not only Bessarabia but northern Bukovina as well.   In deliberately choosing the two-front war for which he had sharply criticized the leadership of Imperial Germany, Hitler acted out of a growing conviction that Britain's persistent reluctance to make peace rested in the hope of winning Russia to her side.   In a decisive conference at the Berghof on 31st July 1940 he declared, according to Halder's notes, that 'with Russia smashed, Britain's last hope will be shattered. . . . Russia's destruction must therefore be made a part of this struggle.   *Spring 1941:*   The sooner Russia is crushed the better.'   As Churchill had foreseen, balked in the west, Hitler recoiled eastwards, resolved, eleven months after the conclusion of the non-aggression pact which had brought him immunity during the campaigns in 1939 and 1940, to shatter the Russian state.   His decision was 'directly connected with the war on England and the failure to bring that war to a speedy conclusion. . . . Embittered by the refusal of England to acknowledge defeat, he hoped to encompass her collapse by first crushing Russia and thus making himself stronger.' [1]

The decisions of 31st July were at once translated into military and political action. The large-scale reduction in the army planned as early as the end of May was abandoned in the face of Hitler's demand for 120 divisions for the east.   Forty new divisions were to raise the total to 180.   On 9th August the order *Aufbau Ost* provided for improved transportation and supply facilities to the east.   Increasingly stronger numbers of troops were moved eastward, and on 17th August Keitel ordered commencement of the new armaments programme required for the operation.   At the same time Hitler took diplomatic counter-measures which outmanœuvred the Soviet Union.   He first forced Rumania to make extensive cessions to Hungary and then, having won the position of arbiter in both Budapest and Bucharest, gave the rump of Rumania with its vital Ploesti oil wells a territorial guarantee.   He now occupied a salient through Hungary to the Black Sea, and Germany and Russia were face to face on the Lower Danube in defiance of the Moscow agreement of 23rd August 1939.   Similarly, on the northern front of the projected attack Finland was propelled by the Soviet Union and enticed by Germany into the Axis camp, with Finnish agreement to the purchase of German armaments and the passage of military personnel and supplies to northern Norway.   On 27th September the so-called Tripartite Pact was signed in Berlin by Germany, Japan, and Italy.   Though directed primarily against England and the United States, this league of the three anti-Comintern powers was also naturally viewed as contrary to the 1939 agreement.   Two months later Hungary, Rumania, and Slovakia joined.   In mid November, a few days after Mussolini had invaded Greece, Molotov came to Moscow for talks on Balkan and Baltic affairs.   But though offered participation in the Tripartite Pact, he was unable to deflect the Germans from their course. On the very day of his arrival Hitler signed an order declaring that, 'irrespective of the results of these discussions, all preparations for the east which have already been ordered verbally will be continued.'   On 18th December

[1] Gerhard L. Weinberg, *Germany and the Soviet Union, 1939–1941* (Leiden, 1954), pp. 116–17.

he issued his directive for Operation *Barbarossa* '*to crush Soviet Russia in a quick campaign.*'

While *Barbarossa* was being prepared, Hitler attempted to force a decision against Britain both by intensified sea warfare and by trying to mobilize his continental partners into the struggle. At the beginning of the war the German Navy possessed only fifty-seven U-boats, of which only twenty-two were suitable for Atlantic operations, and of these only about one-third could be continuously maintained in the battle areas. The U-boat fleet grew rapidly, and after the defeat of France the whole coast with the Channel and Atlantic ports was available for the construction of virtually bomb-proof shelters and air bases from which shipping could be attacked. Though jealousy between Goering and the naval commanders prevented maximum air-sea co-operation, British shipping on the east coast was subjected to ever-increasing attack; and from July onwards all traffic from abroad was diverted north of Ireland to the Mersey and the Clyde. The toll taken mounted steadily. 'The only thing that ever really frightened me,' Churchill wrote later, '. . . was the U-boat peril.' But the British lifeline was also threatened by armed merchant cruisers which sank large tonnages, dislocated shipping movements, and forced the dispersion of hard-pressed British escort and patrol resources. In addition in October the pocket battleship *Scheer*, and a month later the *Hipper*, slipped through the blockade and inflicted heavy damage on British shipping. The extension and intensification of sea and air warfare in the Atlantic drove the United States to follow up the hasty shipments of rifles and ammunition to help Britain meet the threat of invasion with the first of a series of unneutral acts in the Atlantic which marked the passage from strict neutrality to non-belligerency: a bargain involving long leases for bases off the Atlantic coast from British Guiana to Newfoundland and the transfer of fifty World War I destroyers to Britain. It required many months for these to come into service, and by the end of 1940 German aircraft, U-boats, and surface raiders had sunk nearly four million tons of Allied shipping, and British resources had to be diverted from the bombing of Germany to concentrate on the desperate threat to the Atlantic lifeline. When, however, on 10th March 1941, within nine months of the fall of France, the Lend-Lease Act became law, 'British hopes had been underpinned with a solid foundation of American acts,'[1] and the *Reich*'s hopes of ultimate victory dimmed.

In the meantime, as an alternative to the invasion of Russia which he disliked or to the invasion of Britain which he feared, Raeder, strongly supported by Goering, had tried to interest the *Führer* in a major advance into the Mediterranean and the Middle East. Hitler rejected this alternative strategy, but he was attracted by the prospect of using his continental partners to close the Mediterranean to British shipping and to ward off any possible threat from Britain or the United States via Europe's southern flank. For him, however, the Mediterranean was never contemplated as more than a secondary

[1] A. and V. M. Toynbee, *The Initial Triumph of the Axis: Survey of International Affairs, 1939–1946* (London, 1958), p. 276.

theatre.   Though in June, at the flood tide of German victory, Franco had expressed a willingness to enter the war, he later insisted on both territorial concessions at the expense of French Africa and difficult economic conditions. In a meeting at Hendaye on the French frontier on 23rd October Hitler found Franco (forewarned by Pétain) unimpressed with his exposition of the hopelessness of England's position and unwilling to sign the treaty providing for Spain's entry into the war and the seizure of Gibraltar by German air-borne troops.   From an interview at Montoire Hitler also came away empty-handed.   A reticent Pétain was resolved to preserve France's balanc-ing position until the outcome of the Anglo-German struggle should be decided.

Mussolini was the only one of Hitler's partners to make a military move, and this only to Hitler's embarrassment.   Since July Italian forces had been skirmishing on the Sudan-Abyssinian border, and in mid September Graziani had pushed fifty miles inside the Egyptian frontier from Libya.   In a search for a quick success, and out of pique at Hitler's moving German troops into Rumania without notice, Mussolini resolved, as he told Ciano, that the *Führer* would 'find out from the newspapers that I have occupied Greece.' The consequences for Hitler of this petulant and ill-conceived attack were serious.   Just at the time when he had pacified the Balkans by a virtual occupation of Rumania, Mussolini had set it in turmoil again.   It invited Stalin's intervention, and by enabling Britain to occupy Crete and Lemnos increased the aerial threat to the Ploesti oilfields.   Hitler could only pledge aid to Mussolini's 'regrettable blunder' and order the *Wehrmacht*, 'in the event of its becoming necessary, to occupy that part of the Greek mainland north of the Aegean, operating from Bulgaria.'   As this projected Operation *Marita* could not take place until spring, for the next few months Hitler was compelled to look on while stubborn Greek resistance checked the Italian invasion and drove deep into Albanian territory.   For the first time in Europe forces of the Axis met defeat.   Further blows rained on Germany's Italian ally, as on 11th November British carrier-based aircraft struck a heavy blow at the fleet at Taranto, and a month later a mechanized force struck westward along the North African coast at Sidi Barrani, and in two months destroyed an Italian army and advanced 500 miles to Benghazi.   To bolster his failing ally Hitler on 10th November ordered German air force units into southern Italy to attack British supply routes and naval installations; and began the preparation and training of the *Afrika Korps*.

By the end of 1940 Hitler had achieved only an inconclusive victory.   In the West, though Denmark, Norway, Belgium, Luxembourg, and France had fallen victim to the *Blitzkrieg*, Britain still held out, increasingly sustained by U.S. aid and encouraged by naval and military victories over the hapless Italians in the Mediterranean.   Where force could not be applied, German diplomacy had been unsuccessful.   Vichy France had proved elusive and unreliable, and part of the colonial empire was in de Gaulle's hands.   Franco had shamelessly taken advantage of the changed aspect of the war to avoid the attack on Gibraltar.   In the east the picture was more promising.

Poland had been erased from the map, the northern flank had been strengthened through agreement with Finland, the Russians had been outmanœuvred
along the Danube and in the Balkans, and the stage was set for the fateful
operations which were once more to drive the British into the sea and allow
the Germans to overrun the Balkans and to penetrate deep into the Soviet
Union.

In the wake of conquest western Europe had taken on as shapeless an aspect
as German strategy since Compiègne. The campaigns had been preceded by
an astonishing dearth of political planning. Though Hitler occasionally used
the term 'New Order,' he thought, as Arnold Toynbee has remarked, 'only
in terms of conquest, followed, wherever possible, by direct annexation.'[1]
His party propagandists were more voluble. The first considered statement of
what the New Order meant was on 25th July 1940, when Funk, *Reich* Minister
of Economics, presented a picture of a Europe exploited for the benefit of
Germany. Not until after the signing of the Tripartite Pact on 27th September 1940—proclaimed by the *Kölnische Zeitung* to be the 'Magna Carta
of the New Order'—were the economic aspects supplemented by Rosenberg's
contention that the New Order stood for the delimitation of *Lebensräume*,
with the Greater German *Reich* serving as a link between the Baltic and the
Mediterranean. Italian emergence as a theoretically equal partner tended to
make Eurafrica into a single German-Italian sphere, but the problem of
fitting Russia into this pattern could not be solved until after the attack in
June 1941.

Hitler's Europe thus emerged through a process of improvisation and trial
and error, and presented a varied pattern. In Denmark, where the king,
parliament, and army remained, the Germans attempted to establish a 'model
protectorate,' controlling the country through the German minister in
Copenhagen. Increasing German pressure led the king to make a number of
important concessions from July 1941, in the hope of averting direct military
rule or power for the Danish Nazis. In Norway, after the king escaped to
England on 7th June with his government, a crude attempt was made to use
the Nazi Vidkun Quisling as an instrument of German policy. This only
served to crystallize opposition, and power was put into the hands of the
Reich Commissioner, Joseph Terboven, *Gauleiter* of Essen and a close friend
of Goering's. He declared the king dethroned, dismissed the government,
dissolved political parties except Quisling's, and ultimately formed a puppet
government under Quisling behind which he held real power. In the
Netherlands supreme power was also vested in a Nazi proconsul, Dr Artur
Seyss-Inquart. After Queen Wilhelmina and the government left the country
on 13th May he suspended the legislature and formed the administrative
heads of the government, soon to be replaced by Dutch Nazis, into a kind of
sub-cabinet under his own authority. *Gleichschaltung* into the *Reich* soon
followed, as the Netherlands was the first west European country to feel the
impact of Nazism with the dismissal of Jews from the civil service and the

[1] A. and V. M. Toynbee, *Hitler's Europe: Survey of International Affairs, 1939–1946* (London, 1954), p. 56.

aryanization of commerce. In Luxembourg too parliament and the parties were dissolved in the wake of the flight of the Grand Duchess, and the Duchy was steadily absorbed into the *Reich*. In February 1941 it was united with Koblenz-Trier in a renamed *Gau Moselland*, and an intensive programme of Germanization was pursued. At the start Belgium fared better. The long-disputed districts of Eupen, Malmédy, and Moresnet on the frontier were promptly annexed, but the fact that the king was a prisoner of war put full power into the hands of the occupation forces. As Belgium was both a vital base for operations against Britain and a rich economic area to be exploited, the administration was a purely military one, though the Gestapo and other agencies of the *Reich* extended their tentacles into the country. In occupied France the picture was more complicated. In an ominous threat to French territorial integrity the two northern *départements* of Pas de Calais and the Nord were joined to Belgium for occupational administration. The bitterest pill was the Germanization of Alsace and Lorraine and, in August 1940, the incorporation of Alsace into the *Reichsgau Moselland* and of Lorraine into *Westmark*. The zone remained an administrative morass, divided under a military rule in which the Armistice Commission, the Army High Command (O.K.H.), Hitler's own headquarters (O.K.W.), and the Foreign Office all had a part. A harsh occupation policy, with the introduction of the usual Nazi measures, economic exploitation in the interests of the *Reich* and the retention of French prisoners, alienated French opinion and confirmed the fears of Britain and the United States.

Hitler's victories had consolidated his domestic position and discouraged the opposition. After Compiègne there was no possibility that Halder or Brauchitsch, the Commander in Chief, or any field commander would raise a hand against the *Führer*. In the victory ceremonies at the Kroll Opera House on 19th July Hitler had lavished promotions and decorations on the victorious *Generalität*, and in so doing debased their ranks and robbed them of independence. Most were content to leave politics to the *Führer* who had brought glory and conquest. Only a few, together with the army's elder statesmen, Ludwig Beck and Freiherr von Hammerstein, and a handful of civilians, kept alive the embers of resistance. Though they realized that the unparalleled victories had made their position hopeless, they understood even in the heyday of Germany's success that the failure to subjugate Britain had condemned the *Reich* to a prolonged war, and they sought to bring it to an end through a tolerable peace. But they recognized that even this limited objective could not be achieved until Hitler's military fortunes began to ebb. Still, as Goerdeler's biographer has written, 'it says much for the genuineness of the convictions which sustained the Opposition that on nearly all of them the victory had a shattering effect, making them see the future with despair rather than hope.'[1] From 'a happy and lasting peace,' wrote Goerdeler in a memorandum for army officers on 1st July 1940, 'we are farther away than ever—this war serves the ends, not of constructive design, but of fantastic

[1] Gerhard Ritter, *The German Resistance: Carl Goerdeler's Struggle against Tyranny* (London, 1958), p. 170.

scheming . . .' and he predicted the collapse of the Nazi system 'sooner or later.' As a *Putsch* appeared impracticable for the moment, attention focused on planning for the Germany which should emerge after the elimination of the Nazi regime.

Hitler's determination to invade Russia found both supporters and defenders in the army; but the chiefs of the conspiracy were appalled at the prospects of mounting losses, economic hardships, and extension and prolongation of the war into a conflict in which the ultimate defeat of Germany could not be in doubt. Hitler's notorious injunction that the war in the east would be conducted 'with unprecedented, merciless, and unrelenting harshness,' and his *Kommissarbefehl*, the order for the liquidation of the commissars as 'bearers of an ideology directly opposed to National Socialism,' provoked, according to Brauchitsch, protests from the generals and horror and dismay when it became known among the conspirators. 'This kind of thing,' von Hassell wrote in his diary, 'turns the German into a "Boche", a type of being which had existed only in enemy propaganda.' A conference of the chief conspirators concluded sadly that 'nothing was to be hoped for now.' In the Foreign Office, experts of the old school like State Secretary von Weizsäcker also opposed the projected attack on the grounds that 'it will do us no good,' while economic experts argued that trade agreements for the procurement of raw materials obviated the need for war.

The most dramatic instance of disaffection came not from the resistance or conservative officials but from inside the Nazi Party. Early on 10th May 1941 Rudolf Hess flew to Scotland in a vain attempt to bring about peace between the *Reich* and the British government. His crazy venture had no effect on Hitler's military plans or on German foreign policy; but it shocked and mystified the *Führer* and shattered the uneasy equilibrium within the Party. The removal of Hitler's Deputy and, after Goering, his successor, opened the way to power for Martin Bormann, Hess's assistant and special liaison officer at the *Führerhauptquartier*. Within two days Hitler appointed this ruthless schemer Head of the Party Chancery (as the *Führer*'s Deputy was now called), and on 29th May conferred on him all the powers which Hess had exercised as *Reich* minister. As Hitler became more and more immersed in military matters internal affairs fell increasingly into the hands of Bormann, who could determine which matters were to go through to Hitler for decision and could intervene, in the name of the *Führer*, in any issue of party or government. His advent to power reactivated the Party and led to increasing tension and struggle with the S.S., which had had an edge on political power from 1935 to 1940. The S.S. remained the stronger of the two organizations, though the Party was catching up, and Bormann had greater influence with Hitler than did Himmler. Bormann's succession was promptly followed by a further stage in the Nazi assault on the Christian churches, on the grounds that, as Bormann put it in a circular to the *Gauleiter* in June 1941, 'All influences that could infringe upon the leadership of the nation, as exercised by the *Führer* with the help of the N.S.D.A.P., must be eliminated.'

In the meantime planning for the campaigns of 1941 proceeded. Balked once again in his designs for 'striking at Britain in the simplest manner' at Gibraltar, Hitler had to wait for the worst of the winter to abate before launching the attack on Greece and *Barbarossa*, now scheduled for 15th May. By the end of February an army of nearly 100,000 had been built up in Rumania.   In the meantime, to the growing chagrin of their outmanœuvred Russian allies, German troops infiltrated into Bulgaria and on the night of 28th February they crossed the Danube from Rumania and occupied the country peacefully.   The next day, to the impotent rage of the Russians, Bulgaria acceded to the Tripartite Pact.   The base for the attack on Greece was now in German hands.   Pressure on Yugoslavia, on whom Hitler believed the whole Balkan position depended, if his long right flank was to be secure, did not yield such easy fruits.   The Regent delayed and, though he succeeded in extracting concessions, acceded to the Tripartite Pact on 24th March.   This produced a storm in Serbia and Montenegro and led to the overthrow of the Regent three days later.   An enraged Hitler at once ordered an immediate and pitiless attack.   Ten days later, at dawn on 6th April, German forces, soon assisted by Hungarian and Bulgarian units, crossed Yugoslavia's long, exposed frontiers in concentric attacks directed on Belgrade, which was reduced to rubble by systematic attacks from low-flying Stukas.   With only an exhausted Greece and a distant Britain as allies, Yugoslav resistance soon crumbled, and following capitulation the country was broken up into its constituent parts in the interests of its former enemies. The collapse of Yugoslavia carried with it the fall of Greece.   Outflanking the defenders of Salonika the Germans forced the Greeks and the newly arrived British troops back for a last stand at Thermopylae.   German tanks rolled into Athens on 27th April.   British forces were evacuated, the King retired to Crete with his ministers, and General Tsolakoglu signed the capitulation and remained as head of an Axis-protected regime.

Other victories followed.   On 31st March, in command of a mixed Italian-German force, to which Hitler had reluctantly contributed an armoured division, Rommel attacked eastwards along the North African coast, pushed the British out of Benghazi, invested Tobruk, and by mid April stood on the frontiers of Egypt.   To the north the Italians were in the Dodecanese, and Crete was taken in fierce fighting following mass landings by parachute and airborne troops.   But the cost was so heavy that their commander, Student, afterwards referred to Crete as 'the grave of German parachutists.'   The German strategic position in the eastern Mediterranean had thus been dramatically improved.   Though Turkey obstinately clung to neutrality, Iraq, where Raschid Ali became Prime Minister following a *coup* on 3rd April, presented an attractive opportunity for weakening the British position.   Hitler promised and furnished air support, but the revolt was quickly crushed by the intervention of British forces, and, fearful of large-scale German intervention in Vichy-held Syria, where German and Italian planes were based, British and Free French forces crossed the frontier from Palestine and by mid July occupied the whole country.   If the British position in the Middle East now no longer presented the 'immense emergency' which Churchill had seen, it remained precarious. Raeder had understood this and revived his demand for a decisive offensive. There seems little doubt that a quarter of the forces then being assembled for the invasion of Russia could have dealt the British position in the Middle East a fatal blow. Raeder's preference for a more direct attack on Britain than the roundabout route via Moscow was also strengthened by success in the Battle of the Atlantic. Under U-boat and surface attacks the toll of British and Allied shipping mounted ominously in June 1941 to a peak relative to replacements which was never to be reached again. The *Scharnhorst* and *Gneisenau* broke out and sank 115,622 tons of shipping before withdrawing to Brest, where they were immobilized by persistent British bombing. The 45,000-ton *Bismarck*, Germany's newest battleship, slipped out of the Baltic and on 24th May sank the British battle cruiser *Hood* and terrorized the Atlantic before itself falling victim to a concentrated attack by the Royal Navy.

But Hitler was not to be dissuaded. He had already ruled that 'an offensive against the Suez Canal could not be considered until Operation *Barbarossa* is completed.' In these last weeks German leadership was, as Weizsäcker records, 'moving along a one-way street against Russia.' All military and political decisions were circumscribed by the forthcoming attack. From April onwards Stalin gave repeated demonstrations of appeasement that went far beyond anything attempted by Chamberlain. Valuable supplies, including oil and rubber, continued to flow into Germany, often by special trains, right up to the last hours before the attack. Despite the absence of any threat from the east, Hitler was determined to reverse the relationship inaugurated on 23rd August 1939. 'The partnership with the Soviet Union,' he wrote to Mussolini on the eve of *Barbarossa*, 'seemed to me to be a break with my whole origin, my concepts, and my former obligations. I am happy now to be delivered from this torment.'

Delayed by the campaign in Yugoslavia and Greece, Hitler had rescheduled *Barbarossa* from 22nd June. Troop concentration for it was camouflaged in an elaborate double bluff as a feint for the invasion of Britain. On 14th June Hitler reviewed plans with his commanders for the attack at which, he had earlier promised, 'the world will hold its breath.' Though some of the generals had questioned the wisdom of the tremendous operation, and the ambivalent Halder, while striving to ensure its success, faithfully confided his reservations to his diary, this time no doubts were expressed. The generals shared Hitler's confidence in a speedy victory. This was based on Hitler's belief that 'we have only to kick in the door and the whole rotten structure will come crashing down.' This in turn led to an astonishing neglect of positive political planning beyond, that is, exploitation in the interests of the *Reich*. As Hitler's strategy was geared to a rapid destruction of Soviet forces, all that was required was a set of rules for administration of the occupied territories and the eradication of 'undesirables' in the occupied areas. The army was instructed to concern itself only with a limited area behind the front lines. For the rest Alfred Rosenberg, the Balt-born former editor of the *Völkische Beobachter* and author of *The Myth of the Twentieth*

Century, was named in April to direct all questions of the 'east European space.' Characteristically, a few weeks earlier Hitler had already given to Himmler (since 1939 *Reich* Commissioner for the Strengthening of German-ism, with virtually unlimited authority to adjust the map of Europe ethnically and demographically) a blank cheque to act 'independently and on his own responsibility . . . in the preparation for political administration,' accountable to no one but the *Führer*. Between these two the struggle for power was to become increasingly intense, with the army, the Foreign Office, and other agencies also competing for influence.

By 21st June about three million troops were assembled along a 2,000-mile front close to the Soviet border. The 153 German divisions included 19 *Panzer* and 15 motorized—all that fuel and equipment would permit—and were supported by 2,700 aircraft. Six Rumanian divisions were included in Rundstedt's Army Group South which was to strike south of the Pripet Marshes, through the Ukraine to the Black Sea and towards the Caucasus. The *Schwerpunkt* lay to the north. Here von Bock's Army Group Centre was to strike through Minsk and Smolensk towards Moscow, while von Leeb's Army Group North was to clear the Baltic states and, with the assistance of the Finns, seize Leningrad and prepare for a gigantic pincer movement enveloping Moscow.

At 4 a.m. on 22nd June 1941 Ambassador Schulenburg in Moscow and Foreign Minister von Ribbentrop in Berlin handed over notes charging that the Soviet Union had 'intensified its attempts to undermine Germany and Europe' and had 'concentrated all its forces in readiness at the German border.' Even before these diplomatic formalities were concluded German artillery had opened up and the great attack began with a rapid push over the frontier. Though the Russians had taken various precautionary measures they had not expected a *Blitzkrieg* and were caught completely unprepared. Many important bridges were captured intact and, as in Poland two years earlier, hundreds of aircraft were destroyed on the ground.

With his allies—Rumania, Italy, Finland, and Hungary—Hitler's 'grand alliance' outnumbered the Soviet Union and far exceeded it in war potential. The fate of the Soviet Union and of Hitler's hopes for speedy victory depended in no small measure on the reaction of Japan and the Anglo-Saxon powers. Instead of plunging into the Russian rear Japan pursued its plans for south-ward expansion; and Hitler's fate was sealed when Churchill instantly and unequivocally pledged British aid, and the United States pledged 'all economic assistance practicable.' In 1939 Hitler had provoked a European war; in 1941 he became involved in a world one.

Still, the consequences lay in the future. And in the summer of 1941 few competent observers, in the *Reich* or in the West, believed that the Soviet Union could survive more than a few weeks. Armoured divisions drove deep into Russian territory, encircled Russian armies, inflicted heavy casualties, captured hundreds of thousands of prisoners. But the Russians fought tenaciously even when encircled. As Halder wrote in his diary on 11th August, 'we underestimated the strength of the Russian Colossus.' Fresh divisions were thrown in to replace those lost, and the Germans, fighting ever farther from supply bases and without customary air supremacy, met in the T34 a tank off which their anti-tank shells burst harmlessly. By 8th September von Leeb, together with the Finns, began the siege of Leningrad, whose fall appeared imminent. By mid July von Bock had advanced to Smolensk, only 200 miles west of Moscow. Even more striking were the successes in the south, where von Rundstedt drove rapidly towards Kiev and the Dnieper. Hitler became obsessed with Leningrad and the sweeping victories in the Ukraine and rejected the army's plan for a decisive blow towards Moscow, the centre of the Russian road and rail network. He ordered elements of von Bock's forces northward to assist in the assault on Leningrad and others southward beyond the Pripet marshes to assist von Rundstedt's encirclement east of Kiev. In what Hitler termed 'the greatest battle of world history' 665,000 prisoners were taken. But Hitler had committed a costly strategic blunder. By the time the battle east of Kiev ended autumn rains turned the poor Russian roads into quagmires.

Winter was thus perilously close when, on 2nd October, von Bock's forces, reinforced by the armoured divisions recalled from the south, resumed the drive towards Moscow in what Hitler called 'the last great battle of the year.' Relentlessly the Germans drove towards the capital while Hitler proclaimed that 'the enemy in the east has been struck down and will never rise again.' But even while Hitler belatedly agreed to the all-out attack against Moscow, he again dispersed the German effort. Von Leeb was ordered to take Leningrad, which, Hitler said, he had decided to have 'wiped off the face of the earth.' In the south von Rundstedt was ordered to clear the Black Sea coast and strike eastward of Rostov to the Volga and the Caucasus. Leningrad continued to resist with courage and endurance, and though Army Group South managed to seize Rostov on 21st November, five days later it was forced out in a headlong retreat which cost Rundstedt his command. By the end of October German spearheads were sixty-five miles from Moscow and the pincers were beginning to close round the city. But the Russians fought tenaciously, and with the unexpectedly early onset of winter (the first snow fell on 6th October) German troops, lacking either winter clothing or equipment thanks to Hitler's gamble on a quick campaign, suffered cruelly. By the end of November casualties amounted to 750,000, almost a quarter of the force originally committed. The sub-zero weather caused thousands of cases of frostbite, froze fuel, immobilized tanks and guns. No one who fought before Moscow in the winter of 1941–2 and survived was likely to forget the experience. Elements of von Kluge's Fourth Army actually penetrated the suburbs and caught sight of the Kremlin towers on 2nd December, but were forced to pull back. By 5th December the last reserves had been committed and the attack had broken down. 'All the sacrifices and endurance of our brave troops had been in vain,' wrote Guderian. 'We had suffered a grievous defeat.'

As German forces pulled back Hitler announced that operations would close down for the winter. But on 6th December Zhukov launched a massive counter-attack on a two-hundred-mile front with a hundred fresh divisions trained and equipped to fight in the sub-zero temperatures of the Moscow front. The exhausted German armies faced the terrible prospect of the disaster which overwhelmed the Grande Armée in 1812. Hitler met his generals' counsel of a retreat to prepared positions with the order 'No withdrawal,' and dismissed and disgraced commanders who retreated in defiance of orders. His action undoubtedly saved the army from disintegration, but at terrible cost. It was accompanied by a further critical stage in the subordination of the army to the *Führer*'s will. On 19th December he announced that he was taking over active command from von Brauchitsch. 'The little affair of operational command,' he told Halder, 'is something that anyone can do.' The front was stabilized a hundred miles west of the capital. But *Barbarossa* was dead, and with it the overwhelming offensive power of the Third *Reich*. As Halder commented, 'The myth of the invincibility of the German Army was broken.'

The war in the East and the grandiose prospects of constructing a new empire out of the conquered lands absorbed all Hitler's thoughts and energies, and helped to accentuate the turn of the *Reich* Government from 'a cabinet to a court' and to make of the *Reich* administration ever more 'a confusion of private empires, private armies, and private intelligence services.' [1] In the second half of 1941 control by the Party was tightened up and it was given 'supervisory powers over, and sometimes executive function within, the state administration.' On Goebbels's urging Hitler summoned the *Reichstag* in April 1942, and from it secured a formal assertion of his right 'without being tied to existing legal regulations' to appoint, dismiss, or punish any German who failed in his duty as Hitler interpreted it. Two months earlier he had had the good fortune to appoint, as Minister for Armament and Munitions, the able Albert Speer, who soon became the virtual dictator of German war production and who, together with Fritz Saukel, the Plenipotentiary General for Manpower, greatly increased a falling labour force and produced a sensational rise in German war production.

The triumph of Party over army in the winter of 1941–2 was paralleled by the enhanced position of the S.S. By the mid thirties the ambition of Himmler and Heydrich to amalgamate the S.S. with the various police forces had resulted in the absorption of the (state) *Gestapo* into the S.S. and its virtual union with the (Party) S.D. under Heydrich's *Reichssicherheitshauptamt* (R.S.H.A.). It was this office which directed the formidable network of agencies which terrorized wartime Germany and the occupied countries with its arbitrary arrests, tortures, and separate system of courts. The purpose of the concentration camps, divided from January 1941 into three classes 'according to the personality of the prisoner and the degree of his danger to the state,' was changed increasingly to the employment of their inmates in private industry or in mammoth works constructed and owned by the S.S. 'This employment,' Himmler decreed in the spring of 1942, 'must be, in the true meaning of the words, exhaustive. . . . There is no limit to working hours.'

[1] H. R. Trevor-Roper, *The Last Days of Hitler* (London, 1952), p. 10.

HITLER AND MUSSOLINI REVIEWING TROOPS

FIELD MARSHAL ERWIN ROMMEL

FIELD MARSHAL HERMANN GOERING

With the infamous *Nacht und Nebel* decree of 7th December 1941 the *Gestapo*, which had long been an adjunct of criminal justice, became an adjunct of military rule as well, as the severest measures were decreed for quelling opposition in occupied territories. The Armed or *Waffen* S.S. was also constantly enlarged, so that it grew from a small praetorian guard to a force of close on a million men, designed after battle seasoning to act as a 'military State police' and probably, after victory, as the standing army.

The attack on Russia in the summer of 1941 was combined with the idea of using this formidable weapon of terror to exterminate the Jewish population. During the first year of the war the miseries of German Jews had been intensified. Many smaller cities expelled their Jewish communities and proudly proclaimed themselves *judenrein*. In Poland Heydrich's men had encouraged pogroms and a quarter of a million Jews were murdered by the end of 1939. To prepare space for the return of Germans from the Baltic state, half a million Jews were expelled from the western Polish provinces incorporated into the *Reich* and crowded first into a reservation around Lublin and then into the Government General and, later, into the ghettos of Warsaw and Lodz. Plans for the 'final solution' were evolved in the summer of 1941. The '*Führer* Order' for the extermination of the Jews was communicated to those responsible for its execution orally and in stages.' On 31st July, six weeks after the invasion began, Goering charged Heydrich to make 'all necessary preparations [to bring about] a complete solution of the Jewish question in the German sphere of influence in Europe.' The R S.H.A. went into operation immediately. In mid June Himmler had already authorized the construction of the great gas chambers at Auschwitz which were to set their mark on the whole operation. The *Gestapo* began the preparation of the mass deportations to the East, with responsibility falling chiefly on a little-known major of the S.S., Adolf Eichmann. Not until the spring of 1942, however, were the killing facilities in the extermination camps ready. But close behind the German armies rolling eastward into the Soviet Union moved four *Einsatzgruppen*, composed of efficient killers who rounded up and shot Jews still dazed by the battle passing over their heads. By November their victims numbered half a million. For his larger operation Heydrich had run into a maze of knotty problems. These were smoothed out at a conference of high civil servants from various ministries which he assembled in Berlin on 20th January 1942. To this Wannsee meeting Heydrich explained that responsibility for the final solution of the Jewish question lay without regard to geographical boundaries with him as *Reichsführer* S.S. and Chief of the German police, and outlined the manner in which Europe would be 'combed from West to East,' the weakest allowed to die in the mass labour columns, the survivors 'treated accordingly,' and a few of the aged sent to the privileged Theresienstadt camp.

While the curtain was gradually being lifted on the 'Final Solution,' the Nazi 'New Order' was taking shape in the conquered Soviet territories. The assault had been preceded by agreement on little more than overthrowing the Soviet regime, securing some economic advantages, and annexing some

O

Soviet territory. Not until 25th November 1941, at the 'first European Congress,' as the Wilhelmstrasse termed it, was the New Order identified with the anti-Bolshevik 'crusade' in the East. In a basic decree of 17th July Rosenberg was named to head the *Ostministerium*, responsible for the administration of all the territories except those to be incorporated into Germany, Rumania, or Finland. Six weeks later Hitler turned over to civil rule the two *Reich* Commissariats: Ostland, including the Baltic states and Byelorussia; and the Ukraine, stretching to the Black Sea. As Rosenberg's deputy and Commissioner for the Ukraine he named Erich Koch, a known opponent of Rosenberg's policy of encircling the hated Muscovy with a ring of satellites accorded some degree of local autonomy. Koch's appointment ushered in an era of terror and oppression, so that his name became a symbol of German brutality and stupidity in the East. Hinrich Lohse, Commissioner for the Ostland, though less fanatical, was no less determined to strive for an empire independent of Berlin, so that, he said, his son could 'some day put the hereditary ducal crown on his head.' Though the picture of a wellnigh unanimous welcome from the population of the western periphery of the Soviet Union is overdrawn, it seems clear that 'a skilful effort to win the population, civilian and military alike, to oppose the Soviet regime could have yielded substantial, and during the first months of the war perhaps decisive, results.'[1] But this advantage was thrown away; and by the end of 1941 German policy was marked beyond reversal by the dismay and terror spread by the *Einsatzgruppen*, and by the wholesale deaths of prisoners of war, either by outright murder or through neglect.

The end of 1941 ushered in a new phase of the war. While 1940 had ended in a strategic question mark, with brilliant success succeeded by stalemate, by the end of 1941 the *Wehrmacht* had sustained its first major defeat. Its significance was to some extent obscured by the renewed tide of victory in 1942. Ironically, however, at precisely the same time as the *Wehrmacht* was being driven back from the gates of Moscow, Hitler took a step which sealed the ultimate doom of the Third *Reich*. Evidently giving vent to hitherto suppressed resentment and underestimating American strength, Hitler went far beyond the obligations of the Tripartite Pact and on 11th December declared war against the United States. Once the rapidly mobilizing U.S. power could be applied, German resources would be overwhelmed and defeat brought sooner and made more certain.

That critical winter Hitler's attention was still directed to the Russian front. Despite his 'no withdrawal' orders the front was pushed steadily westward from Moscow, until by the end of March spring thaws brought a relative quiet to the whole line. The *Wehrmacht* had paid a terrible price. At the end of February Halder calculated German casualties at over a million, nearly one-third of the force originally committed. At the end of March only eight of 162 divisions were ready for offensive action, and the sixteen armoured divisions had only 140 serviceable tanks.

---

[1] Alexander Dallin, *German Rule in Russia, 1941–1945: A Study of Occupation Policies* (London, 1957), p. 65.

Even before the Russian winter offensive had been checked, Hitler's thoughts were turning to the campaigns for 1942. In the east his main effort was to be in the south: a drive between Kursk and the Sea of Azov to break into the Caucasus, and seize its oil and to wrest from Russian hands the industries of the Volga. For all his boasting that 'the Russian Colossus will be fought by us until he is smashed,' gone now was the confidence of an easy victory. 'We Germans have everything to win in this struggle,' he warned the *Reichstag*, 'for the loss of this war would be simply the end of us.' Before the eastern front broke into full fury again, Hitler was rewarded by a striking series of victories elsewhere. As part of Raeder's plan to pierce the British-held Middle East and link up with Japan, the *Afrika Korps* drove eastward and by the end of June had reached El Alamein, only sixty-five miles from Alexandria. In the Atlantic, Doenitz's U-boat fleet, now built up to nearly 250, was ravaging American waters virtually uncontrolled. Though Allied counter-measures gradually improved, U-boat losses were exceeded by new construction. When pressed in one area Doenitz easily shifted the weight of his effort elsewhere. The toll of Allied shipping grew week by week, reaching a peak of 173 ships grossing 834,196 tons in July alone. Earlier a humiliating defeat had been inflicted on the British when the *Scharnhorst* and the *Gneisenau*, with the cruiser *Prinz Eugen*, escaped from Brest and, though damaged by air-laid mines, succeeded in reaching Norwegian waters after a daring daylight passage up the Channel. This concentration of the whole of German naval strength in what Hitler quixotically persisted in regarding as 'the zone of destiny in this war,' however, removed a potential threat to the convoys moving to assault North Africa in November.

The only cloud in the German sky in the spring of 1942 was the resumption by the R.A.F. of its offensive against centres such as Rostock and Lübeck, and especially the blows against the Ruhr and the Rhineland. On 30th May Cologne was hit by 1,046 bombers in a raid which tore vast holes in the inner city, sent smoke clouds spiralling five miles high, and rendered 45,000 people homeless. Thanks to the efficiency of the air defence organization and the stoicism displayed by the German people (similar to that of the British in 1940–1), help was brought in from the outside, and within a fortnight the city was functioning normally. German night fighters continued to exact a heavy toll, and British resources were not yet adequate for a sustained effort on this level.

Few of the difficulties presaged by stirring U.S. strength, anti-U-boat measures, or improvements in bombing techniques were discernible as the Nazi legions struck out in what was to be the last great conquering campaign of Hitler's war. Reinforced by fifty-two 'allied divisions'—constituting one-third of the force—striking successes were achieved. By mid July Russia again appeared on the brink of defeat. In the Crimea Kerch was retaken and Sebastopol seized. Farther north, after turning back a Russian spoiling offensive at Kharkov, the Germans attacked towards Voronezh on 28th June and then drove rapidly south-east between the Don and the Donetz. Despite strong Russian resistance List's Army Group A seized

Rostov on 24th July, crossed the Don at the end of the month, and raced on another 450 miles towards the Caucasus. By 8th August German forces had reached the destroyed ruins of the most westerly oilfield at Maikob. The swastika was hoisted over Mt Elbrus, the highest peak in the Caucasus, on 21st August. But the attempt to drive to Grozny, Baku, and the Caspian was beyond the strength of the over-extended German forces. More serious was the costly battle for Stalingrad which began in September after having been delayed by Hitler's dispatch of armour to assist the drive to the Caucasus and of Manstein and his siege train north to join in the assault on Leningrad. The cities named after the two giants of Bolshevik history exerted a fateful fascination for Hitler; at Stalingrad he became engaged in a battle of prestige which was to prove a turning point in the war.

By autumn 1942 Hitler was undisputed master of Europe from the Volga to the Channel, and stood on the threshold of the Caspian and the Nile. But El Alamein, Mt Elbrus, and Stalingrad represented the flood tide of Nazi conquest. The German advance had ground to a halt at Stalingrad, in the Caucasus, and in North Africa, and for the first time since he had proclaimed rearmament in 1935 the initiative passed from Hitler's hands. On 23rd October Montgomery's Eighth Army began the battle at El Alamein which in twelve days led to a break through the lines which Rommel, hastily recalled from sick leave in Austria, attempted vainly to hold. On the night of 7th–8th November Anglo-American forces landed on the coasts of Morocco and Algeria, and within a few days occupied the whole of French North Africa as far as the Tunisian frontier, threatening the rear of the *Afrika Korps* which Rommel, in defiance of Hitler's wishes, was drawing back rapidly beyond Benghazi. On 19th and 20th November, when Paulus's Sixth Army had succeeded in capturing most of Stalingrad, the Russians launched powerful counter-attacks and within five days had encircled twenty-two divisions between the Volga and the Don.

Hitler's response to the surprise Allied landing in North Africa (which found him *en route* to Munich for the annual speech commemorating the 1923 rising) could delay but not defeat Allied plans. On 11th November the *Wehrmacht* invaded unoccupied France. Sixteen days later, as German mechanized units raced towards the harbour, the last great French fleet was scuttled at Toulon. Vichy France came to an end. , Hitler also poured supplies and troops into Tunisia with instructions to hold it at all costs. Gradually, however, the Germans were pushed into a gigantic trap. By 13th May 1943 the last surrendered. The vain attempt to deny the Allies the free use of the Mediterranean had cost 250,000 prisoners.

In the east the siege of Leningrad was partially lifted on 18th January 1943, and at Stalingrad the *Wehrmacht* suffered a more significant defeat. From late November the net around the encircled Sixth Army was steadily tightened, as Manstein's effort to open a corridor was defeated and Hitler refused permission for Paulus to abandon the Volga and drive to meet the relieving force. Ultimately, on 31st January, with his ammunition virtually expended, the toll of wounded and frostbitten mounting catastrophically, and the remains of his force exhausted by the prolonged and senseless resistance, Paulus at last disobeyed the *Führer*'s call to the Sixth Army to 'do its historic duty at Stalingrad until the last man' and surrendered. Of its original strength of 220,000, some 30,000 or 40,000 wounded had been evacuated by air. Those who remained either fell in battle or were marched eastwards to the prison camps from which it has been estimated no more than 5,000 returned.

This disaster, with the defeat in North Africa, marked a turning point in the war. With them the offensive power of the *Wehrmacht* had been dissipated, and the tide of conquest was never to flow in its direction again. Gradually the ring was tightened as the Third *Reich* was crushed under the rain of ever-intensifying blows. Despite Goebbels's attempt to paint the disaster in heroic colours, the confidence of the German people was shaken not only in the *Führer*'s military genius but in his humanity. The names and addresses of 90,000 German prisoners were broadcast by Soviet radio and carried into many German homes. Deep depression settled over the *Reich*, and for the first time doubt and despondency spread among high military and civilian official circles as well as through the civilian population. To many Hitler was now revealed as a megalomaniac corporal, whose ambition demanded the cold-blooded destruction of thousands of his loyal subjects.

When the inevitability of disaster on the Volga was realized, the leaders of the conspiracy attempted to effect the *Putsch* which Hitler's earlier victories had precluded. For a time they pinned their hopes on Paulus, but he neither committed suicide in response to Hitler's wishes nor gave the signal for revolt as the conspirators hoped. In the universities Stalingrad made a deep impression. In Munich students howled down the *Gauleiter* of Bavaria and demonstrated in the streets. On 19th February, encouraged to believe that they were giving the signal for revolt, Sophie Scholl and her brother, students deeply influenced by the moral and religious idealism of the Catholic Professor Kurt Huber, scattered leaflets which Huber had himself drafted proclaiming that 'the name of Germany will be sullied for ever unless German youth now at last rises to crush its tormentors and to restore the spirit of Europe.' The sequel was swift and brutal. Condemned to death three days later by the People's Court under the notorious Friesler himself, they were hanged within a few hours. That evening on the walls of many Munich houses appeared the inscription '*Ihr Geist lebt weiter.*'

The student group had no direct connection with the conspirators, but these too were stirred by Stalingrad into new life. General Friedrich Olbricht, the strategically placed Chief of the *Allgemeines Heeresamt*, agreed to work with Oster in building up troops of the Home Army ready to take control following a *Putsch*. The opposition of Beck and Goerdeler to the assassination of Hitler—partly on moral grounds, partly out of fear of a new stab-in-the back legend—was largely overcome. When in March 1943 Hitler was lured from the unapproachable and strongly guarded *Wolfsschanze* near Rastenburg in East Prussia, to von Kluge's headquarters near Smolensk, two gallant officers—Fabian von Schlabrendorff and Henning von Tresckow—contrived to place a time-bomb disguised as bottles of brandy in Hitler's plane. For some mysterious reason it failed to go off. The plotters resumed their planning. But the *Gestapo*, never far behind, raided Oster's office soon afterwards. A number of valued conspirators were arrested—Dietrich Bonhoeffer, Joseph Müller, Hans von Dohnanyi. Oster and Canaris were too compromised to be of further use, Hammerstein died, and Beck was incapacitated by illness. Leadership fell to Goerdeler, with only Olbricht as his military organizer.

In the east the prolongation of the war necessitated some degree of concession in order to achieve a minimum *modus vivendi* behind the German lines. In the process the contest over *Ostpolitik* became increasingly bitter. Though in 1941 Hitler had welcomed Soviet proclamation of partisan warfare as enabling the eradication of any opponents, by mid 1942 the partisan force had reached a strength of well over 100,000. Systematically supplied with Soviet aid, and skilfully taking advantage of difficult terrain and the relative scarcity of German troops, the force was sufficient to create, in Stalin's phrase, 'a second front in the enemy's rear.'[1] Farther back, when Heydrich was murdered by Czech partisans in June 1942, Lidice was razed to the ground and some 1,700 summarily executed as a revenge. The constant and barely concealed aim of Nazi policy was to exploit the East for the benefit of the *Reich*. With the bombing of the homeland and the steady using up of men and materials, the pressure of demand on the East increased. But the amounts of food which the Germans extracted fell short of expectations, and most went to feed the armies in the east. The rewards in raw materials were little better. Besides this failure to make the East contribute substantially to the German war effort, it was ironical that despite the claim that the *Reich* was over-populated, Germany had no one available for migration to the new *Lebensraum*, and had to resort to uprooted ethnic Germans in the limited resettlement operations which were possible before Stalingrad signalled retreat. Like the occupied countries in the west, Russia was turned into a vast labour camp. Nearly two million Russians were seized and transported hundreds of miles to the west, often horribly treated and suffering cruelly, especially in the most heavily bombed centres.

All through 1942 and 1943 S.S. trucks rumbled through Berlin and other cities, collecting human freight for the concentration and extermination camps. From France, Belgium, Holland, from Germany, Austria, and Czechoslovakia, from Hungary and the Balkans the transports moved eastward and northward. During the early months of 1942, immediately after the Wannsee conference, the character of the 'appropriate treatment' was not yet clear. By spring the ambiguity was resolved with the erection of the gas-chamber camps in Poland: Treblinka, Lublin, Belzec, and the rest. In the centre of the huge crescent from which the victims were drawn stood Auschwitz. Here under the energetic direction of Rudolf Höss highly efficient killing installations were devised by which 2,000 people could be exterminated by Zyklon B (hydrogen cyanide) within four minutes.

As hopes of speedy victory ended and the war was extended in June and

---

[1] Ibid., p. 209.

December 1941 the pressure of the system on the German people increased. Gürtner, the Minister of Justice, who was only nominally a Nazi, died in 1941. After Hitler's speech on 26th April 1942, and the subsequent resolution placing him above the law, the radicals led by Goebbels, Thierack, Friesler, and the S.S. organ, *Das Schwarze Korps*, intensified their demand for a complete subordination of justice to the ends of Nazi policy. Though in August Hitler appointed Thierack, formerly president of the People's Court, to succeed Gürtner with instructions to build up 'a National Socialist administration of justice' in agreement with Bormann, the protests of the traditional judiciary were never completely silenced. Belts on the home front were also progressively tightened. As early as 1941 Christmas greetings were banned, many small businesses were closed down, and conscription was ordered for agriculture. The German diet was monotonous and not very palatable, but the distribution system succeeded in dividing a not too adequate food supply reasonably satisfactorily, and sickness and absenteeism were the result of overwork and the dislocation of life under the air bombardment rather than the lack of foodstuffs.

The draft age was lowered in the summer of 1942 from eighteen to seventeen, and with the disaster at Stalingrad Saukel undertook a new manpower comb-out with a decree compelling all men and women employed less than forty-eight hours to register for war work. Two days later a further closing of small businesses and factories was ordered. On 30th January 1943, the tenth anniversary of the seizure of power, a proclamation was issued declaring that 'the force of the National Socialist idea' would 'hold everyone to the fulfilment of his duties and would annihilate everyone who tried to shrink from those duties.' The German labour force reached its peak at the beginning of 1943, despite further mobilization for the armed forces. Speer, in continual conflict with Saukel, succeeded in raising production of armaments 55 per cent between February and July 1942. Civilian production was cut back and total production for 1942 was 50 per cent higher than in 1941.

The efforts of Speer and Saukel to increase war production, and of Goebbels to sustain German morale, ensured that the disasters of the autumn and winter of 1942–3 were not followed by immediate collapse. The year 1943 was to be a year of almost continuous defeat for the *Reich*, as the Allies fought towards the borders of Germany, and prepared the way for the decisive campaigns of 1944 and 1945. A Russian attempt to cut off the dangerously exposed German forces in the Caucasus was defeated by a skilfully conducted retreat, but Kursk fell on 8th February and Rostov a week later. When winter yielded to spring, and a lull settled over the front, the Germans had been pushed over the Don and the Donetz, and the line stabilized from Leningrad via Smolensk and Kharkov to the Sea of Azov west of Rostov, still deep in Russian territory. The sinister silence lasted until 5th July, when the Germans launched their most powerful armoured assault against the Russian salient at Kursk with a force of 500,000 men, including seventeen armoured divisions equipped with the formidable new Tiger tank. Within ten days, having achieved only local success, the attack was broken off in the

face of the Russian summer offensive which had been coolly launched on 12th
July, in the midst of the Kursk battle, against the salient covering the great
'hedgehog' farther north at Orel.   Orel fell on 4th August.   A day earlier
the Russians had attacked at Kharkov, and by September the *Wehrmacht*
was in general retreat.   Smolensk fell on 25th September, the Donetz Basin
was lost, German forces in the Crimea were cut off, and Russian forces surged
across the Dnieper.   Kiev, of immense political significance, was abandoned
by the Germans on 6th November.   By December the weakened German
armies stood westward of the Dnieper, vulnerable to the winter campaign at
which the Russians had proved so effective.

More dramatic than this steady pressing back and consuming of German
military power were the events in 1943 in the Mediterranean.   On 10th July,
two months after the end of the costly campaign in Tunisia, and while the
Kursk offensive was at its height, Allied forces landed on the beaches of Sicily.
By 17th August the island had been seized, 150,000 prisoners taken, and only
the narrow Messina Straits separated the invaders from the European mainland.   Hitler sought to stiffen the resistance of the Italians, about whose
reliability he had increasing doubts.   Unmistakable evidence that Italy had
lost the war cost the Duce the support of powerful forces, including the Crown,
the army and the bureaucracy which had hitherto profited from it.   On 25th
July, spurred on by Mussolini's failure to disengage from the impending fate
of the *Reich*, and by a massive precision bombing attack on Rome's freight
yards by the entire Allied Mediterranean strategic air force, the King dismissed Mussolini, placed him under arrest, and formed a non-fascist government under the aged Marshal Badoglio.

What Goebbels described as these 'almost unbelievable' events afforded
too obvious a precedent for Germany, and constituted a pattern which many
of the anti-Hitler conspirators had dreamed of repeating.   Hitler realized
that Badoglio's proclamation that 'the war continues' concealed preparations
for a separate peace, and he determined to secure Italy with German forces,
rescue Mussolini, and reconstitute the fascist state.   When Allied forces
crossed the Straits of Messina on 3rd September German preparations
were ready.   On 8th September news of an armistice, concluded five days
earlier with Marshal Badoglio, was made public.   The next day Allied
forces landed in the Bay of Naples.   Speedily the sixteen German divisions
south of the Alps disarmed the much more numerous Italian formations
and, aided by the fact that the Allies had landed no farther north than
Salerno, seized Rome and secured two-thirds of Italy, including the industrial
north.   An 'Italian Social Republic' was created under the puppet leadership of Mussolini, who had been rescued in a spectacular airborne operation
from his place of imprisonment high in the Abruzzi Mountains.   By energy,
determination and luck Hitler had retrieved a dangerous situation and
had set the stage for prolonging resistance in the south for another year and
a half.

In the west 1943 saw the Germans lose the Battle of the Atlantic.   At the
start of the year Doenitz (who had replaced Raeder as Commander in Chief in

January) had 212 operational U-boats and was able to keep 100 constantly at sea. Hunting in packs they claimed a heavy toll, reaching a total of nearly 700,000 tons in March, of which over three-quarters were in the Atlantic alone. By increasing use of radar, the closing of the air surveillance gap south-east of Greenland, and persistent air attacks on U-boats in transit in the Bay of Biscay, the Allies swiftly changed the outlook. In April 235 U-boats the greatest number ever achieved, were in action, but in May forty fell victim to Allied counter-measures in the Atlantic, and by June Allied shipping losses fell to the lowest figure since the United States entered the war. At the end of May Doenitz was forced to withdraw his fleet from the North Atlantic for rest or for battle in less hazardous waters. Kept under water and continuously harried, the toll taken by Allied aircraft and naval forces steadily mounted. When the U-boats returned in September in a determined bid to regain ascendancy in the North Atlantic, they succeeded in sinking no more than sixty-seven vessels at the prohibitive cost of sixty-four submarines. 'The enemy holds every trump card, covering all areas with long-range air patrols and using location methods against which we still have no warning,' wrote Doenitz despairingly on 12th November.

More obvious to the individual German was the steadily increasing weight of the air bombardment directed on his cities and the mounting level of destruction and casualties. With the growing strength of the U.S. daylight bomber force, trained and equipped for precision attacks, and by late 1943 protected to the most distant target by long-range fighters, German cities came increasingly under almost continuous day as well as night attack. Throughout 1943 the greatest weight of bombs was delivered at night by the R.A.F. From March to July attacks centred on the Ruhr, beginning with highly destructive blows on Essen and the Krupp complex, and including two heavy attacks on Dortmund, where destruction, Goebbels noted in his diary, was 'virtually total.' From July to November Hamburg received a greater weight of bombing than any other city at this time. In four major raids over 3,000 bombers dropped nearly 9,000 tons of bombs in a skilfully devised pattern which produced simultaneous fires over a large area. The result was the unique and terrible phenomenon of fire-storm, which, with the rush of air produced by the intense heat, rendered useless the normal means of defence and trapped thousands in shelters which had become furnaces, where they were burnt or, more mercifully, asphyxiated. 'The catastrophes of Chicago and San Francisco,' the Police President reported, '. . . pale beside the extent and uniqueness of the Hamburg fire. . . . Its horror is revealed in the howling and raging of the fire-storms, the hellish noise of the exploding bombs, and the death cries of martyred human beings as well as in the big silence after the raids.' [1] From Hamburg the attacks shifted to Berlin, but here the distance gave German night fighters more opportunity to attack enemy bombers, and the destruction was less severe.

In 1943, 200,000 people were killed in bombing attacks; from March 1943

[1] Sir Charles Webster and Noble Frankland, *The Strategic Air Offensive Against Germany* (London, 1961), vol. iv, p. 314.

to March 1944 (when the weight of attack was transferred briefly to targets of more direct relevance to the forthcoming invasion) an estimated 212,000 buildings were destroyed. Worse was to come as German air defences crumbled in the summer of 1944. Yet German cities were neither destroyed nor paralysed by these aerial blows. Even in Hamburg, where production was for a month reduced by half, much was gradually restored. Throughout the country armament production was not only maintained but increased in the first half of 1943, and after levelling off rose steeply again in the first half of 1944, with spectacular increases in tanks and, after February 1944, in fighter aircraft. This was due mainly to the reorganization of German armament production which Speer had almost completed by mid 1944, despite the opposition of Bormann, Goebbels, Saukel, and Himmler, though he never succeeded in eliminating the large quantities of unnecessary consumer goods which were being produced almost to the end of the war. But it also owed much to the German (and foreign) worker, who endured the appalling ordeal of bombing with stoicism, courage, and even heroism, and who, as Speer said in 1944, 'after every attack, even after his own dwelling had been heavily damaged, was again at his place of work within three days at the most.'[1]

Yet German leadership was concerned about the impact on morale. 'A great deal of unrest has been created in Berlin,' Goebbels noted in his diary on 29th July 1943. 'The state of depression because of air-raids has increased as a result of the most recent heavy attacks,' he wrote on 11th September. The eastern front was also 'causing the German people considerably greater worry,' and the fall of Mussolini had made them 'uneasy and distressed.' Yet Hitler's broadcast speech of 10th September—his first since Memorial Day—coupled with the dramatic rescue of the Duce and the capture of Rome acted, so Goebbels noted, 'like champagne on the people.' 'Morale . . . at present is excellent,' he wrote in mid November. It was not only propaganda but an intensification of terror which prevented the rot. Frick, the aged and ineffectual *Reich* Minister of the Interior, was succeeded by Himmler, who went about the task with customary ruthlessness. Critics of the war or of Hitler's conduct of it were proceeded against with 'unflinching determination,' as nearly two thousand death sentences were imposed for 'high treason' within the next year, and energetic measures were instituted against backsliders inside the Party itself.

By the end of 1943, as Halder later wrote, it was 'unmistakably clear that the war had been lost,' and the question was now whether the inevitable defeat would amount to complete destruction as well. Hitler refused to contemplate any initiative to escape from the war. Bringing German foreign policy to a complete state of paralysis, his only prescription was to wait—wait for the chance of military victory in the field before embarking on negotiations, while pinning his hopes on secret weapons to turn the tide or on the break-up of the Allied coalition. More realistic than his *Führer*, Goebbels recognized that Germany would not be able 'in the long run' to

[1] Ibid., vol. ii, p. 225.

stand the two-front war, and that 'sooner or later we shall have to face the question of inclining toward one enemy or the other.' But Hitler refused to respond to overtures which appear to have been made by the Soviet Union, and Goebbels distorted the Casablanca formula of unconditional surrender to persuade the Germans that the Allies intended to destroy them and so lashed them into continued resistance.

While the effect of the unconditional surrender formula on the resistance has been variously estimated, it did not deter the conspirators from making desperate efforts to eliminate Hitler and avert the catastrophe to which he was manifestly leading the *Reich*. In October 1943 the conspiracy acquired its first natural leader in Lieutenant-Colonel Claus Schenk von Stauffenberg. Possessed of a passionate hatred of Hitler, he was shocked into resistance not by the impact of defeat but by an opposition to totalitarianism which had a deep spiritual and Christian basis. Young, daring, and dynamic, despite crippling wounds he had received in the desert, he galvanized the opposition into fresh activity. Building on the plans of Tresckow and Olbricht, by November he had worked out detailed plans for a *coup*. Inclining politically to the left, and with close links to the Kreisau Circle of Helmut von Moltke, Stauffenberg was responsible for the fact that the projected, broadly based interim government with Beck as Regent and Goerdeler as Chancellor should include the socialist Leuschner as Vice-Chancellor and Julius Leber as Minister of the Interior. Though Goerdeler still opposed political assassination, von Hassell spoke for the majority when, on 27th December, he wrote prophetically that 'with Hitler the war will be lost because it will be fought to a catastrophic end by both sides,' and underlined that only by Hitler's elimination could a way to end the conflict be opened. It became increasingly difficult to get near the *Führer* in view of tight security provisions. A series of attempts at assassination were made but all failed. Meanwhile, in January 1944 the *Gestapo* penetrated a peripheral group known as the Solf Kreis. The subsequent arrests included von Moltke, and provided an opportunity for the dismissal of Canaris, whose *Abwehr* had long provided a tent for the conspirators, and also opened the way for Hitler and Himmler to create a new Party-dominated intelligence service under Kaltenbrunner.

Time was thus running out for the conspirators, as the *Gestapo* was hot on the trail and the military situation was becoming increasingly menacing. Despite fierce resistance at Salerno the Allied foothold was made good and British and Canadian forces, moving up from the 'toe,' linked up with the bridgehead. Kesselring was able to check the Allied advance north of Naples, but the important Foggia airfields from which Rumanian oilfields as well as targets in Austria and southern Germany could be bombed had been lost, and Hitler was obliged to maintain valuable divisions not only in the line but in northern Italy against possible seaborne landings. An Allied attempt to turn his winter or Gustav line, running from Carigliano to the Sangro, with a landing farther up the coast at Anzio, was coolly met by Kesselring by sealing off the bridgehead. It was not until 11th May that a concentrated assault pierced the line at Cassino and, savagely punished by the

Allied air forces, the Germans were driven back.   On 4th June 1944 the Allies entered Rome, the first European capital to be liberated.

In the East the Russian winter offensive, which opened on Christmas Eve, gave the Germans little respite.   On 27th January 1944 the siege of Leningrad was definitely lifted and the advance pursued to the frontier of Esthonia. Farther south the Russians attacked south of the Pripet Marshes and early in January were over the Polish frontier.   In March and April the whole of the southern Ukraine was recaptured, the isolated Crimea was cleared (with Sebastopol being taken on 9th May), and the Germans were pushed westward over the Bug and the Dniester.   When the thaw came Soviet armies stood in Rumania and a hundred miles into Poland.   By the end of May the outlook was bleak, and with the opening of the Russian summer offensive disaster ensued.   The first Russian attacks on 10th June were aimed at driving Finland from the war.   A fortnight later, almost exactly three years after Hitler had launched *Barbarossa*, strong forces broke through between Vitebsk and Gomel in White Russia, captured Minsk on 6th July, and reached the Niemen at Grodno by the end of July.   South of the Pripet Marshes the whole German front was broken as the Russians drove over the San and crossed the upper Vistula at Sandomir.   When the Russian forces paused for regrouping they were threatening to break into East Prussia and to encircle the divisions in the Baltic states.

On 6th June 1944, two days after the loss of Rome and in the midst of the lull on the eastern front front which preceded the Russian summer offensive, came the long heralded Allied assault in the West.   That a cross-Channel invasion was on the Allied programme had long been apparent to the Germans, but where and when the blow would fall remained in doubt.   In the the spring of 1944 the assembly of troops in England, the concentration of shipping, the shift of strategic bombing to the French communication and transportation network all suggested that invasion was not far off, but for the most part German intelligence could only speculate on Allied plans, and became convinced that the main assault would be in the Calais-Boulogne area. The Germans had occupied the French coast since 1940, and Hitler's first directive for its fortification was dated 23rd March 1942.   Despite desperate efforts in the spring of 1944 to strengthen the 'Atlantic Wall,' on 6th June the defences of the shores of Normandy were 'a coastal ribbon, entirely without depth.' [1] Though in April and May 1944 Hitler insisted on strengthening German forces in Normandy and Brittany, the bulk of the troops which met the first weight of the Allied assault were inferior static divisions.   The German position was further weakened by a 'confused and chaotic' command organization.   Von Rundstedt, as Commander in Chief West, complained that his only authority was 'to change the guard in front of my gate.' Rommel, as Commander of Army Group B, with operational command over the Seventh Army in Normandy and the Fifteenth Army north of the Seine, also had and used the right of direct access to Hitler; various naval, air force,

---

[1] C. P. Stacey, *The Victory Campaign: The Operations in North-West Europe, 1944–1945. (Official History of the Canadian Army in the Second World War)* (Ottawa, 1960), p. 61.

and S.S. formations, though under Rundstedt's tactical control, were also under Doenitz, Goering, or Himmler; and the most efficient mobile reserves were placed in O.K.W. reserve and could not be moved except under the personal authority of Hitler.

When British, Canadian, and American forces landed on the beaches of the Bay of the Seine they achieved complete tactical and strategic surprise. Though it was heralded by a night of bombing and mass parachute landings, the Germans were slow to appreciate that this was the main effort, and for nearly two months continued to anticipate a further landing north of the Seine. When in mid afternoon Hitler's consent was belatedly given for the use of the precious armoured reserve, it was accompanied with the instruction that 'the enemy bridgehead be destroyed by the evening of 6th June.' This was not to be. The weight of the Allied attack, backed by strong naval and air bombardment, overwhelmed the coastal defences and drove rapidly inland. Within a week, despite powerful local counter-attacks, the bridgeheads were linked up and extended to a depth of twenty miles, and the invading forces were built up to 300,000 men. Faced with the fact that the Allies had made good their lodgement area, Rundstedt and Rommel confronted Hitler on 17th June at Margival near Soissons, in the command post which had been constructed for the invasion of Britain in 1940. But the two field commanders were unable to make him realize the seriousness of the situation. Despite bad weather in the Channel to their rear, the Allies cut the Cotentin Peninsula, seized Cherbourg on 26th June and battled into Caen on 9th July. In a further conference at the Obersalzburg on 29th June the Field Marshals again attempted to impress on Hitler that the line could not be held. But his reply was to order that 'the present positions are to be held,' and to replace Rundstedt by Kluge, with instructions to prevent the expected break-out towards Paris. Rommel survived, but not for long. On 15th July, two days before he was critically wounded by British aircraft, he wrote to Hitler that 'the situation in the Normandy front is growing worse and is approaching a grave crisis. . . . The troops are everywhere fighting heroically, but the unequal struggle is approaching its end.' With the Russian summer offensive in full swing, Hitler was threatened with a major crisis in the West at precisely the same time as in the East.

These imminent crises came at the moment when the resistance was struggling desperately to strike its most ambitious blow. Paradoxically, whereas earlier the conspirators felt powerless so long as Hitler rode the crest of victory, they had been anxious to strike before an Allied landing in the west so as to give their new government a reasonable lease of life and to avoid contributing to a stab-in-the-back legend. After 6th June the question was: To proceed or not? As disasters multiplied in the ensuing weeks some of the leaders felt that it was already too late. 'There is no deliverance,' Beck had told Friedrich Meinecke. 'We must now drain little by little the bitter cup to the bitterest end.' But von Tresckow's answer was unequivocal: 'The assassination must be attempted at any cost. Even should that fail, the attempt to seize power in the capital must be undertaken. We must prove to the world and to future generations that the men of the German resistance movement dared to take the decisive step and hazard their lives upon it. Compared with this object, nothing else matters.' A new accretion of strength was Rommel. His letter of 15th July, with its conclusion that 'it is urgently necessary for the proper conclusion to be drawn from this situation,' meant that if this last appeal to reason were rejected, as appeared certain, he, Kluge, and Stülpnagel, the three highest commanders in the West, would take 'independent action.' Rommel's opposition was military, not political; [1] and it was Tresckow's view that dignity and self-respect demanded action that drove the Berlin conspirators on. They were aided by Stauffenberg's appointment as Chief of Staff to the Home Army, which carried with it the opportunity to attend daily conferences at the *Führer*'s headquarters. The stunning blow of the arrest on 5th July of his friend Julius Leber determined him to undertake the assassination himself. After two unsuccessful attempts he succeeded on 20th July 1944 in the *Wolfsschanze* at Rastenburg in fusing the concealed bomb with a pair of tongs held in the three remaining fingers of his left hand, and unobtrusively left the room. A few minutes later a violent explosion shattered the conference building. Word of the success of the attempt was telephoned to Berlin, communications were interrupted for several hours, and Stauffenberg set off on the three-hour flight to Berlin to take charge of operations there which, unaccountably, had been delayed pending his arrival.

Though Stauffenberg's energy and determination at once set the plans in operation, the three or four hours' delay had seriously prejudiced an enterprise which depended for its success on rapid moves while Rastenburg was still paralysed by his act. It was condemned to failure when it became clear in Berlin that Hitler had survived. After Stauffenberg's departure the brief case containing the bomb had been inadvertently moved so that Hitler was protected by the stout oak supports of the conference table and received no more than a bad shaking up. Under the direction of Goebbels and Himmler the conspirators were rounded up. Olbricht and Stauffenberg were executed by firing squad in the courtyard of the Bendlerstrasse the same evening. Beck committed suicide. Many others were arrested. By dawn on 21st July the plot, which had ironically achieved transitory success only in Paris, had ended everywhere in failure. The reasons for this were many. They included ineptness in executing Stauffenberg's meticulously drafted plans and the near-impossible dual role he had imposed on himself. Lack of courage was not among them. Bad luck, which dogged the conspiracy from the start, played its part, but nowhere more cruelly than in the strange accident which enabled Hitler to survive. The historical significance of the tragedy lies in the fact that it was undertaken without assurance of special consideration from the Allies and without hope of averting defeat or deflecting the consequences of unconditional surrender. Just as Stauffenberg and Tresckow had argued that it was necessary for the attempt to be made, *coûte que coûte*, so too the tragic and costly fact remained that the future development of

[1] Ritter, *The German Resistance*, p. 277.

Germany demanded that it fail, so that the full consequences of the catastrophe which ensued might be clearly ascribed to Hitler and his henchmen, and post-war reconstruction of German democracy remain untroubled by a Nazi movement nourished by a fresh stab-in-the-back legend.

In a broadcast soon after midnight on 20th July Hitler referred to the 'tiny clique of traitors and saboteurs' who had been responsible for the attempted *coup*. But to his dismay *Gestapo* reports progressively showed—and recent historical research has abundantly confirmed—that the conspirators were part of a movement extending into a broad spectrum of German life, involving not only high army officers but many civilians, middle-class officials, representatives of the socialist parties and of labour, of the churches, intellectuals, and even former officials of the Party. Hitler's determination to extirpate the last vestiges of opposition led to vigorous action by a special force of the S.S and *Gestapo*. Some 7,000 were arrested. The net included families of participants and many merely suspected of lack of enthusiasm for the regime. Prisoners were tortured and degraded before being brought for 'trial' before the People's Court, presided over by the satanic Friesler. Execution by hanging—in some cases by slow strangulation by piano wire suspended from meat-hooks—followed in almost 5,000 cases. Goerdeler, betrayed in mid August, was kept imprisoned until 3rd February, 1945, when he too heard the dread summons in the Prinz Albrechtstrasse, '*Kommen Sie! Kommen Sie!*' The day before, an American bomb had blown Friesler and the People's Court to pieces and enabled Fabian von Schlabrendorff to join the small company of conspirators who survived.

The heaviest blows fell on the army. Guderian, now Chief of the General Staff, echoed Hitler's description of the plotters as a few officers who out of cowardice and weakness had chosen the path of disgrace, and pledged to the *Führer* and the German people 'the unity of the Generals, of the Officer corps, and of the men of the Army,' and active co-operation 'in the political indoctrination of younger commanders in accordance with the tenets of the *Führer*.' At the army's request a Court of Honour expelled the arrested (as well as those already executed or who had committed suicide) from the army, thus transferring them to the jurisdiction of the People's Court. The army was required to accept Himmler as Commander in Chief of the Home Army. The Nazi salute and political commissars were introduced. Military resistance of any form ceased. The army, the last stronghold of independent power in the *Reich*, suffered a crushing humiliation, as its *Gleichschaltung*, begun in 1933, was completed. From now on its commanders dared not question the *Führer*'s orders, but numbly carried out the duties which they saw with unmistakable clarity were leading swiftly and inevitably to catastrophe.

For Hitler the failure of the plot bred a new sense of confidence in his mission. 'After my miraculous escape from death to-day,' he told Mussolini the same afternoon, 'I am more than ever convinced that it is my fate to bring our common enterprise to a successful conclusion.' His escape, he told the German people, was 'a confirmation of the task imposed upon me by

WORLD WAR II

WESTERN FRONT

German advances
Allied advances
Major aerial conflict

Scale of Miles
0   100   200   300

Atlantic Ocean

NORWAY

SWEDEN

Oslo

Stockholm

FINLAND

Helsinki

Lake Onega

Dvina

Lake Ladoga

Leningrad

Scale of Miles

0   100   200   300

ESTONIA   *Lake Peipus*

Pskov

Volta

Riga

LATVIA

Moscow

Copenhagen

LITHUANIA

Vilna

Smolensk

Hamburg

Danzig

Grodno

EAST PRUSSIA

Minsk

U.S.S.R.

GERMANY

Berlin

Spring 1945

Vistula

Warsaw

Brest Litovsk

Lodz

POLAND

Summer 1944

Desna

Kursk

Orel

SUDETENLAND

Kiev

Kharkov

Prague

UPPER SILESIA

Dnieper

Stalingrad

BOHEMIA

MORAVIA

UKRAINE

Don

Munich

Danube

Bratislava

RUTHENIA

Rostov

Vienna

Budapest

CARPATHIANS

BESSARABIA

Odessa

Spring 1945

TRANSYLVANIA

Sea of Azov

Grozny

RUMANIA

Sevastopol

Trieste

Fiume

CROATIA

Bucharest

Black Sea

Yalta

DALMATIA

BOSNIA

Black Sea

Batum

YUGOSLAVIA

Belgrade

DOBRUJA

ITALY

Adriatic

SERBIA

BULGARIA

TURKEY

Rome

Sofia

Constantinople

WORLD WAR II

EASTERN FRONT

Axis penetration:

December, 1941

November, 1942

Russian counteradvance

August, 1943

Spring, 1944

Providence.'   In addition to wreaking vengeance on its authors, he proceeded to make use of the failure of the plot for a fundamental overhaul of the apparatus of state.   The ensuing months witnessed the final stage of the imposition of Nazi totalitarian rule; 20th July 1944, as one Nazi commentator put it, was to be the completion of 30th January 1933.   Five days after the attempt Goebbels was named *Reich* Commissioner for Total War, with far-reaching authority to dictate the contribution of Germans to the war effort.   All theatres, music halls, cabarets, and most orchestras were banned. Book production was restricted to Party works; postal services were cut; railway services reduced; newspapers placed under further restrictions; many institutions of learning closed.   In a last-minute effort to mobilize all possible reserves for the armed forces and war production the draft age was lowered from seventeen to sixteen, and the length of the working week was extended from forty-eight to sixty hours.   On 18th October, the anniversary of the Battle of Leipzig, all men between the ages of sixteen and sixty were called upon to serve in the *Volkssturm* which, raised and commanded by the *Gauleiter*, was to serve as a Party army alongside the *Wehrmacht* in defence of the Fatherland.   In a last successful propaganda campaign Goebbels openly appealed to fear, linking the fate of the regime with that of the German people, citing the Morgenthau plan as evidence of what unconditional surrender meant, and playing on terror of what would follow when the Red tide swept in from the east.

The collapse which Goebbels tried to avert appeared imminent as the summer and early autumn brought a succession of disasters.   At the end of July the Americans broke out of the western end of the Normandy bridgehead, drove rapidly south, and turned eastward behind the investing forces.   A counter-attack by massed armour soon fell victim to Allied air superiority. With the retreating Germans caught at Falaise between the Americans driving north and the Anglo-Canadians driving south, and the air forces raining destruction from the sky, half of the million-strong Seventh Army and most of its equipment were destroyed.   Von Kluge was abruptly replaced by Field Marshal Walter Model on 17th August, and fearing (probably rightly) that his recall to the *Reich* meant that his part on 20th July had been discovered, he committed suicide.   Before doing so he wrote to the *Führer*, pointing out that 'the German people have borne such untold suffering that it is time to put an end to this frightfulness.'   Despite Hitler's determination to hold south of the Seine the Germans were forced rapidly back.   On 25th August General Leclerc's tanks rolled into Paris.   Fighting a delaying action on the Seine the remnants of the Seventh Army, together with the Fifteenth Army, belatedly withdrawn from the Pas de Calais, retired rapidly over the Somme and the Belgian border.   'Broken and defeated columns are pouring over the roads, side by side with staffs which are of no use to them.   They don't know where to go and have no way of receiving orders.'   So Model described the situation.   British forces seized Brussels on 3rd September and the port of Antwerp, with its installations undamaged, the next day.   A week later Allied forces which had landed on the Mediterranean coast and advanced

CHANCELLOR ERHARD

WILLI BRANDT

PRESIDENT HEUSS

FORMER CHANCELLOR ADENAUER

up the Rhone met Eisenhower's armies near Dijon and advanced towards Strasbourg. On 17th September, in what a German intelligence report described as 'the largest airborne operation ever seen,' Allied forces seized the crossings of the Maas and the Waal but were defeated in their attempt to capture the bridges at Arnhem. By this time Allied forces had outrun their supplies, and under the leadership of Rundstedt, again recalled to command in the West on 4th September, and of Model, now commanding Army Group B, the beaten and disordered elements of the *Wehrmacht* succeeded in restoring a continuous front and delaying the advance. Not until the end of November were the Germans driven from the Channel ports and the approaches to Antwerp, and over the Maas. Not until 21st November did the Americans succeed in piercing the West Wall and capturing Aachen, the first German city to fall, while to the south it took attacks in November and December for the Allies to cross the German frontier at Saarbrücken and break through the Vosges to Strasbourg and the Rhine. At the end of 1944 the Allied armies stood on the approaches to the *Reich*, but Hitler had won a winter's breathing space.

In the meantime, with the end of the Battle of France, the weight of British and American bombing had shifted back to Germany. In the last three months of 1944 the cities of the *Reich* sustained devastating blows, as, aided by secrecy of approach over occupied territory and meeting defences declining in effectiveness (from at least November the *Luftwaffe* lacked the necessary fuel to use the pilots and planes at its disposal), heavy bombers ranged over the *Reich* almost with impunity by day and night. A higher percentage of high-explosive bombs was dropped and destruction was correspondingly greater. Once again the Ruhr was a primary target. Duisburg alone sustained within twenty-four hours the same weight of bombs as were dropped on London during four years of war. Industrial cities in the north and south, oil refineries, and railway marshalling yards were also targets. The Dortmund-Ems and Mittelland Canals were breached, and breached again as soon as damage was repaired. In November the *Tirpitz* was destroyed in Tromsö Fjord. Armament production, which under Speer's skilful leadership had reached a peak in July 1944, declined with increasing speed under the hail of bombs.

In the East the Soviet summer and autumn offensives of 1944 brought the Red Army to the frontiers of the *Reich* and achieved decisive results on its satellites. The offensive north from Leningrad drove the Finns to sign an armistice in September, leaving the German Lapland army to fight its way back against the pursuing Finns. In the north by early October the Red Army was also across the East Prussian frontier and had broken through to the coast south of Riga between Memel and Libau, severing land connections with the German divisions in Courland. As Russian drives north and south of the Pripet Marshes forced the Germans out of Brest Litovsk and Lvov and approached the Vistula, the Polish underground in Warsaw was provoked into a premature rising on 1st August. Although put down during subsequent weeks while Model held off the Russians, who had exhausted their strength during a long and rapid advance, it was a prelude to the escape of the peoples of south-east Europe from German domination. For with German reserves concentrated in the north and centre, barring the way to the Vistula, the Soviet Army crossed the Pruth, captured Jassy, and virtually encircled the opposing Germans. On 23rd August King Michael of Rumania dismissed Antonescu, accepted an armistice, and declared war on Germany. As the German front collapsed Malinovsky's columns swept down on the un-damaged Ploesti oilfields and entered Bucharest on 31st August. On 5th September the Soviet Union declared war on Bulgaria and, aided by a *coup* four days later, occupied the country without opposition. Bulgaria too quickly changed sides and attacked the flanks of the German armies retreating from Greece and Albania, already harried by Yugoslav partisans. At the beginning of October the Russians crossed the frontier of Hungary which the Germans had occupied early in March, and within a fortnight were at Debrecen, 120 miles east of Budapest. A request by the Regent for an armistice was the signal for Veesenmayer, the S.S. German minister and since March the real ruler of Hungary, to stage a *coup* which was carried out by Otto Skorzeny, Mussolini's rescuer. While the Germans were trying to keep the Russians out of Budapest, the Russians crossed the Danube to the south near its confluence with the Drava and opened the way to the encirclement of the Hungarian capital by Christmas Eve. In the space of half a year the situation had been transformed. The Soviet Union had replaced the *Reich* as the dominant power in south-east Europe, and had unveiled a whole new threat to southern Germany.

The Russian advance in the autumn of 1944 brought the first of the massive westwards flights of the German people. Under the weight of the air raids, especially from 1943, there had been a major shift of population from city to countryside, and, as Allied bombers penetrated farther into the *Reich*, from west to east. Until the summer of 1944 the provinces east of the Oder with their swollen populations had been far from the front, relatively free from air raids, and untroubled by the continual retreats of the *Wehrmacht* hundreds of miles away from Memel and the Vistula. But with the Soviet advances in the autumn of 1944, an estimated half-million Germans fled the advancing Soviet armies in East Prussia, some only to experience further flight and terror in the wake of Russian advances in 1945.

Soviet advances to the Vistula coincided with the end of the extermination camps, some of which were overrun. Treblinka, Sobibor, and Belzec had been evacuated in the autumn of 1943. Lublin was hastily abandoned in July 1944 shortly before it was overrun by the Soviet Army, which imme-diately publicized its discoveries to the world press. During the latter part of 1944 only Auschwitz was still operating to full capacity. From May to September its gas chambers claimed 600,000 victims; in May, June, and July the Jews of Hungary, a ghastly but inevitable consequence of the March *coup*; in August the survivors of the Lodz ghetto; in September and October the Jews of Slovakia and Theresienstadt. In August 1944 Eichmann reported his estimate of Jews killed as six million. In November Himmler decided that for all practical purposes the problem had been solved and ordered the dismantling of the killing stations.[1] 'We have lanced the Jewish abscess,' Hitler remarked ten weeks later. 'The world of the future will be eternally grateful to us.'[2] The cost in Jewish lives has been estimated to lie between 4·2 and 5·1 million.[3]

At the end of 1944 Hitler had succeeded in restoring German defence lines in East and West. In the West he had checked the Allied advance into Holland on the Maas and barred the way to the *Reich*. In the East there had been no advance by the Russians from the Vistula, and hastily dispatched reinforcements from the Polish front blocked the road to Vienna. In Italy Kesselring still denied Bologna and the Po Valley to the Allies. Only at Aachen and in East Prussia had enemy forces succeeded in crossing the German frontiers. Encouraged by this momentary success, Hitler planned a bold gamble: a drive from the Eifel through the Ardennes and over the Meuse to the great port of Antwerp, which was just beginning to emerge as the major Allied supply base. For it he assembled a powerful force by ruthlessly denying other fronts. It included the newly raised *Volksgrenadier* and the rebuilt *Panzer* divisions, two-thirds of the *Luftwaffe*'s strength and precious reserves of the rapidly dwindling petrol supply. Though known as the 'Rundstedt offensive,' the plan was prepared in Hitler's headquarters and was delivered to the Commander in Chief West with the written warning 'Not to be changed.' 'If we had reached the Meuse,' Rundstedt commented later, 'we should have gone down on our knees and thanked God—let alone try to reach Antwerp.' Launched on 16th December and aided by bad weather which grounded Allied reconnaissance planes, the ten armoured divisions of the fifth and sixth *Panzer* armies tore a gaping hole in the American lines. But the Allies swiftly recovered, and, though Hitler ordered Model to make a second attempt, on 8th January 1945 he authorized withdrawal of the armour from the Ardennes front.

For there were ample indications that the lull in the East would soon be broken. Guderian had repeatedly urged on Hitler the necessity to withdraw useless divisions from Norway, the Baltic, and Italy, and to transfer armour from the western front to protect Silesia. This was the only major industrial area in the *Reich* that was intact, almost entirely undisturbed by Allied bombing, and its retention was essential for the continuance of the war. But during the late autumn and early winter Hitler gave priority in the assignment of fresh divisions and equipment to the West, and squandered his resources in the Ardennes and in vain attempt to relieve Budapest. On 9th January, when Guderian reported to Hitler after a tour of the East that 'the Russians had vast forces ready to attack and that the German troops in the East could not hold them,' he met with only a hysterical outburst of rage.

On 12th January 1945 the Soviet offensive on the frozen plains of Poland

[1] Raul Hilberg, *The Destruction of the European Jews* (Chicago, 1961), pp. 630–1.
[2] *The Testament of Adolf Hitler: The Hitler-Bormann Documents, February–April 1945* (London, 1962), p. 66.
[3] Gerald Reitlinger, *The Final Solution: The Attempt to Exterminate the Jews of Europe, 1939–1945* (London, 1953), p. 501; Hilberg, *Destruction of the European Jews*, p. 767.

began when Konev broke out of the bridgehead over the upper Vistula between Cracow and Sandomir. The attack, which soon spread to other sectors, rapidly gained momentum, as the Red Army tore great gaps in the lines manned by seventy-five German divisions—less than half the Russian strength, starved for equipment, and denied any reserve. Warsaw was encircled and taken on 17th January. In the second half of January the Russian offensive—the greatest of the war—swept to the Baltic near Danzig, cutting off the twenty-five divisions in the narrowing pocket of East Prussia. Driving beyond Warsaw, Zhukov crossed the German frontier on 27th January and reached the Oder at Küstrin, a scant forty-five miles east of Berlin. Farther south Konev broke into Silesia, overrunning many industries which had been transferred from the west. To the south Soviet forces bypassed besieged Budapest and stood across the Austrian frontier before Vienna. In terror the Germans fled the battle and the depredations of vengeful Soviet soldiery, thronging the roads in the bitter January cold, frequently cut off by the speed and suddenness of the Russian advance. Many thousands had fled as far as Dresden, the last virtually undamaged major city of the *Reich*, when the Allied air forces struck it on 13th, 14th, and 15th February in a series of attacks which utterly devastated the city. In scenes reminiscent of Hamburg an estimated 135,000 people perished. Morale throughout the *Reich* suffered a severe blow.[1] In the face of this rapidly deteriorating situation Hitler reluctantly agreed to the evacuation of Memel but refused to abandon Courland. Responding to the threat to Berlin (where he had established his headquarters in mid January), he belatedly stripped the West of half its armoured divisions, and in February sent the bulk of the new and repaired tanks and assault guns to stabilize the front on the Oder.

By early February 1945 Russian armies were thus closing up to the Oder-Neisse and approaching Prague and Vienna. The cities of the *Reich* were being pulverized from the air. And on 8th February Eisenhower's forces launched an offensive designed to strike deep into the heart of the *Reich* and bring the war to an end. Preceded by the most concentrated artillery bombardment of the war in the West, British and Canadian troops attacked east of Nijmegen, between the Rhine and the Maas. German forces from the slender reserve and other sectors were drawn into battle and destroyed, as Hitler determined to fight west of the great river and forbade any withdrawal to its eastern bank. The attacks spread to the south as the Americans pierced the Siegfried Line, burst through into the Pfalz, and closed up to the Rhine. On 5th March American troops captured a railway bridge intact at Remagen and quickly seized a bridgehead. On 22nd March Patton's forces made a surprise crossing at Oppenheim, south of Mainz, in an area where there were few German troops to bar the advance. The next evening Montgomery began an assault crossing at Wesel. Supported by airborne landings, it penetrated rapidly beyond the river, and burst out into the Westphalian plain with

---

[1] Webster and Frankland, *The Strategic Bomber Offensive*, vol. iii, pp. 108–9, 224 n. David Irving, *The Destruction of Dresden*, (London, 1963), p. 7.

twenty divisions and 1,500 tanks. By 1st April Model's Army Group B was trapped in the Ruhr as Allied forces met at Lippstadt; on 12th April American spearheads secured bridgeheads over the Elbe. In the east Königsberg fell on 9th April, Vienna was captured four days later, and on 16th April the Russians launched massive attacks on the Oder directed towards encircling the capital.

By March it was unmistakably apparent that the days of the *Reich* were numbered. But Hitler, who had long since lost control of events and the capacity to face facts, was determined to fight on. Two and a half years earlier he had told the anniversary celebration of the 1923 *Putsch* that 'all our enemies may rest assured that while the Germany of [1918] laid down its arms at a quarter to twelve, I on principle have never finished before five minutes past twelve.' On 19th March he proclaimed a 'scorched earth' policy and ordered the *Gauleiter* to destroy 'all industrial plants, all important electrical facilities, waterworks, gasworks . . . all food and clothing stores . . . all bridges, all railway installations, the postal system . . . also the waterways, all ships, all freight cars, and all locomotives . . . without consideration for our own population.' To Speer's protests he replied with genuine nihilism that 'if the war is lost, the German nation will also perish. . . . Those who remain after the battle are those who are inferior; for the good will have fallen.' However, Speer and others flouted these senseless orders in an attempt to salvage the essentials of food and transportation. Encircled in the Ruhr, which Hitler ordered to be held as a fortress, Model prohibited major destruction and on 21st April, three days after the pocket surrendered with 325,000 prisoners, shot himself in a wood near Duisburg.

Propaganda and terror were the last weapons in the Nazi armoury. Both were used to maintain the desperate, hopeless resistance. Goebbels rang all the changes on the V-weapons which were to bring deliverance, wove fantasies around the mythical march of General Wenck to relieve Berlin, appropriated the *Werewolf* movement—designed to maintain guerrilla warfare behind the Allied lines—to the ideological nihilism of National Socialism, promised a last stand in the 'Alpine Redoubt' in the mountain fastness around Berchtesgaden, all in an effort to convince the Germans that the war could still be fought to a stalemate if not to victory. The widespread defeatism and desertion were met by brutal S.S. retaliation. Dismissal and even execution were the penalties for failure to comply with the *Führer*'s orders for 'no withdrawal' or for leaving a combat zone unlawfully. The last number of the *Völkische Beobachter* on 24th April proclaimed that 'everyone who commits or even advocates measures which would weaken our resistance is a traitor. He is to be summarily shot or hanged.' Terrorized by the ever harsher Nazi measures, angered by the rain of bombs from the sky which kept up until the closing gap between the armies advancing from East and West eliminated worth-while targets, terrified by the depredations of the Red Army which Goebbels painted in lurid colours, fearful of the consequences of occupation by the western Allies, German soldiers and civilians struggled in hopeless, unthinking confusion. 'Helplessness combined with faith gripped the nation when it saw its inexorable fate approaching,' wrote Speer later. 'A paralysing fear preceded the "twilight of the gods" and cast its spell over almost everyone. There was a hopefulness with which many clung to the slightest chance, but also a fatalism and numbness to which many more were driven by the destruction of their cities, by lack of sleep, and by fear of their very lives.' [1] There was some last-ditch resistance, as in Berlin, from members of the *Volkssturm* and the Hitler Youth. But for the most part there was no bitter underground campaign, no serious sabotage, as passively, and with a kind of sullen relief, Germans hung out white flags, and from cellars or behind barricaded doors watched the progress of the Allied advance.

As the *Reich* was being destroyed by concentric blows, Hitler had established himself in the *Führerbunker*, the lower floors of the air-raid shelter in the Chancellery garden. On 20th April, five days before American and Russian forces met on the Elbe, the Nazi hierarchy were together for the last time to celebrate Hitler's birthday. In view of the impending division of the *Reich*, Hitler allocated full responsibility in the north to Doenitz, in the south to Kesselring, who had replaced Rundstedt after the Remagen fiasco. Though he had been expected to move to the 'Alpine Redoubt,' to which certain ministries, some commands, and later Keitel and Jodl were dispatched, and to which a number of misled units attempted to battle, Hitler announced on 22nd April that he would remain in Berlin to the end. Others in the Party leadership were convinced of the need for seeking capitulation which even the *Führer* in the fateful conference of 22nd April deemed inescapable, but which, with complete disregard for the fate of the German people, he declined to pursue. In January and again in March Guderian had attempted to persuade Ribbentrop of the need to demand an armistice in the West. Away in the Obersalzburg Goering, long in eclipse, was misled by reports of the conference in the bunker and wirelessed to ascertain if he were to take over negotiations for capitulation as Hitler's deputy in accordance with the succession decree of 1941. Persuaded by Bormann to interpret this as high treason, Hitler ordered Goering dismissed from all his offices and arrested for high treason. A week later the news that Himmler, *der treue Heinrich*, had been negotiating surrender terms with Count Bernadotte of Sweden, caused Hitler to order his arrest at all costs, and crystallized his resolve to commit suicide. On 30th April, as Soviet soldiers hoisted the Red Flag over the ruined *Reichstag*, he fired a revolver into his mouth. The next day Goebbels, whom Hitler had invited to share the final macabre scene, shot his wife and himself in the Chancellery garden. For two days after Hitler's suicide fighting in Berlin went on. Then on 2nd May General of Artillery Weidling, the military commander, signed the capitulation of the city. The same day the German armies in Italy capitulated. In the west Doenitz, whom Hitler had nominated at his successor, held out as long as he could in order, as he told the German people in a broadcast, to save German men and women 'from being destroyed by the advancing Bolshevik.' On 5th May German

[1] Chester Wilmot, *The-Struggle for Europe* (London, 1952), pp. 679–80.

forces in the north-west capitulated. The next day Doenitz dismissed Himmler, Goebbels (of whose death he was ignorant), Rosenberg, and Thierack from their offices in the government which Hitler had bequeathed him. On 7th May Jodl was authorized to sign the acceptance of unconditional surrender at Rheims. At Stalin's insistence a second formal capitulation took place a few minutes after midnight on 8th–9th May at Zhukov's headquarters in Berlin Karlshorst.

The Germany which was unconditionally delivered into Allied hands was, as a leading German historian has described it, 'a burnt-out crater of great power politics.' [1] The physical destruction under the bombing and the desperate resistance as the Allied armies had fought across the country was enormous. The piles of rubble in the centre of many towns and cities made them unrecognizable. In Cologne 66 per cent of the houses were totally destroyed; in Düsseldorf 93 per cent were uninhabitable. Schools, churches, offices—all were ravaged. All bridges over the Rhine were destroyed, all waterways closed, only a few disconnected sections of railway were operating. In human terms the cost was high. An estimated 3·1 million Germans died with the *Wehrmacht* and 100,000 civilians in the course of the fighting. One million prisoners were in the U.S.S.R., many never to return. A half-million civilians died in air raids. Defeat in 1945 was catastrophic, far beyond the scale of a Jena or a Sedan. What was destroyed was not only Hitler's 'Thousand Year *Reich*' but Bismarck's more modest creation which had survived the collapse of 1918. It was perhaps pardonable to ask whether German history had not come to an end.

[1] Friedrich Meinecke, *The German Catastophe* (Cambridge, Mass., 1950), p. 111.

CHAPTER XIV

THE GERMAN PHOENIX, 1945–63

'WITH THIS signature,' Colonel-General Alfred Jodl declared on signing the capitulation at Rheims, 'the German people and the German armed forces are, for better or worse, delivered into the victors' hands.' The 7th of May 1945 opened a new chapter in German history, in which all the major decisions were, for a time, made by non-Germans. How the victors proposed to exercise the responsibility which victory and unconditional surrender had brought to them had been the subject of prolonged debate in Allied capitals and in a series of war-time conferences. By the capitulation many of the lines which were to mould the shape of post-war Germany had been traced out. Yet anxiety to avoid problems which might strain or break the 'strange alliance' resulted in a policy of postponement [1] of decisions on the post-war treatment of Germany until the collapse of the *Reich* made decision unavoidable. The most striking exception was the programme for 'pastoralization' sponsored by U.S. Secretary of the Treasury Henry Morgenthau, but the retreat from this inhumane and impractical scheme began almost as soon as it had been given an incautious approval in principle by Roosevelt and Churchill at Quebec in September 1944. At Yalta the following February, Stalin still pressed for harsh and definitive decisions on Germany's future. But Roosevelt and Churchill, by now concerned at the extent of Russian power, were inclining towards more moderate treatment of a defeated Germany. Once again decision on dismemberment and possible territorial exactions in east and west was postponed. On the related questions of reparations and de-industrialization agreement was reached on no more than that a reparations commission should take as a basis of discussion the figure of £20 billion and that 50 per cent should go to the Soviet Union.

These issues could wait; but arrangements for the occupation and control of Germany could not be long delayed. The pattern of the occupation as it was implemented in 1945 (and the clear outlines of post-war Germany) were set forth in a British report in the summer of 1943. It recommended that Germany should be divided into three zones of occupation, each under the control of one of the major powers, with Berlin as a separate zone, jointly occupied by all three. The British proposal was introduced into the three-power European Advisory Commission (E.A.C.) in January 1944 and approved with little discussion. It assigned to the Soviet Army 40 per cent of German territory, enveloping Berlin and extending to within 100 miles of the Rhine. Yet in the light of war-inflicted sufferings and the relative military balance (this was still six months short of D-day and the Russian

---

[1] John L. Snell, *Wartime Origins of the East-West Dilemma Over Germany* (New Orleans, 1959), especially ch. ii.

armies were already on the Soviet-Polish frontier) the U.S.S.R. might well have claimed a larger share.   The key paragraph of the protocol of 12th September 1944 read that 'Germany, within her frontiers as they were on the 31st December 1937, will for purposes of occupation be divided into three zones, one of which will be allotted to each of the three Powers, and a special Berlin area, which will be under joint occupation by the three Powers.'   On 14th November, following agreement that the British would occupy the north-western zone including the Ruhr, the United States the south-western including Bavaria and the Rhineland, agreement was also reached that supreme authority following surrender would be vested in a Control Council consisting of the Allied Commanders-in-Chief.   At Yalta it was agreed to provide France with a zone and a sector in Berlin (both carved out of the areas already allotted to the western powers), but drafting the details was not completed until after the capitulation.   By this time the question of dismemberment was still buried in the committee to which it had been referred at Yalta, and the term was not in fact mentioned in the surrender document hastily improvised at Eisenhower's headquarters.   Though rejected as a policy by all three powers for different reasons, *de facto* partition and the isolation and division of Berlin were to emerge from the arrangements worked out in the E.A.C. and given a final blessing at Yalta.

On 23rd May 1945 the Doenitz regime was liquidated and its members arrested.   Two weeks later, on 5th June, the Allied commanders—Montgomery, Eisenhower, Zhukov, and de Lattre de Tassigny—signed in Berlin a 'Declaration Regarding the Defeat of Germany' by which they assumed an unprecedented 'supreme authority' over Germany, including all powers formerly possessed by the central, state, or municipal governments, and the right to 'determine the boundaries of Germany.'   The apprehension of the principal Nazi leaders or of those suspected of war crimes was ordered, and the Germans were informed of the details of the occupation zones and of the special arrangements for Berlin, together with the conditions to which they were obliged to submit during the initial phase of the occupation.   With this Declaration the history of the Third *Reich* came to an end, and the legal basis for the occupation was established.

The transition to the occupation regime took many weeks.   At the capitulation the Russians were in sole occupation of Berlin, while to the west the British and Americans had conquered a broad belt stretching from near Lübeck to the Austrian border which had been assigned to the Soviet zone. The advancing Allies had for the most part found the Germans in a dazed condition, physically and psychologically exhausted, resigned to whatever fate lay ahead.   Though the eradication of Nazism had been placed in the forefront of war aims, the Nazis seemed to melt away.   There were only a few isolated instances of sabotage and little open hostility.   In each area conquered the Allied forces acted independently.   In their day-to-day relations with the German population the French began by being much more harsh than the British and Americans, and de Lattre's extravagance in the use of German labour and materials, and his arbitrary decisions, aroused strong antipathies.[1] Disorder, looting, and rape followed on a large scale in the wake of the Soviet occupation, not least in Berlin.   Yet in all occupied areas, as rapidly as possible, the local administration was re-created and placed in the hands of those whom such investigation as was possible indicated were non-Nazis.   Occasionally technical skill furnished grounds for over-looking political backgrounds.   By the end of June local executive authorities up to the *Regierungsbezirk* (sub-provincial) level had been nominated in all four zones.   Though the Western military authorities were cautious about allowing local political units to exercise authority, in the Soviet zone the formation of 'anti-fascist' parties and trade unions was quickly authorized to assist the establishment of Soviet control.

Even before fighting stopped, steps were taken to restore essential services, reorganize ration distribution, clear rubble, improvise bridges, repair slightly damaged houses.   Prisoners of war and senior officials of state and Party were rounded up.   Foreign workers were returned home or assembled in camps.   Factories were started up in a small way where stocks of fuel and raw materials permitted.   The re-emergence or refounding of trade unions was encouraged by all the occupying powers.   Political groups began to coalesce, often continuing their clandestine discussions and planning under the Third *Reich*.   Newspaper publication was resumed; radio stations were taken over and operated almost without a break.   Theatres and cinemas reopened.   Schools and universities reopened despite the handicaps of destruction of buildings, libraries, and laboratories, the shortage of suitable textbooks, and the removal of thousands of teachers and professors through denazification.   In August 1945 an assembly of Protestant church leaders at Treysa in Hesse decided to merge the three representative forces in German church life into a new Evangelical Church in Germany (E.K.I.D. or E.K.D.), which received its constitution a year later at Eisenach.   Two months later at Stuttgart a number of its leaders, including Wurm, Dibelius and Niemöller, with dignity and courage issued a declaration which, while avoiding any imputation of collective guilt, recognized that 'through us [i.e. the German Christians] endless suffering has been brought to many peoples and countries.' [2] The joint sufferings of war and persecution had brought a new understanding between Catholic and Protestant, and Cardinals Faulhaber and Frings and Bishop Galen continued to provide bold leadership in the difficult circum-stances of foreign occupation as under the Nazis.

Though life slowly returned to a defeated and devasted country, conditions in the weeks after surrender were grim.   Infant mortality climbed astro-nomically; deaths from tuberculosis rose sharply.   Despite the prompt arrival of Allied shipments of grain, the average rations available dropped well below subsistence level.   The food shortage was aggravated by Soviet action in the east.   In the face of the agreement at Yalta that the decision on Poland's western frontier was to be left to a peace conference, the Russians in May amputated one-fifth of 1937 Germany by handing over to Polish

[1] F. Roy Willis, *The French in Germany, 1945–1949* (Stanford, 1962), pp. 71, 76.
[2] Stewart Herman, *The Rebirth of the German Church* (London, 1946), pp. 136–7, 142–3.

administration the entire area up to the Oder and the western Neisse Rivers, with the exception of Königsberg, which was incorporated into the U.S.S.R. itself. Many Germans who had not fled the Red Army's advance were promptly dispossessed by the Poles and fled westward, 'bringing their mouths with them,' as Churchill put it at Potsdam.[1] Besides adding to the mouths to be fed in the more crowded and less agricultural west, they contributed to the 'seething movement of human beings' in the Western zones, where the first expellees from the Sudetenland, Hungary, and Rumania, mingled with the refugees from East Prussia and Silesia, with demobilized soldiers, foreign workers, released prisoners, and evacuated city dwellers seeking their homes.

In Berlin and the Soviet zone Russian forces did not wait for Potsdam to begin seizing reparations. Factories were stripped of machinery, railway lines were lifted, typewriters and telephones were carted off by the truckload. In the battered capital steps were taken to secure effective control of political life, hastened by knowledge that rule would soon be shared with the Western powers. Their entry was delayed until the withdrawal of British and American forces behind the western boundary of the Soviet zone. Churchill was anxious to postpone this retreat, which he saw 'bringing Soviet power into the heart of Europe and the descent of an iron curtain between us and everything to the eastward,' until political differences had been resolved at the forthcoming Potsdam Conference. But on 1st July the Anglo-American armies began their withdrawal, followed by a mass of refugees. At the same time Western garrisons moved into the capital, their communications with the west 110 miles away—a main highway, a railway, and an air corridor—passing through or over Soviet held territory and insecurely based on verbal agreements. On 7th July the *Kommandatura* was established 'to exercise the administration of all Berlin zones.'

The war-time Allies had agreed to occupy Germany, but they had not yet agreed on the common policies they were to pursue. This was a central purpose when the leaders of the three major powers (France was not invited though expected to abide by the decisions reached) assembled for the last major war-time conference in the Cecilienhof Palace in Potsdam from 17th July to 2nd August. Of the items on the agenda three were of especial importance for Germany: 'The Principles to Govern the Treatment of Germany in the Initial Control Period'; Reparations; and Poland's western frontier. The principles for the occupation were hardly Carthaginian and demonstrated the extent of the retreat from the Morgenthau Plan. No central government was to be established, but the idea of dismemberment disappeared once and for all, and the political recovery of Germany was to be encouraged within a decentralized, democratic framework. On the contentious reparations issue Western reluctance to agree to any fixed sum was strengthened by increasing awareness of the extent of Soviet removals and by the effect on Germany's capacity to pay after the transfer of so much territory to Poland. This ultimately led to agreement on no more than that each power should satisfy its reparation claims by removing surplus 'productive capacity' from its

---

[1] James F. Byrnes, *Speaking Frankly* (New York and London, 1947), p. 81.

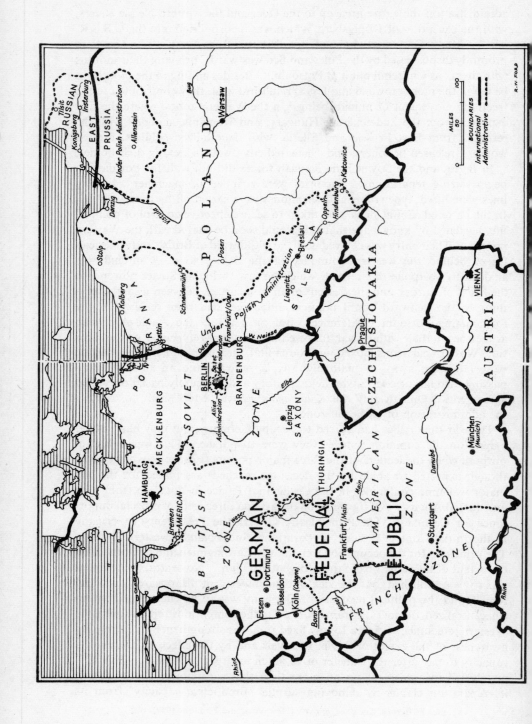

own zone. In addition, the U.S.S.R. was to receive from the Western zones 25 per cent of such 'complete industrial capital equipment . . . as is unnecessary for the German peace economy,' of which 15 per cent was to be paid for by reciprocal deliveries of food and raw materials. No provision was made for Soviet reparations from current Western production. The percentage formula was thus substituted for the definite figure desired by the Russians. Only productive capacity not needed to maintain in Germany 'average living standards not exceeding the average of the standard of living of European countries' was available for reparations. This clearly required the formulation of and adherence to a general economic plan for the whole country. Yet, while Germany was to be treated as 'a single economic unit,' in implementing the required 'common policies' account was to be taken of 'varying local conditions.' The reparation provisions were thus ambiguous and contradictory, and their conflicting interpretation was to be the subject of bitter dispute later on. It remained to be seen, moreover, whether the economy of the Western zones, dislocated by war damage and strained by the swelling influx of refugees, could produce reparations on the scale sought by the U.S.S.R. and yet enable the German people to subsist 'without external assistance.'

The conference was also preoccupied from beginning to end with the Soviet effort to secure approval of the *fait accompli* of advancing the Polish frontier to the line of the Oder and the western Neisse. British and American protests were met with assurances that all the German population had fled, although in the period before Potsdam it appears that only some 250,000 had been expelled over the Oder. Ultimately the Western powers agreed to support the incorporation of Königsberg into the Soviet Union and to accept the fact that the Soviet zone up to the Oder and the western Neisse was under Polish administration. In return they secured agreement that transfers of German populations from Poland, Czechoslavakia, and Hungary which would 'have to be undertaken . . . should be effected in an orderly and humane manner.' Though balked in the attempt to secure final approval for the Oder-Neisse frontier, the Soviet Union had succeeded in excluding the territories east of this line from the occupation regime. Yet the conference represented more of a stalemate than a victory for Stalin, for the nettle of East-West differences was still not fully grasped. Since Yalta the Western powers had conquered more than half of Germany, and in consequence were able to frustrate many of the plans which he had been maturing since 1941, and to reserve final decisions for an eventual peace conference. Yet evasion of the issues at Potsdam opened the door to a postponement which became permanent and to *de facto* partition.

The Anglo-American withdrawal from the Soviet zone at the beginning of July satisfied the Soviet condition for the establishment of the Control Council which met for the first time on 30th July. At first the focal point in its organization was the Co-ordinating Committee, consisting of the Deputy Military Governors, who devoted their full time to the task of administering Germany. Below it the Control Commission was split into a number of functional directorates composed of representatives of each of the occupying armies. The Council continued to meet until March 1948. For the first year and a half it gave an outward appearance of smooth functioning and succeeded in agreeing on a number of matters, including the 1946 agreement establishing the Berlin Air Safety Centre and the three air corridors to the west. Most agreements, however, were of a negative, anti-Nazi character, and from the start the Council disagreed over the nature and scope of German institutions, and especially over the related problems of reparations and the level of industry bequeathed it by Potsdam.

Denazification proved one of the most controversial aspects of the occupation. It was highlighted by a ten-month-long trial of the major war criminals at Nuremberg in accordance with the repeated Allied war-time pledges to 'bring all war criminals to just and swift punishment.' Hitler and Goebbels had committed suicide in Berlin before the capitulation. Himmler, dismissed from Doenitz's government on 6th May, committed suicide soon after his arrest. Bormann, who was never seen after he set out from the bunker following Hitler's suicide, and was not officially declared dead until 1954, was tried in absentia. Robert Ley succeeded in hanging himself in his cell before the trial· began. Gustav Krupp was judged too ill and senile to be tried. But twenty-one others who had held high posts in party or government faced the four-power International Military Tribunal, created in accordance with an agreement reached in London during the summer of 1945: the party leaders Goering, Hess, Rosenberg, Schirach, Streicher, Fritzsche; the pro-consuls Seyss-Inquart and Frank; Frick and Kaltenbrunner; Funk and Schacht; Sauckel and Speer; Neurath, Papen, and Ribbentrop; Keitel and Jodl; Raeder and Doenitz. Each was provided with a German counsel. Most were arraigned on four charges of crimes against peace and waging offensive war, war crimes, and crimes against humanity. The judgment was read on 30th September and 1st October 1946. The S.S. and the S.D., the Gestapo, and the Leadership Corps of the Nazi Party were declared criminal organizations; the S.A., the Reich Cabinet, and the General Staff and the High Command of the Armed Forces were acquitted, as were Papen, Schacht, and the insignificant Fritzsche. Raeder was found guilty on three charges and sentenced to life imprisonment; Doenitz on two and sentenced to ten years. Hess, his mind deteriorating, and Funk, were sentenced for life; Speer and Schirach for twenty years, the elderly Neurath for fifteen. Goering, Ribbentrop, Keitel, Jodl, and Rosenberg were found guilty on all counts, Frick, Seyss-Inquart, Sauckel, Bormann, Kaltenbrunner, Frank, and Streicher on two or more counts, and all twelve were sentenced to death by hanging. After confirmation by the Control Council the sentences were carried out soon after 1 a.m. on 16th October. Goering succeeded in cheating the hangman by swallowing poison shortly before. Those sentenced to imprisonment were confined to Spandau jail in Berlin under four-power control.

The validity of the Nuremberg trials has been disputed both inside and outside Germany, especially on the grounds that new law was formulated to cover crimes already committed. Yet, as was stated at the time, the enormity of the Nazi crimes was such as to demand steps to bring 'our laws in balance with the universal moral judgment of mankind,' [1] and a recent authority has written that 'the International Military Tribunal represents an important milestone in the development of international criminal law towards . . . a permanent international penal court.' [2] Yet as the court was composed exclusively of victors, and included representatives of Hitler's alliance partner of 1939, German objections were inevitably strengthened.

The trials of the major war criminals, their Nuremberg successors, and those of offenders before courts in the countries overrun by the *Wehrmacht*, provided only a partial answer to the 'rooting out nazism' envisaged as a major objective of the occupation. The virtual and unexpected disappearance of the Party at the close of the war was due in part to the stringent security precautions taken. A certain number of prominent Nazis went underground, but by the end of 1945 nearly 70,000 had been interned in each of the British and American zones, and many more had either been removed from office or rejected for employment because of Nazi backgrounds. It was not until October 1946, however, that agreement was reached on a Control Council Directive for a uniform policy of arrests and removals. Even then neither the French nor the Russians paid much attention to it, the former out of scepticism at the whole process, the latter using denazification as a device to pursue the class struggle and strengthen the *K.P.D.* With exemplary thoroughness in the American zone, and rather less in the British, all Germans over eighteen were required to complete a 133-question *Meldbogen*, and offenders were punished according to a scale by fine or imprisonment up to ten years. Higher *Wehrmacht* officers, S.S., *Gestapo* and Party leaders were either brought before special Allied tribunals or released to normal denazification procedures. In February 1948 Marshal Sokolovsky ordered all denazification commissions in the Soviet zone dissolved; by the end of the year the process was virtually completed in the Western zones. It had gone on too long after capitulation, had spread the net too widely, and had absorbed a disproportionate amount of the time and attention of the occupation authorities and of the Germans who manned the commissions. Yet it was inevitable after all that had gone on during the war that some attempt should be made to punish Nazi leaders and to eliminate National Socialism; and despite the criticisms which can be levelled at the programme, it is hard, as one authority has recently put it, to see what better alternative was available.[3]

The emphasis on working through German authorities hastened the re-creation or re-fashioning of local administration. In all zones local councils appointed in the summer of 1945 were replaced after elections at the *Gemeinde* and *Landkreise* level the next year. The most lasting change introduced by the occupation regime was at the *Land* level. In the British zone, well in

[1] Henry L. Stimson, quoted in Whitney R. Harris, *Tyranny on Trial: The Evidence at Nuremberg* (Dallas, 1954), p. 537.
[2] Robert K. Woetzel, *The Nuremberg Trials in International Law* (London and New York, 1960), p. 244.
[3] Michael Balfour and John Mair, *Four-Power Control in Germany and Austria, 1945–1946* (London, New York, Toronto, 1956), p. 184.

P

advance of the Control Council Law of 25th February 1946, abolishing the state of Prussia, two former Prussian provinces, North Rhine and Westphalia, were combined into a single *Land*.   Hanover, Oldenburg, Brunswick, and Schaumburg-Lippe were combined to form Lower Saxony.   With Hamburg and Schleswig-Holstein there were thus four *Laender* by the end of 1946, each with a government and a nominated council.   In the American zone Bavaria, parts of Wurtemberg and Baden, and Hesse and Hesse-Nassau were organized as *Laender*, with Bremen becoming a fourth in March 1947. At this level too the Americans moved more swiftly in handing responsibility back to the Germans' than did the British.   Advisory Assemblies were nominated in January 1946, and constitutions drafted by June.   In the French zone Baden and the southern half of Wurtemberg formed one *Land*, and the territories farther north grouped to form Rhein-Pfalz.   Consultative Assemblies were formed in November 1946, and constitutions ratified in May 1947.   The Saar, first administered as a separate *Land*, was brought within the French customs system in December 1946, and Kehl, on the Rhine opposite Strasbourg, was incorporated within France. In the Soviet zone Brandenburg, Saxony, and Thuringia were left untouched, but Pomerania, cut in half by the Polish 'occupation,' was joined to Mecklenburg, and Anhalt and the Prussian province of Sachsen were joined to form a new *Land*.   *Land* governments were set up as early as July 1945, with elections in October for assemblies to draft constitutions in which Russian control was 'democratically disguised.' [1]

Above the *Land* level it had originally been envisaged that there would be no need for more than the central administrative departments provided for at Postdam.   Between July and October 1945, however, the Russians set up twelve central administrative departments for their zone.   The Americans also began working towards a zonal authority as early as October 1945, and by the spring of 1947 the United States zone council of Ministers-President was reinforced by an advisory committee drawn from the *Land* Assemblies.   The British moved more slowly.   A Zonal Advisory Council met first in March 1946, and after the *Land* elections in June 1947 was reconstituted to consist of members chosen by the *Land* Assemblies.   While the Russians appeared to impose a pre-arranged plan on their zone, the British and Americans moved cautiously and empirically towards evolving some co-ordinating authority in their zones which even the French, with their rooted opposition to centralization as a 'manifestation d'une renaissance du *Reich*,' found necessary.

This development of German administration was accompanied by an unexpectedly early revival of political parties, as all four occupying powers decreed their revival.   Once again it was the Russians who led the way, and, by deliberately making politics of key importance in the Soviet zone, influenced political development throughout the country.   Though the Communists (*K.P.D.*) were first in the field and secured important initial

---

[1] J. P. Nettl, *The Eastern Zone and Soviet Policy in Germany, 1945–50* (London, New York Toronto, 1951), p. 97.

advantages, all democratic parties benefited from the Russian desire 'to cultivate political activity ostensibly as a weapon against the remnants of National Socialism.' [1] A group of Moscow-trained German Communists under the leadership of Walter Ulbricht, principal agent of the Stalinization of the German Communist Party, was brought to Bruchmühle, twenty miles east of Berlin, on 30th April 1945, the day of Hitler's suicide.[2] The *K.P.D.* emerged on 11th June, the day after Soviet Order No. 2 authorized the formation of 'anti-fascist parties' and 'free trade unions.' The revival of other parties soon followed in east and west. Parties were authorized in the British zone in September. In the American zone organization on a district basis was approved in August, on a *Land* basis in November, and on a zonal basis in February 1946. Development in the French zone was slower.

This perhaps premature revival naturally fostered the restoration of the pre-1933 party system, as surviving leaders, programmes, and followers largely reappeared. The first appeal of the *K.P.D.* was signed by Wilhelm Pieck, a venerable pre-1933 Communist, Ulbricht, destined to be its strong man, and fourteen other functionaries most of whom had emigrated in 1933. Though in 1945 the *K.P.D.* was one of the 'big three,' it inevitably became tagged with the pro-Soviet label. Based on the Russian zone it was unable to exploit the pitiful conditions of the time, and Max Reimann's western branch of the party soon dwindled to an insignificant fragment. Continuity was even more marked in the revived Socialists (*S.P.D.*), which issued its first appeal on 15th June. Though Otto Grotewohl was its Berlin leader, its most dynamic figure was Kurt Schumacher, a tough, zealous figure, whose health had been wrecked by ten years in a Nazi concentration camp, but whose oratorical skill made him the unchallenged leader of the Social Democratic masses. He laboured to win middle-class support, and, mindful of what his party had suffered in the past from being labelled internationalist, he made a powerful appeal to nationalist sentiment. The most original development was the emergence of the Christian Democratic Union (*C.D.U.*) A heterogeneous political grouping, it included prominent Catholics but also veterans and left-overs from Liberal, Protestant, nationalist, and other parties and movements, who had come together 'from the realization that their old political party traditions were either inadequate or completely unviable.' [3] It was founded in Berlin on 22nd July, with other groups emerging in Cologne, Frankfurt, Munich, and the north. Though varying in social composition from trade unionists to Rhineland industrialists, and offering widely differing interpretations of the adjective 'Christian,' the name Christian Democratic Union was generally adopted by most by the end of 1945, though the Bavarian *Land* Party has retained the name Christian Social Union (*C.S.U.*). Konrad Adenauer, before 1933 Oberbürgermeister of Cologne, quickly rose to leadership in the British zone and challenged the ambitious and well-financed operations of the Berlin *C.D.U.* under Jacob Kaiser, former secretary-general

[1] Ibid, p. 81.
[2] Wolfgang Leonhard, *Child of the Revolution* (London, 1957), p. 287 ff.
[3] Arnold J. Heidenheimer, *Adenauer and the C.D.U.* (The Hague, 1960), p. 31.

of the Christian trade unions, and Ernst Lemmer.   The fourth of the major parties was the Liberal Democratic Party (*L.D.P.*), or as it was known in some areas the Free Democratic Party (*F.D.P.*) or the German People's Party (*D.V.P.*).   Reacting against the economic policies of the *S.P.D.* and the religious-cultural programme of the *C.D.U.*, it stood for traditional liberal goals of free enterprise economy and anti-clericalism.   To it, as to the *C.D.U.*, however, the main body of German conservative opinion was attracted in the absence of any genuine conservative party.

The decisive stage in the evolution of German political life came at the same time as (and as a by-product of) the growing East-West split, and the progressive breakdown of four-power control.   This had its immediate source in the economic dilemma faced by the Western powers and particularly in the dispute over reparations and the permitted level of industry.   Though neither the expected anarchy nor the anticipated widespread hunger followed the collapse, the situation in all four zones remained bleak, with much real hardship.   Late in 1946 2,700 people in Düsseldorf had no permanent shelter whatsoever, and 13,000 were living in shelters and cellars of ruined houses; three-quarters of a million children in Schleswig-Holstein were without shoes; and it was estimated that there were 10,000 hunger oedema cases in Hamburg alone.   More plant and machinery had survived the bombing and the fighting than had been anticipated.   But shortage of fuel and raw materials paralysed industry, and though basically sound the German economy was reduced to a truncated and primitive level where the best efforts of military government were unavailing.   'The attempt to run the economies of the different occupation zones by detailed military orders only perpetuated the paralysis of the economy,' commented a U.N. report.   'Money ceased to a great extent to function. . . .   Individual barter, compensation trade, wage payments in kind, and other atavistic forms of economic communication took its place.'   Relatively easy food conditions in the countryside contrasted with near starvation in the towns.   There were sharp social inequalities.   The black market flourished.   The cigarette acquired a near universal currency.   The standards of German morality and civil conscience sustained a severe blow.   Despite the *crescendo* of ominous predictions the abnormally mild winter of 1945–6 passed off without undue complaint.   But the assumption that thereafter things would improve was not fulfilled, and the second post-war winter was in every way harder than the first.   Though the 1946 harvest was good the British and American zones were burdened with a fresh, enormous burden of refugees and expellees—an estimated two million from Silesia, Pomerania, and East Prussia alone in 1946—which added nearly 20 per cent to the population seeking a livelihood in an area condemned at Potsdam to lose its surplus industrial capacity as reparations.

French opposition to the creation of the five central German administrative departments, envisaged in the Potsdam agreement as the indispensable requirement for achieving a unified economic administration, made each power increasingly responsible for formulating and executing policy in its own zone.

As a result zonal boundaries hardened into something resembling state frontiers, the zones becoming virtually states in themselves. The whole basis on which the Potsdam agreement was based had thus been challenged by the time the level of industry plan was approved on 26th March 1946. Fourteen industries, especially those of a military character, were to be prohibited, eleven others restricted. Steel capacity, despite British efforts to achieve a realistic figure, was set at 7 million tons, with production limited to 5·8 million tons annually. (Pre-war production was 19 million tons, and in the last year of the war 9·6 million went for civilian uses.) The planned reduction in the level of industry to 'about 50 or 55 per cent of the pre-war level in 1938,' together with the significantly higher proportion of a more restricted output directed to exports, meant that the internal standard of living would be at best austere.

Agreement on the level of industry plan coincided with a continuing food crisis in the Western zones and an open conflict over reparations. Despite strenuous efforts to increase German production of food, massive imports were necessary which, in the absence of sizable exportable quantities of coal or industrial goods, were being paid for by the United States and British taxpayer. At the same time reparations were beginning to flow eastward, including reparations from current production in the Soviet zone. If the country had been administered as an economic unit, these would have assisted in balancing needed exports. In the face of French and Russian resistance to establishing the central agencies and a uniform export-import policy, the Americans suspended reparation deliveries from the American zone on 3rd May 1946, and on 5th September agreed with the British to merge their two zones. The next day at Stuttgart the U.S. Secretary of State, James F. Byrnes, called for the establishment of central German administrative agencies to develop nation-wide economic policies so that Germany could exist 'without assistance from other countries.' 'The American people want to return the government of Germany to the German people,' he concluded. 'The American people want to 'help the German people to win their way back to an honorable place among the free and peace-loving nations of the world.' What the then U.S. Deputy Military Governor, General Lucius Clay, later described as 'the first constructive note which had come from the Western occupying power' [1] indicated that the picture of Russian reparations being drawn from an impoverished Germany which could only be sustained by the United States taxpayer had persuaded the United States to take the lead out of British hands in resisting Russian demands in the interests of a viable Germany.[2]

Though the creation of Bizonia on 1st January 1947 provided the essential step for rebuilding the economy of western Germany, it did nothing for the moment to relieve the British and American taxpayer, and it came too late to save Germany from the troubles of the exceptionally severe winter of 1946–7, when the cold began in mid December and continued until March.

[1] Lucius D. Clay, *Decision in Germany* (New York, 1950), p. 80.
[2] Balfour, *Four-Power Control in Germany*, p. 142.

The food shortage grew critical, with difficulties over imports and the reluctance of German farmers to part with scarce supplies for worthless currency. Barter and evasion became widespread, and the black market almost as important as legitimate business. Shortage of coal, on which the whole industrial recovery depended, persisted. The lot of German civilians was hard, and the prestige of the occupying powers, and with it the prestige of democracy, sank, despite the sacrifices made in the interests of German recovery. If decisive results were to be achieved, incentive must be found, and this appeared to require placing recovery in German hands.

Encouraging German leadership in economic recovery meant facilitating German political responsibility, and on this level too East-West differences had become more marked. Characteristically, developments within the *S.P.D.* and in Berlin and the Soviet zone anticipated those in the rest of Germany. Towards the end of 1945 the Russians resolved on fusion of the *K.P.D.* and the *S.P.D.* The merger was pushed by the Soviet Military Administration (*S.M.A.*), and was actively promoted by Grotewohl, the *S.P.D.* leader in Berlin and the Soviet zone. But, strongly assisted by Schumacher, and with the belated backing of the Western military authorities, the anti-merger forces outvoted Grotewohl and secured a party referendum. In the three Western sectors of Berlin the opponents of the merger won a landslide victory. Nevertheless the Socialist Unity Party of Germany (*S.E.D.*) was formed on 21st–22nd April 1946. It was promptly recognized by the *S.M.A.*, and the *S.P.D.* was banished from the Soviet zone. In Berlin both the *S.E.D.* and the *S.P.D.* continued to compete for the votes of the left. In advance of the elections due on 20th October the *S.E.D.* was shown open favouritism by the *S.M.A.*, and every obstacle was placed in the way of the *C.D.U.*, the *L.D.P.*, and the *S.P.D.* in East Berlin. The results gave the *S.E.D.* a substantial victory, with 4·6 million votes against a combined total of 4·8 million for its opponents, and this put the *S.E.D.* in control of the *Landtäge* and ministries in the five *Laénder*. But the extent of Russian favouritism and coercion was suggested by the simultaneous elections in Berlin—the first and last free elections for the whole city—where the *S.E.D.* received less than 20 per cent of the vote, and the *S.P.D.* emerged triumphant at the head of an overwhelmingly strong 'Western' bloc. This 'catastrophic defeat,' as an official of the *S.E.D.* later described it,[1] gave the Russian leaders a severe jolt. Together with the rapid implementation of the new regime in the British and American zones it appeared to indicate that hopes of uniting Germany under Communist leadership had evaporated. The *S.M.A.* in consequence was forced back on the tactic of building up its position in its own zone while seeking to extract what advantages it could from four-power control. In Berlin, as the *Kommandatura* was progressively reduced to impotence, the importance of the *Magistrat*, now securely in anti-Communist hands, was correspondingly enhanced, and the cold war was fought out in microcosm within the borders of a single city. In the zone the *S.E.D.* built up an elaborate òrganization of the totalitarian kind, aided by higher rations for its

---

[1] Leonhard, *Child of the Revolution*, p. 359.

functionaries, special issues of food and clothing, and a generous allocation of newsprint; and backed by the trade unions, the Farmers' Co-operative, and mushrooming organizations such as the Cultural Union, the Democratic Women's Union, and the Free German Youth, whose membership by the end of 1947 had risen to nearly 800,000. Within the *S.E.D.* the bitter struggle between its two components continued, until by the end of 1947 voluntary desertions and forced resignations resulted in Communist triumph. The two bourgeois parties in the anti-fascist bloc, forbidden to dissolve, provided a cloak for Communist activities and were increasingly compromised through association with all major actions of the *S.E.D.* Assimilation into the East bloc proceeded, and a clear step towards the establishment of a separate government came in June 1947 with the establishment of the German Economic Council.[1] Through land reform, denazification, dismantling, and direct Russian control, the economy was organized on the Soviet model with mining, metal production, and other enterprises being taken into State hands.[2]

Political developments in Berlin and the Soviet zone had a far-reaching impact on the alignment of political parties in the West. With the *S.P.D.* torn apart by the East-West struggle, the Socialist leadership in the Western zones made it clear that they intended to fight any extension of the merger programme, and by the end of 1946 they had formed a tightly disciplined organization under Schumacher. Formal contact with the Soviet zone was lost and, strongly reinforced in their anti-Communism, they made clear their determination to exploit the political opportunities in the West. This placed the *C.D.U.* under pressure to create a supra-zonal party, and to end the rivalry between Adenauer and Kaiser. The final stages of the emergence of the *C.D.U.* and of Adenauer as its unchallenged leader were fought out against a background of sharply deteriorating East-West relations. Differences on issues extending from Berlin to Manchuria became increasingly acute in the spring of 1947, and the new U.S. Secretary of State, George S. Marshall, was confronted with the need to check what his Under Secretary, Dean Acheson, described as the 'aggressive and expansionist' policy of the U.S.S.R. on a worldwide scale. President Truman's 12th March pledge of assistance against Communist expansion was by no means confined to Greece and Turkey, and in Germany involved a stiffening of resistance and a reluctant but determined abandonment of belief in the possibility of co-operation with the U.S.S.R.[3] The breach between the recent Allies was made flagrant by the meeting of the Council of Foreign Ministers which opened in Moscow on 10th March, two days before the proclamation of the Truman Doctrine. Preceded by six weeks of fruitless discussions by their deputies, the Foreign Ministers could agree on little beyond endorsing the Control Council's abolition of the Prussian state 'as the bearer of militarism and reaction.' On the pressing question of economic unity, reparations, and the level of

[1] Nettl, *Eastern Zone*, pp. 132–3.
[2] Hans Herzfeld, *Berlin: Behauptung von Freiheit und Selbstverwaltung, 1946–48* (Berlin, 1959), pp. 14–15.
[3] Peter Calvocoressi, *Survey of International Affairs, 1947–1948* (London, New York, Toronto, 1952), p. 62.

industry, complete deadlock ensued. Neither Bevin nor Marshall would accept Russian claims which would involve either making Germany 'an economic poorhouse in the centre of Europe' or the payment of reparations to Russia by the Western powers. They were prepared to consider some reparations out of current production, but only after their own advances and occupation costs had been met. To the Russians this could only mean indefinite postponement.

The disagreement at Moscow, coupled with the American conviction that 'the patient [i.e. Europe] is sinking,' had two important sequels: the strengthening of Bizonia and the Marshall Plan. In an effort to avoid the appearance of creating a separate West German government the various economic boards had been dispersed geographically from Minden to Stuttgart and subordinated to a committee composed of the Ministers-President of the eight *Laender* in the combined zones. There had been no elected legislature. Immediately after Moscow the military governors were authorized to strengthen this machinery and to raise the level of industry towards a self-sustaining basis. The steps taken were hesitant, however, as British and American authorities still had one eye on the forthcoming London Conference and wanted to avoid the impression of a separate governmental authority and a Western capital. The agencies were concentrated in Frankfurt and subordinated to an Economic Council consisting of fifty-four members of the various *Landtäge*. The Council, which met first on 25th June 1947, began to act like a parliament, with *C.D.U.*, which had fared better in the 1946 elections in the West than in Berlin and the Soviet zone, as the dominant party, the *S.P.D.* as the opposition. Though Kaiser and his Berlin associates struggled for a 'unification first' policy, and in March launched a movement for a council representing the major parties of all four zones, Soviet pressure increasingly dictated the necessity for taking sides. 'It would be Utopian,' he told the Berlin executive on 12th July, 'to talk of mediation at a time when we are literally in danger of being torn to pieces in the play and counter-play of world powers.' [1]

Kaiser's effort to avoid a choice between East and West came precisely when Marshall's proposals were being debated in Paris. Russian rejection for itself and its satellites drew a line down the centre of Europe, splitting Germany and isolating Berlin. To the east the Soviet Union ruthlessly consolidated its political and economic position; to the west American aid was decisive in resuscitating and to some extent uniting Europe. In their report on 12th July the sixteen nations assembled in the Palais Rose declared that 'in order for European co-operation to be effective, the German economy should be integrated in the European economy in such a way as to contribute to an improvement in the general standard of living.' For this an increase in the production and export of Ruhr coal was essential, and 'to this end, West Germany, like the participating countries, should be assisted.' [2] This marked a decisive reversal of the Morgenthau thesis that Europe could prosper

---

[1] Heidenheimer, *Adenauer and the C.D.U.*, p. 111.
[2] André Piettre, *L'Économie allemande contemporaine (Allemagne Occidentale) 1945–1952* (Paris, 1952), p. 475.

independent of Germany. Yet German recovery was still limited to serving Europe, and aid was to be channelled through the occupying powers who were to set the new level of industry. On 29th August agreement was reached between the Western powers on raising the limit of steel production to 10·7 million tons. It was also envisaged that within three years Germany could pay its way and reach a standard of living 25 per cent below that of 1936. In October, in accordance with the new plan, the number of plants which were classified as surplus was reduced from 1,636 to 682.

Though the French acquiesced in the Anglo-American programme only with reluctance, it was evident that the Soviet stand was driving the Western powers together and disposing them to greater co-operation with the Germans. At the same time Soviet pressure in the East was intensified. In mid 1947 Berlin was torn with the Bürgermeister crisis as the *S.M.A.* vetoed the election of Ernst Reuter, the power of the police under the Communist Markgraf continued to grow, and kidnappings became more frequent. Controls on the zonal border were tightened, and after the abortive Munich conference of *Land* delegates in July East-West contacts were narrowly confined. On 6th December the *S.E.D.* assembled in Berlin a 1,500-strong 'German People's Congress for Unity and a Just Peace.' Designed as a form of *Vorparlament*, it included representatives from both the *L.D.P.* and the *C.D.U.*, but Kaiser and Lemmer declined to participate. A deputation under Pieck, Grotewohl, and the *L.D.P.* leader Dr Kulz was selected to go to London to urge that a peace treaty for all Germany on the basis of the Yalta and Potsdam agreements should be negotiated with a reconstructed central German government. A fortnight later, on 20th December, Kaiser and Lemmer paid for their opposition to the People's Congress with dismissal by the *S.M.A.* The Berlin party's ties (and those of the *L.D.P.*) with the zone were cut. With their hopes for a 'Berlin synthesis' dashed, Kaiser and Lemmer had perforce to transfer their activities to the West, and to help to construct the separate institutions which they had so persistently sought to avoid.

When the Foreign Ministers assembled in London on 25th November the French had abandoned their opposition to the new level of industry, and the Council agreed to a steel production of 11·5 million tons. But though the British and Americans seemed prepared for another hazardous and costly attempt to make the Potsdam agreement work, there was no evidence that the Russians would make the necessary concessions. The conference was dominated by the demand for the magical figure of $10 billion in reparations and by attacks on the construction of a West German state around Frankfurt and on the Marshall Plan. Molotov tried on 15th December to secure a hearing for the delegation from the German People's Congress, but the three Foreign Ministers declined to meet a delegation from so haphazard and unrepresentative an assembly. The same day the Council adjourned *sine die*, with the East-West gap over Germany wider than ever.

Failure in London quickened the consolidation of existing institutions in the West and the creation of new ones. The Bizonal Economic Council had

[1] Nettl, *Eastern Zone*, pp. 262–3.

proven ineffective in part because it lacked the necessary powers, and on 9th February 1948 agreement was reached on a new 'constitution' known as the 'Frankfurt Charter.' The Council's members were doubled by the addition of fifty-two members elected by the *Landtäge*; a *Laenderrat* composed of representatives appointed by each *Land* government was added, with an executive committee responsible for 'executing and administering the legislation enacted.' Christian Democrats were elected president of the Economic Council and chairman of the Executive Committee. Meanwhile, at the very time when Czech democracy was being smothered, representatives of the three Western powers, soon joined by those of Benelux, met in London on 23rd February to discuss trizonal fusion and the establishment of a West German government. Bidault's declaration in the National Assembly ten days earlier that the only solution to the German problem lay in 'the integration of a peaceful Germany in a united Europe, a Europe where the Germans, feeling secure in their position, will have been able to get rid of the idea of dominating Europe,'[1] foreshadowed a shift in the French attitude. Yet they fought a stubborn rearguard action to secure political and economic guarantees, insisting on economic incorporation of the Saar, international control of the Ruhr, and a federal political structure. Before recessing on 6th March the conference agreed that 'the economic reconstruction of western Europe, including Germany, and [the] establishing [of] a basis for the participation of a democratic Germany in the community of free peoples, could no longer be delayed by four-power disagreement,' though ultimate four-power agreement was in no way precluded.

In the six-week interval before the conference resumed events moved rapidly. On 17th March Britain, France, and the Benelux countries agreed in the Treaty of Brussels to stand jointly against the Communist threat. The same day the second session of the People's Congress assembled in Berlin 2,000 strong, claiming to be the only representatives of Germany. A German People's Council of 400 was elected with a presidium which looked like an embryonic government, and an *S.E.D.* proposal for an all-German plebiscite for 'Unity and a Just Peace' was 'unanimously' accepted. In a counter-gesture a day later, on the hundredth anniversary of the revolution of 1848, 80,000 Berliners gathered in the Platz der Republik before the ruined *Reichstag* to hear Reuter tell them that the Communist flood would break on their iron will. On 20th March Marshal Sokolovsky, since November 1945 Commander-in-Chief, read the Control Council a long prepared statement recapitulating Soviet charges, and, in a move which was clearly prearranged, left the meeting followed by the remainder of the Soviet delegation. By this time Soviet policies in Berlin had become more menacing. As early as January Sokolovsky had claimed that Berlin was part of the Soviet zone and that the Western powers had acted in a manner 'to prejudice their right to remain in Berlin.'[2] Ten days after Sokolovsky left the Control Council, Russian experiments with obstacles to road and rail traffic in and out of

[1] Willis, *The French in Germany*, pp. 51-2.
[2] Clay, *Decision in Germany*, p. 351.

Berlin became more threatening, when new regulations on military traffic were imposed at twenty-four hours' notice.

By the time the London Conference reassembled on 20th April the lines had been more clearly drawn, with the implementation of the Marshall Plan and the final preparations for reform of the German currency. On 30th April President Truman signed the Foreign Assistance Act under which the French zone was to receive $100 million in aid, the Bizone $414 million. When the Organization for European Economic Co-operation (O.E.E.C.) was formed on 16th April both were included as full members. Though a *Bank Deutscher Laender* had been created in February to act as a bank of issue, no further steps had been taken towards currency reform in the hope that four-power agreement might yet be reached. Reluctance to lose control over the volume of note issue led to Western rejection of the Russian condition for printing notes in the Soviet zone, and the British and Americans determined to proceed in their own zones on 1st June. The move was subsequently postponed for three weeks to secure French participation. By this time the resumed London Conference had reached a substantial measure of agreement. The *communiqué* issued shortly after it dispersed announced that the six powers had agreed that 'it would be desirable that the German people in the different states should be free to establish for themselves the political organization and institutions which will enable them to assume those governmental responsibilities which are compatible with the minimum requirements of occupation and control.' The Ministers-President were accordingly to convene a constituent assembly to draft a constitution which would protect the rights of the states while providing for an adequate central authority. A seven-power International Ruhr Authority was to supervise the allocation of coal, coke, and steel as between Germany and abroad and to oversee marketing practices.

The Western determination to proceed with these plans induced a shriller tone in Soviet counter-blasts. The People's Congress plebiscite held between 23rd May and 14th June was on the whole a failure, but Soviet denunciation reached a climax with the Warsaw Declaration issued by eight Foreign Ministers from central and eastern Europe on 24th June. This charged that the Western powers were splitting Germany and transforming their zones into 'an instrument for the rebuilding of Germany's war potential,' and demanded 'completion' of German demilitarization, four-power control over the Ruhr, conclusion of a peace treaty, withdrawal of occupation forces, and the formation of 'a provisional democratic and peaceable German government, composed of representatives of German democratic parties and organizations. . . .' Eight days earlier, on 16th June, the Soviets walked out of the Berlin *Kommandatura*. The previous day restrictions on communications with the West were tightened when the Elbe bridge on the *Autobahn* was closed for repairs.

Currency reform, though clearly foreseen as a challenge to the Soviets, could not be longer delayed if the pace of Western recovery was to be stepped up. On 18th June the Western commandants informed Marshal Sokolovsky that the new currency would be introduced on 20th June, but not in Berlin 'unless it becomes unavoidable.' The conciliatory intention to exclude Berlin had been taken in the face of strong representations by a Berlin delegation led by Reuter and by the *Laenderrat* in the West.[1] The immediate Soviet reply was to impose fresh restrictions on foot and freight traffic and to declare that the new currency would not 'be permitted to circulate in the Soviet zone of occupation and in the area of Greater Berlin which comes within the Soviet zone of occupation and is economically part of the Soviet zone.' On 23rd June Marshal Sokolovsky announced new currency for the Soviet zone and 'Greater Berlin.' The Western powers at once extended their currency to Berlin. This decision was backed by the city Assembly despite Communist menaces and violence, and on 24th June Berliners were faced by two currency reforms. The same day the railways to the West were closed, barge traffic was cut, and electricity supplies from the East were abruptly cut off.

The Western response to the blockade of Berlin was to halt all shipments to the Soviet zone and to institute an airlift to supply food and fuel for West Berlin's 2·2 million inhabitants and the Western military contingents. All available aircraft were switched to the Berlin route. By 7th July the first Skymaster landed at Tempelhof with ten tons of coal; early in August tankers began to fly in petrol and fuel oil. The capacity of the airlift doubled and redoubled. At first it was seen as a means of gaining time in which to negotiate. Approaches to Sokolovsky in Berlin and protest notes to Moscow both elicited the response that the blockade was a response to the alleged breaches of four-power agreements for the treatment of Germany in Berlin and the Western zones. In Moscow Stalin suggested that agreement could be reached on a formula for introducing, under quadripartite control, East zone currency into West Berlin, simultaneously with the lifting of the blockade and the resumption of negotiations on the German question as a whole. Agreement was eventually reached on a directive to the Military Governors, but Sokolovsky failed to honour the Moscow undertaking.

As the blockade tightened and Soviet pressure on the city intensified, its institutions were gradually split. By September the police, the food administration, and the banks had been divided. On 6th September Communist mobs forced the Assembly to move to the Western sector, where a new administration was constructed. The biennial elections, planned long before the blockade, were held on 25th December, though naturally confined to West Berlin. Despite Communist threats 86·3 per cent of the electorate turned out and 83·9 voted for the democratic parties, nearly 65 per cent for the *S.P.D.*, the most vocal of the Communists' opponents. In reply a 'special meeting' of the rump Assembly, composed of *S.E.D.* dominated organizations, elected a new *Magistrat* under Fritz Ebert, son of Weimar's first president. The division of the city was thus daily becoming sharper, as the eastern half was increasingly drawn into the Soviet zone, the west developing

---

[1] Philip Windsor, *City on Leave: A History of Berlin, 1945–1962* (London, 1963), pp. 95, 101–2.

separate and radically different institutions. The division of the country was hardly farther off.

The Berlin blockade had not been allowed to delay either the evolution of the West German state or the pace of Western economic recovery. On 1st July the Military Governors presented the Ministers-President with documents dealing with the drafting of the constitution by a constituent assembly, modifications in state boundaries, and an Occupation Statute to regulate the relationship between the new government and the Allied authorities. These allayed German fears that the constitution was to be framed and imposed by the Western powers, but the advantages of improved economic prospects through increased aid and the opportunity for achieving a greater share in the regulation of their own affairs were offset by the unhappy prospect of contributing to the division of Germany and provoking the Soviet Union. The Ministers-President were informed that they must either accept the London agreements substantially as they stood or face the prospect of indefinite delay. The Military Governors agreed, however, to use the term 'basic law' instead of constitution, and to call the forthcoming assembly a 'parliamentary council' instead of constituent assembly.[1]

A detailed draft constitution had been prepared by a committee of experts by the time the Parliamentary Council assembled in the *Pädagogische Akademie* in Bonn on 1st September. 'We meet today,' Christian Stock, Minister-President of Hesse, told the gathering, 'for the first time in the new era of German history since the capitulation, not by *Diktat*, but as a result of agreements. . . .' The Council consisted of sixty-five delegates chosen by the *Landtäge* on the basis of one for every 750,000 inhabitants. Most were present or former *Land* ministers or officials. The *C.D.U.* and the *S.P.D.* each had twenty-seven deputies, the *F.D.P.* five, with two each to the revived *Zentrum* (Centre), the conservative *Deutsche Partei* (German Party), and the *K.P.D.* Five non-voting delegates came from West Berlin. Schumacher did not enter the Council, but Adenauer was elected chairman. The weakness of the heterogeneous *C.D.U./C.S.U.* coalition forced the extreme clerical and federalist enthusiasts in its ranks to moderate their demands, and this made easier agreement with the *S.P.D.* and the *F.D.P.*, both of whom favoured a strongly centralized government. The debates were complicated by differences between the occupation powers which delayed agreement on the Occupation Statute, and this had the curious result that, except for omission of provision for defence and the references to German areas not incorporated in the Federal Republic, the Basic Law read as though the occupation powers had never existed.

Planning for a West German government took place against a background of a dramatically improved economic situation following the currency reform. At a single blow West Germany escaped the bonds of poverty, as on the very morrow of the conversion agricultural products and manufactured foods which had hitherto been kept off the market suddenly appeared in the shops.[2]

[1] John Ford Golay, *The Founding of the Federal Republic of Germany* (Chicago, 1958), pp. 13–17.

[2] Piettre, *L'Économie allemande*, p. 206.

'The black market suddenly disappeared,' two French observers wrote. 'Shop windows were full of goods, factory chimneys were smoking, and the streets swarmed with lorries. Everywhere the noise of buildings going up replaced the deathly silence of the ruins. . . . In all sectors of economic life [recovery] began as the clocks struck on the day of currency reform. . . .'[1] The immediate impact of the currency reform was exploited by the neo-liberal policies of the Bizonal Director of Economic Affairs, Professor Ludwig Erhard. Given wide powers to decontrol freely by a law enacted on 26th June, he had the satisfaction of seeing the index of industrial production (on the basis of 1936 equalling 100) climb from 54 in June to 60 in July and to 79 by December. While unemployment climbed steeply, employment also rose, and the cost of living, after climbing from June to October, levelled off and soon started to decline. The fact of recovery was indisputable, but, although the workers were now receiving payment in real purchasing power, there was a marked inequality of income, and pensioners were 'the real step-children' of this first phase of the German recovery.[2]

Meanwhile the airlift had enabled Berlin to survive. Though the winter of 1948–9 was a thin one for Berliners, their courage in the face of danger and privation, and their support and indeed leadership of the occupation powers, had administered the Soviets a severe defeat both at Berlin and in the West, where the continuation of the blockade seemed to be furthering the very measures of consolidation which it had been designed to check. The threat implicit in the blockade had also deepened the currents of anti-Soviet hostility,[3] and largely silenced the critics of Allied separatist policy in West Germany. It had also radically altered the relationship between Germans and the Western Allies from that between occupiers and occupied to something approaching partnership in a joint enterprise. The Soviet Union was thus forced into a drastic alteration in its German policy. While accepting the division of Berlin and of Germany, it had perforce to take steps to prevent the emerging West German state from becoming an active, armed Western ally. This purpose lay behind the peace offensive and the stepped-up campaign for German unity, which was pursued at the same time as the Soviet zone emerged as a nominally independent member of the Soviet satellite system.

This shift in tactics required a liquidation of the Berlin blockade. A hint to an American journalist early in 1949 was followed by Russo-American negotiations at the United Nations. After discussions with the other Western governments, agreement was announced on 5th May providing for the simultaneous lifting of the blockade and the Allied counter-restrictions, followed by a meeting of the Council of Foreign Ministers. Just after midnight on 11th May West Berlin's long night ended as Soviet power-stations resumed transmission across the boundary, and road and rail traffic between the city and the West began again.

---

[1] Jacques Rueff and André Piettre, cited in Ludwig Erhard, *Prosperity through Competition* (London, 1960), p. 13.
[2] Henry C. Wallich, *Mainsprings of the German Revival* (New Haven, 1955) pp. 47–52.
[3] W. Phillips Davison, *The Berlin Blockade* (Princeton, 1958), pp. 281–7.

The Council of Ministers met from 23rd May to 20th June, but beyond renewing the agreement of 5th May no progress was made on either Berlin or general German issues. It seemed to have served no other purpose than to fulfil the terms required for lifting the blockade, and to permit the restatement of positions on either side. It was followed by developments in East and West which further crystallized the division.

On the same day that the Foreign Ministers assembled in Paris the Basic Law was signed in Bonn. Differences among the German political parties over Allied demands for strengthening the powers of the *Laender* had delayed agreement, and not until the Western Foreign Ministers assembled at Washington at the beginning of April to sign the North Atlantic Treaty were the terms of the Occupation Statute and the Statute for the Ruhr agreed to. Once the Military Governors had approved the Basic Law on 12th May it was ratified by all the *Laender* governments. Though twice described as 'provisional,' the Basic Law signed on 23rd May 1949 remained the constitution of the German Federal Republic. Drawing on the experience of the Weimar Republic it provided for the election of the President not by popular vote but by a *Bundesversammlung* composed of members of the *Bundestag* and an equal number of members of the *Landtäge*. His reserve powers were also circumscribed. To counterbalance the weakened Presidency and to avoid the instability of the 1920's the Chancellorship was strengthened. Elected by a majority vote of the *Bundestag* he could only be replaced by a 'constructive vote of no-confidence'—the election of another Chancellor—and if defeated in the *Bundestag* he was empowered to secure a dissolution. The strong influence of the occupying powers was revealed in the federal emphasis on the distribution of powers, the structure of the *Bundesrat* or upper chamber, and in the provisions for constitutional amendment. Schumacher had, however, succeeded in assigning primacy in taxing powers and financial administration to the central government. The Basic Law made no reference to defence. Disarmament and demilitarization, controls in the Ruhr, foreign affairs, and control over foreign trade and exchange were among the powers reserved to the occupying powers by the Statute published on 8th April 1949. They also reserved the general right 'to resume, in whole or in part, the exercise of full authority' if they considered this 'essential to security or to preserve democratic government in Germany or in pursuit of the international obligations of their governments.' By Article 23 of the Basic Law, Greater Berlin was included as one of the original *Laender*. Mindful of their four-power responsibilities the occupying powers decreed that Berlin must not be 'governed by the Federation,' and permitted it only a small number of observers in Bonn. Paralleling the Occupation Statute they promulgated on 14th May a 'Statement of Principles' granting broad authority to the West Berlin government and reserving only decisions over foreign trade and exchange, and supervision of the police.

The dominant theme in the electoral campaign for the first *Bundestag* was economic policy. The *C.D.U.* stood squarely behind the *Sozialmarktwirtschaft* policy of Ludwig Erhard, and were assisted by a steady increase

in industrial production and, by summer, by gradually falling prices.   The
S.P.D. attempted to woo the large masses of electors whom the first phase of
German recovery had bypassed, and were expected to emerge as the largest
party.   But when the votes were counted after 14th August the *C.D.U.*
received 139 seats to the *S.P.D.*'s 131, having won a narrow lead thanks only
to a decided triumph in the predominantly Catholic French zone.   Fifty-
two seats went to the *F.D.P.*, twelve to the *D.P.*   On 12th September the
Bundesversammlung elected Professor Theodor Heuss as *Bundespräsident*
over Schumacher on the second ballot.   A well-known historian and a
former member of the Weimar Democratic Party, he had made a distinguished
contribution to the drafting of the Basic Law.   The bitterness of the election
campaign and the hostility between the leaders of the two major parties
precluded the formation of a 'grand coalition' of *C.D.U.* and *S.P.D.*, and
after prolonged negotiations the *Bundestag* elected the seventy-three-year-
old Adenauer on the first ballot though by a single vote.   With the *F.D.P.*
and the *D.P.*, he formed a right wing coalition cabinet, four of whose thirteen
members had not been elected to the *Bundestag*.   Important posts went to
F.D.P. members Blücher and Seebohm.   Erhard received the vital Economic
Ministry, Fritz Schäfer, another Bavarian, the Finance Ministry.   Apart
from Kaiser, who became Minister for All German Affairs, none of the *C.D.U.*
members had opposed Adenauer on serious issues; all were men he could
trust to follow his initiative.   On 21st September 1949 the Occupation
Statute came into force, the functions of the occupying powers were transferred to the Allied High Commission, and the Federal Republic of Germany
came into being.

East of the Iron Curtain the Soviet Union was pursuing a dual policy
designed to frustrate the consolidation in the West, while at the same time
preparing in secret plans for the erection of an East German state.   The
principal agents of the vociferous propaganda compaign directed against
the West were the National Front and the People's Congress movement.   In
a series of manifestoes directed against 'the Schumacher spying centre in
Hanover' and the 'separatists circled around Adenauer,' and against the
Western powers as robbers of the Ruhr and splitters of Germany, the *S.E.D.*
called for a united Germany, a peace treaty, and the withdrawal of occupation
troops.   The final version of the constitution which had been approved in
principle by the People's Council in October 1948, providing for a bicameral
legislature and every ostensible feature of parliamentary democracy, was
endorsed by the People's Council in March 1949.   In advance of elections
for a third *Volkskongress* scheduled for 15th–16th May, Ulbricht proclaimed
a 'National Front' of all parties and groups, including the National Democratic Party, which had been created a year earlier to provide a haven for
ex-Nazis following the political amnesty.   The *S.E.D.* had meanwhile, in
January 1949, been remodelled on the Russian pattern with a *Politburo* under
Ulbricht.   The bourgeois parties were powerless and kept alive only because
of their usefulness to the *S.E.D.*   The blatant appeal to German nationalism
had only qualified success.   Though the ballots contained rigged party lists

and a request for approval of German unity, and counting was at best questionable, the results gave the Russians a rude shock.   Over one-third (and in Berlin over two-fifths) voted 'No.'

When the Congress assembled at the end of May it resolved to send a delegation to the Foreign Ministers then meeting in Paris, and elected a new People's Council.   Though the effort to influence the Foreign Ministers was a failure, the campaign for unity and peace continued throughout the summer. By autumn, with the emergence of the Federal Republic, it became clear that nothing was to be gained by further postponing the establishment of a separate government for East Germany, whose spontaneous appearance had been long and carefully prepared.   Following a seies of press articles and factory resolutions demanding a German Republic with Berlin as its capital, the People's Council obliged by merely declaring itself to be the provisional *Volkskammer* foreseen in the constitution approved earlier.   Grotewohl became Prime Minister, with Ulbricht and the eastern *C.D.U.* and *L.D.P.* leaders, Nuschke and Kastner, as Deputy Prime Ministers.   An upper house (*Laenderkammer*) was elected by the assemblies of the five provinces, with five observers from East Berlin.   On 11th October it unanimously elected Wilhelm Pieck, the only candidate, as president.   The *Deutsche Demokratische Republik* (*D.D.R.*) came into being on 7th October, with a constitution which demonstrated an outward concern for legality, mentioning 'all that was lacking in human rights in the Soviet zone, while omitting the real factors governing political life.' [1]   Despite the transfer on 10th October of the administrative functions of the *S.M.A.*, and its supersession by a Soviet Control Commission, power remained securely in Russian hands.   The new regime was promptly denounced by the Western powers, as 'without legal validity or foundation in popular will.'   At the first elections, postponed to October 1950, even Nazi records were shattered: of the 98·539 per cent of the electorate which voted, 99·719 cast their votes in favour of the single list of candidates presented by the National Front.[2]

By the end of 1949 separate German states had thus emerged in East and West, each associated with a rival power group.   In the divided former capital, still nominally under four-power control, East Berlin was increasingly drawn within the *D.D.R.*, of which it was the capital; West Berlin, though isolated geographically, was closely linked with the Federal Republic, which provided it with a subsidy and its allocation of E.R.P. (European Recovery Programme) aid.   In the ensuing decade and a half German history became increasingly compartmentalized into the story of the Federal Republic, of the *D.D.R.*, of divided Berlin, and of relations between these parts and with the outside world.   The old question, 'What is Germany?' took on a new dimension, as German history became a fragmented tale on which it is difficult for the historian to impose a unity.

For the Federal Republic the years after 1949 were a period of reviving

---

[1] Nettl, *Eastern Zone*, p. 112.
[2] Peter Calvocoressi, *Survey of International Affairs, 1949–1950* (London, New York, Toronto, 1953), p. 214.

German decision, based on a striking economic recovery and a resurgence of political power.   The new state took on a stability remarkable considering the circumstances of its birth, the weakness of the German democratic tradition, the suddenness of the transition from occupation following defeat to rearmed ally.   The continuing pace of economic recovery—'one of the most impressive performances of the post-war scene' [1]—made the term 'economic miracle' commonplace.   By 1950 industrial production passed the 1936 mark, and exports climbed rapidly as the 'dollar therapy' of the E.R.P. provided capital for expansion and helped to sustain the balance of payments.   The emphasis on recovery brought with it the end of the reparations programme.   The outbreak of the Korean War in 1950 brought the second boom within two years, and the production index once again shot upwards.   Though a good part of the rising national income went into new investments, *per capita* consumption soon surpassed the pre-war level. Unemployment fell gradually, and most of the population was probably better off than before the war.   There remained, however, large distressed classes—pensioners and recipients of some form of public relief who in 1951–2 amounted to between twelve and thirteen million people, or a quarter of the total.[2]   Contrary to many fears, the influx from the Polish occupied 'eastern territories' of eight million expellees and by the mid 1950's of nearly two million refugees from the Soviet zone, proved an aid to recovery rather than a hindrance, providing an abundant labour force, important skills, and new industries, and contributing to the spirit of competition and enterprise.[3] Recovery was also aided by the attitude of the trade unions.   The *Deutscher Gewerkschaftsbund* (*D.G.B.*) was formed on 13th October 1949 as a federation of sixteen unions and by 1952 had a membership of six million.   In the interests of national revival they pursued a policy of restraint both as to wages and hours, and attached importance rather to steady prices and full employment, and to securing a share in industrial management.   An early victory was the passage by the *Bundestag* on 10th April 1951 of a law providing for *Mitbestimmungsrecht* (co-determination) in the iron, steel, and coal industries.[4]

The experiment in parliamentary democracy was greatly facilitated by this growing prosperity, though in the heavy eagle of the Republic's flag which hung behind the president's chair in the new parliament house in Bonn many saw the symbol of the economic miracle, its weight pressing on the parliamentary labours.[5]   The *Bundestag*'s sessions proved dull and formal, with the best work being done in committee.   During its first four years it passed 545 laws.   In addition to completing its own organization and confirming the attractive if provincial city of Bonn as the provisional capital, it had to approve numerous measures for which the Basic Law had made but general provision, and to deal with exceptional problems such as refugees and economic reconstruction.   Chancellor Adenauer took unchallenged leadership

[1] Wallich, *Mainsprings of the German Revival*, p. 106.
[2] Richard Hiscocks, *Democracy in Western Germany* (London, New York, Toronto, 1957), p. 85.
[3] Wallich, *Mainsprings of the German Revival*, pp. 281–2.
[4] Herbert J. Spiro, *The Politics of German Codetermination* (Cambridge, Mass., 1958), p. 38.
[5] Alfred Grosser, *Die Bonner Demokratie* (Düsseldorf, 1960), p. 91.

of his cabinet and treated the *Bundestag* in an aloof, rather cavalier manner. Yet by providing stable and effective government he accustomed the German people to relatively unfamiliar institutions and aided the growth of political democracy. In general he favoured the economic policy of the right and the social policy of the trade unions, in order to secure the growth of both groups for his foreign policy.[1]

Foreign affairs provided the source of political division in the first *Bundestag*, as the *S.P.D.* opposed Adenauer's espousal of European integration and reunification through the backing of a strengthened West. Within a few weeks of its creation the Federal Republic became a member of O.E.E.C., and negotiation of the first Petersberg agreement in November 1949 with the Allied High Commission represented a significant advance in Bonn's status. The imaginative proposal for pooling steel and coal production put forward by French Foreign Minister Robert Schuman in May 1950 was quickly accepted in Bonn, and in August the same year the Federal Republic entered the Council of Europe as an associate member. Membership in other international organizations followed. 'Germany's sick leave from world history,' a German later commented, 'was over.'[2] On 27th September Adenauer recalled to the *Bundestag* that 'in the German people's name unspeakable crimes have been committed, which demand material and moral reparation.' An agreement, reached after long and difficult negotiations, for large payments in goods to Israel over twelve years was approved by the *Bundestag* in March 1953 by a large majority. Behind most of the Republic's foreign policy (conducted without Foreign Office or Foreign Minister) lay the problem of reunification. It was understandable that Communist propaganda, spearheaded by the National Front, should find a receptive audience beyond Communist circles in the West. The Western powers' belated campaign for free elections as the basis for forming an all-German government competed with Grotewohl's demand, in a letter to Adenauer in November 1950, for 'Germans around one table.'

The outbreak of the Korean war had momentous consequences. It provoked sobering thoughts among West Germans at what might have ensued had they succumbed to the National Front's lure of unity at the price of the withdrawal of the occupation forces; it provoked near panic and silenced much criticism of the occupying powers; it bred demands from Bonn for increased provision for the defence of the Republic; and when long-standing rumours of impending German rearmament were given substance it precipitated a bitter political struggle. Though the Petersberg agreement of 1949 had reiterated the Allied intention to prevent the re-creation of German armed forces, and the overwhelming majority of German opinion and its leaders opposed any rearmament, it was evident by the summer of 1950 that N.A.T.O.'s post-Korean planning for integrated European defence required some German contribution. At Strasbourg in August, a few days after the German members took their seats, the Consultative Assembly of the Council of

[1] Alfred Grosser, *Western Germany from Defeat to Rearmament* (London, 1955), p. 203.
[2] Cited in Hiscocks, *Democracy in Western Germany*, p. 52.

Europe called for a European army in which, Mr Churchill explained, German units would be included. In New York in September, the three Western powers agreed to end the state of war with Germany, to reinforce their forces in Germany, and to meet in part German requests by authorizing the establishment of mobile *Land* police formations. In a move designed to prevent the formation of a national German army French Prime Minister René Pleven proposed on 24th October a European army in which German units would be merged at the lowest possible level. This was welcomed by Chancellor Adenauer, who against Schumacher's bitter opposition argued inside and outside the *Bundestag* that it was reasonable for Germans to make a contribution to their own defence, provided they were not merely required as cannon fodder. In December the N.A.T.O. Council endorsed an immediate beginning of German rearmament and the creation of a European army in which the basic national unit would be a combat group of 5,000 to 6,000 men. Aggression in Korea had thus pointed the way to the reconstruction of German armed forces a bare five years after the *Wehrmacht*'s destruction, as the full partnership of West Germany—militarily as well as politically and economically—had become essential to the survival of the Western world. Soviet alarm at this fateful step opened up a prolonged diplomatic dialogue between East and West, and led ultimately to a meeting of the deputies of the Foreign Ministers. After failing to agree on an agenda, however, they adjourned on 21st June 1951.

Early in 1952 the Occupation Statute was amended to permit establishment of a West German Foreign Ministry, and on 15th March Chancellor Adenauer, in the face of much criticism, added control of the Foreign Ministry to his other duties. The Allies ended the state of war with Germany the same year. On 18th April the European Coal and Steel Community Treaty—keystone of the new Europe—was signed, and following approval by the *Bundestag* in April 1952 came into effect on 5th July. But negotiations for the European Defence Community (E.D.C.) and the associated agreements on which West German rearmament depended, were prolonged. In the meantime the campaign for reunification continued. In September 1951 the *Bundestag* approved all-German elections supervised by a neutral commission, but in December investigation by a U.N. Commission was rejected by Grotewohl as an 'intervention in the domestic affairs of the German people.' On 10th March 1952, as the E.D.C. negotiations drew to a close, Russia proposed the withdrawal of foreign troops and the early conclusion of a peace treaty which would restore ex-Nazis full equality of rights, bind a future united Germany to neutrality vis-à-vis the U.S.S.R., and ominously prohibit 'organizations hostile to democracy and to the cause of peace.'

Despite Communist threats and demonstrations the treaties, known as the 'Bonn Convention' or the 'Contractual Agreements,' were signed in Bonn on 26th May 1952, with Schuman commenting simply: 'We must learn slowly to trust each other again.'[1] The primary 'Convention on Relations between the Three Western Powers and the Federal Republic' restored to Germany

[1] Alistair Horne, *Back into Power* (London, 1955), p. 11.

sovereignty alike in internal and external affairs, and officially brought the occupation to an end. Yet in unprecedented fashion important rights relating to the stationing of troops, Berlin, and the negotiation of a final peace treaty were withheld, and the Republic was to pay for its sovereignty by being irrevocably bound to the Western military alliance through the E.D.C., approved by a treaty signed in Paris on 27th May. The Russian reaction was swift. The ring around Berlin was tightened, and the Eastern zone was sealed off behind a ten-metre death strip designed to bring home to Germans the extent of the division of their country wrought by the Contractual Agreements.

For more than two years the future of the treaties was in doubt. Their constitutionality was tested in time-consuming references to the Federal Constitutional Court in Karlsruhe; the shadow of Franco-German hostility rose again over France's determination to maintain her special economic relation with the Saar; but above all the cry for rearmament so soon after Germans had been persuaded that any form of militarism was evil and that German rearmament would not be tolerated bred among German youth a widespread attitude of *ohne mich* (count me out) and a bitter struggle against the treaties led by Schumacher until his death in August 1952. It was March 1953 before the *Bundestag* approved the treaties. In the *Bundesrat* the key was held by Reinhold Maier, Minister President of the newly created *Land* of Baden-Wurtemberg, formed by the reunion of territories formerly divided by the French and American zones. Following a bargain with the newly created Refugee Party (*B.H.E.*), *Bundesrat* approval was obtained on 15th May.

At the time plans for rearming Western Germany were frequently justified by reference to the remilitarization of the Soviet zone. The precise extent of East German military preparations was difficult to discern, as from 1947 on the zonal border was progressively sealed and the chief channel of information was the open frontier in Berlin. Available evidence indicated that it was considerable, especially since the formation of the *Volkspolizei* (People's Police) in 1947, highly centralized and with weapons and organization which emphasized its para-military character. By early 1950 the *Kasernierte Polizei* (Barrack Police), with a solid backbone of former officers and N.C.O.'s, had a strength of some 50,000 and was organized in *Bereitschaften* (Alert Units) along military lines. On 1st July 1952 Grotewohl formally announced the creation of an East German army, known as the *Kasernierte Volkspolizei*, 'in the interests of peace.' It made its first appearance in olive green uniform at the 7th October anniversary parade. By the end of 1952, years before a single West German soldier had been recruited, the new East German force had a strength of more than 100,000, and was equipped with tanks and other heavy Russian equipment.

The early 1950's were on the whole grey days for the seventeen million inhabitants of the *D.D.R.* Though '*Mitteldeutschland*' had suffered less than the western districts, reconstruction and economic progress had been slower, in part because of the reparations, estimated by Western sources in 1953 at $18 billion, extracted by the U.S.S.R. In addition the flow of refugees to the West produced a labour shortage, and much needed land reform undertaken early in the occupation resulted in the creation of many small, uneconomic farms.   Primary emphasis was on the production of basic and capital goods, with consumer goods and food and tobacco lagging behind or only slightly exceeding the pre-war level.   At the second *S.E.D.* Congress in July 1952 Ulbricht announced that the *D.D.R.* would embark on an all-out programme of 'building socialism in East Germany,' with a speeding up of industrialization and a ruthless collectivization of agriculture.   The chief instrument was to be state power—already highly centralized with the abolition a year earlier of the *Laender*.   The East German economy, however, was in no condition to withstand new burdens.   Despite draconic efforts to exact food deliveries from the farmers the winter of 1952–3 was a hungry one.   The food shortage, the rapid collectivization, the campaign against the churches, the waves of arrests and the direction of labour led to an unprecedented flow of refugees to the West, most of them through the escape hatch of Berlin. In April 1952 just over 9,300 left; by January 1953 the figure was over 22,000; in March, following a fresh wave of repressive measures, it reached a peak of 58,000, nearly 2,000 a day.   Soviet alarm brought stringent measures to prohibit flight and then, after the uneasy interregnum following the death of Stalin, the 'New Course.'   This was signalled by the appointment of Vladimir Semeonov to the new post of High Commissioner, and involved a reversal of the policy announced by Ulbricht a year earlier.   It came too late to prevent the explosion.   On 17th June a demonstration, begun by building workers in the grotesque *Stalinallee* housing project in East Berlin to protest against an increase in work norms, turned into rebellion which spread like wildfire to Leipzig, Halle, Brandenburg, and other centres.   For half a day the regime appeared to be tottering.   But the outcome was decided by the massed intervention of Soviet tanks.   Martial law was proclaimed, and despite some examples of desperate courage Berlin and the other scenes of insurrection were reduced to an angry silence.   Fearful of extending the conflict, the Western powers were unable to assist this bitter, futile protest against Communist tyranny with more than sympathy and unavailing protests to the Soviet authorities.   The *Bundestag* declared 17th June the 'Day of German Unity,' and in the ensuing weeks hungry East Germans made their way to West Berlin from the farthest ends of the zone to receive parcels of American food.

The rising of 17th June had important consequences.   It facilitated the end of Soviet reparations exactions and started the transition to a policy of beginning to create better living standards.   Though the concessions announced late in June were extremely modest, the will to resist had been broken. Late in August the screw was tightened again, and Frau Benjamin, the dreaded 'Red Hilde,' became Minister of Justice.   It also appears to have delayed progress towards the four-power talks by which the U.S.S.R. hoped that E.D.C. could be defeated.   When they were finally held in January 1954 the Communist position in East Germany had been re-established.   Finally, it embarrassed Adenauer's advocacy of first E.D.C., then reunification, just when the life of the first *Bundestag* was coming to an end.

The elections, scheduled for 6th September 1953, were the first genuinely 'free' national elections and provided an early test of the success of West German democratization. A fair but complicated new electoral law provided each voter with two votes, one for a particular candidate, the second for a party list. To avoid the danger of a multiplicity of splinter parties it also provided that a party required a minimum of one candidate elected from a constituency or 5 per cent of all votes cast in order to gain representation at Bonn. The campaign turned very largely on foreign policy. The seventy-seven-year-old Adenauer adopted American whistle-stop techniques, and, unmoved by threats or blandishments from the East, tirelessly argued that reunification could only come from Western strength and that the E.D.C. was the only way for Germany to contribute to it. In contrast to this simple, clear programme the Social Democratic alternative, put forward under Erich Ollenhauer, the colourless party functionary who had succeeded Schumacher, of rejecting the Schuman Plan and E.D.C. in the interests of German reunification through a broad security organization, was woolly and unconvincing. Their cry for higher wages and nationalization met with little response from a country clearly prospering. Industrial production was nearly 60 per cent above 1936, unemployment was down, prices remained steady. Though the struggle was primarily between these two a new feature of the campaign was the part played by the *Block der Heimatvertriebenen und Entrechteten* (*B.H.E.*), a party established in 1951 to appeal to the ten million refugees and expellees who had settled in the Republic. To reinforce its interest in central and eastern Europe the words *Gesamtdeutscher Block* (*G.B.*) were added to the party's title.

Though the *C.D.U.* and the *S.P.D.* both benefited from the increased poll (86·2 per cent), the *C.D.U.* increased its lead from eight seats to 94 and, by a single seat, secured the first absolute majority in German parliamentary history, winning 244 out of 487 seats. The *S.P.D.* won 150, the *F.D.P.* 48, the *G.B.*/*B.H.E.* 27, and the *D.P.* 15. If it was hardly surprising that the *K.P.D.* suffered a shattering defeat, it was a cause of satisfaction that the success of the major parties had been achieved at the expense of the splinter and radical parties, with the neo-Nazi German Reich Party getting a bare 1·1 per cent of the vote. Instead of the danger of instability the cry was now that the young German democracy would be endangered by what *Der Spiegel* described as 'too complete' a victory for an authoritarian-prone chancellor. However, with his eye on the possible need for a two-thirds majority in the *Bundestag* which had overwhelmingly re-elected him Chancellor, Adenauer formed a cabinet which included representatives of his two former partners (the *F.D.P.* and the *D.P.*, both of whom had lost seats) and of the *G.B.*/*B.H.E.*, which had signally failed to attract mass refugee or extremist support, and barely survived the 5 per cent rule. It took five weeks to complete the cabinet with its delicate balance of party and confessional interests. New faces among its nineteen members included Gerhard Schroeder as Minister of the Interior and Franz-Josef Strauss as Minister without Portfolio.

Following the election attention was riveted on the international plane.

Preceded by prolonged diplomatic exchanges, a stepped-up campaign for reunification, and the final Russian overture of the repatriation of 10,000 bedraggled prisoners of war, many of them in the most pitiable condition, the four-power conference opened in Berlin on 25th January 1954. The West presented the 'Eden Plan' for free elections, the formation of an all-German government, and the negotiation of a peace treaty; the East the demand for the withdrawal of all foreign troops and the neutralization of Germany. Both differed little from the plans advanced in 1952. All four participants repeated the frequently rehearsed and familiar arguments. On 19th February it adjourned, having failed to agree even on a basis for discussion. This was a blow to the *S.P.D.* and all who had argued the advantages of negotiations with the U.S.S.R. It also adversely affected German morale, as in the West it was widely believed the Western powers had not really tried to reach agreement, while in the East hope of deliverance appeared to stretch off into an indefinite future. This conclusion was reinforced when the Soviet Government announced on 25th March that it was establishing with the *D.D.R.* 'the same relations . . . as with other sovereign states.' The summer of 1954 brought further blows to Adenauer. Delay in reaching agreement with France on the Saar contributed to growing doubts at the Chancellor's European and German policies. The spectacular defection to East Germany of Otto John, head of Bonn's counter-intelligence, brought his prestige to a new low. And finally at the end of August the French National Assembly, undissuaded from its fear of being called upon to 'mourir pour Königsberg,' by Adenauer's assurances that all Germans wished to effect reunification 'only by peaceful means,' rejected E.D.C. by a simple procedural vote before the debate was completed.

Unless the West was prepared to abandon its plans for a German defence contribution, the end of E.D.C. could only lead to its being made in the context of the full sovereignty for which a disillusioned and disappointed Adenauer called when the shattering news from Paris reached his Black Forest holiday retreat. Though Ollenhauer and the *S.P.D.* gloated that the Chancellor's policy was 'completely wrecked,' and Adenauer himself expressed fears that the blow administered by France to the European idea might mean 'a return in Germany to an exaggerated nationalism,' a rescue operation was promptly launched. A nine-power conference in London (28th September–3rd October) unexpectedly agreed on a scheme to restore German sovereignty, provide for the defence of Europe within an enlarged Brussels Treaty, and invite the Federal Republic to join N.A.T.O. Detailed agreements, which involved redrafting those reached in 1952, were worked out in Paris and signed on 23rd October 1953. The same day a Franco-German agreement provided that, pending a German peace settlement and subject to the approval of its inhabitants, the Saar would be Europeanized under a Western Union which was to be formed out of the Brussels Treaty. Though the supra-national character of the E.D.C. had gone, the size of the German defence contribution was fixed, its general staff was limited by placing the power of location of its forces, 'higher training,' and logistics under the jurisdiction of the Supreme Allied Commander (S.A.C.), and the Federal Republic pledged itself not to manufacture atomic, bacteriological, or chemical weapons.

Opposition to the Paris agreements opened up bitter political divisions which, in the case of the Saar, extended into the ranks of the coalition and the *C.D.U.* itself.   The *S.P.D.*, backed by the trade unions and powerfully reinforced by threats and blandishments from East Germany and the U.S.S.R., argued that reunification must precede rearmament, and that a reunited Germany must not ally itself with West or East, while standing ideologically with the Western world.   The deepening division of the country and the extent of the Sovietization of the *D.D.R.* was underlined by the 'elections' of 18th October, when 99·3 per cent of the voters endorsed the single list, with only 280,000 out of twelve million finding a way to record a negative vote.   On 15th January 1955 the Soviet Union issued a last warning that 'ratification would perpetuate the partition of Germany for years,' but that abandonment of the treaties could be followed by all-German free elections before the end of 1955, on the basis of an electoral law drafted 'in the light of existing electoral legislation' in the two German states.   But neither the warning nor the apparently attractive though vaguely worded offer deterred the West German Government.   On 27th February, after four days' debate, the *Bundestag* ratified all but one of the agreements by an overwhelming majority. On the Saar a Free Democratic minister joined the opposition, and Kaiser abstained.   On 5th May Germany became a sovereign, independent power, and four days later a member of N.A.T.O.   The Soviet answer was the 'Treaty of Friendship, Co-operation, and Mutual Assistance', signed at Warsaw on 14th May, though for the time the *D.D.R.* was not asked to contribute armed forces to its unified command.

Though Adenauer was anxious to take immediate steps towards setting up the new armed forces, progress was extremely slow.   A law passed by the *Bundestag* on 15th July allowed the enlistment of only 6,000 men up to 31st March 1956, when definitive legislation would be passed.   By the end of the year only 800 soldiers had been enrolled.   In an effort to ensure democratic control of the defence forces, the *Bundestag* created a civilian board to vet all officers with the rank of lieutenant-colonel and above, and by amendments to the Basic Law made the Defence Minister Commander-in-Chief in peacetime and the Defence Committee of the *Bundestag* into a permanent 'watchdog.'   Within the army efforts were made to implement the reformist ideas for 'citizens in uniform' advanced by Colonel Graf von Baudissin.   A prolonged struggle over conscription was not resolved until late 1956, when the normal period was reduced from a planned eighteen months to twelve.

The events of 1955—the creation of two German states integrated into the rival alliance systems—deepened and widened the division of Germany, and, however unavoidable, gave ample justification to the fears of those who believed that East-West disagreement was prolonging the division—with the precarious isolation of West Berlin—into an indefinite future.   This posed for the Federal Government twin dilemmas: how to avoid creating the impression that it was acquiescing in the permanent partition of Germany, while at the same time doing nothing that would arouse the suspicion of its new allies in response to the persistent attempts of the U.S.S.R. to break the Republic's ties to the West.   At the Geneva summit conference in July the Russians clung tenaciously to the position that the only approach to German reunification lay in the creation of a European security system in which both Germanys would participate, but agreed to a directive to the Foreign Ministers to discuss 'the reunification of Germany by means of free elections.' When Adenauer was invited to Moscow in September, he agreed to the resumption of diplomatic relations and secured the release of a small number of prisoners.   But a week later a Russian treaty concluded with the *D.D.R.* purported to bring the occupation to an end and to grant sovereignty in return for an undertaking to contribute to the defence forces of the Warsaw Treaty powers.   It was followed in January 1956 by the abandonment of the fiction that the *D.D.R.*'s armed forces consisted only of police, when the formation of the *Nationale Volksarmee* was announced with Willy Stoph, a protégé of Ulbricht's, named Colonel-General and. Minister of Defence. Meanwhile at Geneva in November Molotov repudiated the principle of free elections and made it clear that the Soviet Union was aiming at nothing less than the bolshevization of Germany, and in the meantime preferred to prolong the division indefinitely.   This was a devastating blow to the hopes of West Germans, and by revealing the Soviet hand and demonstrating the futility of another four-power conference seemed to drive the German parties together in the realization that reunification was a distant goal.   Paradoxically, at the very moment when the conferences of 1955 had stimulated interest in reunification, the solution to the problem had been made more remote.

Henceforth the stalemate became increasingly intractable, despite repeated efforts to break it.   The diplomatic link between Bonn and Moscow proved unfruitful.   Proposals for thinning out troops as part of a general disarmament programme served only to underline the difficulty of reaching agreement on a formula for reunification.   Events in Poland and in Hungary in 1956 produced understandable anxiety in Bonn and Berlin lest unrest in the *D.D.R.* should involve a repetition of 17th June 1953.   A new note in the prolonged diplomatic debate was the threatening warning in April 1957 against the stationing of atomic weapons on German soil.   German attachment to the West had meanwhile been progressively tightened.   In January 1957 General Hans Speidel, who had been Rommel's Chief of Staff in 1944, was appointed to command N.A.T.O.'s central sector.   The same month registration for military service finally began.   In June the first of three light divisions was handed over to N.A.T.O.   By the end of the year the new German army had a strength of 122,000.   Progress of German integration into Europe was also underlined by the signature on 25th March 1957 of the Rome Treaty bringing into being the European Economic Community (E.E.C.), and the treaty establishing Euratom, designed to organize collaboration among the 'Six' on the peaceful use of atomic energy.   *Rapprochement* with France—especially after de Gaulle's accession to power in May 1958—was facilitated by the end of the dispute over the Saar.   In October 1955 the Saarlanders had rejected the European Statute which Adenauer had accepted only with reluctance. A new agreement signed in October 1956 provided for restoration of German political sovereignty on 1st January 1957. Economic reunification of the Saar with the Federal Republic was completed on 5th July 1959.

Soon after the regaining of sovereignty Adenauer's coalition was in difficulties and his personal prestige was in decline. Late in 1955 he had lost his two-thirds majority in the *Bundestag* when the *G.B./B.H.E.* went into opposition, though its leaders—Oberländer and Kraft—remained in the cabinet. Bluntly expressed opposition to the Chancellor's foreign policy by the mercurial *F.D.P.* leader, Thomas Dehler, led to a split in February 1956. Sixteen members, including Blücher, the Vice-Chancellor, and two other ministers remained in support of the coalition, forming the *Freie Volkspartei* (*F.D.P.*), which later merged with the *D.P.* Adenauer reshuffled his cabinet on 16th October, taking advantage of the occasion to replace the ineffectual Minister of Defence, Theodor Blank, the 'father of the Bundeswehr,' with the energetic and able Bavarian, Franz-Josef Strauss. Though the prestige of the aged Chancellor—he celebrated his eighty-first birthday on 5th January 1957—had declined, and Bonn was already preoccupied with the succession problem, his position was somewhat strengthened by the brutal suppression of the revolution in Hungary and by the unceasing attacks on him from East Germany, and he was determined to lead the party in the impending elections.

The elections of 15th September 1957 were of special significance as the first since the end of the occupation and the regaining of sovereignty. They were widely regarded as a test for political maturity. It was expected that conscription, the stalemate on reunification, and the threat of inflation would cost the Chancellor dear. But the *C.D.U.* campaigned on the slogan, 'No Experiments,' and based its appeal on the country's undoubted prosperity. Its stock was also raised by the timely enactment early in the year of an extensive and enlightened new system of national insurance. Despite intense *D.D.R.* propaganda, foreign affairs played less part than in 1953, and the issue of atomic weapons was peripheral, despite the strong opposition to them by much German opinion, highlighted by an outspoken statement by eighteen leading atomic scientists. The *S.P.D.* expected to profit from the dislike of conscription and its espousal of reunification, but it suffered from the success of Erhard's *Sozialmarktwirtschaft* (which led the *S.P.D.* to de-emphasize its Marxism and omit all reference to socialization) as well as from the lack of inspiring leadership to challenge the personal appeal of the Chancellor.

The result was surprising only in the extent of Adenauer's victory. The *C.D.U.* won an absolute majority of 270 seats in a 497-member Bundestag. Moreover, they won more than 50 per cent of the popular vote, the first time in German history any party had done so. The Social Democrats increased their share of the vote to 32 per cent and their seats to 169, disappointingly low but sufficient to prevent the *C.D.U.* from securing the two-thirds majority necessary for constitutional amendment. The *F.D.P.* secured 41 seats, the *D.P./F.V.P.* 17. The *G.B./B.H.E.* fell victim to the 5 per cent rule and to the successful integration of refugees and expellees into the fabric of the Republic. The Communist Party had been banned in 1956, and the right-wing neo-Nazi parties succeeded in garnering only a few thousand votes. Re-elected Chancellor following the opening session of the *Bundestag*, which symbolically was held in West Berlin, Dr Adenauer formed a cabinet consisting of *C.D.U.* apart from two *D.P./F.V.P.* members. Erhard, to whose policies so much of the victory was due, remained Minister of Economics and became Vice-Chancellor as well.

The vote of 15th September 1957 was an impressive personal triumph for Adenauer. The electorate, like Oliver Twist, had asked for more, and the ensuing years were to see the continuation of the two trends which were already evident in 1957: expanding prosperity and the hardening of lines of division, with the evaporation of the rather naïve hopes fostered by the Chancellor that a strong West Germany, integrated into western Europe, and tightly linked with the United States, would somehow compel or persuade the U.S.S.R. to relinquish its grip on East Germany. The target of 500,000 troops, originally promised for 1957, was repeatedly postponed. Soon after the 1957 elections the question of atomic weapons for the *Bundeswehr* became acute. Early the next year the Chancellor rejected the Rapacki plan for an atom-free zone in central Europe, arguing that the objective should be comprehensive controlled disarmament, and it became clear, as Strauss made explicit in 1960, that the government had no objection to the *Bundeswehr* being armed with nuclear weapons and regarded it as of importance that it should possess weapons to match any opponent. Though the *S.P.D.* took a strong stand against atomic weapons, and were backed by public opinion, the *C.D.U.* succeeded in 1958 in recapturing the state of North Rhine-Westphalia from which it had been ousted in a humiliating *coup* two years earlier. Relations between government and opposition improved, in part in consequence of the more conciliatory attitude of Dr Heinrich von Brentano, who became Foreign Minister late in 1955. But the *S.P.D.* differed over the question of the 'summit' for which the U.S.S.R. began to press from the end of 1957. The government continued to insist on its formula of reunification through free elections. As the Soviet Union had manifestly rejected this course, which would involve sacrificing its East German satellite, and pushed instead the idea of a confederation of the two Germanies which the *D.D.R.* had advanced on 27th July 1957, the stalemate persisted.

East of the zonal frontier the *D.D.R.* developed as 'the foremost bastion of the socialist camp,' increasingly linked by a network of ties—political, economic, and ideological—to the U.S.S.R. and the east European satellites. Economic troubles persisted, as production targets were not met and deliveries to the U.S.S.R. fell behind. None the less the long promised and repeatedly delayed end of rationing came on 20th May 1958, and the rate of economic growth by the late 1950's was not far short of that of the Federal Republic. With a late start, however, it had far to go to catch up. There was some improvement in the standard of living, but with emphasis remaining on the development of heavy industry consumer goods were scarce and life drab.

Every attempt to speed up socialization of industry and to extend collectivization of agriculture led to an increase in the flow of refugees to the West. 'Liberal' elements were purged, and contacts with the West were increasingly cut off.   Barriers along the frontier were strengthened, detection of refugees aided by increased numbers of watch-towers.   From the end of 1957 the campaign against the Church was intensified.   At the fifth *S.E.D.* Congress in July 1958 Ulbricht ominously announced that the development of the economy of the *D.D.R.* would soon demonstrate the superiority of the 'socialist order of the *D.D.R.* to the rule of the imperialist·forces in the Bonn state,' and forecast increases in all industrial targets.

Consolidation of the *D.D.R.*, in Ulbricht's view, required the elimination of West Berlin—'a hotbed of fascists and subversive agencies,' as he described it at a meeting on 27th October 1958.   A fortnight later Khrushchev challenged the whole right of the Western powers to be in the former capital, and on 27th November proposed transforming the Western sectors into a demilitarized free city guaranteed by the four powers.   West Berliners showed unmistakably how they interpreted this superficially attractive proposal by rallying strongly in the elections of 7th December to the support of their youthful, socialist mayor, Willy Brandt.   The Western powers similarly rejected the Soviet scheme, while proposing negotiations within the framework of a general German settlement and security arrangements for Europe as a whole.   On 10th January 1959 the Soviets suggested a peace conference to meet within two months in Warsaw or Prague, and produced a draft treaty which West Germans rightly feared would legalize the partition, create a third partition out of Berlin, and cost Germany the territories beyond the Oder-Neisse line without any *quid pro quo*.   In Bonn all parties were united in their determination to maintain the position in Berlin, but the *S.P.D.* came close to approaching the Communist position with support for steps by the two German states towards reunification through an all-German commission.   Ultimately the firm stand by the Western powers led to agreement on a conference of Foreign Ministers as a first step towards the 'summit.' It met in Geneva, with an interval, from 11th May to 5th August.   The admission of representatives from both Germanys to sit at separate tables was regarded in Bonn as a setback for its policy of denying recognition to the *D.D.R.*, and in Pankow as *de facto* recognition.   After nine dreary weeks, in which familiar plans and arguments were rehearsed, the Foreign Ministers dispersed without achievement.

The Geneva conference of 1959 served to convince many Germans that the Russians merely desired to consolidate the zonal frontier.   Welcome as might be the thaw which followed the visit of Khrushchev to the United States, and the understanding that negotiations were to be continued under 'the spirit of Camp David,' Germans were anxious lest the Western powers make a deal which would lead to a settlement at the expense of prolonged and acknowledged partition.   In the months before the 'summit' the German Government was primarily concerned to secure acceptance of its views by its allies.   By the time the 'summit' was to take place on 16th May 1960,

Khrushchev was probably convinced that he could not extract from the Western powers either changes in the position of Berlin or recognition of the *D.D.R.* At any rate the meeting was torpedoed before it met. From Paris Khrushchev went directly to East Berlin, but did not, as expected, announce immediate conclusion of a separate treaty with the *D.D.R.* Instead, more moderate than the aggressive Ulbricht, he announced his willingness to postpone the settlement for six to eight months 'until the dust had settled,' and a new 'summit' could be arranged with a new U.S. president. Though relations between Bonn and Pankow deteriorated to the level of a cold civil war, the inter-zonal trade agreement was renewed on the last day of the year, and linked with free access to Berlin through the *D.D.R.*

If Bonn failed to make progress on the national question or even towards the more limited objective of securing improved conditions in the Soviet zone, the economic progress continued unabated—a considerable factor with the approach of the 1961 elections. In 1960 industrial production climbed 11 per cent, unemployment disappeared, and industry absorbed thousands of foreign workers. Despite fears, prices rose only moderately, and wages and salaries increased by 12 per cent in a single year, in spite of shorter working hours. Few groups were untouched by the high level of prosperity. At the same time the Chancellor's prestige suffered a damaging blow in a crisis over the related questions of succession to the presidency and to the chancellorship. With the approaching end of President Heuss's second distinguished term, the majority of the *C.D.U.* parliamentary party attempted to 'unfreeze' the political position which Adenauer's authoritarianism and subordination of policies and personalities to his foreign policy had imposed, by persuading him to move upstairs to the presidency.[1] After an intensive campaign he reluctantly yielded, but only after he had been persuaded that he could control foreign policy just as well from the Villa Hammerschmidt. This disastrous perversion of the constitution was averted at the cost of prolonging the 'Adenauer era.' After a bitter intra-party struggle in which the party, with its eye on the approaching elections, declined to consider any other candidate than Ludwig Erhard, the Chancellor withdrew his candidacy. On 1st July the *Bundesversammlung*, meeting in Berlin, elected the Minister of Agriculture, Heinrich Lübke, over Professor Carlo Schmid, one of the ablest *S.P.D.* leaders. Though little known he soon proved a modest but worthy successor to Theodor Heuss. Adenauer's abandonment of his presidential candidacy, and his announcement that he would remain in office indefinitely, marked an astonishing single-handed triumph. Once again it was clear that he held the party firmly in his hand. Though his vigour continued undiminished, there was a strong feeling that he was too old and too authoritarian, and in its election appeal the *C.D.U.* emphasized 'Adenauer, Erhard, and the Team.'

In advance of the elections the *S.P.D.* acquired a new leader and a new policy. Following the dismaying third defeat in 1957 the reformists remoulded the party to a form they hoped would capture a substantial segment

---

[1] Heidenheimer, *Adenauer and the C.D.U.*, pp. 222–3.

of the middle-class vote. In 1959 the Godesberg programme eliminated the last vestiges of Marxism and declared that free enterprise and free competition were important functions of a socialist economy. The next year at Hanover the party abandoned its opposition to N.A.T.O. and rearmament, and largely adopted Adenauer's foreign policy. Ollenhauer had announced as early as 1959 that he would not be a candidate for the chancellorship, and at Hanover Willy Brandt, who had made a highly successful world tour to rally opinion behind his beleaguered Berlin, was named as the *S.P.D.* standard bearer.

The outcome was strongly influenced by a fresh Berlin crisis which preceded the elections by five weeks. The storm signal was raised in a long note to Bonn in January 1961, in which the Soviet Government warned that if no peace treaty were signed 'within the agreed time limit,' the Soviet Union would proceed to conclude a treaty with the *D.D.R.* which would end the occupation regime in Berlin. On 4th June, in a memorandum handed to President Kennedy in Vienna, Khrushchev set the time limit at six months. In mid August a dramatic week-end *coup* by the *D.D.R.* opened up the most critical phase. Behind it lay a serious domestic crisis in what was notoriously the unhappiest of all the satellites. Industrial production was falling short of targets, consumer goods were scarce, and collectivization had resulted in a declining agricultural production and a serious food shortage. Since the start of the year the already limited contacts with the West had been progressively choked off. The ban on the meeting of the *E.K.I.D. Kirchentag* in East and West Berlin was a sharp blow at one of the few institutions which linked East and West. Since the death of Pieck in September 1960 and the abolition of the presidency, Ulbricht as head of a new Council of State had become in name as well as in fact dictator of East Germany. Political pressure and the grey drabness of life under an alien regime produced a state of latent opposition which was attested to by the large numbers who fled across the still open frontier into West Berlin. In the summer of 1961 the threat that this route might be closed caused panic in the East, and the flow became a flood. In July 30,000 entered West Berlin. It was clear that the 'building of socialism' could not be accomplished so long as desperately needed young workers, doctors, teachers, and other specialists merely moved westward when the pressure became too great. During the night of 12th–13th August the government of the *D.D.R.* built wire and wall through the heart of Berlin, putting an end to freedom of movement and dealing a near mortal blow to four-power control. There was no interference with the access routes, and the Western powers took no action beyond protests and measures to strengthen the morale and defences of West Berlin.

In West Germany the 'wall of shame' evoked a wave of indignation. The Chancellor's failure to appear promptly in Berlin strengthened the widespread belief that at eighty-five he was too old to cope with a national crisis. Events in Berlin also naturally thrust Brandt into the limelight. Its more attractive leader, more coherent programme, and better organized campaign enabled the *S.P.D.* to pass the magic figure of one-third of the popular vote to win 36·2 per cent and 190 seats in a 499-member *Bundestag*.   The *C.D.U.* lost 5 per cent of its vote and its absolute majority, winning 248 seats.   The union of the *D.P.* and the *B.H.E.* proved disastrous as it failed to gain the required 5 per cent.   The chief gainer from this and the *C.D.U.* losses appeared to be the rejuvenated *F.D.P.* under its new leader, Erich Mende, which won 67 seats.   After the elections he attempted to use his key position to secure what the *C.D.U.* had failed to accomplish in 1959: a coalition under Erhard.   For seven weeks Bonn was without a government while the crisis in Berlin was at its height, with Russian and American tanks facing each other over a chalk line in the Friedrichstrasse.   Adenauer steadily resisted pressure to step down in such a time of tension, and at the end of October succeeded in forming a *C.D.U.-F.D.P.* coalition.   The price extracted was a pledge to resign before the end of his four-year term, the replacement of Brentano as Foreign Minister by Gerhard Schroeder, the former Minister of the Interior, and a more active 'German' policy.   On 7th November, by a small majority, Adenauer was elected Chancellor for the fourth time.

The crisis over the Berlin wall thus contributed towards weakening the *C.D.U.* and brought closer the long overdue end of the Adenauer era.   On the other hand the prolonged and unedifying political manœuvring in Bonn weakened the West German hand in the negotiations directed towards resolving the crisis.   The crude campaign of nuclear blackmail and the continuing of hostile propaganda directed at the Federal Republic reinforced Soviet demands, but tension abated as Khrushchev lifted the time limit on 27th October.   When Adenauer flew to Washington in November, immediately after his election as Chancellor, it was agreed that negotiations should be confined to the narrow issue of Berlin.   Once again Bonn was concerned to ensure that in the negotiations, which the N.A.T.O. Council entrusted to the U.S. ambassador in Moscow, the Republic's links with Berlin should not be weakened, and that recognition of the *D.D.R.* should be avoided.   No progress was recorded, and in an exchange of notes with Moscow, Bonn was also unsuccessful in achieving any agreement which would improve the lot of the inhabitants of the *D.D.R.*

Meanwhile West Berliners recovered their nerve, and by the end of 1961 the initial flight from the city was checked and labour recruited in the West to replace the *Grenzgängers*, those who had formerly worked in West Berlin but lived in the East.   If in constructing the wall Ulbricht aimed to strike at the viability of West Berlin, he failed.   For the city survived the crisis and actually achieved a sharp increase in industrial production through a programme of rationalization.   Though West Germans were sometimes inclined to regard West Berlin as a costly burden to be subsidized, as Germany's largest industrial city it continued to provide a large market for West German products and to contribute substantially to West German supplies and export trade.   Though 1961 largely deprived the city of its role as outpost, showplace, refuge and token of four-power obligation for German reunification, Berliners soon learned to live with the wall, despite the brutalities perpetrated along it, and appeared determined to ride out the storm indefinitely.

Across the wall, which after 13th August was progressively strengthened
into a formidable barrier over which only a handful succeeded in escaping,
and with the zonal frontier also strongly reinforced, Ulbricht had acquired a
certain freedom of action for more ruthless policies inside a form of gigantic
Konzentrationslager. Conscription was introduced on 24th January 1962.
But Ulbricht failed to end the domestic crisis which had largely inspired the
wall's construction. The shortage of teachers, doctors, and technicians could
not quickly be made good, the ageing population structure meant a continued
decline in the labour force. Industrial production, organized for the benefit
of the Soviet bloc rather than the *D.D.R.* itself, continued to lag behind targets.
Agricultural production dropped and livestock declined. An acute food
shortage led to the reintroduction of rationing of meat and potatoes. Discontent and disaffection were widespread, as much on material as on political
grounds, but understandably there was little overt resistance. While some
East Germans undoubtedly made peace with the regime when the Berlin
gate slammed shut, most appeared to turn their backs on it and to concentrate
on surviving apolitically as best they could.

Though the Federal Government might, with reason, continue to deny
formal diplomatic recognition to the *D.D.R.* while engaging in contacts with
it on the official level over trade and other matters, the fact of division was
clear and, many Germans feared, daily becoming more permanent. A dozen
and a half years after its close the *Reich* was still reaping the consequences
of the war which Hitler had unleashed—Königsberg, cradle of the Prussian
monarchy, absorbed into the Soviet Union; the remainder of East Prussia
and Silesia incorporated into Poland; ten million Germans driven westward
from homes in territories German for generations or even centuries. East of
a line drawn from the Baltic to the Czech frontier, an area including Weimar
and Wittenberg, Dresden and Stettin, Potsdam and the historic part of Berlin,
was absorbed into the Soviet empire and reduced to a satellite status, which
rested on terror, barbed wire, and the other apparatus of Communist power.
The name 'Germany' disappeared from the map save as a geographical
expression. Only in the Federal Republic—embracing an area differing
little in extent from that of German settlement before the great colonization
eastward began after 1200—with its unique extension to the truncated and
encircled West Berlin, were the essential elements of a free society preserved
and, with its strengths and weaknesses, the traditions of a thousand years
of German history carried on.

The early 1960's found this new bearer of German traditions in a puzzled,
restless mood. It was not only that more than a dozen years after its creation it had been unable to produce even a token fulfilment of the aims of
reunification and the recovery of the eastern territories, nor the feeling that
the 'economic miracle' was an insufficient basis to justify the state's existence.
The arrest of Adolf Eichmann in 1960, coming almost at the same time as the
publication of a highly successful popular history of the Third *Reich*,[1] again

---

[1] William L. Shirer, *The Rise and Fall of the Third Reich: A History of Nazi Germany* (New
York, 1960).

Q

confronted Germans with the spectre of Germany's unhappy past.   Many
had dealt with this through a widely noted form of mass amnesia, though
many, too, had met it with a courageous attempt to analyse and to understand, but not to excuse, as the record of German historical scholarship and
of such institutions as the Munich *Institut für Zeitgeschichte* amply demonstrated.   Eichmann's trial and his execution on 3rd May 1962 also triggered
off the first and large-scale attempt by the Federal Government to bring Nazi
murderers to trial,[1] and inspired an overdue attempt to cleanse the stables
of German justice with a law which, ironically, came into effect on 1st July
1962, at precisely the moment when the State Attorney Frankel was being
driven from office following publication of serious charges against him in
East Berlin.   An even more serious blow came following the outspoken
criticism of the *Bundeswehr* in the weekly news magazine *Der Spiegel*.[2]   The
occupation of its offices by night, and the arrest of its editors in a manner too
clearly reminiscent of the methods of the Third *Reich*, evoked a storm of
protest at home and abroad, and a political crisis which, following that
produced by the Berlin wall and the manœuvring after the 1961 elections, disrupted the coalition and all but drove the Chancellor from office.   Though the
heavy hand of the authoritarian state was checked, the affair did great damage,
and the process of reconstruction after it promised to be long and difficult.
In the end Adenauer secured a reprieve, but the price paid for Free Democratic support for the coalition cabinet reconstructed on 11th December was
the ousting of Strauss, despite his position of strength as head of the Bavarian
C.S.U., and a pledge on the part of the Chancellor to resign in the autumn of
1963.   A few weeks later he was forced to bow to the decision of the party to
nominate as his successor Ludwig Erhard, the man whom he had struggled
consistently to keep out of the *Palais Schaumburg*.   At the same time the
rigidity of the Chancellor's views brought him into sharp opposition to the
more flexible diplomatic stance of President Kennedy, and resulted in a
deterioration in U.S.-German relations.   His single-minded pursuit of
Franco-German reconciliation, culminating in the Franco-German Treaty
signed on 22nd January 1963, appeared to make the Federal Republic an
accomplice in the exclusion of Britain from Europe, at the risk of weakening
if not destroying the life-sustaining ties of Washington.   Opposition to the
treaty, and a widespread desire for British membership in the E.E.C.,
encouraged by the anglophile trio of Erhard, Schroeder, and the new Defence
Minister, von Hassell, resulting in approval of the treaty only after the addition of a protocol which largely robbed it of its intended exclusive purpose.

By the summer of 1963, with the Chancellor in his eighty-eighth year, it
seemed safe at last to write that the 'Adenauer era' was nearing its close.
His unique achievements in fourteen years of office can, as a Swiss writer has
recently pointed out,[3] only be measured by recalling the beginnings of the
Bonn Republic and the magnitude of the challenge which lay ahead.   At

---

[1] Hannah Arendt, *Eichmann in Jerusalem* (New York, 1963), pp. 11 ff.
[2] 16: No. 41, 10th October 1962.
[3] F. R. Allemann, 'The End of the Adenauer Era,' *Encounter*, XX, No. 2, February 1963, p. 59.

the cost of imposing a stern authoritarian rule he provided the nascent state with the political stability and economic wellbeing which enabled the new democratic forms to survive and develop roots of as yet unmeasured depths— though the sobriety of the German electorate and the reaction of democratic forces to the challenge of the *Der Spiegel* affair were encouraging signs. From defeat and the status of international pariahs he led the Germans back into power and sovereignty within a decade of the end of the war, and 'made of the Republic a respected bastion of freedom on the frontiers of a divided Europe. His burying of the Franco-German hatchet was an immense historic achievement, which was hardly predictable in 1945, and his resolute pursuit of European integration and westward orientation helped to bridge the long-standing gulf between Germany and the West, and to provide Germans, and particularly young Germans, with an alternative target to the lost territories to the east on which to fix their gaze. As, in Winston Churchill's oft-quoted and well-deserved phrase, 'the greatest German statesman since Bismarck,' he fashioned the new state in his own image and identified it with his own personality. By 1963 it had outgrown his grasp, and it is only to be regretted that, towards the close of an extraordinary career which began nearly a decade after he had reached the age when most men seek retirement, he inflicted serious damage on his own promising creation.

In contrast to the eras of Bismark and William II, of Weimar and Hitler, the Adenauer era alone achieved a 'normal' end. On 11th October the old Chancellor resigned. Five days later the *Bundestag* elected Professor Ludwig Erhard, the sixty-six year old father of the 'economic miracle' whom Adenauer had sought to eliminate from the succession. Among the few new faces in the reshuffle coalition cabinet was the *F.D.P.* leader, Dr Erich Mende, who in 1961 had declined to serve under Adenauer. Kurt Schmuecker, a small businessman from Oldenburg, succeeded Erhard as Minister of Economics. With the new leadership a new spirit seemed to prevail in Bonn, but the change appeared to be in style rather than in substance. Much of the new government's declaration of policy was devoted to the familiar problems of German unity and Berlin. The West German public was soon reminded of the very different conditions in the *D.D.R.*, when on 20th October 99·25 per cent of eligible voters participated in 'elections' and 99·95 per cent approved the single list presented to them. At the same time repeated Soviet obstruction of Western military convoys along the *Autobahn* emphasized how precarious were the links to West Berlin. 'We are told', the new Chancellor had said in the *Bundestag*, 'that the division of our country is a reality which must be accepted. Of course it is a reality, but an unbearable one . . .' How the 'far stronger reality' of 'the will of the German people to restore its unity' was to be made to prevail remained for Erhard, as for Adenauer, an unresolved dilemma.

SELECT BIBLIOGRAPHY

THE LITERATURE on German history is enormous, as is shown in the standard and outstanding German publication Dahlmann-Waitz, *Quellenkunde der deutschen Geschichte* (9th edition, Leipzig, 1932). A new edition is in preparation at the Max Planck Institute, Göttingen. In the meantime it can be supplemented by the *Jahresberichte für deutsche Geschichte* (Leipzig, 1927–40, 1949 ff.). Günther Franz's *Bücherkunde zur deutschen Geschichte* (Munich, 1951) furnishes a briefer list. For English readers there is a useful section on Germany by Hajo Holborn in *The American Historical Association's Guide to Historical Literature* (New York, 1961). Here it is intended to list only some of the more important and helpful books in English and French, with a few references to books in German which are of outstanding value.

GENERAL

F. W. Putzgers, *Historischer Schul-Atlas*, Bielefeld and Leipzig, 1923; *Westermanns Atlas zur Weltgeschiche Teil III, Neuzeit*, Brunswick, 1953; R. E. Dickinson, *Germany, A General and Regional Geography*, New York, 1953; K. A. Sinnhuber, *Germany, its geography and growth*, London, 1961; K. Pagel, *Deutsche Geschichte in Bildern*, Berlin, 1928; Bruno Gebhardt, *Handbuch der deutschen Geschichte*, 4 vols., Stuttgart, 1960–1; M. Dill, Jr, *Germany, A Modern History*, Ann Arbor, 1961; E. F. Henderson, *A Short History of Germany*, rev. ed., New York, 1937; H. Holborn, *A History of Modern Germany*, vol. i, *The Reformation*, New York, 1959 (vol. ii forthcoming); H. Pinnow, *History of Germany*, trans., London, 1933; K. S. Pinson, *Modern Germany, its History and Civilization*, New York, 1955; H. S. Steinberg, *A Short History of Germany*, Cambridge, 1944; E. Vermeil, *Germany's Three Reichs*, trans., London, 1945; V. Valentin, *The German People, their History and Civilization*, trans., New York, 1946; G. P. Gooch, *Studies in German History*, London, 1948; Fritz Hartung, *Deutsche Verfassungsgeschichte vom 15 Jahrhundert bis zur Gegenwart*, 6th ed., Stuttgart, 1954; *Cambridge Medieval* and *Cambridge Modern Histories*, and *New Cambridge Modern History*.

CHAPTER I. THE REFORMATION ERA AND ITS RESULTS

J. Bryce, *The Holy Roman Empire*, rev. ed., London, 1927; W. Stubbs, *Germany in the Later Middle Ages, 1200–1500*, London, 1908; G. Barraclough, *Medieval Germany 911–1250: Essays by German Historians*, trans., Oxford, 1938; *The Origins of Modern Germany*, 2nd ed., Oxford, 1949; J. W. Thompson, *Social and Economic History of Europe in the Later Middle Ages*, New York, 1931; J. Janssen, *History of the German People at the Close of the Middle Ages*, trans., vol. i, London, 1896; L. Ranke, *History of the Reformation in Germany*, trans., London, 1845; Preserved Smith, *Age of the Reformation*, New York, 1920; *Life and Letters of Martin Luther*, New York, 1914; J. Lortz, *Die Reformation in Deutschland*, 3rd ed., 2 vols., Freiburg im Breisaau, 1949; E. G. Schweibert, *Luther and his Times*, St. Louis, 1950; R. Bainton, *Here I Stand: A life of Martin Luther*, New York, 1951; T. M. Lindsay, *History of the Reformation*, vol. i, London, 1906; A. Hyma, *Luther's Theological Development from Erfurt to Augsburg*, New York, 1928; H. Treitschke, *Luther and the German Nation*, trans., New York, 1915; R. Ehrenberg, *Capital and Finance in the Age of the Renaissance*, trans., London, 1928; R. W. Tawney, *Religion and the Rise of Capitalism*, London, 1926; *The Fugger News Letters*, ed. V. Klarwill, London, 1924–6; R. Pascal, *The Social Basis of the Reformation*, London, 1938; K. D. Macmillan, *Protestantism in Germany*, Princeton, 1917; J. S. Schapiro, *Social Reform and the Reformation*, New York, 1909; W. L. McElwee, *The Reign of Charles V*, London, 1938; K. Brandi, *The Emperor Charles V*, trans., London, 1939; C. V. Wedgwood, *The Thirty Years War*, London, 1938.

CHAPTERS II AND III.   THE RISE OF PRUSSIA (TO 1786)

L. Ranke, *History of Prussia*, trans., London, 1847–8; F. L. Carsten, *The Origins of Prussia*, Oxford, 1954; O. Hintze, *Die Hohenzollern und ihre Werke*, Berlin, 1915; A. Waddington, *Histoire de Prusse* (to 1740), Paris, 1912; *Le Grand Electeur*, Paris, 1905; S. B. Fay, *The Rise of Brandenburg Prussia to 1786*, New York, 1937; G. Schmoller, *The Mercantile System*, trans., New York, 1896; R. R. Ergang, *Potsdam Führer*, New York, 1941; R. A. Dorwarts, *The Administrative Reforms of Frederick William I of Prussia*, Cambridge, Mass., 1953; C. T. Atkinson, *History of Germany, 1715–1815*, London, 1908; T. Carlyle, *Frederick the Great*, vol. i; P. Gaxotte, *Frederick the Great*, trans., London, 1941; G. P. Gooch, *Frederick the Great*, London, 1947; G. Ritter, *Friedrich der Grosse: ein historisches Profil*, 3rd ed., Heidelberg, 1954; Mirabeau, *De la Monarchie Prussienne sous Frédéric le Grand*, London, 1788; H. Rosenberg, *Bureaucracy, Aristocracy, and Autocracy: The Prussian Experience, 1660–1815*, Cambridge, Mass., 1958; Gordon A. Craig, *The Politics of the The Prussian Army, 1640–1945*, Oxford, 1955.

CHAPTER IV.   THE INTELLECTUAL AND LITERARY REVIVAL OF THE
EIGHTEENTH CENTURY

Histories of German Literature: by K. Francke, trans., New York, 1896; W. Scherer, trans., New York, 1890; J. G. Robertson, London, 1931; W. H. Bruford, *Germany in the Eighteenth Century*, Cambridge, 1935; *Culture and Society in Classical Weimar 1775–1806*, London, 1962; F. L. Carsten, *Princes and Parliaments in Germany from the Fifteenth to the Eighteenth Century*, Oxford, 1959; K. Hillebrand, *German Thought from the Seven Years War to Goethe's Death*, London, 1880; H. Hoffding, *History of Modern Philosophy*, trans., London, 1924; J. G. Hibben, *The Philosophy of the Enlightenment*, New York, 1910; E. M. Butler, *The Tyranny of Greece over Germany*, Cambridge, 1935; F. Paulsen, *German Universities and University Study*, New York, 1906; H. Kohn, *The Idea of Nationalism: A Study of its Origins*, New York, 1944; K. S. Pinson, *Pietism as a Factor in the Rise of German Nationalism*, New York, 1934; L. A. Willoughby, *Classical Age of German Literature, 1748–1805*, London, 1926; T. W. Rolleston, *Life of G. E. Lessing*, 1894; F. McEachran, *The Life and Philosophy of Johann Gottfried Herder*, Oxford, 1939; A. Gillies, *Herder*, Oxford, 1945; R. R. Ergang, *Herder and the Foundations of German Nationalism*, New York, 1931; G. H. Lewes, *The Life and Works of Goethe*, Everyman's Library; P. H. Brown, *Life of Goethe*, London, 1920; B. Fairley, *A Study of Goethe*, Oxford, 1947; C. Thomas, *Life and Works of Friedrich Schiller*, New York, 1906; F. Ungar, *Friedrich Schiller*, New York, 1959; W. Wallace, *Life of Kant*, London, 1911; T. M. Green, *Kant*, selections, New York, 1929; C. J. Friedrich, ed., *The Philosophy of Kant*, New York, 1949.

CHAPTER V.   THE REMAKING OF GERMANY THROUGH THE FRENCH REVOLUTION
AND NAPOLEON

H. von Treitschke, *History of Germany in the Nineteenth Century*, trans., vol. i, London, 1915; A. Sorel, *L'Europe et la revolution française*, vol. i, Paris, 1885; G. P. Gooch, *Germany and the French Revolution*, London, 1920; J. Droz, *L'Allemagne et la révolution française*, Paris, 1949; R. Aris, *History of Political Thought in Germany from 1789 to 1815*, London, 1936; H. A. L. Fisher, *Studies in Napoleonic Statesmanship: Germany*, Oxford, 1903; A. Rambaud, *Les Français sur le Rhin, 1792–1804*, Paris, 1891; J. R. Seeley, *Life and Times of Stein*, 3 vols., London, 1878; G. S. Ford, *Stein and the Era of Reform in Prussia*, Princeton, 1922; G. Ritter, *Stein, ein politische Biographie*, 3rd ed., Stuttgart, 1958; Ricarda Huch, *Stein*, Leipzig, 1932; Mme de Staël, *Germany*, trans., Boston, 1883; G. Brandes, *The Romantic School in Germany*, London, 1902; L. A. Willoughby, *The Romantic Movement in Germany*, London, 1930; H. S. Reiss, *Political Thought of the German Romantics, 1793–1815*, Oxford, 1955; A. G. Pundt, *Arndt and the Nationalist Awakening in Germany*, New York, 1935; R. Adamson, *Fichte*, London, 1903; Fichte, *Addresses to the German Nation*, trans., Chicago, 1922; F. Meinecke, *Weltbürgertum und Nationalstaat*, 7th ed., Munich, 1928; E. N. Anderson, *Nationalism and the Cultural Crisis in Prussia, 1806–1815*, New York, 1939; H. Kohn, *The Mind of Germany*, New York, 1960.

CHAPTER VI.   CONSERVATIVES, LIBERALS, AND NATIONALISTS, 1815–40

H. von Treitschke, *History of Germany in the Nineteenth Century*, trans., vols. ii–vii, London, 1916–19; H. von Sybel, *The Founding of the German Empire*, trans., vol. i, New York, 1890; E. Brandenburg, *Die Reichsgründung*, Leipzig, vol. i, 1922; A. W. Ward, *Germany, 1815–90*, 3 vols., London, 1916; F. Schnabel, *Deutsche Geschichte im neunzehnten Jahrhundert*, 4th ed., 4 vols., Freiburg im Breisgau, 1948; E. J. Passant, *A Short History of*

Germany, 1815–1945, Cambridge, 1959; A. J. P. Taylor, *The Course of German History since 1815*, London, 1945; *The Habsburg Monarchy, 1815–1918*, 2nd ed., London, 1948; Metternich, *Memoirs*, trans., vols. iii–v, 1815–35, London, 1881–2; A. Herman, *Metternich*, London, 1932; C. de Grunwald, *Metternich*, trans., London, 1953; A. Cecil, *Metternich*, London, 1933; W. M. Simon, *The Failure of the Prussian Reform Movement, 1807–19*, Ithaca, 1955; J. G. Legge, *Rhyme and Revolution in Germany, 1813–50*, London, 1918; F. C. Sell, *Die Tragödie des deutschen Liberalismus*, Stuttgart, 1953; L. Krieger, *The German Idea of Freedom*, Boston, 1957; J. H. Clapham, *Economic Development of France and Germany, 1815–1914*, Cambridge, 1923; T. S. Hammerow, *Restoration, Revolution, Reaction: Economics and Politics in Germany, 1815–1871*, Princeton, 1958; W. O. Henderson, *The Zollverein*, London, 1939; J. Bowring, *Report on the Prussian Commercial Union*, London, 1840; E. Corti, *The House of Rothschild*, New York, 1928; G. Goyau, *L'Allemagne religieuse: le Catholicisme*, vol. i, 1800–48, Paris, 1910; Goethe, *Conversations with Eckermann*, Everyman's Library; E. Caird, *Hegel*, London, 1883; R. Macintosh, *Hegel and Hegelianism*, Edinburgh, 1903; M. Lowenthal, *The Jews of Germany*, New York, 1936.

CHAPTER VII. THE REVOLUTION OF 1848–9

G. Brandes, *Young Germany*, London, 1923; E. M. Butler, *The Saint-Simonian Religion in Germany*, Cambridge, 1926; Heine, *Prose Writings*, trans., London, 1887; H. G. Atkins, *Heine*, London, 1929; V. Valentin, *1848: Chapters of German History*, London, 1940 (part trans. of the larger work in German); J. Droz, *Les révolutions allemandes de 1848*, Paris, 1957; P. Robertson, *Revolutions of 1848, A Social History*, Princeton, 1952; R. Stadelmann, *Soziale und politische Geschichte der Revolution von 1848*, Munich, 1948; P. Matter, *La Prusse et la révolution de 1848*, Paris, 1903; E. H. Carr, *Karl Marx*, London, 1938; G. Mayer, *Friedrich Engels*, trans., London, 1936; F. Engels, *Revolution and Counter-Revolution in Germany in 1848* (formerly attributed to Marx), London, 1920; K. Marx and F. Engels, *Correspondence, 1846–93*, London, 1934; K. Schurz, *Reminiscences*, vol. i, New York, 1909; L. B. Namier, *1848: The Revolution of the Intellectuals*, London, 1944; M. L. Hansen, *The Atlantic Migration, 1607–1860*, Cambridge, Mass., 1940.

CHAPTER VIII. THE UNIFICATION OF GERMANY

E. Brandenburg, *Die Reichsgründung*, vol. ii; H. von Sybel, *The Founding of the German Empire*, trans., vols. ii–vii, London, 1891–8; E. Denis, *La Fondation de l'Empire Allemande, 1852–71*, Paris, 1906; W. H. Dawson, *The German Empire, 1867–1914*, vol. i, London, 1919; O. Pflanze, *Bismarck and the Development of Germany, The Period of Unification, 1815–1871*, Princeton, 1963; F. Darmstaedter, *Bismarck and the Creation of the Second Reich*, London, 1948; *Germany and Europe*, London, 1945; P. Matter, *Bismarck et son temps*, Paris, 1905–8; E. Eyck, *Bismarck*, 3 vols., Zürich, 1941–4; *Bismarck and the German Empire*, London, 1950 ('a summary of the salient points of my larger work'); C. G. Robertson, *Bismarck*, London, 1918; A. J. P. Taylor, *Bismarck, The Man and the Statesman*, London, 1955; Bismarck, *Reflections and Reminiscences*, trans., 2 vols., London, 1898; R. Morier, *Memoirs and Letters*, 1826–76, 2 vols., London, 1911; Beust, *Memoirs*, trans., 2 vols., London, 1887; E. N. Anderson, *The Social and Political Conflict in Prussia, 1858–1864*, Lincoln, Neb., 1954; H. Oncken, *Napoleon III and the Rhine*, trans., New York, 1928; W. E. Mosse, *The European Powers and the German Question, 1848–71: With Special Reference to England and Russia*, Cambridge, 1958; M. Friedjung, *The Struggle for Supremacy in Germany, 1859–66*, trans. (shortened), London, 1935; R. H. Lord, *Origins of the War of 1870*, New York, 1924; L. D. Steefel, *Bismarck, the Hohenzollern Candidacy, and the Origins of the Franco-Prussian War*, Cambridge, Mass., 1962.

CHAPTER IX. ECONOMIC, SOCIAL, AND CULTURAL TRENDS IN THE MIDDLE OF THE NINETEENTH CENTURY

H. Lichtenberger, *The Evolution of Modern Germany*, trans., London, 1913; J. H. Clapham, *Economic Development in France and Germany*, Cambridge, 1923; H. Oncken, *Lassalle*, Stuttgart, 1912; W. H. Dawson, *German Socialism and Ferdinand Lassalle*, London, 1891, and *Evolution of Modern Germany*, London, 1908; J. Kuczynski, *Short History of Labour Conditions in Germany, 1800 to the Present*, London, 1945; W. Sombart, *Socialism and the Socialist Movement*, trans., London, 1909; M. E. Hirst, *Friedrich List*, London, 1909; J. T. Merz, *A History of European Thought in the Nineteenth Century*, vol. i, 1907; W. C. Dampier, *A History of Science*, London, 1943; G. P. Gooch, *History and Historians in the Nineteenth Century*, London, 1920; E. Kohn-Bramstedt, *Aristocracy and the Middle Classes in Germany*, London, 1937; E. K. Bennet, *A History of the German*

'*Novelle*,' Cambridge, 1934; G. Freytag, *Reminiscences*, trans., London, 1890; E. Newman, *Wagner as Man and Artist*, New York, 1924; W. H. Hadow, *Richard Wagner*, London, 1934; G. Weston, *The Protestant Church in Germany and Sweden*, London, 1940; G. Goyau, *L'Allemagne religieuse*, *Le Catholicisme*, vols. iii–iv; *Le Protestantisme*; W. Wallace, *Life of Schopenhauer*, London, 1893; Schopenhauer, *Philosophy*, ed. I. Edman, New York, 1928.

CHAPTER X. THE BISMARCKIAN EMPIRE: I. 1871–90

It is a great pity, if only because Bismarck was a master of style, that so small a proportion of his speeches and writings is available in English. The big collected works (*Die Gesammelte Werke*, 1924 seq.) contain 9 vols. of Political Writings, 3 vols. of Conversations, 4 vols. of Speeches, 2 vols. of Letters, and 1 vol. of the Reminiscences. There are also single volumes of selections such as those of H. Rothfels, *Bismarck, Deutscher Staat, Ausgewählte Dokumente*, Munich, 1925; T. Klein, *Der Kanzler*, Munich, 1943; as well as selections from his speeches and his letters. A new anniversary edition began to appear in 1962; *Bismarck, Werke in Auswahl*, ed. G. A. Rein *et al.*, 8 vols., Stuttgart, 1962–. But in English, apart from quotations in histories and biographies, we have only the *Reflections and Reminiscences*, with the additional volume, *New Chapters of Bismarck's Autobiography*, trans., London, 1920, two volumes of *Correspondence of William I* (and others) with Bismarck, ed. J. A. Ford, New York, 1903, and a selection of the letters to his wife.

Eyck, Matter, Taylor, Robertson, as for Chapter VIII; J. Ziekursch, *Das Zeitalter Bismarcks, 1871–90*, Frankfurt on Main, 1927; H. Lichtenberger, *The Evolution of Modern Germany*, trans., London, 1913; W. H. Dawson, *The German Empire, 1867–1914*, 2 vols, 1919; B. E. Howard, *The German Empire*, London, 1906; G. Stolper, *The German Economy, 1870–1940*, New York, 1940; W. H. Dawson, *Protection in Germany*, London, 1904; E. Brandenburg, *From Bismarck to the World War*, trans., London, 1927; G. P. Gooch, *Studies in German History*, London, 1948; E. M. Carroll, *Germany and the Great Powers, 1866–1914*, New York, 1938; W. L. Langer, *European Alliances and Alignments*, 2nd ed., New York, 1950; A. J. P. Taylor, *The Struggle for Mastery in Europe, 1848–1918*, Oxford, 1954; F. W. Foerster, *Europe and the German Question*, London, 1940; J. W. Fuller, *Bismarckian Diplomacy at its Zenith*, New York, 1922; P. Wiegler, *William the First*, trans., London, 1929; J. Redlich, *Francis Joseph I*, trans., 1925, New York; M. Busch, *Bismarck, Secret Pages of his History*, trans., 3 vols., London, 1908; N. Rich and M. H. Fisher, *The Holstein Papers*, 4 vols., Cambridge, 1955–63; W. Taffs, *Lord Odo Russell, Ambassador to Bismarck*, London, 1938; A. Bebel, *My Life*, trans., London, 1912; H. W. C. Davis, *Political Thought of H. von Treitschke*, London, 1914; A. Dorpalen: *Heinrich von Treitschke*, New Haven, 1957; *The Philosophy of Nietzsche*, Modern Library, contains most of his major works in translation; C. Brinton, *Nietzsche*, Cambridge, Mass., 1945; W. A. Kaufmann *Nietzsche, philosopher, psychologist, antichrist*, Princeton, 1950.

CHAPTER XI. THE BISMARCKIAN EMPIRE: II. THE ERA OF WILLIAM II, 1890–1918

E. Eyck, *Das persönliche Regiment Wilhelms II*, Zurich, 1948; J. A. Nichols, *Germany After Bismarck*, Cambridge, Mass., 1958; W. F. Bruck, *Social and Economic History of Germany 1888–1938*, Cardiff, 1938; A. Gerschenkron, *Bread and Democracy in Germany*, Berkeley, 1943; P. Gay, *The Dilemma of Democratic Socialism, Eduard Bernstein's Challenge to Marx*, New York, 1953; C. E. Schorske, *German Social Democracy, 1905–1917*, Cambridge, Mass., 1955; A. Rosenberg, *The Birth of the German Republic, 1871–1918*, trans., New York, 1931; J. P. Mayer, *Max Weber and German Politics*, London, 1944; H. Delbrück, *Government and the Will of the People*, trans., London, 1923; F. Stern, *The Politics of Cultural Despair*, Berkeley, 1961; M. S. Wertheimer, *The Pan-German League, 1890–1914*, New York, 1924; L. W. Muncy, *The Junker in the Prussian Administration, 1888–1914*, Providence, R.I., 1944; M. E. Townshend, *The Rise and Fall of Germany's Colonial Empire, 1890–1914*; W. L. Langer, *The Diplomacy of Imperialism, 1890–1902*, 2nd ed., New York, 1951; E. T. S. Dugdale, *German Diplomatic Documents*, 4 vols., London, 1929–1931; H. C. Meyer, *Mitteleuropa in German Thought and Action, 1815–1945*, The Hague, 1955; S. B. Fay, *The Origins of the World War*, 2 vols., 2nd ed., New York, 1930; B. E. Schmitt, *The Coming of the War, 1914*, 2 vols., New York, 1930; A. J. P. Taylor, *The Struggle for Mastery in Europe, 1848–1918*, Oxford, 1954; L. Albertini, *The Origins of the War of 1914*, trans., 3 vols., Oxford, 1953–7; E. M. Carroll, *Germany and the Great Powers, 1866–1914*, New York, 1938; T. Wolff, *The Eve of 1914*, trans., New York, 1936; G. Ritter, *The Schlieffen Plan*, trans., New York, 1956; H. W. Gatzke, *Germany's Drive to the West*, Baltimore, 1950; J. W. Wheeler-Bennett, *Brest-Litovsk, The Forgotten Peace*, London, 1938; A. Mendelssohn Bartholdy, *The War and German Society*, New Haven, 1937; R. H. Lutz (ed.), *Causes of the German Collapse*, Stanford, 1934, and *The Fall of the German Empire, 1914–1918*, 2 vols., Stanford, 1932; B. von Bülow, *Memoirs*, 4 vols., London,

1931–2; *The Memoirs of Prince Chlodwig of Hohenlohe-Schillingfürst*, 2 vols., trans., London, 1906; Tirpitz, *My Memoirs*, 2 vols., trans., London, n.d.; *The Memoirs of Prince Max of Baden*, 2 vols., trans., London, 1928; P. Scheidemann, *Memoirs of a Social Democrat*, 2 vols., trans., London, 1928.

CHAPTER XII. THE WEIMAR REPUBLIC AND THE NAZI DICTATORSHIP

A. Rosenberg, *A History of the German Republic*, trans., London, 1936; S. W. Halperin, *Germany Tried Democracy, a Political History, 1918–33*, New York, 1946; G. Scheele, *The Weimar Republic*, London, 1946; E. Eyck, *A History of the Weimar Republic*, trans. of first half of his *Geschichte der Weimarer Republik*, Cambridge, Mass., 1962; A. Luckau, *The German Delegation at the Paris Peace Conference*, New York, 1941; J. T. Shotwell, *What Germany Forgot*, New York, 1940; W. M. Jordan, *Great Britain, France, and the German Problem*, London, 1943; H. J. Gordon, *The Reichswehr and the German Republic, 1919–1926*, Princeton, 1957; J. H. Morgan, *Assize at Arms*, New York, 1946; P. Waite, *Vanguard of Nazism. The Freecorps Movement in Post-war Germany, 1918–1923*, Cambridge, Mass., 1952; W. Kaufmann, *Monarchism in the Weimar Republic*, New York, 1953; R. Fischer, *Stalin and German Communism*, Cambridge, 1948; Klaus Epstein, *Matthias Erzberger and the Dilemma of German Democracy*, Princeton, 1959; H. W. Gatzke, *Stresemann and the Rearmament of Germany*, Baltimore, 1954; J. W. Wheeler-Bennett, *The Wooden Titan, Hindenburg*, London, 1936; *G. Stresemann: Diaries, Letters and Papers*, trans. and ed. E. Sutton, 3 vols., London, 1935–40; R. d'O. Butler, *The Roots of National Socialism*, London, 1941; K. von Klemperer, *Germany's New Conservatism*, Princeton, 1957; G. Freund, *Unholy Alliance*, London, 1957; R. T. Clark, *The Fall of the German Republic*, London, 1934; K. D. Bracher, *Die Auflösung der Weimarer Republik*, 3rd ed., Stuttgart, Düsseldorf, 1960, Eng. Trans. forthcoming; K. Heiden, *Der Führer, Hitler's Rise to Power*, Boston, 1944; A. Bullock, *Hitler, A Study in Tyranny*, rev. ed., London, 1962; H. Heiber, *Adolf Hitler, A Short Biography*, trans., London, 1961; Hitler, *Mein Kampf*, unexpurgated ed., trans., London, 1939; N. H. Baynes, ed., *Hitler's Speeches*, 2 vols., London, 1942; *Hitler's Table Talk, 1941–1944*, London, 1953; *The Trial of the Major War Criminals before the International Tribunal, Proceedings*, vols., i–xxiii, Nuremberg, 1947–9; *Documents in Evidence*, vols., xxiv–xlii, Nuremberg, 1947–9; *Nazi Conspiracy and Aggression*, 8 vols., plus 2 supplementary vols., Washington, 1946–8; *Trial of German Major War Criminals*, London, 1946–50; *Documents on German Foreign Policy*, trans., Series C, 1933–7, Series D, 1936/7–40, London, Washington, 1949–, 1957– ; H. Mau and H. Krausnick, *German History, 1933–45*, trans., London, 1959; H. Buchheim, *The Third Reich*, trans., Munich, 1961; W. L. Shirer, *The Rise and Fall of the Third Reich*, New York, 1960; T. L. Jarman, *The Rise and Fall of Nazi Germany*, London, 1955; International Council for Philosophy and Humanistic Studies, *The Third Reich*, London, 1955; K. D. Bracher, W. Sauer, G. Schulz, *Die nationalsozialistische Machtergreifung*, Cologne, 1960; E. Mathias and R. Morsey, *Das Ende der Parteien*, Düsseldorf, 1960; S. H. Roberts, *The House that Hitler Built*, London, 1937; F. Neumann, *Behemoth. The Structure and Practice of National Socialism*, New York, 1942; J. Goebbels, *My Part in Germany's Fight*, London, 1935; H. Rauschning, *The Revolution of Nihilism*, New York, 1939, and *The Voice of Destruction*, New York, 1940; C. W. Guillebaud, *The Economic Recovery of Germany, 1933–1938*, London, 1939; E. N. Peterson, *Hjalmar Schacht, For and Against Hitler*, Boston, Mass., 1954; N. Micklem, *National Socialism and the Catholic Church*, London, 1939; R. H. Samuel and R. H. Thomas, *Education and Society in Modern Germany*, London, 1949; T. Taylor, *Sword and Swastika*, New York, 1952; J. W. Wheeler-Bennett, *The Nemesis of Power, The German Army in Politics*, London, 1954; W. Hofer, *War Premeditated*, trans., London, 1955; A. J. P. Taylor, *The Origins of the Second World War*, London, 1961.

CHAPTER XIII. TRIUMPH AND CATASTROPHE, 1939–45

C. Falls, *The Second World War*, 3rd ed., London, 1950; K. von Tippelskirch, *Geschichte des Zweiten Weltkrieges*, Bonn, 1951; *H.*-A. Jacobsen and H. Dollinger, *Der Zweite Weltkrieg in Bildern und Dokumenten*, Munich, 1963; A. Bullock, *Hitler, a Study in Tyranny*, rev. ed., London, 1962; F. H. Hinsley, *Hitler's Strategy*, Cambridge, 1951; Felix Gilbert (ed.), *Hitler Directs his War*, New York, 1951; Fritz Halder, *Hitler as Warlord*, London, 1950; T. Taylor, *The March of Conquest: The German Victories in Western Europe, 1940*, New York, 1958; Louis de Jong, *The German Fifth Column in the Second World War*, London, 1956; R. Wheatley, *Operation Sea Lion*, Oxford, 1958; R.I.I.A., *Survey of International Affairs, 1939–1946*: A. and V. M. Toynbee (eds.), *Hitler's Europe*, and *Documents*, ed. M. Carlyle, London, 1954; A. and V. M. Toynbee, *The Initial Triumph of the Axis*, London, 1954; R. Aron, *The Vichy Régime, 1940–44*, London, 1958; *Ciano's Diary, 1939–1943*, London, 1947; *The Goebbels Diaries*, London, 1948; G. L. Weinberg, *Germany and the Soviet Union, 1939–1941*, Leiden, 1954; *Nazi-Soviet Relations, from the Archives of the German Foreign Office*, Washington, 1946; A. Dallin, *German Rule in Russia, 1941–1945*, London, 1957; G. Reitlinger, *The Final Solution*, London, 1953; Raul Hilberg, *The Destruction of the European Jews*, Chicago, 1961; E. Kogon, *The Theory and Practice of Hell*, trans., New York, 1958; G. Reitlinger, *The S.S.: Alibi of a Nation*, London, 1956; E. Crankshaw, *Gestapo, Instrument of Tyranny*, London, 1956; *The Schellenberg Memoirs*, London, 1956; W. Frischauer, *Himmler*, Boston, 1953; R. Manvell and H. Fraenkel, *Herman Goering*, London, 1963; H. Rothfels, *The German Opposition to Hitler*, trans., London, 1961; G. Ritter, *The German Resistance*, trans., London, 1958; E. Zimmermann and H.-A. Jacobsen, *Germans against Hitler, July 20, 1944*, 3rd ed., trans., Bonn, 1960; J. W. Wheeler-Bennett, *Nemesis of Power*, London, 1963; H. Guderian, *Panzer Leader*. London, 1952; A. Kesselring, *A Soldier's Record*, New York, 1954; *The Rommel Papers*, London, 1953; C. Wilmot, *The Struggle for Europe*, London, 1952; F. W. Deakin, *The Brutal Friendship*, London, 1962; D. Irving, *The Destruction of Dresden*, London, 1963; G. Blond, *The Death of Hitler's Germany*, New York, 1954; H. R. Trevor-Roper, *The Last Days of Hitler*, 2nd ed., London, 1952; F. Meinecke, *The German Catastrophe*, trans., Cambridge, Mass., 1950.

Chapter XIV. The German Phoenix, 1945–63

J. L. Snell, *Wartime Origins of the East-West Dilemma Over Germany*, New Orleans, 1959; E. McInnis, R. Hiscocks, R. Spencer, *The Shaping of Post-war Germany*, London, New York, Toronto, 1960; H. Feis, *Between War and Peace: The Potsdam Conference*, Princeton, 1960; M. Balfour and J. Mair, *Four-Power Control in Germany and Austria, 1945–1946*, London, 1956 (R.I.I.A *Survey of International Affairs, 1939–1946*); R.I.I.A., *Survey of International Affairs, 1947–1948*, ed. P. Calvocoressi, London, 1952; *1949–1950*, ed. P. Calvocoressi, London, 1953; thereafter annual volumes, each with companion volume of documents, various editors; W. Friedmann, *The Allied Military Government of Germany*, London, 1947; E. H. Litchfield, ed., *Governing Post-war Germany*, Ithaca, New York, 1953; E. Davidson, *The Death and Life of Germany*, New York, 1959; L. D. Clay, *Decision in Germany*, New York, 1950; B. Ruhm von Oppen, *Documents on Germany Under Occupation, 1945–1954*, London, 1955; *Germany, 1947–1949, The Story in Documents*, Washington, 1950; J. P. Nettl, *The Eastern Zone and Soviet Policy in Germany, 1945–50*, London, New York, Toronto, 1951; W. P. Davison, *The Berlin Blockade*, Princeton, 1950; A. Grosser, *Western Germany from Defeat to Rearmament*, trans., London, 1955; H. C. Wallich, *Mainsprings of the German Revival*, New Haven, 1955; J. F. Golay, *The Founding of the Federal Republic of Germany*, Chicago, 1958; E. Alexander, trans., *Adenauer and the New Germany*, New York, 1957; P. Weymar, *Konrad Adenauer*, trans., London, 1957; R. Hiscocks, *Democracy in Western Germany*, London, 1957; A. Grosser, *Die Bonner Demokratie*, Düsseldorf, 1960; E. Plischke, *Contemporary Government of Germany*, Boston, 1961; B. Connell, *Watcher on the Rhine*, London, 1957; W. Stahl (ed.), *The Politics of Post-war Germany*, New York, 1963; H. Kohn, *German History, Some New German Views*, London, 1954; W. G. Grewe, *Deutsche Aussenpolitik der Nachkriegszeit*, Stuttgart, 1960; H. Speier and W. P. Davidson, *West German Leadership and Foreign Policy*, Evaston, Ill., 1957; G. Freund, *Germany Between Two Worlds*, New York, 1961; W. Brandt, *My Road to Berlin*, New York, 1960; P. Windsor, *City on Leave: A History of Berlin, 1945–1962*, London, 1963; C. B. Robson (ed.), *Berlin, Pivot of German Destiny*, Chapel Hill, N.C., 1960; H. Speier, *Divided Berlin*, London, 1961.

INDEX OF PLACES AND PERSONS

AACHEN, 164, 165, 245, 423, 425
Abbeville, 391
Abdul Hamid II, Sultan of Turkey, 313
Abel, 170
Abyssinia, 383
Acheson, Dean, 443
Addison, Joseph, 82
Adenauer, Konrad, 439, 443, 449, 452, 454, 455, 456, 458, 459, 460, 461, 462, 463, 464, 466, 467, 468, 470
Adrianople. *See* EDIRNE
Adriatic, 322, 330, 331, 332, 385
Aehrenthal, 322, 331
Aeneas Sylvius (Piccolomini), 1
Afghanistan, 293, 320
Africa, 282, 292, 293, 294, 312, 317, 325, 329, 334, 381, 382, 396
Agadir, 329
Agram. *See* ZAGREB
Agricola, 9
Aisne, 392
Albania, 331, 332, 339, 396, 424
Albert I, 'The Bear,' Margrave of Brandenburg, 30
Albert Achilles (Albert III), Elector of Brandenburg, 31, 45
Alexander I, Tsar, 117, 119, 120, 122, 128, 131, 132, 136
Alexander II, Tsar, 210, 278, 282, 283, 291
Alexander III, Tsar, 210, 291
Alexandria, 407
Alfieri, Vittorio, 68
Algarotti, Francesco, 69
Algeciras, 319, 320
Algeria, 319, 408
Alsace, 3, 20, 38, 73, 109, 110, 111
Alsace-Lorraine, 238, 245, 250, 271, 274, 275, 278, 282, 284, 294, 295, 297, 306, 311, 318, 328, 329, 337, 339, 349, 350, 358, 363, 386, 398
Altenstein, 155
Altmark. *See* OLD MARK
Ancillon, Frederick, 151
Andes, 255
Andrassy, Julius, Count, 236, 284, 285
Angora, 314
Anhalt, 150, 438
Ansbach, 30, 118
Antonescu, 424
Antwerp, 422, 423, 425
Anzio, 415
Archimedes, 255
Arctic, 390
Ardennes, 390, 425
Armenians, 313
Arndt, E. M., 122, 140, 156, 158, 166, 185
Arnhom, 423
Arnim, Achim v., 122
Arnim, Count, 276, 282, 309
Arnold, Matthew, 107
Ascanian dynasty, 30
Asia, 283, 292, 312, 317, 320, 382
Asia Minor, 313
Aspern, 120
Atlantic, 401, 407, 413
Atlantic ports, 395
Auerstadt, 118, 122, 128
Augsburg, 11, 22, 80
—, Diet of, 6
—, Peace of, 16, 18
—, see of, 8
Augustenburg, Duke of, 215, 216, 217
Augustus, Elector of Saxony, King of Poland. *See* FREDERICK AUGUSTUS

Augustus the Strong. *See* FREDERICK AUGUSTUS
Auschwitz, 405, 410, 424
Auslanddeutsche, 380
Austen, Jane, 134
Austerlitz, 117, 118
Australia, 274, 293
Austria (and Austria-Hungary), 3, 14, 17, 18, 36, 37, 39, 46, 48, 58, 63, 65, 66, 67, 75, 85, 109, 110, 111, 112, 114, 115, 116, 117, 119, 120, 121, 122, 128, 129, 130, 131, 132, 133, 134, 136, 140, 141, 142–9, 150, 153, 155, 159, 172, 177–84, 190, 191, 192, 193, 200, 201, 202, 208, 209, 210, 213, 214, 215, 216, 217, 218, 219, 220, 221, 223, 225, 232, 234, 235, 236, 242, 260, 263, 265, 270, 271, 281, 282, 283, 284, 290, 291, 297, 303, 310, 312, 319, 320, 321, 322, 323, 327, 329, 330, 331, 332, 334, 335, 336, 337, 339, 340, 362, 369, 379, 381, 382, 384, 385, 386, 410, 415
Austrian Netherlands, 218
Avignon, 210
Azov, Sea of, 407, 411

Bach, Austrian minister, 200
Bach, Sebastian, 26, 77
Bacon, Francis, 373
Baden, Prince Maximilian Alexander Friedrich Wilhelm of, 343, 344
Baden, 79, 86, 115, 116, 117, 133, 140, 144, 148, 149, 153, 154, 166, 170, 172, 175, 176, 177, 185, 191, 202, 220, 223, 230, 232, 239, 243, 246, 263, 267, 304, 438
Baden-Wurtemberg, 457
Badoglio, Pietro, Marchese del Sabotino, Duke of Addis Ababa, Marshal, 412
Bagdad, 303, 314, 334, 339
Baku, 408
Bakunin, Michael Alexandrovich, 191
Balkans, 236, 275, 282, 283, 284, 289, 291, 303, 320, 322, 323, 329, 330, 331, 332, 334, 336, 338, 385, 396, 397
Ballenstedt, 30
Baltic, 215, 222, 251, 397, 401, 425, 426
— States, 387, 393, 402, 405, 406, 416
Bamberg, see of, 8
Bamberger, Ludwig, 293
Banse, Ewald, 377
Barth, Karl, 378, 380
Basel, 298
—, Council of, 8, 118
—, Peace of, 112
Basra, 339
Bassermann, Friedrich Daniel, 149, 169, 185, 187, 188
Baudissin, Graf v., Col., 461
Bauer, Bruno, 162
Bauer, Gustav, Chancellor, 351
Baumgarten, Alexander, 225
Bautzen, 128
Bavaria, 3, 5, 7, 18, 19, 20, 21, 30, 45, 63, 73, 112, 116, 117, 129, 131, 132, 133, 134, 136, 137, 141, 146, 148, 153, 170, 191, 193, 202, 218, 220, 221, 223, 230, 232, 233, 234, 237, 238, 239, 240, 242, 246, 252, 253, 263, 265, 267, 269, 270, 288, 304, 331, 344, 345, 347, 348, 355, 358, 371, 372, 431, 438
Bayreuth, 30
Bazaine, Achille, Maréchal, 238
Bebel, August, 225, 231, 250, 251, 278, 285, 292, 304, 324, 328
Beck, Ludwig, Gen., 389, 398, 409, 410, 415, 417, 418

Beckerath, Hermann v., 169, 187
Beethoven, Ludwig van, 99, 141, 262
Belfort, 238
Belgium, 66, 112, 155, 221, 223, 235, 245, 292, 303, 337, 341, 342, 349, 358, 363, 390, 396, 398, 410
Belgrade, 335, 400
Belzec, 410, 424
Benedetti, Vincent, 223, 237
Benelux countries, 446
Benghazi, 396, 400, 408
Benjamin, Frau, 458
Bennigsen, Rudolf v., 226, 231, 271, 275, 277, 280, 289, 290
Berchtesgaden, 427
Berchtold, Leopold Count, 331, 335, 336
Bergen, 10
Bergmann, Professor Ernst, 380
Berlin, 27, 30, 31, 41, 45, 50, 51, 55, 57, 58, 59, 70, 78, 80, 87, 118, 121, 122, 128, 135, 149, 151, 154, 155, 162, 165, 167, 175, 176, 179, 180, 181, 182, 183, 184, 186, 188, 204, 210, 213, 219, 224, 230, 231, 237, 241, 243, 245, 247, 248, 249, 250, 254, 255, 256, 257, 260, 270, 275, 278, 279, 283, 286, 291, 293, 294, 295, 301, 302, 303, 308, 313, 333, 334, 336, 342, 344, 345, 347, 348, 352, 358, 363, 368, 369, 383, 385, 393, 394, 414, 418, 426, 428, 430, 431, 432, 433, 436, 439, 442–8, 450, 451, 453, 457, 458, 460, 462, 465, 466, 467, 468, 469
— Assembly, 184, 186
— Decrees, 120
—, East, 442, 453, 466, 467, 470
— Karlshorst, 429
—, West, 448, 449, 450, 451, 453, 461, 465, 467, 468, 469
Bernadotte, Count, 428
Bernhardi, Friedrich v., 332, 377
Bernstein, Eduard, 304
Berthold, Archbishop of Mainz, 5
Bessarabia, 394
Bessemer, Henry, 245
Bethmann-Hollweg, J. J., 203, 204
Bethmann-Hollweg, Theobald v., 321, 323, 326, 327, 328, 331, 333, 334, 335, 336, 339, 341, 342, 365
Beust, F. F. v., 202, 236
Bevin, Ernest, 444
Beyens, Baron, 332
Biarritz, 210, 221
Bidault, Paul, 446
Biscay, Bay of, 413
Bismarck, Prince Herbert v., 295
Bismarck, Prince Otto v., 28, 31, 47, 58, 75, 76, 86, 109, 114, 131, 138, 139, 142, 151, 155, 158, 166, 174, 182, 184, 192, 193, 194, 200, 201, 202, 203, 204, 205, 206, 207, 208, 209, 210, 213, 214, 215–27, 230–41, 243, 256, 262, 264, 265, 269, 270–98, 303, 305, 306, 309, 311, 312, 316, 317, 321, 323, 324, 326, 329, 332, 337, 340, 341, 351, 379, 385
Bismarck Archipelago, 293
Bitzius, Gotthelf, 260
Björkoe, 319
Black Forest, 175, 260
— Sea, 198, 223, 394, 402, 403, 406
Blank, Theodor, 463
Blomberg, Werner v., 385
Blondel, Georges, 333
Blücher, Gebhard Leberecht v., 128
Blum, Robert, 170, 172, 175, 177, 179, 186
Bock, Fedor v., 391, 402, 403
Bodelschwingh, 169, 181
Bodmer, 83
Boers, 293
Bohemia, 3, 17, 19, 132, 145, 171, 178, 189, 221, 259, 283, 389
Bohle, 381

Böhme, Jakob, 25
Bologna, 425
Bonhoeffer, Dietrich, 410
Bonn, 267, 272, 298, 381n., 449, 451, 454, 456, 459, 462, 465, 468
Bordeaux, 392
Bormann, Martin Ludwig, 399, 411, 414, 428, 436
Born, Stephen, 176
Börne, Ludwig, 163, 192
Borneo, 293
Borsig, Johann, 295
Borsig, 165
Bosnia-Herzegovina, 283, 322, 323, 329, 334
Boswell, 87
Bötticher (Lagarde), 315
Boulanger, Georges, Gen., 289, 290
Bourbons, 19, 36, 66, 116
Bowring, John, 154
Boyen, 152
Brahms, Johannes, 262
Brandenburg, minister, 183, 184
Brandenburg, province, 3, 7, 9, 18, 21, 27, 29–76, 118, 120, 149, 207, 258, 263, 438, 458
Brandt, Willy, 465, 467
Brauchitsch, Walther Heinrich Alfred Hermann, Field Marshal, 398, 399, 404
Braun, Otto, 344, 372
Bremen, 20, 80, 113, 118, 133, 149, 199, 292, 301, 344, 438
Brenner, 385
Brentano, Clemens, 122
Brentano, Heinrich v., 464, 468
Brentano, Lujo, 287
Brentano, revolutionary, 187, 191
Breslau, 163, 180, 245, 261, 278, 286n.
Brest, 401, 407
Brest-Litovsk, 340, 341, 344, 349, 362, 388, 423
Briand, Aristide, 361
Brion, Friderike, 94
Britain, 55, 66, 112, 114, 117, 125, 128, 134, 152, 186, 189, 210, 215, 217, 220, 235, 236, 238, 245, 246, 247, 250, 257, 279, 282, 284, 286, 291, 292, 302, 303, 304, 310, 312, 314, 315–23, 329, 330, 333–7, 339, 355, 358, 359, 363, 367, 377, 381, 382, 383–7, 389, 392, 393, 394, 395, 396, 398, 400, 401, 446, 470
British Guiana, 395
Brittany, 392, 416
Bruchmühle, 439
Bruck, 155
Bruges, 10
Brünning, Heinrich, 365, 368, 369, 370, 378, 382
Bruno, 25
Brunswick, 3, 8, 46, 80, 118, 119, 136, 141, 149, 154, 255, 261, 262, 438
Brusiloff, Alexei Alexeivich, 338
Brussels, 166, 390, 391, 422
Bucharest, 394, 424
Bucher, Lothar, 237, 296
Buchlau, 322
Büchner, Ludwig, 256
Budapest, 394, 424, 425, 426
Buffon, Georges Louis Leclerc de, 9
Bug, 416
Bukovina, 338, 394
Bulgaria, 283, 289, 322, 330, 331, 332, 335, 337, 338, 340, 396, 424
Bülow, Prince Bernhard v., 281, 290, 303, 306, 313, 315, 317, 318, 319, 321, 322, 323, 324, 325, 326, 334
Bunsen, Christian, 168, 191
Buol (Schauenstein), Count, 143, 200
Burckhardt, Jakob, 258, 271, 298
Burgundy, County of, 3, 27
Burke, Edmund, 122, 131
Burns, Robert, 98
Busch, Moritz, 275, 276n., 296n.

Byelorussia, 406
Byrnes, James F., 441

Caen, 417
Calvin, Jean, 25
Cambon, Paul, 318
Cameroons, 293
Camphausen, Otto v., 164, 165, 169, 182, 183, 279
Campo Formio, Peace of, 112
Canaris, 410, 415
Canitz, Friedrich Rudolf Ludwig, 169
Canossa, 274
Cape Colony, 292
Caporetto, 339
Caprivi de Caprera de Montecuccoli, Georg Leo v., 303, 306, 310, 324, 326
Carigliano, 415
Carinthia, 3
Carlsbad, 144
Carlstadt, 14
Carniola, 3
Carnot, Hippolyte, 340
Caroline Islands, 314
Casablanca, 415
Caspian Sea, 408
Cassel, 243
Cassino, 415
Castlereagh, Henry Robert, Viscount, 132, 134
Catherine II, Tsarina, 55, 73, 90
Caucasus, 198, 340, 402, 403, 407, 408, 411
Cavaignac, Louis Eugène, 177
Cavour, Camillo Benso, Count, 172, 202, 222
Celle, 253
Celtis, Konrad, 24
Chad, Lake, 329
Chamberlain, Houston Stewart, 316, 366
Chamberlain, Joseph, 313, 318
Chamberlain, Neville, 386, 401
Channel, the, 395, 407, 408, 417
— ports, 423
Charlemagne (Charles the Great), 2
Charles, Archduke of Austria, 120
Charles, Duke of Brunswick, 146
Charles I, King of England, 211
Charles II, King of England, 39, 47
Charles IV, Holy Roman Emperor, 3, 30
Charles V, Holy Roman Emperor, 4, 6, 18, 22, 27, 31
Charles VI, Holy Roman Emperor, 58, 65
Charles XII, King of Sweden, 48, 57, 63
Charles Augustus, Duke of Saxe-Weimar, 79, 94
Charles Eugene (Karl Eugen), Duke of Wurtemberg, 98
Charles Frederick, Grand Duke of Baden, 79
Chateaubriand, François René, 137
Chaumont, Treaty of, 131
Chemnitz, 250
Cherbourg, 417
China, 312, 313
Christ, Johann Friedrich, 85
Christian IX, King of Denmark, 215
Churchill, Winston, 320, 392, 394, 395, 401, 402, 430, 433, 456, 471
'Cicero,' Elector of Brandenburg, 31
Clarendon, 219
Clay, Lucius, Gen., 441
Clemenceau, Georges, 291, 320, 355
Cleves-Jülich, 19
Clyde, 395
Cobden, Richard, 154, 155
Coblenz, 113, 150, 159, 203, 237, 349
Cocceji, Samuel, 55, 69
Cologne, 2, 3, 8, 11, 19, 134, 140, 150, 157, 158, 164, 165, 167, 172, 175, 180, 182, 188, 266, 349, 363, 407, 429, 439
Compiègne, 392
Congo Free State, 293, 313
—, River, 293

Conrad v. Hoetzendorf, Gen., 322, 331, 332, 335
Constance, 267
—, Council of, 30
Constantinople, 201, 283, 313, 317, 331, 332
Copenhagen, 215
Copernicus, 25, 103
Cotentin Peninsula, 417
Courland, 338, 423, 426
Cousin, Victor, 110
Cracow, 134, 171, 426
Crete, 313, 396, 400
Crimea, 282, 407, 412, 416
Croats, 322
Croce, Benedetto, 162
Cromwell, Oliver, 36
Cuba, 314
Cuno, Wilhelm, Chancellor, 358, 359
Custozza, 179, 221
Czechoslovakia, 363, 380, 382, 383, 384, 385, 386, 410, 435
Czechs, 222
Czernin, Count Ottakar, v. u. zu Chudenitz, 335

Dahlmann, Frederick Christopher, 140, 147, 162, 187, 189
Dalberg, Karl Theodor Anton Maria v., Archbishop of Mainz, 115, 116, 117
D'Alembert, Jean le Rond, 64
Damascus, 314
Danckelmann, 48, 49
Danilevsky, Nikolai Yakovlevich, 283
Danube, 200, 315, 394, 397, 400, 424
Danzig, 34, 119, 350, 382, 386, 387, 426
Dardanelles, 283, 322, 338
Darré, Walter, 373, 376
Darwin, Charles, 256, 264
Dawes, Charles Gates, 360
Deák, Ferencz, 171
Debrecen, 424
Defoe, Daniel, 83
De Gaulle, Charles, Gen., 396, 462
Dehler, Thomas, 463
Dehmel, Richard, 297, 308
Delbrück, Hans, 276n., 326, 344
Delbrück, Rudolf, 154, 231
Delcassé, Théophile, 318, 319
De Maistre, Joseph Marie, Comte, 137
D'Enghien, Louis Antoine, Duc, 116
Denmark, 10, 47, 48, 171, 182, 189, 209, 215, 216, 217, 218, 222, 279, 390, 396, 397
Dernburg, 325
Descartes, René, 103, 104
Dijon, 423
Dilthey, Wilhelm, 307
Disraeli, Benjamin, 226, 282
Dittmann, 343
Dnieper, 403, 412
Dniester, 416
Dobrudja, 331
Doenitz, Karl, Adm., 407, 413, 417, 428, 429, 436
Dohnanyi, Hans v., 410
Dollfuss, Engelbert, 382
Döllinger, 258, 266, 267, 268, 272
Don, 407, 408, 411
Donauwörth, 19
Donetz, 340, 407, 411, 412
Dorpat, 33
Dortmund, 245, 413
Dortmund–Ems Canal, 423
Drava, 424
Dresden, 80, 84, 86, 175, 198, 242, 262, 426, 469
Drexler, Anton, 367
Droste-Fischering, Baron Klemens August v., Archbishop of Cologne, 158
Droysen, Johann Gustav, 48, 202, 258
Dubois-Raymond brothers, 256
Duhan, Charles Gilles, 62
Duisburg, 45, 423, 427

Dunkirk, 391, 392
Düppel, forts, 217
Dürer, Albrecht, 9, 24
Düsseldorf, 249, 261, 429, 440
Dyle, 391

East Friesland, 66, 72, 124
East Germany, People's Republic, 453, 458, 461, 463, 464, 467
East Prussia, 34, 37, 38, 39, 40, 41, 62, 75, 79, 81, 89, 102, 104, 106, 118, 126, 128, 151, 167, 168, 386, 387, 416, 424, 425, 426, 433, 440, 469
Ebert, Friedrich, 344, 347, 348, 351, 352, 353, 360
Ebert, Fritz, 448
Eckart, Dietrich, 365
Eckart, Meister, 370
Eckermann, Johann Peter, 142, 255
Edirne, 331
Egypt, 293, 317, 318, 400
Eichel, 71
Eichmann, Adolf, 405, 424, 469, 470
Eichhorn, Johann Albrecht Friedrich, 154, 168, 257
Eifel, 425
Einstein, Albert, 378
Eisenach, 250, 432
Eisenhower, Dwight David, Gen., 423, 426, 431
Eisleben, 14
Eisner, Kurt, 344, 348
El Alamein, 407
Elba, 129, 133, 159
Elbe, 427, 428
Elberfeld, 165
Elbrus, Mt, 408
Elizabeth, Tsarina, 66, 75
Emden, 66, 72
Ems, 237
Engels family, 164
Engels, Friedrich, 161, 166, 171, 174, 176, 192, 248, 251
England, 4, 13, 17, 22, 29, 40, 46, 49, 57, 58, 64, 77, 80, 81, 110, 111, 116, 118, 119, 139, 140, 147, 150, 155, 165, 166, 416
Erasmus, 24, 25
Erfurt, 120, 251, 304
Erhard, Ludwig, 450, 451, 452, 463, 464, 466, 468, 470
Ernest Augustus, King of Hanover, 175
Erzberger, Matthias, 343, 349, 358
Essen, 245, 413
Esthonia, 416
Ethiopia. . See ABYSSINIA
Eugène, Prince of Savoy, 62, 63
Eugénie, Empress of France, 214
Eulenberg, Prince Philipp, 309
Eupen, 398
Europe, 282, 288, 301, 305, 306, 312, 313, 314, 319, 321, 331, 336, 340, 344, 372, 373, 382, 383, 385
—, Central, 220, 221, 222, 240, 281, 315
—, Eastern, 283
—, Middle-Eastern, 383
—, South-Eastern, 377, 383

Falaise, 422
Falk, Adalbert, 273, 274, 279
Falkenhayn, Eric v., Gen., 338, 341
Far East, 312, 313
Fashoda, 317
Faulhaber, Cardinal, 379, 432
Favre, Jules, 238
Feder, Gottfried, 367
Fehrbellin, 39
Ferdinand I, Austrian Emperor, 179
Ferdinand, Archduke, later Ferdinand II, Holy Roman Emperor, 19
Ferdinand III, Holy Roman Emperor, 13

Ferry, Jules, 289, 293
Feuerbach, Ludwig, 162, 262, 263
Fez, 329
Fichte, Johann Gottlieb, 13, 50, 79, 82, 85, 91, 122, 128, 135, 245, 249, 254, 262, 263, 298, 315
Fielding, Henry, 83
Fiji, 293
Finland, 382, 390, 393, 394, 397, 402, 406, 416
Flanders, 29, 338
Flaubert, Gustave, 307
Fleurus, 112
Foch, Ferdinand, Maréchal, 355
Foggia airfield, 415
Fontane, Theodor, 258, 260, 346
Forkenbeck, 226, 231, 280
Forster, Georg, 113
Fouqué, 137
France, 4, 10, 17, 20, 22, 27, 38, 39, 42, 46, 48, 51, 57, 58, 62, 66, 77, 79, 85, 86, 90, 93, 97, 99, 103, 108–35, 136, 138, 140, 147, 149, 150, 155, 166, 169, 172, 185, 186, 188, 189, 202, 203, 207, 209, 210, 215, 218, 220, 221, 222, 223, 232, 234, 235, 236–40, 242, 243, 244, 245, 247, 250, 252, 253, 257, 261, 270, 271, 272, 275, 276n., 281, 282, 283, 284, 289, 290, 291, 292, 293, 294, 297, 298, 301, 302, 306, 307, 310, 312, 313, 314–23, 327, 328, 330, 332, 333, 334, 336, 337, 341, 349, 355, 358, 359, 361, 363, 367, 369, 377, 381, 382, 383, 385, 386, 387, 389, 390, 392, 396, 398, 408, 410, 431, 433, 438, 446, 460
Franche Comté, 3
Francis II, Holy Roman Emperor, first Austrian Emperor, 117, 131, 145, 171
Francis Ferdinand, Austrian Archduke, 331, 334
Francis Joseph, Austrian Emperor, 179, 202, 213, 216, 219, 222, 236, 283, 321, 335
Francke, A. H., 49, 81
Franco, Gen., 396
Franconia, 2, 5, 122
Frank, Hans, 389, 436
Frankel, State Attorney, 470
Frankfurt on Main, 11, 79, 80, 93, 96, 98, 117, 133, 152, 162, 171, 172, 174, 176, 179, 180, 184–94, 198, 203, 208, 209, 210, 213, 216, 222, 230, 232, 238, 246, 265, 285, 301, 326, 354
Frantz, Constantin, 315
Frederick, Elector of Hesse, 146
Frederick I (Barbarossa), Holy Roman Emperor, 113, 301
Frederick I, Grand Duke of Baden, 202
Frederick I, King of Prussia, 45–50, 51, 53, 56
Frederick II ('The Great'), King of Prussia, 33, 36, 45, 52, 54, 56, 57, 58, 59, 60–76, 78, 87, 103, 106, 111, 118, 122, 125, 126, 151, 166, 204, 208, 221n., 224, 297, 385
Frederick II, Elector of Brandenburg, 31
Frederick III, Holy Roman Emperor, 3, 4, 8
Frederick III, King of Prussia, first German Emperor, 295, 297
Frederick VII, King of Denmark, 215
Frederick Augustus, Elector of Saxony, King of Poland, 45, 47
Frederick William I, Elector of Brandenburg, 35–45, 48, 51, 54, 57, 58, 60, 67
Frederick William I, King of Prussia, 49, 51–60, 65, 67, 81
Frederick William II, King of Prussia, 79, 106, 111, 118
Frederick William III, King of Prussia, 118, 122, 125, 128, 136, 137, 138, 140, 142, 145, 150, 152, 156, 159, 160, 166, 242, 265, 294
Frederick William IV, King of Prussia, 157, 158, 159, 160, 166–72, 175, 180, 181, 182, 183, 184, 188, 191, 193, 195, 201, 203, 204, 208, 209, 264, 266
Frederick of Hohenzollern, Elector of Brandenburg, 30

Frederick the Wise, Elector of Saxony, 14
Freiburg, 428
Freiligrath, Ferdinand, 163
French Equatorial Africa (French Congo), 329, 330
Frenssen, Gustav, 308
Freytag, Gustav, 258, 261, 301
Frick, Wilhelm, 367, 371, 373, 414, 436
Friedland, 118
Friedrichsruh, 208
Friesler, 409, 411, 419
Frings, Cardinal, 432
Fritsch, Werner Freiherr v., 385
Fritzsche, 436
Froebel, Frederick, 213
Fuggers, 11, 22, 23
Fulda, 119
— Abbey, 8
Funk, 397, 436
Fürth, 242

Gagern, F. v., 140, 145
Gagern, H., 185, 187, 188, 191, 193
Galen, Clemens August, Count, Bishop of Münster, 432
Galicia, 120, 145, 171, 178, 179, 338
Galileo, 25
Gallipoli, 338
Gambetta, Léon, 238, 277
Gastein, 219
Gauss, F. C., 255
Geissel, Johannes v., Cardinal of Cologne, 266
Gellert, Christian Fürchtegott, 82, 86
Geneva, 382, 462, 465
Gentz, Friedrich v., 122, 137
George II, King of England, 66
George V, King of Hanover, 230
George, Stefan, 307
George William, Elector of Brandenburg, 35, 36
Gerhardt, Paul, 25
Gerlach, 182, 197, 203, 208, 209, 217
German East Africa, 293, 294, 310
— South-West Africa, 294, 325
Gervinus, Georg Gottfried, 147, 162, 258
Gesner, Johann Matthias, 82, 85, 144
Gessler, Otto, 349, 362
Gibbon, Edward, 90
Gibraltar, 396, 400
Giesbrecht, Wilhelm v., 257
Giessen, 253
Gladstone, William Ewart, 282, 294
Gneisenau, August Wilhelm Anton, Count Neithardt v., 121, 124, 127
Gobineau, Joseph Arthur, Count, 315
Goebbels, Josef, 368, 371, 373, 377, 379, 388, 393, 404, 409, 411, 412, 413, 414, 415, 418, 422, 427, 428, 429, 436
Goerdeler, Carl, 389, 398, 409, 410, 415, 419
Goering, Hermann, 367, 370, 371, 373, 377, 379, 388, 390, 395, 397, 405, 417, 428, 436
Goethe, Johann Wolfgang, 27, 70, 78, 79, 81, 82, 83, 84, 85, 86, 88, 89, 90, 91, 92, 93–7, 98, 99, 100, 101, 102, 104, 112, 120, 121, 134, 141, 142, 162, 163, 199, 225, 255, 260, 286, 292, 352, 378
Goltz, Colmar v. der, 313
Gomel, 416
Gooch, G. P., 317
Görres, Ludwig, 113, 122, 140, 158, 159
Gortshakoff, Prince Alexander, 210, 233, 283, 284
Gotha, 251
Gothland, 33
Gotthelf, Jeremias, 260
Göttingen, 82, 85, 140, 144, 147, 162, 255
Gottsched, Johann Christoph, 82, 83, 86
Grätz (Graz), 25
Graziani, Rodolpho, Marchese de Neghelli, Gen., 396

Great Elector. See FREDERICK WILLIAM I, ELECTOR OF BRANDENBURG
Greece, 313, 330, 331, 332, 335, 338, 386, 394, 400, 401, 424, 443
Greenland, 413
Gregorovius, Ferdinand, 221n., 258
Gregory XVI, Pope, 267
Grey, Sir Edward, 306, 320, 321, 327, 331, 334, 336
Grillparzer, Franz, 177
Grimm, Jacob, 190
Grimm brothers, 147, 167
Grimmelshausen, Christoffel, 26
Grodno, 416
Groener, Wilhelm, 224, 347
Gropius, Walter, 378
Grotewohl, Otto, 439, 442, 445, 453, 455, 457
Grozny, 408
Grumbkow, Friedrich Wilhelm v., 56
Grün, Karl, 166
Guderian, Heinz, Gen., 391, 403, 419, 425, 428
Guelders, 57
Guelph family, 46, 136
Guericke, Otto v., 26
Guernica, 383
Guinea Coast, 43
Gürtner, 411
Gustavus Adolfus, King of Sweden, 35
Gutzkow, Karl Ferdinand, 261

Haase, Hugo, 343
Habsburg, 3, 4, 5, 19, 36, 38, 46, 47, 66, 78, 112, 117, 120, 134, 136, 177, 178, 187, 188, 372, 382
Habsburgs, Spanish, 19, 37, 74
Haeckel, Ernest, 256, 263, 307
Hague, The, 320, 391
Halberstadt, see of, 8, 37
Haldane, Richard Burdon, 320, 336
Halder, Franz, Gen., 393, 394, 398, 401, 402, 404, 406, 414
Halle, 49, 50, 55, 59, 63, 80, 81, 82, 119, 128, 144, 254, 458
Haller, K. L. v., 137, 138, 157
Hamann, Johann Georg, 83, 102
Hambach, 141, 145, 148
Hamburg, 2, 23, 27, 79, 80, 86, 87, 116, 118, 120, 133, 149, 176, 199, 292, 301, 344, 358, 413, 414, 438, 440
Hammerstein, editor, 295
Hammerstein, Freiherr v., 398, 410
Hanover, 46, 49, 50, 59, 66, 74, 79, 116, 118, 119, 120, 132, 134, 137, 144, 146, 147, 149, 153, 154, 155, 175, 191, 202, 221, 222, 226, 230, 231, 232, 243, 438, 467
Hansa, 2, 10, 11, 27, 33, 34, 80, 126, 292
Hansemann, D., 140, 165, 169, 182, 185
Harden, Maximilian, 325
Hardenberg, Friedrich v. See NOVALIS
Hardenberg, Karl August v., 117, 120, 124, 125, 126, 128, 134, 150, 152, 159, 252
Harkort, Frederick, 164, 242, 245
Harzburg, 369
Hasse, E., 316
Hassell, v., 389, 399, 415, 470
Hatzfeld, Sophie, Countess, 248
Hauer, W., 380
Haugwitz, Christian August, 125
Hauptmann, Gerhard, 286n., 297, 301, 307, 308
Haushofer, Karl, 381
Häusser, 202
Haussmann, 351
Hebbel, Friedrich, 261
Hecker, Friedrich Karl Franz, 166, 170, 175, 176, 185
Heckscher, Johann Gustav Moritz, 187
Hegel, Georg Wilhelm Friedrich, 85, 92, 93, 103, 111, 138, 141, 156, 162, 192, 209, 249, 254, 255, 256, 257, 263

Heidelberg, 122, 144, 185
Heine, Heinrich, 102, 137, 158, 162, 163, 166, 186, 249
Heinitz, 124
Heligoland, 120, 292, 310
Helmholtz, Hermann v., 256
Hendaye, 396
Henlein, Konrad, 382
Henry IV, Holy Roman Emperor, 274
Henry the Lion, Holy Roman Emperor, 30, 46
Heppenheim, 185
Herder, Johann Gottfried, 78–81, 83–6, 89–93, 94, 95, 96, 102, 104, 121, 122, 260, 286, 378
Hermes, Georg, Professor, 267
Herreros, 325
Herriot, Édouard, 360
Hertling, Count, Chancellor, 341
Herwegh, Georg, 161, 162, 164, 176, 198
Hess, Rudolf, 367, 373, 388, 399, 436
Hesse, 3, 7, 120, 136, 141, 143, 170, 185, 187, 197, 304, 438
Hesse-Cassel, 79, 116, 119, 149, 154, 196, 213, 221, 222, 243
Hesse-Darmstadt, 116, 140, 153, 197, 222, 223, 230, 239
Hesse-Homburg, 133
Hesse-Nassau, 438
Heuss, Theodor, Professor, 452, 466
Heydrich, Reinhard, 404, 405, 410, 415
Heyne, Christian Gottlob, 82, 144
Heyse, Paul, 260
Himmler, Heinrich, 373, 388, 389, 399, 402, 404, 405, 414, 417, 418, 419, 424, 428, 429, 436
Hindenburg, Paul v. Beneckendorf u., 338, 340, 341, 353, 361, 362, 364, 365, 369, 370, 372, 382
Hirsch-Duncker, 304
Hitler, Adolf, 86, 351, 358, 362, 366–74, 376, 377, 388–404, 406–12, 414–21, 423–7, 436, 439, 469
Hofer, Andreas, 120
Hoffmann v. Fallersleben, August, 163
Hohenlinden, 112
Hohenlohe, Prince Karl, Chancellor, 233, 237, 256, 276n., 284, 285, 295, 311, 312, 317, 324
Hohenstauffen, 27, 281, 301
Hohenzollerns, 5, 30, 31, 40, 47, 58, 63, 72, 73, 74, 128, 136, 150, 160, 166, 184, 207, 301, 345, 365
Holbein, Hans, 24
Hölderlin, Johann Christoff Friedrich, 95
Holland, 17, 20, 22, 23, 38, 39, 40, 42, 57, 80, 116, 119, 125, 150, 152, 157, 235, 292, 315, 344, 390, 391, 410, 425
Holstein, Friedrich v., 309, 310, 312, 318, 319, 325
Horace, 63
Höss, Rudolf, 410
House, Col., E. M., 333
Hoverbeck, Leopold, Baron, 226, 280
Huber, E. R., 380
Huber, Kurt, 409
Huch, Ricarda, 162, 308
Hugenberg, Alfred, 364, 369, 371
Huguenots, 39, 62
Humboldt, Alexander v., 245, 253, 255, 292
Humboldt, Wilhelm v., 128, 132, 137, 139, 141, 159, 255, 286
Hume, David, 104
Hungary, 3, 17, 18, 47, 132, 145, 171, 179, 201, 348, 385, 386, 394, 402, 410, 424, 433, 435, 462, 463
Hutten, Ulrich v., 13, 24

Ibsen, Henrik, 301, 307
Illyria, 132, 134
Immermann, Karl Leberecht, 261
India, 317, 334
Indo-China, French, 317
Ingolstadt, 26

Ionescu, 320
Iraq, 400
Ireland, 198, 336, 395
Isabella II, Queen of Spain, 237
Israel, 426
Italy, 2, 3, 10, 24, 26, 46, 48, 84, 93, 95, 108, 109, 112, 114, 116, 117, 121, 132, 171, 177, 179, 202, 209, 220, 221, 222, 225, 232, 236, 271, 272, 282, 290, 291, 298, 301, 305, 315, 318, 319, 321, 323, 330, 331, 336, 337, 338, 363, 367, 268, 375, 382, 383, 386, 394, 396, 402, 412, 412, 415, 425, 428
Itzstein, 149, 170, 185
Izvolsky, Alexander Petrovitch, 322, 336

Jablonski, Daniel Ernest, 49
Jacobi, C. G. F., 255
Jacoby, Johannes, 182
Jagellonian Dynasty, 34
Jagow, Gottlieb v., 331, 335, 336
Jahn, Friedrich Ludwig, 167, 185
James II, King of England, 39
Jameson, Dr. (later Sir) L. S., 313
Japan, 312, 313, 318, 322, 383, 394, 402, 407
Jassy, 424
Jellačić, Ban Josef, 178
Jena, 26, 54, 94, 97, 98, 99, 101, 111, 118, 121, 122, 125, 128, 144, 256
Jerome (Buonaparte), King of Westphalia, 119
Joachim I, Elector of Brandenburg, 31
Joachim II, Elector of Brandenburg, 31
Jodl, Alfred, Gen., 428, 429, 430, 436
Joffre, Joseph Jacques Césaire, Maréchal, 337
John, Archduke of Austria, 188, 192
John Sigismund, Elector of Brandenburg, 31
John, Otto, 460
Johnson, Samuel, 87
Jordan, 64, 189
Joseph II, Holy Roman Emperor, 79, 111
Jülich-Berg, 58, 65
Julius Caesar, 258
Jung, 182
Jutland, 217, 339

Kaiser, Jacob, 439, 443, 444, 445, 452
Kaiser Wilhelmsland.   See NEW GUINEA
Kalckstein family, 41
Kaliningrad.   See KOENIGSBERG
Kaltenbrunner, 415, 436
Kamenz, 86
Kant, Immanuel, 78, 79, 81, 85, 86, 87, 89, 91, 92, 93, 97, 99, 101–7, 111, 122, 192, 225, 254, 259, 260, 296
Kapp, Wolfgang, 348
Karl.   See CHARLES
Karlsruhe, 172, 457
Kastner, 453
Katte, 62
Kaunitz, Wenzel Anton, 66
Kautsky, Karl, 304, 343
Kehl, 438
Keitel, Wilhelm, Field Marshal, 394, 428, 436
Keith, George, Earl Marischal, and James, 69
Keller, Gottfried, 260
Kellog, F. B., 363
Kempten Abbey, 8, 12
Kennedy, John F., 467, 470
Kepler, Johann, 24, 26
Kerch, 407
Kerrl, Hans, 373
Kesselring, Albert, Field Marshal, 415, 425, 428
Ketteler, W. E., Bishop of Mainz, 266, 267
Kharkov, 407, 411, 412
Khrushchev, Nikita Sergeyevich, 465, 466, 467, 468
Kiao Chau, 312
Kiderlen-Wächter, 320, 322, 323, 326, 329, 331
Kiel, 140, 219, 222, 344
— Canal, 292

Kiev, 403, 412
Kinkel, 198
Kirdorf, 302, 303, 363
Kitchener, Herbert, Lord, 317
Kleist, Heinrich v., 122
Kleve, 31, 40, 41, 63, *and see* CLEVES-JÜLICH
Klopstock, Frederick, 81, 82, 83, 89, 93
Kluge, Gunther Hans v., Field Marshal, 403, 409, 417, 418, 422
Kniephof, 208
Kniprode, Winrich v., 34
Koblenz-Trier, 398
Koch, Erich, 406
Koenigsberg (since 1946 Kaliningrad), 33, 40, 41, 45, 47, 55, 79, 102, 103, 104, 169, 172, 181, 255, 311, 427, 433, 435, 460, 469
Konev, Marshal, 426
Konia, 314
Königgrätz, 221, 222, 225
Königsberg. *See* KOENIGSBERG
Korea, 456
Kossuth, Louis, 171
Kotzebue, August Friedrich Ferdinand, 144
Kremsier, 179, 191
Kruger, Paul, 313
Krupp, Alfred, 245, 247, 302, 322
Krupp, Gustav, 436
Krupps, 142, 164
Kuhlmann, 373
Kulm, 33
Kulz, Dr. 445
Kursk, 407, 411, 412
Küstrin, 426
Kyffhäuser, 301

Lagarde. *See* BÖTTICHER
Lamprecht, 316, 373
Langbehn, 316
Lange, F., 316
Lansdowne, Marquis of, 318
Laplace, Pierre Simon, Marquis de, 103
Lapland, 423
Lasker, Edmund, 206, 226, 231, 274, 278, 280, 289
Lassalle, Ferdinand, 194, 206, 225, 231, 248–51, 262, 278
Lattre de Tassigny, Gen., 431
Latvia, 388
Lauenburg, Duchy of, 217
Lausanne, 376
Leber, Julius, 415, 418
Leclerc (de Hautecloque), Philippe, Gen., 422
Ledebour, Georg, 331
Leeb, Wilhelm v., Field Marshal, 402, 403
Leibnitz, Gottfried Wilhelm, 20, 45, 49, 50, 104
Leiningen, Prince Karl, 170, 187
Leipzig, 27, 49, 80, 82, 83, 85, 86, 87, 93, 99, 129, 144, 172, 175, 176, 242, 249, 250, 261, 275, 278, 298, 458
Lemmer, Ernst, 440, 445
Lemnos, 396
'Lenin,' Vladimir Ilyitch Ulianov, 343
Leningrad, 402, 403, 408, 411, 416, 423
Leo, H., 162, 166
Leo XIII, Pope, 274
Leopold, Prince of Hohenzollern-Sigmaringen, 237
Leopold I, Holy Roman Emperor, 47
Leopold II, Holy Roman Emperor, 111
Leopold II, King of the Belgians, 293, 391
Leopold of Anhalt, 56
Lessing, Gotthold Ephraim, 64, 68, 70, 78, 79, 82, 83, 85, 86–9, 90, 93, 94, 95, 96, 105, 286n., 378
Leuschner, 415
Leuthen, 66
Ley, Robert, 367, 373, 375, 436
Libau, 423
Libya, 396

Lichnowski, Prince, 320, 322, 334, 336
Lidice, 410
Liebig, Justus, 162, 253, 255, 256
Liebknecht, Karl, 328, 343, 346, 348
Liebknecht, Wilhelm, 231, 250, 251, 278
Liège, 390, 391
Liman v. Sanders, 332
Lincoln, Abraham, 200
Lindner, R. W., 141
Linnaeus, Karl, 91
Lippstadt, 427
List, Frederick, 148, 162, 165, 198, 242, 293
List, Gen., 407
Lithuania, 33, 34, 315, 338, 386, 388
Lloyd George, David, 330
Locarno, 363, 383
Locke, John, 104
Lodz, 198, 405, 424
Lohse, Hinrich, 406
Loire, 392
Lombardy, 171
London, 10, 166, 215, 235, 302, 331, 393, 445, 460
Longwy-Briey, 339
Lorraine, 3, 5, 73, *and see* ALSACE-LORRAINE
Lorraine (French part after 1871), 302
Louis XI, King of France, 37
Louis XIV, King of France, 22, 36, 38, 39, 43, 47, 50, 51, 79
Louis XV, King of France, 66
Louis XVI, King of France, 93, 101, 111
Louis XVIII, King of France, 139
Louis-Philippe, King of France, 172
Louise, Queen of Prussia, 118, 122
Louvain, 391
Lower Saxony, 438
Lübeck, 11, 133, 174, 260, 308, 344, 407, 431
Lübke, Heinrich, 466
Lublin, 405, 410, 424
Lucius v. Ballhausen, 285
Ludendorff, Eric, 338–41, 343, 347, 358, 377
Lüderitz, 292, 293
Ludwig, Otto, 260
Ludwig I, King of Bavaria, 148, 170, 171, 174
Ludwig II, King of Bavaria, 220, 233, 239, 240, 260, 267
Lunéville, Treaty of, 112, 114, 115, 116
Lusatia, 30, 31
Luther, Chancellor, 359, 360
Luther, Martin, 1, 3, 9, 12, 13, 21, 24, 26, 82, 94, 111, 120, 137, 144, 155, 265, 286
Lüttwitz, Gen., 348
Lützen, 128
Luxemburg, Rosa, 328, 348, 349
Luxemburg, Grand Duchy of, 3, 30, 134, 149, 155, 221, 223, 233, 235, 396, 398
Lvov, 423

Maas, 423, 425, 426
Maassen, Karl Georg, 153
Maastricht, 391
Macedonia, 322, 330, 331
Machiavelli, Niccolò, 8, 64, 76, 209
Mackensen, August v., Marshal, 339, 362
Mackinder, Sir Halford John, 381
MacMahon, Marie Edmé Patrice, Maréchal, 282
Madrid, 237
Magdeburg, 23, 26, 31, 35, 55, 116, 119, 196, 242, 321, 411, 414, 432
—, see of, 8, 39, 115
Magenta, 202
Mahomet, 366
Maier, Reinhold, 457
Maikob, 408
Main, 230, 232
Mainz, 3, 8, 9, 112, 113, 116, 144, 176, 190, 223, 266, 349
Malinovsky, Marshal, 424

Mallinckrodt, Arnold, 266
Malmédy, 398
Malmo, Truce of, 189
Malplaquet, 57
Manchuria, 312, 443
Mann, Thomas, 174, 308, 378, 381
Mannheim, 170
Manstein, Erich v., Gen., later Field Marshal, 408
Manteuffel, Edwin, Freiherr v., 294, 295
Manteuffel, Ernst Christoff, 59
Manteuffel, Otto Theodor, Freiherr v., 183, 184, 203, 204
Marburg, 26
Marcks, Erich, 33, 296n.
Marengo, 112
Margival, 417
Maria Theresa, Empress, 65, 66, 79, 111
Marianne Islands, 314
Marie Antoinette, Queen of France, 111
Marie Louise, Archduchess of Austria, 131
Marienburg (Prussia), 33
Mark, County of, 31, 40
Marne, 337, 338, 392
Marschall v. Bieberstein, 310, 312, 313
Marshall, George Catlett, Gen., 443, 444
Marwitz, F. A. L. v. d., 127
Marx, Chancellor, 359, 360, 363
Marx, Karl, 142, 162, 166, 167, 172, 176, 225, 248, 249, 251, 254, 271, 279, 304
Masaryk, T. G., 210
Mathy, Karl, 149, 170, 185, 187
Matthias, Holy Roman Emperor, 19
Maupertuis, Paul Louis Moreau de, 69
Maurice, Elector of Saxony, 18
Maximilian I, Holy Roman Emperor, 3, 4, 13
Maximilian II, King of Bavaria, 220, 267
Maximilian Joseph, King of Bavaria, 148
Mayer, R., 256
Mecklenburg, 3, 8, 31, 119, 147, 252, 260, 262, 270, 438
Mecklenburg-Schwerin, 149
Mediterranean, 291, 319, 330, 335, 395, 397, 400, 408, 412
Mehemet Ali, 166
Mehring, Franz, 304
Meinecke, Friedrich, 287, 417
Melanchthon (Schwarzerd), Philipp, 14, 25, 26, 31, 82, 84
Memel, 33, 134, 149, 350, 386, 423, 424, 426
Mencken, 208
Mende, Erich, 468
Mendelssohn, Felix, 262
Mendelssohn, Moses, 70, 87
Mersey, 395
Mesopotamia, 334, 338
Messina Straits, 412
Metternich, German Ambassador, 320, 334
Metternich, Prince Klemens, 97, 109, 121, 122, 128–32, 137, 142, 145, 146, 151, 153, 161, 168, 171, 175, 177, 181, 200, 214, 290
Metz, see of, 20, 238
Meuse, 390, 391, 425
Mevissen, Gustav, 165, 166, 169
Mexico, 198, 220
Meyer, Conrad Ferdinand, 258
Meyr, Melchior, 260
Michael, King of Rumania, 424
Michaelis, Georg, Chancellor, 341, 342
Middle East, 395, 400, 401, 407
Mieroslawski, Ludwik, 171, 191
Mikulov, 221
Milan, 134, 173
Milton, John, 45, 83
Minden, city, 444
—, see of, 37
Minsk, 402, 416
Miquel, Johann v., 225, 231, 275n., 277, 280, 310

Mirabeau, 68, 75, 249
Mittelland Canal, 423
Model, Walter, Field Marshal, 422, 423, 425, 427
Moeller van den Bruck, 347, 372
Mohrungen, Heinrich v., 89
Molotov, Vijacheslav Mikhailovich, 394, 445, 462
Moltke, Helmuth, Count v., 218, 223, 231, 235, 236, 238, 282, 295, 297, 313, 333, 415
Moltke, Wilhelm Ludwig v., 333, 336, 338
Mommsen, Theodor, 202, 258
Monte Cassino. See CASSINO
Montenegro, 330, 339, 400
Montesquieu, Charles de Secondat, 91, 92, 209
Montevideo, 390
Montez, Lola, 170, 174
Montgelas, Maximilian v., 137
Montgomery, Sir Bernard Law, Gen., 408, 426, 431
Montoire, 396
Moravia, 179, 221, 283, 389
Moresnet, 398
Morier, R. B. D., 216, 285
Morgenthau, Henry, 430
Morocco, 303, 309, 318, 319, 323, 329, 330, 333, 408
Moscow, 394, 401, 402, 403, 406, 443, 444, 448, 462
Möser, Justus, 83
Motz, F. C. A. v., 242
Müller, Adam, 122, 137, 146
Müller, Hermann, 363, 364, 365
Müller, Johannes, 111, 256
Müller, Joseph, 410
Müller, Ludwig, 379
Müller, R., 343
Munich, 135, 176, 177, 220, 243, 253, 260, 267, 308, 344, 348, 359, 366, 368, 379, 381, 386, 409, 439
Münster, Count, Ambassador, 290
Münster, see of, 8, 150, 159
Münzer, Thomas, 14
Mussolini, Benito, 382, 385, 387, 392, 394, 396, 401, 412, 414, 419

Namur, 391
Nantes, Edict of, revocation, 39, 43
Naples, 415
—, Bay of, 412
Napoleon I, Emperor of the French, 13, 74, 77, 78, 97, 101, 108–35, 109, 144, 204, 257
Napoleon III, Emperor of the French, 202, 209, 210, 215, 216, 219, 220, 221, 222, 223, 234, 236, 237, 238, 254
Narvik, 390
Nassau, 116, 124, 125, 148, 153, 154, 175, 222
Naumann, Friedrich, 285, 304n., 313, 365
Near East, 283, 313, 317, 381
Neisse, 426, 433, 435
Netherlands, 3, 30, 46, 48, 57, 73, 109, 111, 112, 134, 145, 149, 397
Neudeck, 361
Neufchâtel, 48, 171
Neumark. See NEW MARK
Neurath, Constantin, Freiherr v., 371, 384, 436
Newfoundland, 395
New Guinea, 293
New Mark, 31, 33
Newton, Sir Isaac, 103, 255
New York, 166, 302, 456
Nice, 220
Nicholas I, Tsar, 182, 186, 201
Nicholas II, Tsar, 318, 319, 320
Nicholas of Cusa, 5
Nicolai, F., 70, 87
Niebuhr, Reinhold, 128, 138, 257
Niemen, 416
Niemöller, Martin, Pastor, 380

Nietzsche, Friedrich, 151, 258, 264, 298, 300, 307, 308, 380
Nijmegen, 426
Nikolsburg, 221, 223
Nile, 408
Nord, 398
Nordlingen, 19
Normandy, 416, 417, 422
North Africa, 290, 407, 408, 409
North Mark. *See* OLD MARK
North Rhine-Westphalia, 438, 464
Norway, 297, 307, 390, 394, 396, 397, 425
Noske, Gustav, 344, 347, 349, 351
Novalis, 121, 122
Novgorod, 10
Nürnberg (Nuremberg), 11, 22, 24, 27, 80, 117, 242, 384, 436
Nuschke, 453

Obersalzburg, 417, 428
Odenwald, 175
Oder, 424, 426, 427, 433, 435
Oder-Neisse line, 465
Offenburg, 166, 185
Olbricht, Friedrick, Gen., 409, 410, 415, 418
Oldenburg, 119, 134, 149, 202
Old Mark, 30, 39, 119
Olive, Peace of, 38
Ollenhauer, Erich, 459, 460, 467
Olmütz, 200, 203, 209
Opitz v. Boberfeld, Martin, 24
Oppenheim, 426
Orange River Free State, 292
Oregon, 198
Orel, 412
Oslo, 390
Ossian, 83, 90
Oster, Hans, Maj.-Gen., 391, 409, 410
Ostland, 406
Otto I, Holy Roman Emperor, 29

Pacific Islands, 292, 293, 294, 312, 314, 317
Paderborn, see of, 8
Palatinate, 3, 7, 18, 30, 111–14, 133, 134, 137, 141, 148, 191
Palestine, 400
Palmerston, Henry Jonathan Temple, third Viscount, 215
Pankow, 465
Papen, Franz v., 369, 370, 371, 372, 436
Paris, 97, 102, 111, 113, 115, 129, 166, 167, 172, 174, 176, 177, 183, 192, 238, 239, 249, 253, 255, 276, 278, 281, 282, 290, 333, 347, 350, 363, 392, 418, 422, 444, 453
—, Treaty of (May 1814), 129
—, Treaty of (Nov. 1815), 129
Pas de Calais, 398, 422
Patton, George Smith, Gen., 426
Paulus, Friedrich, Field Marshal, 409
Percy, Thomas, Bishop of Dromore, 83
Persia, 320, 334
Persian Gulf, 334, 339
Pertz, G. H., 257
Pétain, Henri Philippe Benoni Omer Joseph, Marshal, 392, 396
Peter the Great, Tsar, 47, 48, 57, 63
Peters, Karl, 293, 325
Pfalz, 426
Pfitzer, Paul, 140, 148
Pforta College, 298
Philippines, 317
Piave, 339
Pieck, Wilhelm, 439, 445, 453, 467
Piedmont, 172
Pillersdorff, 178
Pillnitz, Declaration of, 112
Pius IX, Pope, 167, 267, 268, 274, 279
Pleven, René, 456
Ploesti, 394, 396, 424

Po Valley, 425
Poincaré, Raymond, 336, 355, 360
Poland, 10, 19, 29, 34, 35, 36, 38, 41, 47, 48, 75, 97, 106, 110, 111, 114, 117, 118, 119, 126, 131, 132, 133, 136, 140, 171, 181, 188, 192, 213, 214, 215, 219, 223, 252, 265, 272, 294, 315, 326, 338, 341, 350, 362, 363, 380, 383, 386, 387, 388, 389, 397, 405, 410, 416, 425, 432, 433, 435, 462, 469
Polenz, Wilhelm v., 308
Pomerania, 12, 20, 30, 31, 35, 36, 37, 42, 47, 55, 57, 67, 134, 233, 252, 261, 272, 438, 440
Pomerelia, 34, 67, 72, 75, 119, 134, 151
Pompadour, Mme de, 66
Popitz, 389
Port Arthur, 312
Portugal, 120, 292, 334
Posen, 134, 169, 171, 273
Potsdam, 55, 68, 70, 72, 105, 182, 183, 242, 286n., 433, 435, 469
—, Edict of, 39
Prague, 19, 178, 179, 223, 232, 264, 465
Pressburg, Treaty of, 114, 177
Preuss, Hugo, 347, 351, 352
Pripet Marshes, 402, 403, 416, 423
Prussia, 20, 24, 28, 29–76, 85, 90, 97, 101, 102, 106–12, 115, 117–21, 125, 136–42, 143, 144, 145, 147, 149–60, 175, 177–84, 188, 191, 193, 200–40, 242–5, 247, 249, 250, 252, 258–71, 273–8, 280, 281, 282, 285, 286, 292, 294, 296, 302, 304, 305, 306, 308, 310, 325, 327, 332, 338, 341–7, 352, 361, 365, 369, 372, 376, 379
Prussians, aboriginal, 33
Pruth, 424
Pufendorf, Samuel, 21, 45
Pultawa, 48
Puttkamer, Maria v., 208
Puttkamer, R. V. v., 285, 295, 325

Quebec, 430
Quedlinburg Abbey, 8
Quinet, Edgar, 141, 155, 167, 223
Quisling, Lauritz Vidkun Abraham, 397

Raabe, Wilhelm, 260, 261
Racine, Jean, 45, 62
Radetzky, Josef, Count, Marshal, 177, 179
Radowitz, Josef Maria v., 168, 170, 187, 194, 195
Raeder, Erich, Grand Admiral, 390, 395, 401, 407, 436
Ranke, Leopold v., 2, 4, 67, 159, 162, 257, 258, 346
Rapallo, 363, 363
Raschid Ali, 400
Rastadt, 113, 115
Rastenburg, 409, 418
Rathenau, Emil, 288
Rathenau, Walter, 305, 317, 341, 351, 358, 362
Ratzel, Friedrich, 381
Ravensberg, County of, 32
Ravenstein, Lordship of, 32
Rebenac, Ambassador, 39
Rechberg u. Rothenlöwen, Count J. B. v., 216
Regensburg, Diet of, 20
Reichensberger brothers, 266
Reimann, Max, 439
Reinke, 231
Remagen, 426
Rembrandt van Rijn, 45
Renan, Ernest, 271
Reuchlin, Johann, 24
Reuss, 134
Reuter, Ernst, 445, 446, 448
Reuter, Fritz, 260
Reval, 33
Rheims, 429
Rheinsberg, 63, 64

Rhenish League, 10
— Prussia, 29, 38, 40, 51, 55, 57, 59, 65, 124, 140, 150, 151, 159, 164–7, 172, 180, 210, 230, 245, 246, 249, 252, 272, 294, 303, 339, 355, 358, 363, 364
Rhine, 391, 423, 426, 429, 430
Rhineland, 407, 431. *See also* PALATINATE and RHENISH PRUSSIA
Rhine-Pfalz, 438
Rhône, 392, 423
Ribbentrop, Joachim v., 384, 387, 428, 436
Richardson, Samuel, 83
Richelieu, A. J. du P de, Cardinal, 20, 36, 223
Richter, Eugen, 280, 285, 289, 293, 294, 311
Ried, Treaty of, 129
Riehl, W. H., 241, 260
Riga, 23, 423
Rilke, Rainer Maria, 307, 308
Riquetti de Mirabeau, Count, 60
Ritter, Karl, 162
Rodbertus, J. K., 182, 249
Roehm, Ernst, 367, 368, 374
Romanov dynasty, 382
Rome, 4, 9, 26, 67, 91, 111, 135, 157, 158, 178, 221n., 236, 266, 267, 271, 274, 379, 380, 381, 383, 412, 414, 416
Rommel, Erwin Johannes Eugen, Maj.-Gen., later Field Marshal, 400, 408, 416, 417, 418, 462
Roon, A. T. E., Count, Marshal, 205, 206, 207, 210, 217n., 218, 231, 236
Roosevelt, Franklin Delano, 430
Roscher, W. G. F., 162
Rosegger, Peter Kettenfeier, 260
Rosenberg, Alfred, 367, 371, 372, 378, 379, 390, 397, 401, 406, 429, 436
Rossbach, 66, 122
Rostock, 407
Rostov, 403, 408, 411
Roth of Königsberg, 41
Rothenburg, 10
Rothschild, Meyer Amschol, 246
Rotteck, K. W. R. v., 140
Rotterdam, 391
Roumelia, Eastern, 289
Rousseau, Jean-Jacques, 82, 83, 90, 92, 102
Ruge, Arnold, 187
Ruhr district, 302, 303, 358, 359, 361, 407, 413, 423, 427, 431, 446, 447, 452
Rumania, 290, 303, 305, 330, 331, 332, 335, 337, 338, 349, 382, 386, 394, 396, 400, 402, 406, 416, 433
Rundstedt, Karl Rudolf Gerd v., Gen., 391, 392, 402, 403, 416, 417, 423, 425, 428
Russell, Lord Odo, 273, 281, 282
Russia, 10, 29, 33, 36, 48, 55, 57, 58, 75, 89, 110, 111, 112, 115, 117, 120, 128, 129, 131, 134, 136, 140, 169, 188, 201, 208, 214, 215, 220, 222, 223, 235, 236, 242, 243, 270, 271, 276, 281, 282, 283, 284, 290, 291, 293, 296, 298, 303, 304, 307, 310, 311, 312, 314, 317–23, 327, 329–37, 340, 341, 343, 346, 349, 353, 362, 363, 371, 373, 381, 390, 393, 394, 397, 399, 401, 405, 407, 410, 444. *See also* SOVIET UNION (U.S.S.R.)
Ryswick, 47

Saar, 129, 245, 350, 377, 382, 438, 446, 460, 461, 462
Saarbrücken, 423
Sadowa, 221
St. Gall Abbey, 8
St. Petersburg, 210, 214, 307
Saint-Simon, C. H. de R., Comte de, 165, 249
Salerno, 412
Salisbury, Marquess of, 291
Salonika, 331, 400
Salzburg, see of, 8, 120, 134
Samoa, 314

San, 416
Sandomir, 416, 426
Sangro, 415
San Stefano, 283
Sarajevo, 334
Sas, Col., 391
Saukel, Fritz, 404, 411, 414, 436
Saverne (Zabern), 328
Savigny, Friedrich Karl v., 128, 138, 257
Savoy, 220
Saxe-Weimar, 79, 144, 146, 262
Saxony, 3, 5, 7, 9, 16, 21, 26, 31, 35, 45, 65, 66, 73, 74, 79, 86, 98, 102, 116, 118, 119, 128, 129, 131–4, 136, 144, 146, 149, 153, 154, 170, 175, 177, 180, 183, 191, 220, 221, 222, 223, 231, 242, 245, 250, 263, 275, 276, 302, 304, 308, 348, 358, 438
Schacht, Hjalmar, 369, 376, 436
Schäfer, Fritz, 452
Scharnhorst, Gerhard Johann David v., Gen., 121, 124, 127
Schaumberg-Lippe, 438
Scheffel, Victor v., 258
Scheidemann, Philipp, 325, 344, 348, 351, 352
Schelling, Friedrich Wilhelm Josef v., 122, 254, 255
Schenkendorff, Max v., 156
Schiller, Friedrich, 78, 79, 80, 82, 83, 84, 85, 86, 93, 94, 95, 97–101, 104, 134, 252, 260, 276
Schirach, Baldur v., 379, 436
Schlabrendorff, Fabien v., 409, 419
Schlegel, August Wilhelm, 121
Schlegel, Friedrich, 121, 137, 138, 141, 146
Schleicher, Kurt v., 369, 370, 374
Schleiden, Matthias J., 256
Schleiermacher, Friedrich, 121, 128, 141, 155,
Schleswig, 171
Schleswig-Holstein, 182, 188, 192, 200, 206, 214–19, 222, 230, 250, 261, 283, 284, 294, 308, 350, 438, 440
Schlieffen, Alfred, Count, 337
Schlözer, A. L. v., 82
Schlüter, Andreas, 50
Schmalkaldic League, 18
Schmerling, Anton v., 187, 216
Schmid, Carlo, 466
Schmoller, Gustav v., 287
Schnaebelé affair, 295
Schoen, Theodor, 126, 329
Schönbrunn, Peace of, 114, 120
Scholl, Sophie, 409
Schopenhauer, Arthur, 162, 198, 259, 260, 262, 263, 298, 299
Schouvaloff (Shuvalov), Piotr Andreivich, 284
Schrader, Henrietta, 297
Schroeder, Gerhard, 459, 468, 470
Schrötter, 126
Schubert, Franz, 142, 203, 206, 262
Schulenberg, Ambassador, 402
Schultze-Delitzsch, Franz Hermann, 226
Schumacher, Kurt, 439, 442, 443, 449, 451, 452, 456, 457, 459
Schuman, Robert, 455, 456
Schumann, Robert Alexander, 262
Schurz, Karl, 198
Schwann, Theodor, 256
Schwarzburg, 134
Schwarzburg-Sondershausen, 153
Schwarzenberg, Prince, 179, 191
Schwarzenberg, minister, 135, 191, 195, 197, 200
Schwarzerd. *See* MELANCHTHON
Schweinitz, 285
Schweitzer, J. B. v,. 231, 250
Schweninger, Dr., 295
Schwerin, Otto v., 42, 43
Schwiebus, 46
Scotland, 98
Sebastopol, 407, 416

Sedan, 238, 390, 391
Seeckt, Hans v., Gen., 354, 362
Seine, 392, 416, 417, 422
—, Bay of the, 417
Semeonov, Vladimir, 458
Semler, Johann, 82
Serbia, 290, 322, 323, 330, 331, 332, 335, 336, 338, 339, 400
Severing, Karl, 372
Seyss-Inquart, Artur, 389, 397, 436
Shakespeare, 83, 85, 87, 90, 225, 306
Shuvalov. See SCHOUVALOFF
Siam, 317
Sicily, 118
Sickengen, Franz v., 8, 14
Sidi Barrani, 396
Siemens, Werner, 246
Siemens, William, 246
Siemens & Halske, 246, 361
Sigismund, Holy Roman Emperor, 5, 30, 31
Silesia, 27, 46, 65, 66, 69, 71, 73, 75, 87, 119, 151, 210, 245, 246, 248, 252, 294, 302, 308, 351, 355, 425, 426, 433, 440, 469
Simon, Ludwig, 187
Simson, M. E. S. v., 187
Skagerrak, 339
Skorzeny, 424
Slovakia, 394, 424
Smith, Adam, 137, 139
Smolensk, 402, 403, 409, 411, 412
Sobibor, 424
Socrates, 88, 286n.
Sokolovsky, Vassili Danilovich, Gen., later Marshal, 437, 446, 447, 448
Solferino, 202
Sombart, Werner, 276, 316
Somme, 392, 422
Sonnemann, 285
Sophia, Electress of Hanover, 50
Sophia Charlotte, Queen of Prussia, 50
South Africa, 313, 314, 317
South America, 255, 303
Soviet Union (U.S.S.R.), 402, 415, 424, 433, 435, 443, 444, 449, 450, 452, 457, 458, 461, 462, 464, 467, 469. See also RUSSIA
Spa, 344
Spain, 4, 23, 42, 58, 120, 129, 237, 314, 318, 319, 383, 384, 396
Sparta, 67
Speer, Albert, 404, 411, 414, 423, 427, 428, 436
Speidel, Hans, Gen., 462
Speier, 12, 20
—, see of, 8,
Spener, P. J., 49, 81
Spengler, Oswald, 347
Spiegel zum Desenberg, F. v., Archbishop of Cologne, 158
Spielhagen, Friedrich v., 242, 261, 263
Spinoza, Benedict de, 91, 107
Spitzweg, 142
Sprenger, 313
Stadion, J. P. K., Count, 120, 178
Staël, Mme de, 79, 122, 373,
Stahl, F. J., 157
Stalin, Josif Vissarionovich, 388, 393, 396, 401, 410, 429, 430, 435, 448, 458
Stalingrad, 408, 409
Stapel, 172
Stassfurt, 253
Stauffenberg, Claus Schlenk v., Lieut.-Col., 415, 418
Stehr, Hermann, 305
Stein, Frau v., 94
Stein, Karl, Freiherr vom u. zum, 8, 116, 118, 121, 122, 124–7, 128, 130, 131, 132, 134, 144, 150, 155, 159, 160, 187, 252, 257
Stein, Lorenz, 165
Stephan, Martin, 198
Stephenson, George, 245

Sterne, Lawrence, 83
Stettin, 43, 55, 57, 469
Stifter, Adalbert, 259, 260
Stinnes, Hugo, 302, 354, 363
Stock, Christian, 449
Stockholm, 343
Stoecker, Adolf, 295, 316
Stoph, Willy, 462
Storm, Theodor, 260, 263
Strafford, 211
Stralsund, 57, 242
Strasbourg. See STRASSBURG
Strassburg, 83, 90, 93, 95, 423, 455
—, see of, 8, 12
Strasser, Gregor, 367, 374
Strasser, Otto, 367
Strauss, David, 162, 263, 298
Strauss, Franz-Josef, 459, 463, 464, 470
Streicher, Julius, 367, 380, 436
Stresemann, Gustav, 351, 359, 360, 362, 363, 364
Struve, Gustav v., 166, 170, 172, 175, 176, 185, 186, 190
Student, Kurt, Gen., 400
Stülpnagel, 418
Stumm, Karl (-Halberg), 302
Stuttgart, 432, 441, 444
Stüve, J. K. B., 175
Styria, 3, 19
Suarez, Francisco, 69
Sudan, 317
Sudermann, Hermann, 297, 301, 307, 308, 385
Sudeten Germans, 377, 382
Sudetenland, 433
Suez Canal, 292, 401
Swabia, 2, 5, 122, 134, 232, 260
Swabian League, 10
Sweden, 20, 35, 36, 37, 38, 39, 47, 51, 57, 189, 215, 388
Swift, Jonathan, 82
Swiss, 12
Switzerland, 20, 22, 43, 48, 101, 147, 171, 176, 177, 190, 199, 232, 259, 260, 262, 279, 305
Sybel, Heinrich v., 202, 258
Syria, 400

Tacitus, 9
Talleyrand (-Périgord), C. M. de., 115, 132
Tanganyika, Lake, 293
Tangier, 316, 319
Tannenberg, 34, 338
Taranto, 396
Teplitz, 129
Terboven, Joseph, 397
Thaer, Albrecht v., 253
Theresienstadt, 405, 424
Thermopylae, 400
Thierack, 411, 429
Thiers, Louis Adolphe, 187, 238, 281–2
Thoma, Ludwig, 243
Thomas à Kempis, 9
Thomasius, 49, 81
Thorn, 83, 134
Thuringia, 23, 80, 134, 153, 260, 301, 336, 352, 438
Thyssen, August, 302, 354, 361, 369, 376
Tibet, 320
Tieck, Ludwig, 121
Tilsit, Peace of, 110, 119, 122
Tirpitz, 309, 315, 318, 320, 321, 332
Tisza, Stephen, Count, 335
Tobruk, 400
Togoland, 293
Tolstoy, Leo Nicolaevich, Count. 307
Tonking, 293
Toul, see of, 20
Toulon, 408
Tours, 392
Toynbee, Arnold. 216
Transvaal, 313

Treblinka, 410, 424
Treitschke, Heinrich, 34, 47, 134, 145, 157, 159, 167, 209, 219, 225, 235, 258, 271, 277, 286, 292, 293, 307, 315, 316
Trent, Council of, 18
Trentino, 336
Tresckow, Henning v., 409, 415, 417, 418
Treysa (Hesse), 432
Trier, 3, 8, 150, 158
Tripoli, 318, 330
Troeltsch, Ernest, 351
Tromsö Fjord, 423
Trondheim, 390
Truman, Harry S., 443, 447
Tschirschky u. Bözendorff, 335
Tsushima, 319
Tunis, 290
Tunisia, 408
Turkey, 111, 168, 283, 303, 313, 322, 329, 330, 331, 334, 337, 338, 340, 386, 400, 443
Turks, 4, 6, 11, 21, 36, 47
Twesten, Karl, 206, 224, 226, 231
Tycho Brahe, 25, 102
Tyrol, 3, 22, 129, 134, 385

Uhland, Ludwig, 148
Ukermark, 30
Ukraine, 402, 406, 416
Ulbricht, Walter, 439, 452, 453, 458, 462, 465, 466, 467, 468, 469
Ulm, 11, 117
Ulster, 336
United States of America, 131, 139, 142, 164, 177, 199, 200, 242, 244, 246, 247, 248, 255, 258, 259, 363, 364, 381, 382, 394, 395, 398, 402, 406, 413, 464, 465
Unruh, Hans Viktor v., 182, 206, 226
Ural, 292
Utrecht, Peace of, 48, 51
U.S.S.R. See SOVIET UNION

Valentin, Viet, 174, 321n.
Valmy, 112
Varnbüler, v. u. zu Hemmingen, F. K. G., 233
Varzin, 208, 233, 272, 277
Vatican, 267
Venetia, 132, 171
Venice, 23, 33, 45, 134, 221
Verdun, 338, 339
—, see of, 20
Versailles, 22, 45, 237, 238, 349, 350, 368, 380, 381, 384
Vessenmayer, 424
Vicari, Bishop of Freiburg, 267
Victoria, Queen of England, 256, 297
Vienna, 2, 21, 27, 38, 47, 65, 77, 79, 81, 96, 114, 146, 171, 172, 175, 176, 177, 178, 179, 181, 183, 186, 188, 201, 213, 217, 219, 222, 261, 332, 335, 366, 382, 425, 426, 427
—, Congress of, 120, 124, 129–35, 143, 145
Villafranca, Peace of, 202
Vincke, 169, 187, 206, 275n.
Virchow, 206, 226, 256, 272
Vistula, 416, 423, 424, 425, 426
Vitebsk, 416
Vögler, 361
Vogt, Karl, 187, 256
Volga, 403, 407, 408
Vollmar, 304
Voltaire, François Marie Arouet de, 62, 64, 68, 72, 83, 91, 92
Voronezh, 407
Vosges, 423

Waal, 423
Wackenroder, 121
Wagner, A., 287
Wagner, Richard, 77, 191, 220, 259, 261, 262, 298, 316

Wagram, 120
Waitz, 257
Waldeck, 182, 206, 226
Waldersee, Gen., 295, 306
Walfisch Bay, 292
Wallenstein, 35, 100
Warsaw, 38, 39, 214, 389, 405, 423, 426, 461, 465
—, Grand Duchy of, 119, 170
Wartburg, 14, 144
Wartenburg, 49
Washington, 451, 468, 470
Waterloo, 129, 133
Watteau, 63
Weber, historian, 22, 142, 287
Weber, Carl Maria, 262
Weber, E. W., 256
Weber, Max, 297, 351
Wedekind, Frank, 297
Weidling, Gen., 428
Weiland, Christoph Martin, 79, 81, 83, 85
Weimar, 27, 80, 83, 89, 90, 93, 94, 98, 101, 177, 259, 352, 451, 469
— Republic, 224, 246, 348, 354, 355, 359, 360, 364, 368, 371, 372, 373, 378
Weitling, William, 166
Weizsäcker, Ernst, Freiherr v., 399, 401
Welcker, K. T., 140, 149, 187
Wenck, Gen., 427
Wends, 30
Wesel, 426
Wessenberg (-Ampringen), I. H. K., Bishop of Constance, 267
West Germany, Federal Republic of, 444, 449, 450, 451, 452, 453, 455, 461, 464, 467, 468, 469, 471
West Prussia. See POMERELIA
Westarp, Count, 369
Westphalia, 48, 119, 120, 137, 150, 164, 166, 169, 175, 180, 183, 230, 245, 246, 249, 252, 272, 294, 303, 339, 355, 358, 363, 364, 382, 426
—, Peace of, 13, 17, 19, 37, 38
Wettin dynasty, 136
Wetzlar, 20
Wilhelmina, Princess, 52, 56
Wilhelmina, Queen of the Netherlands, 397
William, Elector of Hesse, 35, 100, 146
William I, King of Prussia, later German Emperor, 202, 203, 204, 205, 206, 207, 208, 210, 213, 214, 215, 217, 219, 222, 223, 230, 233, 237, 239, 278, 282, 284, 295, 296, 305, 321
William II, German Emperor, 204, 217n., 244, 295, 301, 306, 307, 309, 310, 312, 313, 314, 315, 316, 317, 319, 320, 321, 323, 324, 325, 326, 327, 328, 329, 331, 332, 335, 336, 338, 344
William III, Prince of Orange, King of England, 36, 38, 39, 45
William 'the Russ,' Prince of Prussia, 168, 170
Wilson, Woodrow, President, 333, 349, 355
Wimpheling, 8
Winckelmann, J. J., 70, 78, 80, 84, 85, 88, 95, 105
Windischgrätz, 179
Windthorst, Ludwig, 231, 272, 274, 275n., 293, 310
Wirth, A., 313, 316
Wirth, Josef, 358
Wittelsbach dynasty, 30, 136, 345
Wittenberg, 26, 27, 156, 265, 469
Wittgenstein, W. L. G., 151
Wöhler, Friedrich, 256
Wolf, F. A., 254
Wolfenbüttel, 87
Wolff, Christian, 59, 63, 81, 144
Wolff, O., 361
Woltmann, Alfred, 316
Worms, Diet of, 6, 14, 17, 18
Wrangel, F. H. E., Marshal, 183

Wurtemberg (Württemburg), 3, 7, 21, 22, 23, 81, 98, 117, 131, 132, 133, 141, 148, 153, 185, 195, 202, 223, 230, 233, 234, 237, 239, 240, 243, 252, 263, 265, 267, 438
Württemberg. *See* WURTEMBERG
Würzburg, 266
—, see of, 8, 12, 19, 134

Xanten, Convention of, 32

Yalta, 430, 431
Yangtse valley, 313
Yorck, 127, 128
Young, Arthur, 83

Young, Owen D., 363
Yugoslavia, 382, 385, 400, 401

Zabern. *See* SAVERNE
Zagreb, 178
Zanzibar, 293
Zedlitz, 85
Zetkin, Clara, 325
Zhukov, Georgiy Konstantinovich, Marshal, 403, 426, 429, 431
Zola, Émile, 238, 307
Zoroaster, 299
Zürich, 80, 81, 83, 164, 166, 279

DATE D

Sudawn	
NOV 3 '67	
JAN 3 '68	
JAN 17 '68	
JAN 24 '68	
OCT 15 '70	
JAN 22 '78	
NOV 1 0 1980	
DEC 1 1981	
MR 7 '88	
GAYLORD	